Bilingual Education in the 21st Century

Para Ricardo Otheguy
por tu paciencia, generosidad y amor

For Joshua A. Fishman
for sharing your insights and lessons

Bilingual Education in the 21st Century:
A Global Perspective

Ofelia García
with contributions
by Hugo Baetens Beardsmore

WILEY-BLACKWELL

A John Wiley & Sons, Ltd., Publication

Library of Congress Cataloging-in-Publication Data

García, Ofelia.
  Bilingual education in the 21st century : a global perspective / Ofelia García ; with contributions by Hugo Baetens Beardsmore.
     p. cm.
  Includes bibliographical references and index.
  ISBN 978–1–4051–1993–1 (hardcover : alk. paper) — ISBN 978–1–4051–1994–8 (pbk. : alk. paper)   1. Education, Bilingual.   I. Beardsmore, Hugo Baetens.   II. Title.
III. Title: Bilingual education in the twenty-first century.

LC3715.G37 2008
370.117—dc22

2008017214

A catalogue record for this book is available from the British Library.

Set in 10/12.5pt Sabon by Graphicraft Limited, Hong Kong

13   2017

Contents

List of Figures

List of Tables

Preface and Acknowledgments (and a Caveat)

This book has been the result of a long trajectory. Originally, the book was conceived as a co-authored work with Hugo Baetens Beardsmore. The finished book contains two chapters that are solely authored by Hugo Baetens Beardsmore, and two which he co-authored. These chapters contain his name, and his role may be visible to the readers. What may not be visible, however, is the extent of Hugo Baetens Beardsmore's contributions to the entire book. Hugo read, commented, gave of his expertise, and expanded on all the chapters. And we negotiated much. When he generously decided that his name should not appear as author, I intended to alert the reader whenever he had made an addition. I soon discovered that this was impossible because his contributions are so extensive. Because his voice is intertwined with mine throughout, there is a "we" voice across the book, which I have chosen to retain. I owe much gratitude to Hugo Baetens Beardsmore. This book could not have been written without your support and encouragement. You have been a faithful email correspondent and a wonderful teacher. I am grateful for your extensive knowledge and experience, your generosity, and, especially, your sense of humor.

Although this book was written during my years at Teachers College, Columbia University, much about bilingual education was learned during the years I spent in two other institutions: the City College of New York and the Brooklyn Campus of Long Island University. At the City College, my colleague and husband, Ricardo Otheguy expanded my vision of bilingual education. And progressive educators such as the late Lillian Weber, the late Miriam Dorn, as well as my early colleagues in the bilingual education field, Gerardo Torres and Carole Berotte Joseph, shaped my first conceptualizations of how to educate language minorities. During my years at Long Island University, I was blessed with a colleague and good friend, Cecelia Traugh. Cecelia taught me to use language carefully and descriptively, to observe children's work deeply, to work collaboratively with others. Her impact has been extensive.

The work done with colleagues in International and Transcultural Studies at Teachers College, Columbia University has greatly influenced my thinking in the last years. I want to thank particularly the four colleagues with whom I have closely collaborated – Lesley Bartlett, JoAnne Kleifgen, Hervé Varenne, and María Torres-Guzmán, my colleague in the bilingual education program. Another colleague, Patricia Velasco, read the chapter on practice in this book and offered suggestions. But it is perhaps the students at Teachers College to whom I owe the greatest debt. During the fall of 2007, my graduate students read part of the manuscript and commented on it extensively; this text incorporates some of their observations. Some of my students couldn't be held back. Cristina Muir and Yesenia Morales insisted on developing "Myths and Realities," that is here adapted and included as appendix. Yi-Sheng Lin developed the original questions for the first few chapters. Lori Falchi, always willing to do more, gave me valuable comments on the last four chapters, developed the original questions for those, and extended "Myths and Realities." Ameena Ghaffar-Kucher and Jeehyae Chung read and commented on Part I of the book. Zeena Zakharia ensured that the Arabic context received attention by authoring a section which is here included in chapter 11. Elizabeth Huaman Sumida insisted that Native Americans be given space and shared information. My colleague and doctoral student, Tori Hunt, an expert on practice, commented extensively on the relevant chapters and gave me suggestions. Kate Menken, my first doctoral student at Teachers College, and now a professor at CUNY and language-policy scholar, read those chapters carefully. I could not have done this without the exchange with all my students. I thank all of you who read and commented on it.

During the course of the preparation of the manuscript I had four graduate Research Assistants – Cambria Russell, Debra Cole, Robert Werner, and Carmina Makar. Each of them had particular strengths and worked at different times. Cambria started the bibliography, and read and commented on the early chapters. Debra, a scholar on Deaf bilingual education, taught me much about the education of the Deaf, questioned my writing and my assumptions, and continued building the bibliography.[1] She insisted that the Deaf be treated like all others – integrated throughout, and not treated separately. She wrote a section on the Deaf which appears in chapter 11. Rob Werner has been a most careful reader of the entire manuscript. He caught all kinds of infelicities, and finalized the bibliography. He worked with attention to detail, often with tight demands. Carmina Makar came to me towards the end of the process, but her help has been invaluable. These four graduate students have received very little financial compensation for the enormous work they have done. My only hope is that they have learned from me, as much as I have learned from them. I am very grateful to the four of you. Arsen Babaev, the Bilingual Education Secretary, kept my administrative load light while I paid attention to this book – thank you. The book also benefited greatly from the comments of six anonymous reviewers. I thank you for your careful reading and generous recommendations.

During my years studying bilingual education, I have collaborated with many different colleagues, all of whom have influenced me in a variety of ways. You know who you are and I thank you. I have to especially mention Jim Cummins, Christine Hélot, Nancy Hornberger, Tove Skutnabb-Kangas, and Guadalupe Valdés as people who have taught me much and whose friendship I value. And I would be remiss if I didn't express my gratitude to Colin Baker. Many years ago, before he had written *Foundations of Bilingual Education*, Colin visited me in New York; I was touched by his insightfulness and his generosity. And perhaps no other book on bilingual education has been more influential to my students and to myself than his *Foundations*. His friendship and support have been a gift.

I have had the blessings of family throughout my life – a tight Cuban family with roots and branches here, there; in Puerto Rico and Mexico. My immediate family – my son, Eric, my two daughters, Raquel and Emma, and my husband, Ricardo – have taught me what it is to be a bilingual Cuban American family in New York, with all its vicissitudes and wonders. Many times you waited for dinner and other things, as I worked on this and many other writings. *Los quiero mucho. Les agradezco mucho el que me quieran, se quieran, y quieran a los demás.* Flying hearts to all of you!

The last words are always saved for those who have had the most influence in one's work, the two men to whom I dedicate this book – Ricardo Otheguy and Joshua A. Fishman. Almost thirty years ago I studied with Joshua A. Fishman. I often remark that everything I know, I learned in Fishman 101. I always take refuge in Fishman's work and words to think about bilingual education. It is not often that one has a most generous mentor who also becomes a good friend. As I have gotten older, I often model my manner with my students on how Fishman treated me as a young and inexperienced graduate student – always trusting and pushing me beyond my limits. The lessons have been well learned.

And how can I talk about a husband and colleague? Ricardo walked into my life as a colleague, but we have been a family for over a quarter of a century. Ricardo has been a most patient listener, and he has given me room to disagree, to hold different views. He has never complained about the attention I pay to my students and my work, even though sometimes it takes away from things that we both hold dear. I have learned more from him than from any other, about language, but also about history, politics, and life in general. *Aunque te admiro como intelectual, es tu dulzura y tu generosidad lo que más valoro. Es lo que me da el sentido de esperanza, lo que me permite que mi imaginación vuele, y lo que me ayuda a tener fe en un mejor futuro – uno de paz, de amor, de compromiso social y de tolerancia – regalos que tú me has dado.*

Finally, a caveat for the readers. This book has many limitations, but among the most serious are the western and speaking lenses that dominate. Although bilingual and somewhat traveled, both Hugo and I are hearing, and we are both products of European and North American scholarship. And although we strove to extend beyond our geographical and intellectual limits, it is not a completely global and inclusive picture that emerges. My only hope is that it will stimulate scholars from around the world, and in particular from all non-dominant contexts, to challenge and expand what we discuss here.

Part I
Bilingual Education for All

1

Introducing Bilingual Education

Scenarios

A Bilingual Education Classroom in New York, U.S.

"Go to the computers in your head," Ms. Acuña says, as twenty-five pairs of hands grasp their heads and begin making motions. Children tap their foreheads intently, determined to find "their computer." This is a bilingual kindergarten classroom in Queens, New York. Ms. Acuña's class is comprised of U.S. Latino students of different backgrounds who are learning English. Her students speak Spanish at home, but Ms. Acuña will focus on promoting literacy and numeracy in both Spanish and English. She continues, "Find your mouse and press English only. Okay? Is everybody there? English only, *no español*." Now that the kindergarten class is set on English only, Ms. Acuña reads a book in English, asks questions in English, and expects her students to respond accordingly. Patricia tells Ms. Acuña that the first thing to do when it is time to read is to "look at the title." Yuniel raises his hand and says, "I see a bear." The comments begin with a flood – "I see a basket." "I see two bugs." "I see *un carruaje*."

When it is time for the math lesson, Ms. Acuña tells the students to go back to their computer, this time to switch to Spanish. The class will count backwards and forwards, using their *dedito señadito* to track the numbers on the page – "*cero, uno, dos, tres . . .*" They learn the value of a penny, and one student counts five pennies. "*Son cinco* pennies," he says. To this, Ms. Acuña responds, "*Sí, tienes razón, pero estamos en español. ¿cómo se dice* pennies *en español?*" (That's right, but remember we are in Spanish. So, how do we say "pennies" in Spanish?) This gentle reminder acknowledges a correct answer without complaining about the language in which it is given.

In this classroom, both languages are correct. They are valuable tools the children access, via the computer in their brains, to learn reading, writing, and arithmetic. A glance at the walls reinforces this idea. The room is adorned with posters, calendars, wall charts, alphabet, and other visuals labeled twice, in red and blue – blue for English, red for Spanish. And there's a poster that reads "*Te lo digo, y no hay engaño, ser bilingüe es una dicha que nos dura todo el año*" (I tell you, and it's no joke, being bilingual is a happiness that lasts throughout the year). Bilingualism is highly valued in Ms. Acuña's class. Although all of the children are Spanish speakers, the class spends each school day toggling back and forth from one language to the other without so much as a flinch.

Written by Kristin Jefferson, December 11, 2006

A Bilingual School in Japan

On the floor of a second-grade classroom, Atsuko and Michiko are working on math problems in English. One of them says: "We start with four. We take away one. How many are left?" The other one replies: "Three are left." Afterwards, the other child initiates the dialogue and changes the numbers. They are in an immersion program in Katoh School where, in the first three grades, approximately two thirds of the instruction takes place in English, whereas one third of the time is devoted to developing Japanese language and literacy. In fourth grade, approximately 50 percent of the instruction is in English and 50 percent is in Japanese. Atsuko and Michiko will continue into high school where they will follow both the Japanese curriculum and that of the International Baccalaureate. They will then be taking most of their classes in English.

For more on this school, see www.
bi-lingual.com/School/ElementaryProgram.htm.

Overview

In this introductory chapter, we consider the following features of bilingual education:

*   its definitions and characteristics;
*   its beneficiaries and reasons;
*   its geopolitics and language orientations.

Introduction

This chapter develops the main thesis of this book: that bilingual education is *the only way* to educate children in the twenty-first century. In this chapter, we develop an integrated plural vision for bilingual education, by which bilingualism is not simply seen as two separate monolingual codes – a vision that goes beyond "one plus one equals two." This plural vision depends upon the reconceptualization of understandings about language and bilingualism, further developed in Part II of this book – Bilingualism and Education.

Here we reconstitute the activity known as "bilingual education;" we reposition bilingual education for the twenty-first century, while building on the scholarship of the past; and we outline how this inclusive plural vision of bilingual education has the potential to transform the lives of children and adults throughout the world.

We also introduce the reader to the ways in which sociohistorical positionings, geopolitical forces, and language ideologies interact to sustain different kinds of bilingual education policies throughout the world. In considering this, the chapter introduces another complexity to the topic of bilingual education: states, nations, and social groups have different histories, needs, challenges, and aspirations for their children; therefore different educational options need to be available. This point will be further developed in Part III of this book – Bilingual Education Policy – where bilingual education theoretical frameworks and types, as well as language-in-education policies throughout the world, will be reflected upon.

In considering definitions of bilingual education, we also approach another main thesis of this book: that bilingual education practices must be extended to reflect the complex multilingual and multimodal communicative networks of the twenty-first century. Part IV of this book – Bilingual Education Practices – suggests curricular, pedagogical, and assessment practices that respond to this complexity.

What Is Bilingual Education?

Definitions and characteristics

What is bilingual education? We think immediately of someone who has a good command of two languages as bilingual; and of the use of two languages in education as bilingual education. But, as Cazden and Snow (1990) point out, bilingual education is "a simple label for a complex phenomenon." Colin Baker (1993: 9), one of the most perceptive scholars in the field of bilingual education, suggests that sometimes the term bilingual education is used to refer to the education of students who are already speakers of two languages, and at other times to the education of those who are studying additional languages. Some students who learn additional languages are already speakers of the majority language(s) used in their society, while sometimes they are immigrants, refugees, Indigenous peoples,[1] members of minoritized groups,[2] or perhaps even members of the majority group,[3] learning a different language, the dominant language, in school. Bilingual education refers to education in more than one language, often encompassing more than two languages (Baker, 2001). Because of the complexity surrounding bilingual education, many people misunderstand it. In the United States, for example, many lay people think that teaching immigrants using only English is bilingual education.

Bilingual education is different from traditional language education programs that teach a second or a foreign language. For the most part, these traditional second- or foreign-language programs teach the language *as a subject*, whereas bilingual education programs use the language *as a medium of instruction*; that is, bilingual education programs teach content through an additional language other than the children's home language. For example, in the scenarios at the beginning of this chapter, Spanish and English are media of instruction in Ms. Acuña's kindergarten, whilst Japanese and English are used in instruction in the program in Japan. More than anything else, bilingual education is a way of providing *meaningful and equitable education*, as well as an education that builds tolerance towards other linguistic and cultural groups. In so doing, bilingual education programs provide a general education, teach in two or more languages, develop multiple understandings about languages and cultures, and foster appreciation for human diversity. Traditional second- or foreign-language programs often aim to use only the target language in instruction, whereas bilingual education programs always include some form of more than one language in at least some parts of instruction. Although the approach may be different, the development of some type of bilingualism is accomplished in both *language-teaching programs*[4] and *bilingual education programs*.

Depending on the type of language-teaching and bilingual education program followed, it may be difficult to differentiate between bilingual education and second- or foreign-language teaching programs. As we shall see, language-teaching programs in the twenty-first century increasingly integrate language and content, therefore coming to resemble bilingual education; and bilingual education programs are paying more attention than ever to explicit language instruction, therefore coming to resemble language-teaching programs. And although many second-language and foreign-language programs pay lip service to using only the target language in instruction, in reality bilingual ways of using languages (more on this below) are very often present in these programs – in the instructional material used, in the language use of the teacher, and certainly in the language use of the children. Moreover, sometimes in bilingual education programs one finds a language ideology that is very similar to that found in language-teaching programs, with teachers attempting to use only the target language in instruction: that is, no translation is provided and the teacher never uses both languages within the same lesson. But what continues to separate these two kinds of programs has to do with the broader general goal of bilingual education – the use of two languages to *educate generally, meaningfully, equitably, and for tolerance and appreciation of diversity*[5] – and the narrower goal of second- or foreign-language teaching – to learn an additional language. In educating broadly, bilingual education focuses not only on the acquisition of additional languages, but also on helping students to become global and responsible citizens as they learn to function across cultures and worlds, that is, beyond the cultural borders in which traditional schooling often operates. In educating equitably, bilingual education focuses on making schooling meaningful and

Table 1.1   Differences between Bilingual Education and Language Education

	Bilingual Education	*Foreign or Second-Language Education*
Overarching Goal	Educate meaningfully[6] and some type of bilingualism	Competence in additional language
Academic Goal	Educate bilingually and be able to function across cultures	Learn an additional language and become familiar with an additional culture
Language Use	Languages used as media of instruction	Additional language taught as subject
Instructional Use of Language	Uses some form of two or more languages	Uses target language mostly
Pedagogical Emphasis	Integration of language and content	Explicit language instruction

comprehensible for the millions of children whose home languages are different from the dominant language of school and society. This last aim is particularly relevant for the education of immigrants, refugees, Indigenous peoples throughout the world (for example, Tribal peoples in India and Bangladesh), autochthonous minorities, and many African and Asian children. The differences between bilingual education and language education programs are displayed in Table 1.1.

Even the widely accepted definition of bilingual education being the use of two languages in education is not straightforward. As Baker (2001: 4) points out, "the ownership of two languages is not so simple as having two wheels or two eyes." And being educated bilingually cannot be equated to being given two balanced wheels like those of a bicycle: bilingual education is not simply about *one language plus a second language equals two languages*. The vision of bilingual education as a sum of equals reduces bilingual education to the use of two or more separate languages, usually in different classroom spaces, time frames, contexts, or as spoken by different teachers. In this reductive view, bilingual education has been often interpreted as being the simple sum of discrete monolingual language practices. Separate and full competencies in each language are expected of students. Furthermore, these "idealized" bilingual education practices take little account of how languages are used in society, or of real bilingual and multilingual practices.

Throughout this book, we refer to the language ideologies that support language practices in bilingual education as being like the two balanced wheels of a bicycle, as "monoglossic." Monoglossic ideologies of bilingualism and bilingual education treat each of the child's languages as separate and whole, and view the two languages as bounded autonomous systems. We contrast this monoglossic language ideology to one based on Bakhtin's (1981) use of *heteroglossic* as multiple voices. A heteroglossic ideology of bilingualism considers multiple language practices in interrelationship, and leads to other constructions of bilingual education, which we consider in the next section.[7]

A new angle

In the twenty-first century, our complex multilingual and multimodal global communicative networks[8] often reflect much more than two separate monolingual
codes. More than a bicycle with two balanced wheels, bilingual education must
be more like a *moon buggy* or *all-terrain vehicle*, with different legs that extend
and contract in order to ground itself in the ridges and craters of the surface.
Communication among human beings, and especially of children among themselves
and with their teachers, is full of craters, ridges, and gaps. And when this communication occurs among children speaking different languages, or among children
speaking one language and the teacher speaking the other, these features are particularly salient. A bicycle just would not do for this terrain. And so, a bilingual
education that values only disconnected wholes and devalues the often loose parts,
and insists on the strict separation of languages is *not the only way* to successfully
educate children bilingually, although it is a widely conducted practice.

As will be seen in Part III of this book, there are many paths (and types of
programs) that lead to differentiated levels of bilingual practice and use. Bilingual
education that is adaptive, able to expand and contract, as the communicative
situations shift and as the terrain changes, is precisely what all children in the twenty-
first century need. What is important for bilingual education, then, may not always
be the full language parts in isolation, but the quality and the effectiveness of the
integrated sum. *One plus one does not always equal two.*

The complex networks in which children participate require us to have a different
vision than the linear and directional one embodied in the traditional sum.
Language practices are not unidirectional but polydirectional. We could compare
today's language practices to the South Asian banyan trees,[9] which grow up, out,
down, horizontally, or vertically through the air until they come upon something
solid. The language practices of bilinguals are interrelated and expand in different
directions to include the different communicative contexts in which they exist. The
varied bilingual practices in schools protect identities, communities, and relationships, much in the same way that the roots of banyan trees in, for example, the
doorway in the Ta Prohm Temple at Angkor Wat in Cambodia, help preserve
the structure.

Children do not enter school as cohorts with static and homogeneous language
uses. Their language practices cannot be added to in linear fashion, since the children
come and go into schools at different times, in different grades, having different
language resources. And they bring a variety of language practices to the classroom
that interact with the language practices of school, changing their own and those
of the schools. What is needed today are practices firmly rooted in the multilingual
and multimodal language and literacy practices of children in schools of the
twenty-first century, practices that would be informed by a vision starting from the
sum: an *integrated plural vision*.

Educating children bilingually enables language practices that, like the banyan
trees, build on each other in multiple ways and directions – up, out, down, across –
but yet rooted in the terrain and realities from which they emerge. Bilingual education, for us, is simply any instance in which children's and teachers' communicative

practices in school *normally include the use of multiple multilingual practices that maximize learning efficacy and communication*; and that, in so doing, *foster and develop tolerance towards linguistic differences, as well as appreciation of languages and bilingual proficiency.* Our definition, then, does not depart greatly from the ways in which others have defined bilingual education. Where we perhaps differ is in grounding bilingual education firmly on the language and literacy practices that we observe in schools, on what has become widely known as "bilingual encounters" (Martin, 2003), instead of on theoretical frameworks of how language ought to be and ought to function, frameworks that have little to do with actualizing the potential of children's intellect, imagination, and creativity. In other words, we aim to have bilingual education reconceptualized in response to the social interaction among students, teachers, and other members of the educational community, using two or more different languages, not merely as abstract language practices devoid of the complex social realities of multilingualism. These more complex understandings of languages and bilingualism, or, rather, of the way that people use languages, are the topic of Part II of this book. And this reconceptualization also has important implications for curriculum, pedagogy, and assessment in bilingual education, the subject of Part IV of this book.

Reimagining

Bilingual education in the twenty-first century must be reimagined and expanded, as it takes its rightful place as a meaningful way to educate *all* children and language learners in the world today. In this book we have chosen to use "bilingual education," rather than "multilingual education," as the umbrella term to cover a wide spectrum of practice and policy. Bilingual education, as we shall see in future chapters, takes on many different forms, and increasingly, in the complexity of the modern world, includes forms where two or more languages are separated for instruction, but also forms where two or more languages are used together in complex combinations. All of these are, to us, instances of bilingual education. For the sake of brevity, and for continuity with past practice, we have decided to both reimagine and extend the term, and show "the entire beast as a multisplendored thing" (Fishman, 1976: p. x). Our use of "bilingual education" encompasses what many have referred to as "multilingual education" (see, for example, Cenoz and Genesee, 1998; García, Skutnabb-Kangas, and Torres-Guzmán, 2006). The European Commission also uses the term "multilingual education" to refer to its policy of "mother tongue plus two other languages for all" (European Commission, 2003). UNESCO adopted the term "multilingual education" in 1999 in the General Conference Resolution 12 to refer to the use in education of at least three languages: the mother tongue, a regional or national language, and an international language (UNESCO, 2003). Our use of the term "bilingual education" also includes these instances of *trilingual* and *multilingual education.* Bilingual education is here used to refer to education using more than one language, and/or language varieties, in whatever combination.

In today's globalized world, bilingual education is at times criticized, on the one hand, because it is seen as maintaining separate linguistic enclaves, and, on the other, because it does not accommodate the linguistic heterogeneity of the times. For example, in the United States bilingual education is often blamed, first, for the ghettoization[10] of U.S. Latino[11] students in segregated classrooms, and, second, for the lack of attention paid in these programs to ethnolinguistic minorities other than Latinos. But although U.S. Latinos are often educated in segregated classrooms, these arrangements have much more to do with residential and social class segregation than with bilingual education per se. And although it is important to pay attention to *all* children with different ethnolinguistic profiles, it is Latino children who are often most in need of bilingual education programs in the U.S., for they constitute the greatest proportion of English-language learners in the country (approximately 75 to 79 percent), and yet receive but scant attention. Besides, as we will see in Chapter 8, there are bilingual education programs in the United States in many languages besides Spanish and English.

Bilingual education is also often blamed because nations and states[12] seeking legitimacy in the twentieth century have often claimed an immutable relationship between language and identity, using bilingual education as a means to strengthen that link (Heller, 1999). For example, referring to some of the nations of Spain, such as Galicia and Catalonia, Del Valle and Gabriele-Stheeman (2002) explain that, as nation-states had done since the Enlightenment, the Spanish entities that achieved some autonomy following the end of the dictatorship of Francisco Franco based their language-in-education policy on an ideology that linked their identity and language strictly and unidirectionally.

Although all these criticisms are taken on board, they do not constitute reasons for abandoning the many practices associated with bilingual education, but are rather arguments for expanding them. In fact, now more than ever, the world recognizes the importance of bilingual education; although it chooses, many times, to call it by other names, as we will see in Part III of this book.

In the United States, the growth of immigration and migration, especially of Spanish speakers, has unleashed a reaction against bilingual education, leading to the substitution of the term "bilingual" by the term "English language acquisition."[13] The states of California, Arizona, and Massachusetts have declared bilingual education illegal. And the term "bilingual education" is often attached only to programs for recently arrived immigrants that are *transitional* in nature, and not to programs that include speakers of English and where two languages are used throughout the child's education. In fact, these two-way bilingual education programs in the United States are now called, in many instances, *dual language education*, again silencing the word "bilingual."

Within the European Union, bilingual education is being promoted under the banner of CLIL/EMILE, acronyms which refer to "Content and Language Integrated Learning/*Enseignement d'une Matière par l'Intégration d'une Langue Etrangère*" (CLIL/EMILE, 2002). The choice of CLIL/EMILE responds to the fact that the term "bilingual education" is politically loaded for certain European countries, even though these are bilingual programs that use more than one language in instruction.[14]

In Canada, the persistent voices of First Nations peoples, and their efforts to revitalize and maintain their languages, continue to challenge the limitation of bilingual education only to the languages of power: English and French (see, for example, Heller, 1999, for Canada). And the recognition of the multilingualism of many countries in Africa and Asia in particular has also served to question the viability of bilingual education in only two languages in a more complex socio-linguistic order.

Throughout the world, bilingual education practices are becoming more popular than ever, and we use the term "bilingual education" because it enables us to link to the research, scholarship, policy, and practice of the last fifty years. We also use it because bilingual education is centered in schools[15] where curriculum and assessment are mostly linear, inducing educators to think of language acquisition in similar ways. Thus, usually children are initially schooled bilingually, that is, in two languages, even when the intent is to develop proficiency in more than two languages, or even when many more than two separate languages are used in instruction. There is much scholarship on bilingual pedagogy, bilingual curriculum, and bilingual assessment, and "multilingual" only refers to its multiplicity. Programs that educate teachers to use more than one language in instruction are also most often referred to as bilingual education programs. Another reason for using the term "bilingual education" is that it remains appropriate, as we will see in future chapters, for ethnolinguistic groups who live in bilingual contexts where two languages predominate, or for whom the use of two languages in schooling seems sufficient.

In sum, although we recognize that in some instances bilingual education is simply not enough, we prefer the term "bilingual education" here because it is more grounded in theory, research, practice, and reality than "multilingual education." We also think that it is easier to understand the complexity of bilingual education if we start with a discussion of two languages, and then extend these notions when considering more multilingual possibilities. In what follows we briefly consider the reasons for bilingual education, which will be expanded upon in Chapter 5.

Beneficiaries and Reasons

Beneficiaries

The overarching principle of this book is that some form of bilingual education is *good for all education, and therefore good for all children, as well as good for all adult learners.* This is a principle that we have always held; one that was well established by Fishman (1976). Bilingual education is good for all – language majorities, that is, powerful ethnolinguistic groups, as well as language minorities, those without power. An education that is bilingual is good for the rich and the poor, for the powerful and the lowly, for Indigenous peoples and immigrants, for speakers of official and/or national languages, and for those who speak regional languages. Bilingual education is not only good for children in gifted and talented programs, but also good for children in vocational and technical education, as well as for those in special education. It is important for hearing children, as well as Deaf children. Bilingual education is also good for adults in lifelong language-learning situations, since bilingual individuals enjoy cognitive and social advantages over monolinguals (see Chapter 5). As Fishman (1978b: 47) has said: "In a multilingual world it is obviously more efficient and rational to be multilingual than not, and that truism increasingly applies to the whales, as well as the minnows."

Although the state and particular ethnolinguistic groups might benefit collectively from bilingual education,[16] the value of bilingual education is in what it offers children, youths and adults in general. Bilingual education has the potential of being a *transformative* school practice, able to educate all children in ways that stimulate and expand their intellect and imagination, as they gain ways of expression and access different ways of being in the world. Speaking specifically about the potential of bilingual education for the United States, Fishman (1978b: 1) states: "Bilingual education is a celebration of liberation from provincialism for those who know only English and liberation from self-doubt for those who haven't yet learned English."

Reasons

It has been long recognized that schools play a key role in social and cultural reproduction (Apple, 1982). The French sociologist Pierre Bourdieu (1991) has linked education to reproduction of the social order. Bourdieu proposes that we view education as capital, an asset of quantifiable value. At schools, students acquire *cultural capital*, that is, knowledge, abilities, and strategies related to the presentation of self; as well as *symbolic capital* having to do with respectability and worthiness. Also valuable is *linguistic capital*, the ability to use appropriate norms of language. Being able to use languages effectively, Bourdieu argues, increases one's "wealth" because it allows one to interact with others in various social contexts. In a sense, knowing how to use a language is a way of gaining cultural and symbolic capital. By using a language effectively, one can gather information and build self-worth through social interactions. Bourdieu believes that the ability of students to build linguistic capital is dependent mostly on the education they receive, and thus schools play a major role in regulating language as capital and mediating access to it.

Monolingual education has at times been used as a way to limit access and legitimate the linguistic practices of those already in power. Bilingual education has *the potential* to give access to languages of power.[17] And bilingual education can also legitimize language practices in a minoritized language, giving authenticity to the bilingual practices of many. As such, bilingual education can be *transformative*. As Lewis says (1978: 20, our italics): "Bilingual education has been advocated for entirely pedagogical reasons, while the fundamental rationale for the proposal is to bring about *greater political, economic, and social equality* [. . . A]ll forms of education are concerned with the redistribution of power or the maintenance of its current distribution." As we will see throughout this book, bilingual education can bring about greater social equality. The tensions surrounding bilingual education often have to do with dominant groups protecting their power.

Before we start critically examining our views of languages, bilingualism, and bilingual education in Part II of this book, it is important to consider how geopolitical and sociohistorical forces have shaped *the study* of bilingual education. We offer here a general historical perspective of how the field of bilingual education has evolved. But geopolitical forces affect states or social groups differently, so bilingual education options co-exist in the twenty-first century, as we will further consider in Part III of this book.

Geopolitics and Language Orientations

In the beginning . . . enrichment

The use of two languages in education is not new. Mackey (1978: 2–3) describes how the 16,000 tablets unearthed in Aleppo, Syria, in 1977, indicated that bilingual schooling is at least 4,000 to 5,000 years old. The tablets were used to teach children to read and write in Eblaite (a language closely related to Akkadian, spoken in Ancient Mesopotamia and written in cuneiform script[18]) and Sumerian, which by then was a classical sacred language.

After the people of the Mediterranean port of Ugarit developed a sequential alphabetic form of writing around 1500 BC, bilingual education spread throughout the ancient world. In the East, this sequential alphabet became the Aramaic alphabet which brought about the Persian, Indian, Arabic, and Hebrew scripts. In the West, it became the Greek alphabet, which gave rise to the modern Roman and Cyrillic alphabets (Mackey, 1978). E. Glyn Lewis (1977) has shown how in the West, from the second century onward, Greek–Latin bilingual education was the way to educate boys from Roman aristocratic homes, who were expected to learn the language of the admired Hellenic civilization. Bilingualism was seen as a form of enrichment.

Many schools have always practiced some form of bilingual education. It has always been common, for example, for the school text to be written in a language or a register different from that spoken by the school children. Translation of classical texts into vernaculars, one form of bilingual education, has always been central to the notion of schooling. And the reading of sacred texts in one language, with the study of commentaries written in another language, and discussion in yet another language, has also been a traditional way of schooling many ethnolinguistic groups. It has also been common for teachers, whether bilingual themselves or not, to teach in a language other than the one the children speak with each other. The purpose of schooling, and the bilingual practices observed, has been often related to the oscillation between the language practices of the home and community and those of the sacred and classical texts studied in school.

Bilingual education has come into its own especially since the second half of the twentieth century, as schools have acknowledged the linguistic heterogeneity of children. But positionings and ideologies towards bilingualism in school have shifted in different contexts even at the same historical juncture. Ruiz (1984) has offered a framework with which to examine different language orientations: 1) language as a problem, 2) language as a right, and 3) language as a resource. We use the lens of language orientations to discuss the geopolitical forces that have promoted one or another perspective on bilingualism, and, therefore, on bilingual education (for a summary, see Table 1.2 below).

As a problem

It is important to situate the emergence in the twentieth century of bilingual education for the masses as a result of *modernist development ideological frameworks* that imagined, constructed, and narrated a "nation-state" into being in one language,[19] and thus considered bilingualism to be a problem. Rooted in structural-functionalist concepts, modernization theory posits that the development of an independent, modern nation-state calls for urbanization, secularization, and the citizens' transformation from a traditional to a modern disposition (Peet, 1999; Tsai, 2005). As a result of industrial and urban developments in the nineteenth century, languages became "modern;" that is, languages which symbolized national identity were standardized, codified, and used in schools, to the exclusion of others.

Especially after World War I and II, nations within the constructed "nation-state," whose languages did not coincide with the one elevated to privileged status, became cause for concern. This was the case, for example, of Latvians in the former Soviet Union who were forced to learn Russian and to give up Latvian; the nations and their languages were viewed as a problem. Bilingual education became an instrument, in some cases, of improving the teaching of the language chosen for modernization, and, in others, of linguistically assimilating all people.

At the same time, in 1953, UNESCO, responding to the educational failure of children in colonial situations, issued an important resolution declaring that it was axiomatic that a child be taught to read in their home language. The resolution stated:

> On educational grounds we recommend that the use of the mother tongue be extended to as late a stage in education as possible. In particular, pupils should begin their schooling through the medium of the mother tongue, because they understand it best and because to begin their school life in the mother tongue will make the break between home and school as small as possible.

Based on this principle, efforts to use the children's language in education, especially in the early grades, gained strength, leading to the first official uses of what has since been termed "transitional bilingual education," that is, the use of the child's heritage language in the early grades and *only* until the child is fluent in the majority or colonial language. Despite the transitional and temporary aspects of this type of bilingual education, transitional bilingual education opened the door for schooling the masses, providing for the use of local languages, in addition to the other language, at times a colonial one, in the education of the young. Bilingual education was recognized around the world as being capable to do for the masses, and their children, what it had so well done for the elite – ensuring the acquisition of the languages of power through schooling while educating. But the potential of bilingual education for all children did not fully materialize because language difference, in this modernist conceptualization, was seen as a problem.

As a right

The worldwide economic downturn of the 1970s, and the ensuing widening of social inequities, led to an acknowledgment that modernization had failed and that decolonization did not necessarily translate into self-determination or sovereignty (Pepper, 1996; Tsai, 2005). The ability of a state's bilingual education policies to transform citizens and societies, espoused by theories of modernization, was called into question (Fagerlind and Saha, 1989). The role of sociohistorical processes in shaping particular forms of bilingual education, and in particular the role of class, ethnicity, race, language, and gender in such shaping, was given increased atten- tion (Skutnabb-Kangas and Phillipson, 1994; Tollefson, 1991, 2002; Wiley, 1996b, 1999; Wright, 2004). Some forms of bilingual education, especially transitional bilingual education, were increasingly criticized, as language minorities claimed their language rights and developed their own forms of bilingual schooling. Language minorities who had lost their home languages developed bilingual educa- tion programs that supported the revitalization of these languages. Other language minorities who felt threatened linguistically were able to set up programs to develop their home languages. In differentiating what came earlier from the way in which language-in-education policies were increasingly *critically* conceived, Ricento (2000: 208, our italics) says: "It seems that the key variable which separ- ates the older, positivistic/technicist approaches from the newer critical/postmodern ones is *agency*, that is, the role(s) of individuals and collectivities in the processes of language use, attitudes, and ultimately policies." Language difference was seen more and more as a right which had to be negotiated (Skutnabb-Kangas, 2000), and language minorities started gaining agency in shaping their own language policies and practices in the education of their children.

As a resource[20]

The end of the Cold War, the development of globalization, and the growing role of international organizations, have accelerated the movement of peoples and have challenged the sovereignty of states in the twenty-first century. With the increasing awareness of other languages, and the dominance, especially, of English, but also of Chinese, Spanish, and Arabic throughout the world (Graddol, 2006), bilingual education has taken yet another turn, now growing often without the direct inter- vention of the state, and including forms that respond to a much more dynamic language use.

In supporting bilingual or multilingual education for all children in the world, UNESCO (2003: 17–18) emphasized the importance of both the global and the national and declared:

> the requirements of *global and national* participation, and the specific needs of particular, culturally and linguistically distinct communities can only be addressed by multilingual education. In regions where the language of the learner is not the official or national language of the country, bilingual and multilingual education can make mother tongue instruction possible while providing at the same time the acquisition of languages used in larger areas of the country and the world (our italics).

UNESCO also proposes (2003: 30) three basic guiding principles, no longer simply focused on the mother tongue as it was in 1953, but on intercultural multilingual education as a resource for all:

1. *Mother tongue instruction* as a means of improving educational quality by building upon the knowledge and experience of the learners and teachers;
2. *Bilingual and/or multilingual education* at all levels of education as a means of promoting both social and gender equality and as a key element of linguistically diverse societies;
3. Language as an essential component *of inter-cultural education* in order to encourage understanding between different population groups and ensure respect for fundamental rights.

Bilingual education is increasingly seen as a means through which children and youth can interact within their own ethnolinguistic community, as well as with others. This lens of complex linguistic interactions has been termed "linguistic ecology" (Haugen, 1972; Mühlhäusler, 1996).[21] The challenge of bilingual schools in the twenty-first century is to prepare children to balance their own linguistic ecology (Fettes, 2003), enabling them to go freely back and forth in their overlapping languages and literacies. Mühlhäusler's "ecological approach" (2000, 2002) calls for "a situation of equilibrium whereby languages automatically readjust themselves to fit into the environment, and perpetuate themselves through language contact, rather than isolation" (quoted in Tsai, 2005: 11). Children and educators have to be made aware of their ability to "self-regulate," as languages take on complementary and overlapping roles in different domains of communication (Mühlhäusler, 2000, 2002), but without external language management by the state or even the school itself. Fettes has shown how today's linguistic "geostrategies" which he defines as strategies designed to ensure the co-existence of particular languages or language types (2003: 44) are different from the "politico-strategies" of the twentieth century, in which one language was imposed on others in the state. This ecological approach to bilingualism has very different consequences for bilingual education. We will expand on this in Parts II and III of this book.

One of the biggest changes in the globalized community of the twenty-first century is the blurring of territory that was clearly demarcated by language and culture. Although many territories had only given the appearance of being homogeneous, they provided a context, even if imagined, to enforce monolingual schooling. In the twenty-first century, however, we are aware of the linguistic complexity of the world in which monolingual schooling seems utterly inappropriate. Language differences are seen as a resource, and bilingual education, in all its complexity and forms, seems to be the only way to educate as the world moves forward.

Summary

Table 1.2 provides an overview of the geopolitical changes that have occurred since the end of World War II and their impact on theoretical perspectives for studying language use, as well as language orientations.

Table 1.2   Sociohistorical and Sociolinguistic Orientations and Bilingualism[22]

Stages	*Stage I: The End of WWII until the early 1970s*	*Stage II: The 1970s–1980s*	*Stage III: The mid-1980s to present*
Geopolitical Climate	Independence of Asia and African countries	Economic downturn and widening of social inequalities	Globalization; end of Cold War; growth of NGOs; technological advances
Theoretical Perspective	Structural-functionalist	Critical	Ecological
Language Orientations	Language diversity as problem	Language diversity as right	Language diversity as resource

Conclusion

It is the goal of this book to show how the theories and practices of bilingual education, and the underpinnings that inform it, have grown and developed. From a monoglossic view of bilingual education as a bicycle with two balanced wheels, we propose a bilingual education that is more like an all-terrain vehicle in its heteroglossic possibilities. This book tells the story of that development.

It is also the purpose of this book to offer a critical reading of the current conversations (or lack of them) around bilingual education and multilingualism, and to imagine and construct a paradigm of bilingualism that is not always linear and that reflects the linguistic fluidity present in the discourse of the twenty-first century (this concept will receive more attention in Chapter 3).

In this chapter we distinguished stages which roughly correspond to the three orientations of language-in-education planning that Ruiz (1984) has identified – language as problem, language as right, and language as resource. But we demonstrated how the three conceptions and the different kinds of bilingual education types that reflect these orientations *co-exist* in the twenty-first century, depending on the wishes of peoples and societies, as well as their histories and needs.

It is precisely because (depending on the angle from which we look) bilingual education is seen as a problem, as a right, or as a resource, that we have decided to refer to the enterprise as bilingual education. Adopting more complex, more fluid terms to refer to the educational enterprise that we study here under the rubric of bilingual education would fail to acknowledge different societal realities. We believe that monolingual education is no longer adequate in the twenty-first century, and that every society needs *some* form of bilingual education. Our view of bilingual education is complex, like the banyan tree, allowing for growth in different directions at the same time and grounded in the diverse social realities from which it emerges. Just as bilingualism gives speakers choice, bilingual education gives school systems more choice, for there are many alternatives. Before we turn to the education element of bilingual education in Parts III and IV, we pay some attention to the language and bilingual elements in Part II of this book.

Parts II, III, and IV are interrelated. Part II examines languages and bilingualism as individual and societal phenomena, within a sociocultural framework that pays attention to how bilingualism develops in different social and cultural contexts. Part III presents program types and variables in bilingual education, as well as policies that are related to the different understandings of bilingualism developed in Part II. Finally, Part IV looks at practices, especially language arrangement, pedagogies, and assessments, which are related to the different understandings held by individuals, communities, and states about bilingualism and bilingual education.

Although Part IV will be more pertinent for classroom teachers, Part III for school systems and societies, and Part II for scholars of bilingualism, it would be useful to read all parts in sequence. Understanding the nature and purpose of language and bilingualism, and the bilingual education options available, is important in order to develop adequate pedagogies and practices.

Questions for Reflection

1. What is bilingual education? How does it differ from language education?
2. Explain the difference between the bicycle and the all-terrain vehicle in thinking about bilingualism.
3. What is the relevance of the image of the banyan tree to this treatment of bilingual education?
4. What are some of the reasons why the term "bilingual education" has become contested, and why have we adopted it in this book?
5. What are some possible benefits of bilingual education? Who are the potential beneficiaries?
6. What is the difference in viewing language as a problem, as a right, and as a resource, and how has this impacted on the development of bilingual education?

Further Reading

Baker, C. (2006). *Foundations of Bilingual Education and Bilingualism*. Multilingual Matters, Clevedon, UK. Fourth edn.

Baker, C., and Prys Jones, S. (1998). *Encyclopedia of Bilingualism and Bilingual Education*. Multilingual Matters, Clevedon, UK.

García, O., and Baker, C. (eds.) (2007). *Bilingual Education: An Introductory Reader*. Multilingual Matters, Clevedon, UK.

Part II
Bilingualism and Education

2
Languaging and Education

A Child's Language Use: A Scenario

Follow 14-year-old Tatyana as the computer is turned on. The web-based program Tatyana uses has a drop-down menu making it possible to switch between the Ukrainian in which her schooling is conducted, the Russian her father speaks to her, and the French she wants to learn. And when the computer's microphone is turned on, Tatyana avidly listens to the different voices of the many games that are available, in Ukrainian, Russian, French, English, or any other language she fancies. Watch the screen as the child sends messages back and forth, with multiple signs, words, and visuals combining to communicate effectively with the many participants on the other end, sometimes nearby, but many other times far away.

Now listen to Tatyana as she speaks to her other teenage sisters. The Ukrainian she uses is very different from that which she speaks with her mother or the Russian which she speaks to her father. The language she hears on television and radio depends on who in the home is holding the remote control. Different channels often bring other languages, other varieties, as the characters change from professional to working-class, from rich to poor, from adults to children, and as programs originate in different geographical areas for specific populations.

Now enter Tatyana's school, but stop at the playground. There you see children of the same language-background interacting, sometimes going back and forth from language practices of play and friendship to those of schoolwork. Other times, children of different language backgrounds are together – playing, talking, engaging in language practices as they relate to their peers.

Then walk into a classroom. Tatyana, who was chatting comfortably with many friends in the playground, is now sitting quietly at a desk. Sometimes, the teacher calls for group work and Tatyana is asked to complete a task with classmates. But the task is directed, the language is controlled, and only "accountable talk"[1] on the subject of the lesson and in the standard language of instruction at the particular time is allowed by the teacher.

If Tatyana is lucky, she is in a bilingual classroom, but even there she's not allowed to use her multiple language practices to complete school tasks, to communicate with others, to think clearly, to show the understandings acquired, the knowledge internalized. The teacher carefully controls the language that is to be used during instruction. Assessment is done only using paper and pencil tasks, and often just in the dominant school language. Even when technology supports assessment, the academic tasks usually require only written language, devoid of sounds, of visuals, of other signs and language practices that may be in the child's linguistic repertoire.

The teacher's talk is often very different from that of the children. And the discourse used in the classroom is very different from the authentic, multiple communication that takes place in the children's home and in informal settings. Even teachers who pride themselves on using an innovative pedagogy fall prey at times to the Initiation–Response–Feedback (IRF) sequence (also referred to as IRE: Initiation–Response–Evaluation) that has been identified in the literature (Cazden, 1988; Sinclair & Coulthard, 1975) as common in classroom discourse, with the teacher questioning, the student responding, and the teacher evaluating and giving feedback.

Overview

In this chapter, we will discuss:

- language constructions;
- languaging in different contexts.

Introduction

Before we examine the concept of bilingualism that underlies all understandings of bilingual education in Chapters 3 and 4, it is important to think about language itself, because language is both the *medium* through which school subjects are taught and is also an important *subject* studied in school. Bilingual education often involves educating in languages of unequal positions and power, so it is important first to discuss how certain languages have come to have the powerful role that they have today.

Educators and scholars of bilingual education also need to be aware of the purposes for the imposition of certain language codes, and especially the standard academic language. Juxtaposing these notions with the fluid ways in which languages are used in the twenty-first century, what we will here call "languaging," allows us to understand the changes that we must make conceptually in our thinking about language to support the children's language practices in classrooms.

In this chapter, we focus on the complex role that bilingual schools play regarding language. Whereas all schools, even monolingual ones, must negotiate the standard language that they use and promote, and the intricate language practices of students, it is in bilingual schools that this complexity comes to the fore. In bilingual schools the heterogeneity of language practices involving two or more languages is much more intricate than the two standard languages in isolation that schools use and promote. It is precisely this tension between the heteroglossic language practices of emergent bilingual[2] and bilingual students, and the standard language promoted in school, that makes bilingual education such a fertile ground for thinking about language. It is the task of any bilingual school to build on this tension, as it acknowledges and utilizes the child's complex linguistic practices to ensure that the use of two or more standard languages are incorporated into the child's linguistic repertoire.

Language Constructions

Constructing language

Makoni and Pennycook (2007) have proposed that our present conception of language was originally constructed by states that wanted to consolidate political power, and in so doing established language academies, encouraged the preparation of grammars, dictionaries, and treatises to strengthen and standardize languages, and encouraged the enumeration of languages in ways that masked their differences or similarities.[3] With regard to language academies, among the first was the Accademia della Crusca, founded in Florence in 1572 to uphold the Tuscan dialect of Dante and Petrarch. In 1635 Cardinal Richelieu founded the Académie Française to promote clarity, simplicity, and good taste in French. And in 1713, the Real Academia Española was established in Spain with its motto of "*limpia, fija y da esplendor*" (cleans, stabilizes, and gives splendor), championing Spanish (Castilian[4]) and keeping it uncontaminated. Throughout the eighteenth century, other language academies flourished in Europe, and Arabic bodies were established in several countries, including Syria, Iraq, Egypt, and Jordan. Academies in Damascus, Cairo, Baghdad, Amman and Rabat all work for their own interest in the standardization and spread of Arabic (Laroussi, 2003). Official and semi-official agencies in multilingual African and Asian countries are concerned with both language purification, as well as language selection. In Malaysia, Indonesia, and Singapore, where Malay is used, *The Handbook for the Formation of Technical Terms* was agreed upon in 1975.

In contrast to these efforts to control language, there has never been an official English language academy. The major repository for standard English is in dictionaries, though there have been many individual guidebooks on usage (one of the more famous being *Fowler's Modern English Usage* [1968, revised by Sir Ernest

Gowers, Oxford, Oxford University Press]). In 1755, Samuel Johnson published his great dictionary, stabilizing English, but rejecting what he called linguistic "embalming." In the United States, Noah Webster published his dictionary in 1827, removing "improprieties and vulgarisms," but staying away from prescription.

That the construction of language, as we know it today, is tied to political control is evident, for example, in the case of Spanish. The year of the encounter between the Old and the New World, 1492, is also the year of the conquest of the last Arab kingdom of the Iberian Peninsula in Granada and of the expulsion of Jews by the Catholic monarchs; it is also the year of publication of Elio Antonio de Nebrija's grammar, the first grammar of a modern European language. Nebrija's work explicitly links the standardization of language, through a grammar, to the consolidation of political power, as it claims: "*siempre la lengua fue compañera del imperio*" (language was always the companion of empire).

The social construction of language was not simply limited to Europe. In Korea, for example, King Sejong invented Hangul, the phonemic alphabet organized into syllabic blocks in the fifteenth century. Hangul replaced the Chinese characters that had been used.

In the case of colonized populations, "constructed" state languages were then "administratively assigned" to them (Makoni and Pennycook, 2007). Beyond states, there were missionaries and colonial officers who evangelized, converted, controlled, and administered colonized populations. Errington (2001) has shown how missionaries and colonial officers imposed these "invented" monolithic languages onto specific territories. For example, Batibo (2005) describes how the rivalry between two missionary organizations led to separate orthographies for two languages in Cameroon – Ewondo and Bulu – which are mutually intelligible. The same happened when missionaries developed different signing systems for schools for the Deaf in the African context (Miles, 2005).

Mühlhäusler (2000: 38) has said that the "notion of 'a language' makes little sense in most traditional societies where people engage in multiple discursive practices among themselves." Mühlhäusler (1996: 5) explains that "the identification of languages and their subsequent naming is far from being an act of objective description." And speaking of the Pacific region, he continues: "The notion of 'a language' is one whose applicability to the Pacific region, and in fact most situations outside those found within modern European nation-states, is extremely limited" (1996: 7). Romaine concurs with Mühlhäusler when describing the complex language use in Papua New Guinea; she says (1994: 12): "the very concept of discrete languages is probably a European cultural artifact fostered by procedures such as literacy and standardization. Any attempt to count distinct languages will be an artifact of classificatory procedures rather than a reflection of communicative practices." Regarding Africa, Samarin (1996) has referred to it as "a continent without languages." In general, languages have been constituted separately "outside and above human beings" (Yngve 1996: 28) and have little relationship to the ways in which people use language, their discursive practices, or what Yngve also calls their "languaging." Languaging, as Shohamy (2006b) says, refers to language practices of people.

Languages are socially constructed – this is the reason why there is no consensus on the number of languages in the world. According to *Ethnologue*, collected by

SIL International, a Christian-faith-based language-preservation society, there are 40,000 names for different languages, although the society counts close to 7,000 languages (Grimes, 2000). *Ethnologue* (Gordon, 2005: no pag.) again notes that "the definition of language one chooses depends on the purpose one has in identifying a language."

Language is truly a social notion that cannot be defined without reference to its speakers and the context in which it is used (Heller, 2007). It is also true, however, that language is a psychological and grammatical notion. For example, the mental grammars of person A and person B may be more similar to the grammars of person A and person C, although whether A and B end up speaking the same language is a sociopolitical decision. It is important then to recognize that, despite the fact that language has a psychological and linguistic component, it is the social context in which it is used, and the wishes and power of its speakers, that determines its role – especially in schools.

The state

It is common practice to associate a state with a single language. For example, it is generally thought that French is spoken in France whereas Spanish is used in Spain; and that Danish Sign Language is used in Denmark, whereas Costa Rican Sign Language is used in Costa Rica. However, with multilingualism being the norm in many countries, such an association has been called into question. Since the publication of Anderson's influential *Imagined Communities* (1983), it has been widely accepted that nation-states were imagined and narrated into being. A nation-state is a mental construct made up of affinities such as language with imagined people. Anderson (1983: 15) explains that these nation-states are imagined communities because "the members of even the smallest nation will never know most of their fellow members, meet them or even hear of them, yet in the mind of each lives the image of their communion." But although these nation-states unite "imagined" communities, they often divide "real" communities that share language and culture. Perhaps the most obvious example here is that of African nations. At the Berlin Conference of 1885, political boundaries were drawn at right angles to the coastline, and neither linguistic areas nor former kingdoms were considered.

That nation-states are constructed is confirmed by the fact that in the beginning of the twentieth century there were only sixty sovereign states. At the end of World War II there were seventy-four states; today there are approximately 200, with the number changing frequently. The constructions continue.

The linguistic consequences of the construction of nation-states have been great. Few states have ever been monolingual in their makeup, and even today there are very few countries in the world that can be considered linguistically homogeneous (see Lewis, 1981). Iceland and possibly Korea are probably the only clear-cut cases where the entire autochthonous population uses one and the same language for the majority of its social interaction. The rest of the world, whether countries in the Americas, Africa, Asia, Europe, or Oceania, and without taking into account recent immigration patterns, have almost never been inhabited by people who share one common language. And yet, the predominant ideology tends to associate monolingualism with the norm, whereby the dominance of one language within the borders of a political entity is considered as more natural, more desirable, more efficient, and more productive for the sake of cohesion than reality warrants.

In 1967, Mackey wrote that "bilingualism, far from being exceptional, is a *problem* which affects the majority of the world population" (11; our italics; an unfortunate way of presenting the issues involved). In the early 1980s Grosjean (1982: vii) estimated that at least half the world's population was bilingual, since there were thirty times as many languages as there were countries. In 2000, Grimes listed 6,809 languages in over 200 countries.

Mackey (2003) has pointed out that, in the past, a language used to be the property of its users, indicated by the name itself; for example, *lingua anglica, lingua romana rustica*. But with the rise of the state, language became associated with the land in which it was spoken. Less than 25 percent of the world's 200 or so countries recognize two or more official languages (Tucker, 1998). This has important consequences for education, since it turns out that although there are more bilingual and multilingual individuals in the world than monolinguals, and more languages than states, the fact that education takes place in the *de jure* or *de facto*[5] official language means that most children in the world are educated in a language other than that of the home. Although nation-states may have been mental and imagined constructs, its consequences are not imaginary for minoritized language communities within it.

Today, as we discuss further in the next section, globalization and the mobility of populations has made us conscious of the fact that specific languages do not belong to territories or states. Rather, languages belong to the people who speak them, who are in different geographical spaces. But this creates challenges to political states that organize educational systems and that increasingly have to educate children who do not speak the school language at home.

Globalization

The norms in the organization of work and methods of production brought about by new communication technology and globalization have greatly impacted languaging practices in the twenty-first century (Maurais and Morris, 2003; New London Group, 2000). Fettes (2003: 37) summarizes the geopolitical and technology changes and their effect on language communities:

> National economies have become far more integrated in the global economy; money and workers have become much more mobile; the pace of technological change has accelerated to an unbelievable extent; and the explosive growth of communication and information networks is on the verge of "annihilating space." Increasingly, every language community must become aware of its position in a "dynamic world system of languages" characterized by vast and expanding differences in status and use.

In the twenty-first century, we have witnessed the creation of new economic trading blocs and new socioeconomic and sociopolitical organizations that have affected how language is used – for example, the European Union, Mercosur (South American Common Market or Mercado del Sur, see Hamel, 2003), the North American Free Trade Area and the World Trade Organization, and the controls exercised by the International Monetary Fund and the World Bank. The European Union, a transnational democracy, is poised to replace old models of democracy in the nation-state. There has been a redrawing of political states along ethnic and linguistic lines in Eastern Europe. The linguistic diversity of Africa, Asia, and even Latin America has become well recognized.[6]

These sociopolitical and socioeconomic changes have also resulted in dramatic population shifts. For example, between 1960 and 2000, the total number of international migrants doubled to 175 million, representing nearly 3 percent of the world's population (Graddol, 2006: 28). And this immigration is characterized by *transnationalism*; that is, the ability to go back and forth to the country of origin, aided by improved transportation and technology (Castles, 2000). Migrant workers and immigrants are not the only ones who move back and forth. Refugees and asylum seekers, business and expatriate workers, international students, and even tourists, all contribute to population movement making bilingualism important in the twenty-first century. At present, there are 32.8 million refugees and internally displaced persons, the result of conflicts over scarce resources and marginalization. Tourism accounted for 763 million international travelers in 2004, and three quarters of those tourists were from non-English speaking countries traveling to countries where English was not spoken (Graddol, 2006: 29). It has been estimated that between 2 and 3 million students travel to another country to study each year. The United States and the United Kingdom account for over a third of all international students in the world (Graddol, 2006: 76), but increasingly there are other countries involved. China, for example, receives students from Korea and Japan. All these population movements bring about changes in language use, and amplify the presence of bilingualism, as people need to communicate or access information outside their primary language group.

Inexpensive communication technology in this globalized world has also made possible the outsourcing of services to countries with cheaper labor costs, with bilingualism as an important resource. Voice over Internet Protocol (VOIP), available to consumers at no cost, and mobile phones with their capacity for Short Text Messages (SMS or Short Message Service), make it possible for many more people to communicate across national borders, not only in different languages, but using different *modalities*, with language bound up with visual, audio, and spatial semiotic systems. The ability to download multimedia files through podcasting is enabling many to share their own languages, and others to learn them on their own without the help of schools or other intermediaries.

The internet has also increased our contact with other languages and bilingualism. Although English continues to be used most often on the web (68% in 2000, according to Catalan ISP VilaWeb [cited in Graddol, 2006: 44]), this figure is declining. Table 2.1 displays the top ten languages used in the web; that is, the number of internet users by language:

Table 2.1   Internet World Users by Language

Language	Millions of Users	% Represented
English	427	30%
Chinese	233	17%
Spanish	122	9%
Japanese	94	7%
French	67	5%
German	63	4%
Arabic	60	4%
Portuguese	58	4%
Korean	35	2%
Italian	34	2%
Rest of languages	213	15%

Miniwatts Marketing Group, 2008

Between 2000 and 2008, the greatest language growth on the internet was experienced by Arabic (2,062%), followed by Portuguese (668%), Chinese (622%), and then French (452%). English experienced only a 201 percent growth in the last decade (Miniwatts Marketing Group, 2008). According to an analysis made in Ireland about the demand and supply of foreign language skills in the enterprise sector (Expert Group on Future Skills Needs, 2005), approximately 50 percent of users worldwide choose a language other than English to access the Google web-search utility (based on data sourced from Google Inc.; www.google.com/press/zeitgeist.html, August 2004). And new software has made the availability of different scripts easier. Many websites are using multilingual strategies, allowing consumers and users to access information in the language they prefer. Machine translation is readily available. There are even websites that allow internet users to communicate with each other in sign languages. And Internet programs such as Camfrog, MSN Messenger or Skype allow Deaf people to reach out beyond national boundaries and see different sign languages in use. For the Deaf community, the improvement in cochlear implant technology has changed the boundaries of the community, and sign language has had to be renegotiated as important in the education of the Deaf.

Although English is widespread in the media, and in news in particular, with BBC and CNN predominating, other languages are used more and more. Since the establishment of Al Jazeera in Qatar in 1996, Arabic has had an important international presence in the news media. In 2003, Al Arabiya was launched from Dubai, with Saudi backing. And in 2005, Telesur started its transmission in Spanish from Caracas. In Canada, on September 1, 1999, the Aboriginal Peoples Television Network (APTN), with programming relevant to First Nations and Indigenous communities around the world, was launched. Approximately 30 percent of all programming is in Indigenous languages.[7]

With the advent of DVDs, viewers have options of languages or subtitles, using this as a way to develop bilingual proficiency. Secondary Audio Programming (SAP), available on television sets since 1990, enables one to see a television program that is close-captioned; that is, has text that accompanies the video, or is in different languages. Whereas the close-captioning is especially useful for the Deaf community,[8] the language option of SAP allows for a bilingual television experience. For example, starting fall 2005, all prime-time television shows on the second largest U.S. television network, ABC, are available in SAP dubbed in Spanish or close-captioned. This not only makes it possible for U.S. Latinos who prefer Spanish to watch these programs, but also for Anglophones to improve their Spanish. In addition, subtitles allow U.S. Latino viewers to strengthen their English skills, while the dubbing of television programs develops their formal Spanish. An American woman married to a Deaf Italian and living in Rome watches movies on DVD with English dialogue and Italian subtitles. But sometimes, languages are switched so that the American woman can hear Italian and the Italian man can practice his reading of English print (Cole, personal communication, November 26, 2006). In Japan, TVs and VCRs have a button similar to the SAP button which allows the viewer to turn off the Japanese dubbing and listen to the program in its original language (Rob Werner, personal communication, October 12, 2006). It is then possible to watch Yankee games in English, Al Jazeera in Arabic, or the network news channels of France, Spain, Korea, and others, all in their original languages.

Because of improved technology and better public funding for services, people who are Deaf can communicate with hearing people over the internet, video relaying,[9] and other forms of written communication. A person may use American sign language and borrow signs from other sign languages during a single conversation, and another person may use a webcam to sign with another viewer and, at the same time, send instant messages in a written language to that viewer (Cole, written communication, January 3, 2007).

The technologies of the twenty-first century have enabled discursive constructions that function simultaneously in space and time. What is different today from the ways in which people languaged in the nineteenth and twentieth century is that we can simultaneously and collaboratively engage in many different language practices at the same time, as happens in electronic instant messaging and chatting. And in so doing, there is a measure of "agency" that did not exist prior to the technological revolution. That is, speakers are now free to choose a broader range of language practices than those offered by the immediate community and the school; and they can use them in ways that are not reflected in more institutionalized language practices of schools and official publications.

Lingua francas are one way in which communication across the state borders has been achieved. Lingua francas are often either numerically powerful languages such as Arabic, Chinese, English, or Spanish, or a planned international language such as Esperanto. Esperanto, an artificially constructed language, was invented by L.L. Zamenhof at the end of the nineteenth century to serve as a second language, in order to foster international peace and understanding. An international sign system for Deaf language users has also been developed. None of these artificial lingua francas has been completely successful.

English, Graddol (2006) tells us, is a growing lingua franca, especially in Asia (see Tsui and Tollefson, 2007). In many countries the learning of English is considered a basic skill, to be taught in school alongside Math and Literacy. And yet

English does not enjoy complete hegemony in the world. Mandarin is also grow-ing as a lingua franca. And there are other languages experiencing growth. In North Africa and West Africa, Arabic is growing much more quickly than English. In the United States, Spanish competes with English. Global English may be on the rise, but so is global Chinese, global Arabic, and global Spanish. As a first language, English is being challenged by both Spanish and Hindi-Urdu, and is said to be falling from second to fourth place (Chinese holds the first place). Demographically, Arabic is growing faster than any other world language (Graddol, 2006).

That the linguistic flow, even in the media, is not now unidirectional or favoring English has been much discussed by Graddol (2006). Graddol gives some interest-ing examples. In East Asia, Chinese and Japanese viewers are more interested in soap operas from Korea than those from the United States, and Japanese Manga comics are more important than English comics. The influence of Bollywood, the Hindi-language film industry in India, competes with Hollywood in all of Asia. And Spanish *telenovelas* (soap operas) are increasingly seen by North American housewives. In fact, the Spanish-language *Univisión*, the fifth largest television station in the U.S., has a growing Anglophone viewing audience.

In terms of second-language users, Putonghua (Mandarin) holds first place, and is emerging as extremely important in other East Asian countries, such as South Korea. The first Confucius Institute dedicated to teaching Putonghua opened in Seoul, South Korea, in November 2004, and others have opened in the United Kingdom, the United States, Africa, Australia, and Continental Europe. Table 2.2 displays the ten written languages which have the most second-language users (expressed in millions).

We should end this section on globalization by pointing out the persistent import-ance of the local (Canagarajah, 1999, 2005a), of what Appadurai (1996) calls "global-ization from below." Recently, the term "glocalization" has been coined to note the presence of the local in the global and vice versa.[10] At a 1997 conference on "Globalization and Indigenous Culture," Roland Robertson defined glocalization as "the simultaneity – the co-presence – of both universalizing and particularizing tendencies."

As national identities have become fragmented through the weakening of the nation-state construction, the relationship between language and identity is more relevant

Table 2.2   Second-Language Users

1	Mandarin	1,052
2	English	508
3	Hindi	487
4	Spanish	417
5	Russian	277
6	Bengali	211
7	Portuguese	191
=8	German	128
=8	French	128
10	Japanese	126

From: Figure 1.37, Graddol, 2006, based on Ostler, 2005

today than ever (Canagarajah, 2005b). Responding to scholars and critics who view the process of globalization as making ethnicity and language differences unnecessary, Fishman (2001: 460) notes:

> Some of the very processes of globalization and post-modernism that were supposed to be most deleterious to purportedly "parochial" identities have actually contributed most to their re-emergence as "part-identities." The increasing ubiquity of the civil state, of civil nationalism and, therefore, of a shared supra-ethnic civil nationalism as part of the identity constellation of all citizens, has resulted in more rather than less recognition of multiculturalism at the institutional level and a more widespread implementation of local ethnicity as a counterbalance to civil nationalism at the level of organized part-identity.

Language plays a vital role in today's globalized world, and it is more important than ever in education.

Languaging

Languaging and languages

Close your eyes and listen with your "inner ear" as Patricia Carini (2000) has taught us to do, to children talking to each other in a classroom, in a playground. Or open your eyes and see Deaf school children signing. Bring to your mind's eye the words of characters in a movie, a television show, a play, or the words of Shakespeare, Cervantes, and Proust on a page, or even those of a person you love, or of the email you have just exchanged. Or hear the words of a prayer uttered in a Native American language. People language for many purposes. They language for expression, for interaction, and to express reference (Ager, 2001). But language practices can also be turned into something about which people, communities, and states have opinions and feelings (Ager, 2001). That is, language practices or languaging also act as a *symbol system* (Fishman, 1996); they can become symbolic of the speech community itself or of sacredness. Thus, languaging practices are codified into languages. For example, Urdu has become an important identity marker for Pakistanis after independence, although only a minority of Pakistanis actually speaks it. Likewise, the way in which people use Caribbean Creole has important symbolic significance for many (see for example Willis, 2002). Some languages have acquired a sanctity dimension. Examples of sacred languages are Biblical Hebrew; Qur'anic Arabic; Sanskrit, the language of Hinduism and the Vedas; Latin, used by the Roman Catholic Church; Old Church Slavonic, used in some Orthodox Eastern Churches; Avestan, the language of the Zoroastrian[11] holy book, the *Avesta*; Coptic, the liturgical language of the Coptic Orthodox Church; Old Tibetan; Ge'ez, used in the liturgy of the Ethiopian Orthodox Church; Pali, the language of the Theravada Buddhism scriptures (the Pali Canon); several scriptural languages of the Eastern Orthodox Churches; and the ceremonial languages of Indigenous peoples. For many Native Americans, their language practices are instruments of communication with living and ancestral or spiritual entities as well, and language and the notion of "spirit" are intertwined.[12] The Anishinaabe, also known as Ojibwe, believe that their language, Ojibwemowin, was given to them at their time of creation as human beings. Their language is therefore viewed as a gift which must be honored, and is the only language that can be used in their ceremonies. Kipp (2002: 17) explains:

> Tribal languages contain the tribal genesis, cosmology, history, and secrets within. Without them we may become permanently lost, or irrevocably changed. I am a Pikuni and know why. In our language, I am a *nizitapiwa*, a real person. It derives from how my language treats the form for "I" or "me" spoken as "*niz*," a derivative of *nostum*, or my body. When I speak Pikuni, my body and spirit speak to *kizitapiwa*, another real person.

Furthermore, language for many Native American communities defines place – the ecology of homeland can be spoken and understood through Native languages. For example, Zuni Pueblo member Enote (2002: 30) states: "Our language tells us about our umbilical cords that go out across the landscape, the valleys, the texture of the mountains, canyons, climate, the creation of beings. Because we have been in the same place for a very, very long time, through this language, we can affect something. My understanding is in my vocabulary."

Some languages are oral and are not written, for example some Amerindian languages or some of the "tribal languages" of India. And then there are languages that are signed and not written. A sign language is a linguistic system of manual/visual, not vocal/aural, communication with its own phonological, morphological, syntactic, and semantic rules (Cole, forthcoming).[13] Just like all children, Deaf children grow up and language as they participate in social interactions and as they network with relatives, friends, and members of the community in different ways. Deaf children do not all communicate in the same ways: some prefer to speak and use assistive devices to hear others, some use mainly signing, and then there are some who use both speech and signing. For written communication, Deaf children operate pretty much in the same way as other children. They read newspapers, write letters or emails, send text messages over the phone, and skim through textbooks.

Languages are not fixed codes by themselves; they are fluid codes framed within social practices.[14] Hopper (1998: 157–8), for example, argues: "There is no natural fixed structure to language. Rather, speakers borrow heavily from their previous experiences of communication in similar circumstances, on similar topics, and with similar interlocutors. Systematicity, in this view, is an illusion produced by the *partial settling or sedimentation* of frequently used forms into temporary systems" (our italics). According to this conceptualization, it is not languages that exist, but *discourses*; that is, ways of talking or writing within a context. Following Michel Foucault, discourse conceives language as a form of social practice that naturally occurs in connected speech and written text with those who participate in the event.[15] Yngve (1996), Shohamy (2006), and Makoni and Pennycook (2007) go beyond discourse to say that there is only *languaging*: social practices that are actions performed by our meaning-making selves. What we have learned to call dialects, pidgins, creoles, and academic language are instances of languaging: social practices that we perform. In the section below, we turn our attention to these practices as they have been studied within traditional language conceptualizations.

Dialects

In considering the role of language practices in bilingual education, the notion of dialect is of special importance. For linguists, the term "dialect" is a neutral term used for variants of a specific language. Romaine (1994) defines dialect as "a subordinate variety of a language," and refers to *regional dialects*, associated with a place, *social dialects*, associated with social class, and *historical dialects* referring to ancestors of present language varieties. There are also *ethnic dialects* spoken by ethnolinguistic groups.

However, lay people often reserve the term "dialect" for languages or ways of using language that are socially stigmatized. For example, many people think that what they speak to friends and families in informal settings is a dialect, and what they speak in school is a language. Indeed, when states want to ensure that people who engage in certain languaging practices remain oppressed, these practices are often referred to as dialects; although when the speakers of these so called dialects achieve political power, they are then often designated as languages. Max Weinreich is often quoted as having said that "a language is a dialect with an army and a navy" (see Romaine, 1994: 12). This serves well to remind us that the difference between what people call a dialect and a language is most often not linguistic, but social, and having to do with the power of its speakers.

Afrikaans, the regional languages of Spain and most of Europe, Quechua, and Luxemburgish are examples of this process. Afrikaans in South Africa was considered a dialect of Dutch until the 1920s when the language was standardized and its status raised as a result of the success of the Afrikaner political movement. During the dictatorship of Francisco Franco, Catalan, Basque (Euskara[16]) and Galician (Gallego) were referred to as dialects by many in the Spanish-speaking world. They were not taught in schools, except in "underground" efforts such as the *ikastolas*[17] in the Basque country. Upon Franco's death, the new Spanish Constitution of 1978 recognized Spanish as the official language of the state, and named Catalan, Euskara, and Galician as official regional languages in the respective regions. Recently, the term *lengua regional* (regional language) has been replaced by *lengua propia* (own language), indicating that Catalan, Euskara, and Galician are even more than regional languages; they are official languages of those nationalities just as Castilian (Spanish[18]), and all others are Spain's own. In much the same way, many of the dialects of Europe, as they have previously been called, have now received institutional support and a change of status to "regional language," as a result of the Council of Europe's European Charter for Regional or Minority Languages.

In Latin America, Quechua, spoken by 8 to 12 million speakers across Peru, Ecuador, Bolivia, Argentina, Chile, and Colombia, is often designated as a dialect. Only recently, and with its officialization in Peru, Ecuador, and Bolivia, has Quechua achieved status as a language, even though this designation also obscures the fact that there are multiple varieties of Quechua, many of which are not mutually intelligible (Hornberger and Coronel-Molina, 2004). Similarly, according to the constitution of Luxembourg, Luxemburgish is a language, although linguistically some consider it a Rhennish dialect.

Many lay people also assume that dialects are varieties of a language that are *mutually intelligible*, that is, speakers are able to understand each other. But, of course, mutual intelligibility has little to do with language, and more to do with people, since it is people who understand each other. And many cases contradict the assumption that dialects are mutually intelligible whereas languages are not. For example, Swedish, Norwegian, and Danish are considered different languages, although they are mutually intelligible and the differences are not linguistic, but political and cultural (Romaine, 1994). We speak of dialects of Chinese even though at least eight of them are mutually incomprehensible. Hindi, Punjabi, and Urdu are all closely related and, for the most part, mutually intelligible, although they use different scripts. After India became independent, Hindi leaders claimed that Urdu and Punjabi were dialects of Hindi. With the independence of Pakistan, Urdu became recognized as a totally different language adopting an Arabic script, with Punjabi also receiving regional recognition in India.

In the context of Africa, Batibo (2005: 2) gives us the example of the Chagga people at the foot of Mount Kilimanjaro, who consider themselves speakers of one language, although linguistically there are three different speech forms which are not mutually intelligible. In contrast, speakers of Sesotho, Setswana, and Sepedi in southern Africa see themselves as speaking three different languages, although they are mutually intelligible and could be considered varieties of one language.

Because the differences between what people call language and what they call dialects are often socially constituted, it is better to use the term "varieties" of language practices when speaking of different ways in which people language, whether in standard or non-standard ways. It is important to emphasize, though, that these varieties are not isolated wholes, but consist of features that come in and out of the languaging that people do, with the different linguistic features that make up their linguistic repertoire.

Pidgins and creoles

Another language topic that is important for bilingual educators are *pidgins* and *creoles*. Pidgins are defined by linguists as languages that come into being in contact situations, and are used by speakers with different language backgrounds to communicate, typically to trade or in plantation contexts. For us, they are just another manifestation of how people language. Structurally speaking, pidgins are simplified; that is, they have little morphology and limited syntax, and they are not mutually intelligible with the language from which they derive their lexicon. Pidgins are always learned as second languages.

In contrast, when pidgins become nativized and standardized, and adopted as the language of the home by the entire population, they are known as *creoles*. Creoles are said to be lexically and structurally complex, and are learned as first languages.

Two major groups of creoles are usually distinguished – Atlantic creoles and Pacific creoles. Atlantic creoles were established primarily during the seventeenth and eighteenth century in West Africa and the Caribbean, as a result of the slave trade.

Pacific creoles were developed in the nineteenth century with recruited and indentured laborers. The creolization of these later pidgins was more gradual than the abrupt change with Atlantic creoles.

The best-known Atlantic creole is Haitian Creole, the co-official language, alongside French, of Haiti since 1987, and widely spoken by the vast majority of Haitians. In the Pacific area, Tok Pisin, an English-based creole spoken by more than half the population of Papua New Guinea, Hiri Motu, an indigenous creole, and English all share official status in Papua New Guinea, although English is the official medium of education. Bismala is the national language of Vanuatu, but it is forbidden in school, where English and French are used (Romaine, 1994). Despite being well-accepted language systems that are part of the languaging of many, creoles, as other stigmatized practices, have very little official place in school. A significant exception is the Jamaican Bilingual Primary Education Project where language practices that include Creole are being used to educate (Devonish and Carpenter, 2005). Yet classrooms in Jamaica, Haiti, Papua New Guinea, and Vanuatu have always been bilingual in reality, since creoles are part of the languaging practices of children, and of the teachers.

Michel De Graff (1999) has argued against what he calls "creole exceptionalism," that is, the idea that because creoles had no time to incorporate the parent-languages' complex grammars, and because they are so new, creoles are similar to each other and different from other languages.[19] In fact, if you compare the evolution and structures of English with that of Creoles, De Graff argues, there is no way to distinguish one from the other. This is the same claim made by Muysken (1988: 300) when he says: "The very notion of a Creole language from the linguistic point of view tends to disappear if one looks closely; what we have is just a language." In this reconstituted view, a creole may just be the partial settling of language practices, of languaging by people with different language backgrounds, and under certain social circumstances.

The languaging of creole speakers takes different features from their entire linguistic repertoire. They often move closer to the standard, speaking what linguists refer to as an *acrolect*. Other times, their languaging has more features of the creole itself, leading linguists to refer to this variety as a *basilect*. The choice of words to describe this languaging positions the acrolect as superior to the basilect. But viewed from the perspective of the speaker, and not from the language itself, creole-speakers choose and blend features from their entire linguistic repertoire, making their languaging more responsive to standard or creole features depending on their communicative intent and its function.

Language in school

Academic language

If our conception of language has been constructed, often through socio-political rather than linguistic criteria, then the language of school, especially what we have learned to call the "standard academic language," is the ultimate creation. Coulmas (2005: 215) defines standard as "a prestige variety of language, providing a written institutionalized norm as a reference form for such purposes as language teaching and the media." Wright (2004: 54) says: "A standard language is the means by which large groups become and remain communities of communication. The norm is decided and codified by a central group, disseminated through the institutions of the state such as education and then usage is constantly policed and users dissuaded from divergent practices, both formally and informally." Standardization occurs by fixing and regulating such features as the spelling and the grammar of a language in dictionaries and grammar books which are then used for prescriptive teaching of the language. What is important is to recognize that standardization is not an inherent characteristic of language, but an "acquired or deliberately and artificially imposed characteristic" (Romaine, 1994: 84). The term often used in opposition to standard is "vernacular:" the local language practices.

The standard that is taught in school is sometimes not spoken anywhere. For example, a Moroccan native speaker of Tamazight (Berber)[20] may also be fluent in colloquial Moroccan Arabic. In school, however, he is taught to read and write only in modern standard Arabic (MSA). Furthermore, to read the Qu'ran, as well as to pray, this Moroccan uses classical Arabic.

It is important to emphasize that the results of the construction of a standard language are very real. In schools, even bilingual ones, it is the standard language that is valued for teaching, learning, and especially to assess what is being learned. Schools pay a lot of attention to the teaching of language itself, sometimes to the internal mechanics that characterize the language – what some call "grammar" – other times to its use in meaningful contexts, especially in reading and writing. But language is central in school because it is also the means through which teaching and learning occurs. Oftentimes, however, this use of language in school, as controlled by the teacher and limited to what is considered "the standard," has little to do with encouraging children's intellectual inquiry and creativity or with children's languaging. The ability to use the standard language is a developmental goal of education, but restricting the languaging of students may severely limit their communicative and intellectual potential, and their possibilities of becoming better educated.

Standardization and literacy are intrinsically linked, because, as Romaine has pointed out, "the acquisition of literacy presupposes the existence of a codified written standard, and standardization depends on the existence of a written form of language" (1994: 86). Because literacy relies on the standard, the standard language itself is taught explicitly in school, and *it certainly needs to be taught*. Wright (2004: 44) has pointed out that "a standard is more easily acquired than an in-group variety that is not codified." We are not questioning the teaching of a standard language in school; without its acquisition, language minority children will continue to fail and will not have equal access to resources and opportunities. But we have to recognize that an *exclusive* focus on the standard variety keeps out other languaging practices that are children's authentic linguistic identity expression. In Chapters 13 and 14 we will turn to how to teach the standard language in linguistically and culturally relevant ways, and in Chapter 12 we suggest ways of building on the languaging of bilingual children in classrooms.

The *exclusive* use of a standard variety for school has important implications for bilingual education. As we shall see, the language practices of immigrants, but also of Indigenous peoples and other minoritized and Deaf communities, are influenced by contact with dominant language practices, as well as by the exclusion of home language practices from all formal domains, and most especially schools, sometimes for generations. As a result, the minoritized language practices of the home often have little to do with the standard minority language taught in school. Without a lot of caution, the school's insistence on using only the standard variety of the home language can be detrimental, and may even aggravate the linguistic insecurity that many minority speakers feel.

Characteristics

Skutnabb-Kangas and Toukomaa (1976), working with Finnish immigrants in Sweden, proposed that there is a difference between the way in which language is used in academic tasks and in conversation and intimacy. The *surface fluency* so evident in conversational language is most often supported by cues that have little to do with language itself. For example, in playing ball in a playground, children will gesture, point, ask questions, repeat the same commands, use their body, their faces, their hands. In writing to someone we know intimately, much can be left unsaid because the meaning is often carried by what we know about the other person. In personal dialogue, we often ask the other person to repeat, to clarify, and to provide an example. Cummins (1981b) has called this use of language – language practices that are supported by meaningful interpersonal and situational cues – "contextualized language." Contextualized language, supported by paralinguistic cues, is what one uses for *basic interpersonal communication*, what Cummins calls "BICS."

Contextual support, Cummins (2000) explains, can be *external*, having to do with aspects of the input itself, as in cases where language use allows for redundancy, and is spoken clearly. But contextual support can also be *internal*, having to do with the experiences, interests, and motivations that interlocutors have. The more students know and understand, the easier it is for them to make sense of academic language, since there is internal support for understanding the messages.

To complete school tasks, and especially assessment tasks, another different set of language skills is needed. Students in school need to be able to use language without any extralinguistic support, in ways that are very different from the way in which we use language most of the time in real life. That is, *decontextualized language* is what is needed in order to participate in the IRE/IRF (Initiation–Response–Evaluation/Feedback) cycle that is so common in classroom discourse, in order to read texts that are devoid of pictures and other cues, or texts that are about things students know nothing about. Decontextualized language is also what students need in order to write the academic essays that require an unknown audience with whom communication is important, and in taking multiple-choice tests that force only one answer. In speaking about the need for these decontextualized language skills, Cummins (1981b) calls them *Cognitive Academic Language Proficiency* (CALP).

Cummins (2000: ch. 2) posits that academic language, both oral and written, is associated with higher-order thinking, including hypothesizing, evaluating, inferring, generalizing, predicting, or classifying. And yet, Cummins argues that CALP is not superior to BICS, and that developmentally they are not separate but develop jointly within a matrix of social interaction. A major goal of schooling is to expand the use of decontextualized language that characterizes academic registers, but to do so, Cummins tells us, social interaction and the contextualization of academic language practices is most essential.

Reasons

In order to reflect on why the standard language is imposed in schools, we have to first describe how certain languages or specific varieties are forced on particular groups. It is obvious that more powerful groups impose their language on the less powerful. This is the case, for example, of Sámis and Roma in Finland who have to learn Finnish, whereas Finns do not need to speak the other languages present in their territory. Similarly, children in the United States do not have to learn Spanish or Chinese, whereas U.S. Latino, Chinese, or Native American children are expected to learn English.

In some countries, children are schooled in a language spoken only by a powerful minority within the country, and not by the majority of speakers. This is the case, for example, of Haiti, where until recently children were schooled solely in French, although only the elite were French-speakers, with most Haitians speaking Haitian Creole. This educational practice privileged those who spoke French at home, severely curtailing educational opportunities for those who were schooled in a language they did not understand. Likewise, in many African and Asian countries, during colonial times, education took place only in the colonial language, educating an indigenous elite to serve as brokers between the colonial power and the Indigenous population, and ensuring that only a few became educated. The practice continues today in many African countries, guaranteeing that the power stays in the hands of the Indigenous elite.

Corson (2001) points to how prejudice against users of non-standard varieties of a language is as old as the history of language itself. For example, the Bible recounts how pronunciation of the word "Shibboleth" was used to distinguish the conquered Ephraimites, whose dialects lacked an /ʃ/ sound, from the victorious Gileadites. Whenever an Ephraimite tried to pass for a Gileadite, "the men of Gilead asked him, 'Are you an Ephraimite?' If he replied, 'No,' they said, 'All right, say "Shibboleth."' If he said, 'Sibboleth,' because he could not pronounce the word correctly, they seized him and killed him at the fords of the Jordan. Forty-two thousand Ephraimites were killed at that time" (Book of Judges 12: 5–6).

Thinking about the situation of what has been called African American Vernacular English (AAVE) or Ebonics[21] is instructive in this regard. Although many scholars (see especially Labov 1972) have clearly shown that AAVE is logical and regular, and that its grammatical and phonological characteristics cannot be the cause of poor academic performance, the features that characterize this variety continue to be stigmatized. Even in schools with many African American teachers and in neighborhoods where most are African Americans, only an English standard is accepted, developed, and used in assessment. The widespread bias against non-standard varieties of English, especially bias against features associated with AAVE or Ebonics has much to do with racism, as shown in the research of Baugh (1997).

This racism that is associated with language is what Tove Skutnabb-Kangas (2000) has termed "linguicism."

There are many other examples worldwide of using language to limit educational and occupational opportunities. Makoni and Pennycook (2007) propose that when the "constructed" African languages were introduced into local communities as official languages, they actually accentuated social differences, since they could only be acquired through formal education and not everyone had access to school. Likewise, Pennycook (2002) has shown how language use in education in colonial Hong Kong were responsible for creating "docile" people, able to cooperate in their own exploitation. Roots (1999) has provided examples of how hearing educators have maintained their control over Deaf communities by imposing signing bans. Ricento (2003) has demonstrated how policies against bilingual education in the United States may have much to do with controlling the state's growing bilingualism and ensuring that opportunities remain in the hands of monolinguals. In the same way, García (2003), García and Menken (2006) and Menken (2008) have suggested that the growing insistence in the use of standard written English in high-stakes assessment in the United States has to do with gate-keeping; that is, the ability to control who goes forward, and ensuring that only those who can write English natively, and without any features of language contact, can access higher education and professional positions. Written standard English in U.S. school assessments is increasingly used to create differences between monolinguals and bilinguals which are then used as gate-keeping mechanisms for promotion, high-school graduation, and college entrance (for more on assessment, see Chapter 15).

The obsession with language categories, as well as the school's insistence in using only "the standard" to teach, learn, and assess, has then much to do with the concept of *governmentality* as proposed by Foucault (1991). Foucault focuses on how language practices "regulate" the ways in which language is used, and establish language hierarchies in which some languages, or some ways of using language, are more valued than others. This has to be interpreted within the framework of "hegemony" developed by Antonio Gramsci (1971) which explains how people acquiesce to invisible cultural power. Erikson (1996: 45) defines "hegemonic practices" as "routine actions and unexamined beliefs that are consonant with the cultural system of meaning and ontology within which it makes sense to take certain actions, entirely without malevolent intent, that nonetheless systematically limit the life chances of members of stigmatized groups." Our routine language practices become "regulatory" mechanisms which unconsciously create categories of exclusion. Thus, our discursive practices are one of the most obvious examples of hegemony in which we all, and especially educators, participate.

As the preceding sections have shown, our conceptualization of language is often limiting and does not reflect the complex ways in which people *language*. As far as bilingual education is concerned, it is essential that efforts be made to incorporate these features of people's languaging in policy, curriculum, and instructional planning. It is most important to understand the important role different language varieties and language practices, including pidgins and creoles, have in education.

Conclusion

Language is an important aspect, although by no means the most important, in considering the topic of bilingual education. Because language is so familiar, we operate with a series of assumptions about language that have to be questioned in order to think about bilingual education. In this chapter, we have considered how our conception of standard language has been constructed through sometimes oppressive practices, and other times discursive practices. Through these practices, many of us have become convinced of the naturalness of the standard language and of its neutrality.

In this chapter we deconstructed language as a concept so as to enable us to understand its power and potential as a discursive tool. In so doing, we have questioned practices that on the surface seem natural, but that have the effect of exerting control and restricting opportunity. That language is a social construction, linked to the construction of the nation-state, is a fact. But that language, as socially constructed, has real implications for children's education is a most important reality. Despite the changes to our conception of nation-states as a result of globalization, language in school continues to operate mostly as it has in the past, distanced from the real ways in which children *language*.

We reimagine language as language practices, languaging as a resource of imagination, languaging without bridles, languaging without prejudices, in its full *realia* of modes and meanings that are supported by technology today. We focus here not on language per se but on the multiple discursive practices that constitute what we call languaging. The language use in bilingual schools is determined mostly by states that control whether all children are to be educated in one language or the other or in many, or whether the children's languaging is to be valued. But bilingual schools that act on their potential to be transformative must build on the children's complex languaging to also develop the languaging practices of schools, what we have learned to call "standard academic language."

In Chapters 3 and 4, we turn to examining the concept of bilingualism itself, changing emphasis to a more sociopolitical level in Chapter 4, but always considering bilingualism in the interrelationship created by languaging, and the agency of those who language.

Questions for Reflection

1. What does it mean for languages to have been constructed? Give some examples.
2. How have globalization and technology impacted on the ways in which language is used?
3. What does languaging mean? How does it differ from a language?
4. What is academic language and what are some of its characteristics? What is its role in schools?
5. Discuss "language" and "dialect" as presented in this chapter. Give examples of its social construction.

6. What are pidgins and creoles? Do they have a role in bilingual education?
7. Reflect on your personal experiences with language practices. What factors influence your decision to language in one way or another?

Further Reading

Corson, D. (2001). *Language Diversity and Education.* Lawrence Erlbaum, Mahwah, NJ.

Coulmas, F. (2005). *Sociolinguistics. The Study of Speakers' Choice.* Cambridge University Press, Cambridge.

Graddol, D. (2006). *English Next. Why Global English May Mean the End of "English as a Foreign Language.'* The British Council, London. Available at: www.britishcouncil.org/learning-research-english-next.pdf.

Makoni, S., and Pennycook, A. (2007). *Disinventing and Reconstituting Languages.* Multilingual Matters, Clevedon, UK.

Maurais, J., and Morris, M.A. (eds.) (2003). *Languages in a Globalising World.* Cambridge University Press, Cambridge.

Mühlhäusler, P. (1996). *Linguistic Ecology. Language Change and Linguistic Imperialism in the Pacific Region.* Routledge, London.

Romaine, S. (1994). *Language in Society: An Introduction to Sociolinguistics.* Oxford University Press, Oxford. Second edn. 2001.

3

Bilingualism and Translanguaging

A Bilingual Child: A Scenario

Recently, a very concerned and veteran teacher in a New York City school did a descriptive review[1] of Pablo, a kindergarten child whom she described as a "second-language learner." But it turns out that Pablo was born in New York of Cuban-born parents who have lived in the United States for a long time. The language issues she described had to do with language use of a *bilingual kindergartener*, but certainly did not have anything to do with a second-language learner, for indeed, this child was most comfortable in English. For example, the teacher questions how in tracking the words of the rhymes of "Jack and Jill," Pablo twice reads "pear of water" without questioning its meaning. The teacher asks herself: "Does he think pear is pail?" The teacher, knowing that Pablo speaks Spanish at home, focuses on language issues that although different, may be also present in the emergent reading of many monolingual children. It is common for monolingual children to rely on rhymes and sound in beginning reading without attaching too much sense to what they are reading. And certainly in the case of rhymes, where meaning sometimes is nonsensical, children often rely only on sound. Furthermore, it has been ascertained, as we will see in Chapter 5, that bilingual children tend to have more metalinguistic skills and divergent thinking than monolingual children, thus enabling them to play with words and sounds of words much more than those who are monolingual. The teacher, ignorant of this fact, dismisses this gift of bilingual children and sees it instead as a burden.

This bilingual five-year-old has an incredible imagination. On another occasion, in retelling how they had made rice the week before, Pablo draws for the teacher how they got started. He says: "First, I'm going to make a tube . . . . . . A tube, everything of water has a tube." The teacher is perplexed, but it soon emerges that the child, cognizant of the fact that they started by putting water in a pot, is truly starting from the beginning, by drawing first the plumbing, the "tube" from which water flows. But in the tube there's a story for all of us who study bilingualism. Pablo selects the word "tube" based on his knowledge of the Spanish word *tubería* for plumbing. But this is not an instance of a second-language learner who does not know the term for plumbing. This is a common bilingual use, drawing from different signs in unique combinations. That Pablo is able to transform *tubo* with the Spanish morphology, to "tube," is in itself indicative that this child is familiar with the English language. That Pablo uses a word that is close in meaning to "plumbing" is also indicative of his language expertise. If this teacher had been made aware of bilingualism not as a deviation from the norm, but as a common communicative repertoire used by most people in the world, she would not be viewing the child's language use as troublesome. In fact, Pablo shows signs of promise, of his ability to delve deep into himself in order to draw on understandings that especially in early childhood come straight from the home.

Overview

This chapter focuses on bilingualism, especially the bilingualism of individuals. In this chapter we will discuss:

- bilingualism and translanguaging;
- new models of bilingualism – *recursive* and *dynamic* – and traditional models of bilingualism – *additive* and *subtractive*;
- terms and concepts associated with bilingualism;
- bilingual abilities;
- bilingual development;
- neurolinguistic and psycholinguistic considerations of bilingualism.

Introduction

Chapter 2 considered the complexities surrounding language. We analyzed the relationship between language, states, and globalization, and we introduced the concept of *languaging* to talk about speakers' discursive practices. We also discussed the differences between language practices at home, in communities, and in academic contexts.

This chapter will describe the many ways, and the many settings throughout the world in which languaging bilingually is the usual way of languaging, and in which bilingual individuals are the norm. Individuals and communities in settings throughout both the developed West and the developing world usually language bilingually, that is, they *translanguage* when they communicate. In many, perhaps most, settings in the world, it is normal and unmarked to translanguage in inter-actions between individuals who belong to the same bilingual culture. Sometimes translanguaging takes place across cultures. Translanguaging, or engaging in bilingual or multilingual discourse practices, is an approach to bilingualism that is centered, not on languages as has been often the case, but on the practices of bilinguals that are readily observable. These worldwide translanguaging practices are seen here not as marked or unusual, but rather are taken for what they are, namely the normal mode of communication that, with some exceptions in some monolingual enclaves, characterizes communities throughout the world.

Centered, then, on the translanguaging practices of bilingual communities, our considerations of bilingualism go beyond the traditional practices discussed in the literature. We expand the models of bilingualism to include those that respond to more complex realities. In so doing, we question some of the assumptions that have been made in the study of bilingualism and the terms that have been used to describe it. After discussing bilingual abilities, we end by reviewing recent neurolinguistic and psycholinguistic evidence with regard to bilingualism.

As will become evident in this chapter, the complexities of bilingualism and the resulting translanguaging are seldom acknowledged in schools, even in bilingual education programs. This chapter lays the groundwork for thinking differently about how we approach educational policies and practices to educate children bilingually, which will be the subject of Part III and Part IV of this book.

Bilingualism and Translanguaging

Not one plus one

Bilingualism, according to Baker (2001), is the ability to use more than one lan-guage.[2] Early scholars of bilingualism, in particular Bloomfield (1933), only con-sidered native-like control of two languages as a sign of bilingualism. But later scholars, such as Einar Haugen and Uriel Weinreich, had much broader definitions of bilingualism, perhaps because as bilinguals themselves they were aware of its complexity, and they had worked in immigrant U.S. contexts where different forms of bilingualism were common.[3] Haugen (1953) considered even minimum proficiency in two languages a sign of bilingualism. Weinreich (1953) labeled some-one who alternated between the two languages as a bilingual. Diebold (1964) speaks of "incipient bilingualism" to designate those who are at the very beginnings of acquiring some competence in another language, thereby providing a minimalist definition of bilingualism.

Balanced bilingualism presents a picture of children and adults who are equally competent in two languages in all contexts and with all interlocutors. Although this is still a widely accepted idea, especially among educators, it has long been recognized that such a form of bilingualism does not exist. The belief in balanced bilingualism holds that a bilingual is like two persons, each fluent in one of the two languages. But more realistically, a bilingual is a person that "languages" differently and that has diverse and unequal experiences with each of the two languages. Since the emergence in 1960 of the field of sociolinguistics, that is, of the study of how language and language use varies in different social contexts and because of the various social characteristics of interlocutors, the concept of bilingualism itself has been extended beyond the traditional "balanced" conception of the bicycle with two perfectly round wheels. The languages of an individual are rarely socially equal, having different power and prestige, and they are used for different purposes, in different contexts, with different interlocutors. As we said in Chapter 1, bilingualism is not like a bicycle with two balanced wheels; it is more like an all-terrain vehicle. Its wheels do not move in unison or in the same direction, but extend and contract, flex and stretch, making possible, over highly uneven ground, movement forward that is bumpy and irregular but also sustained and effective.

Translanguaging

When describing the language practices of bilinguals from the perspective of the users themselves, and not simply describing bilingual language use or bilingual contact from the perspective of the language itself, the language practices of bilinguals are examples of what we are here calling *translanguaging*. We borrow this term from Cen Williams (cited in Baker, 2001) who used it to name a pedagogical practice which switches the language mode in bilingual classrooms – for example, reading is done in one language, and writing in another. For us, translanguagings are *multiple discursive practices* in which bilinguals engage in order to *make sense of their bilingual worlds*. Translanguaging therefore goes beyond what has been termed code-switching (more on this concept below), although it includes it, as well as other kinds of bilingual language use and bilingual contact. Translanguaging for us extends what Gutiérrez and her colleagues have called "hybrid language use," that is, a "systematic, strategic, affiliative, and sense-making process" (Gutiérrez, Baquedano-López, and Alvarez, 2001: 128).

Bilingual families and communities must translanguage in order to construct meaning. Take, for example, a meal in a bilingual family. Families are constituted by bilinguals with different degrees of abilities and sometimes monolingual family members. Translanguaging is thus the only discursive practice that can include all family members. In bilingual communities, it is also important to translanguage in order to make sense of signs written in the two or more languages of the community, often communicating different messages. Additionally, translanguaging is an important practice among language minority children who serve as translators for their parents who do not speak the majority language. Orellana, Reynolds, Dorner, and Meza (2003) and Valdés (2002) have shown the value of the multiple literacies in which youth engage while translating for their families. Bilinguals translanguage to include and facilitate communication with others, but also to construct deeper understandings and make sense of their bilingual worlds.

Bilingual communities translanguage extensively, sometimes using their languages for different modalities. For example, in the United States Latino children often select English for reading since more children's literature in English is available. However, the same children pray in Spanish since it is the language that the parents use in their bedtime prayers. In speaking to me about his participation in a religion class, a bilingual Latino fifth-grader in a two-way bilingual education program tells me about his translanguaging as he translanguages:

> *Yo estaba en español porque yo no sé como rezar en ingles. [...] Este año mi amigo E.M. en la clase de Ms. S., él me dijo cómo se persignaba en inglés. [...] Yo no sé, yo tengo una vida muy loca porque yo sé cómo rezar en español pero no en inglés, pero sé como más de inglés que español. [...]*
>
> *Cuando estoy en St. G. la misa está como en transmisión, una oración en español y otra en inglés. [...]* For me it's easier in English, well because I feel more comfortable in English, but when I talk to my parents I speak in Spanish. And sometimes I only speak in Spanish, then Spanish and a little bit of English.
>
> (I was in Spanish because I don't know how to pray in English. [...] This year my friend E.M. in Ms. S.'s class, he told me how to make the sign of the cross in English. [...] I don't know, I have a very crazy life because I know how to pray in Spanish and not in English, but I know, like, more English than Spanish [...]
>
> When I'm in St. G., the mass is like in *transmission*, a sentence in Spanish and another in English [...] [continues in English].)
>
> November 5, 2007

The child's choice of the word *transmisión* (transmission) for *traducción* (translation) when he describes a Catholic mass in which one sentence is in English and another one in Spanish is perhaps significant. It turns out that it is precisely the translanguaging that makes the transmission of the message possible.

This translanguaging also occurs between written and signed languages. Deaf students also often translanguage, as they select which mode (signed or written) to use that may be most appropriate for one's social needs or social conditions (Cole, personal communication, November 18, 2006).

Technology-enabled communication facilitates complex languaging practices that question monolingual realities. In bilingual speech, Lüdi (2003: 175) tells us, "rules and norms are activated that overlap single languages and govern the harmonic, i.e. the 'grammatical' mixing of elements from different languages." What we have is multiple discursive practices or translanguaging.

Despite the ability of bilinguals to translanguage, monolinguals are often oblivious to the presence of these bilingual practices (what Hélot, 2003, 2006, 2007 calls "invisible bilingualism"), or dismissive of their significance, with any difference in language practices often evaluated as a deficiency. In the United States, for example, the concept of *Spanglish* (Stavans, 2004) is used to explain the many ways in which Latinos use Spanish differently from the ways in which Spanish is used in both Spain and Latin America. But as Otheguy (1995, 2001, 2003) has clearly shown, the communicative practices used by U.S. Latino communities draw creatively on both their linguistic knowledge of the Spanish language system and their cultural knowledge of the United States. Reducing this to Spanglish puts U.S. Spanish speakers in a position of deficiency, seen from a monolingual Spanish or English perspective, and denies their agency as speakers engaged in complex linguistic practices that express their new realities. Bilingual language practices frequently, but not always, differ from the language use of two separate monolinguals. These practices are in no way deficient, they simply reflect greater choices, a wider range of expression than each monolingual separately can call upon, and convey not only linguistic knowledge, but also combined cultural knowledge that comes to bear upon language use.

For us, translanguaging includes but extends what others have called language use and language contact among bilinguals. Rather than focusing on the language itself and how one or the other might relate to the way in which a monolingual standard is used and has been described, the concept of translanguaging makes obvious that there are no clear-cut boundaries between the languages of bilinguals. What we have is a languaging continuum that is accessed. The sections below describe how bilingual use and bilingual contact have been traditionally studied and propose how we might view these concepts within a translanguaging framework.

Bilingual use

Studies have shown that the language use of bilinguals responds to their communicative and affective intent, as well as to the situation and the interlocutor. Fishman *et al.* (1971) proposed the construct of *domains* which "summate the major clusters of interaction that occur in clusters of multilingual settings involving clusters of interlocutors" (1971: 586). As such, domains are "an abstraction which refers to a sphere of activity representing a combination of specific times, settings, and role relationships" (Romaine, 1994: 43). For example, in the study of the Puerto Rican community conducted by Fishman *et al.* in 1971, and on the basis of observation and interviews, it was determined that the domains of family, friendship, and religion were mostly carried out in Spanish, whereas employment and education were domains in which English was used. Likewise, Batibo (2005: 1) describes the language use of a Tshivenda speaker in South Africa:

> he may speak Tshivenda to his parents but use IsiZulu to address his workmates, and then receive orders from his employer in Afrikaans. But he may use English in a bank or when talking to educated strangers, and finally use Fanagalo in a pub with colleagues. To this Tshivenda speaker, each of these languages would provide not only a communicative function but also a social role.

Domains allow scholars to make connections between, on the one hand, clusters of interaction and interlocutors, and on the other, more concrete social situations.[4]

The use of stable domains or different values and attitudes to explain language use has been questioned recently, especially as the lens has expanded to include the concept of languaging. For example, Heller (1999) calls our attention to interactions among discursive patterns that are socially constructed, rather than pre-determined. Speaking of Franco-Canadians, Heller (1999: 6) invites us to:

> Look closely at the patterns and what you see is people interacting with each other, drawing creatively on their linguistic and cultural resources to position themselves and each other as they struggle to redefine what it means, in this case, to be francophone and to speak French, as well as to define the value of the linguistic resources each possesses.

Translanguaging includes languaging bilingually within the same domain.

It is true, however, that bilinguals usually have differentiated use and competence in the languages in which they translanguage, having had exposure to various language practices. Sometimes, this differentiated use and competence has to do with personal preference. Grosjean (1997) refers to this language use of bilinguals as the "complementarity principle" and explains that any bilingual is never two monolinguals in one person, and any child, regardless of circumstances or education, will never be able to become two monolinguals in one person.

In one of the earliest books on bilingualism, Hugo Baetens Beardsmore (1982: 11) explains: "although many bilinguals' performance in two languages may well differ distinctively from that of two separate monoglots, in terms of the totality of the range of abilities, the bilingual may well achieve a similar, if different repertoire." Describing the many different ways that bilinguals weave their two languages as in a piano–violin duet, Walters (2005: 1) says: "The child of a two language home, the native-born child of immigrant parents, the hearing impaired user of ASL and spoken English, the hotel desk clerk, the hospital intake nurse, the fruit vendor in the open market, the airport control tower operator, and the student on a study abroad program all play the tune in clearly different ways." *Bilinguals are not double monolinguals*, and as Grosjean (1982) and Romaine (1989), among others, have repeatedly stated, they should not be studied from monolingual perspectives. Cenoz and Genesee (1998: 27) conclude that "multilinguals may not need the same levels of proficiency in all of their languages in all of the same discourse domains as monolinguals."

Auer (1995: 115–16) states that bilingualism affords the bilingual speaker "resources not available to monolingual speakers for the constitution of socially meaningful verbal activities." Thus, "research on linguistics should be centered on the *multilingual speaker as a norm*, not on the monolingual individual" (Herdina and Jessner, 2000: 1; emphasis mine). The bilingual child whom we described in the scenario at the beginning of this chapter, Pablo, uses the Spanish-based language practices of his home and the English ones of his school as resources for articulating his understanding of rice balls, but often integrating his language practices. Bilingualism is not about 1 + 1 = 2, but about a plural, mixing different aspects or fractions of language behavior as they are needed, to be socially meaningful.

Because the range of the linguistic repertoire of bilinguals is more differentiated than that of monolinguals, the linguistic choices[5] for bilinguals are also greater. Gumperz (1982) has shown how language use of bilinguals has much to do with the desire to be socially distinct, as well as assimilating. Early on, Blom and Gumperz (1972) studied the use of two varieties of Norwegian – Ranamål symbolizing local values, and Bokmål associated with more Pan-Norwegian attitudes. The fact that speakers select one variety or another, or even both simultaneously, has to do with different values and attitudes, but also with different communicative intent and possibilities. And in the twenty-first century, as languaging possibilities become more complex, translanguaging is increasingly a mode of choice for bilinguals.

Bilingual contact

Traditionally, bilingual language use has been studied from the perspective of the language itself, and not of its speakers, leading scholars to characterize bilingual speech as reflecting language contact.[6] In his classic study, Weinreich (1953) referred to this with the term "interference." Since Weinreich, research has also shown that many features that were originally considered as so-called interference, or contact phenomena, were in fact developmental features not at all due to the other language in the speaker's environment, but similar to deviations from the norm that native-speaking children go through as they acquire a given language. Also, studies of bilingualism have shown that language contact phenomena may at times be a result of *volition*, that is, of intent, a way of giving emphasis or finding the right word, or of responding to intimacy with the interlocutor or changes in content. Scholars nowadays prefer the term "transference" to refer to language contact phenomena at all linguistic levels.

All speech is characterized by *borrowing*, that is, the taking of individual lexical items from other languages (as when English speakers say "au revoir" or "delicatessen," or when New Yorkers use the Yiddish word "schlep" to refer to a tiresome walk or carrying something which is difficult). Japanese has an alphabet, called *katakana*, devoted to words of foreign origin. For example, *arubaito* means "a part-time job" (from the German word *arbeit*), *hochikisu* means "stapler" (from the English word *Hotchkiss*, a company name and early maker of staplers), and *furaido poteto* (from the English words "fried potatoes") are very popular at *Makudonarudo* (McDonald's) (Rob Werner, personal communication, November 13, 2006). But the speech of bilinguals often reveals more *borrowings* or *loans* than that of monolinguals.

Sometimes, bilingual speakers borrow the form of a word from another language, along with its content. This is the case, for example, of bilingual Latinos who in New York refer to *bíldin* in speaking about the red-brick New York buildings in which they live, and reserve the Spanish word *edificio* for the buildings, usually a government office or school, that they found in their Caribbean country of origin (Otheguy and García, 1993). Some of these borrowings are *phonologically assimilated*, that is, they become part of the sound system of the language into which they come, as in the case of *bíldin*. Other times, these borrowings are *morphologically assimilated* and take on the grammatical characteristics of the borrowing language. This is the case, for example, of *rufo* or *lonchar* in the practices of U.S. Latinos, where the words are from English – "roof," "lunch" – but Spanish morphology is used. Haugen (1953) has referred to this phenomenon as "loan blends." Other times, bilingual speakers borrow only the meaning of a word. This is the case of U.S. Spanish *registrarse*, used in Spanish with the English meaning of "to register," when in Spanish the word *registrar* means to search. Haugen (1953) has referred to these cases as "loan shifts."

Sometimes bilinguals do not choose one language-based practice or the other, but select from both in one and the same speech act. This process of going back and forth from one language to the other is generally referred to as *code-switching*. Code-switching is defined as "the juxtaposition within the same speech exchange of passages of speech belonging to two different grammatical systems or subsystems" (Gumperz 1982: 59).

Code-switching may be of at least two types. The first type, *intrasentential*, refers to instances in which the switch occurs within the boundaries of a clause or a sentence. An example, given by Martínez (2006: 95) is:

Sí, y luego es una trampoline *así; pero aquí vienen los* ropes *así. Y nomás de ese tamaño. Esa era para brincar. No era* to . . . it wasn't a big trampoline. (Yes, and there was a *trampolín* like this, and the *sogas* come like this here. No more than this size. That was for jumping. It wasn't *para . . . no era un trampolín grande.*)

The second type, *intersentential*, describes when the switching occurs at clause or sentence boundaries, as in this example by Martínez (2006: 95): "Anyway, I was in and he was, you know, the one that would let you out. And he was laughing cause he saw me coming in. *Se estaba riendo de mí*." (He was laughing at me.)

As Auer (1995) points out, code-switching is a contextualization cue available only to bilinguals. Furthermore, one of the social functions of code-switching, the negotiation of language choice, is also unique to bilingual situations. Edwards (2004: 20) calls bilinguals "speakers whose twin bow-strings allow them not only the style-shifting available to monolinguals but also full language-shifting." And he concludes by saying that this ability is a valuable addition to the linguistic repertoire of speakers.

Code-switching often occurs spontaneously among bilingual speakers in communication with others who share their languages. Far from being a sign of inadequacy or sloppy language usage or lack of knowledge, it has been shown that code-switching is a sophisticated linguistic skill and a characteristic of the speech of fluent bilinguals (see Milroy and Muysken, 1995; and Auer, 1995, for an overview).

In studying bilingual communities, Myers-Scotton (1990, 1993) has shown how code-selection in a code-switching environment is used to negotiate interpersonal relationships. Choice of code is motivated according to whether a given available code is marked,[7] that is, whether it has social meaning, or not (Myers-Scotton calls this the "Markedness Model"). It assumes that when two or more codes are available, selecting a particular one is marked in the environment of the other that is not marked. The negotiating principle posits: "Choose the form of your conversational contribution such that it symbolizes the set of rights and obligations which you wish to be in force between speaker and addressee for the current exchange" (Myers-Scotton: 1990, 58). Through experiencing language in their community, speakers develop a sense of which code is unmarked for a given interaction. Unmarked choices are the most frequent. And a marked choice implies a renegotiation of rights and obligations between participants.

Studying the South African context, Finlayson and Slabbert (1997) have shown that in the case of the six male friends in their study, code-switching among seven languages – Zulu, Xhosa, Southern Sotho, Tswana, Afrikaans, Tsotsitaal, and English – may be a way of constructing social meanings. Zentella (1997) shows how for the bilingual girls in the *bloque* of her study, concepts of race, ethnicity, and class, intersect with setting and topic as speakers draw from their full range of linguistic features to code-switch.

A few scholars distinguish between *code-switching* and *code-mixing*. For some, code-switching refers to the bilingual's ability to select the language in response to external cues and according to the properties of the linguistic system; code-mixing on the other hand, refers to combining elements from each language because the speaker does not know how to differentiate between them (Meisel, 1989).

Code-mixing is usually accompanied by reduction in the linguistic forms and the uses of that language (De Bot and Clyne, 1994), as a result of a process of language attrition or loss.

Michael Clyne (2003a, b) has shown how the field of language contact studies has shifted in the past decade as a result of globalization and increased migration. As we said before, the language practices of bilinguals may bear little resemblance to the way in which languages are taught in schools. In the twenty-first century traditional *language contact* studies, as originally handled by the pioneers in the study of bilingualism, such as Haugen and Weinreich, have been extended to include internal and external motivations for contact and change, cross-cultural and intercultural discourse, and pragmatics,[8] all disciplines that did not exist when the pioneers embarked on their investigations. Since the 1980s, studies of transfer, borrowing, and interference tend more to be referred to under the term "cross-linguistic influence" (Sharwood Smith and Kellerman, 1986).

Our concept of translanguaging shifts the lens from cross-linguistic influence, proposing that what bilinguals do is to intermingle linguistic features that have hereto been administratively or linguistically assigned to a particular language or language variety. Translanguaging is thus the communicative norm of bilingual communities and cannot be compared to a prescribed monolingual use.

Models of Bilingualism

Because social groups and individuals have dissimilar needs, aspirations, and resources, bilingualism has adopted different forms at various times and in different places. Traditionally two models of bilingualism have been advanced in the scholarly literature to reflect these different forms – subtractive and additive – which we review below. But especially in the twenty-first century, other forms of bilingualism have been constituted that have not received scholarly attention. In this book, we name and describe two additional models of bilingualism – *recursive* and *dynamic*.

Subtractive

When monoglossic ideologies persist, and monolingualism and monolingual schools are the norm, it is generally believed that children who speak a language other than that of the state should be encouraged to abandon that language and instead take up only the dominant language. The model of individual bilingualism that follows is subtractive as in Figure 3.1:

$$L1 + L2 - L1 \rightarrow L2$$

Figure 3.1 Subtractive Bilingualism

In this model, the student speaks a first language and a second one is added while the first is subtracted. The result is a child who speaks only the second language.

This bilingualism is characterized by increasing loss of linguistic features of the first language. Immigrants to the United States, and other social contexts that do not favor bilingualism, usually follow this pattern. As a result, the bilingualism of the second generation of the immigrant group gives way to the monolingualism of the third generation.[9]

Perhaps no harsher school measure to achieve this subtractive bilingualism has been known than the one followed by many states in the education of Indigenous children. In the U.S., as in many other countries, Indigenous children were sent to boarding schools where they were effectively cut off from communication with parents and communities who spoke their home languages. This led to the silencing of the children's languages, rendering them monolingual and subtracting the possibility of their bilingualism. As we will see in later chapters, this monolingual approach to the education of these children led to the death of many Indigenous languages throughout the world.

Additive

Bilingualism for prestigious groups and the elite has always been additive, a model under which the second language is added to the person's repertoire and the two languages are maintained. This additive bilingualism model can be rendered as in Figure 3.2:

$$L1 + L2 = L1 + L2$$

Figure 3.2   Additive Bilingualism

Despite the benefits of this approach, bilingualism here is still seen from the perspective of a monolingual norm. That is, bilingualism within this model is simply double monolingualism, a category different from monolingualism, but with bilingual individuals expected to be and do with each of their languages the same thing as monolinguals. The model of additive bilingualism was proposed by Lambert (1975) as he and his colleagues developed bilingual school programs in Canada that responded to the country's declared bilingual identity in 1969 (more on this in Chapter 6).

Recursive

In cases when bilingualism is developed after the language practices of a community have been suppressed, the development of the community's mother tongue is not a simple addition that starts from a monolingual point. When a community engages in efforts to revitalize their language practices, as, for example in the case of the Māori of Aotearoa/New Zealand, individuals are not starting from scratch and adding simply a second language. The ancestral language continues to be used in traditional ceremonies and by many in the community to different degrees. Therefore, bilingualism is not simply additive, but recursive. These bilingual individuals and communities often move back and forth along a bilingual continuum. And in so doing, the language is not added whole, but in bits and pieces, as ancestral language practices are reconstituted for new functions. Indeed in these cases bilingualism is recursive because it reaches back to the bits and pieces of an ancestral language as it is reconstituted for new functions and as it gains momentum to thrust itself forward towards the future.

This recursive bilingualism does not stem from a monoglossic vision that starts out from monolingualism (as does additive bilingualism), but it originates in already heteroglossic languaging practices, in bilingualism per se. We call this model of bilingualism *recursive* as rendered in Figure 3.3:

Bilingual

Figure 3.3 Recursive Bilingualism

Dynamic

The model of recursive bilingualism is also insufficient to reflect the complex bilingual competence needed in some societies in the twenty-first century. A more heteroglossic conception of bilingualism recognizes its adjustments as it shifts and bounces. Bilingualism is not simply linear but *dynamic*, drawing from the different contexts in which it develops and functions. More than ever, categories such as first language (L1) and second language (L2), base and guest languages, host and borrowing languages, are not in any way useful (more on this in the section Questioning Assumptions, below), because the world's globalization is increasingly calling on people to interact with others in ways that defy traditional categories. In the linguistic complexity of the twenty-first century, bilingualism involves a much more dynamic cycle where language practices are multiple and ever adjusting to the multilingual multimodal terrain of the communicative act, as in Figure 3.4:

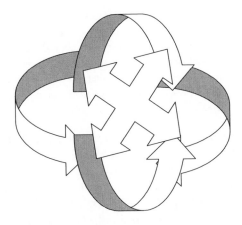

Figure 3.4 Dynamic Bilingualism*

* The intermingling of the arrows, some linear, some elliptical, some shaded to indicate one language, others blank to indicate the other languages, does not indicate directionality, but simultaneous multiplicity of multilingual discourses

With language interaction taking place on different planes including multimodalit-ies, that is, different modes of language (visuals as well as print, sound as well as text, and so on) as well as multilingualism, it is possible for individuals to engage in multiple complex communicative acts that do not in any way respond to the linear models of bilingualism proposed above. The all-terrain vehicle of bilingualism that we illustrated in Chapter 1 moves along communicative ridges and craters created by multiple conditions dealing with individuals, societies, contexts, and language practices. This dynamic model of bilingualism is also applicable to multilingual African and Asian contexts in which children engage in multiple discursive practices that incorporate the many language practices that they have available. But it is increas-ingly applicable in the developed West. For us, this model of dynamic bilingualism is closely related to the concept of plurilingualism which we consider next.

Dynamic bilingualism and plurilingualism
We use the term "dynamic bilingualism" in ways similar to the ways in which European scholars use the term "plurilingualism," referring to the understanding that language use in the twenty-first century requires differentiated abilities and uses of multiple languages as citizens cross borders either physically or virtually. The Language Policy Division of the Council of Europe[10] proposes the concept of plurilin-gualism as:

- The intrinsic capacity of all speakers to use and learn, alone or through teaching, more than one language. *The ability to use several languages to varying degrees and for distinct purposes* is defined in the Common European Framework of Reference for Languages (p.168) as the ability "to use languages for the purposes of com-munication and to take part in intercultural action, where a person, viewed as a social agent, has proficiency, of varying degrees, in several languages and experi-ence of several cultures." This ability is concretized in a repertoire of languages a speaker can use. The goal of teaching is to develop this competence (hence the expres-sion: plurilingualism as a competence).
- An educational value that is the basis of *linguistic tolerance*: Speakers' awareness of their plurilingualism may lead them to give equal value to each of the varieties they themselves and other speakers use, even if they do not have the same func-tions (private, professional or official communication, language of affiliation, etc). But this awareness should be assisted and structured by schools since it is no sense automatic (hence the expression: plurilingualism as a value). (Our emphasis, Council of Europe, 2000a)

The concept of plurilingualism has at its core the idea that European citizens in the twenty-first century must have at their disposal a varying and shifting repertoire of language practices to fulfill different purposes. But besides having *plurilingual competence*, European citizens are encouraged to develop *linguistic tolerance* as they learn to value different language practices. Although it is acknowledged that plurilingual competence may be developed either through schooling, private study, or even participation in public life, the school is given a primary role in the develop-ment of *plurilingualism as a positive value*. This acknowledges that the educational system needs to develop citizens who are capable of linguistic tolerance towards speakers who "language" differently.

The concept of plurilingualism is helpful in that it enables us to shed concepts of balanced bilingualism, or the idea that children be equally competent in two languages in all contexts and with all interlocutors. We also value the idea of plurilingualism because it extends mastery of two or more standard languages to include hybrid language practices. Thus the concept of plurilingualism confirms the idea proposed in Chapter 1 that one plus one does not always equal two.

Increasingly, the world seeks to develop bilingual citizens who function within the plurilingual dynamics of the twenty-first century. For example, Posner (1991) suggests the concept of *polyglot dialogue* with everyone speaking their language, but understanding everyone else's. A similar concept, that of *Receptive Multilingualism* (RM), is proposed by Braunmüller (2002, 2006) for speakers of genetically closely related languages. He gives the example of Scandinavia where speakers of Danish and Swedish, for example, would speak to each other in their own vernacular, probably pronounced a little more distinctly and/or more slowly. Braunmüller (2006) believes that RM would work well for Europe, and would stop the rise of English as a lingua franca, since only Finnish/Estonian, Latvian/Lithuanian, Hungarian, Greek, Albanian, Basque (Euskara), and the Celtic vernaculars are not part of larger European language families. Since the mid-1990s, the European Union has supported the production of the *EuroCom-series*, focusing on helping students acquire reading comprehension of genetically related languages in a short time and without much additional language-specific learning.

Summary

In the twenty-first century, we need to reshape our concept of bilingualism and bilingual individuals in order to fit the communicative exigencies of the bilingual languaging needed in today's interdependent and technologically enriched world. We need to move from ways of looking at bilingualism as two separate languages. But because communities, nations, and states have different needs, aspirations, resources, and power, different kinds of bilingualism exist and all are considered in this book. Thus, we do not use the term "plurilingualism," useful as it may be in many contexts, and prefer instead to speak about various models of bilingualism that are inclusive of the different circumstances in which people language throughout the world.

Table 3.1 summarizes the four models of bilingualism that educators must think about as they establish bilingual education programs. Only the first – subtractive –

Table 3.1 Models of Bilingualism

Subtractive	*Additive*	*Recursive*	*Dynamic*
Moves towards monolingualism	Attempts *balanced bilingualism*	Accepts the *flows of bilingualism*	*Encourages communicative and dynamic bilingualism*

has monolingualism as its goal, with the other three offering different positions with regards to bilingualism.

Questioning Assumptions

Viewing bilingualism as social practices of individuals (Heller, 2007) with trans-languaging as its core, and not simply as two languages that are spoken whole, leads us to problematize concepts that have heretofore been accepted in the bilingual educa-tion literature – "semilingualism," "language dominance," "mother tongue," "second-language learners," and "heritage-language learners." We will turn to examining how each of these terms have been used in the literature and give reasons why we should question these concepts. There are two general conceptualizations that run across our discussion. First, that the concepts of semilingualism, language dominance, and mother tongue emerge from a treatment of bilingualism from only a linguistic angle, and not from the perspective of bilinguals themselves who translanguage as common practice. Second, that if we adopt the angle of bilingual speakers who translanguage, then we could substitute the simple word "bilingual" for second-language or heritage-language learner. Putting bilingualism at the center of the dis-cussion by insisting that these students are emergent bilinguals, or bilinguals engaging in complex translanguaging practices, can lead us to abandon a monolingual viewpoint and use a more heteroglossic lens, which would allow for a fuller vision of the range of language practices and experiences that bilinguals bring.

Semilingualism

The obsession with monolinguals as the norm of reference has led to the proposal of the concept of *semilingualism*, referring to the unequal performance of bilingual children in their two languages when compared to monolingual children (see Skutnabb-Kangas and Toukomaa, 1976). The development of sociolinguistics has expanded our understandings of the languaging practices of bilinguals; that is, their discursive practices, and how these in turn are affected by social and political constraints. This increased understanding has led scholars to abandon the concept of semilingualism, no longer considering it a useful characterization. And yet, many bilingual educational programs and bilingual educators, eager to regulate the lan-guage practices of bilingual children and impose monolingual norms, continue to refer to children who engage in translanguaging as semilingual.

It is true that all children deserve an opportunity to develop bilingualism of the kind most applicable for them. It is also important for educators to help all children acquire full proficiency in the academic standard of the language of power in the society in which they live. But characterizing as semilinguals those who engage in naturally occurring translanguaging practices contributes to the linguistic stigmat-ization and language-shaming that is responsible for the academic failure of many bilingual children who are members of minoritized groups. Identity plays an import-ant role in the investment of learners to develop their bilingualism and to engage in schools (Norton, 2000; more on identity in Chapters 4 and 5).

Language dominance

Another concept prevalent in twentieth-century bilingualism studies, that has been increasingly questioned, is that of *language dominance*, tested frequently by psychologists using speed of reaction and translation speed tests. The dominant bilingual was defined as one for whom competence in one of the languages was superior to the competence in the other (Lambert, 1955). Objecting to the use of speed tests to determine language dominance of bilinguals, Fishman *et al.* (1971) argued that where bilingualism is socially constructed, and not merely an occupation or hobby, the concept of language dominance as determined by speed tests is irrelevant. Bilinguals are much more than just two monolinguals, and often, as we will see, it is difficult to disentangle abilities and functioning in one language from that in the other. It is true, however, that for some tasks, and when requested to act monolingually, bilinguals might be more dominant in one language than the other. Language dominance is task-specific. Bilinguals generally translanguage. It is only when bilinguals are forced to choose only one language in carrying out a precise task that we may be able to speak of their language dominance for that exact event.

Mother tongue

A common concept in the literature on bilingualism is that of *mother tongue.* According to Lieberson (1969: 291), the United Nations defines mother tongue as "the language usually spoken in the individual's home in his early childhood, although not necessarily used by him at present." As we saw in Chapter 1, the UNESCO 1953 document that poses the advantages of vernacular education uses the term "mother tongue." So does the 1977 Directive of the Council of the European Community on the education of the children of migrant workers. This directive states that member states should promote the teaching of the mother tongue and the culture of the country of origin in the education of migrant workers' children.

Kroon (2003: 36) gives a reason for the coining and use of the term mother tongue: "The awareness or invention of a common mother tongue plays a central role in the attempt to establish and develop the awareness of a common fatherland, i.e., a nation-state. A fatherland needs a mother tongue, which education has to supply, and generally speaking, this is done by selecting, standardizing and teaching a so-called national or official language." Many minoritized language groups have adopted the term "mother tongue" to refer to their language practices, sometimes the language of their ancestors. Kaplan and Baldauf (1997) give us reasons to question its use. Speaking of a child born to a Tamil-speaking mother in Malaysia possibly acquiring Tamil, Straits Malay, and/or Straits Chinese, and/or Bahasa Malay, and/or English, Kaplan and Baldauf say (1997: 36): "One may be a native speaker of a language even though one's mother was not [. . .]. It is impossible to designate that individual's mother tongue except in the literal sense, and it is not so useful to do so [. . .]. It is not a useful term, but it is, nonetheless [. . .] widely used." Baker and Prys Jones give us yet another reason for why the term has to be questioned (1998: 50): "'Mother tongue' tends to be used for language minorities and much less so for language majorities. The term therefore tends to be a symbol of separation of minority and majority, or those with less, as opposed to those with more power and status."

Skutnabb-Kangas (1981: 18) has shown the difficulties of identifying a mother tongue and refers to four criteria that can be differently identified:

- Origin   The language(s) one learned first
- Competence   The language(s) one knows best
- Function   The language(s) one uses most
- Identification
    ○ Internal   The language(s) one identifies with
    ○ External The language(s) others identify one with

Skutnabb-Kangas (1981) concludes that it is often impossible to identify an individual's single mother tongue. Instead, competence in a language, the function for which it is used, and the identification with that language either by oneself or by others shifts and changes.

Once we consider the language practices of people, the concept of mother tongue itself can be questioned. How does one identify an individual's mother tongue when many are spoken by the mother in the home and acquired simultaneously, and often used in translanguaging ways? And how does one then acknowledge the role of the father and other relatives in societies and social groups in which the mother and the father have different language practices, or in cases, as that of the Indigenous group in the Vaupes area of Colombia and Brazil, where the primary language is that of the father? (See Romaine, 1989.) What the state calls mother tongue may also not necessarily be the language of the home. In China, for example, children will be expected to learn in what is called their mother tongue, Putonghua (Mandarin), which is not always the language of the home. In Singapore, where official policy imposes learning of the child's so-called "ethnic mother tongue," it is ethnicity which determines which languages will be learned in school – Mandarin for the Chinese, Malay for the Malays, and Tamil for those of Indian origin – irrespective of the actual language used in the home. And ironically, the so-called "ethnic mother tongue" is determined by the ethnicity of the father! (Baetens Beardsmore, 1998.) Because the role of the family is changing as rapidly as that of language use itself, we prefer in this book to speak of *home language practices*.

But we warn the reader that the concept of home language is also, at times, limiting. For example, Te Reo Māori is the ancestral language of all Māoris in Aotearoa/New Zealand even if some don't speak the language fluently at home in the present and it is not their mother tongue in the literal sense. At present, those involved in the Māori revitalization movement often refer to themselves as second-language speakers. But Te Reo Māori is neither their second nor first language, nor their home language, nor their mother tongue. Acknowledging, however, that bilingualism is complex, and is never a full ability in two languages, enables us to speak about Māori *bilingualism*.

In some cases, this bilingualism might be *emergent*, revitalizing a language that is no longer a first language or mother tongue, but that has deep ancestral connections and is part of their languaging in ceremonies and rituals. Thus, these Māori learners might be considered emergent bilinguals, and not simply second-language learners.

The same is true of the Deaf community. Most Deaf children are born to hearing parents, and sign language might not be the language of the home. But Deaf children need to develop bilingual practices in both signed and written languages. And although the sign language might not be the language of the home or the "mother tongue" in the literal sense, it is most important for bilingual Deaf children. Bosso and Kuntze (1994: 43) express the concept that Deaf children in the U.S. must be bilingual, saying: "ASL allows deaf students to become literate about their histories, experiences and culture, and it is through a full command of English that deaf students find themselves linguistically empowered to engage in dialogue with the various sectors of the wider society."

Second-language learners/speakers

As the example of Pablo in the beginning of this chapter shows, understanding language only through a monoglossic perspective leads many teachers to assume that children are *second-language learners* or *second-language speakers* in school, just because they engage in different language practices at home or because they have another language background. To be bilingual and speak another language at home certainly does not mean that one is necessarily a second-language learner in school. After having immigrated from Cuba as an eleven-year-old to New York City, García continues to speak Spanish at home. Does that mean that she's a second-language learner, a second-language speaker? Until what point does one remain a second-language learner or a second-language speaker? What aspects of language use make one a second-language learner? We have already determined that Māoris in Aotearoa/New Zealand who are learning their ancestral language cannot be simply second-language learners because of their recursive bilingualism, and the strong presence of bits of their own language practices in rituals throughout.

The literature on English teaching has already shed this construction of native speakers, second-language speakers, and those learning English as a foreign language. In the twentieth century, Braj Kachru (1985) proposed a model of three concentric circles: the *inner circle* representing the native speakers; the *outer circle* consisting of second-language speakers; and the *expanding circle* of people learning English. But, in our globalized world, this model has been challenged since "the traditional definition of 'second-language user' (as one who uses the language for communication within their own country) no longer makes sense" (Graddol, 2006: 110). Acknowledging the growing bilingualism with English in the world, and the impossibility of distinguishing between second-language speakers and learners, Pakir (1993) refers to Kachru's second group as *English-knowing bilinguals*, and to the third group as *English-using bilinguals*.

Language learning is a continuous developmental process that occurs throughout a lifetime and is recursive and circular. In that sense, we are all language learners at certain times, under certain conditions, with certain people. Characterizing bilinguals as second-language learners robs bilingualism of its possibilities of being considered as the norm for large sections of the world's population.

In the globalized context of the twenty-first century, the concept of a second-language learner must be replaced by the concept of the bilingual whose communicative practices include translanguaging. Those who are learning a second language should be considered emergent bilinguals so that educators can understand that it will be impossible for their students to leave their home language practices behind if they are going to succeed in learning the additional language (for more on this, see García, Kleifgen, and Falchi, 2008). Conceptualizing emergent bilinguals as sliding across a bilingual continuum enables us to move away from artificial categorizations such as second-language learner vs. fluent speakers – which are difficult to determine.

The concept of a second-language speaker is also problematic. Is a second-language speaker someone who speaks with an accent? When does one stop being a second-language speaker? Terms such as "second-language learner" and "second-language speaker," when studied from a heteroglossic and bilingual perspective, make little sense. Instead, we should speak about "bilinguals," giving the term a full range of possibilities, and taking away the negative connotations associated with being second, and not first.

Heritage language

The term "heritage language" is also often used to refer to languages spoken by ethnic communities. It became popular in the Canadian context to refer to the educational programs that provincial governments of Canada set up within their elementary school systems, after the passage of its multicultural policy in the late 1960s. Alberta was the first Canadian province to pass legislation in 1971 permitting languages other than English and French to be used and taught in elementary schools (Danesi, McLeod, and Morris, 1993).

Although the term was not used in the United States, it has recently gained favor, as the word "bilingual" has been silenced (for more on this, see Chapter 8).[11] Since 1999, there has been a biennial conference focusing on issues of heritage-language teaching, research, and policy, and the Center for Applied Linguistics and the National Foreign Language Center have been much involved in these efforts.[12]

But who is a heritage-language learner? Someone who has some ability in a language that their parents, grandparents, or distant ancestors speak? Or is it someone whose parents, grandparents, or distant ancestors spoke that language, although s/he no longer does? What proficiency in that language must one have in order to be categorized as a heritage-language learner? And what connotations does the term "heritage" have? We think of old, ancient, in the past, when in fact, we are speaking about languages of the future. And what does focusing simply on the heritage language mean for the speaker? Doesn't it rob the child or adolescent of his bilingual identity and translanguaging possibilities by insisting on only one language? For these reasons, we think that bilingualism for these students is a much better focus, one that recognizes the fluidity of bilingual language use, the possibilities of bilingual acquisition and the potentiality of accessing a full range of expressive and communicative possibilities now and in the future (see O. García, 2005b).

Bilingual Abilities

Depending on the reasons for using their languages, bilinguals may have only *oracy* abilities in one language or the other – the ability to listen and speak – and not *literacy* abilities – the ability to read and write either language or vice versa.[13] Or they may have, as the Deaf do, *signacy*, that is, the ability to interpret or attend to, and produce signs (Nover and Andrews, 1999). But any one of these language abilities may be manifested in different combinations among bilingual individuals, as in Table 3.2:

Table 3.2   Language Abilities

Oracy	Literacy	Signacy
Listening	Reading	Attending[14]
Speaking	Writing	Producing

Sometimes bilinguals only have *receptive bilingual abilities*, that is, they may understand, read or attend to, or interpret, signs in more than one language, although they can't speak, write, or produce signs in more than one language. Other times bilinguals also have *productive bilingual abilities*, that is, they are capable of also speaking, writing and producing signs in more than one language, as in Table 3.3:

Table 3.3   Type of Bilingual Ability and Language Ability

	Oracy	Literacy	Signacy
Type of Bilingual Ability			
Receptive	Listening	Reading	Attending
Productive	Speaking	Writing	Producing

There are four circumstances that often produce *receptive* or *passive* bilinguals:

1. *Children of immigrant, Indigenous, or autochthonous minority background,*[15] whose home languages are not promoted in the wider society and who are often able to understand their parents and elders, but are incapable of speaking the language themselves.
2. *Deaf children* who are born to hearing parents, and whose education excludes the use of sign language, may not develop the ability to productively sign standardized sign languages.
3. *Those that have learned a language in traditional language programs* may understand, read, and interpret the language learned well, although they may be incapable of speaking, writing, or producing signs. In the United States, for example,

throughout the first half of the twentieth century and up to the language awareness brought about by Sputnik in 1959, foreign-language study was limited to two years and focused only on reading (García, 1997b). Many though not all programs of English for Specific Purposes (ESP) throughout the world, of the type geared towards engineers and technicians, aim to teach students only to read and comprehend written texts which may be needed in their professions.

4. *Scholars of extinct languages* also have biliteracy skills but may never be in a position to develop oracy in a language that they have never heard. This is especially true for dead languages that have sacred functions, such as Latin and Sanskrit. Although some scholars of Hebrew, the language of the Torah, also develop only literacy in Hebrew, the fact that Hebrew has been revived as a result of Zionism and the establishment of the state of Israel, means that many scholars of Hebrew also have developed productive ability.

The distinction between being a receptive and a productive bilingual has to do with levels of *language ability or skills*. But bilingualism can also be a consequence of *language function*, that is, the use to which one puts either language. In fact, language ability and language function are often interrelated, since one has to have the possibility to function and use a specific language or two languages in order to develop ability to engage in language practices that use either or both of the languages. Cenoz and Genesee (1998: 17) tell us that "language proficiency changes as a result of adjustments to interacting linguistic subsystems that reflect the user's communicative needs." Bilinguals have a different and distinct range of linguistic abilities, but their bilingual functioning is more subjected to social and political pressures than the language functioning of monolinguals.

For example, Deaf children may study only the written language of the majority community. In Moscow, they may study the Russian language, whereas in Quebec they study French. But their signing ability may be limited because schools rob them of the opportunity to function as bilingual signers. But in other societies, and even in some schools or areas, Deaf children are encouraged to learn a sign language *as well*. At some schools in Moscow, Russian Deaf children also study Russian Sign Language – a system that has its own structure, grammar, and norms distinct from the Russian language. Whether a Deaf Russian child is a competent user of sign language has much to do with the opportunities that school and society afford her or him (Debra Cole, personal communication, October 13, 2007).

Because sign languages are not heavily tied to national identity, and because Deaf children are often dismissed as disabled and their complex language use not understood, bilingual education for the Deaf has received less attention by governments than bilingual education for other minoritized populations. The little governmental attention that bilingual education for the Deaf receives means that there is often greater flexibility in policy and curriculum development with regards to bilingualism at schools for the Deaf than for other minoritized groups. This is not to say that these schools have full control; they are also bounded by politics, research, available resources, and societal norms and views at the local, national, and international levels (Cole, forthcoming).

Bilingual Development

Elective or obligatory?

Some individuals *choose* to develop bilingual abilities, often the result of studying the language in school or through personal effort. That is, their bilingualism is optional. This type of bilingual has been referred to as "elite bilingual" by Fishman (1977b) and "elective bilingual" by Valdés and Figueroa (1994). Other individuals are *forced* to develop bilingual abilities. That is, their bilingualism is obligatory. For example, for many Deaf sign language users, possessing oracy skills does not come naturally (Graney, 1997); yet, they are compelled to study and develop oracy skills at many schools. There is nothing elective about these Deaf bilinguals. The same can be said of immigrants, Indigenous peoples, and autochthonous minorities who are forced to learn and use only language practices that are not those of the home. Fishman (1977b) refers to these forced bilinguals as "folk" bilinguals, while Valdés and Figueroa (1994) call them "circumstantial bilinguals." Whether people are elective bilinguals or folk bilinguals is also related to whether they become bilingual as children or adults, the topic of the next section.

Children's bilingual development

Many guides for bilingual parenting have been published over the last few years,[16] including the *Bilingual Family Newsletter*, from Multilingual Matters. Different websites are devoted to helping parents embark on bilingual upbringing for the first time.[17] Interesting official developments to help future parents have taken place, for example, in Wales, where all parents attending family-planning clinics are now also given a kit-box with information on language planning for their future children, in an attempt to stimulate them to reflect as seriously on the bilingual future of their children as on their physical well-being (Edwards and Newcombe, 2006). In Scotland, too, there is official support of the same kind, with the promotion of guidebooks entitled *The Family Language Action Plan*, addressed to families. There is also a call center to give parents encouragement to place their children in a full-time nursery from birth to five years, with the clear indication that neither parent nor child need be a Gaelic speaker to join a Gaelic nursery. In Finland and Sweden, there is legal support for parents of Deaf children to learn sign languages during their children's very early years. What these initiatives show is that there are incentives and encouragement to become bilingual at least in some parts of the world; whereas in others, there is still often discouragement and denigration.

It is important to understand concepts of bilingual development. "Acquisition" of an additional language is distinguished from "learning" another language. Acquisition, according to Krashen (1981b) refers to "picking up" a language, as is done in the family, in the street or community, or in informal ways. Most people who acquire a language develop oracy first. The term "learning" a second language is used to indicate the study of the language as is done in school or other formal settings.

Another important concept is whether children become bilingual either *simultaneously*, acquiring the two languages more or less at the same time in the home, or *sequentially*, that is, acquiring the second language at a later stage and usually once they go to school. Simultaneous bilingualism has been referred to as the acquisition of "bilingualism as a first language" (Swain, 1972).

In the twenty-first century, the concepts of sequential and simultaneous bilingualism seem to work less well, as some children go to school earlier and participate in complex multilingual encounters, in reality and virtual reality, with ease and frequency from an early age. Clyne relates how when his daughter was seven, one of her friends, noting that she spoke German to her father, asked whether she was German. "Oh no," she replied, "I'm bilingual." Some scholars now often refer to *childhood bilinguals* (those who develop bilingualism in childhood) and *emerging bilinguals* (those who develop bilingualism later) instead of speaking of simultaneous and sequential bilingualism (Clyne, 2003a).

The scholarship on *bilingual acquisition* or *bilingual first-language acquisition* (BFLA) (as opposed to first- or second-language acquisition) has blossomed since the 1980s (for a review, see Genesee, 2003; see also De Houwer, 1990; Hoffman, 1991; Meisel, 1989; Romaine, 1989). Research during the last two decades indicates that infants possess the ability to discriminate language-related differences in auditory input very early, as well as the ability to remember such information; abilities that make the acquisition of bilingualism possible (see Boysson-Bardies, 1999). As concluded in the review by Genesee (2003: 212), the "rate of bilingual development and/or age of emergence of certain language phenomena in bilingual children [is] comparable to or within the age range reported for monolingual development." Bilingual development in early childhood mirrors monolingual development. De Houwer (2006: 782) summarizes:

> The "milestones" of bilingual development and their timing are the same as those for monolingual children. Bilingual children's comprehension precedes their production, babbling is typical toward the end of the first year, then comes a period in which single-word utterances are produced, to be followed by a short or drawn-out period of two-word utterances. Then come multiword utterances, soon to be followed by multiclausal ones. There is no evidence that the fact that children growing up with two languages have to process more variation in the input has an effect on the rate of acquisition: on the whole, bilingual and monolingual children reach the milestones of development within similar age ranges.

There is no evidence that bilingual children differ from monolingual children except for the fact that they produce mixed utterances in addition to monolingual ones; that is, they translanguage from an early age. And young bilingual children know usually by the second year of life how to make the choice of whether to use one language or the other, or a mix of the two. Some children growing up with bilingual input produce only one language. In fact, this is the most common pattern of interaction between bilingual immigrant parents and their bilingual children. This seems to offer support for the *Intentionality Model for Language Acquisition* that places agency of the child at the center of the developmental process (Bloom and Tinker, 2002).

The natural simultaneous development of the bilingualism of children has always been prevalent in many countries of Asia and Africa, for example in India or South

Africa. In the western world, however, most documented cases of simultaneous bilingualism are of middle-class children with whom one parent spoke one language, and the other parent spoke the other language (see Deuchar and Quay, 2000). In fact, the most detailed cases of children's bilingual development have been those of the children of linguists. Ronjat (1913) was the first to introduce the concept of *one person – one language* in developing simultaneous bilingualism in children. Leopold (1939), who meticulously noted the bilingual development of his daughter, Hildegard, in English and German, also made special efforts to balance the use of two languages by carefully separating them: he only spoke German to his daughter, and his wife used only English. Volterra and Taeschner (1978) document two sisters acquiring Italian and German simultaneously, and determine that they went through three stages.[18] These stages have been questioned by more recent scholarship that has documented bilingual development that is less linear and more complex, involving the child's ability to categorize the variation in speech sounds into two main ways of speaking (De Houwer, 1990, 2006; Meisel, 1989; Paradis and Genesee, 1996). In reality, many cases of bilingual development of children take place in mixed-language families where parents are bilingual. This is the case of Zentella's (1997) study of language use in *el bloque* by Puerto Rican girls growing up bilingual not only in bilingual homes, but also in a bilingual community.

There are ever more cases of reconstituted families where there may be no common language shared between the new partners and their respective offspring in the nuclear family. This new sort of family cell is fairly frequent in international circles such as the headquarters of the European Union in Brussels, where mixed-language marriages among the civil servants from all over Europe are commonplace. Since all these civil servants are expected to be trilingual and they send their children to European Schools where they too are led to trilingual competence, when marriages break up and new partnerships are formed, deciding on what language patterns to follow in private home life may be complex and not always easy to solve (Baetens Beardsmore, personal communication, March 2007). Another complexity is raising Deaf children who migrate to another country and have to learn new languages (both signed and written) when their parents may not know either language. *The Bilingual Family Newsletter* publishes ever more question-and-answer articles in its columns about complex cases such as these.

Adults' bilingual development

Although the development of bilingualism in infancy and continuing through early childhood is ever more understood, it is also possible to develop bilingual and biliteracy competence in adolescence and in adulthood. Many adolescents who immigrate become bilingual through participation with their peers and through schooling. Adults also can develop bilingual and biliteracy fluency, and reach high levels of competence when they study a second language in a well-designed educational program (Rivera and Huerta-Macías, 2008). Extremely successful programs for adults have been noted with the case of Ulpan in Israel, intensive programs of Hebrew language learning funded and required by the state of Israel for all newcomers. In 1987, the European Commission introduced Erasmus, an exchange program that encourages university students from different European countries to study for part of their degree in a different language in another country. This has now been extended to other parts of the globe under the name Erasmus-World. In answering whether students need to be fluent in the language of the university in which they plan to study, the website says:

> If you are starting from scratch, do not be put off. Learning a new language will show that you are the kind of person who can take on a challenge. [. . .] And do not despair – everyone can learn languages. You will find that it is easier and more fun when you are living and studying in the country than when you are in the classroom at home! So, do not let lack of a language deter you. Many students have started with no knowledge and, at the end of their degree, acquired a good working knowledge of another language. (Erasmus, 2007)

Tribal Colleges that are fully accredited and operated by American Indian tribes in the United States offer Native American language and culture courses. For example, at Lac Courte Oreilles Ojibwa Community College in Wisconsin, Ojibwemowin language is offered to adult learners and is a requirement for the Native Studies associates degree (Sumida, personal communication, April 2007). Language programs such as this meet the historical mission of Tribal Colleges in the United States, which is based on the need to serve American Indian college students and honor their cultures. In many instances, the spaces that these Tribal Colleges create for language are the only formal classroom time available for the language in the community. The same can be said of the growing number of "heritage-language study" at universities in the United States.

Child vs. adult bilingualism

Many have proposed that there are advantages to the early introduction of a second language in school (Cenoz and Genesee, 1998: 28). This is based on the widespread belief that earlier is better for bilingualism (Birdsong, 1999; Genesee, 1978; Harley and Wang, 1997; Long, 1990). And yet, there seem to be no age-related differences in the process of language learning. Starting to acquire a second language in childhood is not in itself a sufficient condition for the development of full bilingualism (Meisel, 2004). Genesee (2004: 555) summarizes the arguments saying: "Notwithstanding some compelling arguments (e.g., Long, 1990; Scovel, 1988), empirical evidence in favor of a critical period for L2 acquisition has been equivocal, with some studies claiming evidence for the critical period and others evidence against it (White and Genesee, 1996)." The development of bilingualism in school often has much more to do with pedagogical and student factors than with biological predispositions to acquire language (Genesee, 2004). So findings, for example, on the effects of starting to teach children in kindergarten vs. secondary schools through the medium of a second language (what in Canada are known as early-immersion and late-immersion programs)[19] have been equivocal. Whereas some report the impressive progress of students starting at the secondary level (Krashen, Long, and Scarcella, 1982; Genesee, 1988), others find that students starting at kindergarten do better (Genesee, 1981; Wesche, Towes-Janzen, and MacFarlane, 1996). But even

Wesche, Towes-Janzen, and MacFarlane (1996) propose that the differences between early onset and late onset of bilingualism in school are negligible by the time students are in secondary school. Older students can make quick progress. Singleton (2001) has also shown that early second-language learners are neither more successful nor more efficient in acquiring a second language. The same has been found in foreign-language learning contexts (Muñoz, 2006).

Because children have more time to practice and develop their bilingual competence, and because often the social and educational settings in which they participate are more conducive to authentic practice, it turns out they often appear to be more successful in developing their bilingualism. Yet, in formal educational settings, adults, able to use their metalinguistic skills in a first language more efficiently, learn more quickly than younger learners. Children's communicative needs are also simpler than those of adults, and children's language practices are often supported through gestures and visuals. Thus, the language that children need is less complex and more contextualized than that needed by adults, leading many to think that they are better bilingual acquirers. In short, there is little evidence for a "critical period" for second-language learning, except perhaps for the development of a native-like accent, and adults are quite capable of becoming bilingual. Johnstone (2002: 20) summarizes the findings by saying: "given suitable teaching, motivation, and support, it is possible to make a success of language learning at any age and stage, though older learners are less likely to approximate to the levels of a native speaker."

In the next section, we consider how bilingualism has been studied from a neurolinguistic and psycholinguistic perspective.

Neurolinguistic and Psycholinguistic Considerations

Brain processing

Neurolinguistic studies suggest that there might be a different cerebral organization that is specific to the bilingual (Fabbro, 1999). This evidence is mostly drawn from studies of *aphasia*, that is, the loss or impairment of language skills as a result of brain damage (for a review, see Paradis, 1983). Long before PET scans and MRI techniques were used to study the brain, dichotic listening and tachistoscopic presentations[20] were used to examine the relationship between brain and behavior in bilingualism. Albert and Obler (1978) were among the first to say that there was more right-hemisphere brain activity in the language processing of bilinguals and that the bilingual brain may be lateralized differently.

In the last two decades, the evidence seems to suggest that there are processing differences in bilinguals. For example, loss of one language and its subsequent recovery in aphasic bilinguals seems to occur differently from the loss and recovery of the other language (Goral, Levy, Obler, and Cohen, 2006; Levy, Goral, and Obler, 1999). Most neuropsychologists agree that bilingual experience has some influence on brain function, although they disagree on the neuro-psychological consequences of their experiments (see Abutalevi, Cappa, and Perani, 2001; and Klein, Milner, Zatorre, Evans, and Meyer, 1994). Abutalevi, Cappa, and Perani (2001) conclude that the bilingual brain is certainly not the sum of two monolingual language systems. Cook (1992) summarizes the evidence saying that bilinguals are "multicompetent" and process language in ways that differ essentially from those of monolinguals.

This difference in language processing has large consequences for voice-onset times in each language, that is, the length of time that passes between when a consonant is released and when the vibration of the vocal folds begins, or the voicing (see for example Zampini and Green, 2001). Bilinguals also have different levels of vocabulary (Pearson, Fernandez and Oller, 1992, 1993), and their speech acts are encoded differently (Walters, 2005). These psycholinguistic differences of bilinguals may have enormous consequences as we think about their schooling.

Psychological state

Hamers and Blanc (1983) have studied what they call the *bilinguality* of bilinguals which they define as: "the psychological state of an individual who has access to more than one linguistic code as a means of social communication; the degree of access will vary along a number of dimensions which are psychological, cognitive, psycholinguistic, social psychological, social, sociological, sociolinguistic, sociocultural and linguistic" (Hamers and Blanc, 1989 translation: 6). Bilinguality includes multiple aspects of a bilingual identity – emotions, preferences, anxiety, personality, social influence, and reference groups (Pavlenko, 2005, 2006; Pavlenko and Blackledge, 2004). In the rootlessness of globalization, attention has to be paid not only to bilingualism itself, and bilingual speakers, but also to the psychological, physiological, and social environments that the concept of bilinguality makes evident (Aronin and Ó Laoire, 2003).

Increasingly, what today distinguishes the study of bilingualism is the interface between the sociolinguistics of bilingualism and psycholinguistics (Walters, 2005). The study of bilingualism must integrate the broader question of social and political relations and organizations (the subject of the Chapter 4) with the psycholinguistic level, so that we can link language practices to larger-scale analysis of bilinguals in school.

Psycholinguistic constructs

Perhaps no other scholar of bilingualism has contributed as much to the field of bilingual education as Jim Cummins. Based on the constructs of BICS (contextualized language skills and practices) and CALP (decontextualized language skills and practices) considered in Chapter 2, Cummins (1979, 1981b, 2000) proposes that it takes *five to seven years* to develop in an additional language the decontextualized academic language skills and practices of CALP.

Cummins (1979, 1981b) further considers the construct of the *interdependence of the two languages* of a bilingual. He explains the concept of linguistic interdependence by saying: "To the extent that instruction in Lx is effective in promoting proficiency in Lx, transfer of this proficiency to Ly will occur provided there is adequate exposure to Ly" (Cummins 2000: 38). He has also argued (2000: 26) that if the conditions are right, "transfer across languages is two-way," so that his theoretical construct of interdependency is multi-directional and recursive, acknowledging the different directions that linguistic interdependency takes. That is, Cummins does not posit that the first language needs to be fully developed before the second language is introduced in school. Cummins (2000: 25) argues: "Rather the first language must not be abandoned before it is fully developed, whether the second language is introduced simultaneously or successively, early or late, in that process." He also insists that transfer will not happen automatically, but that schools are responsible for guaranteeing the child's adequate exposure to each language.

Cummins' interdependence hypothesis leads him to posit a *Common Underlying Proficiency* (CUP). Cummins says that the two languages of a bilingual individual are not stored separately in the brain (as in the model of Separate Underlying Proficiency with competition among languages), but co-exist and rely on a common, and not separate, underlying language proficiency as in Figure 3.5 (taken from Baker and Hornberger, 2001, pp. 131 and 132).

To help us understand what this might mean, Cummins gives us the image of a *dual iceberg*, with the surface features of the two languages separated at the top level where they are visible, but like an iceberg, emerging from the same source. Thus, a bilingual individual might have different phonology (sounds), morphology (word formation), syntax (arrangement of words in sentences), and lexicon (words) in each of their languages, but the motor that makes language use and practices possible is exactly the same for each language. Students who have developed literacy in one language will tend to make stronger progress in acquiring literacy in an additional language since knowledge of linguistic practices, as well as prior knowledge of the world, transfer across languages. Also, what is learned in one language does not have to be re-learned in another, since conceptual knowledge transfers, and it is just linguistic labels that might have to be taught.

Linguistic interdependence is present in the case of bilingualism in linguistically congruent, as well as linguistically distant languages. But it is stronger in the case

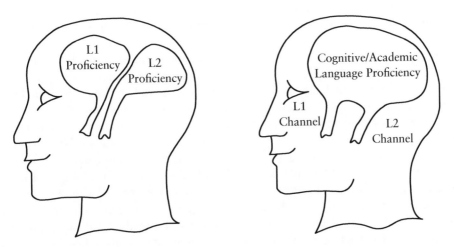

Figure 3.5   Separate Underlying Proficiency/Common Underlying Proficiency

of linguistically congruent languages where the interdependence can derive from linguistic factors, as well as familiarity with language and literacy practices and ways of using language. Yet, even in cases where the two languages are not linguistically congruent, for example, Chinese and English, English-speaking students learning Chinese will benefit from the familiarity with literacy use in English because they will understand, for example, that reading is really about making meaning from print, and that writing requires the ability to communicate to an unknown and distant audience. In addition, they will have had practice in decoding, directionality of print, the mechanics of writing in their own language, all useful for literacy practices in another language.

Insisting on the interdependence of the two languages of a bilingual child, and on the role of the Common Underlying Proficiency, Cummins' hypotheses also refute the fact that time spent in teaching in one language in particular has a direct relationship to the development of that particular language. Instead, these hypotheses posit that what is important for linguistic and academic development is time spent in meaningful instruction that will develop the cognitive base and the language and literacy practices from which academic language develops, and not the specific time that is spent teaching through one language or the other. Cummins (1981a), however, makes very clear that transfer of academic skills across languages does not happen automatically. Instead, it is most important that students be given extensive practice using both languages in academic ways.

Another one of Cummins' major contributions to the theoretical frameworks of bilingualism is his *threshold hypothesis*. The threshold hypothesis posits that high bilingual proficiency in two languages is associated with more positive cognitive effects (more on this in Chapter 5). When the threshold hypothesis has been tested with children learning Euskara, Spanish, and English in primary schools in the Basque Country, it has been found that Cummins' threshold level hypothesis can also be applied to trilingual situations (Lagabaster, 1998).

Cummins has never specified the threshold level that would be appropriate for developmental benefits. It has also remained unclear whether the threshold level is for each of the two languages or for both languages jointly. Despite its limitations, the threshold hypothesis has stimulated support for developing bilingualism, and has helped to disentangle issues of language proficiency from issues of academic functioning. For example, the threshold hypothesis warns us that a bilingual child who has reading difficulties in one of his languages may not have reached an adequate threshold of language proficiency. That is, the problem may not lie in reading ability per se, but on the language proficiency level acquired.

Cummins' psycholinguistic constructs have important consequences for bilingual education and schooling that will be considered in later chapters. His threshold hypothesis is useful because it posits that development of bilingualism, (whether additive, recursive, or dynamic) where the additional language is acquired at no cost, can lead to improved linguistic outcomes and academic success. In contrast, subtractive bilingualism, with children acquiring a second language at the expense of their first language, would most likely impair the possibility of developing the second language appropriately, since learners could not use their first language in making sense of new linguistic and cognitive situations. Cummins' interdependence hypothesis provides the basis for advancing our understandings of bilingualism in ways that fit the exigencies of twenty-first-century translanguaging.

Conclusion

This chapter has looked at bilingualism from different perspectives, but always insisting that *bilingualism is not monolingualism times two*. We looked at the broader communicative range that bilingualism provides over monolingualism, and we proposed that translanguaging is the normal mode of languaging when bilingual individuals are the norm. Translanguaging, or engaging in bilingual or multilingual discourse practices, is an approach to bilingualism that is centered, not on languages as has been often the case, but on the practices of bilinguals that are readily observable. These worldwide translanguaging practices are seen here not as marked or unusual, but rather are taken for what they are, namely the normal mode of communication that characterizes communities throughout the world.

This chapter has also made evident that bilingualism is strongly linked to social and political constructions, and cannot therefore be analyzed without reference to the social order. We expand the traditional models of bilingualism, suggesting that deficit models of subtractive bilingualism, or more prestigious models of additive bilingualism, may be insufficient in some contexts today. We proposed a recursive model of bilingualism, applicable especially to speakers in communities which are in the process of revitalizing their languages. We also identified a dynamic model of bilingualism that captures the complexity of bilingualism and multimodalities. This model of dynamic bilingualism has much to do with the concept of plurilingualism that has been advanced in the European context, but that has always been prevalent especially in many African and Asian contexts.

The various uses to which speakers put their bilingualism creates differences in language ability. The neurolinguistic and psycholinguistic evidence with regards to bilingualism is also explored. The chapter ends by discussing Cummins' theoretical constructs which combine psycholinguistic perspectives with social perspectives that enable us to see the effects of the social context on bilingualism.

In the next chapter we focus on the sociopolitical context of societal bilingualism, paying particular attention to language revitalization efforts and language ideologies, and reviewing the study of language planning and policy.

Questions for Reflection

1. What is meant by "bilingualism is not monolingualism times two"?
2. What do we mean by "translanguaging"? Describe some of the language practices of bilinguals, including language-contact phenomena.
3. Explain the four models of bilingualism considered in this chapter.
4. Discuss the concept of plurilingualism. How does it differ from the traditional definitions of bilingualism? What does it add to the concept of bilingualism? Why does this book insist on talking about dynamic bilingualism instead of adopting the term "plurilingualism"?

5. Discuss the difficulties with terms such as "mother tongue," "second-language speaker," "heritage speaker." Why would the term "bilingual" be more appropriate?
6. Identify different types of bilingual development and discuss the differences between child and adult bilingual development.
7. Discuss the theoretical constructs of bilingualism proposed by Jim Cummins, specifically the difference between contextualized and decontextualized language development, the interdependence hypothesis, and the threshold hypothesis.

Further Reading

Albert, M., and Obler, L.K. (1978). *The Bilingual Brain: Neuropsychological and Neuro-linguistic Aspects of Bilingualism.* Academic Press, New York.

Baetens Beardsmore, H. (1982). *Bilingualism: Basic Principles.* Multilingual Matters, Clevedon, UK. Second edn. 1986.

Cummins, J. (2000). *Language, Power and Pedagogy: Bilingual Children in the Crossfire.* Multilingual Matters, Clevedon, UK.

Grosjean, F. (1982). *Life with Two Languages.* Harvard University Press, Cambridge, MA.

Heller, M. (ed.) (2007). *Bilingualism. A Social Approach.* Palgrave Macmillan, New York.

Hélot, C. (2007). *Du bilinguisme en famille au plurilinguisme à l'école.* L'Harmattan, Paris.

Li Wei (2000). *The Bilingualism Reader.* Routledge, London.

Myers-Scotton, C. (2006). *Multiple Voices. An Introduction to Bilingualism.* Blackwell, Malden, MA.

Romaine, S. (1994). *Bilingualism.* Blackwell, Oxford.

Yip, V., and Matthews, S. (2007). *The Bilingual Child. Early Development and Language Contact.* Cambridge University Press, Cambridge.

4

The Sociopolitics of Bilingualism

People say you've become a man of letters, but where are your poems that I can sing at night when I miss you? [. . .] And, if you were Javanese, you would be able to write in Javanese. You write in Dutch, Gus, because you no longer want to be Javanese. You write for Dutch people. Why do you honor them so greatly? They drink and eat from the Javanese earth. You do not eat and drink from the Dutch earth. Why, why do you honor them so greatly?
Pramoedya Ananta Toer, This Earth of Mankind, *(1975) 1990: 309*

Overview

In this chapter we will consider societal bilingualism, especially with regards to four recent developments:

- transglossia;
- language revitalization;
- language ideologies;
- language policy as right and resource.

Introduction

Chapter 3 considered the theoretical construct of bilingualism in its sociolinguistic and psycholinguistic complexity. This chapter pays more attention to the *sociopolitics* of societal bilingualism. Societal bilingualism is a result of social and political forces that go beyond individuals, but that deeply affect them too. Not only is the banyan tree of bilingualism complex, but banyan trees take on different shapes depending on the societal context in which they grow. Although the concepts covered in this chapter are at the macro-level of society, they are important for educators because schools reflect society and the bilingual policies and practices that we find in school are a direct result of societal bilingualism.

Clyne (1997: 302) delineates five ways in which societal bilingualism comes about:

1. *Sprachinseln*; that is, ethnolinguistic enclaves that exist in political states;
2. colonialism;
3. international migration;
4. international borders;
5. spread of international languages.

This chapter complements Chapter 3 since individual bilingualism is always a function of the speech community in which the speaker participates. Fishman (1972b: 22) defines speech community as "one, all of whose members share at least a single speech variety and the norms for its appropriate use." Romaine (1994: 22) points out that a speech community is not necessarily coextensive with the language community. She adds "[a] speech community is a group of people who do not necessarily share the same language, but share a set of norms and rules for the use of language." Speech communities constitute what Wenger (1998) calls "communities of practice," that is, groups of people who interact and communicate regularly. Schools constitute speech communities and communities of practice.

According to Fishman (1991) the study of societal bilingualism – of the bilingualism of speech communities – has focused on three aspects:

1. habitual language use;
2. behavior towards language;
3. sociocultural change processes.

Although much attention was devoted in the twentieth century to the first aspect, as manifested in the question that grounds Fishmanian sociolinguistics – "Who Speaks What Language to Whom and When" – and some to the second aspect, it is the third aspect, that of *sociocultural change processes* and their relationship to language, that has received the least attention. Twenty-first-century scholarship has increasingly turned to this dimension, what we are calling the *sociopolitical dimension*. As we have said before, this is a result of the increased movement of people, the expansion of communication and transportation technology, the birth of transnational democracies, the redrawing of political states along linguistic lines in parts of Europe, the ascendancy of Asia in the world markets, and the spread of English. As a result of the unprecedented mobilization of speakers and their language practices, multiple discursive practices and translanguaging have increasingly assumed a central role.

The study of societal bilingualism has developed as it has adapted to the bilingualism of the present century around four clusters:

1. The extension of Fishman's approach towards diglossia,[1] a core concept in the study of societal bilingualism heretofore, and the reconceptualization of a transglossia.

2. The extension of the study of language maintenance and language shift to the study of language revitalization or reversing language shift.
3. The extension of studies of language and identity to language ideologies.
4. The development of language planning and policy away from the focus on language as a problem towards that of language as a right and a resource.

As we will see in Parts III and IV of this book, each of these four dimensions is important to the planning of bilingual education programs and curricula. Language planning is at the core of educational planning, and especially bilingual education planning. And whether to maintain or revitalize a minoritized language or to add another language is an important consideration in planning bilingual education programs. The language identities of groups, as well as the language ideologies of societies, have much to do with the kinds of bilingual education programs that are developed. Finally, the way in which bilingualism is conceptualized greatly impacts language use in the classroom. These conceptualizations also affect the type of bilingual methodology that is used. We begin here by considering each of the theoretical dimensions separately.

Transglossia

Diglossia and bilingualism[2]

The meaning of the Greek roots of the word di-glossia corresponds to the Latin roots for bi-lingual, and it is the term generally used to study bilingualism at the societal, rather than individual level. In a now-famous article by Ferguson (1959), the term was developed into a convincing conceptual model for the analysis of societal differentiation in the use of varieties of language.[3] It refers to cases of society that use a H(igh) variety of one language for certain prestigious functions, and a L(ow) variety of the same language in ordinary functions, such as those carried out in the home and informal work sphere. Diglossia is usually annotated as follows:

$$\frac{\text{H}}{\text{L}}$$

with the H above the line indicating the high variety and functions, and the L below the line indicating the low variety. Ferguson gives the example of Switzerland where Swiss German serves as the L variety and is widely used in the home, and Standard High German is the H variety used in education. Egypt is another case in point, with Classical Arabic serving as the H, and Colloquial Arabic as the L.

Fishman (1964) extends Ferguson's definition of diglossia to encompass not only language varieties, but also different languages. Whereas individual bilingualism has to do with language choice that is not fixed, societal diglossia depends, according to Fishman, on the functional distribution of the two languages. Fishman says: "bilingualism is essentially a characterization of individual linguistic versatility while diglossia is a characterization of the societal allocation of functions to different languages or varieties" (1972b: 145). For example, Switzerland is a diglossic country because different languages are spoken in different cantons, but there are individuals within Switzerland who may not be bilingual. Fishman *et al.* (1971: 560) warn that "socially patterned bilingualism can exist as a stabilized phenomenon only if there is functional differentiation between two languages." Fishman explains that without diglossia, stable bilingualism cannot be obtained because "no society needs two languages for one and the same set of functions" (1972a: 140).

Fishman describes two different enduring societal arrangements for bilingualism:

1. *Territorial principle*, whereby a specific geographical territory in a state uses one language for formal functions, whereas the other territory uses the other language, and thus, the state remains bilingual through generations. This is the arrangement that has been worked out in Switzerland, for example, with German, French, Italian, and Romansch having equal official status in different cantons. It is also the arrangement in Belgium, where Dutch is official in the north, French is official in the south, and German in the east. The territorial principle is clearly a geographical concept that usually applies to nation-states.
2. *Personality principle*, whereby a social group decides to use one language for specific functions, and the other language for other functions, usually in separate domains. This is the case of the Old Order Amish in the U.S. who use Pennsylvania German (also known as Pennsylvania Dutch) in the home, English in school, and High German to read the Bible.

According to Fishman, for both the territorial and the personality principles in diglossia to operate, what is needed is strict *compartmentalization*; with each language tied to specific territories in one case, or functions or domains in the other.

Fishman combines bilingualism, what he defines as an individual's linguistic versatility, with diglossia to consider four different societal situations, as explained below:

1. *Bilingualism with diglossia*, where speakers are bilingual and there is a societal arrangement with each of the languages fulfilling a different function. This is the case of the Old Order Amish and the Hassidic Jews in the United States. In Paraguay, a landlocked Latin American country, both Spanish and Guaraní are official and the majority of Paraguayans are bilingual, with Guaraní clearly fulfilling an identity function. This is also the case of Luxembourg where Luxemburgers have Luxemburgish as their first language and language of everyday interaction, but employ French and German in complementary distributions for official purposes. Since 1984 Luxemburgish has shared official status with French and German (Clyne, 1997).
2. *Bilingualism without diglossia*, where there is much individual bilingualism, but there is no societal arrangement for its maintenance and endurance. This is the case, for example, of the United States, a highly bilingual country because of immigration, but with very few societal arrangements for the protection or promotion of the bilingualism of its citizens.
3. *Diglossia without bilingualism*, where there is a political societal arrangement so that different languages are spoken in different territories or by different

groups, but the groups themselves do not have to be bilingual. This is the case in German-speaking Switzerland, as we have previously considered. This was also the case of South Africa during apartheid, as the speakers of Zulu, Sotho, and many of the other African languages were not given access to bilingualism in English or Afrikaans. And it can also be considered the case of Haiti, where most of the population remains monolingual Haitian Creole speakers, although the small elite are bilingual in French and Haitian Creole (Bentolila and Gani, 1981).

4. *Neither diglossia nor bilingualism*, that is, a monolingual society which is a rare and disappearing situation and happens only in very isolated communities. Cuba is perhaps a notable exception, having undergone political isolation through the U.S. imposed embargo since 1961. Seen from a language-majority speech-community perspective, however, this arrangement also describes monolingual speech communities in the English-speaking world.

There are more complex cases of societal bilingual use, such as that of Tunisia where Classical and Tunisian Arabic are in diglossic distribution, but French is also used. Platt (1977) has coined the term *polyglossia* to refer to cases such as Singapore, where there are multiple Hs. In Singapore, for example, standard English, Mandarin, standard Malay, and Tamil share co-official status, but non-standard English (also called Singlish), Hokkien, Cantonese, non-standard Malay, and Indian languages other than Tamil may be used for everyday purposes. Hence, a Hokkien-speaking child may be educated in Mandarin Chinese, in addition to English (Baetens Beardsmore, 1998). In Africa, many states are *triglossic*, with a prestigious code used for government, and other official functions; a middle-level code used as lingua franca for inter-ethnic medium in local administration, local trade, and mass media; and a language of limited communication used for intra-ethnic communication, family interaction, and cultural expression (Abdulaziz-Mkilifi, 1978). T'Sou (1980) refers to the triglossic distribution of languages in places such as Singapore, China, and Malaysia where political changes have superimposed Mandarin over a regional High language such as Cantonese, and where the local or regional language is used only in informal and intimate spheres.

Although the concept of diglossia, as proposed by Fishman, has proven useful for analyzing societies and social groups that want to protect and develop their bilingualism, Fishman himself has loosened some of the strictures of compartmentalization in the original model. Diglossia, Fishman (1985b) warned, requires control, but not the "freezing of intercultural boundaries."

Fishman's updated diglossic model (1991) moves away from the designation of languages and domains as being High and Low, concepts that contribute to the linguistic hierarchies that respond to differential power. Instead, Fishman insists on the protection and stability of what he calls the *Xish functions*, in the face of *Yish functions*, with X designating co-territorial threatened (X) languages, and Y designating unthreatened or less threatened (Y) languages.[4] Fishman explains that "Bilingualism is protective of Xishness and *interactive* with Yishness" (our italics, 1991: 85).

In promoting a program of action to revitalize threatened languages, Fishman (1991) recognizes the importance of using that language for some of the social functions that had previously been attributed to the more powerful language, for example, secondary education or local employment. However, Fishman insists that it is important to guard against the invasion of the non-threatened powerful language into the less powerful domains, especially the family, where it can destroy the possibility of intergenerational transmission and obliterate the possibility of developing home language speakers within one generation. Fishman represents this new diglossic relationship, with powerful functions above the line for both the *n-Th* (non threatened or powerful language) and the *Th* (threatened language), but with only the *Th* language below the line in more informal domains, and specifically the home, as:

$$\frac{n\text{-}Th/Th}{Th}$$

This perspective attempts to bring attention to both the Threatened and Non-Threatened language and considers ways of balancing the use and value of both.

Transglossia

Increasingly the concept of diglossia has been called into question. Woolard and Schieffelin (1994: 69) call diglossia "an ideological naturalization of sociolinguistic arrangements," claiming that the use of the term has made linguistic hierarchies seem natural. Likewise Williams (1992) criticizes the concept of diglossia for stressing its consensual nature, rather than the conflict underlying it. This has been underlined in an article on the stresses between the use of French and of Occitan in southern France (Gardy and Lafont, 1981). Romaine (2006) has also questioned the validity of the concept of stable diglossia in a globalized world, insisting on "societal bilingualism" as the preferred term, and separating it from the concept of diglossia. She quotes Calvet (1993: 45), who criticizes diglossia for tending to "obfuscate the conflicts that characterized diglossic situations and to present as normal a situation of domination." Other scholars point to cases of "broad diglossia" or "leaky diglossia" that were often ignored in the early literature (Fasold, 1984: 54): cases where the boundaries between languages leak as people translanguage.

The Language Policy Division of the Council of Europe (2003a) prefers the term "multilingualism" to diglossia. It defines multilingualism as referring "exclusively to the presence of several languages in a given space, independently of those who use them: for example, the fact that two languages are present in a territory does not indicate whether inhabitants know both languages or one only" (Council of Europe 2003: 19–20). Unlike diglossia, languages are no longer assigned separate territories or even separate functions, but they may co-exist in the same space. Another difference is that languages are not placed in a hierarchy according to whether they have more or less power.

In reality, ethnolinguistic groups do not have strict divisions between their languages, and there is often much overlap. Batibo (2005) gives the example of a woman trader in a Lagos market who may choose to address her client in standard

Yoruba, dialectal Yoruba, Pidgin English, or, if she is educated enough, Standard English. The same phenomenon is documented in the Puerto Rican community of East Harlem where Spanish and English are used without compartmentalization of domains (Pedraza, Attinasi, and Hoffman, 1980). As we have said, translanguaging characterizes most encounters among bilinguals.

The "imagined" conceptualization of political states as clearly demarcated by language and culture has given way to a more fluid conceptualization of language practices, centered not on personal spaces or territories, but on trying to maximize *efficiency and equality* among speakers themselves, despite the fact that much inefficiency and inequality still exists (Fettes, 2003). The French sociolinguist Louis-Jean Calvet (1999) has proposed a *gravitational model* of bilingualism that acknowledges that today's spread of global powerful languages can co-exist with official and national languages, with regional lingua francas, and with local vernaculars; and not threaten them in any way. Calvet then posits that for individuals this means being able to use two or three languages without any competition whatsoever.

Mühlhäusler's *ecological approach* (2000, 2002) calls for "a situation of equilibrium whereby languages automatically readjust themselves to fit into the environment, and perpetuate themselves through language contact, rather than isolation" (quoted in Tsai, 2005: 11). This is done through the self-regulation or the agency of the speakers themselves. Rather than externally imposed mechanisms of control to separate each of the languages as in the concept of diglossia, the co-existence of languages in stable societal bilingualism has to do with internally imposed *self-regulation* by the speakers themselves, and the *functional interrelationships*, for mutual benefits, among languages (Martí, Orega, Idiazabal, *et al.*, 2005). Annamalai (2005: 111) says: "When multilingualism is taken as the norm, the functional (or ecological) relationship between languages in a multilingual network (or linguistic ecology) defines the nature of each language in the network."

"Transglossia" might be a better term to describe societal bilingualism in a globalized world: a stable, and yet dynamic, communicative network with many languages in *functional interrelationship*, instead of being assigned separate functions. Fishman himself (1999) concedes that today's identities may be multiple, and that different languages could be co-present in individuals and societies to give each of these identities appropriate expression: "The global and the specific are now more commonly found together, as partial (rather than as exclusive) identities, because they each contribute to different social, emotional, and cognitive needs that are co-present in the same individuals and societies and that are felt to require and to benefit from different languages in order to give them appropriate expression" (Fishman, 1999: 450).

One of the most important challenges for bilingual education today is to ensure that languages do not compete with each other, but that they be developed and used in functional interrelationship. Given the changing ways in which languages now function and in which people translanguage, complete compartmentalization between languages of instruction may not always be appropriate. We shall turn to this in Chapter 12, as we discuss language arrangements in the bilingual classroom, as well as the language practices of students.

Language Maintenance, Shift and Revitalization

Language maintenance and shift

Fishman (1968: 76) conceptualizes *language maintenance* and *language shift*, saying: "The study of language maintenance and language shift is concerned with the relationship between change (or stability) in language usage patterns, on the one hand, and ongoing psychological, social or cultural processes, on the other hand, in populations that utilize more than one speech variety for intra-group or for inter-group purposes." Language shift or maintenance does not happen in a vacuum, it occurs only when certain societal conditions are present:

1. co-existence of more than one language – bilingualism;
2. differences in power, value, and status conferred on each of the two languages that lead the group to maintain or abandon the home language;
3. pressure in political, economic, or social forms from one of the two language groups (see Batibo, 2005; and Paulston, 2000).

The process of *language shift* among immigrant populations tends to take place over three generations in countries such as the United States or Australia. In situations of language shift, forms and uses are reduced (De Bot and Clyne, 1994) and eventually this leads to groups shifting their use of one language to another. In cases of minoritized languages, this may lead to *language death*.

Well-known examples of language shift are the Anglification of the North American content, the Arabization of the Maghreb, the Russification of Siberia and the Caucauses, the Hispanization of Latin America, and the Sinoization of the Chinese interior. This was also the case of many Māoris in Aotearoa/New Zealand who shifted from Te Reo Māori to English, and of many Native American groups. The ascendancy of English through globalization may or may not produce language shift, as it has done in Singapore but not in Brunei, even though both countries educate through the medium of English (Baetens Beardsmore, 2003).

In reality, the study of language shift has received more attention than that of *language maintenance*. This has to do with the fact that minoritized groups receive intense pressure from dominant groups to linguistically assimilate, making language shift a more frequent phenomenon. The language maintenance of minority groups has not been looked upon favorably, whereas the language maintenance of majority groups has been considered natural and uninteresting.

Many bilingual education programs for minoritized groups have goals of either language shift or language maintenance. For example, in the United States, what has become known as transitional bilingual education programs for language minorities encourages mostly Spanish-speaking children to shift quickly to English only; most bilingual education programs in Africa are of the transitional kind. And yet, in many parts of the world, language-minority children attend bilingual education programs that have the maintenance of the home language as a goal, at the same time that the state or national language is developed.

The description of language shift situations was the purview of much research in the twentieth century, but increasingly scholarship has turned to trying to do something about it. The situation of minoritized languages has become dire to the point that many have become endangered, and scholars have had to take on activist positions.

Language revitalization

The change from description of language shift situations to diagnosis and action is the purview of what Fishman (1991) has called *Reversing Language Shift* (RLS) and others have called *language revitalization* (Hinton, 2001, 2002; Hinton and Hale, 2001; King, 2001; Nettle and Romaine, 2000).

In Fishman's *Graded Intergenerational Disruption Scale* (GIDS) (1991), the higher the score, the lower the language maintenance prospects of a group. The GIDS provides a way by which ethnolinguistic groups can assess the threatened state of their languages (X) and mobilize resources on their behalf:

Stage 8: X spoken by socially isolated old folks;
Stage 7: X spoken by socially integrated and ethno-linguistically active, but beyond child-bearing age;
Stage 6: X is normal language of informal spoken interaction between and within all three generations of family, with Y reserved for greater formality and technicality than those common in daily family life;
Stage 5: X is also used for literacy in home, school, and community, but such literacy is not reinforced extra-communally;
Stage 4: X is used in lower education that meets requirements of compulsory education laws;
Stage 3: X is used in lower work sphere, outside of the community, and involving interaction between both speech communities;
Stage 2: X is used in lower governmental services and mass media, but not higher levels;
Stage 1: X is used in higher level educational, occupational, governmental, and media efforts.

Fishman posits that the crucial stage beyond which there is no intergenerational mother-tongue transmission, and therefore, no possibility of language maintenance, is Stage 6: "Without intergenerational mother tongue transmission, [. . .] no language maintenance is possible. That which is not transmitted cannot be maintained" (Fishman, 1991: 113). He later adds: "Face-to-face interaction with real family embedded in real community is the real secret weapon of RLS" (2001: 458).

RLS is especially important in the twenty-first century as a way to balance globalization. Fishman (2001: 6) states: "RLSers aim at nothing more than to achieve greater self-regulation over the processes of sociocultural change which globalisation fosters. They want to be able to tame globalisation somewhat, to counterbalance it with more of their own language-and-culture institutions, processes and outcomes." The concept of RLS has been questioned by Romaine (2006), who contends that because we cannot go back in time, there is no reversal. King (2001) also distinguishes between RLS and language revitalization, pointing out that the efforts are not about bringing the language back to former patterns, but bringing it forward to new users and uses.

Although RLS is of interest to Indigenous language communities, as Hinton (2003: 52) has noted, Fishman's work is primarily focused on threatened languages in Europe and European languages in the Americas. Hinton discusses several differences between RLS as posited by Fishman and what Indigenous communities need. Because of the small numbers of speakers, Stages 3, 2, and 1 of the GIDS would be unlikely to be a goal. And because many Indigenous languages are not written, the emphasis of RLS on literacy functions is also of questionable value (Brandt and Ayoungman, 1989; Hinton, 2002, 2003; Hinton and Hale, 2001).

Bilingual education is being increasingly used today for language revitalization purposes. Often those bilingual education programs start in early childhood and have become known as *language nest* programs (more on this in Chapters 6 and 11). Bilingual education has an important role to play not only in language acquisition, but also in language shift, language maintenance, and language revitalization.

Language Ideologies[5]

Language and identity

Nationalist ideologies throughout the world continue to link language to identity unidirectionally. Sue Wright (2004: 44) gives several examples[6]:

> Kurdish speakers in Turkey, Iran, Iraq and Syria are still battling for the right to use their language. Macedonian speakers have been recently prosecuted by the Greek state. Russian speakers in Estonia are denied citizenship until they acquire some competence in Estonian. [. . .] The English Only Movement in the United States employs these arguments. The Conseil Constitutionnel in France did so recently too.

As we said before however, language, as constructed, is not only a simple identity marker, but is capable of generating imagined communities and of constructing particular loyalties (Anderson, 1983: 133). Language, then, has much more than a *semiotic* and *symbolic* function; it also has a *rhetorical* function, used to discursively construct identity and solidarity.

In the rootlessness that has come about as a result of globalization, language and identity have taken center stage. Aspects of identity beyond attitudes have become foregrounded in the study of bilingualism – emotions, preferences, anxiety, personality, and social influence (Dorian, 1999; Liebkind, 1999; Pavlenko, 2005, 2006). For example, the growing interest in revitalizing Indigenous languages and regional languages has much to do with looking for authentic meaning in local identity.

Today we have adopted a much more fluid positioning of identity, because of multiplicity, managed through discursive practices. The unidirection between language and identity has been questioned. Liebkind (1999), for example, shows that there is a reciprocal role between language and identity; that is, language use influences the identity formation of the group, while at the same time, the identity of the group influences the patterns of attitudes and language uses. Le Page and Tabouret-Keller (1985: 181) show how individual and social identity are mediated by language, with speakers creating speech acts as *acts of projection* in which "the individual creates for himself the patterns of his linguistic behaviour so as to resemble those of the group or groups with which from time to time he wishes to be identified, or so as to be unlike those from whom he wishes to be distinguished." That is, unlike Giles's theory of *accommodation*, Le Page and Tabouret-Keller propose that speakers do not adapt to the style of the interlocutor; rather they adapt to the *image* they have of themselves in relationship to the interlocutor. Heller (1999) points out that ethnolinguistic minorities in a globalized economy pragmatically access their multiple linguistic and cultural resources, as they participate in plural social networks. That is to say, they decide who they want to be and choose their language practices accordingly. Pennycook (2003) introduces the concept of *performativity* which indicates that people do not use language based on their identity, but instead perform their identity by using language (Pennycook, 2000).

Postcolonial identity involves not only "sameness" but by extension "otherness" and the development of hybrid identities which involve plural language practices. Hybrid identities, are, as Holt and Gubbins (2002: 4) say "an attempt to link or acknowledge the past in the light of a different cultural environment rather than a mark of disloyalty." The construction of these multiple and hybrid identities rest on multiple factors beyond language, such as race, social class, age, generation, sexual orientation, geopolitical situation, and institutional affiliation (Bhabha, 1990; Pavlenko and Blackledge, 2004).

In the United States, *border theory* (Anzaldúa, 1987; Elenes, 2002; Saldívar-Hull, 1997) growing out from people's "border narratives" as subaltern communities, is being used to study the hybrid identities of youth of Mexican American descent (Bejarano, 2005). Bejarano (2005: 28) explains:

> The experience of living and breathing the geopolitics of the border, the literary, linguistic, and cultural forms and embeddedness of the border, means understanding the distinct languages that come from this area, the cultural practices and nuances of the region, the social, cultural, and political messages and lessons displayed in art, performances, writings, and languages, and how people live their lives in these spaces. People *en la frontera* (on the border) or people who have had the border experience comprehend the hybrid nature of their existence – their situatedness within representations of *mestizaje*.[7]

As we will see in Part IV of this book, identity is a most important concept in bilingual education, for it is necessary for students to invest in language learning (Norton, 2000). Furthermore, Cummins (2000, 2006) has identified the negotiation of identity as one of the most important principles when teaching language minority students. Educators must be aware of the different and complex links between language and identity and the ways in which students' language practices construct and perform multiple identities.

Language ideologies

The field of *linguistic ideology* has emerged as a way to link linguistic practices to broader sociopolitical systems (see for example Gal, 1989; Woolard and Schieffelin, 1994; Schieffelin, Woolard, and Kroskrity, 1998; Irvine and Gal, 2000; Pavlenko and Blackledge, 2004). For Irvine (1998: 255) linguistic ideologies represent the cultural system of ideas about social and linguistic relationships, in addition to political and moral interests. For these scholars, attitudes, values, and beliefs about language are always ideological, and are enmeshed in social systems of domination and subordination of groups, relating to ethnicity, class, and gender. There are therefore some ideologies that are more privileged than others, and language represents some of these better and more consistently than others. Therefore, language itself is capable of constituting some notions of identity, and not others (see, for example, French 1999: 279, on Guatemala).

One of the most popular ideologies is precisely that there is, or that there has to be, a link between language and identity, but it is important to recognize that this is a result of the homogenizing work of school in imposing a national standard. This is linked to Bourdieu's concept of linguistic practices as *symbolic capital*, considered in chapter one. This symbolic capital is distributed unevenly in the speech community, and as such, there is *symbolic violence* because the dominant ideas are naturally assumed and the oppressed recognizes the dominant group as superior.

Linguistic ideologies include the possibility of *agency and resistance* as speakers' abilities and options are recognized. Language is also a place of resistance, of power, and of solidarity (Pavlenko and Blackledge, 2004). Blommaert (1999: 10) says that linguistic ideologies are produced and reproduced through what people say and do not say, and do and do not do, through language itself. The study of language ideologies focuses, then, on the sociohistorical, sociopolitical, and socioeconomic conditions that affect the production of social meanings in relationship to language and to discourses. The social context can prevent individuals from accessing certain linguistic resources or adopting new identities (see Heller, 1982, 1995; Pavlenko, 2002; Woolard, 1998).

The language choices available to children and their parents, as well as the discursive practices that are encouraged and supported in school, have an important impact on children's identity and their possibilities of developing agency or resisting. Bilingual education types and pedagogies have to take into account the more hybrid identities of students, for bilingual students are situated in specific social, historical, and cultural contexts and they can resist or accept the positions offered by those contexts (Norton and Toohey, 2001: 310).

Language Policy as Right and Resource

Language policy[8]

In this book we follow the conceptualization of Spolsky (2004) who subsumes under the term "language policy" what has also been termed language planning.[9] Spolsky (2004: 5) considers three components of *language policy*:

1. *language management* – also known as language planning, language intervention, language engineering, or language treatment, and referring to direct efforts to manipulate the language situation;
2. *language practices* – the habitual pattern of selecting among varieties that make up its linguistic repertoire; related to what Hymes (1967) calls *ethnography of speaking*;
3. *language beliefs* or ideology – the beliefs about language and language use.

The interactive way in which language is planned (or unplanned) and dictated from the top down, and the ways in which it is interpreted, negotiated (or planned) from the bottom up makes it impossible to differentiate between one level and the other. And language beliefs and ideology interact with the two levels. As we will see, all bilingual education is an instance of language policy in education (LiEP).[10]

The field of language policy (LP) grew out of the language "needs" of new "nations" founded as a result of decolonization. As such, early language planners[11] believed that language "problems" could be solved, and focused on the linguistic dimension of modernization, mainly through engaging in the three dimensions of the LP enterprise:

1. *corpus planning*: changing the form of the language itself through standardization (standardizing language forms), graphization (developing a writing system), modernization (coining new words and terms);
2. *status planning*: modifying the status and prestige of the language;
3. *acquisition planning*: developing new users of the language.

Acquisition planning is especially relevant to those of us interested in bilingual education because school is the most important agent in acquisition planning.

According to Cooper (1989), the LP enterprise can be carried out by three different kinds of actors – individuals (for example, Ben Yehuda in the case of the revitalization of Hebrew in Israel, or Samuel Johnson on corpus matters of English, or even mothers and fathers as they plan for the language that they will pass on to their children), by communities and groups (for example, women opposing sexist language or businesses supporting one language or the other), or by governments or other authoritative bodies. Most governmental agencies have been established to disseminate the language of the state beyond that of the native-born community. Examples are the British Council, the Alliance Française, the Goethe Institute, the Confucius Institute, the Japan Foundation, the Korean Foundation, and the Instituto Cervantes. But LP can also be carried out by intergovernmental agents such as the World Bank which offers financial support in exchange for certain policies. For example, it has been said that the policy in Tanzania of shifting from Kiswahili to English at the secondary level is tied to concessions made to the World Bank in exchange for financial aid (Mtesigwa, 2006).

Many scholars have identified the goals of language policy and planning.[12] Ager (2001) discusses seven motives:

1. *Identity*, as when states impose certain languages as a link to specific identities. For example, France has maintained that it is a perfect hexagon and that only

French is tied to French identity, thus silencing, until very recently, the other languages of France – Basque, Breton, Catalan, Corsican, Flemish, German, and Occitan. When Algeria obtained independence from France in 1962, it declared Classical Arabic the sole official and national language, rejecting Algerian Arabic and the Berber languages (also known as *Tamazight*). And in Catalonia, Catalan has become the only language used in the government of the *Generalitat de Catalunya* (the government), and must be used as medium of instruction. Singapore, however, has adopted four official languages – Mandarin, Malay, Tamil, and English. The first three were chosen for identity purposes of the three major ethno-linguistic groups.[13] English, however, was selected as a neutral "other language" to serve as the language of interethnic communication. In Canada, the declaration of the Official Languages Act (1969), made English and French languages of Canadian identity. And yet in 1974 Quebec declared French the sole official language of Quebec, the language of Québecois identity, and Bill 101, the Charter of the French Language in 1977, made French the language of work, business, and education in Quebec.

2. *Ideology*, as when states or groups impose different languages or standards as a result of an ideology. An example is the United States' recent federal law, No Child Left Behind, mandating students' annual progress reports that are based on written standard English assessments (Menken, 2005, 2008). An intriguing case is that of Eurasians (people of mixed Asian and European backgrounds) in Singapore who have English as their home language. Wee (2002) points out that, for them, English is not an accepted "ethnic mother tongue," since it would puncture the official Singaporean ideology that English is no one's mother tongue, has neutral status, and only has a purely pragmatic function within Singaporean bilingual education policy. Another example was the imposition of English and the banning of signing at schools for the Deaf in New York in the 1880s because it was argued that if Deaf children could not speak and pray to God, they would not be saved.

3. *Image creation*, as when states try to ensure that a favorable view is taken of their history and language by projecting its language. It is well known, for example, that the British Council and the U.S. government have supported the greater use of English in international communication (Phillipson, 1992). The Goethe Institute, the Japan Foundation, and the Instituto Cervantes do the same for German, Japanese, and Spanish, respectively.

4. *Insecurity*, as when states or groups are wary of others and their languages. This is the case of the rejection of the Roma and their language, Rom, especially in central Europe. Another example is Namibia, which chose English as its official language even though it is the native language of not more than 3 percent of the population, and is spoken by only 53 percent of the population; instead of Afrikaans and German, the previous two official languages associated with colonialism and oppression, or the many other African languages (Pütz, 1992). Proposition 227, outlawing bilingual education in California, could be considered another example of insecurity-based LP, as voters acted on their Hispanophobia.

5. *Inequality*, as when states or groups act on language in order to correct inequalities in society. This is the case, for example, of non-sexist language that came to be used especially during the 1970s and 1980s. And it is also the case of the European Charter for Regional or Minority Languages (1993), binding countries of the Council of Europe which ratify it to recognize the languages of their linguistic minorities. The U.S. Supreme Court case, *Lau vs. Nichols* (1974, more on this in Chapter 8), can also be considered a case of inequality-based language planning. The Supreme Court ruled that educating English Language Learners in a language they did not understand was not equal educational opportunity and that something had to be done about the language of instruction.
6. *Integration* with a group. This was the case when, for example, in Wales, following the Education Act of 1870, Welsh children were not only required to learn English in school, but prohibited from speaking Welsh.
7. *Instrumental* motives, as when groups or individuals acquire a second language because it will give them advantages, usually economic ones, in the market or in careers. This is the case especially of English throughout the world. In Africa, it is the case of Swahili in Eastern Africa, Wolof in Senegal, Akan in Ghana, Hausa in Northern Nigeria, and Lingala in Zaire (Bamgbose, 1994).

Fishman (2000, 2006) has pointed out that all language planning boils down to a super-factor of *independence vs. interdependence*: whether the social group wants to be considered independent of another, or affiliated with another one. Fishman suggests four processes by which the forces of independence or interdependence might be carried out:

Table 4.1   Independence vs. Interdependence in Language Planning

Independence	*Interdependence*
Ausbau, or building away from another language for distancing; as in Noah Webster's 1783 American English dictionary, or Urdu and Hindi's adoption of different scripts.	*Einbau*, or bringing together two languages; as in the current Romanian treatment of Moldavian.
Uniqueness, or making a language uniquely one's own; as when Johannes Aavik (1880–1973) selected "artificial" syllables for Estonian, ensuring that it would not be mistaken for Finnish or be swallowed up by Russian.	*Internationalization*, for example when Ataturk westernized Turkish through French influences and by adopting the Roman script.
Purification, driven by fear of contaminant. An example would be the Loi Toubon in France enacted in the 1990s to protect French from English. Another would be the revival of Hebrew, careful not to be contaminated by Yiddish.	*Regionalization*, to connect to other languages in the region. Bahasa Malay and Bahasa Indonesia influence each other and borrow broadly.
Classicization, that is, keeping certain languages very close to their classical source – Hindi to Sanskrit, Tamil to Old Tamil, Urdu to Classical Persian.	*Vernacularization*, favoring popular usage.

With regards to acquisition planning, the purview usually of schools, Kaplan and Baldauf (1997) outline the different kinds of LP activities that schools must carry out:

1. determining which languages are to be taught within the curriculum;
2. defining the teacher-supply and identifying who would teach language;
3. determining what segment of the population will be exposed to language education;
4. determining the model and methodology that will be employed, the materials to be used, how and by whom the material will be prepared, and how it will be disseminated;
5. defining the assessment processes used for initial placement, in-course testing, and output summative testing;
6. defining the assessment processes for teacher performance and system performance;
7. determining how to support the activity fiscally and physically.

Deciding on the type of education that is offered is language policy (Shohamy, 2006b). Most of the educational decisions and activities that are carried out within bilingual education programs are also instances of language policy. (We will explore this further in Chapters 8 through 12.) Thus, understanding language policy is very important for bilingual educators.

As a right

Beginning in the late 1970s and through the 1990s, language planning was criticized because it was conducted mostly by elites who governed in their own self-interest and reproduced inequalities (Tollefson 1991; Luke, McHoul, and Mey, 1990). As we stated in Chapter 1, the role of sociohistorical processes in shaping language use and policy, and in particular the role of class, ethnicity, race, language, and gender in such shaping, was given increased attention in the last decade of the twentieth century (Tollefson, 1991, 2002; Wiley, 1996a, 1999; Wright, 2004). During this time, theories of *linguistic imperialism* in language planning (Phillipson, 1992) received attention, as modernization and the role of the state were called into question. *Critical theory* was adopted to study the role of language in asymmetrical power relations between speakers. As such, *language rights* became an important field of study (Skutnabb-Kangas, 2000), with an individual's right to use and learn his or her home language becoming recognized as a basic human right.

May (2001, 2006) provides four reasons why the study of minority language rights has become popular in the twenty-first century:

1. The decline and loss of many of the world's languages (Nettle and Romaine, 2000; Krauss, 1992).
2. The historical, social, and political construction of certain languages as minoritized, for example, the case of Spanish in the United States.
3. The questioning of language shift and in particular the idea that one learns languages at the expense of one's home language.

4. The need to accord minoritized languages the same protections and institutional support that majority languages enjoy.

Skutnabb-Kangas and Phillipson (1994) have identified two broad categories of Linguistic Human Rights:

1. *Individual rights*: the right of every person "to identify positively with their mother tongue, and to have that identification respected by others" (1994: 2). This includes an individual's right to learn and use their home language, including in education, as well as to learn one of the official languages in one's country of residence.
2. *Community rights*: "the right of minority groups to exist" (1994: 2). This includes the right to establish and maintain schools and other educational institutions, with control of curricula.

Skutnabb-Kangas (2000, 2006) then proposes that there are two kinds of LHRs:

1. *Expressive, or non-instrumental* rights which ensure people's capacity to enjoy a secure linguistic environment in their home language and a group's fair chance of cultural self-reproduction.
2. *Instrumental rights* which ensure that language not be an obstacle to meaningful participation in the democratic process and public institutions, and to social and economic opportunities.

Skutnabb-Kangas (2006) also proposes that Linguistic Human Rights can be negative or positive. *Negative linguistic human rights* refer to the right not to be discriminated against on the basis of language. *Positive linguistic human rights* refer to the maintenance and development of identity through the freedom to practice unique aspects of minority life, and specifically language (Skutnabb-Kangas, 2006).

Skutnabb-Kangas (2006) posits a hierarchical order relative to linguistic human rights for different groups.

1. Linguistic majorities.
2. Linguistic minorities in the following order:
    a. *national autochthonous minorities*, referring to a group smaller in number than the rest of the population of a state whose members have ethnic, religious, or linguistic features different from those of the rest of the population and want to safeguard those features;
    b. *Indigenous peoples*, referring to those who inhabited the region or country at the time of conquest or colonization;
    c. *Immigrant minorities*;
    d. *Refugee minorities*;
    e. *Sign language minorities*.[14]

Skutnabb-Kangas's (2000) model of Linguistic Human Rights for linguistic minorities rests on three principles:

1. For proper integration, positive *promotion-oriented rights* are necessary. That is, language minorities must both enjoy a secure linguistic environment in their home language, as well as be able to use that language to participate meaningfully in a democracy.
2. For proper integration, both *territorial and personal rights* are necessary; attention must be paid to the home language of individuals, as well as that of groups in defined geographical territories.
3. For proper integration, both *traditional "hard law" rights* codified in covenants and conventions, *and "soft law" rights* such as those in declarations and recommendations are necessary.

A number of important laws, both hard and soft, have been signed in the last twenty years to protect the linguistic rights of minoritized groups. For example, the UN Declaration on the Rights of Persons Belonging to National or Ethnic, Religious and Linguistic Minorities (1992) says: "States should take appropriate measures so that, wherever possible, persons belonging to minorities have adequate opportunities to learn their mother tongue or to have instruction in their mother tongue." The Delhi Declaration and Framework for Action adopted in 1993 at UNESCO's Education for All Summit, supports, "initial instruction in the mother tongue, even if it may in some cases be necessary for the students to subsequently master a national language or other language of wider usage if they are to participate effectively in the broader society of which they are part" (p. 8).[15]

In 1996, at a meeting in Barcelona, the Universal Declaration of Linguistic Rights was signed by UNESCO and several non-governmental organizations (see www.egt.ie/udhr/udlr-en.html). Article 23 establishes that education must be at the service of linguistic and cultural diversity and of harmonious relations between different language communities throughout the world. Article 24 states: "All language communities have the right to decide to what extent their language is to be present, as a vehicular language and as an object of study, at all levels of education within their territory: preschool, primary, secondary, technical and vocational, university, and adult education." The Council of Europe's European Charter for Regional or Minority Languages (1993), which entered into force in 1998, promotes the use of these languages in education and the media in the member states of the Council of Europe. But only autonomous minorities are included in these provisions, while immigrants and others are excluded (Clyne 1997: 304). The European Charter of Fundamental Rights (2000), Article 22, states: "The Union shall respect cultural, religious and linguistic diversity" (quoted in Wright, 2004: 195) (more on this in Chapter 9).

At the first conference on African languages and literatures ever held on African soil in Asmara, Eritrea in January 2000, the Asmara Declaration on African Languages and Literatures was passed. Article 5 states: "All African children have the inalienable right to attend school and learn in their mother tongues. Every effort should be made to develop African languages at all levels of education" (quoted in Mazrui, 2004: 130). The UN Convention on the Rights of Persons with Disabilities (2006) includes in Article 24 on Education a clause (3b) that ensures an inclusive education system for Deaf students, the facilitation of the learning of sign language, and the promotion of the linguistic identity of the Deaf community.

As a resource

The recent changes in global geopolitics has led to further shifts in LP studies, as it has become accepted that the power of the state is constrained by internal and external pressures having to do with economic forces and transnational migration (Ricento, 2006). Inter- and supranational bodies, such as the United Nations, NATO and International Courts, as well as the IMF and the WTO have increasingly challenged state political and economic sovereignty (Wright, 2004).

The stronger claims of linguistic imperialism posited by Phillipson (1992) and the view that English is a "killer language" (Skutnabb-Kangas, 2000) have been questioned by some (Brutt-Griffler, 2002; Spolsky, 2004) who claim that English is mixing with local linguistic forms and that it is being used as a lingua franca without overtaking local languages. But scholars throughout the world have continued to raise a voice of alarm over the growing role of English, especially as it connects to global economic and political interests and links to Anglo-Americanization (see, for example, Fishman, Conrad, and Rubal-López, 1996; Pennycook, 1998).

In Africa, the World Bank and local partners have funded the use of former colonial languages in education rather than African languages (Brock-Utne, 2000; Mazrui, 2004). And in Asia, there are places such as Singapore where English has overtaken the local languages. Within the European Commission, English is threatening French as first internal working language, leading to the setting up of a vigorous watchdog committee. Phillipson (2003) argues that to safeguard a multilingual Europe from English, more active language policies are needed.

Language policy efforts have turned to making evident the power of discourse that reflects different ideologies. Ricento (2006: 17) describes this change of focus of LP activities saying that it: "became concerned with the role of language – materially and discursively – in the production, exercise, and contestation of power at all levels of society, and the effects of power on language practices." It is important for bilingual educators to understand that any language policy adopted by a school reflects different ideologies, not only linguistic ones, but also sociopolitical ones. As Cummins (2000) often reminds us, school language policies and practices are intricately tied to the production, exercise, and contestation of power within a school.

Conclusion

It is clear from the foregoing discussion that bilingual educators must clearly understand the sociopolitical context that creates bilingualism, and that represses it, or nurtures it and develops it. Language hierarchies and diglossic relationships among languages are not inevitable; they are the products of sociopolitical contexts and of language ideologies. Many languages today are more endangered than ever.

As we will see in Part III of this book, bilingual education has been used by states and communities to plan language use and to increase or decrease the users of certain languages. The kind of bilingual education program that is developed has important consequences for language acquisition, shift, maintenance, or revitalization. But before we turn to examining bilingual education programs in Part III of this book, it is important to consider the cognitive and social benefits of bilingualism, as well as the factors that intervene to promote or hinder these advantages. This is the subject of our next chapter.

Questions for Reflection

1. Identify the relationship between diglossia and bilingualism in different social contexts. Give some examples.
2. How is diglossia to be understood today?
3. What is the connection between language and identity? Please provide examples.
4. What are language ideologies? Why are they important?
5. Discuss the three components of language policy according to Spolsky.
6. What are Linguistic Human Rights? What are some of the covenants and declarations that support them?
7. Do you agree or disagree with the following statement: "Language hierarchies and diglossic relationships among languages are not inevitable; they are the products of sociopolitical contexts and of language ideologies" (p. x). Why? Reflect on your personal experiences.

Further Reading

Calvet, L.J. (1987). *La guerre des langues et les politiques linguistiques*. Payot, Paris. Translated by M. Petheram (1998). *Language Wars and Linguistic Politics*. Oxford University Press, Oxford.

Ferguson, G. (2006). *Language Planning and Education*. Edinburgh University Press, Edinburgh.

Fishman, J.A. (1991). *Reversing Language Shift. Theoretical and Empirical Foundations of Assistance to Threatened Languages*. Multilingual Matters, Clevedon.

May, S. (2001). *Language and Minority Rights. Ethnicity, Nationalism and the Politics Of Language*. Pearson, Essex.

Rassool, N. (2007). *Global Issues in Language, Education and Development. Perspectives from Postcolonial Countries*. Multilingual Matters, Clevedon.

Ricento, T. (ed.) (2006). *An Introduction to Language Policy. Theory and Method*. Blackwell, Malden, MA.

Shohamy, E. (2006b). *Language Policy: Hidden Agendas and New Approaches*. Routledge, London.

Skutnabb-Kangas, T. (2000). *Linguistic Genocide in Education – or Worldwide Diversity and Human Rights?* Lawrence Erlbaum, Mahwah, NJ.

Skutnabb-Kangas, T., and Phillipson, R. (eds.) (1994). *Linguistic Human Rights: Overcoming Linguistic Discrimination*. Mouton, Berlin.

Spolsky, B. (2004). *Language Policy*. Cambridge University Press, Cambridge.

Tollefson, J.W. (1991). *Planning Language, Planning Inequality*. Longman, London.

Wright, S. (2004). *Language Policy and Language Planning. From Nationalism to Globalisation*. Palgrave, New York.

5

Benefits of Bilingualism

Learning English could lead into the way and that is a good thing, but you shouldn't forget your Spanish. We're very lucky to learn Spanish for when we're trying to get a job. [Pointing to another student] She's even luckier because she's black. [. . .] Spanish is everywhere. They could face Spanish in the future, so why not learn it now?

Latino sixth-grader boy, Amistad Dual Language School,
New York City, February 2005

El español es muy importante para mí porque es uno de los lenguajes que corren por mi sangre. Es el lenguaje de la tierra cual mi mamá caminó cuando chiquita. Es el lenguaje de la comida que mi papá comió para ponerse grande y fuerte. Y como yo no pude criarme en la tierra de mis padres se criaron, todavía puedo hablar el lenguaje de las palmas, el mar y el sol.

Latino sixth-grader boy, Amistad Dual Language School,
New York City, May 2005

Overview

In this chapter we will discuss:

- Cognitive advantages of bilingualism:
  - metalinguistic awareness;
  - divergent thinking;
  - communicative sensitivity;
  - ability to learn multiple languages.
- Social advantages of bilingualism:
  - socioeconomic benefits;
  - maximum global interactions;

- ○ maximum local interactions;
- ○ potentializing acts of identities;
- ○ cultural awareness.
- • Factors that intervene in maximizing or minimizing advantages:
  - ○ social: socioeconomic status, dominance and power, ethnicity, race, nationality, gender, identity, and age;
  - ○ linguistic: linguistic threshold and linguistic hierarchies supported by language ideologies.

Introduction

As we have seen in Chapters 2, 3, and 4, languaging bilingually is the usual way of languaging in the world, and bilingual individuals are the norm. But bilingualism is often misunderstood by lay people. School systems are often ignorant about the advantages that bilingualism might accrue for the children themselves, as well as for their communities, their states, and the world. Parents are continuously instructed by educators, school psychologists, and speech therapists to speak to their children solely in the language of school, and not to bother raising children bilingually. As a result, the language interactions between these parents and children suffer, with parents unable to language in ways that seem natural and intimate. This chapter reviews the advantages that children might obtain from being bilingual and being raised and educated bilingually.

We start by discussing cognitive benefits for individuals: advantages relating to higher mental processes such as knowledge, thinking, problem-solving, conceptualization, and symbolization, which might result in academic advantages in school. We then discuss the social advantages of bilingualism: economic potential and character development which will result in better world citizens and community members.

But because, as we have explored above, language practices are socially constructed, the benefits of bilingualism are often maximized or diffused depending on external social and linguistic factors. We end the chapter by considering some of the factors that may mitigate the cognitive and social advantages of bilingualism.

Cognitive Advantages

Since the seminal article by Peal and Lambert (1962), the literature showing that bilingualism is an important factor in cognitive development is extensive. The bilingual ten-year-olds included in Peal and Lambert's study in Montreal outperformed the monolingual children in verbal and non-verbal intelligence tests, leading the authors to conclude that bilingual children "are more facile at concept formation, and have greater mental flexibility" (1962: 22). However, it is important to point out that Peal and Lambert also noted: "it is not possible to state from the present study whether the more intelligent child became bilingual or whether bilingualism aided his intellectual development" (1962: 20). Since then, many empirical studies have detailed various aspects of cognitive advantages for bilingual children (for a review of these, see Hamers and Blanc, 1989, and Hakuta, 1986, chapter 2; see also Hakuta and Diaz, 1985). Positive cognitive advantages have also been demonstrated among Deaf students who are instructed bilingually (see for example Hoffmeister, 2000).

Bialystok (2004: 579) has pointed out that thirty years prior to Peal and Lambert's study, Vygotsky in *Thought and Language* (1934, translation 1962) had noted that children's knowledge of two language systems resulted in greater linguistic awareness and linguistic flexibility. Vygotsky (1962: 110) explained that being able to express the same thought in different languages enables the child to "see his language as one particular system among many, to view its phenomena under more general categories, and this leads to awareness of his linguistic operations." Bilingual children's ability to use two languages makes language structures more visible as children have to organize their two language systems. It is as if bilingualism provides x-ray vision, allowing the children to conceptualize underlying structures and to incorporate them into one functioning communicative system (Bialystok, 2004). Thus, bilingual children develop a more analytic orientation to language, in other words, greater *metalinguistic awareness*.

Metalinguistic awareness

Metalinguistic awareness is the ability to treat language as an object of thought. As Tunmer, Pratt, and Herriman say (1984: 12), it is to look at language "with the mind's eye and taken apart." Cazden (1972) defines it as "the ability to make language forms opaque and attend to them in and for themselves." Bialystok (2001, 2004) divides metalinguistic awareness into word awareness, phonological awareness (awareness of the sound system), and syntactic awareness (awareness of word order).

In 1961, Leopold, studying the development of the bilingualism of his daughter, Hildegard, attributed her ability to recognize and appreciate the arbitrary nature of meaning, that is, the looseness of the link of word and meaning, to her bilingualism. Ten years later, Ianco-Worrall (1972) confirmed the bilingual children's greater word awareness, as bilingual children were more willing to change the names of objects than monolingual children. When asked, "Which is more like *cap, can* or *hat*?", bilinguals tended to respond to meaning, monolinguals to sound. Ianco-Worrall concluded that bilingual children's semantic development happened faster than that of monolingual children. Ben-Zeev's (1977) concluded that bilingual children were superior to monolingual children also in sentence construction. Bialystok (1987) found that bilingual children were able to accurately judge the grammaticality of a sentence, independent of meaning, much better than monolingual children. Bilingual children seem to hold form apart from meaning at greater levels than monolingual children, whether this happens at the word level or at the syntactic level.

Baker (2001) has pointed out that recent studies of metalinguistic awareness in bilinguals have shifted from thinking as a product to the actual *process* of thinking. Instead of looking at what children are capable of as a result of having received a bilingual education, we look at how their logic operates as they learn two or more languages. Bilinguals are studied not necessarily for comparisons with monolinguals but because bilinguals offer the possibility of more critically discerning cognitive and language processing.

Bilingual children's cognitive functioning appears to impact not only their language knowledge, but also their critical thinking and sociolinguistic development in many aspects of their education and lives in general. For example, Bialystok (2001) considers that metalinguistic awareness is an important factor in the development of reading in young children. And because bilingual children see words printed in two separate ways they are capable of faster understanding the symbolic representation of words in print. Bialystok (2004: 597–8) concludes:

> Sometimes, bilingual children excel in specific tasks that measure their progress in coming to understand the structure of language and in learning how to read but there is little evidence that their overall achievement in these skills is significantly different from that of monolinguals. Instead, *their advantages make it easier to master these skills by giving them more refined cognitive process with which to approach them*, and the possibility of transferring the effortful learning of these abilities from one language to the other (our italics).

Bialystok's conclusion is important because it supports the idea that bilingualism in and of itself is not a determinant of superior achievement. Instead, however, Bialystok reminds us that bilingual children's advantages in understanding the structure of language have to be built upon in order for these advantages to result in academic achievement. This is an important idea because it enables us to propose that schools, and specifically bilingual education, might have a lot to do with building bilingual children's metalinguistic awareness.

Divergent thinking

In the 1930s, Vygotsky had also noted that bilingual children had two ways to describe the world and thus more flexible perceptions and interpretations. Psychologists have since referred to this ability as *divergent or creative thinking*. Tests of divergent thinking often ask respondents to generate a list of uses of an object or solutions to a problem. An example given by May, Hill, and Tiakiwai (2004) is: "think of a paper clip and tell me all the things you could do with it." Bilinguals have been shown to be able to come up with more innovative solutions to problems, able to think with creativity and flexibility (for a review of this literature, see Baker, 1988, and Ricciardelli, 1992). Baker (1988) gives us an example of how divergent thinking may be tapped by asking the child: "How many interesting and unusual uses can you think of for cans?" Bilingual children tend to give more responses, and replies that are more varied, original, and elaborate.

Communicative sensitivity

Although all speakers have choices, bilinguals with two codes or more at their disposal constantly have to understand and decide on the linguistic choices they have in particular situations. This practice in gauging the communicative situation gives bilinguals what is known as more *communicative sensitivity*. Ben-Zeev's (1977) studies suggest that the Spanish–English bilinguals and Hebrew–English bilinguals in her study show more sensitivity to the content of the verbal stimulus than monolinguals, perhaps because they constantly have to evaluate whether the language is correct or incorrect. Studying the Konds in Orissa, India, Mohanty (1994) concludes that bilinguals are more sensitive to messages: they are better able to discern the content of the message. Bilingual children in immersion bilingual programs in Canada have also been found to be more sensitive to the needs of listeners (Genesee, Tucker, and Lambert, 1975).

Ability to learn multiple languages

It turns out that bilinguals have a different type of language competence than monolinguals, and, as experienced language learners, they show improved ability to learn a third language. Hawkins (1986) has developed the concept of "language apprenticeship," or the value of becoming bilingual as a basis for acquiring other languages. Studies of third-language acquisition have proliferated in recent years as the spread of global languages and the increasing mobility of peoples have promoted the learning of more than two languages (see for example Cenoz and Genesee, 1998; Cenoz, Hufeisen, and Jessner, 2001; Hoffman and Ytsma, 2004). Bilingual learners are more competent at learning additional languages than monolingual learners.

Social Advantages

The research literature on bilingualism has also pointed to the social development advantages that bilingual children accrue.

Socioeconomic benefits

Bilingualism is an important resource that accrues socioeconomic benefits.
Breton (1978) explains how bilingualism could be conceptualized as a form of capital that, like all capital, can depreciate or gain in value. García and Otheguy (1994: 100) have also held that bilingualism is a form of capital used to "negotiate social goods and benefits." The benefits of speaking English are well known throughout Europe, Asia, Africa, and Latin America. Grin (2003) concludes that in Switzerland, English-speaking workers earn approximately 12 percent to 30 percent more than those who do not speak English. But it is interesting to note that the value of English depends on the region of Switzerland in which it is spoken. For example, in German-speaking Switzerland, English proficiency yields higher earnings than proficiency in French. However, in French-speaking Switzerland, German proficiency yields higher earnings than proficiency in English (Grin, 2003).

Mandarin proficiency is becoming increasingly important especially for business in Asia. And bilingualism in Welsh and English, as well as Catalan and Spanish are also important for participation in the economy in Wales and Catalonia respectively.

There are socioeconomic benefits associated with bilingualism, even when the language is not a global one.

In the United States, despite the stigmatization of Spanish, proficiency in Spanish has been shown to lead to more employment opportunities in the service sector. The presence of a large Spanish-speaking population makes it important for teachers, social workers, police, doctors, and many others to be bilingual. Villa (2000) and Carreira (2000) have shown that Spanish-speakers in the United States consume approximately US$400 billion annually and they constitute 23 percent of the purchasing power. The earnings of Spanish-language ads, for example, have grown exponentially. Whereas in 1970, Spanish-language ads yielded US$14.3 million, in 2000, they yielded US$786 million (García, 2008b).

García (1995) has shown that, although for U.S. Latinos Spanish monolingualism has negative socioeconomic consequences, the same can be said of English mono-lingualism. For U.S. Latinos, English monolingualism, that is, giving up Spanish in favor of English, has a negative effect on income. This is especially the case for Cuban Americans in Miami-Dade County where Spanish has negotiated for itself not only a communicative role, but also economic value (García, 1995). This finding was confirmed by Boswell (2000) who concluded that in Florida there was a clear economic advantage for Latinos who spoke English very well and also spoke Spanish. In fact, U.S. Latinos who were English monolinguals earned less than those who were proficient in English and Spanish.

Linton (2003) has shown that among U.S. Latinos there is a positive relationship between upward mobility and bilingualism. Portes and Rumbaut (1996, 2001a, b) have referred to this as a process of *selective acculturation* where immigrants consciously make choices about their language use as they try to adapt to a new life. They posit that when ethnic networks and strong communities support children to deal with prejudice, navigate the education system, and find a place in the labor market for the ethnic language, bilingualism can bring equal, if not greater, benefits.

Global interactions

The ability to communicate flexibly, through different media, and in more than one language is increasingly important in today's globalized world. As technology has brought the world closer together and enabled global instantaneous inter-actions, the ability of children to speak, read and write in multi-discursive fashion is an increasingly important commodity in the world's social, political, and economic development.

As a result, bilingualism is an asset for the social development of all children. The European Commission, in its official policy document on language and educa-tion (The Action Plan for Language Learning 2004–2006, 2003), argues that bilin-gualism is insufficient, and that education in the twenty-first century should aim to develop plurilingualism for all citizens. Plurilingualism, as we have seen, has been defined as "proficiency, of varying degrees, in several languages and experience of several cultures" (Council of Europe, 2000a: 168). Children today need to be fam-iliar with very different discourse modes and codes, and ways of using these through different modalities. The need is no longer to be dominant in two languages, but rather to be familiar with many discourse modes and codes. Translanguaging has become essential to participate in global and local interactions. For example, it is important to be able to read in one language and speak in another, or vice versa. It is also important to be able to switch between codes, to translate, to be able to mix and choose appropriate norms.

Heller (1999) has proposed that international market forces are redefining the value of languages. Many youths, for example, adopt a transnational perspective, and in many cases, bilingualism might not only be an asset in the local marketplace, but also in the larger transnational community. For example, in the United States, Spanish is becoming increasingly important not only to sell to the U.S. Latino community, but to sell internationally to the entire Spanish-speaking world (García, 2008b; García and Mason, forthcoming). And bilingual Dominican businessmen will benefit from their bilingual practices not only in the Dominican heartland of New York – Washington Heights – but also in the Dominican Republic.

A report published in Ireland for the Minister for Enterprise, Trade and Employment and the Minister for Education and Science (Expert Group on Future Skills Needs, 2005) points out that there is empirical evidence from a number of recent international surveys that there is a link between linguistic ability and export success. Foreign managers who worked in Ireland considered lack of cultural awareness and language competency to be significant shortcomings in Irish management capability. The report also underlined the fact that in planning future skills needs, the "English is enough" viewpoint, while superficially appealing, is seriously flawed and needs to be strongly countered. Seventy-five percent of the world's population does not speak any English, and 94 percent do not speak it as their mother tongue. The report concluded that for Ireland, a National Language Policy should be formulated to provide an integrated and coherent approach to language education, in all learning contexts. Finally, it stressed that language skills are complementary to other skills such as science, engineering and technology and are not in competition with them, nor are these skills mutually exclusive.

Local interactions

The social development of bilingual children also relies on their ability to communicate in more local and situated circumstances. Children need to be able to communicate with their parents, their caregivers, their extended families wherever they may be, their friends, their communities. Technology has enabled this communication to be easier, faster, and more frequent. Certainly parents in technologically advanced societies today are in frequent contact with their children through cell phones and email. And friends and families in different geographical regions communicate more frequently and simultaneously through instant messaging. Technology enables group communication, rather than one-to-one communication. But without common language practices, the different technology available would be meaningless. And for many children whose parents or caregivers speak minoritized languages at home, or who live in residentially segregated communities that mostly use a minoritized language, or whose families are members of organizations, clubs, or religious institutions where a minoritized language is spoken, the ability to participate in these local networks depends on their degree of bilingualism.

Potentializing "acts of identities"

Hall (1996: 4) studies identities not as "who we are" or "where we came from", so much as "what we might become." This is an important definition because it fits squarely with what education is all about – what children might become. Children are immersed in practices of very different worlds – those of the family and those of school – and through these, children construct identities in relation to those communities (Wenger, 1998; Lave and Wenger, 1991). A multiple identity developed through participation in different communicative networks gives children the possibility of developing more broadly, of drawing from many multiple perspectives.

A bilingual identity constitutes just one dimension of the many that make up a child's identity – their gender, social class, ethnicity, race, nationality, community. But without the added dimension of bilingualism, some of these identities will never be constructed, developed, or represented. Le Page and Tabouret-Keller (1985) refer to the potential of language to index identity, to function as "acts of identity." Certainly, bilingualism gives children a greater range of expression and thus more freedom in constituting or *performing*, as Pennycook (1998, 2002) might say, their own acts of identity (see the section on language and identity in Chapter 4, and the section on identity below).

Cultural awareness and construction

Being or becoming bilingual, if successfully achieved, enhances cultural awareness, both in the culture(s) of origin and the culture of the additional language. When one is confronted with another way of looking at things, as if through a different pair of spectacles, one becomes more aware of one's culture of origin, as well as that of others. In an unpublished paper, Skutnabb-Kangas (1987) posited the notion of *cultural competence* as an added dimension to communicative competence. Baetens Beardsmore (1994) developed this into a frame of reference for the cultural dimension of bilingualism in Asian contexts. In his study of bilingual Asian communities, Baetens Beardsmore identifies four aspects of cultural competence – *knowledge, feelings, behavior,* and *metacultural awareness* – and applies them to the Singaporean context.

Knowledge is a cognitive feature covering information about the relevant cultures, including language, history, traditions, and institutions. For example, in Singaporean schools, the compulsory other language requirement concentrates on these aspects of cultural competence, as can be seen from an analysis of textbooks and teaching practice. Although important, this may not be enough, since the approach is hardly dissimilar from what occurs in traditional language lessons across the world, and may do no more than scratch the surface.

Feelings are an affective component referring to attitudes towards, and identification with, a culture. This component is more evidently present in Singapore, transmitted by family and environmental factors. However, the shift towards

English dominance that is being witnessed at present in Singapore may well transform the affective relationship with the Indigenous languages.

Behavior refers to the capacity to act in a culturally appropriate way. Here again, the component is usually present in Singapore. However, urbanization, technological changes, and advances in levels of (English-dominant) education may well be affecting behavioral patterns away from what are considered as traditional Asian core values, for example, filial piety, respect for authority.

Metacultural awareness refers to an understanding of the distinctiveness of cultures, and a tolerance toward cultural diversity. The multi-ethnic composition of Singapore society, for example, makes metacultural awareness inevitable.

Interviews with European secondary school learners in a bilingual education program where they learn history through an additional language clearly reflect these cultural advantages and students' awareness of them. Students express their pleasure in receiving the topic from a different cultural perspective than the one used in their first language history courses (European Commission, 2006).

Oksaar (1989) shows how bilingual and bicultural people may at times coalesce their language and cultural usage into a mixture of both, where one language, LA, coincides with a particular culture, CA, and the additional language, LB, with another culture, CB, leading to a new use of language which coincides with elements from both cultures, giving culture X:

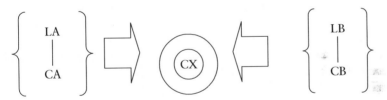

Figure 5.1 Relationship between Language and Culture

Bilingualism enables individuals to become aware of differences in culture, as well as to construct their own hybrid culture that enables them to negotiate both cultural systems. This view is consistent with the concept of *transculturation*.[1]

Intervening Factors

All findings on the positive effects of bilingualism on cognitive development and social development signal the importance of *intervening factors* that maximize or minimize cognitive and social development. There are *social intervening factors* such as socioeconomic status, dominance and power in society, ethnicity, race, nationality, gender, identity, and age; as well as *linguistic ones* such as thresholds of bilingualism and linguistic hierarchies. We discuss each of these intervening factors below.

Social factors

Socioeconomic status

Although the cognitive and social advantages of bilingualism have been aptly demonstrated when research studies carefully match children on *socioeconomic status*, the same does not obtain when children's social status has not been carefully controlled. In fact, prior to Peal and Lambert's carefully controlled 1962 study, bilinguals were rendered as mentally confused and inferior to monolinguals (see, for example, Saer, Smith, and Hughes, 1924). Socioeconomic status has nothing to do with children's intellectual development, but the social conditions of children in different socioeconomic contexts do shape these children's opportunities and access to language and bilingualism development.

Poor children rarely have access to well-equipped schools with excellent teachers. Often, poor children attend schools in the communities in which they live, and the schools may reflect some of the poverty of the community – educational resources are of poor quality, classrooms are overcrowded, class size is large, and the school building is in need of repair. Although there are some very committed teachers and principals in the schools of the poor, many teachers in poor schools are uncertified and may themselves have received a poor education.

Poor families also cannot relocate to ensure that their children are receiving an adequate education. Poor bilingual families have to settle for the educational program that their local school offers, whether it is a monolingual or bilingual program. This is particularly relevant for the Deaf community. Often poor Deaf children remain isolated in communities with few resources or services more appropriate for the Deaf – such as bilingual schools and interpreting services (Cole, forthcoming).

Poor families also cannot afford the resources to support their children's education outside of school. They can rarely pay for tutoring and after-school or weekend supplementary classes or summer camps. There are also fewer computers and less technology in the homes of the poor. All of these are ways that allow middle-class families to enhance the possibility of their children becoming well educated and bilingual.

Throughout the world, the educational gap between rich and poor has only grown larger. In the United States in 2002, for example, 27.4 percent of Latino families and 30.0 percent of African American families had income levels below the poverty line (U.S. Census Bureau, 2002), compared to 9 percent of white families. In the same year, Latino and black students performed about four grades below the national average in reading achievement (Au, 2006: 16).

When poor children are bilingual, their bilingualism is often *subtractive* because it is almost never supported and developed in schools. Often they are immigrants. And because their home language is not in any way supported in school or majority society, poor children can rarely enjoy the full range of cognitive and social benefits afforded to middle-class bilingual children.

Dominance and power

Socioeconomic status is directly related to power, for it often determines who controls the educational system itself, and whose children get to benefit from such education. Gramsci (1988) has advanced the idea that schools are engaged in *hegemonic* practices that keep power in the hands of the dominant group. Powerful dominant groups also have greater options of which schools their children attend and the education they receive.

As far as educating their children bilingually, dominant groups often have a choice. Their bilingualism is *optional*. And their children are bilingually educated in bilingual schools where children acquire a second language not to replace, but to add to their own linguistic repertoire. These students can then become fully bilingual and biliterate. In contrast, non-dominant groups have no choice but to become bilingual in order to interact with the powerful group. Thus, their bilingualism is *obligatory*. But their children are most often educated in monolingual schools that cater to the dominant group. Thus, their bilingualism is *subtractive*, and eventually leads to shift to the dominant language. Sometimes, if they are fortunate, these children receive some kind of bilingual education. But as we will see, this education is most often transitional and temporary.

It then turns out that non-dominant children fare less well than dominant children in obtaining the cognitive and social advantages of bilingualism, precisely because their bilingualism is not extended, valued, or respected. Often, their translanguaging is debased, considered inappropriate or "mixed." This negative and subtractive treatment of the bilingualism of non-dominant children has important cognitive and social consequences for it prevents them from building on their existing translanguaging practices to incorporate into their linguistic repertoire standard ways of using dominant languages.

Ethnicity

Glazer and Moynihan (1975: 1) have defined ethnicity as "the character or quality of an ethnic group." The German Romantics, and in particular Johann Gottfried Herder (1744–1803), had defined ethnic identity as natural and not movable. But more recent scholarship has signaled the situational and subjective construction of ethnicity. Barth (1969), for example, sees ethnicity not as unchanging cultural traits, but as situational and in relationship to the ethnic boundaries that define social interactions and, in turn, maintain these boundaries. Eriksen (1993) has considered ethnicity an "aspect of relationship, not a property of a group." Ethnicity can be a social and political resource, and can be both "adopted and adapted."[2] But Max Weber (1946) has warned that ethnicity is not solely the *process* of identity construction, but is also the *product* of the characteristics resulting from such a process. Language facilitates the group's formation, as it adds to the group's subjective belief in a common descent.

Recent postmodern scholarship has shifted the attention from ethnicity to more hybridized identities (Bhabha, 1994), and to the *mestizaje* and plurality of ethnicities affected by new local and global identities. As May (2001: 42, 43) states, however, although one can acknowledge the "fractured and fracturing identities" of the postmodern world, ethnicity can not always be hybrid or invented. He then raises a most important question (2001: 43): "If ethnicity is invented, why is it that "at the same time the news is full of ethnic cleansing and genocide?", to which he finds the answer by referring to the concept of *habitus* that Bourdieu (1991) developed to study social class. Habitus is "a system of dispositions common to all products of the same conditionings" (1991: 59) by which the material form of life is "embodied and turned into second nature" (1991: 63). According to Bourdieu, habitus is not simply an ideological construction; it is a way of viewing and living in the world that members of social groups acquire as a result of social-ization. For Bourdieu, as May (2001) states: "Habitus is both shaped by, and also shapes, objective social and cultural conditions which surround it." Habitus does not determine behavior, although it orients action by presenting a range of choices.

Children's ethnicity then, is both a construction of their socialization in the world, as well as a way of living and being in the world. Their language practices are an important part of their ethnicity. And children's bilingual and biliterate develop-ment is deeply affected by the constraints and options in their socialization, as well as in the social and political circumstances of their ethnicity construction. Those children, then, whose language practices match the dispositions that have been turned into second nature in a particular social context have more range of choices and practices than those whose language practices do not. Given the greater range of choice that bilingual children of dominant groups have, they will obtain greater cognitive and social advantages from their bilingualism than those whose choices are more restricted by their social and historically situated conditions.

Race

Weber (1978) suggests that race is a social construction that establishes social and political hierarchies. Ethnolinguistic groups are often spoken about as racial groups. In her study of Puerto Rican experiences of language, race, and class in the United States, Bonnie Urciuoli (1996: 15) explains: "When people are talked about as a race [. . .], the emphasis is on natural attributes that hierarchize them and, if they are not white, make their place in the nation provisional at best. When groups are seen in racial terms, language differences are ideologically problematic." *Racializing* involves race discourses[3] that emphasize the sociopolitical dimension of race as a natural group that is dangerous or unwilling to work on nation-building. Language in this racialized discourse is seen as an impediment to class mobility and to the welfare of nation-states.

Language groups who are subject to racialization are those that are poor and non-dominant – often those who have been subjected to conquest, colonization, slavery – and who may indeed be in the process of, or have completed, shift to a dominant language. Thus again, their bilingualism is subtractive.

Regrettably, it is sometimes teachers in schools who carry out this linguistic racial-ization. Walsh (1991: 106) quotes a teacher as saying: "those poor kids come to school speaking a hodge podge." A bilingual Latino college student reflects on his fourth-grade teacher for an assignment and says: "One time she told me, in front of whole class, to wash my face just because I was dark and she thought I was dirty. She actually gave me a bar of soap and made me wash my face in the sink in class. When I was done she said, 'Oh, you must be naturally dirty.' Actually made me cry" (Double Entry Journal, p. 1). Bilingual children are often victims of this racialization. As a result, they deny that they speak any language other than the dominant one. Thus, race and, especially, racialization are important factors in understanding why children who are racialized rarely have opportunities to build on their bilingualism for cognitive or social benefits.

Nationality and immigration status

A nation simply refers to a group of people who are conscious of forming a distinct community because they share historical and cultural memories, a homeland, and a desire of some social and/or political self-determination (Guibernau, 1996). The state, however, is an entity with political sovereignty over a territory, having control of legitimate force and loyal citizens (Weber, 1978; Giddens, 1984). The nation-state, then, is the forced and constructed confluence of both nation and state.

In his influential book entitled *Imagined Communities*, Benedict Anderson (1983) points to print technology as the mechanism through which the nation-state, developed in the last two centuries, became equated with the nation. Gellner (1983) suggests that the rise of nationalism in the modern era was a result of industrialization, which demanded cultural and linguistic continuity, with school becoming the most important agent of the monolingual stance. Children whose nationality, then, is congruent with that of the state will have greater possibilities of using their home language in school and developing their potential for full bilingualism, allowing them improved cognitive and social benefits.

Immigrants, and especially undocumented immigrants, are often the least successful in getting bilingual educational services that would support their bilingualism. When this is the case, immigrant children undergo language shift, robbing them of the potential to access the cognitive and social benefits that bilingualism might bring.

Gender

Women and men have been shown to speak differently and to have different communicative practices (Lakoff, 1973; Ochs, 1992; Tannen, 1990). Lakoff (1973), for example, has shown how women are more tentative in speaking than men. Ochs (1992) has studied how images of women are constructed through communicative practices that socialize children. Norton (2000) looks at the effects of the inequities of gender on possibilities of speaking. All other factors being equal, girls seem to have fewer opportunities to engage in bilingual practices, and fewer possibilities of developing their full bilingualism than boys.

And yet, recent evidence suggests that among some groups, and in certain contexts, girls have a greater rate of participation than boys in higher education. For example, there are more Muslim girls of Maghreb origin in Belgian universities than boys (Beatens Beardsmore, personal communication, November 2006). Also in Brussels, Moroccan immigrant girls have been shown to have more Belgian friends and be more bilingual than Moroccan immigrant boys, who have more Moroccan social networks, are less fluent in French, and tend to maintain more use of Tamazight or Berber languages (Hassani, 2001). In bilingual additive programs in Central Europe, the girls far outnumber the boys. In the United Kingdom, in standard second-language lessons, girls far outnumber boys, and the boys drop the foreign language more readily than the girls when this is possible. One interesting exception has been Ireland, where boys were reported to take up the study of Japanese as a second language more frequently because of the craze of electronic games, especially the handheld Game Boy! (*Profile on Language Education Policy: Ireland*, 2008).

Identity

Heller (1987) has shown how language is not simply a tool for communication, but is also an instrument of identity negotiation which facilitates or restricts access to powerful social networks. Likewise, Norton (2000: 13) argues that language is constitutive of and constituted by a speaker's identity.

Krashen (1981b, 1982) has proposed that the *affective filter* comprising the learner's motivation, self-confidence, and anxiety, is the most important factor in second language acquisition. Norton (2000: 120–3), however, proposes that Krashen's affective filter can only be understood in relationship to social structures of power that are constructed by the "lived experiences of learners." The learner's identity is a site of struggle between the subjectivities produced in different social sites – home, school, community, and thus it is diverse and changing. When children's language identities converge in the practices they engage in at home, in school, and in the community, bilingualism develops in additive, recursive, or dynamic ways, giving children more opportunity to obtain the cognitive and social advantages of bilingualism. This has been clearly demonstrated in the study of school-developed multilingualism with adolescents from the European School network (Housen and Baetens Beardsmore, 1987). But most often, the language identities of bilinguals are complex, conflicting, contradictory. And in situations of unequal language power, bilingualism develops poorly, or not at all, and cognitive and social advantages are not forthcoming.

Linguistic factors

The threshold

The *threshold* of bilingualism has been shown to be an important factor in determining the cognitive and social advantages of the child's bilingualism. As discussed in Chapter 3, Cummins (1976) has postulated his *Threshold Hypothesis*, which posits that in order to reap the cognitive advantages that have been associated with bilingualism, bilinguals have to be able to use their two languages in complex ways, thus passing a second threshold.[4] All positive effects of bilingualism on cognitive development have been associated with children who have reached this second threshold. All have been children *not* in subtractive bilingual situations.

For children, it is generally *school* that is capable of developing their bilingual abilities beyond a second threshold. As children engage in complex language and literacy practices in two languages, their range of cognitive and social options increase, and so do the benefits they can obtain from their bilingualism.

Language hierarchies

Some languages are more dominant than others. This has to do with the power of its speakers. Oral languages, for example, have more power than sign languages. Among oral languages, languages that have print literacy are more dominant than those that do not. And those that have global currency, for example, English and Mandarin, are more powerful (Crystal, 1997; Graddol, 1997). Oral languages of Indigenous peoples are also more entitled to rights than languages of immigrants.

Among sign languages, languages that are spoken by more dominant groups, such as American Sign Language (ASL), are more powerful than those sign languages that have fewer signers. Deaf students who know ASL are less likely to develop bilingual skills in other sign languages than those who use a sign language of less prestige. Deaf students in the United States are mostly waived from studying a second language, whereas Deaf students in other parts of the world are encouraged to develop bilingual skills in other written languages. For example, Malaysian students who are Deaf study not only Malaysian Sign Language and Malay, but also other written languages, especially English.

The prestige of the additional language has much to do with the development of bilingualism, with languages of higher prestige being more likely to be acquired than languages of lower prestige. For example, among English-speakers in the Anglophone world, it is much easier to find one who has learned French than one who has learned Haitian Creole.

Speakers of languages with high prestige have less inclination to develop bilingual competence than speakers of languages with low prestige since they do not perceive a need for bilingualism. This is especially the case of the Anglophone world where English-speakers rarely develop bilingual abilities. The rank or pecking order of the bilingual's languages has much to do with the development of bilingualism and the ability to enjoy cognitive and social benefits.

Conclusion

It is important to recognize the cognitive and social advantages that bilingualism accrues and that bilingual children have at their disposal. By addressing the many intervening factors that maximize or minimize these advantages, this chapter makes evident that the relationship between bilingualism and cognitive and social advantages is not always clear cut, having much to do with the sociocultural and sociopolitical context in which the child lives and is educated.

Now that we understand languaging and translanguaging practices, as well as the advantages that may be enjoyed by engaging in languaging bilingually, we are ready to consider how these language practices and cognitive and social aspirations match, or do not match, the bilingual education programs that have been developed in the last half century. Part III of this book will focus on how different groups have constructed different types of bilingual education programs, and how a range of societies have adopted and adapted these bilingual education types to meet their societal needs. Bilingual education policy as constructed from the top down by states and social groups will then be the subject of Part III. We will have to wait until Part IV of this book to understand how practices at the level of classroom curricula and pedagogies negotiate these policies from the bottom up.

Questions for Reflection

1.   What are possible cognitive advantages of bilingualism, as discussed in this chapter?
2.   What are possible social advantages of bilingualism, as discussed in this chapter?
3.   What are some factors that intervene in maximizing or minimizing the cognitive and social advantages of bilingualism?
4.   Reflect on your personal bilingual learning experiences. Has being bilingual been beneficial? Why and how?

Further Reading

Bialystok, E. (2001). *Bilingualism in Development: Language, Literacy, and Cognition.* Cambridge University Press, New York.

Kroll, J.F., and de Groot, A.M.B. (eds.) (2005). *Handbook of Bilingualism: Psycholinguistic Approaches.* Oxford University Press, Oxford.

Part III
Bilingual Education Policy

6

Bilingual Education: Frameworks and Types

We cannot remake the world through schooling but we can instantiate a vision through pedagogy that creates in microcosm a transformed set of relationships and possibilities for social futures; a vision that is lived in schools. This might involve activities such as simulating work relations of collaboration, commitment and creative involvement; using the school as a site for mass media access and learning; reclaiming the public space of school citizenship for diverse communities and discourses; and creating communities of learners that are diverse and respectful of the autonomy of lifeworlds.

New London Group, 2000: 19

Overview

In this chapter we will discuss:

- Bilingual education models.
- Theoretical frameworks for bilingual education today:
  - two new ones – recursive and dynamic;
  - two traditional ones – subtractive and additive.
- Types of bilingual education:
  - transitional;
  - maintenance;
  - prestigious;
  - immersion;
  - immersion revitalization;
  - developmental;
  - poly-directional and two-way (dual language education);
  - CLIL and CLIL-type;
  - multiple multilingual education.

Introduction: The Social Context

Mid-twentieth century

Perhaps the greatest advance of the twentieth century has been the extension of an education that was previously reserved for the social elite to the masses. Compulsory education, at least through the primary years of schooling, has become an established axiom, although a free education is not by any means universal. But bringing education to the masses has meant that schools have had to contend with issues of linguistic heterogeneity, especially because the masses often speak languages that are different from those of dominant groups in which education has hereto taken place.

By the mid-twentieth century, colonial empires started to collapse, as African and Asian countries gained their independence. Most of these countries had used the colonial languages in education, effectively denying an education to most of the children. As we pointed out in Chapter 1, in 1953, the UNESCO resolution declared that it was axiomatic that a child be taught to read in his or her mother tongue. Efforts to use the children's language in education, especially in the early grades, started to gain strength.

As we have said, the social elite have always had experience with bilingual education. In colonial contexts, their children were often made bilingual in the language of power through schooling (Rassool, 2007). In Europe, Latin America, Asia, and Africa, the elite often send their children to bilingual schools in order to learn one of the prestigious languages – French, German, or English. But no such thing had occurred with the masses, for whom school had been mostly monolingual in the language of power. This had the effect of encouraging language shift and homogenizing differences in order to uphold linguistic hierarchies and maintaining power.

In the second half of the twentieth century, especially in the 1960s, there was a worldwide rise in ethnic activism. This ethnic revival has been well documented by Fishman (1985a). In the United States, this ethnic revival coincided with the civil rights era, offering through Title VI of the Civil Rights Act equal educational opportunity to all. In Canada, the Royal Commission on Bilingualism and Biculturalism was established in the 1960s in response to the notion of two founding nations (the French and the English). The recognition of inequalities and the awareness that language education played an important part in social opportunities was responsible for the surge of different kinds of bilingual education programs throughout the world, and especially in North America.[1]

Into the twenty-first century

If the twentieth century extended the privilege of universal education to the masses, and did so primarily by incorporating their languages into educational systems, even if only initially, the turn of the century extended the masses themselves, as people, goods, and information move across borders at a speed previously unheard of. If the twentieth century was about extension, the twenty-first century is about *movement*, a dynamism that through technology enables simultaneity in space and time of languages and cultures. Whereas McLuhan's work, the *Gutenberg Galaxy* (1967), posits that the coming of the press came to influence linear thoughts and language, today we have moved towards a hypertextual way of cognitive organization, and language is expanding and intertwining with different elements of culture. It is technology that enables the world to understand in unprecedented ways the language and cultural differences that engulf us all, as well as the realization that not all of us are caught up in the same dynamism. Because of the co-existence of many realities side by side, and the greater agency of some groups and peoples, issues surrounding bilingual education today are more complex than in the past. The banyan trees of bilingual education keep expanding.

As we have seen in Part II of this book, bilingualism is today not only about one language following the other and existing exclusively in states. The concept of translanguaging provides a more fitting description of the ways in which many people "language," that is, use language in action, in the twenty-first century. Of course, this bilingual languaging has always been with us, as is evident in the many pidgins and creoles that have resulted from the intense language and cultural contact of traders. But what is different now is that this translinguistic contact and use also exists between ordinary people of equal power and that the direction of contact is multi-way, affecting more than one group. A monolingual education cannot offer children who live in this greater linguistic dynamism the opportunities to develop cognitively, socially, or linguistically. Bilingual education in the twenty-first century needs to do more than simply shift or maintain minority languages or add languages of power; it needs to be attentive to the dynamics of bilingualism itself.

Bilingual Education Models?

It is traditional in bilingual education circles to speak of *models*. Hornberger (1991: 222) differentiates between the concept of *model*, which she defines as a broad category having to do with goals with respect to language, culture, and society; and program *types*, relating to contextual characteristics (students characteristics and teacher characteristics) and structural characteristics (the kind of program structure, languages in the curriculum, and classroom language use). Following Fishman (1976), Hornberger (1991: 223), proposes three models of bilingual education:

Table 6.1   Bilingual Education Models According to Hornberger (1991)

	Transitional Model	*Maintenance Model*	*Enrichment Model*
Linguistic Goal	Language shift	Language maintenance	Language development
Cultural Goal	Cultural assimilation	Strengthened cultural identity	Cultural pluralism
Social Goal	Social incorporation	Civil rights affirmation	Social autonomy

Hornberger (1991: 224) then goes on to specify contextual and structural characteristics, as in Table 6.2:

Table 6.2   Contextual and Structural Characteristics According to Hornberger (1991)

Contextual Characteristics	*Structural Characteristics*

• Nature of students
  ○ numbers
  ○ stability
  ○ voluntary or involuntary placement
  ○ socioeconomic status
  ○ immigrant or involuntary minority status
  ○ first language background
• Background of teachers
  ○ ethnicity
  ○ degree of bilingualism
  ○ training
	• Location of BE program in school
	  ○ school-wide or targeted
	  ○ one way or two-way
	• Allocation of languages
	  ○ across the curriculum
	  ○ patterns of language in the classroom

In this book we recognize that models are artificial constructs that are divorced from the day-to-day reality of school language use, and the teaching and learning of an additional language. There is no tight representation of systems, and the same model may have very different features depending on how the many variables interact with each other. Besides the fact that models are gross generalities, there is another danger in considering them. This has to do with the fact that decision-makers and policy-makers may import models: whole systems that have nothing to do with the context in which their children live and go to school. Early on, William F. Mackey (1978: 6) cautioned about the "exporting of a model of bilingual schooling as a magic formula for education success." And he adds:

> Abstract or generalized discussion on whether this model is better than that one can be both meaningless and harmful. It is meaningless because what is desirable education for any group depends on *the particular context* in which its children will have to live and work. It is harmful because any assumption that there is a best and universally applicable model is bound to lead some people to *pick the wrong one*. Moreover, in trying to make a model operational, even though it be the wrong one, the institution (university or school or class) tends to become a system the purpose of which is to make the system work (our italics).

Most typologies[2] of bilingual education incorporate broad goals, as well as contextual and structural characteristics (see for example Baker, 2001; Baker and Prys Jones, 1998; Brisk, 2006; Fishman and Lovas, 1970; García, 1997a; Skutnabb-Kangas, 1981, 2000; Skutnabb-Kangas and García, 1995; Spolsky, 1978). For example, the *Encyclopedia of Bilingualism and Bilingual Education* (Baker and Prys Jones, 1998) lists ten *types/models* of bilingual education programs and ninety *varieties* around the world.

One of the best known, most elaborate, and useful typologies of bilingual education, that is, a classification of types, was proposed by Mackey in 1970. Mackey's typology distinguishes ninety different variables depending on four intersecting factors:

1. relationship between the language(s) of the home and the schools;
2. curricular organization of languages: the medium of education, their pattern of development, the distribution of the languages in the curriculum, the transition from one language to the other;
3. the linguistic character of the community and the country;
4. the function, status, and differences, both regionally and internationally, of the various languages.

Before we turn to our own analysis of variables in bilingual education in Chapter 7, we identify here types of bilingual education. We do so while acknowledging that these types also "leak" into each other. But we think a typology is useful for educators. Because we recognize the *fluidity of the types*, we include a treatment of variables and their entanglements, much the same way as a banyan tree, in Chapter 7.

Bilingual Education Theoretical Frameworks

Monoglossic

The types of bilingual education programs that were developed in the twentieth century responded to the way in which societal bilingualism was then defined, with diglossia as the theoretical construct to operationalize it, and monolingualism in each one of the two languages as the norm. In other words, the desired outcome was either proficiency in the two languages according to monolingual norms for both languages, or proficiency in the dominant language according to monolingual norms. These kinds of programs respond to what we have called a *monoglossic belief* which assumes that legitimate linguistic practices are only those enacted by monolinguals.

Those who want to ensure that language-minority children would shift to a majority language organize *non-diglossic bilingual education types* where the two languages are only initially used without any functional compartmentalization. Given the differential power of the two languages and the devaluing of the children's home language, these programs promote a *subtractive* type of bilingualism.

On the other hand, societies or groups which are concerned with the acquisition, maintenance and development of the children's bilingualism in both the home and the majority languages generally set up *diglossic bilingual education types* where each language is carefully compartmentalized. These types of bilingual education programs promote an *additive* type of bilingualism.

Thus, these two kinds of bilingual education theoretical frameworks can be considered as either:

- subtractive
  or
- additive.

Subtractive
This framework supports language shift to the more powerful language of instruction. It does so by using the two languages interchangeably, that is, in non-diglossic ways, *temporarily*, and results in children developing a feeling that the home language is useless at school, and that only the school language is valued and assessed. It corresponds to the *transitional model* proposed by Fishman (1976) and Hornberger (1991). This theoretical framework has a monoglossic orientation, considers minority students only as monolingual, sees their bilingualism as a problem, and supports linguistic and cultural assimilation, having monoculturalism as a goal. Following the subtractive bilingualism model that we defined in Chapter 3, children come in speaking one language, the school adds a second language, and children end up speaking the school language and losing their own language. Figure 6.1 displays this.

$$L1 + L2 - L1 \rightarrow L2$$

Figure 6.1   Subtractive Bilingual Education Theoretical Framework

Additive
The second kind, the additive bilingual education theoretical framework, advances the bilingualism of children by insisting that the two languages be functionally compartmentalized, maintaining diglossia. It corresponds to both Fishman and Hornberger's *maintenance and enrichment models*. This theoretical framework also has a monoglossic orientation, working towards the development of the students' bilingualism according to two monolingual standards, and views this bilingualism as an enrichment possibility. Despite developing bilingualism, monoculturalism is cultivated for language majorities, whereas biculturalism – the ability to function in two separate cultures – is expected for language minorities. Following the additive bilingualism model that we defined in Chapter 3, children come in speaking one language, the school adds a second language, and they end up speaking both. Figure 6.2 displays this additive BE theoretical framework:

$$L1 + L2 = L1 + L2$$

Figure 6.2   Additive Bilingual Education Theoretical Framework

Heteroglossic

But the bilingual ecology today has shifted in some, although not all, contexts. During the last decades of the twentieth century, western scholarship has slowly become aware of the vast linguistic complexity of the East, of Africa, of the developing world, and of the Deaf community. Eastern and Deaf scholars, and those in the developing world, have started to make their mark about their own complex bilingualism, a topic they know so well. And with the world enmeshed in the complexity of globalization and the interrelationships between states and regions, bilingualism has become a welcomed resource for global understanding. Views of *heteroglossic linguistic practices and beliefs*,[3] or the realization of multiple co-existing norms which characterize bilingual speech, of bilinguals' translanguaging, have started to compete with monoglossic ones.

Some schools, in some societies, have started to adapt in order to recognize the multilingualism in their midst. They continue to use bilingualism as a way to more effectively teach a dominant language and to add an additional one, but at times, bilingualism is used to educate profoundly and globally, giving parents, both minority and majority, options that had not been previously available. The very neat frameworks and types of bilingual education that were developed in the second half of the twentieth century started to *leak*, as the concept of diglossia itself was questioned, and as features of one type were combined with features of another to better fit the situation at hand, and especially to adapt to the complex bilingualism of the students. And the top-down language-in-education policies of states started to be resisted as communities and families experimenting with bilingual education acted on their renewed agency.

Besides language shift, language maintenance and language addition, bilingual education programs have increasingly had as sociolinguistic aims:

1. *Bilingual revitalization*: an understanding that children of groups of minoritized languages that have suffered language loss must have the possibility of recovering their languages, as well as developing bilingual proficiencies.
2. *Bilingual development* rather than language maintenance: the understanding that all children, including those who are speakers of a minority language, whether immigrants, autochthonous minorities, Indigenous, or Deaf peoples, need more than just to maintain proficiency in a home language. Language-minority children, as well as language-majority children, have different degrees of proficiency in the home language and all need to develop academic proficiency in that language, not just maintain it as spoken in the home.
3. *Linguistic interrelationships* or the understanding that relationships between two or more languages are never competitive, but are strategic, responding to functional needs. As such, children of different ethnolinguistic groups need to have contact with each other, to be educated together, in polydirectional ways that respect differences,[4] and children of all groups need to develop strategic multilingual competence, using the entire spectrum of their languaging capabilities.

This leads us to recognize that there are types of bilingual education, that because of the more gravitational nature of their bilingualism, cannot be seen through a traditional diglossic lens, and that because of their non-linear nature are neither subtractive nor additive. We can then identify two further theoretical frameworks for bilingual education programs, neither of them relying solely on monolingual children for language shift, language addition or language maintenance:

- recursive;
- dynamic.

Recursive

This theoretical framework acknowledges that even a single ethnolinguistic group's bilingualism is complex and not static, and, therefore, depending on personal and sociohistorical circumstances, bilingualism can take different directions at various times from that of simple shift, addition, or maintenance (Cummins, 2000; García, Morín, and Rivera, 2001). The comings and goings of bilingual use and proficiency are recognized by schools, as different children, families, and communities find themselves at various points on a bilingual continuum depending on life circumstances, and as they interact with other speech communities.

A recursive bilingual education theoretical framework supports the possibility of *language revitalization* through education in the ways described by King (2001): acknowledging that language revitalization is not about going back to a past linguistic state, but about recapturing a lost language and culture in the context of the present and in imagining the future. In this way, bilingual education programs with a linguistic revitalization goal are of the recursive type, going back and forth between discourse modes and the bilingual continua of the community in question.

This theoretical framework supports a heteroglossic vision, focuses on the bilingual continuum of students as they come into classrooms, sees their bilingualism as a right, and works towards the acceptance of all of their linguistic and cultural differences. This type of theoretical framework therefore promotes biculturalism, as groups develop understandings of their histories and reconstruct their cultures, but also as they develop competencies in the other languages and cultures with which they are in contact.

Generally, these programs tend to protect and nurture the language undergoing revitalization, but in so doing, classroom language practices show much hybridity since teachers themselves are often not fluent speakers of their ancestral language. Bilingualism is not the endpoint or the goal, but the core, the center, of what these programs are about, even when their language policy seems to be monolingual in the ancestral language. The children are not second language learners, but emergent bilinguals. They have strong ethnic identification with a language that survives in rituals and ceremonies, and among some in their community, especially the elders. It could be displayed as in Figure 6.3:

Bilingual

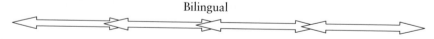

Figure 6.3   Recursive Bilingual Education Theoretical Framework

Dynamic

This theoretical framework supports language interactions taking place on different planes including multimodalities, and other linguistic interrelationships. These types of programs develop the ability to move along the communicative ridges and craters created by the multiple linguistic interrelationships of the many individuals along the many points of the bilingual continuum. The bilingual education programs activate the all-terrain vehicle of bilingualism that we presented in Chapter 1.

A balanced form of bilingualism as with the bicycle is not the endpoint. Instead, plurilingualism, or a dynamic form of bilingualism, is at the core of this type of program. This theoretical framework considers all students as a whole, acknowledges their bilingual continuum, sees their bilingualism as a resource, and promotes *transcultural* identities; that is, the bringing together of different cultural experiences and contexts generating a new and hybrid cultural experience.[5]

A dynamic theoretical framework of bilingualism allows the simultaneous co-existence of different languages in communication, accepts translanguaging, and supports the development of multiple linguistic identities to keep a linguistic ecology for efficiency, equity and integration, and responding to both local and global contexts (Calvet, 1999; Fettes, 2003; Mühlhäusler, 1996). This theoretical framework supports the integrated education of children at different points of the bilingual continuum, sometimes from different linguistic and cultural backgrounds. It supports the education of children to use languages for *functional interrelationships*, and not simply for *separate functional allocations*. Figure 6.4 displays this framework:

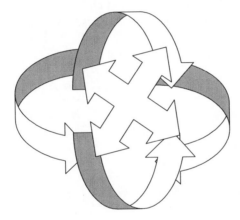

Figure 6.4   Dynamic Bilingual Education Theoretical Framework*

* The intermingling of the arrows, some linear, some elliptical, some shaded to indicate one language, others blank to indicate the other languages, does not indicate directionality, but simultaneous multiplicity of multilingual discourses

Co-presence

Although the last two theoretical frameworks can be traced to recent geopolitical and technological changes, all four theoretical frameworks are prevalent today throughout the world. It is important to recognize that not all social groups or states have the same resources, degree of agency, or aspirations for their children's education.

In many societies only the first two frameworks are applicable or accepted, and, in some, even those are questioned. For many groups, in many contexts, the first two frameworks for bilingual education are still quite relevant. This has to do with the fact that not all societies and groups have been touched by globalization in the same way. Nor have they the same degree of power to develop schools in which they have control over how language practices are enacted. Some societies and social groups, many of them bounded by cultural and religious identities, insist that their languages and cultures remain separate from those of others, while at times wanting access to the benefits that bilingualism in more global languages might bring. And there are ethnolinguistic groups throughout the world that continue to be segregated, despite the ending of open apartheid in South Africa, through residential and economic separation. In Africa today, and in many countries of Asia, it is transitional bilingual education that is being developed as an alternative to monolingual instruction in many former colonial languages. There are also elite groups that continue to view language as static in order to protect their status and power. They continue to base their bilingual education programs in an additive theoretical framework. Thus, all four theoretical frameworks, and the types of bilingual education programs emanating from each, co-exist in the twenty-first century.

Frameworks and principles

In this section we consider the characteristics of the four theoretical frameworks of bilingual education – language ideologies, linguistic goals, linguistic ecology, bilingual orientation, cultural ecology, and the type of children they serve – as they appear in Table 6.3. Each of the six principles following is based on these six characteristics:

Table 6.3   Theoretical Frameworks of Bilingual Education

	MONOGLOSSIC IDEOLOGIES		*HETEROGLOSSIC IDEOLOGIES*	
	Subtractive Bilingual Ed. Theoretical Framework	*Additive Bilingual Ed. Theoretical Framework*	*Recursive Bilingual Ed. Theoretical Framework*	*Dynamic Bilingual Ed. Theoretical Framework*
Language Ideology	Monoglossic	Monoglossic	Heteroglossic	Heteroglossic
Linguistic Goal	Monolingualism	Bilingualism	Bilingualism	Bilingualism
Linguistic Ecology	Language shift	Language addition; Language maintenance for minorities	Language revitalization	Plurilingualism
Bilingualism Orientation	Bilingualism as problem	Bilingualism as enrichment	Bilingualism as right	Bilingualism as resource
Cultural Ecology	Monocultural	Monocultural to bicultural	Bicultural multiplicity	Transcultural
Type of Children	Exclusively minority	Exclusively majority (maintenance and prestigious); Exclusively minority (maintenance)	Mostly non-dominant groups	All

Language ideologies
In the subtractive and additive bilingual education theoretical framework, the norm for bilingual education types is *monoglossic*: it values each of the languages according to monolingual standards. It results in a simple monolingual duality. These two theoretical frameworks view children as starting out as monolingual only, whether speakers of majority or minority languages. Bilingual education is seen through a monoglossic lens responding to a diglossic conceptualization with bilingualism only understood as $1 + 1 = 1$ (in the case of a subtractive framework) or $1 + 1 = 2$ (in the case of an additive framework). That is, the linguistic ecology is either of language shift in the subtractive framework, or of language addition (plus maintenance for language minorities) in the additive framework.

In the recursive and dynamic bilingual education theoretical framework, bilingualism itself is of a more complex kind, the result of a heteroglossic position that recognizes multiple co-existing norms. Children educated in these schools demonstrate a range of bilingual and multilingual proficiencies even as they start school, since they are positioned in different points of a bilingual continuum (in the case of the recursive framework) or use their bilingualism dynamically as they try to make sense of the language continuum of the classroom (in the case of the dynamic bilingual framework).

Linguistic goals
All but the subtractive bilingual education theoretical framework have bilingualism as a goal. That is, a subtractive bilingual education theoretical framework leads to *monolingualism*, while an additive, recursive, or dynamic one leads to *bilingualism*. A subtractive bilingual education theoretical framework results in a weak form of bilingual education (Baker, 1995), while additive, recursive, and dynamic bilingual education theoretical frameworks result in strong forms of bilingual education.[6] The difference is the type of languaging bilingually that each of the models support.

Linguistic ecology
Because the language goal of the subtractive bilingual education theoretical framework is monolingualism, its linguistic ecology responds to one of *shift*. Although the language goal of the other theoretical frameworks and the type of bilingual education that they produce is bilingualism, their linguistic ecology is different, with additive bilingual frameworks responding to *linear addition* of languages, while the recursive bilingual framework acknowledges the *bilingual continuum of language revitalization*, and the dynamic bilingual framework builds on *plurilingualism*.

Bilingualism orientations
Each of the theoretical frameworks for bilingual education responds to different *bilingual orientations*. A subtractive theoretical framework for bilingual education views bilingualism as a *problem*, while the additive one sees it as *enrichment*, the recursive one recognizes it as a *right* of the minority language community that wants to revitalize their language and of communities that want to be bilingual, and the dynamic one considers it as a *resource* for all.

Cultural ecologies

Because language is always related to culture, each of these bilingual education frameworks also responds to different actualizations of how culture is conceived for bilingual students. The cultural ecology of subtractive and additive theoretical frameworks also responds to monoglossic beliefs. In the subtractive framework, monoculturalism is imposed. In the additive framework, sometimes monoculturalism is maintained or biculturalism is nurtured. However, in this biculturalism each culture is viewed separately and whole, as cultivated in an additive framework.

The cultural ecology of recursive and dynamic plurilingual frameworks differs from the above in acknowledging the complex multiplicities of cultural parts as they are either revitalized or recovered on the one hand, or blended in the other. In the recursive framework, cultural parts are conceived as the colors in a kaleidoscope, with different parts coming in and out as enacted by the participants, producing reflections of biculturalism that are more about cultural multiplicity. But in the dynamic plurilingual framework, cultural parts are often blended to enable transculturalism.

Types of children

While our conceptualizations of bilingualism itself have shifted as we have become more familiar with it, the language orientation of education remains, for the most part, tied to the kinds of children being schooled:

1. Bilingualism is considered a *problem* when educating powerless language-minority children in isolation.
2. Bilingualism is considered a *privilege for enrichment* when educating the elite.
3. Bilingualism is considered a *right* when educating language-minority students who have considerable agency because they have gained power and rights.
4. Bilingualism is considered a *resource* in two situations:
   • when educating students in integrated and mixed classrooms where language-majority and language-minority children are educated jointly;
   • when educating bilingually *all* students in a given region or state.

There are, of course, many exceptions to these trends. For example, there are excellent bilingual education programs where the bilingualism of powerless language-minority children who are taught in isolation is considered an asset, a privilege, a right, and a resource (see for example García and Bartlett, 2007, for a description of a secondary school for Latino newcomers in the U.S.). All bilingual education frameworks that have bilingualism as a goal always consider bilingualism an enrichment activity, whether it is for majorities or minorities.

The next section proposes different types of bilingual education programs that correspond to the four theoretical frameworks explained above. We offer here brief descriptions of the different types of bilingual education. We expand upon these types of bilingual education in Chapters 10 and 11, and refer the reader there for more details.

Bilingual Education Types

We start by matching the types of bilingual education that we develop in this book to the four proposed theoretical frameworks. Table 6.4 displays this relationship:

Table 6.4   Theoretical Framework and Bilingual Education Types

	Subtractive Bilingual Ed.	*Additive Bilingual Ed.*	*Recursive Bilingual Ed.*	*Dynamic Bilingual Ed.*
Language Ideology	Monoglossic	Monoglossic	Heteroglossic	Heteroglossic
Linguistic Goal	Monolingualism	Bilingualism	Bilingualism	Bilingualism
Types	• transitional	• maintenance • prestigious • immersion	• immersion revitalization (heritage language immersion) • developmental	• poly-directional or two-way (dual lang., bilingual immersion; two-way immersion) • CLIL and CLIL-type • Multiple multilingual

The descriptions that follow are in themselves theoretical. In practice, all bilingual education types look different from the way in which they are described by scholars and teachers, as schools adapt them to the sociolinguistic landscape in which they exist, the diverse wishes of communities and parents, the realities of the teaching force, of instructional material, and of the children's social and age situations. The complexity of contextual and structural characteristics differentiates programs within each type category. Although we present them as categories, these types are much more fluid in reality, and sometimes can be considered continua of each other. Often, in practice, it is difficult to identify the type of bilingual education program a school is following. The banyan tree of bilingual education adapts to each context in different ways, as educators and parents act on their wishes, aspirations, and resources.[7] Chapters 10 and 11 give evidence of how different social groups have appropriated these types to plan bilingualism differently.

Monoglossic types

We start by discussing bilingual education types that are based on monolingual lenses and ideologies that support the acquisition of a second language and its development as separate from that of the other language. In all these program types, the assumption is that children start as monolinguals from the same linguistic point.

Transitional[8]

Transitional bilingual education types are those that use the child's language in instruction *only* until the child is fluent in the majority language, most often the language of the state. Although the use of the child's language to educate and impart values is as old as civilization itself, the popularity of transitional bilingual education really started with the growing concern about colonized groups in the early twentieth century. The temporary nature of transitional bilingual education programs, as well as the fact that they usually involve the youngest children, makes the programs appealing to many.

Transitional bilingual education is based on the philosophy that education is about building on children's strengths, their language and culture being their greatest assets. But it is also based on the superiority of the majority language and culture and the mandate to teach it well to the child. Transitional bilingual education ultimately supports and values monolingualism and permits bilingualism only as a temporary measure.

Transitional bilingual education programs tend to hire bilingual teachers, most often members of the ethnolinguistic group themselves, who are deeply familiar with the home language practices and culture. As members of bilingual communities, and without a clear language policy of when one language or the other is to be used, bilingual teachers code-switch back and forth, working especially hard to communicate with the children. Teachers are often conflicted about their roles in enabling communication with their children and teaching the majority language, the only language in which valid assessment takes place.

Joshua A. Fishman has been critical of the transitional nature of bilingual education in the United States, comparing it to a vaccine. Speaking about the use of languages other than English in transitional bilingual education he said (1976: 34):

> If a non-English mother tongue is conceptualized as a disease of the poor, then in true vaccine style this disease is to be attacked by the disease bacillus itself. A little bit of deadened mother tongue, introduced in slow stages in the classroom environment, will ultimately enable the patient to throw off the mother tongue entirely and to embrace all-American vim, vigor, and stability.

Transitional bilingual education programs usually have no clear language policy. Teachers are given a charge – *to teach children the majority language and to use the children's home language to facilitate and speed up the process.* The home language only becomes a tool to assist in the acquisition of the majority language. With this vague charge, the language use of transitional bilingual education teachers varies immensely, depending on their own language proficiencies, those of the children, the difficulty of the content they are trying to teach, the instructional material they have, and their own values towards bilingualism.

And yet, transitional bilingual programs provide, "safe houses" (García 2006b) in the sense given to the term by Mary Louise Pratt (1991), that is, a social and intellectual space where the group is able to constitute itself as "horizontal, homogeneous, sovereign communities with high degrees of trust, shared understandings, temporary protection from legacies of oppression" (1991: 39). Hernández-Chávez

(1978: 536) also points to some of its advantages: "The cognitive and educational retardation, the culture shock, and the alienation that often accompany early school experiences through an unknown tongue can be tempered or even largely eliminated by the use of the child's home language." It is clear that bilingual education, even of the transitional kind, is more beneficial to language-minority children than a monolingual education. In the last decade, there has been a growth of Newcomers' schools and programs to support the transition of immigrant children to the dominant language. These programs are all of the transitional kind.

Maintenance

Maintenance Bilingual Education programs include educational programs mostly for language minorities who speak their languages at home when they enter school and want to maintain them while they develop proficiency in a dominant language. Besides teaching academic subjects through two languages, these programs reflect community cultural values, and often are interested in the community's self-determination. Maintenance programs not only maintain the group's home language while teaching the dominant language, but also instill a strong bicultural identity in children.

Schools of this type often make choices of how to arrange the languages based on practical considerations, such as the number of teachers of each language, their qualifications and interests, the instructional material they have, the parents' wishes, the community's sociolinguistic profile and that of the students. In general, however, these programs use one language as medium of instruction for some period of time, and the other language for another, of equal or unequal length (more on language arrangements in Chapter 12).

Referring to the United States context, where maintenance bilingual education programs in public schools are now rare (more on this history in Chapter 8), August and Hakuta (1998: 20) define maintenance programs thus: "Most students in the program are English-language learners and from the same language background. They receive significant amounts of their instruction in their native language. Unlike transitional programs, these programs aim to develop English proficiency, but also to develop academic proficiency in the native language." In general, maintenance bilingual education programs are now referred to as developmental bilingual education programs, since it has become accepted that most language minorities need much more than just language maintenance, with language shift and loss a common aspect of their experiences.[9]

Prestigious

In prestigious bilingual education programs, majority children are taught through the medium of two languages of prestige, mostly with two teachers, with each one teaching in a different language. Mejía (2002) calls these programs "elite bilingual education." Usually, the languages are clearly separated by teacher on the principle of one person, one language, although both languages are usually explicitly taught in Language Arts classes. These programs often compartmentalize the use of the two languages, ensuring that children add on a language, but guaranteeing that they keep the add-on language distinct from their own ethnolinguistic identity. Thus, the emphasis is on adding a language, separate and different from that which identifies them as an ethnolinguistic group.

Throughout the world, language-majority speakers who want their children to become bilingual have organized these bilingual education programs, often educational efforts that function outside of the state system and that are funded by parents' tuition.

Immersion

In immersion bilingual education, for at least a period of time, language-majority children are taught exclusively in the language that they are trying to acquire.[10] This second-language teaching philosophy rests on the principle that languages are best learned when used in authentic communication than when they are explicitly taught, as in second-language education programs. To that end, the additional language is used as medium of instruction. Generally, immersion bilingual education programs not only use two different teachers for each of the languages, but children often switch rooms which are carefully allocated to a specific language.

As a bilingual/diglossic additive type of education, the term "immersion" must always be put *alongside* that of bilingual education. Despite the immersion of the child in the other language for education, the child's home language is honored, respected, used throughout the school, and taught after the immersion period. The immersion period that excludes the child's language tends to last only one year, and even during that time, the home language is extensively used by the children (Swain, 1978).

It is also instructive to realize that immersion bilingual education is for children whose home language has some degree of power and will be reinforced in society at large. Children immersed in another language in school must have the benefit of continuing to hear the home language used not only at home, but also in the media and in public, and to see it in print in signs and labels. Without that societal support, a child who is immersed in another language in education starts to undergo language shift and does not become bilingual. Immersion bilingual education is always additive, and builds upon the strength and power that the other language already enjoys in society. The teaching of language-minority children exclusively in the majority language can never be considered an instance of immersion education, despite it being called so. Indigenous peoples, immigrant minorities, autochthonous minority children, or Deaf children being educated in monolingual classrooms are not in immersion education, but rather in what has been called *submersion* or *sink-or-swim*.[11]

Johnson and Swain (1997) identify eight different core features of immersion programs:

1. The additional language is a medium of instruction.
2. The immersion curriculum parallels the local majority language curriculum.
3. Overt support exists for the home language.
4. The program aims for additive bilingualism.
5. Exposure to the additional language is largely confined to the classroom.
6. Students enter with similar (and limited) levels of proficiency in the additional language.

7. The teachers are bilingual.
8. The classroom culture is that of the local majority-language community.

Immersion bilingual education programs differ depending on the stage at which children are exposed to instruction through the medium of the other language. *Early Immersion Bilingual Education* is prevalent in pre-schools and early grades throughout the world. Starting in the earliest grade of school, children are instructed through the medium of the other language with a teacher who is bilingual. Although the teacher speaks to the children solely in the other language, she is able to fully understand and react appropriately as the children speak their home language to her and to each other. It is the teacher, then, and the strategies she uses, that become the mechanism through which children acquire the language of instruction, while being educated. When Early Immersion Bilingual Education programs start in elementary schools, the children are often immersed the first year. By the second year, their home language is often used in developing literacy and in other language arts activities. In the third year, children may spend one half of the time being educated through the medium of the other language and another half in their home language. There are many different arrangements of this distribution of languages in Early Total Immersion programs across the world.

Late Immersion Bilingual Education refers to programs that usually start after the child has already been educated through his or her home language. Some programs start after three years in primary school, others at the middle-school stage, and others at the secondary-school stage, when the children's conceptual base and academic skills have been solidly established.

As immersion bilingual education programs have grown, other adaptations and extensions have been made. Besides the *total immersion bilingual education programs* described above where all instruction is in the language other than that of the child for a period of time, there are also *partial immersion bilingual education programs*. These programs, both early and late, immerse children in the second language only for part of the day and not for the full day as the total programs do.[12]

Heteroglossic types

We now turn to bilingual education types that are based on heteroglossic lenses and ideologies and support the development of bilingualism while recognizing that many children come from homes and communities that have some familiarity with bilingualism. As such, it is accepted that these children do not start out as monolinguals, but have access to diverse languaging practices. Sometimes the differences in languaging between the home and the school have to do with the fact that children come from language communities whose languages have been suppressed, and thus their languaging practices include bits and pieces of what the school considers the standard language. Other times these differences have to do with the fact that children within the same classroom come from a range of language communities. These bilingual education types recognize that even within a single speech community, there is much diversity of languaging practices. And they acknowledge the children's linguistic heterogeneity, both within the same ethnolinguistic group, as well as across different groups. For these bilingual education types, the development of bilingualism depends on the degree to which bits and pieces of the children's languaging practices are extended in the academic context. Heteroglossic bilingual education types support the language interaction of children with different translanguaging practices and build bilingualism accordingly.

Immersion revitalization

Motivated by the success of the Canadian immersion bilingual education programs, ethnolinguistic minorities who have experienced language shift away from their heritage languages have adapted and extended immersion bilingual education programs to fit their needs. In cases where the language shift has been radical, as for example among the Māoris in Aotearoa/New Zealand, immersion revitalization programs start at the pre-school level and are usually referred to as Language Nest Programs (more on these in Chapter 11), One of the best-known educational efforts to revitalize a language through schooling has taken place in Aotearoa/New Zealand since the 1970s. Called Te Kohanga Reo, this Māori language nest immersion program has spread since the 1980s to other Indigenous communities determined to revitalize their languages, including the American Southwest. These programs are also often called "heritage language immersion" because of their emphasis not just on reclaiming their languages, but also of "incorporating local knowledge in school curricula" (Romero and McCarty, 2006: p. i). When the children have undergone a high level of language shift and when the group has sufficient agency and power, immersion bilingual revitalization programs are used.

Developmental

There are three reasons for the shift in bilingual education policies from those that focused only on the maintenance of minority languages at the end of the twentieth century to those targeting the development of languages:

1. The realization that because of the limited domains in which minority languages usually function, more is needed than the simple maintenance of the language as spoken in the homes. Schools have a most important role not only in developing the school language, but also the home language of language-minority students. Otheguy and Otto (1980) have shown why it is insufficient to speak of maintenance bilingual education without referring to its developmental nature. Language is not static, and so the task of bilingual programs is not simply to maintain a language, but also to develop especially its academic functions, as well as to extend the other language.
2. The awareness that because of the language loss and language shift that language-minority communities experience as a result of different degrees of linguistic oppression, their children often come to school with different language proficiencies. A model that relies on plain maintenance of the home language and addition of the school language is therefore insufficient.
3. The recognition that communities and schools have increasingly to contend with much more than one language group, and that it is difficult to reserve maintenance bilingual education programs only for language-minority children. For

example, in the autonomous regions of Spain there is increased immigration from Latin America, the Maghreb, China, and Eastern Europe. The educational question has become not just how to maintain (or revitalize) the languages other than Spanish and equalize them, but how to teach both languages to immigrants in the same schools.

Whereas maintenance bilingual education stems from a monoglossic vision, based on separation from the language-majority community and seeking self-determination for the group itself and biculturalism, developmental bilingual education is more heteroglossic, based on a bilingual/multilingual and bicultural model of community and seeking recognition of equality, but enacting multiple languages and identities. It is sometimes difficult to distinguish between maintenance and developmental bilingual education programs for language-minority populations, leading some to call them "maintenance developmental bilingual education" types (Baker, 2001; Baker and Prys Jones, 1998; García, 1997a). In this book, we have kept the distinction, however artificial, to emphasize the way in which the types have evolved, from a diglossic one based on biculturism and self-determination, to one that recognizes the recursive nature of bilingualism, the cultural multiplicity of its speakers, and the greater range of linguistic differences.

Developmental bilingual education programs are for non-dominant language groups who are reaffirming and developing their minoritized languages. Because their language shift has not been extensive and thus the languages are not endangered, these developmental recovery bilingual education programs are more appropriate than immersion revitalization programs. Through these programs, language-minority children develop academic proficiency in their home languages, as well as in a dominant language. These language-minority groups have received sufficient attention from the state or are organized enough to be able to support these types of bilingual education program. Because of the dynamic nature of migration in a globalized world, children come in and out of these classrooms at all times, thus reflecting the entire bilingual continuum, even if the home language happens to be the same. Deaf bilingual education usually falls under this type.

Poly-directional or two-way (dual language)
These programs are also known as *two-way* dual language, *two-way immersion*, *bilingual immersion*, or simply *dual language*. We prefer to refer to them as poly-directional rather than two-way because it acknowledges that children in these programs do not simply speak either language A or language B, and have to acquire the other language. In the complex interrelationships of the twenty-first century, there is much intermarriage, divorce, and reconstituted families, and children often go to school with a bit of both languages. There are also children who go to schools in different countries with different languages. Some are born in one country, reside for a few years in another one, go to school in a third country, come back to the country in which they were born, for example. There are families that live their entire lives that way – professional families, as well as working-class families. What we often have in these classrooms, then, are children at all points of the bilingual continuum who interact with each other and who share their languaging differences across groups.

U.S. scholars and educators often refer to this kind of bilingual education as "dual language" education, thus avoiding the politics surrounding the ideologically loaded "bilingual" (for more on this, see Chapter 8). But calling this "dual language education" emphasizes two separate languages, taking attention off bilingualism, and negating the reality of bilingual classroom practices, that is, their translanguaging (see Chapters 3 and 12). In the United States these programs immerse children with different linguistic profiles (supposedly 50 percent speakers of English and 50 percent speakers of the language other than English) for a minimum of 50 percent of the time, in studying through another language.[13] (For detailed descriptions of the design and the principles of such programs, see Howard and Christian, 2002; Howard, Sugarman, Christian, Lindholm-Leary, and Rogers, 2007.)

These poly-directional bilingual education programs also refer to, for example, the European Schools for Civil Servants (more on these in Chapter 11), where more than two-language groups are officially involved in learning and studying through each other's languages.

CLIL and CLIL-type

All bilingual education is *content-based language learning* (Brinton, Snow, and Wesche, 1989; Snow, Met, and Genesee, 1989). But in the last decade whole countries, and even supranational bodies, have begun to support bilingual education for all its citizens in the form of teaching one to two subjects in an additional language. Because all the children are involved, there are languaging differences in the classroom from the very beginning, that is, there is plurilingualism within the children themselves.

The European Commission has supported this approach in the development of Content and Language Integrated Learning (CLIL/EMILE) as a form of bilingual education for all (for more on the European Union's language policy in education, see Chapter 9). CLIL is a way of teaching languages in mainstream education from pre-school through vocational education, for all populations (Baetens Beardsmore, 1995, 2002). It is not a special program for some schools, like immersion bilingual education. Its teachers need to have a high level of fluency in the language, although "native" language proficiency is not expected. CLIL protects the development of the first language, while exposing students to the second language for a certain time which may start in primary school. For the European Union, with an understanding that all students should be fluent in their *Mother Tongue + 2 languages* in the near future, CLIL is providing a practical and sustainable way of educating their citizens for plurilingualism (Baetens Beardsmore, 2002). The CLIL-type bilingual education includes all children in the learning of an additional language and builds flexibility in its conception of bilingualism. It does not require equal time for the two languages, nor does it call for "native-like" proficiency of bilingual teachers or bilingual children. CLIL is discussed in detail in Chapter 9.

Although CLIL is a European term, the same type of bilingual education approach is followed by many countries that want to make *all* children bilingual by teaching one to two subjects in an additional language. Increasingly, for example, math and science are taught throughout the world in English. This is the case, as we will see in Chapter 11, of Malaysia. We refer to these types of bilingual education programs as CLIL-type.

Multiple multilingual education
These programs always involve at least three languages and involve groups who manifest a complex multilingualism that creates a bilingual continuum along which children are situated at different points. Sometimes different languages are weaved in and out of the curriculum. These programs exist in societies like India where the linguistic complexity demands that all citizens receive some form of bilingual education, although, as we will see, tribal languages are often ignored (see for example Mohanty, 2006). Most bilingual education programs today, whether for minorities or majorities, and initially of one type or another, are extending themselves to encompass the multiplicity of this type of multilingual education.

Types and principles

In this section, we summarize the different types of bilingual education programs and their characteristics. We start out by describing some of the principles of these types. This section also includes a comprehensive table, Table 6.7, which summarizes the characteristics of the types of bilingual education programs as they correspond with different theoretical frameworks. The reader is reminded that we will expand upon these types of bilingual education programs, and give examples from different social contexts, in Chapters 10 and 11.

Figure 6.5 presents the correspondence between *type of bilingualism* and type of bilingual education program:

Bilingualism	Bilingual Education
Subtractive $L1 + L2 - L1 \rightarrow L2$	Transitional
Additive $L1 + L2 = L1 + L2$	Maintenance Prestigious Immersion
Recursive 	Immersion revitalization Developmental
Dynamic 	Poly-directional or two-way (Dual language) CLIL and CLIL-type Multiple multilingual

Figure 6.5   Type of Bilingualism and Type of Bilingual Education Program

The types of bilingual education programs also respond to the *different kinds of children* being educated, and especially to the position of power which they hold. Table 6.5 summarizes the usual correspondence between type of bilingual program and kind of child:

Table 6.5   Children and Bilingual Education Types

Type of Children	Type of Bilingual Education
For powerless language-minority children	Transitional
For empowered language-minority children	Maintenance
	Immersion revitalization
	Developmental
For empowered language-majority children	Prestigious
	Immersion
For all – different language groups	Poly-directional/two-way (dual language)
	CLIL and CLIL-type
	Multiple multilingual education

Finally, the different types of bilingual education use language differently. In considering monoglossic types of bilingual education, we can safely speak of a first and second language, although the emphasis might be in one or the other, especially at the beginning. But in heteroglossic types, especially because of the broad continuum of linguistic proficiencies present in classrooms, it is often impossible to speak of a first or second language. It is, of course, possible to identify the language of instruction that is used first, second or third. We speak then of the ThL (threatened language) or the DL (dominant). In cases where there is an equitable relationship between the two languages, we speak of X or Y. Table 6.6 summarizes the

Table 6.6   Initial Language Emphasis and Bilingual Education Types*

Type of Bilingual Education	Initial Language Emphasis
Monoglossic	
Transitional	L1
Maintenance	L1 + L2
Prestigious	L1 + L2
Immersion	L2
Heteroglossic	
Immersion revitalization	ThL
Developmental	ThL + DL
Poly-directional/two way (Dual)	X(ThL) + Y(DL)
CLIL/CLIL-type	DL + X
Multiple multilingual	X(ThL) + Y(D)

* For some types, depending on the group in question, the X/Y languages could be threatened or dominant. This situation is indicated with parentheses.

different *initial* language treatment possibilities that correspond to each of the types of bilingual education.

Whereas in transitional bilingual education the initial language used is that of the child, in immersion bilingual education it is the child's second language. In contrast, in maintenance and prestigious bilingual education programs, the child's L1 is usually used in the beginning, with the L2 following quickly. When groups have lost their language and are revitalizing them through bilingual education, an initial emphasis on the threatened language is necessary. But when the group wishes to expand the functions of a language that most of them speak, then both their threatened and the dominant language might be used simultaneously. Depending on the degree of danger to the language, the threatened language might be more emphasized. When two or more groups are schooled jointly, their languages are simultaneously introduced. Sometimes, one of the languages is a threatened language and the other one is dominant. But sometimes both languages have equal status. In CLIL-type programs, an additional language is added, usually after the child has acquired the schools' dominant language. Finally, in complex multilingual situations, the threatened language and the dominant language are usually simultaneously introduced, although perhaps for different functions. For example, in Luxembourg, Luxemburgish is not used in literacy instruction.

Table 6.7 provides the summary characteristics for all the types of bilingual education programs here considered. It displays the principles and characteristics that we have been discussing throughout this chapter.

Deaf bilingual education

Understandably, many educators point to the unique modality (signing) of one of the languages of Deaf students and put the scholarly study of Deaf education aside, depositing it away in the field of special education. Even when bilingual education for the Deaf is included in bilingual education scholarship, it often receives a section of its own. In this book we have tried to integrate the discussion of the Deaf as language minorities and bilinguals throughout, pointing sometimes to differences, as well as to similarities. A bilingual Deaf school might incorporate features from one or more of these types listed above; hence we do not offer a separate category.[14] However, examples of bilingual education practices and policies for the Deaf are given wherever appropriate, and we develop it further in Chapter 11.

As we will see, bilingual education programs for the Deaf are also becoming more complex. One reason for this complexity has to do with improvements in cochlear implants, making the categorization of the Deaf more fluid; although the use of sign language alongside speech becomes ever more important. For this reason, bilingual education programs for the Deaf are more of the developmental kind, acknowledging the heteroglossic conditions of Deaf children in the twenty-first century.

But bilingual education for the Deaf go beyond those of the developmental kind, for just as with other children, Deaf children are increasingly in need of more than just one written language and one signed language. For example, Deaf children at Beijing School Number Four for the Deaf are required to study English starting in

Table 6.7 Types of Bilingual Education and Characteristics*

Type of BE	Linguistic Goal	Linguistic Orientation/ Linguistics Ecology	Cultural Ecology	Type of Children	Initial Language Emphasis
MONOGLOSSIC					
Transitional	Monolingualism	Problem/shift	Monocultural	Lang. minority	L1*
Maintenance	Additive biling.	Enrichment/maintenance	Bicultural	Lang. minority	L1 + L2
Prestigious	Additive biling.	Enrichment/addition	Monocultural to bicultural	Lang. majority	L1 + L2
Immersion	Additive biling.	Enrichment/addition	Monocultural to bicultural	Lang. majority	L2
HETEROGLOSSIC					
Immersion revitalization	Recursive biling.	Right/revitalization of endangered languages	Bicultural multiplicity	Lang. Minority Diff. points of bilingual continuum	ThL
Developmental	Recursive biling.	Right/Revitalization of expanding languages	Bicultural Multiplicity	Lang. Minority Diff. points of bilingual continuum	ThL + DL
Poly-directional or two-way (dual language)	Dynamic biling.	Resource/plurilingualism	Transcultural	Multiple groups Diff. points of bilingual continuum across groups	X(ThL) + Y(DL)
CLIL and CLIL-type	Dynamic biling.	Resource/plurilingualism	Transcultural	All Diff. points of bilingual continuum	DL + X
Multiple multilingual	Dynamic biling.	Resource/plurilingualism	Transcultural	All Diff. points of bilingual continuum	X(ThL) + Y(DL)

* Monoglossic models start out with either the child's first language or the child's second language or both. Because heteroglossic models start out from a bilingual and not a monolingual conception, we do not indicate the languages as being either first or second, but instead indicate whether they are threatened (ThL) or dominant (DL). When the languages do not have a clear power valance, they are indicated simply as X or Y. For some types, depending on the group in question, the X/Y languages could be also be threatened or dominant. This situation is indicated with parentheses.

elementary school. At a school for the Deaf in Rome, the children start studying English at the elementary level, and they also start studying French at the second-ary level (Cole, 2008). Some schools around the world require their Deaf students to study speech in the foreign language, and some require that they also study foreign sign languages. To complicate the matter even further, migration is not limited to non-Deaf populations: Deaf people do migrate too. They may arrive at a new school with the tough task of learning new languages in addition to their own home languages (see for example Gerner de García, 1992, 1993; Christensen and Delgado, 2000). Deaf children are also increasingly going to school with hearing children, and there are two-way dual-language programs for these children. Even outside of the school sphere, Deaf people of various linguistic groups are inter-acting with each other more frequently – at international conferences, in athletic competitions, and on the internet (Moody, 2002). Deaf people in the United States translanguage between American Sign Language, mime, written English, and often International Sign Language.[15] Because of these new complexities about the bilin-gual context of Deaf people, Deaf bilingual education is becoming an important area of study. Brejle's (1999) survey of bilingual programs for the Deaf around the world demonstrates that the number of such programs is on the rise.

Conclusion

This chapter has described four theoretical frameworks for the development of bilin-gual education types; and has identified their ensuing types of bilingual education programs. But we have warned that this conceptualization of bilingual education types is problematic and inaccurate. As bilingual education efforts around the world have expanded, each local context has adapted the type to fit its need. We return to some of these approximations in Chapters 10 and 11, and in so doing, we describe the language-in-education policy (LiEP) of many states and ethnolinguistic groups.

As we have affirmed throughout this book, the changes brought about by modern-day globalization and technology have changed our conceptualizations of bilingualism, from the linear types of the past, to the more recursive and dynamic types of the present. And yet linear bilingual education types continue to exist along-side more dynamic types, sometimes even in the same school. *No one type is better than the other.* The advantages of one type over the other are always related to the lens through which one looks, and the goals, aspirations, and wishes of parents and children, as well as the educational resources that are available. It is important nevertheless to repeat that all bilingual education programs have important advant-ages over monolingual ones for the children, as well as for societies, and our world's social and political ecology. It is also important to understand that those bilingual programs with a goal of bilingualism (all but the transitional type) are much more effective in developing language and academic proficiency than those with a goal of monolingualism.

In the next chapter we discuss the interrelationship of variables in bilingual education while contextualizing with societal examples. Chapters 8 and 9 focus on the language policies in education of two contrasting contexts – the United States and the European Union. The last two chapters in Part III of this book then discuss language policies in education throughout the world as a way to illustrate different types of bilingual education. Some of these policies are espoused by states, others by ethnolinguistic groups themselves, others by groups of parents. Again, the banyan tree of bilingual education is entangled in local contexts.

Questions for Reflection

1. Identify the four theoretical frameworks discussed in this chapter that have shaped types of bilingual education programs. What are the differences between them?
2. Identify different types of bilingual education programs. What are possible benefits of implementing these programs? Who would benefit?
3. Analyze carefully each of the components in Table 6.7. Pay particular attention to the last column. Summarize the Table.
4. Reflecting on personal experiences, are there any existing bilingual education programs and/or schools that you know of? What theoretical framework do they reflect? What type of program would you consider them to be? Why?

Further Reading

Baetens-Beardsmore, H. (1993) (ed.). *European Models of Bilingual Education*. Multilingual Matters, Clevedon.

Baker, C. (2006). *Foundations of Bilingual Education and Bilingualism*. Fourth edn. Multilingual Matters, Clevedon. First edn. 1993; second edn. 1996; third edn. 2001.

Baker, C., and Prys Jones, S. (1998). *Encyclopedia of Bilingualism and Bilingual Education*. Multilingual Matters, Clevedon.

Brisk, M.E. (2006). *Bilingual Education. From Compensatory to Quality Schooling*. Second edn. Lawrence Erlbaum, Mahwah, NJ.

Faltis, C.J., and Hudelson, S.J. (1998). *Bilingual Education in Elementary and Secondary School Communities. Toward Understanding and Caring*. Allyn and Bacon, Boston, MA.

Fishman, (1976). *Bilingual Education: An International Sociological Perspective*. Newbury House, Rowley, MA.

García, O. (1997). "Bilingual Education." In F. Coulmas (ed.). *The Handbook of Sociolinguistics*. Blackwell, Oxford, pp. 405–20.

García, O., and Baker, C. (eds.) (2007). *Bilingual Education: An Introductory Reader*. Multilingual Matters, Clevedon.

Skutnabb-Kangas, T. (1981). *Bilingualism or Not: The Education of Minorities*. Multilingual Matters, Clevedon.

7

Bilingual Education: Factors and Variables

by Hugo Baetens Beardsmore[1]

L'école est un curieux lieu de langage. Il s'y mélange les langues officielle, privée, scolaire, des langues maternelles, des langues étrangères, de l'argot de lycéen, de l'argot de la Cité. À considérer toutes ces langues qui cohabitent, je me dis que l'école est peut-être le seul lieu où elles peuvent se retrouver dans leur diversité et dans leurs chevauchements. Mais il faut être très vigilants et justement tirer partie de cette belle hétérogénéité.

(The school is a curious place for language. In it there is a mixture of official, private and school languages, mother tongues, foreign languages, schoolgoers' slang, the slang from the block. When you look at all these languages living together you say to yourself that the school is perhaps the only place where they can find each other in all their diversity and overlappings. But we need to be vigilant and take advantage of this beautiful diversity.)

Steiner and Ladjali, 2003: 83–4

Overview

In this chapter we review bilingual education variables under three overarching factors:

- the situational factor;
- the operational factor;
- the outcome factor.

Introduction

As we stated in the previous chapter, in his early overview of bilingual schooling, William Mackey (1976) claimed that up to 3,000 variables could potentially intervene to account for the nature of the bilingual classroom. It is evident that the unraveling of those parameters is an immense task for educators. This chapter discusses macro-variables in an effort to help policy-makers, and those wishing to develop educational systems, schools, and programs, to consider what needs to be taken into account. It must be remembered, however, that this chapter enumerates the variables while requiring that each local context takes its own individual cases into account.

The macro-variables that are important to consider cluster under three broad factors: situational, operational, and outcome (Spolsky, Green, and Read, 1974). These three macro-factors, with interdependent variables, form the overarching framework of bilingual education policy (see Table 7.1).

An overview of the literature reveals that this constant set of parameters is reiterated in general discussions on multilingual education. (See Baker, 2001; Baker and Prys Jones, 1998; Brisk, 2006; CLIL/EMILE, 2002; García, 1997a; García, Skutnabb-Kangas, and Torres-Guzmán, 2006; Harley, Allen, Cummins, and Swain, 1990; Hornberger, 1991.) The rest of this chapter considers the different variables. It is important for the scholar, evaluator, or administrator of different kinds of bilingual education programs to distinguish between variables that can be manipulated, and those over which there is no control because of larger global or national policies.

Situational Factor

The situational factor refers to the context in which the bilingual school operates. If we examine the variables in the situational factor in the light of current experience

Table 7.1   Macro-Factors and Interdependent Variables for BE Policies

Situational Factor	*Operational Factor*	*Outcome Factor*

1. Students
  a. Target students
  b. Social background
  c. Linguistic background
2. Population diversity
3. Language policy
4. Opportunity for language use
  a. Geography
  b. Languages out of school
5. Status of languages
6. Linguistic characteristics
7. Attitudes
8. Economics
9. Religion, culture, and ideologies
	1. Curriculum
	2. Subjects
	3. Initial literacy
	4. Exit criteria
	5. Materials
	6. Teachers
	7. Language strategies
	8. Parental involvement
	9. Whole school
		1. Linguistic
		  a. Shift
		  b. Addition
		  c. Maintenance
		  d. Revitalization
		  e. Development minoritized language
		  f. Development multiple languages
		  g. Development plurilingualism
		2. Literacy
		  a. Literacy in majority language
		  b. Receptive biliteracy
		  c. Partial biliteracy
		  d. Full biliteracy
		3. Content-matter
		4. Sociocultural

worldwide, it may help to get a clearer picture of what can be reasonably manipulated in a given context to achieve successful multilingual achievement outcomes
for the largest number of students possible.

Students

Target students

There is a disparity of opinion as to who can best benefit from bilingual schooling,
with very little convincing research to guide policy-makers. Popular wisdom claims
that very young children from stable middle-class backgrounds learning prestigious
languages are the ideal recipients for bilingual education. But when we look around
us, we see *the whole range* of populations, ages, social, and linguistic backgrounds
being successfully catered for in one program or the other. In some countries
such as Luxembourg (Lebrun and Baetens Beardsmore, 1993; Davis, 1994), Malta
(Camilleri, 1995), Lebanon (Duverger, 2005), Brunei Darussalam (Jones, Martin,
and Ozóg, 1993; Jones 2002), and the Philippines (Bernardo, 1999, 2004), it is
the whole school population that is receiving some form of bilingual education.
In others, such as Germany (Mäsch, 1993), self-selected students are engaged in
bilingual education. In still others, such as Canada (Swain and Lapkin, 1982), the
Basque Country (Artigal, 1993; Etxeberria, 1999), and New Zealand (May, 2001),
children are in bilingual education programs at parental request. In other countries,
such as the United States (Casanova, 1991) or Belgium (Leman, 1993), decisions
as to who participates in bilingual education programs mostly have to do with the
perceived needs of immigrants.

Although this great variety in target students implies different types of bilingual
programs, what is clear is that any type of student can benefit from some form of
bilingual education, since the whole range of students is at present being catered for
in bilingual education programs throughout the world. This includes the Deaf who
use sign languages as their dominant mode of communication (Gibson, Small, and
Mason, 1997; Brejle, 1999), as well as those with learning challenges (Bruck, 1984).

*We know of no contemporary research whatsoever that shows that bilingual
education of some type or other is harmful* (see Duverger, 2005: 73, who refers to
the lack of serious and convincing evidence to show that failures in bilingual classes
are due to the use of two languages), though we are aware of vocal subjective
hostility, doubts and warnings of dire consequences, usually from articulate, monolingually handicapped individuals (Baetens Beardsmore, 2003; Crawford, 2004 for
the U.S.).

Social background

Many bilingual education programs in the world today are either for the *social
elite* (for instance, many international schools like the Lycée International de Saint-
Germain-en-Laye or the International School of Geneva), or for deprived *immigrants*
or *refugees* requiring temporary bilingualism for transition to the majority language
(for instance, transitional bilingual education programs in the U.S.). Yet many bilingual
schools can, and do, cater for populations of *mixed social* backgrounds with no

more problems than those faced by similar monolingual schools. For example, this is the case of some of the European Schools designed for European civil servants (Swan, 1996), and Welsh schools (Jones, 1995). This is also the case of many two-way bilingual education programs in the U.S. (Freeman, 1998; Lindholm-Leary, 2001). Success or failure of the education program is more likely to be attributable to social problems in general rather than the languages of instruction. On the other hand, many unsuccessful educational endeavors for minority groups (immigrants, refugees, Indigenous peoples, autochthonous minorities, or the Deaf) can clearly be attributed to a lack of adequate bilingual education, as when language-minority children are given a *sink-or-swim* or *submersion experience* (Cummins, 1984; Skutnabb-Kangas, 1981) in a mainstream monolingual school environment.

It may be more difficult to provide bilingual education for some populations who have been victims of *social stigmatization*, or who are *dispersed* over large areas. This is the case of the Roma who straddle different national borders in central Europe, and who have no standardized Rom language. Yet, there are recent initiatives, for example, The Ghandi Project targeting Rom speakers in Hungary (see Csovcsics and Solymosi, 2006) that are successfully addressing the linguistic and bilingual educational needs of such non-sedentary populations.

Linguistic background

Bilingual education can be successfully provided for language-majority or language-minority children, though differently. *Immersion* programs in Canada where English-speaking children are immersed in French from the beginning, are successful when offered to speakers of a majority language (Swain and Lapkin, 1982), and totally inappropriate if offered to minority-language speakers (Hernández-Chávez, 1984). Alternative strategies for balancing the time and timing of the introduction of an additional language of instruction are recommended according to the status, prestige, and numerical strength of the target population. For example, the Basque Country has developed three different models of bilingual education in order to respond to these differences (Artigal, 1993).

It is the most difficult to find acceptance for bilingual education in communities where there is no perceived need for other-language proficiency, as, for example, in large sections of the Anglo-Saxon world, especially the United States and England.

Population diversity

The development or operation of a bilingual education program also depends on the school population in terms of language abilities and use. Whether students share a common language, or whether they bring to the school many different languages, can affect how a program is created and run. A bilingual program for a school where all children speak the same home language will look different from one at a school where not all students speak the same home language. In the former program, there may be a lot of linguistic comparative analysis of the students' home language and the target language; whereas in the latter type, there may be a greater reliance on activities that encourage authentic conversation in the target language.

Countries such as Cameroon, with over 200 indigenous languages and a school system incorporating French and English (Todd, 1984), and India, with 1,652 mother tongues (1961 census), a much larger number of dialects, and twenty-two constitutionally recognized official languages (Constitution of India, eighth schedule, December 2003; Mohanty, 2006), face insuperable difficulties in providing the type of bilingual development advocated by western theories (Baetens Beardsmore, 1992; Mohanty, 2006).

Although the European Schools for Civil Servants (Baetens Beardsmore, 1992) can provide up to eight mother-tongue sections as the basis of their trilingual development, they too are confronted with up to forty-two nationalities, some of whom are difficult to incorporate into a home language class. Even Luxembourg, with its advanced experience in trilingual education in Luxemburgish, German, and French, admits to problems in incorporating minority immigrant children into its trilingual programs.

The heterogeneity of the student population may leave no choice but to work with restricted lingua francas, though support in the students' languages may help to overcome the dilemma between ideal theoretical foundations and reality. A recent development in Europe has been to encourage *multilingual language awareness programs* in primary schools in order to incorporate all the languages of a classroom population into at least some form of recognition, as illustrated by Young and Hélot (2006) and Candelier (2003) (see also García, 2007c).

Language policy[2]

This parameter is the most polemical because schools are often bound by it. Top-down educational policy can be: *mandatory* in favor of promoting bilingualism for all (as in Luxembourg, the Basque Country, Malta, Brunei); *highly interventionist* as in Singapore where the nature of bilingual development is determined by ethnic origin (Pakir, 1993); *prohibitory* as in Flemish Belgium, California, Arizona, and Massachusetts in the U.S. (see Chapter 8) where, except for pilot projects, bilingual education is illegal; *minimalist*, that is, offering very little, as in Ireland outside the Gaeltacht (the Irish-speaking region); or *indifferent* as in England (Coyle, 2002) where it is mostly ignored.

In spite of the European Commission and Council of Europe's encouragement of bilingual education for autochthonous minorities (see Chapter 9), some European countries do not support bilingual education in their official educational policy. Iceland, for example, although encouraging traditional foreign-language learning, does not allow bilingual education programs, under the fear that they would promote English and might in the long run threaten the Icelandic language. This is also the case of France, reluctant to expand bilingual education offerings (see Hélot and Young, 2006). Most countries will allow small-scale experimental projects in bilingual education, particularly for targeted groups. This is the case, for example, of the use of Yoruba and English in the IFE Primary Education Research Project in Nigeria during the 1970s.

Although the United States does not have an explicit language-in-education policy, it implicitly discourages bilingualism in education. This is done not overtly, but covertly through mechanisms such as tests (more on this in Chapters 8 and 15) (see Shohamy, 2001, 2006a, b). The recent focus of the No Child Left Behind act (2001) in assessing all children, including recent immigrants, through standardized assessment instruments that rely on standard written English to measure annual yearly progress is one example of the mechanisms used by the United States to suppress all bilingualism (see Menken, 2005, 2008).

Opportunities for language use

Geographical location
The success of the Luxembourg trilingual system is partially due to the fact that the three languages involved are widely available throughout the country both *inside and outside* the classroom (Berg, 1993; Davis, 1994). For German and French there is a monolingual hinterland within easy reach of every learner, thereby making the perceived vitality of the target languages self-evident. The motivational variable for other-language acquisition is considerably enhanced since the burden of providing role models is not left to the classroom alone, as is the case in many countries.

Languages out of school
Linked to the above parameter is that of the distribution of language usage outside the school walls. Fishman (1977a) underlined the fact that for successful bilingual development, "School use of a language is not enough" (1977a: 102). This has been shown in the Irish situation, where in spite of enormous good will, the maintenance of Irish (outside the Gaeltacht Irish-speaking areas) is hampered by its lack of use outside the classroom, thereby placing most of the burden for usage on the school itself.

European Schools find that the language of the host environment tends to be the one most successfully developed as a lingua franca among the multilingual population – so French as a second language is automatically developed in the European School in Brussels, English as a second language in the Oxford European School, and Dutch in the European School of Mol, Belgium, even though the latter is not an official second language (Baetens Beardsmore, 1995). Part of the school success of English in many non-English-speaking countries can be attributed to it being so widely available outside the classroom, via the media, advertising, and tourist contacts, that it benefits from automatic promotion. Korea, for example, has gone to many lengths to create a context for speaking English: the government has created English villages with weekend and weekday programs in which English is used to teach drama, music, dance, global awareness, and other subjects, and all store employees speak English. About 200 students in middle school attend the Korean English village every week.

Status of languages

High-status languages can compensate for their lack of prevalence in the out-of-school environment, as witnessed by the success of bilingual programs with English as a component part. Schools using a regional or minoritized language in a bilingual program do in fact help raise the status of threatened languages, as has been successfully achieved in Catalonia with the heavy support for Catalan–Spanish bilingual education in the early post-Franco period, or in Wales, where ever more English-speakers are opting for early total or partial Welsh immersion-type programs. If the perceived status of a language is less prestigious, as was long the case with Dutch, compared to English or German in French-speaking Belgium, it is less easy to introduce bilingual programs. Despite many years of use of Spanish in bilingual education programs in the United States, U.S. Spanish continues to be minoritized, although Spanish has long been a language of global standing, and is becoming ever more popular in Europe and other parts of the world (García, 2008a; Mar-Molinero and Stewart, 2006).

Linguistic characteristics

Languages that belong to the same language family tend to share characteristics, and language relatedness has been shown to be useful in learning an additional language. For example, Romance languages such as Spanish and Italian share characteristics, while Dutch, German, and Danish, as Germanic languages, have some in common. Languages also differ with respect to their basic sentence structures. English, Spanish, and Greek are SVO languages (Subject, Verb, Object), Hebrew and Welsh are VSO languages (Verb, Subject, Object), while Japanese and German are SOV languages (Subject, Object, Verb).

Languages such as English and Spanish use the Roman alphabet, which has relatively few symbols compared to other systems. Arabic orthography taxes students further, requiring changes to the shape of each letter depending on the position in a word. Chinese uses a logographic system requiring a large number of symbols because each character represents a word or morpheme. It is said that Chinese requires learning around 4,000 characters for basic reading (Miller, 2002). There are languages with syllabic systems, for example Korean. These syllabic systems are easy to decode, but it may be difficult to learn to combine syllables for different meanings (more on the impact of script in Chapter 14). There are also sign languages where the handshape, location, and movement are manipulated in different ways to mark phonology and morphology.

Attitudes

The community's and students' attitude towards a language has much to do with the implementation and success of a bilingual education program. Bilingual education in languages viewed more positively may attract more funding and public support than other programs. It is also important to gauge the motivations for learning an additional language in designing a bilingual education program. For example, a bilingual education program for students motivated to learn English in a country whose economy relies heavily on English-speaking tourism, would be very different than one in which there is no tourism.

One of the major justifications for introducing content-matter bilingual teaching is precisely because of its impact on attitudes and motivation. The failure of traditional other-language lessons can be attributed to the fact that learning a language for some long-term and apparently inaccessible goal has had no immediate pertinence for the majority of learners. Content-matter learning through an additional language – bilingual education – makes language acquisition more immediately pertinent, with short-term rewards readily perceived by learners (CLIL/EMILE, 2002; Krashen, 1994, 1996, 1999). As we will later see, content-matter learning through an additional language has to be accompanied with explicit language teaching.

Economics

There are also economic considerations concerning the cost of providing bilingual education. It has long been assumed that bilingual education is more expensive, thereby justifying its parsimonious support. Research evidence on this aspect is beginning to evolve and is revealing intriguing figures. We know that exceptional multilingual provision of the European School type is expensive, but it is inherent to the special structure and organization of these schools. Experimental provisions in pilot projects are also inherently more expensive than provisions in mainstream education. But the question is whether widespread bilingual provision *need* be more expensive than monolingual education.

The Swiss researcher, François Grin (2002, 2003) is developing ever more sophisticated models for the analysis of the role of economics in language-planning issues, including bilingual education. In a study produced for the European Commission, the issue of policy choices in economic terms has been addressed, on the assumption that at present, "As there is no such thing as a 'market' for diversity, there is a need for public intervention" (Grin and Moring, 2002: p. i). What is interesting in this report is that it is not based on the concept of language "rights" but on an analysis that focuses on the effectiveness, the cost, and the cost-effectiveness of policies. Cost-effectiveness estimates are computed by dividing an indicator of outcome by cost figures. Thus, instead of focusing attention on a total cost figure as the sole source of measurement, the technique shows, for example, that the language initiatives which support the use of Welsh in a broad range of community projects in Wales (Mentrau Iaith) work out at an average net cost of €2 (US$2.7 on the current exchange rate) per Welsh speaker.

Economic evaluations of bilingual education should not include the total cost of schooling, since children would have to be schooled anyway, whatever the language may be. The real cost of the policy is only whatever is spent over and above the normal educational costs in order to sustain the bilingual education system. Grin and Moring (2002: 86) say: "Often editorial columns of newspapers and magazines, as well as parliamentary interventions are repositories of pronouncements invoking the 'enormous cost' of such policies – usually with no information whatsoever."

According to economic specialists, a full identification of cost should take into account several theoretical constructs: "opportunity cost" – not a monetary figure, but the value of the best alternative use of the same resource; "non-market costs" – e.g. the psychological distress undergone, for example, by those who feel disenfranchised by the setting-up or not of a policy; the distinction between "total, average and marginal costs" – for example, the cost of the "third" minority-language primary school is likely to be different from the cost of the "second" and "fourth."

Studies of economics of education usually look at input variables and output variables in education. Input variables are either of the *school-kind* (teaching experience, class size, size of school, curriculum) and *non-school-kind* (peer influence, parental socioeconomic levels, poverty, race, sex, family size) or they are of the *manipulable kind* (teaching load, class size, teacher salary) or *non-manipulable-kind* (sex, race, age of students). Output variables are usually those of *consumption* which give short-term individual benefits (enjoyment) or *investment* which give long-term individual and social benefits (acquisition of math and verbal skills, improved health, moral and social values, and improved attitudes).

The new vein of economic research in language education policy issues is posing new questions and shaking conventional wisdom. Bilingual education costs must take into account non-material elements, or the branch known as "cultural economics" which includes non-material or symbolic values, as well as "environmental economics" which weighs up the advantages and drawbacks of different policy options. The costs entailed by language education policy often turn out to be much lower than is commonly assumed, and in the case of minoritized languages, "Granting official status to the minority language may be costly, but these costs should be weighed against those that would have occurred in case of worsening inter-group conflict" (Grin, 2003: 43). In addition, the costs must also be weighed against increasing rates of crime and illiteracy and the soaring rate of dropouts. Bilingual education could bring us both short-term and long-term benefits socially and economically.

Religion, culture, and ideology

These represent important parameters that must be taken into account in bilingual education. It is for *religio-cultural* reasons that Brunei Darussalam introduces the Jawi (Arabic) script next to the Romanized alphabet in its bilingual Malay–English primary schools. Because of the desire to underline the Malay Islamic Monarchy ideology of the state, the authorities of Brunei include the acquisition of reading and writing skills in the Roman alphabet for Malay and English, and Arabic script for Malay and Arabic, thereby making the program trilingual and triliterate.

It is also for religious reasons that the Ojibwe of northern U.S. and southern Canada are developing immersion revitalization programs in Ojibwemowin, the language linked with the religious ceremonies of the Midewiwin, the secret medicine society that has existed since pre-Columbian times. Many of these pre-Columbian religious systems rely on use of Indigenous languages, believed to be the only appropriate language of ceremony, and the language of spirit.

Ideological considerations may help promote the development of a bilingual program. For example, the development of a European identity for children was an important factor in the growth of European Schools for Civil Servants (Müller and Baetens Beardsmore, 2004). On the other hand, ideology may impede the availability of bilingual education programs, as when Flemish linguistic nationalists obstruct the setting up of French bilingual programs in northern Belgium. Similarly, in the United States certain groups oppose bilingual education on ideological grounds relating to xenophobic and anti-immigrant sentiments.

Both Fitouri (1983) and Riquet (1984) discuss the ideological debate around the role of bilingualism in education in Tunisia and reveal how the superimposition of French on Arabic alienates the middle-class elite from the rest of the population, drives a wedge between social groups, and engenders language determined class tensions. Ideological considerations may *help* the development of bilingual education programs (as in the teaching of Hebrew to Jewish children; see Genesee, 1994), may *impede* their availability (as in preventing bilingual education with French in Flemish Belgium), or may represent an *extra problematic dimension* as in Morocco (Bentahila, 1983) or Tunisia (Fitouri, 1983; Riquet, 1984).

Bilingual education programs in Indigenous or Native American languages are deeply linked with American Indian sovereignty; that is, the social, economic, and political recognition that tribes have a unique relationship with the national state. Therefore, language revitalization possible through bilingual education is an "act of self-determination" and of "resistance" (McCarty and Watahomigie, 1999).

Situational variables are not easily manipulated by individual schools. However, schools can react to such variables (except in prohibitory cases), by manipulating school-operational variables, to which we now turn.

Operational Factor

While the variables grouped under the situational factor regard the conditions outside, but surrounding a school, the *operational factor includes variables within the educational system itself*. The variables under the operational factor have many sub-components. Depending on the interaction with the situational variables outlined above, they are easier or more difficult to operationalize.

Curriculum

This covers the time and timing of the introduction of the other language or languages of instruction, together with the proportional distribution of subject and content-matter teaching through more than one language. And it also covers overarching educational goals of the program. Enormous variation exists here, and research findings can generally justify whatever proportional distribution may have been selected for a given population in a specific setting. It would seem that the major question here is of fine-tuning research assumptions to specific conditions, or else of offering alternative paths for achieving similar goals.

Certain programs introduce the other language as a subject prior to its use as a medium (for example in Germany; Mäsch, 1993), whereas others do not (Canadian early total immersion; Swain and Lapkin, 1982). Some programs focus on the language as a subject throughout the curriculum as a support to their use as a medium (European Schools; Baetens Beardsmore, 1995); others gradually phase out the additional language as a subject. Some programs make a radical shift from one language to another, as in Brunei where English as a medium takes over from Malay for most subjects in the fourth year of primary education (Jones, 1996), whereas in Luxembourg the transition from Luxemburgish through German to French is gradual through the whole school program.

Subjects

The nature of the content-matter subjects taught via the additional language also varies, though many programs tend to teach social sciences, geography, history, art, and physical education in the additional language. The sciences are often favored to be taught in English or French in countries where Indigenous languages have not developed scientific academic registers. In Europe, on the other hand, the status of the target language appears to have virtually no bearing on the selection and allocation of subjects. Any subject can be the vehicle of content-matter teaching through the other language, as can be seen from the overview of different forms of bilingual education operating in the European Union (Content and Language Integrated Learning [CLIL-AXIS], 2006).

An interesting case from Peru is reported by Duverger (2005). Apparently in Peru young adolescent poor girls often become pregnant because of the taboo against sex education in schools. In order to limit unwanted teenage pregnancies, a group of Peruvian teachers decided to try out an interdisciplinary approach using the French language to talk about genitalia, boy–girl relations, fecundation, pregnancy, and so on. Apparently this enabled those involved to talk about the above with a certain objectivity which avoided the mental blockages inculcated by the family, social, and religious environment of these lower-level groups of adolescents, without re-activating the mental image taboos and embarrassment associated with the home language in family, church, and outside society. In other words, the second language, French, helped attain the objectivity necessary to access knowledge.

In some programs, which operate on a *modular basis*, certain parts of a content-matter discipline may be taught via the medium of a second language where learners will be expected to handle the subject matter in their home language, even though part of the material may have been taught via the other language. The modular system, where the language of instruction may vary for a period of time, develops the capacity to handle specific content matter in either of the two languages being used. An example of this is the way in which curriculum is organized in Cypress Hills Dual Language School in New York City, with children switching languages of instruction for the same subjects every week (García and Traugh, 2002).

The important factors in selecting the language of instruction for particular subject matter, whatever the phasing or combinations may be, are *progression* and *continuity*. Unsuccessful bilingual development often results from lack of continuity and lack of lock-step development. This has been observed in research in the United States which shows that the least development is reached by those students that go back and forth among English as a second language programs, transitional bilingual education programs and dual language or two-way dual language programs, or who are faced with different language policies in education in the bilingual education programs which they attend (Ramirez, 1992; Thomas and Collier, 1997, 2002).

Initial literacy

Initial reading and writing may occur in totally opposite patterns, depending on situational variables or the status of the languages involved (for more on this, see Chapter 14). It is generally considered advisable to start reading and writing in the child's strongest language, particularly if it is a threatened minority language, as with immigrants, refugees, Indigenous peoples, or autochthonous minorities. Canadian French immersion does the opposite with success, as a result of the omnipresent prestige of English in the all-English out-of-school environment. In cases where the home language has no written standard and no reading materials available, as with some of the Indigenous languages of Borneo for example, it is, of course, not possible to begin reading and writing in the home language.

In French-speaking Belgium where bilingual programs operate, comparisons have been made between young learners who were taught to read first in French, their home language, and later in Dutch, their second language, and others who were first taught to read in Dutch, the second language. It was found, unexpectedly, that the latter developed better reading skills in both languages (and were incidentally slightly better in French when compared with those who were in monolingual French streams, Blondin, 2003). This was explained by the fact that Dutch spelling is far less opaque than that of French, which, like English, is one of the more difficult writing systems to match up with phonological output.

Similar advantages have been noted when children who were taught initial reading skills in Spanish or Italian as their non-home language in bilingual programs, again because the relationship between print and sound is far more regular and less opaque than in languages such as English or French. In French-speaking Belgium, parents were at first upset when reading in French was introduced after initial reading in Dutch had been mastered, since their French-speaking children began by pronouncing the written matter with a Dutch accent. This fear was soon dispelled by the experienced teachers, as it normally took no more than two weeks for these young readers to learn to distinguish the writing systems between the two languages and to link the French written material with their stronger home first language.

It is not clear what the ideal situation is with divergent script systems, an area that still requires research. Very little comparative research has been conducted of the type done in French-speaking Belgium to measure the effects of starting reading and writing skills in Chinese or English, for example, in Arabic script or French in North Africa, in Thai or Cambodian scripts or English, in Cyrillic script or the Roman alphabet for Russians, Bulgarians, or Greeks, in some form of bilingual education. Nor is it clear to what extent different writing systems modify the Common Underlying Proficiency Hypothesis as developed by Cummins (see above in Chapter 3) as applied to literacy skills in bilingual development (more on this in Chapter 14).

Exit criteria

Exit, or evaluation criteria often determine the emphases of what goes on in bilingual education. For example, if oral or speaking skills are not measured in significant examinations they tend not to be developed. If external examining bodies or national standardized tests call the tune, then the school has no choice but to teach towards their examinations.

Various possibilities exist. In Luxembourg foreign and monolingual university entrance requirements impose native-like proficiency on the four linguistic skills, on top of subject-matter specialization as the final sanction. The Luxembourg language requirement is one of the most stringent in Europe. The most liberal is the German situation where the bilingual component is a *complementary plus point* but cannot penalize a student who is adequate in content-matter (see Chapter 15). In between lie the tailor-made examinations of the type offered by the European Baccalaureate and the International Baccalaureate, which appear to be the most appropriately designed for taking bilingual education into account, at least for university entrance level.

In Bulgaria and Romania, in the networks of secondary schools that teach through French as their additional language medium, a system of evaluation has been developed that depends on the presentation of a portfolio of group work on a thematic choice agreed upon with the teachers, and which includes oral and written presentations of independently researched topics incorporating both a science and a humanities aspect. Assessment is carried out along criteria relative to the content-matter subject as well as criteria relating to the language, with higher coefficients for the content-matter subject than for the language (since these programs are considered primarily as courses on the non-linguistic discipline prior to being language courses; Duverger, 2005). These appear to be challenging, yet exciting breakthroughs in bilingual assessment scales for those working through to higher levels of education via a form of bilingual schooling (more on bilingual assessment in Chapter 15).

The least appropriate situation is where evaluation criteria are those for monolingual programs that fail to take into account the specificity of bilingual development – particularly for intermediate stages of development. Unfortunately these appear to be in the majority at present. This is prevalent in the United States where the No Child Left Behind act of 2001 requires states to show the annual yearly progress of all students, including immigrants who are learning English, in standardized tests that are normed on monolingual populations (see Escamilla, 2006; García and Menken, 2006; Menken, 2005, 2008).

Although many minoritized languages are included in bilingual education curricula, they are often not used in assessment, or simply not assessed. This is the case, for the most part, of Spanish in the United States, but also of sign language throughout the world. Both Spanish and sign language are often just seen as media for communication in classrooms, their development is not assessed, and they are not used to assess content knowledge. There are some exceptions to this.

Materials

This is an area in which bilingual education has much to do. There are few specifically designed bilingual materials available, and most schools have to adapt and improvise from monolingual products in order to suit their specific bilingual teaching issues.

The Luxembourg authorities wisely produce all their own primary school materials to take their peculiar situation into account, relying on foreign monolingual second-ary school materials only at the stage where language competence is sufficiently developed. The Landesinstitut für Schule und Weiterbildung in North-Rhineland-Westphalia (Germany) is particularly involved in the development of appropriate materials.

Incompatibilities between the language of a textbook and its content-matter for a given curriculum are one of the major problems (see Drexel-Andrieu, 1993), particularly for culturally loaded subjects such as history and geography. But even sciences such as mathematics can cause problems, as when theorems, which carry the same name in German and French, are interpreted in totally different ways in the mathematics traditions of the countries using these languages, or when math-ematical operations are carried out differently in various countries.

Teachers

A major variable, difficult to meet as bilingual education expands, is finding sufficient qualified subject-matter teachers capable of teaching through another language. Ideally, bilingual education should rest on specialists with fluent competency or having been educated in a country where the language of instruction is spoken. Austria is one country that produces sufficient numbers of teachers competent in both a language and their subject specialty in secondary education, since all future teachers during their initial training are required to select two subjects they will be later teaching, one of which is often a foreign language (Heindler and Abuja, 1996).

But native-speaker competence is not an absolute necessity, if adequate levels of ability are present in the teacher. In the Netherlands, for example, the advice is for there to be at least one native speaker available on a school's premises to serve as a feeder to non-native-speaking teachers working partially or wholly through their weaker language (Fruhauf, 1996). Greater professional mobility might help allevi-ate the shortage, but this variable is likely to represent a major stumbling block to rapid expansion of bilingual education.

A major problem confronting many bilingual education programs, whether in privileged circumstances or not, is the lack of pre-service and in-service education for teachers operating within the systems. Many teachers who have been educated for monolingual schools are required to learn how to adapt to new or evolving bilingual programs once on the job, by trial and error. This lack of training may well account for many of the past inadequacies in outcomes, but even in success-ful programs teachers are often left to fend for themselves. There is no specific education for work in the complex European School system, where teachers are seconded from their national, monolingual programs. Many CLIL-type programs in Europe depend on the good will and enthusiasm of teachers willing to take the plunge in adapting to working through a weaker language (both for them and their students) of instruction. Many reports on the improvement of bilingual education provision in Europe highlight the urgent need for appropriate initial and in-service training (Council of Europe, 2008: *Language Education Policy Profile – Ireland*; Council of Europe, 2008: *Profil des politiques linguistiques éducatives – Val d'Aoste*).

Language strategies

Swain (1996a) has underlined the need for *output* in second-language development within the immersion context. Other studies have shown how content-matter teaching in a second language must be particularly careful to integrate subject-specific language problems with the developmental aspects of second-language acquisition, through co-ordinated cross-curricular teacher collaboration (Baetens Beardsmore, 1995; Christ, 1996; Fruhauf, 1996).

Parental involvement

All successful education relies heavily on parents and schools sharing the same values. Monolingual education does not usually have to contend with parents not necessarily understanding at least some of what their children do. Elite bilingual schools often count on input from parents to help achieve their goals. It is up to schools to manipulate this variable by devising strategies to inform and involve parents as much as possible. This may be particularly important for specific groups, for instance, immigrant minorities. Young and Hélot (2006) have shown how successful the involvement of immigrant parents can be in adapting French primary schools to the reality of their children's mixed ethnolinguistic backgrounds. In the United States, Moll, Amanti, Neff, and Gonzalez (1992) have shown how teachers can use the *funds of knowledge* of language-minority communities as a way to involve families.

Depending on the culture of origin of the parents, some schools have found it difficult to involve immigrant parents who have complete trust, and believe that it is inappropriate to meddle with what goes on in school. Initiatives to overcome such reticence require imagination. One rare bilingual school in Denmark does not allow children to be enrolled unless there is a strong commitment from parents to attend teacher–parent meetings and open days. The Lycée International de Saint-Germain-en-Laye had no problems with parental involvement for Anglo-Saxon sections or those covering northern Europe, but had little parental response from those sections catering for Spanish, Italian, and Portuguese children until the director used indirect techniques. He offered his sports fields on Saturday afternoons to the parents of the less involved sections, using the opportunity to talk with the fathers and onlookers informally during the games. He also invited the mothers from these sections to use the school kitchens for lessons in the cooking of their national specialties, purely as an opportunity to talk to the mothers about the schooling of their children. Both initiatives were aimed at improving the children's school achievement and were successful.

Whole school

Bilingual education cannot succeed unless the whole school is involved in fostering the use of more than one language on the premises. This goes from signs and public announcements reflecting a multilingual environment, to structured collaboration between language and content-matter teachers to smooth out discrepancies between levels and approaches to use of the additional language. All personnel should equally promote a positive approach to multilingualism at all times, particularly avoiding subtle negative feedback to pupils on the part of teachers and staff who might value more the dominant language.

Outcome Factor

Variables under this outcome factor refer to what can be reasonably expected in terms of linguistic proficiency and scholastic achievement from a particular bilingual program in a given context with its specific resources. It may also refer to the sociocultural pattern expected of a group of students.

Linguistic

As we have been saying, bilingualism is a complex concept and is not an absolute. The linguistic goals of a particular bilingual education program may be as follows:

Shift to majority language and loss of the first language. This is the goal of transitional bilingual education programs particularly prevalent in the United States for moving children into mainstream all-English education, and of most bilingual education programs in countries of Africa.

Addition of an additional language at no cost to the first language. This is the goal being promoted for language-majority populations, and especially for majority populations in Canada and all over Europe.

Maintenance of a minoritized language while developing proficiency; that is, adding an additional language. In some ways this is a reflection of the paragraph above, but this time for language-minority populations.

Revitalization of a threatened language. This is the goal of many of the programs for Indigenous peoples whose languages have suffered greatly.

Development of a minoritized language. This is the goal of programs, for example, in Catalonia and the Basque Country, under the linguistic *normalización* policies (Leman, 1993) in order to affirm and reconstitute these languages.

Development of plurilingual proficiency. This is the goal of programs that encourage the use of two or more languages in functional interrelationship and that include all children.

Development of multiple languages. This is the goal of highly multilingual societies such as India, or groups that want to encourage multilingual use. Some programs for Deaf bilingual education which teach more than one written language and a sign language or more fall under this category. This is also the goal of societies or groups that wish to have their citizens develop multilingual proficiencies that include global languages.

Literacy

Not all bilingual education programs promote biliteracy. In fact, many bilingual education programs use one of the two languages only orally or through one medium, such as signing. Bilingual education programs have a broad range of literacy goals and outcomes (for more on this, see Chapter 14).

Monoliteracy
A program might promote literacy in *only one of the languages*, as in some of the developing countries or in countries with immigrant communities in transitional programs.

Receptive biliteracy
A program might merely promote *receptive literacy skills*, as tends to be the case with Irish in the Republic of Ireland, though obviously a proportion of learners of Irish can handle productive literacy skills well.

Partial biliteracy
Canadian immersion programs tend to develop *partial biliteracy* in that writing skills in French are not pushed as a major priority, unlike European School programs where part of the written final examinations must be taken in a second language on criteria similar to those for monolinguals.

Full biliteracy
Many bilingual programs do aim for *full biliteracy*, though not necessarily with native-speaker proficiency for more than one language as the final outcome expectation. Hence *linguistic outcome goals* may well be for:

$$\left.\begin{array}{l} \text{minimal} \\ \text{partial} \\ \text{full} \end{array}\right\} \text{bilingualism}$$

coupled with:

$$\left.\begin{array}{l} \text{minimal} \\ \text{partial} \\ \text{full} \end{array}\right\} \text{biliteracy}$$

Content matter
The expected outcomes of *properly designed* bilingual programs, of whatever type they may be, should be similar to those obtained in monolingual education as far as the non-linguistic content-matter subjects are concerned. This explains why the main focus of attention until recently has been on linguistic outcomes, on the assumption that if the linguistic outcomes are satisfactory, the content-matter outcomes will also be adequate.

One should expect to be confronted with similar proportions of success rates, failure rates, dropouts, problem cases, and special needs in bilingual education, as in similar monolingual programs servicing comparable populations, and where the only major difference in any comparison is that of the use of more than one language in a program. To date this is rarely the case in the documented literature, since many, though not all, bilingual programs are designed to cater for specific categories of learners, where there may or may not be some form of explicit or implicit selection of candidates.

Bruck (1984) studied the suitability of immersion programs in Canada for children classified as having specific learning disabilities. This investigation quite rightly pointed out that when a program as widespread as Canadian immersion had gone beyond experimental or piloting stages, but was reaching out to thousands of children, one should expect to find similar statistical proportions of children with specific learning problems as in monolingual mainstream education. By comparing children with specific learning problems in immersion with those with similar problems in monolingual education, and noting the solutions available, Bruck (1984) found that they broke down into three categories. Some children with learning problems were pulled out of immersion when the difficulties were noted and transferred into mainstream education without any special support, which did not improve their scholastic achievement. A second category were pulled out of immersion and transferred to monolingual schools where special support was available, and where the learning problems were somewhat alleviated. A third category was kept in the immersion program, but was given special support to help alleviate the learning difficulties. This group progressed academically in their subject matter, and also gained some bilingual proficiency.

Bilingual programs aimed at developing minoritized languages such as Catalan, Euskara (Basque), or Welsh must all have satisfactory academic outcomes for considerable numbers of learners involved, since in all three cases it is possible to study subjects from the humanities or the exact sciences through the medium of these languages at university level.

Bilingualism for elite populations usually provides excellent achievement, as witnessed by the impressive scores on the European Baccalaureate for school leavers in the European School Network, where some schools have 100 percent success rates on a very demanding examination system. However, these results are partially explained by some students leaving the network before the final assessment, if they feel incapable of taking the examinations successfully.

Transitional bilingual education programs, especially in the United States, have tended to use linguistic criteria (English language development) as central to judgments about the success or failure of their outcomes on non-language content matter. An exception is the Foyer Project developed in Brussels in a trilingual learning context and involving an immigrant language, plus the school language, Dutch, which happens to be a minoritized one, and the majority language of the out-of-school environment, French. The goal of this program is not primarily for language maintenance, nor is it primarily to produce language shift, though that may well be the non-avowed outcome, but to provide the immigrant children with similar chances of success in their general progress upon transfer to secondary education after completion of a Foyer Project primary school. Results reveal that the immigrant children do not reach French native-speaker levels in comparison with peers. But this is not expected, since they are not in a monolingual home language environment. Nor is their level of Dutch at the end of primary school equivalent to that of native-speaker Dutch peers. Again, this might not be expected, since they are not monolinguals functioning exclusively in Dutch as the peer group tends to do. However, their level of Dutch, the main target language in this particular program, is equivalent to that of immigrant children submersed in monolingual Dutch schools elsewhere in the country. But the criterion considered as most significant is that the immigrant children are distributed across different types of secondary programs in exactly comparable distributions to their Dutch peers upon entry to the mono- lingual, all Dutch, secondary school program, which is the measure retained by the Foyer project for outcome success. And as an incidental bonus, the same immigrant children often outperform their Dutch peers on the compulsory other language intro- duced in primary school – French – probably because they are already bilingual anyway, and in a program that respects and values their language of origin.

Researchers in the United States have repeatedly shown that bilingual education benefits language-minority students (Krashen, Rolstad, and MacSwan, 2007; Ramirez, 1992; Thomas and Collier, 2002). Lindholm-Leary (2001) demonstrated that students in two-way bilingual education programs outperformed transitional bilingual educa- tion students. (For more on this evidence, see the section on "Empirical Evidence" in Chapter 8 of this book.)

Sociocultural

Another important outcome factor is the sociocultural one. Many minority child- ren feel much more motivated and respected in bilingual education programs. For example, it is widely accepted that immigrant Latino students in U.S. transitional bilingual education programs enjoy school more, as shown by their higher rates of attendance (Paulston, 1992). Leman (1993: 94) summarizes: "Additional criteria for rating the success of the bicultural programme are the social and mental matur- ity achieved by the target-group children and their degree of feeling at ease at school. The target-group children score very positively in these respects."

The development of two-way and poly-directional bilingual education programs many times impacts upon children's attitudes towards different language groups, and their ability to work together. García (forthcoming) quotes a Latino boy in a two-way dual language program in New York City who says about the collabora- tion in the class: "A., she came into this school, not learning Spanish, and A., she learned Spanish with people helping her. You get other students to help in Spanish and English, yes." And in the same school, another boy expresses his renewed pride in Spanish: "Spanish is as good as English, and if you don't know in English, you need to learn it in Spanish, became some people can understand what you're say- ing" (García, forthcoming; García and Mason, forthcoming). The work of Teresa McCarty and her colleagues among Native American communities in the United States remind us that the students' great linguistic insecurity is relieved when they participate in bilingual education programs (McCarty, Romero, and Zepeda, 2006).

Much of the discussion on different types of bilingual education tends to con- centrate on linguistic outcomes to the neglect of a proper evaluation of the balance between linguistic and non-linguistic outcomes, especially achievement and socio- cultural outcomes. Further information on achievement outcome of bilingual education programs will be reviewed in Chapters 8 and 9, where U.S. and European bilingual policy is considered.

Integrating Situational, Operational, and Outcome Factors

If we analyze these variables and factors in interrelationship, we can make some general observations about *situational* and *outcome* factors,[3] by discussing some specific cases.

Focusing on the situational factor, we can conclude that it is most important to understand whether the other language of instruction is prevalent in the out-of-school environment or not. If the other language is a *foreign language* not spoken outside, the development of bilingualism depends primarily on the school and perhaps incidentally on the mass media for its acquisition and support. If it is an *immigrant minority language* it may not depend entirely on the school for informal, oral interactions, but may rely entirely on the school for activities that use decontextualized academic language, particularly if the parents have limited literacy.

In some countries where bilingual education is mandated for the entire school population, such as Luxembourg, Malta, Catalonia, or the Basque Country, the languages used as media of instruction are all *available in the wider out-of-school environment*, thereby rendering the school's task easier through constant extra-curricular support. Luxembourg succeeds in high proficiency levels and scholastic outcomes based on a trilingual education system because the situational context is favorable to the spontaneous use of three languages in everyday life, and because the schools can take this into account in operationalizing the educational phasing of each language in the curriculum (Lebrun and Baetens Beardsmore, 1993). Catalonia and the Basque Country are similarly placed with respect to the two languages they use, though the *situational variables* dealing with the distribution and background linguistic knowledge of the school population account for their offering not one model of bilingual schooling, but, in the Basque Country, three different types, according to the perceived needs of the target students (Artigal, 1993).

In Canada, Germany, and the United States, on the other hand, bilingual education *often* cannot rely on extra-curricular support, as the schools generally operate in "constructed" monolingual environments and therefore carry a greater linguistic-instructional burden (Cummins and Swain, 1986; Mäsch, 1993; Swain and Lapkin, 1982).

Moreover, there is a great difference in the *linguistic outcome* expectations between the countries used as illustrations. Luxembourg, Catalonia, and the Basque Country can legitimately expect, and achieve, high and widespread levels of bilingualism for the majority of the population across the four linguistic skills, due to the fact that the schools alone do not carry all the load of inculcating the languages. Canada, Germany, and the United States on the other hand, have different outcome expectations. In Canada it is the receptive skills of reading and understanding that are best developed, while in Germany receptive and productive bilingual competence is expected only from the self-selected volunteers who enter the program; but lack of such competence in no way impedes scholastic progression if the content-matter of the syllabus has been satisfactorily assimilated. In the United States, in the few programs that aim to develop the bilingualism of those who opt into such programs, bilingual competence may be an expectation of parents and teachers, but neither local nor state educational authorities expect bilingualism to be a goal of education.

In designing bilingual education programs, it is important to consider the situational factor and the operational factor, as well as to consider achievement and socio-cultural variables as most important. Linguistic and academic achievement tends to go hand in hand. Language supports learning. And bilingual education for minor-itized groups provides the opportunity to build from the child's strength, his or her home language and culture, to educate deeply, and to multiply knowledge and understanding.

Conclusion

Although not exhaustive, the above factors represent significant interlocking vari-ables that are interrelated. It is important for all these variables to be considered, for neglect of one may result in the failure of the entire program. Yet these variables still represent generalities, and fail to take into account many important features, especially at the local level, that await future investigation.

For example, there is no research on the feasibility of attaining reasonable levels of bilingual competence amongst all pupils, irrespective of general levels of cognitive ability, or precisely what levels of linguistic competence can be legitimately attained from a school-determined bilingual system. We know little about the purely linguistic elements of rate and route of learning two or more languages, depend-ing on phasing and the structure of the curriculum, the effects of transfer, the role of translanguaging, the tolerance level of errors, the nature and quality of teacher-talk and pupil-talk in bilingual programs, to name but a few of the dark spots. The research agenda is vast and represents a rich vein for exploitation in what has developed into a growth industry in educational linguistics.

In the next two chapters we contrast two very different contexts as we exam-ine bilingual education policies – the United States and the European Union. In Chapter 8 we look at the historical development of bilingual education policies in the United States, the country in which more has been done over the years to use bilingual education in the education of immigrants. This is followed by Chapter 9 which analyzes the present bilingual educational policies supported by the Euro-pean Union in the education of its citizens. Both offer contrasting analyses of two important contexts – one national, the other supranational – before we turn to more detailed analyses of other bilingual education policies throughout the world that have resulted in different types of bilingual education programs in Chapters 10 and 11.

Questions for Reflection

1. What are the proposed factors that influence the design and implementation of bilingual education as discussed in this chapter? Are there others not discussed here?

2.   What is the relationship between bilingual education itself and the factors that impact the implementation of bilingual education?

3.   Taking into account both personal experiences and the variables/factors discussed in this chapter, propose strategies to improve the implementation of bilingual education in classrooms. How would these strategies apply to concepts that were discussed in previous chapters, such as language ideology, language use, and language planning?

Further Reading

Baetens-Beardsmore, H. (1993) (ed.). *European Models of Bilingual Education*. Multilingual Matters, Clevedon.

Kaplan, R., and Baldauf, R. (1997). *Language Planning: From Practice to Theory*. Multilingual Matters, Clevedon, ch. 5: "Social Purpose Language Planning: Education and Literacy," pp. 122–52.

Mackey, W.F. (1970). "A Typology of Bilingual Education." *Foreign Language Annals* 3, 596–608.

Skutnabb-Kangas, T., and García, O. (1995). "Multilingualism for All? General Principles." In T. Skutnabb-Kangas (ed.). *Multilingualism for All*. Swets and Zeitlinger, Lisse, pp. 221–56.

8

U.S. Language Policy in Education

There is no equality of treatment merely by providing students with the same facilities, textbooks, teachers, and curriculum; for students who do not understand English are effectively foreclosed from any meaningful education.
Lau vs. Nichols, 1974

Overview

In this chapter, we will review the historical traditions of U.S. language policies: The past:

- restriction of Indigenous and Enslaved languages; tolerance of European languages;
- turning toward restriction, early twentieth century;
- renewed tolerance, second half of twentieth century;
- official English: new restrictions, late twentieth century.

The present:

- linguistic diversity in schools;
- language inequities;
- attacks on bilingual education;
- BE types;
- empirical evidence;
- language education.

Introduction

The United States, a nation made up of people of different origin, has had a long history with bilingualism and bilingual education. This chapter traces the historical traditions of bilingualism and bilingual education in the United States, while providing a current account of bilingual education today. Throughout this chapter we explore the ideologies, events, and actors that have shaped bilingual education policy. The United States, with its rich linguistic tradition, provides an important case study through which to explore how power, race, and class intersect with language ideologies that support or work against bilingualism and their manifestations in bilingual education programs. The historical framework provided in this case study also helps elucidate how the sociopolitical context interacts with the possibilities of bilingual education in a situation that, although rich in language diversity, sees itself as monolingual.

The Past[1]

The beginnings

At the time of the European encroachment, there were approximately 2 million Native Americans speaking over 300 languages North of what is today Mexico. Since the 1700s, the African languages of those who were enslaved were brought to United States shores. And Europeans brought other languages; not only English, but also German, French, Spanish, and Dutch, among others.

In 1790, the first census (which did not include either Native Americans or African slaves) determined that about 25 percent of the inhabitants spoke languages other than English (Lepore, 2002). From the earliest colonial times, different European groups established schools that taught only in their home languages. The Continental Congress translated documents into German and French in order to ensure support for the American Revolution. Although the issue of an official language for the new country was debated by the founding fathers, there was no choice of a single language in the Constitution (Heath, 1976). Castellanos (1983: 4) explains the decision by saying: "Because of the many nationalities represented in Anglo America, as well as the many Indian nations that existed here, knowledge of two or more languages became a decided advantage for trading, scouting, teaching and spreading the gospel, as well as for diplomacy." German had a very different history than Native American languages, Spanish, and French, succeeding in gaining presence in legislation, education, and the press throughout the nineteenth century. The words of Benjamin Franklin with regards to the Germans of Pennsylvania, however, remind us that there was never a policy of complete promotion of languages other than English (LOTEs), but that these LOTEs were *tolerated*[2] as tools in the economic and territorial expansion of the United States. In a letter to a British Member of Parliament dated May 9, 1753, Franklin says:

> Few of their children in the Country learn English; they import many Books from Germany; and of the six printing houses in the Province, two are entirely German, two half German half English, and but two entirely English; They have one German News-paper and one half-German. Advertisements, intended to be general are now printed in Dutch [German] and English; the signs in our Streets have inscriptions in both languages, and in some places only German: They begin of late to make all their

Bonds and other legal Writings in their own Language, which (though I think it ought not to be) are allowed good in our Courts, where the German Business so increases that there is continued need of Interpreters; and I suppose in a few years they will also be necessary in the Assembly, to tell one half of our legislators what the other half say. (Quoted in Crawford, 1992)

Gradually, anti-foreigner sentiment (coupled with an anti-LOTE sentiment) replaced the positive attitude exhibited in welcoming people of different groups. For example, the Know Nothing Party which came into being in the 1850s to oppose the growing Irish Catholic population excluded anyone who was foreign-born from holding political office. For all languages other than English, the period of tolerance came to an abrupt end throughout the entire country in the late nineteenth century. By the early twentieth century, as we will see, *xenophobia*, fear of foreigners, led to a restrictive language policy.

We start by giving an overview of the restriction that was imposed on Native American and the African languages of slaves, especially with regards to schooling. We then turn to the tolerance adopted towards linguistic heterogeneity in early United States, and especially towards German, French, and Spanish.

Restriction of Indigenous and Enslaved languages

Indigenous languages

The Native North American population numbered around 2 million at the time of the European encroachment. By 1890 there were fewer than 250,000 Native North Americans (McCarty, 2004). Although Native Americans were not made U.S. citizens until 1924, and their nations were not states, in 1819 the U.S. Congress passed the Civilization Act, allocating money to operate "mission schools" to "make the whole tribe English in their language, civilized in their habits and Christian in their religion" (quoted in Del Valle, 2003: 281). However, the "Five Civilized Tribes" (the Cherokee, Creek, Choctaw, Chickasaw, and Seminole) were allowed to control their own education until 1898.

Little mention was made of the use of Native American languages in all the early treaties with the U.S. government. The first mention of the use of a Native American language in educating Native American people is the Treaty of May 6, 1828, with the Cherokee Nation. Article Five agreed to pay $1,000 to purchase a printing press "to aid the Cherokees in the progress of education, and to benefit and enlighten them as people, in their own language" (Leibowitz, 1980, p. 57). By 1852, Oklahoma Cherokees operated twenty-one bilingual schools and two academies, and had a higher English literacy level than the white populations of Texas or Arkansas (Leibowitz, 1980).

In 1868, the Indian Peace Commission, appointed by Congress in 1867 to make recommendations about the Indians concluded: "in the *difference of language* today lies two-thirds of our trouble. Schools should be established which children should be required to attend: their barbarous dialects would be blotted out and the English language substituted" (quoted in Castellanos, 1983: 28, our italics). The U.S. government ended all treaties with Indian tribes by 1871 and shifted its policy from relocation of Indians to the West to assimilation to the general population. The 1878 *Report of the Commissioner of Indian Affairs* suggested that children be removed from their parents and put in boarding schools. Between 1879 and 1902 the U.S. government built twenty-five boarding schools where students were forbidden to speak their native languages (Reyhner and Eder, 1989).

J.D.C. Atkins, Indian Commissioner from 1885 to 1888, directed that "no textbooks in the vernacular will be allowed in any school where children are placed under contract or where the Government contributes to the support of the school; no oral instruction in the vernacular will be allowed at such schools – *the entire curriculum must be in the English language*" (Prucha, 1976: 286, our italics). By 1928, the *Merriam Report* concluded that the education of Native Americans was in a deplorable state and urged the closing of boarding schools, although no action was immediately taken (McCarty, 2004).

Enslaved languages

If Native American languages were repressed and persecuted in school, the languages of African slaves were not ever recognized. From the early decades of the eighteenth century until the end of the Civil War in 1865, over 12 million enslaved Africans, speakers of many different languages and mostly from West Africa, were brought to the Americas. Lepore (2002) has estimated that among them were between 2 and 3 million Muslims, literate in Arabic. But the policy of mixing enslaved Africans with different language practices led to massive language shift. The linguistic features that characterize what we know today as African American Vernacular English or Ebonics may be remnants of creolized English-based practices that, through successive contact with English, became decreolized[3] (Roy, 1987).

Tolerance of European languages

German

German was prevalent in Pennsylvania and Ohio during the eighteenth century. The Continental Congress (1774–1779) published its legislative documents and official proclamations in German for the benefit of the German community (Castellanos, 1983). By 1776 there was a sizeable network of German-language schools, including the bilingual interdenominational academy Franklin and Marshall College in Lancaster, Pennsylvania, which was founded in 1787 (Castellanos, 1983). These schools were mostly private parochial elementary schools of the Lutheran and the Reformed churches, although they, at times, received public funds (Castellanos, 1983). By 1830, one third of the white population of Pennsylvania was of German descent, and the documents of the Pennsylvania constitutional convention were published in German (Del Valle, 2003). In 1837, the legislature in Pennsylvania passed a law that permitted the founding of German-language schools as equal with English-language schools (Del Valle, 2003).

Ohio, with a sizable German-speaking population, also passed a law in 1839 which permitted the establishment of German schools. In 1840, the Cincinnati bilingual public school was established, teaching in both German and English. And during the second half of the nineteenth century, children in Cincinnati in the first four grades could split their school week between an English and a German teacher. Other cities in Ohio, and especially St. Louis, established bilingual education programs. In 1837, a year before the first all-English public school opened in St. Louis, a German–English public school was established. In the bilingual public schools of St. Louis, a quarter of the students during the second half of the nineteenth century were *not* of German descent. This can then be considered the beginning of two-way bilingual education in the United States since German-speaking and non-German-speaking students were educated in both English and German. The St. Louis Superintendent of Schools, William Torrey Harris (who later became U.S. Commissioner of Education) defended his city's bilingual education program, saying that "national memories and aspirations, family traditions, customs, and habits, moral and religious observances cannot be suddenly removed or changed without disastrously weakening the personality" (cited in Castellanos, 1983: 23). But by the late nineteenth century, St. Louis terminated its bilingual education policy, restricting the teaching of German to public secondary schools.

Spanish
According to Heinz Kloss (1977), Spanish in the United States could be said to have special rights because it was spoken by original settlers. The Treaty of Guadalupe Hidalgo (1848) which ended the Mexican American War ceded nearly half of the Mexican territory to the United States, what today is California, Arizona, Texas, Nevada, New Mexico, Utah, and parts of Colorado and Wyoming. Article IX of the Treaty guaranteed that Mexicans would enjoy "all the rights of citizens of the United States . . . and in the meantime shall be maintained and protected in the free enjoyment of their liberty and property and secured in the free exercise of their religion without restriction" (quoted in Crawford, 1992: 51).

As the Southwest territories where Spanish was spoken became U.S. states or territories, Spanish was used in legislation, education, and the press. However, as the language of a group that was conquered (or what Ogbu [1998] calls "involuntary minorities", in contrast to "voluntary minorities," such as the German immigrants), Spanish had a much more difficult time gaining acceptance than German did.

When California became a state in 1850, it was decreed that "all laws, decrees, regulations and provisions emanating from any of the three supreme powers of this State, which from their nature require publication, shall be published in English and Spanish" (Del Valle, 2003: 13). But in 1855 English was declared the only language of instruction, the publication of state laws in Spanish was suspended, and court proceedings were required to be in English (Castellanos, 1983).

In 1850, the territory of New Mexico (including present-day Arizona and New Mexico) was added to the Union. When thirteen years later Arizona and New Mexico were separated as territories, the population of New Mexico was around 50 percent Spanish-speaking. New Mexico wasn't admitted to statehood until 1912 when more Anglos had moved in, and the majority was English-speaking. The pressure to assimilate linguistically was carried out, in part, by repressing schooling in Spanish and replacing it with schools in English only. For example, in 1874, 70 percent of the schools were in Spanish, 33 percent were bilingual, and a mere 5 percent were in English only. Fifteen years later, in 1889, 42 percent of the schools were in English only, whereas 30 percent of the schools were conducted in Spanish, and 28 percent remained bilingual (Del Valle, 2003). By 1891 a New Mexico statute required all schools to teach in English. Bilingual editions of laws in New Mexico continued to appear until 1949.

This view of Spanish as the language of conquered Mexicans contrasts sharply with the tradition of teaching Spanish as a foreign language in the United States (for more on this, see García, 1997b, 2003). George Ticknor occupied the first Harvard Professorship of French and Spanish in 1813.[4] This elite Spanish-teaching tradition, focusing on the reading of the literature of Spain, was continued by such well-known American literati as Henry Wadsworth Longfellow, James Russell Lowell, Washington Irving, and William Prescott. The teaching of the literature of Spain was restricted to the university, and consisted of reading the literature in Spanish, while using English for the discussion. Its aim was not bilingualism but merely acquiring literary understandings.

The Modern Language Association, founded in 1883, claimed that the aim of modern language study was "literary culture, philological scholarship and linguistic discipline." Little attention was paid to the languages other than English spoken in the United States.

French

When Louisiana was purchased from the French in 1803, there was a majority of people of French descent and schools were bilingual in French and English. The first State constitution in 1812, as well as the ensuing constitutions of 1845, 1852, and 1864, stipulated the promulgation in French and English of laws and public records. But by 1921, the constitution made no reference to the French language and required that all public schools teach in English (Del Valle, 2003).

Toward restriction: early twentieth century

The end of the nineteenth century and the beginning of the twentieth century brought the outright restriction of languages other than English and bilingual education. By that time, the growing German immigration had been joined by Swedes, Ukrainians, Finns, Lithuanians, Poles, Slovaks, Greeks, Russians, Italians, and Jews coming from many different countries. Between 1890 and 1930, 16 million (mostly European, and increasingly Eastern and Southern European) immigrants entered the United States. Disdain for especially Italian and Jewish immigrants was widespread, anchored in the prejudice against non-Protestants, as well as in their darker complexions. The Deaf were excluded regularly as "undesirables," although preference was given to Deaf immigrants from English-speaking countries (Baynton, 2006). Increasingly, suspicion grew around Germans, as they became the enemy of the United States in World War I.

Between 1820 and 1920, 7 million Germans had immigrated to the United States and they comprised 15 percent of all immigrants. Of the 92 million Americans reported in the 1910 census, 2.5 million had been born in Germany. By the beginning of the century, the number of German Americans and their attention to their language, especially in schools, was beginning to draw criticism. For example, a 1910 *New*

York Times article stated: "Some German-American parents want German to be taught. It pleases their pride, but it does not do their children any good."

Chinese immigrants, who had been coming to the United States since the mid-nineteenth century as a result of the Taiping Rebellion in China and the Gold Rush in California, became excluded in 1882, when Congress passed the Chinese Exclusion Act which was not repealed until 1943. And the Japanese immigration that followed the Chinese was also met with hostility. For example, although there were only ninety-three Japanese students in San Francisco schools where there were 20,000 students, the San Francisco Chronicle suggested that Japanese children were crowding American children out of classrooms (Castellanos, 1983). In 1909 California passed an amendment to allow separate schools for "Indian and Mongolian" children. California prohibited the Japanese from owning land in 1913 and from leasing rights in 1920. The 1924 Immigration Act barred all non-white immigration except those of African descent.

Mexican immigration, both of documented and undocumented people, also increased around the turn of the century. They mostly settled in the Southwest where there was already a sizable population of Mexican descent.

The United States world position was also shifting around this time, as it consolidated its territorial gains. Hawaii was annexed in 1898 and English was made the language of legal documents and the educational system. An English-only rule was imposed in Puerto Rican schools after it was occupied as a result of the Spanish American War of 1898. Eighteen years later, after the total failure of this English-only policy in the schools of Puerto Rico, the use of what we now know as "transitional bilingual education" was established in Puerto Rico. Spanish was used in the first four years of school, Spanish and English were combined in the fifth grade, and English-only was then used from sixth grade on. This transitional bilingual education policy was in effect for thirty-two years until 1948, when Spanish was re-established as medium of instruction in Puerto Rico, with English taught as a required foreign language.

The mood of the time was captured by Theodore Roosevelt when he said that "it would not be merely a misfortune but a crime to perpetuate differences of language in this country" and recommended that immigrants who had not learned English after five years should be returned to their countries (cited in Castellanos, 1983: 40). In 1915, Theodore Roosevelt said:

> There is no room in this country for hyphenated Americanism [. . . The foreign born] must talk the language of its native-born fellow-citizens [. . .]. We have room for but one language here, and that is the English language, for we intend to see that the crucible turns our people out as Americans, of American nationality, and not as dwellers in a polyglot boarding house. (Quoted in Edwards, 1994: 166)

And in 1917, he added: "We must have but one flag. We must also have but one language. That language must be the language of the Declaration of Independence, of Washington's Farewell address, of Lincoln's Gettysburg speech and second inaugural [. . .]. We call upon all loyal and unadulterated Americans to man the trenches against the enemy within our gates" (quoted in Crawford, 1992: 19).

In 1906, the Nationality Act required English proficiency for naturalization as a U.S. citizen.

The teaching of Spanish benefited from the anti-German feelings that surrounded World War I. For example, when the American Association of Teachers of Spanish came into being in 1917, it adopted as its motto: "The war will be won by the substitution of Spanish for German." But although its first president, Lawrence Wilkins, promoted the teaching of Spanish, instead of German, at the secondary level, he prevented its inclusion in the elementary school curriculum and the hiring of "foreign" teachers. Spanish was taught at the secondary level in the same ways that it had been previously taught at the university, that is, with an emphasis on reading (García, 1997b, 2003).

After World War I, bilingual education was abandoned, and the study of foreign languages restricted. This had to do with the isolationism and nationalism of U.S. society after the war, as well as the development of public schools, now with mandatory attendance and no longer supporting church-affiliated schools. In 1903, only fourteen of the forty-eight states had regulations that required that English be the sole language of instruction, but by 1923, that number had increased to thirty-four. Castellanos (1983: 39) describes the situation:

> In some states the laws forbade the use of other languages for instruction in all subject areas except foreign language classes. In seven states, statutes revoked certification of teachers caught in the "criminal act" of using any language except English to teach in the public schools. Students who violated this English-only rule were subjected to sundry indignities, such as small fines or detention. "Spanish detention," for example, became a household word in the Southwest.

Although this restriction of languages other than English in instruction was prevalent in the period surrounding World War I, the tide started to turn in 1923 when the U.S. Supreme Court struck down language-restrictive laws in Nebraska, Idaho, and Ohio. In *Meyer vs. Nebraska*, the U.S. Supreme Court used the Due Process Clause of the 14th Amendment to overturn a 1919 Nebraska statute claiming that "no person, individually or as a teacher, shall, in any private denominational, parochial, or public school teach any subject to any person in any language than that English language." In overturning the Nebraska statute, the U.S. Supreme Court asserted that Meyer, a parochial school teacher in Nebraska had not violated the state's 1919 statute that mandated English only instruction, when he taught a Bible story in German to a 10-year-old child. This court case is significant because it asserted the rights of language minority communities to protection under the constitution.

The Court stated: "The protection of the constitution extends to all – to those who speak other languages as well as to those born with English on the tongue. Perhaps it would be highly advantageous if all had ready understanding of our ordinary speech, but this cannot be coerced with methods which conflict with the Constitution" (quoted in Del Valle, 2003: 37). The more tolerant attitude of the court, coupled with the increasing support for "cultural pluralism," the notion that distinct groups contributed greatly, espoused by John Dewey, and especially Horace Kallen, led to some limited efforts to establish bilingual schools and nurture the teaching of languages other than English. Supplementary ethnic schools of Chinese, Japanese, Greek, and Hebrew were also started around this time. And by 1940 the Franco-American community had a total of 249 bilingual schools "mi-anglais, mi-français, à part égales" (Epstein, 1977: 37). And yet, bilingualism in education throughout this time remained on the backburner, as the nation faced the economic depression of the 1930s.

In 1929 the *Modern Foreign Language Study* issued national recommendations regarding the teaching of languages other than English. The study recommended that reading be the primary aim of foreign language study and that it be limited to two years (Huebener, 1961). By 1934, less than 20 percent of all secondary school students were studying a modern language and only 16 percent were studying Latin. French was the most popular modern language, studied by 11 percent of students in high school, whereas Spanish was studied by only 6 percent of secondary school students (Crawford, 1983).

In 1949, the report *What the High Schools Ought to Teach* characterized foreign-language study as useless and time-consuming. And around the same time, Harvard's *General Education in a Free Society* report commented that foreign-language study was only useful in strengthening students' English (Huebener, 1961). Languages other than English were only recognized as "foreign," and useful to study only as a tool to improve metalinguistic skills in English.

World War II brought a new wave of attacks against bilingual education efforts in the United States, this time especially against Japanese American and Chinese American schools. President Roosevelt issued Executive Order 9066 in 1942 authorizing the roundup of 115,000 *Nikkei* (Japanese Americans). Two thirds of those imprisoned in concentration camps in ten states without trial for the sake of "national security" were *Nisei*, that is, natural-born American citizens of Japanese parents.

In 1942 the Bracero Program was established to bring short-term Mexican contract laborers for agricultural work. Mexican immigrants continued to arrive and their children were typically placed in segregated schools. Reports on the education of Mexican Americans noted that Spanish-surnamed children in general were three years below average academically than their Anglophone counterparts (Castellanos, 1983). Likewise, the other large Spanish-speaking group, the Puerto Ricans, U.S. citizens as a result of the Jones Act of 1917, were also failing in the nation's schools. In the 1960s, the dropout rate among Puerto Rican students in New York City schools was 60 percent. In 1963, only 331 academic high-school diplomas were issued to Puerto Rican students in New York City, and of those, only twenty-eight went on to college (Castellanos, 1983). Many Mexican American and Puerto Rican students were in special education classes meant for disabled students.

It is also interesting that during this time and throughout the first half of the twentieth century, Oralism, that is teaching Deaf students to read lips and talk, was promoted as the only way to teach Deaf students, effectively denying the use of American Sign Language (ASL) in bilingual education programs for the Deaf.

In 1950, the Amendments to the Nationality Act were passed, requiring English literacy for naturalization as a U.S. citizen. But the climate was soon to change. The national origin quotas of the National Origins Act of 1924 (also known as the Johnson-Reed Act) had limited the number of immigrants who could be admitted from any country to 2 percent of the number of people from that country who were already living in the United States in 1890. It significantly restricted immigration of Latin Americans, Africans, Asians, as well as Southern and Eastern Europeans. But in 1965, the Immigration and Naturalization Services Act of 1965 (also known as the Hart Celler or the INS Act of 1965) abolished the quotas. As a result, unprecedented numbers of immigrants from Asia, Latin America, and other non-western nations entered the United States.

Tolerance: second half of the twentieth century[5]

What was the source of the renaissance of bilingual education in the second half of the twentieth century? Castellanos (1983: 71) explains:

> The shortcomings of English as a Second Language when used in isolation, the rapidly increasing enrollment of students of limited English-speaking ability in our schools, the onset of student unrest in the inner cities (the dawn of the Civil Rights era) and the persuasive powers of Cubans all combined to bring about the revival of bilingual education in the United States.

In 1954 the U.S. Supreme Court ruled in *Brown vs. Board of Education* that segregated schools were unconstitutional, ushering in a new era in American civil rights. In effect, *Brown vs. Board of Education* established the precedent that when it came to education, same was not always equal, a principle that was later to be used for the education of language-minority students.

Three years later, in 1957, the Russians launched *Sputnik*, reminding the U.S. that increased knowledge of languages other than English, as well as math and science, were necessary to compete with Russians in airspace. In 1958 the National Defense Education Act was passed, increasing funding for the study of "foreign languages."

With the help of the Ford Foundation, the first bilingual program after World War II was set up in Dade County, Miami, in 1963, at the Coral Way Elementary School. Half of the student population consisted of English-speakers, and the other half of Spanish-speakers. Half of the teaching was done in English, with the other half done in Spanish by experienced Cuban teachers. In the first grades, children received instruction in their native language, with concepts reinforced in their second language. But children were also mixed for music and art classes, as well as in the playground, and lunchroom.

The success of the Coral Way School led to the establishment of other bilingual schools in the Southwest – two in the San Antonio Independent School District and two in other parts of Texas in 1964, another one in New Mexico and Texas in 1965, yet another one in San Antonio and two in other parts of Texas in 1966. In 1966, two bilingual schools were also established in California and one in Arizona, and the following year, yet another one was started in New Mexico (Castellanos, 1983).[6] As Castellanos (1983) remarks, the renaissance of bilingual education started without any federal involvement.

It is instructive to remember that in 1964, Title VI of the Civil Rights Act was passed by Congress, prohibiting discrimination on the basis of race, color, or national origin. The act states: "No person shall, on the grounds of race, color, or national origin, be denied the benefits of, or be subjected to discrimination under any program or activity receiving Federal Financial assistance." Title VI of the Civil Rights Act played an important role in developing bilingual education in the United States.

In 1968, the U.S. Congress passed Title VII of the Elementary and Secondary Education Act – the Bilingual Education Act. The Act was sponsored by Senator Ralph Yarborough of Texas, defined its goal as the quick acquisition of English, and limited its participation to poor students. Yarborough clearly stated: "It is not the purpose of this bill to create pockets of different languages throughout the country [. . .] not to stamp out the mother tongue, and not to make their mother tongue the dominant language, but just to try and make those children fully literate in English" (cited in Crawford, 2004: 107). The situation was dire. In 1960, of all Puerto Ricans 25 years of age and older in the United States, 87 percent had dropped out without graduating from high school and the dropout rate in eighth grade was 53 percent. In the Southwest, the average Chicano child had only a seventh-grade education. In Texas, the high-school dropout rate for Chicanos was 89 percent. And in California, less than a half a percent of college students at the University of California campuses were Chicanos (Mackey and Beebe, 1977: 6).

Title VII of the Elementary and Secondary Education Act (known for the title of section VII: The Bilingual Education Act) did *not* require bilingual education. Rather, Congress put aside money for school districts that had large language minority enrollments and wanted to start up bilingual education programs or create instructional material. The law (PL90–247) read:

> In recognition of the special educational needs of the large numbers of children of limited English-speaking ability in the United States, Congress hereby declares it to be the policy of the United States to provide financial assistance to local educational agencies to develop and carry out new and imaginative elementary and secondary school programs designed to meet these special educational needs.

When the Bilingual Education Act was first reauthorized in 1974, the eligibility for bilingual education was expanded to students of any socioeconomic status who had limited English-speaking ability (LESA) and provided for the first time a definition of bilingual education:

> It is instruction given in, and study of, English and (to the extent necessary to allow a child to progress effectively through the education system) the native language of the children of limited English speaking ability; and such instruction is given with appreciation for the cultural heritage of such children, and (with respect to elementary school instruction) such instruction shall (to the extent necessary) be in all courses or subjects of study which will allow a child to progress effectively through the educational system. (Quoted in Castellanos, 1983: 120)

Meanwhile, in the early 1970s, a group of Chinese American parents had brought a judicial case against the San Francisco School Board on the grounds that their children were not receiving an equitable education. The case was brought under the Equal Protection Clause of the Fourteenth Amendment of the Constitution and Title VI of the

Civil Rights Act. The case, known as *Lau vs. Nichols* eventually went up to the U.S. Supreme Court. Justice William O. Douglas, delivering the opinion of the court wrote:

> There is no equality of treatment merely by providing students with the same facilit-
> ies, textbooks, teachers and curriculum; for students who do not understand English
> are effectively foreclosed from any meaningful education [. . .]. Basic skills are at the
> very core of what these public schools teach. Imposition of a requirement that, before
> a child can effectively participate in the educational program, he must already have
> acquired those basic skills is to make a mockery of public education. We know that
> those who do not understand English are certain to find their classroom experiences
> wholly incomprehensible and in no way meaningful [. . .]
>
> No specific remedy is urged upon us. Teaching English to the students of Chinese
> ancestry who do not speak the language is one choice. Giving instructions to this group
> in Chinese is another. There may be others. (*Lau vs. Nichols*, 414 U.S. 563, 39 L. Ed.
> 2d 1 (1974).

An English-only education was found to be in violation of the equal educational opportunities provision of the Civil Rights Act of 1964. However, the court offered no specific methodology as a remedy. It merely instructed school districts to take "affirmative steps," and called upon the Office of Civil Rights to guide school districts. The Office of Civil Rights set up a Task Force that eventually promulgated guidelines (which became known as Lau Remedies).

When Lau was decided, Aspira, a Puerto Rican civil rights organization, settled out of court a suit they had brought on behalf of Latino limited-English-proficient students in New York City. The agreement on the suit, *Aspira of New York vs. Board of Education* (1975), became known as the Aspira Consent Decree. All children entering New York City schools who were of Latino background were tested in English, and if found limited, were subsequently tested in Spanish. All children who scored higher on the Spanish test were then put into bilingual education programs (Reyes, 2006a).

In 1976 two nationwide studies on bilingual education were conducted: the General Accounting Office Report (GAO, the investigative arm of Congress) and the study of the American Institutes for Research (AIR) (Danoff, 1978). The GAO panel concluded that the research showed positive effects for transitional bilingual education on students' achievement in English and also pointed to more limited data that supported the use of native languages for learning in subjects other than English. The AIR study, on the other hand, concluded that participation in Title VII Spanish–English bilingual education programs did not produce gains in English language arts or mathematics. But a review and analysis of twelve studies performed by Rudolph C. Troike in 1978 concluded that "students in the bilingual programs exceeded the achievement levels of control groups or district norms, and in several instances they exceeded national norms in English, reading, and math" (Troike: 1978: 5).

In 1979, the Lau Remedies were rewritten for release as regulations, mandating bilingual education in elementary schools where there were at least twenty-five children of the same language background in two consecutive grades (Crawford, 2004). As part of the evaluation of the proposed Lau Regulations, the U.S. Department of Education requested an examination of the literature which was carried out by

Keith Baker and Adriana de Kanter. After reviewing twenty-eight studies, Baker and de Kanter (1981) concluded that there was no consistent evidence for the effectiveness of transitional bilingual education. Baker and de Kanter argued that the evidence did not support the necessity of teaching academic subjects in the child's native language, although the curriculum needed to be structured differently from that of English monolingual students. Baker and de Kanter also recommended that immersion programs in English-only be given more attention. The Lau Regulations were never published as official regulations, and in 1981 they were withdrawn by Terrel Bell, the incoming Secretary of Education for Ronald Reagan calling them "harsh, inflexible, burdensome, unworkable, and incredibly costly" (cited in Crawford, 2004: 120).

It is important to point out that from the very beginning, Title VII (the Bilingual Education Act) did not address the maintenance and development of the students' home languages, thus demonstrating the lack of interest in bilingualism itself. From 1968 to 1978, there was little interest in languages other than English. In the late 1970s, only 22 percent of all high school U.S. students were studying a language other than English, and in 1977 only 8 percent of college students were enrolled in language courses. In April 1978, the Carter administration established the President's Commission on Foreign Languages and International Studies, and its recommendations pointed, for the first time, to the contradictions inherent in the Bilingual Education Act with regards to languages other than English. Pointing to "Americans' scandalous incompetence in foreign languages," the Commission (Perkins, 1980: 12, 13) reports:

> The President's Commission believes that our lack of foreign language competence diminishes our capabilities in diplomacy, in foreign trade, and in citizen comprehension of the world in which we live and compete. Americans' unwillingness to learn foreign languages is often viewed by others, not without cause, as arrogance. The melting-pot tradition that denigrates immigrants' maintenance of their skill to speak their native tongue still lingers and this, unfortunately, causes linguistic minorities at home to be ignored as a potential asset. [. . .] The United States is blessed with a largely untapped resource of talent in the form of racial and ethnic minorities who, by being brought into the mainstream of educational and employment opportunities in the areas of foreign language and international studies, can be expected to make rapid, new, and valuable contributions to America's capacity to deal persuasively and effectively with the world outside its borders.

The 1978 reauthorization of the Bilingual Education Act expanded the eligibility of children from "limited English-speaking abilities" (LESA) to individuals with "limited English proficiency (LEP). The 1984 reauthorization specifically approved *developmental bilingual education* in which students can maintain their languages after learning English, bringing back *maintenance bilingual education* under a new label. These programs, however, continued to be rare in the 1980s and beyond. But with the 1984 reauthorization, funding also became available for English-only programs as *Special Alternative Instructional Programs* (SAIPs), although only 4 percent of the funding was reserved for these kinds of programs (Crawford, 2004; Garcia E., 2005). (For more on this entire history, see especially www.ncela.gwu.edu/policy/1_history.html.)

The political climate in favor of bilingual education was beginning to change. Perhaps the words of President Ronald Reagan, shortly after taking office, are indicative of the climate: "it is absolutely wrong and against American concepts to have a bilingual education program that is now openly, admittedly dedicated to preserving their native language and never getting them adequate in English so they can go out into the job market and participate."

In an important judicial case (*Castañeda vs. Pickard*, 1981) the Fifth Circuit substantiated the holding of *Lau* that schools must take "appropriate action," and that such action must be based on sound educational theory, produce results, and provide adequate resources including teachers and materials. The case, however, did not mandate a specific program such as bilingual education or ESL.

In 1985, Willig conducted a meta-analysis of the studies that had been reviewed by Baker and de Kanter in 1981 in which she measured the program effect in each study, even if not statistically significant. Willig (1985) concluded that there were positive effects for bilingual programs for all academic areas. In 1987, The General Accounting Office (GAO) surveyed ten experts who looked favorably on the use of bilingual education to teach language-minority children and were quite critical of approaches that used English only.

The 1988 reauthorization of the Bilingual Education Act expanded the funding for *Special Alternative Instructional Programs* (SAIPs) where only English was used. These SAIP programs could consist of up to 25 percent of programs funded. The 1988 reauthorization also imposed a three-year limit on participation in transitional bilingual education programs. Congress reauthorized Title VII in 1994 (Bilingual Education, Language Enhancement, and Language Acquisition Programs) for the last time, under the *Improving America's Schools Act*. Although it gave increased attention to two-way bilingual education programs, the quota for the Special Alternative Instructional Programs (SAIPs) in which English only is used was lifted.

Official English: new restrictions[7]

In 1981, Senator Samuel Hayakawa introduced the first constitutional amendment to make English the official language of the United States. The Amendment reads: "Neither the United States nor any State shall make or enforce any law which requires the use of any language other than English. This article shall apply to laws, ordinances, regulations, orders, programs, and policies."[8] This could be said to be the beginning of a new stage of restriction of languages other than English in the United States. With Dr. John Tanton, Hayakawa founded U.S. English in 1983. U.S. English claims that it is "the nation's oldest, largest citizens' action group dedicated to preserving the unifying role of the English language in the United States." Closely related to U.S. English, Inc. is the U.S. English Foundation, which has the same advisory board and chief executive officer. Tanton had also founded the Federation for American Immigration Reform. U.S. English was thrown into disarray when in 1988 an internal memo authored by Tanton was circulated. In the memo Tanton speaks about the "threats" of U.S. Latinos, and mentions a tradition of the *mordida* (bribery), their Catholicism, their "low educability" and their high birthrates. Tanton, along with Linda Chavez, resigned as a result.

Since 1981, state after state has passed "Official English" laws or English-only laws. Fishman explains the growth of the Official English movement by saying: "Official English/English Only efforts cannot hide the fact that the power class (as well as those Anglos and non-Anglos who aspire to join its ranks) feels insecure about its own leadership role and its prerogatives in American society" (quoted in Crawford, 1992: 165). In a September 1985 speech, the then Secretary of Education, William J. Bennett, said, "we have lost sight of the goal of learning English as the key to equal educational opportunity" (Bennett, 1985, in Crawford, 1992: 360). As a specific response to William Bennett, the Spanish American League Against Discrimination (SALAD), a civil rights Miami-based organization, issued a statement in 1985 which said in part:

> We fear that Secretary Bennett has lost sight of the fact that English is a key to equal educational opportunity, necessary but not sufficient. English by itself is not enough. Not English Only, English *Plus!*
>
> Bennett is wrong. We won't accept English Only for our children. We want English plus. English plus math. Plus science. Plus social studies. Plus equal educational opportunities. English plus competence in the home language. (Quoted in Combs, 1992: 217)

SALAD and the League of United Latin American Citizens (LULAC) started to use the term "English Plus" as a policy alternative to "English Only," highlighting the importance of a second language for all people in the United States. In 1987, the English Plus Information Clearinghouse (EPIC) was established, under the auspices of the National Immigration, Refugee, and Citizen Forum, and the Joint National Committee for Languages (a coalition of the American Council on the Teaching of Foreign Languages [ACTFL], Teachers of English to Speakers of Other Languages [TESOL], and the National Council of Teachers of English [NCTE]). It is a coalition of more than fifty civil rights and educational organizations (Combs, 1992). The states of New Mexico, Oregon, Rhode Island, and Washington, as well as the cities of Atlanta, Cleveland, Dallas, San Antonio, Tucson, and Washington, DC, have endorsed English Plus resolutions (Combs, 1992).

But it has been at the state level where the English Only laws have been passed. As Table 8.1 shows, in early 2007, twenty-eight states had passed English Only laws, although Alaska's was struck down in court. In 1998, the Arizona Supreme Court had found that Arizona's constitutional amendment measure violated the 1st Amendment guarantee of *freedom of speech* and the 14th Amendment guarantee of *equal protection* of the laws (Crawford, 2006a). The court ruled that not only did state employees and elected officials have a right to express themselves in languages other than English, but that people with limited English proficiency had rights to receive information "when multilingual access may be available and may be necessary to ensure fair and effective delivery of governmental services." But in 2006, an English Only statute was passed.

Three states are bilingual – New Mexico, Louisiana, and Hawaii – although only Hawaii has been declared officially bilingual through a constitutional amendment passed in 1978.

Table 8.1   States that Have Adopted English Only Laws*

State	Means	Date
Alabama	Constitutional Amendment	1990
Alaska	Initiative Statute	1998 (ruled unconstitutional in state superior court, 2002)
Arizona	Constitutional Amendment	1998 (declared unconstitutional, 1998)
	Statute	2006
Arkansas	Statute	1987
California	Constitutional Amendment	1988
Colorado	Constitutional Amendment	1988
Florida	Constitutional Amendment	1988
Georgia	Statute	1986
Idaho	Statute	2007
Illinois	Statute	1969
Indiana	Statute	1984
Iowa	Statute	2002
Kansas	Statute	2007
Kentucky	Statute	1984
Mississippi	Statute	1987
Missouri	Statute	1998
Montana	Statute	1995
Nebraska	Constitutional Amendment	1920
New Hampshire	Statute	1995
North Carolina	Statute	1987
North Dakota	Statute	1987
South Carolina	Statute	1987
South Dakota	Statute	1995
Tennessee	Statute	1984
Utah	Statute	2000
Virginia	Statute	1981, revised 1996
West Virginia**	Statute	2005
Wyoming	Statute	1996

* From information supplemented to that supplied in Crawford, 2004
** This statute was rescinded because of a technical flaw

In 2002, thirty states had statutes allowing native-language instruction (Crawford, 2004). Although seven states still prohibit instruction in languages other than English, the bans have not been enforced to date.

The Present

Linguistic diversity in schools

Before we take a closer look at the situation of bilingual education in the United States today and the consequences of a restrictive language policy in education, it would be instructive to describe the language diversity of U.S. schoolchildren, as well as some of the educational inequities that are the result of English only policy in schools. We start then by describing this diversity in the present, however inadequately, using U.S. Census figures.[9]

Attention is rarely paid to the languages other than English that children speak in the United States, especially once they have become bilingual and able to speak English, in addition to their home language. For example, although most U.S. school districts ask parents to complete a Home Language Survey, these figures are never considered except in the case of those often labeled as English Language Learners (ELLs) or Limited English Proficient Students (LEPs), and that we refer to here as emergent bilinguals.[10] This is because neither the school system nor society considers bilingualism to be a resource. Thus, the bilingualism of U.S. children is seldom an object of study and exact figures are hard to come by. Finally, all emergent bilinguals are lumped into one category in relationship to English, without regard to the home languages they speak.

From the 2000 U.S. Census we can glean, although not determine, the extent of the bilingualism of North American 5 to 17 year olds, the student population in the United States. The large number of undocumented immigrants in the United States has been well established. But even underestimating, and using only official census figures which count, for the most part, only the documented, the figures are staggering, as seen in Table 8.2:

Table 8.2 Language Spoken at Home by 5–17-year-olds

	Number	*% of total*	*% of LOTE* speakers*
Speak English	43,316,237	81.58%	
Speak LOTEs	9,779,766	18.42%	
• Speak Spanish	6,830,100	12.86%	69.84%
• Speak other Indo-European	1,445,063	2.72%	14.78%
• Speak Asian and Pacific Isld	1,158,936	2.18%	11.85%
• Speak other languages	345,667	0.65%	3.53%

Source: 2000 U.S. Census. Summary File 4
* Languages other than English

Although over 80 percent of U.S. schoolchildren speak English at home, almost 19 percent (possibly many more if we consider the undocumented) or one fifth of all schoolchildren in the United States speak a language other than English at home. Almost 13 percent of all U.S. schoolchildren speak Spanish at home, and Spanish represents almost 70 percent of all LOTEs spoken by U.S. children. But other languages are increasingly competing with Spanish. Other Indo-European languages make up 15 percent, and Asian languages make up 12 percent of all LOTEs spoken in the United States.

Today most schoolchildren who speak languages other than English at home (regardless of whether they are emergent bilinguals or not) live in Arizona, California, Florida, Illinois, New Jersey, New Mexico, New York, and Texas, as shown in Table 8.3:

Table 8.3 Languages Spoken at Home by 5–17-year-old Schoolchildren in States with High Concentration of LOTE Speakers

	Arizona	California	Florida	Illinois	New Jersey	New Mexico	New York	Texas
Speak only English	700,732	3,886,749	2,058,387	1,906,780	1,156,705	260,215	2,518,326	2,882,740
Speak LOTEs	284,061	2,879,695	637,410	460,661	366,687	118,218	928,518	1,380,888
% speak LOTEs	28.84%	42.56%	23.64%	19.46%	24.07%	31.24%	26.94%	32.39%
• Speak Spanish	232,395	2,188,434	490,254	321,898	211,243	91,941	540,247	1,254,273
% speak Spanish	81.81%	76.00%	76.91%	69.88%	57.61%	77.77%	58.18%	90.83%
• Speak other Indo-European language	11,653	190,330	113,053	89,345	91,391	2,626	248,174	49,011
• Speak Asian and Pacific Island language	9,150	457,249	23,452	34,439	45,201	1,738	100,085	63,871
% speak Asian and PI lang.	3.22%	15.88%	3.68%	7.48%	12.33%	1.47%	10.78%	4.63%
• Speak other languages	30,863	43,682	10,651	14,979	18,852	21,913	40,012	13,733
Total 5–17-year-olds	984,793	6,766,444	2,695,797	2,367,441	1,523,392	378,433	3,446,844	4,263,628

Source: 2000 U.S. Census. Summary File 4. Table PCT 38

As can be seen in Table 8.3, California is the state with the most speakers of languages other than English, both in terms of absolute numbers and in percentage terms. Languages other than English are spoken by 2,879,695 schoolchildren, representing 43 percent of all California schoolchildren. California is followed by Texas where 1,380,888 schoolchildren representing 32 percent of all Texas schoolchildren, speak a LOTE. The strength of California's and Texas's bilingualism is then followed by New Mexico (31.2%), Arizona (28.8%), New York (26.9%), New Jersey (24%), Florida (23.6%), and, finally, Illinois (19.5%).

Spanish is spoken by three quarters of California schoolchildren who speak languages other than English (76%), but California is also home to the greatest percentage of children who speak Asian and Pacific Islander languages (16% of all children), making the strong multilingualism of this state unique. This is in contrast to Texas, where 90 percent of all Texan schoolchildren who speak languages other than English speak Spanish; making Texas the leading U.S. state in terms of Spanish-speaking schoolchildren. Whereas over three quarters of schoolchildren who speak a LOTE in the Southwestern states speak Spanish, schoolchildren in the two states in the Northeast speak more than Spanish, as shown by the fact that only 58% of New Jersey and 58% of New York students speak Spanish at home. In fact, schoolchildren in both of these Northeast states increasingly speak Asian languages (12 percent in New Jersey and 11 percent in New York). This portrait makes it evident that in the United States, bilingualism is not simply about English + Spanish. Increasingly, and especially outside of the states that were once Mexico, it is English + Many Languages = Bilingualism for the children, and Multilingualism for the state. It is also important to add that approximately an additional 500,000 Americans speak American Sign Language (Padden, 2003).

Speaking a language other than English at home does not reveal any information about English-language proficiency. The U.S. census asks those who claim to speak a language other than English at home to identify whether they also speak English – "very well," "well," "not well," or "not at all." We consider the category of speaking English "very well" or "well" as being *English-proficient bilinguals*.[11] We wish to point out that those children are considered bilingual, since they speak both the LOTE at home, and English "very well" and "well." We consider the category of speaking English "not well" or "not at all" as showing that these schoolchildren are emergent bilinguals, and in the process of becoming bilingual by acquiring English through schooling. Referring to these students as English Language Learners (ELLs) as many school districts presently do, or as Limited English Proficient students (LEPs) as federal legislation such as the No Child Left Behind act does, signals the lack of recognition that in teaching these children English they will become bilingual. English Language Learners are emergent bilinguals. That is, through school and through acquiring English, these children become bilingual and are able to continue to function in their home language as well as in English. Denying the bilingualism that they develop through schooling in the United States has much to do with the unequal conditions in which these children are educated (García, Kleifgen, and Falchi, 2007).

Table 8.4 shows the number of bilinguals and emergent bilinguals for the entire United States:

Table 8.4   Number of Bilinguals and Emergent Bilinguals among Schoolchildren of Different Language Groups

	Numbers	Percentages Bilinguals vs. Emergent Bilinguals[12]
5 to 17-year-olds: total	53,096,003	
Speak only English	43,316,237	
Speak LOTEs	9,779,776	
• Bilinguals	8,457,800	86.48%
• Emergent bilinguals	1,321,976	13.52%
Speak Spanish	6,830,100	
• Bilinguals	5,792,138	84.80%
• Emergent bilinguals	1,037,962	15.20%
Speak other Indo-European	1,445,063	
• Bilinguals	1,314,319	90.95%
• Emergent bilinguals	130,744	9.05%
Speak Asian and Pacific Island languages	1,158,936	
• Bilinguals	1,033,250	89.16%
• Emergent bilinguals	125,686	10.84%
Speak other languages	345,667	
• Bilinguals	318,083	92.02%
• Emergent bilinguals	27,584	7.98%

Source: 2000 U.S. Census. Summary File 4. Table PCT 38

These data are important because of what they tell us about the bilingual resources of U.S. schoolchildren. Of those who speak languages other than English at home, a full 86 percent are English proficient and bilingual. The percentage of emergent bilinguals per language group is clearly higher among Spanish-speakers, but even then, a full 85 percent of Spanish-speaking schoolchildren speak English "very well" or "well."

The number of emergent bilinguals in the United States, that is, those language minority children who are in the process of acquiring English in school, has increased dramatically in the last decade.[13] Over a decade ago, in the fall of 1991, the number of emergent bilinguals in kindergarten to twelfth grade was 2,314,079, accounting for an increase of 1 million over the previous decade (Fleischman and Hopstock, 1993). The largest proportion of emergent bilinguals then were speakers of Spanish (73%), Vietnamese (3.9%), Hmong (1.8%), Cantonese (1.7%), Cambodian (1.6%), Korean (1.6%), Lao (1.3%), Navajo (1.3%), Tagalog (1.3%), Russian, French Creole, Arabic, Portuguese, Japanese, Armenian, Chinese (unspecified), Mandarin, Farsi, Hindi, and Polish (Fleischman and Hopstock, 1993) (For a full account of the demographic characteristics of this population, see García, Kleifgen, and Falchi, 2007).

According to Crawford (2004), from 1990 to 2000 the number of emergent bilinguals doubled to 3.9 million which accounts for more than 8 percent of all school enrollment in the United States. Spanish is the home language of three out of four of all English language learners, but the following languages are spoken by at least 10,000 schoolchildren: Vietnamese, Hmong, Cantonese, Korean, Haitian Creole, Arabic,

Russian, Tagalog, Navajo, Khmer, Mandarin, Portuguese, Urdu, Serbo Croatian, Lao, Japanese, Punjabi, Armenian, Polish, French, and Hindi (Crawford, 2004).

According to the National Center for English Language Acquisition, between 1989–1990 and 2003–2004, the enrollment of emergent bilinguals in Pre-Kindergarten through twelfth grade more than doubled, from 2,030,451 students to 5,013,539. This number represents approximately 10.1 percent of the total public-school enrollment. In fact, in the last fifteen years, the enrollment of emergent bilinguals has increased at nearly seven times the rate of total student enrollment (www.ncela.gwu.edu/expert/faq/08leps.html).

As we saw in Table 8.4 (under Speak LOTE, Emergent Bilingual), the 2000 U.S. Census counts only 1,321,976 schoolchildren as not speaking English at all or not speaking English well. And yet, California alone reported to have enrolled 1,598,535 English Language Learners, the largest number of public-school emergent bilinguals ever, followed by Texas (660,707 emergent bilinguals), Florida (282,066), New York (191,992), Illinois (161,700), and Arizona (144,145) (www.ncela.gwu.edu/expert/faq/01leps.html). The disparity of the figures – that is, those provided by the 2000 U.S. Census and those provided by state reports – is due to two factors. On the one hand, there is the issue of the undercounting of the undocumented. On the other hand, the U.S. Census is clearly based on self-report, and in the case of schoolchildren, on the report of parents who might evaluate their children's English language proficiency inaccurately or differently from what school systems consider to be adequate English proficiency.

The Council of Great City Schools (Casserly, 2006) recently issued a report on emergent bilinguals in urban schools. Table 8.5 reproduces the results of the survey and ranks U.S. cities according to the number of emergent bilinguals enrolled:

Table 8.5   School Districts in Cities and Number and Proportion of Emergent Bilinguals Ranked by Number

	State	*Number of emergent bilinguals*	*Number of students*	*% emergent bilinguals*
1	Los Angeles, CA	328,684	747,009	44%
2	New York City, NY	122,840	1,023,674	12%
3	Chicago, IL	82,540	434,419	19%
4	Miami-Dade, FL	62,767	369,223	17%
5	Houston, TX	61,319	211,444	29%
6	Clark County, NV	53,517	267,585	20%
7	Dallas, TX	51,328	160,400	32%
8	San Diego, CA	38,629	137,960	28%
9	Santa Ana, CA	36,807	59,312	62%
10	Broward County, FL	29,909	271,900	11%
11	Fresno, CA	25,233	81,396	31%
12	Long Beach, CA	24,601	93,589	26%
13	Garden Grove, CA	23,698	49,574	48%
14	Fort Worth, TX	21,690	80,335	27%
15	Denver, CO	21,630	72,100	30%
16	Palm Beach, FL	20,326	169,381	12%
17	Hillsborough, FL	18,129	181,298	10%

Table 8.5   (*continued*)

	State	Number of emergent bilinguals	Number of students	% emergent bilinguals
18	San Bernardino, CA	17,913	58,661	30%
19	Compton, CA	17,496	30,233	58%
20	Austin, TX	17,337	78,807	22%
21	Fontana, CA	16,587	41,930	40%
22	San Francisco, CA	16,326	56,297	29%
23	Pomona, CA	15,826	33,294	48%
24	Sacramento, CA	15,382	51,273	30%
25	Oakland, CA	15,010	50,034	30%
26	St. Paul, MN	14,241	42,510	34%
27	Philadelphia, PA	12,525	189,779	7%
28	Orange County, FL	11,578	165,403	7%
29	Tucson, AZ	8,603	61,448	14%

Source: www.ncela.gwu.edu/expert/faq/02districts.html

However, the linguistic diversity of the United States does not merely exist in the aforementioned. In the last decade, the immigrant population in the United States grew most rapidly in other states, as shown in Table 8.6:

Table 8.6   Increase of Immigrant Population per State, 1990–2000

U.S. state	Percentage increase
North Carolina	274%
Georgia	233%
Nevada	202%
Arkansas	196%
Utah	171%
Tennessee	169%
Nebraska	165%

Especially in the last three decades, the nature of the immigration to the United States has changed radically. Table 8.7 displays the regions from which immigrants have come to the United States since 1910:

Table 8.7   Region of Birth of Foreign-born Population in the U.S., 1910–2000

	1910	1930	1960	1970	1980	1990	2000
Europe	87.4%	83.0%	75.0%	61.7%	39.0%	22.9%	15.8%
Asia	1.4%	1.9%	5.1%	8.9%	19.3%	26.3%	26.4%
Africa	–	0.1%	0.4%	0.9%	1.5%	1.9%	2.8%
Oceania	0.1%	0.1%	0.4%	0.4%	0.6%	0.5%	0.5%
Latin America	2.1%	5.5%	9.4%	19.4%	33.1%	44.3%	51.7%

Source: U.S. Census Bureau, Pop Division No. 29 and Summary File 3

The decline of European immigration accompanied by the growth of especially Latin American, but also Asian and African immigration has been significant.

According to Crawford (2004), one in five students in U.S. elementary and secondary schools is now either an immigrant or the child of an immigrant, and only 16 percent of them are of European or Canadian background. In contrast, in 1970, only one in fifteen students was an immigrant or the child of an immigrant, and 60 percent were from Europe or Canada (Crawford, 2004). Today, a total of 8.6 million students are immigrants themselves (E. García, 2005). Over 20 percent of U.S. students have at least one immigrant parent. Over half of the newcomers speak Spanish (38% from Mexico and 20% from other Latin American countries), and a quarter (23%) are from Asia or the Pacific Islands (Crawford, 2004). Language-minority enrollment has increased from 24 percent in 1977 to 40 percent in 2000. Latino students increased from 3 million to 4.5 million in the same period (a 52% increase), while Asian/Pacific Islanders increased from 553,000 to 1,158,000 (a 116% increase) (Kendler, 2002, cited in E. García, 2005).

According to the National Clearinghouse for English Language Acquisition, over 400 languages were spoken by emergent bilinguals in the United States (see www.ncela.gwu.edu/stats/4_toplanguages/langsrank.pdf). Table 8.8 gives a breakdown of the top fifteen languages in order of importance:

Table 8.8   Languages Spoken by U.S. Emergent Bilinguals

Language	Number of emergent bilinguals speaking LOTE	% represented
1. Spanish	3,598,421	79.05%
2. Vietnamese	88,906	1.95%
3. Hmong	70,768	1.55%
4. Chinese (Cantonese/Yue)	46,466	1.02%
5. Korean	43,969	0.97%
6. Haitian Creole	42,236	0.93%
7. Arabic	41,279	0.91%
8. Russian	37,157	0.82%
9. Tagalog (Pilipino, Filipino)	34,133	0.75%
10. Navajo (Diné)	27,029	0.59%
11. Khmer	26,815	0.59%
12. Chinese, Mandarin	22,374	0.49%
13. Portuguese	20,787	0.46%
14. Urdu	18,649	0.41%
15. Serbo-Croatian	17,163	0.38%

Source: U.S. Department of Education, *Survey of the States' Limited English Proficient Students and Available Educational Programs and Services, 2000–2001.*

Language inequalities

Most emergent bilinguals come from disadvantaged backgrounds. Using the figures for the number of free or reduced-price school lunches among emergent bilinguals, Zehler, Fleischman, Hopstock, *et al.* (2003) suggest that more than 75 percent are poor.

De Cohen, Deterding, and Chu Clewell (2005) report that nearly 70 percent of emergent bilinguals are enrolled in 10 percent of the nation's schools, which are predominantly located in urban poor areas. Their study shows that 72 percent of children in what they call "the High-LEP schools" or schools with a high number of emergent bilinguals qualify for free and/or reduced-price school lunches, as compared to about 40 percent in "Low-LEP schools." We also know that, of the 11 million immigrant children and children of immigrants in the 2000 Census, about half were low-income (Capps, Fix, Murray, *et al.*, 2005). Forty percent of the principals at the High-LEP schools in the De Cohen, Deterding, and Chu Clewell (2005) study cite poverty as a serious issue and identify "serious" and "moderate" student health problems. August and Hakuta (1997) report that 57 percent of the families of Latino emergent bilinguals and 35 percent of families of Asian/Pacific language emergent bilinguals have incomes under US$20,000.

Zehler, Fleischman, Hopstock, *et al.* (2003) estimate that 54 percent of the parents of emergent bilinguals have not completed eight years of schooling. Of the 16- to 24-year-olds, 42 percent had dropped out of school, compared to 10.5 percent of those who spoke English (August and Hakuta, 1998). They frequently attend poor urban schools that are crowded and segregated and where teachers lack adequate credentials.

Speaking of schools that have high concentrations of emergent bilinguals, De Cohen, Deterding, and Chu Clewell (2005: 14) summarize:

High-LEP schools are more likely to be located in urban areas and therefore have many characteristics associated with urban schools: larger enrollments; larger class sizes; greater racial and ethnic diversity; higher incidences of student poverty, student health problems, tardiness, absenteeism, and lack of preparation; greater difficulty filling teaching vacancies; greater reliance on unqualified teachers; and lower levels of parent involvement.

Bilingual education under attack[14]

As the nation's Latino population grew, and Spanish started to be heard in most schools and streets in the United States, Spanish itself came under assault. The most effective attack against bilingual education was spearheaded by a Silicon Valley software millionaire by the name of Ron Unz. Proposition 227 (California Education Code, Section 305–306), which was introduced as "English for the Children," was presented to California voters in June 1998. It stated that: "all children in California public schools shall be taught English by being taught in English. In particular, this shall require that all children be placed in English language classrooms. Children who are English learners shall be educated through sheltered English immersion during a temporary transition period not normally intended to exceed one year" (quoted in Del Valle, 2003: 248). The proposition prohibits the use of native language instruction in teaching emergent bilinguals and mandates the use of Sheltered English Immersion programs, where only English is used for a period not to exceed a year. Parents could request waivers if the child is over 10 years of age, has special needs, and is fluent in English. Sixty-one percent of Californians voted for the proposition. The Latino vote was two to one against the initiative.

Twenty-five percent of California students are not proficient in English. (In California these students are presently referred to as ELs, *English Learners*.) Yet, prior to the passage of Proposition 227, only 30 percent of these emergent bilinguals were in bilingual programs, with the rest in either English as a Second Language programs or regular classrooms (Crawford, 2003a). Of the 30 percent of California emergent bilinguals in bilingual programs, less than 20 percent were being taught by a credentialed bilingual teacher (Cummins, 2003). Four years after Proposition 227 was passed, only 590,289 emergent bilinguals (just 42 percent of the total in 1998) had become proficient in English, and annual redesignation rates, that is, the rates of English acquisition, remain unchanged. Furthermore, 141,428 emergent bilinguals are in bilingual classrooms at parents' requests. And more than half a million of these children have now been "mainstreamed," meaning that they receive no special help, even though they continue to be classified as Limited English Proficient (Crawford, 2003a). According to the California Education Department (2006a, b), today only 7.6 percent of emergent bilinguals in California are in transitional bilingual education classrooms (compared with 30% in 1998). In 1998 the percentage of teachers providing transitional bilingual education to emergent bilinguals in California was 29 percent. Today it is 4.4 percent (California Education Department 2006a, b; Rumberger and Gándara, 2000). Curiously enough, two-way bilingual education programs are growing in California.

A year after California's Proposition 227 was passed, Unz took his efforts to Arizona. In 2000, 63 percent of the Arizona voters approved Proposition 203 (Arizona Revised Statutes 15–751–755) which banned bilingual education. Arizona's proposition is even more restrictive than that of California. It limits school services for emergent bilinguals to a one-year Structured English Immersion Program[15] that includes ESL and content-based instruction in English Only. Waivers are almost impossible to get.

In 2002, the proposition in Massachusetts (Question 2, G.L. c. 71A) to replace transitional bilingual education with Structured English Immersion programs for emergent bilinguals passed by 68 percent. But in that same year, Amendment 31 to Colorado's state constitution that would have made bilingual education illegal was defeated with 56 percent of voters opposing it. Interestingly, the campaign to defeat the amendment focused on the threat that non-English-speaking children would be in the same classrooms as other children. A TV commercial warned that the Unz initiative would "force children who can barely speak English into regular classrooms, creating chaos and disrupting learning" (quoted in Crawford, 2004: 330). As Crawford (2004: 330) says, the approach used could be described as "If you can't beat racism, then try to exploit it."

Zehler, Fleischman, Hopstock, *et al.* (2003) establish that between 1992 and 2002 the number of emergent bilinguals in grades K–12 grew by 72 percent nationwide, and yet, their enrollment in bilingual programs declined from 37 percent to 17 percent. Crawford (2007) estimates that approximately half of emergent bilinguals in

California and Arizona who would have been in bilingual classrooms in 2001–2002 were reassigned to all-English programs. In the first year, California students in bilingual education programs declined from 29.1 percent to 11.7 percent (Crawford, 2007).

In an incisive retrospective article on the Aspira Consent Decree that guaranteed transitional bilingual education to Spanish-speaking English Language Learners in New York City, Reyes (2006a) points to the decline of such programs, coupled with the very slow growth of two-way bilingual education programs, and the massive explosion of ESL programs. For example, although in the 2000–2001 school year approximately half of emergent bilinguals were in transitional bilingual education and half in English as a Second Language classrooms in New York City (48 percent and 52 percent), by 2004–2005, less than a third of the students (29 percent) were in transitional bilingual education, while two thirds (66 percent) were in ESL programs. Only 2.6 percent of all ELL students in New York City were in two-way bilingual education programs in 2004–2005.

As many have remarked, the word "bilingual" (what Crawford has called "the B-Word," 2004: 35) has been progressively silenced (Crawford, 2004; García, 2003, 2006b; Hornberger, 2006; Wiley and Wright, 2004). Crawford (2006b) traces the decline of the use of the term "bilingual education" in the *New York Times*. Whereas from 1981 to 1990, the term appeared eighty-six times, from 1999 to 2006 there were only fourteen references to bilingual education. Crawford (2004: 35) says that instead of the term "bilingual education," "dual language, dual immersion and two-way immersion are increasingly used as 'safer' terms for what was originally known as two-way bilingual education, in hopes that avoiding the 'B-word' will minimize opposition." Even Crawford himself, in an effort to increase readership and have an impact with policy makers, dropped the name of bilingual education from his well-known *Bilingual Education: History, Politics, Theory, and Practice*. The fifth edition of the book was then titled *Educating English Learners. Language Diversity in the Classroom*. García (2008b) portrays this silencing of the word bilingual as follows:

Office of Bilingual Education and Minority Languages Affairs (OBEMLA) →	Office of English Language Acquisition, Language Enhancement and Academic Achievement for LEP students (OELA)
National Clearinghouse for Bilingual Education (NCBE) →	National Clearinghouse for English Language Acquisition and Language Instruction Educational Programs (NCELA)
Title VII of Elementary and Secondary Education Act: The Bilingual Education Act →	Title III of No Child Left Behind, Public Law 107–110: Language Instruction for Limited English Proficient and Immigrant Students, 2001

As the last row of the table above indicates, in 2001, the Bilingual Education Act (Title VII) was repealed. The new legislation, known as No Child Left Behind

(NCLB) contains Title III (Public Law 107–110) which is entitled *Language Instruction for Limited English Proficient and Immigrant Students.* The purpose of Title III is "to ensure that children, who are limited English proficient, including immigrant children and youth, attain English proficiency." The federal competitive grants of Title VII were replaced by formula grants that are administered by states. As such, Wiley and Wright (2004) have observed that bilingual education will be negatively affected because of the high accountability measured by English-only assessments combined with the states discretionary power in allocation of funding. Although it is still possible to obtain funding for bilingual education programs, NCLB requires mandatory, high-stakes tests in English for all children, leading Crawford (2004: 336) to call the act "No Child Left Untested." Crawford (2004: 332) provides an insightful analysis of the consequences of No Child Left Behind: "In the name of 'accountability,' it created new carrots and sticks that may ultimately prove more powerful than Unz' initiatives in pressuring schools to adopt all English instruction."

This climate of restriction of languages other than English affects all ethnolinguistic groups. This is the case of Native American languages. For example, in 1990, The Native American Languages Act (PL101–477) was passed, recognizing the language rights of American Indians, Alaska natives, Native Hawaiians, and Pacific Islanders. And in 1992, under the Native American Languages Act (PL 102–524) Congress established a grant program "to ensure the survival and continuing vitality of Native American languages." Bilingual educational efforts are not sufficient to redress the language shift that has taken place among Native Americans (McCarty, Romero, and Zepeda, 2006). In a post-Unz climate, efforts to use Native American languages in education have also been met with criticism. Recently, H.R. 4777, the Native American Languages Preservation Act, was considered by the U.S. House of Representative. Boulet (2006), among others, criticized the notion that children be immersed in Native American Languages, and stated: "At a time in life when children of Limited English Proficient parents need to hear the most English in order to develop fluency, H.R. 4766 seeks to ensure they will hear far less."

Types of bilingual education

It is clear that in the United States today, the main focus of bilingual education has to do with the education of immigrants, mostly Latinos, but also Chinese, Koreans (Shin, 2005), Russians, Haitians, Vietnamese, and others. And despite the development of two-way bilingual education programs in the last decade, it is the teaching of English to emergent bilinguals that remains the focus of attention.

U.S. scholarship insists on speaking of "models" of bilingual education, and three have been identified as prevalent (some more than others) in the United States today: transitional bilingual education, developmental bilingual education, and two-way bilingual education (dual language).[16] We reproduce here a table with the different approaches to the instruction of language minority students in the United States today. Only the last three are bilingual education program types.

Table 8.9 Language Education Programs in the U.S. Today

Program	Language used in instruction	Components	Duration	Goals
MONOLINGUAL EDUCATION				
Submersion (sink-or-swim)	100% English	Mainstream education; no special help with English; no qualified teachers	Throughout K–12 schooling	Linguistic assimilation (shift to English only)
ESL Pullout (submersion plus ESL)	90–100% in English; may include some home language support or not	Mainstream education; students pulled out for 30–45 minutes of ESL daily; teachers certified in ESL	As needed	Linguistic assimilation; remedial English
Structured Immersion (Sheltered English, content-based ESL)	90–100% English; may include some home language support	Subject-matter instruction at students' level of English; students grouped for instruction; teachers certified in ESL, should have some training in immersion	1–3 years	Linguistic assimilation; quick exit to mainstream education
BILINGUAL EDUCATION				
Transitional Bilingual Education (Early-Exit)	90–50% initially in the home language; increasing percentage of English up to 90%	Initial literacy usually in home language; some subject instruction in home language; ESL and subject matter instruction at students' level of English; sheltered English subject instruction; teachers certified in Bilingual Education	1–3 years; students exit as they become proficient in English	Linguistic assimilation; English acquisition without falling behind academically
Developmental Bilingual Education (Late-Exit)	90–50% initially in the home language; gradually decreasing to 50% or less by grade 4 or 50:50 from beginning	Initial literacy in home language; some subject instruction in home language; ESL initially and subject matter instruction at students' level of English; teachers certified in bilingual education	5–6 years	Bilingualism and biliteracy; academic achievement in English
Two-Way Bilingual Education (Two-way Dual Language, Two-Way Immersion, Dual Immersion, Dual Language)[17]	90:10 model: 90% home language, 10% other language in early grades, moving to 50:50 model: parity of both languages	Emergent bilinguals and native-English speakers taught literacy and subjects in both languages; peer tutoring; teachers certified in bilingual education	5–6 years	Bilingualism and biliteracy, academic achievement in English

Source: adapted from Crawford, 2004: 42

A description of successful bilingual education programs in the United States can be found at www.alliance.brown.edu/pubs/pos/.

Empirical evidence

The results of large-scale evaluation programs (Ramirez, 1992; Thomas and Collier, 2002), and meta-analyses reviewing studies that compared student performance in different types of programs (Willig, 1985) agree that using the home language in instruction benefits language minority students. The Ramirez study (1992) was a longitudinal study of 554 kindergarten to sixth-grade Latino students in five states (New York, New Jersey, Florida, Texas, and California) who were in English-only structured immersion programs, in transitional early-exit programs, and in late-exit developmental bilingual programs. In this study, two-way dual language education programs were not evaluated. The results of the Ramirez study favored late-exit developmental bilingual programs, that is, programs that use bilingual students' home languages for at least five to six years. Although there were no differences between programs among students in the third grade, by sixth grade students in late-exit developmental programs were performing better in mathematics, English language arts and English reading than students in the other programs.

Collier (1995) stresses that four factors are important for the equitable and successful education of emergent bilinguals: 1. a socioculturally supportive environment; 2. the development of the students' first language to a high cognitive level; 3. uninterrupted cognitive development which best occurs through education in the first language; 4. teaching the second language with cognitively complex tasks. Thomas and Collier (1997: 15) provide evidence that development of first-language skills provides a sound foundation for subsequent academic success in and through English as a second language. They state: "The first predictor of long-term school success is cognitively complex on-grade level academic instruction through students' first language for as long as possible (at least through grade 5 or 6) and cognitively complex on-grade level academic instruction through the second language (English) for part of the day."

In 2002, Wayne Thomas and Virginia Collier released a study of the effectiveness of different kinds of educational programs for language-minority student achievement. They compared the achievement on nationally standardized tests[18] of students in different kinds of programs who entered the U.S. school district with little or no proficiency in English in kindergarten to first grade, following them to the highest grade level reached. The results for English Total Reading[19] appear in Table 8.10:

Table 8.10   English Total Reading for Emergent Bilinguals in Different Kinds of Programs

Type of program	Result	When tested
Submersed in English mainstream	15 NCE[20]	Fifth grade
Submersed in English mainstream	25 NCE (12th percentile)	End of eleventh grade
ESL content classes for 2–3 years	34 NCE (23rd percentile)	End of high school
Transitional bilingual education for 3–5 years (50:50)	47 NCE (45th percentile)	End of eleventh grade
Transitional bilingual education for 3–5 years (90:10)	40 NCE (32nd percentile	End of fifth grade
Developmental bilingual education (50:50)	62 NCE (72nd percentile)	After four years
Developmental bilingual education (50:50)	56 NCE (61st percentile)	By seventh grade
Developmental bilingual education (90:10)	41 NCE (34th percentile)	End of fifth grade
Two-way bilingual education (50:50)	58% met Oregon standards	End of third and fifth grades
Two-way bilingual education (90:10)	51 NCE (51st percentile)	End of fifth grade

According to Thomas and Collier (2002) five main results can be gleaned from this table:

1. The use of the students' home languages in bilingual education produces better results in English reading that programs that use English only.
2. Developmental and Two-way bilingual education programs produce better results in English reading than transitional bilingual education programs.
3. Two-way 50:50 programs, or programs that devote equal time to English and the minority program from the beginning and until the end seem to be more effective than two-way 90:10 programs.
4. All 50:50 programs (whether transitional, developmental or two-way) seem to produce better results in English reading than those programs that are 90:10 and where instruction starts out devoting 90 percent of the time to the minority language and 10 percent of the time to English.
5. Developmental 50:50 bilingual education programs, or programs that cater only to one minority ethnolinguistic group,[21] seem to be most effective, although the high results are only after four years, indicating the low incidence of these kinds of programs in the United States.

With regards to Spanish Total Reading[22] for those students in English/Spanish programs, the results are summarized in Table 8.11:

Table 8.11   Spanish Total Reading for Students in Different Kinds of Programs

Type of program	Result	When tested
Transitional bilingual education (90:10)	51 NCE	Fifth grade (in all English curriculum)
Developmental bilingual education (90:10)	55 NCE (60th percentile)	Fifth grade
Two-way bilingual education (50:50)	62 NCE (71st percentile)	After 1–2 years of U.S. schooling, grades 3–6
Two-way bilingual education (90:10)	61 NCE (70th percentile)	Fifth grade

For Spanish Total Reading, the best results are obtained in two-way bilingual education programs. But it is instructive to realize that even in transitional bilingual education classes, students are on grade level in Spanish reading achievement.

Thomas and Collier (2002) also point out that English-speakers in two-way bilingual education did well in English, learned Spanish, and achieved well above the fiftieth percentile in all subject areas on norm-referenced tests. On all measures, they outperformed their comparison groups being schooled monolingually.

Lindholm-Leary (2001) conducted a comprehensive evaluation of programs serving emergent bilinguals in California: 1. English-only programs; 2. transitional bilingual education; and 3. two types of two-way bilingual education (what she called simply Dual Language Education or DLE). There were two types of Dual Language Education programs included: 1. the 50:50 model, meaning that 50 percent of the instruction is in the child's home language, and 50 percent is in the additional language; 2. the 90:10 model, meaning that, *initially* 90 percent of the instruction is in the child's first language and 10 percent in the other language, as it gradually moves to a 50:50 arrangement. Lindholm-Leary concluded that students who were in instructional programs where English was used for only 10 percent to 20 percent of the time (whether transitional or 90:10 Dual Language) did as well on English proficiency tests as those in English-only programs or in 50:50 Dual Language programs. By grade six, however, Latino students in dual language education outperformed transitional bilingual education students. In mathematics all students in dual language education performed ten points higher than those educated only in English.

Oller and Eilers (2002) conducted a large-scale study of these dual language education programs in Miami. They compared 952 bilingual and monolingual students from kindergarten to fifth grade in dual language education and English-immersion classrooms. By the fifth grade, there is no gap in English-language test performance between students, and those in dual language education are bilingual. Their study also found that regardless of school type and age, Latino students spoke predominantly in English.

Recent meta-analyses of the literature on the teaching of emergent bilinguals show that those in bilingual education programs outperform those in all-English programs on tests of academic achievement (Krashen and McField, 2005; Krashen, Rolstad, and MacSwan, 2007). This was also the conclusion of the reviews by Rolstad, Mahoney, and Glass (2005) and Slavin and Cheung (2005). Slavin and Cheung (2005) reviewed sixteen studies comparing structured English-immersion with transitional bilingual education. They found that most of the studies favored transitional bilingual education over structured English immersion, and that no study reviewed significantly favored structured English-immersion programs. Rolstad, Mahoney, and Glass's (2005) meta-analysis found evidence that the use of a child's home language is more beneficial for emergent bilinguals than structured English immersion. Likewise, the National Literacy Panel on Language Minority Children and Youth, chosen by the Bush administration, concluded that bilingual education approaches in which the child's first language is used are more effective in teaching children to read than are English-only approaches (August and Shanahan, 2006).[23] Francis, Lesaux and August (2006: 392) summarize these findings of the National Literacy Panel saying: "it seems reasonably safe to conclude that bilingual education has a positive effect on English reading outcomes that are small to moderate in size."

In their recent synthesis of the research evidence in the education of emergent bilinguals, Genesee, Lindholm-Leary, Saunders, and Christian (2006) repeat that students who are in educational programs providing extended instruction through the medium of their native language – late-exit bilingual education programs (developmental and two-way bilingual education/dual language) – outperform students who only receive short-term instruction through their native language (early-exit transitional bilingual education). They also found that bilingual proficiency and biliteracy were positively related to academic achievement in both languages. Finally, these researchers found that emergent bilinguals who participated in primary school programs that provided first language support had acquired the same or superior levels of reading and writing skills as students in English-only programs by the end of elementary school, while developing their bilingualism and biliteracy.

Despite the evidence that two-way dual language programs are quite successful in developing the academic language of emergent bilinguals, we cannot conclude that they are superior to other forms of developmental bilingual education that are only for one group. In reality, and despite the promise of two-way bilingual education, not all localities can implement these programs because many language-majority communities are not eager to have their children schooled with language-minority students. What is evident from the research is that the use of the child's first language is most important for their long-term academic achievement in English, as well as cognitive growth.

What have been the effects on achievement in states where bilingual education has been outlawed? It seems that in California, Arizona, and Massachusetts, changes to English-only instruction have not in any way improved the education of English Language Learners. Crawford (2006a: 7), citing other sources, summarizes:

- A five-year study, commissioned by the California legislature, found no evidence that all-English-immersion programs had improved academic outcomes for English learners in the state. In 2004–2005, only 9 percent of these students were reclassified as fluent in English – a rate that was virtually unchanged since the year before passage of the English Only law (California Department of Education, 2005).
- Researchers at Arizona State University reported that 60 percent of English learners in Arizona made "no gain" in English in 2003–2004, while 7 percent actually lost ground; all were enrolled in English-only programs (Mahoney, MacSwan, and Thompson, 2005). Another ASU study (Wright and Pu, 2005) found that the academic achievement gap between English learners and other students was widening.
- In Massachusetts, more than half of the students were still limited in English after three years in structured English-immersion classrooms (Sacchetti and Tracy, 2006).

Language education

Despite the great number of bilingual students in U.S. schools, our bilingual capacity as a nation is extremely poor. The attacks on bilingualism and bilingual education have consequences for all of us, and not just for the children of immigrants. For example, in 2002 the *Digest of Education Statistics* reported that only 44 percent of U.S. high school students (ninth to twelfth grades) and 15 percent of junior high school students (seventh and eighth grades) were enrolled in foreign-language classes. Only four states have a foreign-language graduation requirement for all students, and eighteen states have a foreign-language graduation requirement for some students (National Council of State Supervisors for Languages, 2006). Eighteen states reported that the No Child Left Behind act has had a negative impact on their foreign-language programs because schools had to focus on reading and math skills.

A 1997 Center for Applied Linguistic national survey of approximately 3,000 public and private elementary and secondary schools revealed that most foreign-language programs offered only five hours of instruction per week or fewer (Branaman and Rhodes, 1997). Generally, foreign-language programs are offered only at the secondary level by 87 percent of all schools. Only 31 percent of U.S. elementary schools offer instruction in a second language (Branaman and Rhodes, 1997).

In the United States Spanish continues to be the most popular language studied in school by almost 70 percent of the students in grades seven to twelve; while French represents 18.3 percent, German 4.8 percent, Latin 2.7 percent and Italian 1.2 percent (Draper and Hicks, 2002). Arabic, Chinese, Farsi, Japanese, Korean, Russian, and Urdu combined account for less than 1 percent of U.S. high-school-student foreign-language enrollment (Draper and Hicks, 2002). At the tertiary level, the distribution changes somewhat, and is given here as Table 8.12:

Table 8.12   Top Twelve Languages Studied in Colleges
and Universities in the U.S.

Language	Percentage
Spanish	53.0%
French	14.4%
German	7.1%
Italian	4.5%
American Sign Language	4.3%
Japanese	3.7%
Chinese	2.4%
Latin	1.9%
Russian	1.7%
Ancient Greek	1.5%
Biblical Hebrew	1.0%
Arabic	0.7%

Source: *ADFL Bulletin* 35(2–3) (Winter–Spring 2004)

In the case of Spanish, the increase of Spanish-language learners is directly related to the growth of the Spanish-speaking population in the United States, which has created an important market of well over US$800 billion. Spanish has become fashionable, as the language spoken by Penelope Cruz, sung by Shakira and Ricky Martin, and rapped in Reggaetón (García, 2008b). Although Spanish is increasingly studied in school, 70 percent of the students are in Basic Levels (Draper and Hicks, 2002) and drop out afterwards. And there are few serious secondary school programs of Spanish for Spanish-speakers (also known as Spanish as a Heritage Language), as has been made evident by Valdés, Fishman, Chávez, and Pérez (2006) for California.

In the last decade there has also been increased attention given to the teaching of American Sign Language. As of 1997, there were twenty-eight states that had approved ASL as a foreign language, making it possible to study ASL to fulfill a foreign-language requirement (Wilcox and Peyton, 1999).

On September 26, 2001, a report of the House Permanent Select Committee on Intelligence stated that language was the single greatest need in the intelligence community. Former Senator Paul Simon (2001: p. A23) pointed out, "Today, some 80 federal agencies need proficiency in nearly 100 foreign languages. While the demand is great, the supply remains almost nonexistent." To address this critical need, the Foreign Language Assistance Program of 2006 increased funding ($17.8 million to $21.7 million) to improve and expand language study for elementary- and secondary-school students. In addition, the National Security Language Initiative of 2006 aims to have more Americans master "critical need languages" starting at an earlier age. The "critical languages" identified by the initiative include Arabic, Chinese, Hindi, Farsi, and Russian. The $114 million initiative targets higher education, although there is a small amount of funding for new language elementary and secondary programs. The initiative has also allocated $18 million toward the education of teachers, recognizing the need to increase the number of qualified language teachers (Mason, 2006).[24]

Conclusion

Figure 8.1 provides a timeline of U.S. bilingual education policy, summarizing for the readers some of the events that we have been describing:

1954	*Brown vs. Board of Education*
1957	Launching of *Sputnik*
1958	National Defense and Education Act, NDEA
1963	Establishment of Coral Way Bilingual Education Program
1964	Title VI, Civil Rights Act
1968	Title VII, Elementary and Secondary Education Act (ESEA): Bilingual Education
1974	1st reauthorization, Title VII of ESEA. Definition of transitional BE
1974	*Lau vs. Nichols*
1975	Aspira Consent Decree
1976	GAO and AIR Studies
1978	President's Commission on Foreign Languages and International Studies
1978	2nd reauthorization, Title VII of ESEA
1981	Baker and de Kanter Study
1981	*Castañeda vs. Pickard*
1981	Sen. Hayakawa introduced 1st Official English constitutional amendment
1983	U.S. English founded
1984	3rd reauthorization, Title VII, ESEA. Approved developmental BE. Made 4% funding available for Special Alternative Instructional Programs (SAIP) English
1985	Willig study
1987	GAO survey
1987	EPIC established
1988	4th reauthorization, Title VII, ESEA. Expanded SAIPs to 25% of funding
1990	The Native American Languages Act
1992	Ramirez study
1994	5th reauthorization, Title VII, ESEA. Increased attention to two-way bilingual programs. Lifted quota for SAIPs
1998	California's Proposition 227 passed
2000	Arizona's Proposition 203 passed
2001	No Child Left Behind, Title III, Language Instruction for Limited English and Immigrant Students
2001	Lindholm-Leary study
2002	Massachusetts Question 2 passed
2002	Thomas and Collier study
2006	August and Shanahan study
2006	National Security Language Initiative
2007	National Literacy Panel on Language Minority Children

Figure 8.1 Timeline of Bilingual Education Policy in the United States

The United States has had a long history with bilingualism and bilingual education. Not only are over 300 languages spoken in the United States, but speakers of these languages are more in contact with each other than perhaps anywhere else in the world (Finegan and Rickford, 2004). It is not uncommon to listen to an Italian contractor or a Korean grocer speak Spanish to their workers. In a nail salon, one frequently hears a Salvadoran attendant speak Korean to her employer. It is in the United States where speakers of different varieties of Spanish live side by side, and communicate in a language that is no longer the language of one nation, but the language of a continent. And it is also in the United States where Punjabi speakers from India and Pakistan, Mandarin speakers from mainland China and Taiwan, and Persian speakers from Iran and Tajikistan, come into contact with each other.

The bilingual wealth of the United States is seldom recognized officially, although it is often valued by the ethnolinguistic community itself and by parents. For example, although languages other than English are rarely taught in U.S. primary schools, there are large networks of supplementary language and culture programs that teach these languages to children. And the recent growth of two-way bilingual education programs, despite the threats of No Child Left Behind, bears witness to the increasing desire of mainstream U.S. parents that their children not only be academically competent in English, but that they also acquire familiarity with other languages and cultures – especially those that they hear in the street, on television, and on the radio.

As the U.S. educational system falls prey to the reductionist tendencies of the accountability measures of No Child Left Behind, more and more parents are looking for public-education opportunities that challenge children intellectually and that go beyond its testing requirements. It turns out that two-way bilingual education programs often provide such intellectual incentive. Many Gifted and Talented programs in public schools have gone "Dual Language." And many enrichment supplementary educational programs take place in languages other than English. Recently, for example, the first private English–Spanish bilingual pre-school opened in New York City where pre-schoolers compete for placement. The bilingual pre-school, La Escuelita, has proven very popular with middle-class parents, and is giving very young children an opportunity to learn in two languages.

The United States is caught in a double bind. On the one hand, at the national level, anti-bilingual sentiment is running high, tied to anti-immigrant efforts. But on the other hand, informed parents are looking beyond our borders and seeing the world through new eyes and languages. To these parents, it is clear that their children must become competent bilinguals. The greatest test for U.S. public schools in the twenty-first century will not be merely to ensure the English language literacy of all students and the closing of the achievement gap among children of all kinds, as the No Child Left Behind act leads us to believe. The greatest challenge will be how to provide mainstream children an education that prepares them with the global understandings, languages included, that will be required in the twenty-first century.

The next chapter describes the plurilingual policy that is presently being promoted in the European Union and the CLIL/EMILE types of bilingual programs that are gaining strength. The present EU policy of promotion of plurilingualism contrasts sharply with that of the U.S. However, it is to be noted that the European Union trails the United States in including in education the languages of immigrants and refugees that increasingly define it. The EU efforts on behalf of bilingual education that we describe in the next chapter do not support the ways in which immigrants language.

Questions for Reflection

1. Reflect on the history of bilingual education policy up to the present, as discussed in this chapter. What major events have shaped this policy?
2. What are possible rationales for the direction bilingual education policy has taken in the U.S.?
3. Reflecting on previous chapters, how do language ideologies connect to bilingual education policy in the U.S. context? Give examples.
4. How has Proposition 227 affected the development of bilingual education in the California? Has it been effective? Why or why not?
5. How have the current bilingual education policies in the U.S. impacted on the different types of bilingual education programs?

Further Reading

Castellanos, D. (1983). *The Best of Two Worlds. Bilingual-Bicultural Education in the U.S.* New Jersey State Department of Education, Trenton, NJ.

Crawford, J. (ed.) (1992). *Language Loyalties: A Sourcebook on the Official English Controversy.* University of Chicago Press, Chicago, IL.

—— (2000). *At War with Diversity. U.S. Language Policy in an Age of Anxiety.* Multilingual Matters, Clevedon.

—— (2004). *Educating English Learners: Language Diversity in the Classroom*, fifth edn. (Formerly *Bilingual Education: History, Politics, Theory, and Practice.*) Bilingual Educational Services, Los Angeles, CA.

—— (2008). *Advocating for English Learners.* Multilingual Matters, Clevedon.

Dicker, S. (2003). *Languages in America. A Pluralist View*, second edn. Multilingual Matters, Clevedon.

García, E. (2005). *Teaching and Learning in Two Languages. Bilingualism and Schooling in the United States.* Teachers College Press, New York.

González, J. (ed.) (2008). *Encyclopedia of Bilingual Education.* Sage, Thousand Oaks, CA.

Krashen, S. (1996). *Under Attack: The Case against Bilingual Education.* Language Education Associates, Burlingame, CA.

Wiley, T. (1996b). *Literacy and Language Diversity in the United States.* Center for Applied Linguistics, Washington, DC. Second edn. 2005

Wiley, T., and Wright, W. (2004). "Against the Undertow: Language Minority Education Policy and Politics in the 'Age of Accountability.'" *Educational Policy* 18(1), 142–68.

Important Websites

American Council on the Teaching of Foreign Languages www.actfl.org/i4a/pages/index.cfm?pageid=1

Brown Alliance, Portraits of Success www.alliance.brown.edu/pubs/pos

Center for Advanced Study of Language www.casl.umd.edu

Center for Applied Linguistics www.cal.org/

Center for Language Minority Education www.clmer.csulb.edu/

Center for Research on Education, Diversity and Excellence (CREDE) www.crede.ucsc.edu/

Crawford's Language Policy Web Site and Emporium http://ourworld.compuserve.com/homepages/JWCRAWFORD/

Institute for Language Education Policy www.elladvocates.org/

Language Policy Research Unit www.asu.edu/educ/epsl/lpru.htm

National Association for Bilingual Education www.nabe.org/

National Clearinghouse for English Language Acquisition and Language Instruction Educational Programs www.ncela.gwu.edu/

Office of English Language Acquisition, Language Enhancement, and Academic Achievement for Limited English Proficient Students www.ed.gov/about/offices/list/oela/index.html

TESOL www.tesol.org/s_tesol/index.asp

USC Center for Multilingual, Multicultural Research www-bcf.usc.edu/~cmmr/

9

Language Promotion by European Supra-national Institutions

by Hugo Baetens Beardsmore

On n'habite pas un pays, on habite une langue.
(You don't live in a country, you live in a language.)

Cioran: 1995: 1651

Overview

In this chapter, we will discuss:

- The Council of Europe:
  - policies;
  - assessment:
    - the Common European Framework of Reference for Languages (CEFR);
    - the European Language Portfolio (ELP);
  - country profiles on plurilingual education;
  - the European Charter for Regional or Minority Languages.
- The European Commission:
  - the Action Plan for Language Learning;
  - other efforts.
- Bilingual education and CLIL in particular.

Introduction

The previous chapter considered language education policies in one national context – the United States. This chapter discusses the language education policies promoted by two *supra-national institutions* in Europe: the Council of Europe, with its seat in Strasbourg (France); and the European Commission, with its seat in Brussels (Belgium). Even though education is a national prerogative, and neither of these organizations can impose a particular orientation dealing with languages in education, both operate via consensual persuasion on promoting the learning of languages and bilingual education. Individual national policies, their history, and present status, will not be discussed in detail, given the enormous variety of circumstances in the forty-eight countries involved, though at times illustrations of practice in various countries will be given.

It is important to draw distinctions between the United States approach towards language policy – one of *tolerance* toward languages other than English at best, mostly implicit, and outward *restriction* during some historical periods – to that of present practices by these two supra-national bodies of the European Union – explicit *promotion* of bilingualism.[1]

The Council of Europe

The Council of Europe consists of forty-eight member states, and since 1954 has a Convention that provides a framework for developing international co-operation in the field of culture and education to support its core values, based on human rights, democracy, and the rule of law. The Language Policy Division of the Council of Europe has produced a number of pioneering policy documents, backed up by research expertise and underpinned by scientific workshops and conferences that have had considerable impact on many aspects of language education within Europe.

The Council of Europe and its member states believe that the promotion of linguistic diversity should be pursued through *language-in-education policy* (LiEP). This is intended to promote mobility, inter-comprehension, and economic development, as well as maintaining European cultural heritage, of which linguistic diversity is a significant constituent. To this end, the major concern is not only to protect and develop languages, but equally, to enable citizens to develop their linguistic abilities. Consequently, the Council of Europe's actions cover two major orientations. On the one hand, there is the promotion and improvement of language learning for all citizens; on the other hand, there is support for all languages within the member states, be they majority, regional, or minority and lesser-used languages. This support also includes a stance on the protection of sign languages (Council of Europe, 2003), which includes them as part of Europe's linguistic and cultural heritage. Recommendation 1598 declares support for the different sign languages in Europe, as well as the need for education, teacher-training, and training of interpreters in sign languages. The Council of Europe has produced a book (Timmermans, 2005) based on information from twenty-six member-state governments and NGOs indicating policy positions and users' access to their political, social, and cultural rights. There is, however, little official support for immigrant languages, possibly because it is proving difficult to obtain consensus across the member states for a united position on the issues involved. (For more on the situation of immigrant minority languages in Europe, see Extra and Yagmur, 2002.)

Policies

The following extracts from official documents clearly show the ideological basis of the language policy being promoted. (For this and other work of the Language Policy Division of the Council of Europe consult www.coe.int/t/dg4/linguistic/default_en.asp.)

Council of Europe language education policies aim to promote:

PLURILINGUALISM: all are entitled to develop a degree of communicative ability in a number of languages over their first one in accordance with their needs;

LINGUISTIC DIVERSITY: Europe is multilingual and all its languages are equally valuable modes of communication and expressions of identity. The right to use and to learn one's language(s) is protected in Council of Europe Conventions;

MUTUAL UNDERSTANDING: The opportunity to learn other languages is an essential condition for intercultural communication and acceptance of cultural differences;

DEMOCRATIC CITIZENSHIP: Participation in democratic and social processes in multilingual societies is facilitated by the plurilingual competence of individuals;

SOCIAL COHESION: Equality of opportunity for personal development, education, employment, mobility, access to information and cultural enrichment depends on access to language learning throughout life. (Council of Europe, 2006: 5)

The Council of Europe policy documents attach particular importance to the development of a *person's plurilingual repertoire* over time, which is defined as "different languages and language varieties at different levels of proficiency and includes different types of competences. It is dynamic and changes in its composition throughout an individual's life" (Council of Europe, 2006: 6).

To achieve this, the Council of Europe promotes a plurilingual education which involves:

- an awareness of why and how one learns the languages one has chosen;
- an awareness of and the ability to use transferable skills in language learning;
- a respect of the plurilingualism of others and the value of languages and varieties irrespective of their perceived status in society;
- a respect for the cultures embodied in languages and the cultural identities of others;
- an ability to perceive and mediate the relationships which exist between languages and cultures;
- a global integrated approach to language education in the curriculum. (Council of Europe, 2006: 5)

In 1998, Recommendation No. R (98) 6 was passed, encouraging member states to promote widespread plurilingualism:

- by encouraging all Europeans to achieve a degree of communicative ability in a number of languages;
- by diversifying the languages on offer and setting objectives appropriate to each language;

- by encouraging teaching approaches at all levels that use a flexible approach – including modular courses and those which aim to develop partial competences – and giving them appropriate recognition in national qualification systems, in particular public examinations;
- by encouraging the use of foreign languages in the teaching of non-linguistic subjects (for example, history, geography, mathematics) and creating favourable conditions for such teaching;
- by supporting the application of communication and information technologies to disseminate teaching and learning materials for all national and regional languages;
- by supporting the development of links and exchanges with institutions and persons at all levels of education in other countries so as to offer to all the possibility of authentic experience of the language and culture of others;
- by facilitating lifelong learning through the provision of appropriate resources. (Council of Europe, 2006: 9)

The Council of Europe (together with the European Commission) first organized a European Year of Languages in 2001, involving forty-five countries, in a sustained effort to promote linguistic diversity and increased language-learning in order to respond to the "economic, social and cultural changes in Europe" (Council of Europe, 2006: 13). Since then, this has become an annual event.

Assessment

Besides promoting renewal in methodology and materials, the Council of Europe has developed several assessment instruments that are beginning to achieve recognition as member states become more familiar with them. These instruments are not standardized tests, since it would be impossible to produce parallel, comparative instruments across a wide variety of languages, but are intended to produce more transparent and more internationally comprehensible indications of what progress has been achieved after contact with a particular set of languages, including the first language.

The Common European Framework of Reference for Languages (CEFR) is an instrument to assist member states to develop policies for plurilingualism. It is a descriptive scheme which sets out what a competent language user has to do in order to communicate effectively and offers descriptors at six levels of proficiency, from the most basic, A1, to the highest, C2. These six levels describe what the learner can do in positive terms and how well the learner performs along the following criteria, which are presented here in summary form:

A1 Basic User – Breakthrough: Can understand and use familiar everyday expressions and very basic phrases aimed at the satisfaction of needs of a concrete type.

A2 Basic User – Waystage: Can understand sentences and frequently used expressions related to areas of most immediate relevance (e.g. very basic personal and family information, shopping, local geography, employment).

B1 Independent User – Threshold Level: Can understand the main points of clear standard input on familiar matters regularly encountered in work, school, leisure, and so on. Can deal with most situations likely to arise whilst traveling in the area where the language is spoken.

B2 Independent User – Vantage: Can understand the main ideas of complex text on both concrete and abstract topics, including technical discussions in his/her field of specialization. Can interact with a degree of fluency and spontaneity that makes regular interaction with native speakers quite possible without strain for either party. Can produce clear, detailed text on a wide range of subjects and explain a viewpoint on a topical issue giving the advantages and disadvantages of various options.

C1 Proficient User – Efficiency: Can understand a wide range of demanding longer texts, and recognize implicit meaning. Can express him/herself fluently and spontaneously. Can use language flexibly.

C2 Proficient User – Mastery: Can understand with ease virtually everything heard or read. Can summarize information from different spoken and written sources, reconstructing arguments and accounts in a coherent presentation. Can express him/herself spontaneously, very fluently, and precisely, differentiating finer shades of meaning even in more complex situations.

A *Manual* has been developed to assist member states, and national and international providers of examinations in relating their certificates and diplomas to the CEFR. To ensure that the reference levels as set out in the Common European Framework of Reference for Languages are interpreted in the same way by all language professionals, illustrations of these levels in a number of languages are being developed.

Several countries, for example, the Netherlands, have been working on how to calibrate their national examination and assessment materials to fit the Common European Framework of Reference. As familiarity with the matrix grows, more countries are looking into how to use this means of providing a transparent and coherent system of recognition of language skills.

The European Language Portfolio (ELP) is a further instrument intended to measure a person's contact with other languages. The European Language Portfolio has two functions, the first of which is to supplement certificates and diplomas awarded on the basis of formal examinations by allowing the owner to document language-learning that has taken place outside formal education. The terms of reference use the six proficiency scales of the Common European Framework for Languages. Its second aim is to foster the development of learner autonomy and the skills that support lifelong learning. The Portfolio has three components:

- *a language passport* that is regularly updated with a description of the owner's linguistic identity, language-learning achievement, and intercultural experience;
- *a language biography* that sets targets and monitors progress and outcomes;
- *an up-to-date dossier* with a selection of personal work that illustrates what the owner can do in languages other than the first. (Council of Europe, 2006: 15)

The application of the European Language Portfolio to different types of population has been validated for several countries, including Switzerland, the United Kingdom, Hungary, Portugal, the Netherlands, and Georgia.[2]

Reports on the introduction of the CEFR and the ELP are beginning to show the impact they are having as those involved – learners, teachers, administrators – adapt and familiarize themselves with the tools. It is apparent that merely referring to the Common European Frame of Reference does not guarantee the quality of outcomes, that employers and universities do not yet recognize or know how to interpret the tools, and that at present they are likely to function in parallel to national certification methods. Moreover, since the two assessment tools referred to only refer to language skills, they may not cover all aspects of bilingual education programs that deliver part of the content-matter curriculum through more than one language. On the other hand, the European Language Portfolio has been received very favorably by both pupils and teachers as it enabled the invisible factors in language-learning to be taken into account (learning styles, strategies applied), as well as building bridges between the individual dimension of language knowledge (the languages I know) and the group dimension (the languages in my class, my region, the world).

In the Val d'Aoste[3] region of Italy, learners particularly appreciated the fact that the portfolio belongs to them, and that it reveals all their linguistic skills in all the languages and dialects they know, not just those forming part of the school curriculum. The younger children appeared particularly enthusiastic, and involved their families in drawing up the biographical element of their language development. However, many users felt that the portfolio would have little value outside the school environment and would not be taken into account by future employers (Assessorat à l'Éducation et à la Culture, 2007).

Country profiles on plurilingualism
The Council of Europe also provides expertise to countries or regions that request help in critically assessing where they stand with respect to plurilingualism and how they can improve its development (Council of Europe, 2006: 15). To this end, the Council of Europe has produced a *Guide for the Development of Language Education Policies in Europe* (Council of Europe, 2003). It covers the whole of language education, including education in the "mother tongue / first language," official languages of the area in question, foreign, second, or minority languages. The *Guide* helps to analyze the strengths and weaknesses of a region's current language education policy, and to identify the non-linguistic and linguistic factors that may be involved.

Countries or regions in Europe who wish to analyze their own language-in-education policy can submit a self-evaluation to an expert team for analysis and discussion in collaborative dialogue. At no time are the Language Education Policy Profile and the subsequent experts' report considered an external evaluation for comparisons between countries: "It is a process of reflection by the authorities and involves civil society, together with Council of Europe experts who have the function of acting as catalysts" (Council of Europe, 2004: 16). The goal is to integrate all points of view in a description of the current situation and provide options for future developments. Armenia, Austria, Cyprus, Hungary, Ireland, Lithuania, the regions of Lombardy and the Val d'Aoste in Italy, Luxembourg, Norway, Poland, and

Slovenia are among those that have created country profiles. (For these and other language education policy profiles, see www.coe.int/t/dg4/linguistic/Profils1_EN.asp.)

European Charter for Regional or Minority Languages
At a more formal level of implementation, the Council of Europe has produced a European Charter for Regional or Minority Languages (Council of Europe, 1993), which was adopted by the Committee of Ministers of the Member States in 1992. The Charter aims to protect and promote regional or minority languages from a cultural perspective, emphasizing culture, and is not aimed at linguistic minorities as such, or their individual or collective rights. It is therefore not intended to support modifications of borders or problems of nationality, but is a realistic and measured means of alleviating the problems of minorities whose language represents a distinctive feature. The charter deliberately adopts an intercultural and plurilingual approach in which each category of language can find its rightful place. It also does not deal with the new languages present in Europe as a result of immigration. The Charter consists of two major sections, one of which covers general principles applicable to all regional or minority languages, the other covering a set of specific items on the role of these languages in the social life of a particular linguistic community. Individual states can select a certain number of dispositions from the list of alternatives proposed (a minimum of thirty-five sections from the specific items) in a supple combination which takes into account the varied contexts of the languages in question: for example, the number of speakers of a given language, or their degree of fragmentation or dispersal. Finally, the Charter contains a set of application criteria, which includes a committee of European experts, some with a legal background, whose task is to monitor implementation.

   Not all European countries have ratified this Charter. As of this writing, France has not, despite the presence of minority languages such as Euskara (Basque), Catalan, Dutch, German, and Occitan within its borders, and despite the support from the then President of the Republic and several ministers, on objections from the constitutional court. Nor has Ireland ratified the Charter, in spite of Irish being a threatened minority language, on the argument that Irish is constitutionally protected as the first official language of the Republic. Belgium, likewise, has not ratified the Charter, since its 1 percent of the population speaking German is constitutionally protected, with its own parliament and ministry of education, and therefore not considered as requiring further support. Estonia is still debating ratification because of reticence about the support it would give to the Russian language and the potential risk that the 32 percent Russian minority population would not learn the national language, as was the case in the past (Poleschuk and Helemäe, 2006).[4] On the other hand, and merely as examples, Denmark ratified the Charter in 1997 (Kühl and Pedersen, 2006) as did Finland in 1997 (Myntti and Nuolijärvi, 2006).

   Interestingly, Article 65 of the general section of the Charter clearly states that speakers of regional or minority languages are aware that for their own development it is necessary to know the state's official language, but that this should not impede support for the specific language of identity. Article 72 of the general principles also clearly states that the final goal is not to create complete equality between the regional or minority language and the state's official language, or to create linguistic ghettos, but to give the former as much support as is required for non-discrimination.

The major section of the Charter dealing with education, from which states that ratify the document can select a series of options, obliges the authorities to guarantee that the regional or minority languages are available at all the appropriate stages of the education system, leaving it to the organizers to decide whether to offer these languages merely as a subject or to use them as a medium in non-language content-matter.

The Charter represents a model initiative to lend support to linguistic communities (at least those indigenous to Europe) whose very existence is ever more threatened by modernization, globalization, and technological advances. This does not mean to say that its implementation, even in those countries that have ratified the Charter, is as efficient as could be desired. Some countries merely provide minimal instruction of the language as a subject, in compliance with the articles selected for ratification, but little more. An example is that of the United Kingdom, which in 2007 received a warning from the Council of Europe that it must do more to meet its obligations to protect its regional and stateless languages. The call comes as part of the Council of Europe's monitoring of the European Charter for Regional or Minority Languages, which came into force in the UK in July 2001. It commits the government to safeguard and promote Welsh, Scottish Gaelic, Irish, Scots, Ulster-Scots, Cornish, and Manx Gaelic. Hence, the very existence of the Charter, and the increasing number of countries considering ratification, is a welcome sign.

The European Commission

The European Commission of the European Union, based in Brussels, has a much stronger political mandate (stimulated by Resolutions from the European Parliament) than the Council of Europe, though the field of education and culture is less subject to controls from its headquarters than other areas. As of 2007, a Commissioner (the highest level of decision-taking within the European Union) has been nominated with a specific mandate to promote multilingualism. This Commissioner works mainly through consensual persuasion which is channeled through the member-state government experts, campaigns, workshops and conferences, the production of scientific reports, and the promotion of examples of good practice. Unlike other areas of European integration, education and language questions are the independent responsibility of the member states so there is no obligation to implement proposals emanating from the European headquarters. The Commission works informally in collaboration with the Language Policy Division of the Council of Europe so as to avoid duplication. Part of its budget is devoted to funding specific studies on language issues, some of which deal with bilingual education (see for example Grin and Moring, 2002; Euromosaic III, 2004).

The European Commission of the European Union has also offered financial support that goes to specialized centers, for example, the Mercator Network which groups three research and documentation centers specialized in the field of regional and minority languages in the European Union. Mercator Education focuses on minority-language education (www.mercator-education.org) which was recently renamed as Mercator European Research Centre on Multilingualism and Language Learning (www.mercator-research.eu); Mercator Legislation looks at minority language legislation (www.ciemen.org/mercator); and Mercator Media deals with minority language press and media (www.aber.ac.uk/mercator). The European Commission has also subsidized a resource center for teachers involved in bilingual education (see the European Content and Language Integrated Classroom website [EuroCLIC] at www.euroclic.net).

The Action Plan for Language Learning

In Barcelona in 2002, the heads of state and government of the then member states of the European Union requested the European Commission to produce an Action Plan on Education, stating that efforts should be made to improve the mastery of basic skills, in particular by teaching at least two foreign languages from a very early age, so as to help Europe "become the most competitive and dynamic knowledge-based economy in the world" by 2010 (Council of the European Union, 2004: 8).

The Action Plan (European Commission, 2003) emphasizes the encouragement of language-learning for all citizens, and the formulation of clear objectives for language-teaching at all stages of education (for more information, see http://ec.europa.eu/education/doc/official/keydoc/actlang/act_lang_en.pdf).

Primary emphasis is placed on:

- the promotion of the mother tongue and two other languages for all citizens (MT + 2);
- the promotion of linguistic diversity across Europe;
- the extension of different forms of bilingual education for a wide-ranging public.

In order to implement the Action Plan, a working group of experts designated by the Ministries of Education of the member states, together with experts from the pre-accession and associated states, met regularly to exchange information from their countries in five major areas:

- early language-learning;
- languages in secondary education;
- linguistic diversity in the education system;
- lifelong language-learning;
- the initial and in-service training of language teachers.

There is no attempt in any European policy document to promote a single lingua franca to the detriment of any indigenous European language. The position is clear: "Learning one *lingua franca* alone is not enough. Every European citizen should have meaningful communicative competence in at least two other languages in addition to his or her mother tongue. This is an ambitious goal, but the progress already made by several Member States shows that this is perfectly attainable" (European Commission, 2003: 10). To this end, it is important in policy to distinguish between laissez-faire and *vouloir-faire*, or between allowing things to take their course and intervening in a pro-active fashion. The warning given by Robert Phillipson that, "it would be dangerous for Europe to allow language policy to be left to *laissez faire* market forces" (Phillipson, 2003: 5), comes very much to the fore in the preoccupations of both the European Commission and the ministerial experts. "One can standardize commercial goods, but one cannot standardize people's identity" (Euromosaic III, 2004: p. iv). The authorities are well aware of the notion: "*Sous les paves des États Nations, la plage des parlers et des langues*" (Under the paving stones of the nation-states lies the beach of ways of speaking and languages) (Labrie, 1993: 38).

Other efforts

In the 1970s little attention was paid to the situation of regional and minority languages in Europe, but in the 1980s the importance of the first language as a symbol of cultural identity was stronger within Europe than among many communities outside Europe. In the 1990s policy-makers attempted to guarantee all citizens of the European Union a means of non-confrontational identity with the culture of their home countries. Indeed, the bilingual citizens of the European Union are recognized as having multiple identities, that of their home language and culture, and a wider identity on the regional, national, and European levels (Euromosaic III, 2004: p. iv).

In 2000, 47 percent of Europeans did not believe that the enlargement of the European Union would mean that a common language should be spoken. Around seven out of ten Dutch, Danes, and Finns think this way. Yet, 38 percent did believe Europeans would have to speak a common language, especially Italians (63%) and Greeks (45%). On the other hand, a majority (63%) believed that it is necessary to protect their own languages more, as the enlargement of the European Union is envisaged. This view is shared by 90 percent of the people in Greece and Finland, and three quarters of Portuguese, Spaniards, and Luxemburgers (Eurobarometer, 2000).

Given that linguistic diversity is one of the defining characteristics of the European Union, attempts are made, via a flexible approach to the concept of having everyone learn their mother tongue plus two additional languages (MT + 2), to reconcile the complexity of the linguistic reality with the positions each member state opts to defend (European Commission, 2002).

The information provided by member-state ministries experts reveals that support for linguistic diversity is proving one of the more difficult areas to address. At the eighth meeting of the language group (February 2004) mention was made of the necessity to take account of the fluctuating needs of migrant language groups, for example Rom.[5] A significant issue raised was the tension that exists between the desire to promote linguistic diversity on the one hand, and the need to guarantee continuity of language learning provision from primary to secondary education on the other, particularly in less densely populated areas and with ever greater mobility of children between school networks.

Eurydice, one of the European Commission's specialist organizations for information gathering and statistics, provides information on languages taught in over thirty European countries. (See the reports in www.eurydice.org/ressources/eurydice/pdf/0_integral/049EN.pdf.) A recent study of the available data on language teaching (Eurydice, 2005: 9–12) reveals the following:

- Throughout the countries, 8 percent of schoolgoers aged 15 claim to speak a language other than the language of instruction at home, with 0.7 percent as the proportion in the United Kingdom (Northern Ireland) and up to 34 percent in Flemish Belgium – the latter figure representing not only people of immigrant origin but also dialect speakers of standard Dutch.
- Almost all countries provide language-support measures for immigrant children, but this rarely goes beyond measures to strengthen the host country language and in many cases does not even consist of transitional bilingual education (for more information, see Eurydice, 2005).
- Throughout Europe compulsory teaching of another language is beginning at an increasingly early stage, and in several countries, such as Spain and Luxembourg, even in the first year of schooling. In the majority of countries half of all pupils in primary education (more in certain countries) learn at least one foreign language. In the majority of countries all pupils are offered the possibility of learning a minimum of two foreign languages during compulsory education, and in twenty countries they are even obliged to do so for at least one year (for more information, see Eurydice, 2005).
- The proportion of time allocated to foreign languages as a compulsory subject varies from 9 percent (Poland) to 34 percent (Luxembourg) of the total curriculum. English, French, German, Spanish, and Russian represent 95 percent of all foreign languages learned, and the dominant position of English in both primary and secondary education is becoming ever stronger. In thirteen European countries pupils are obliged to learn English during compulsory education, leading to a proportion of almost 90 percent learning the language at some time in their education. German and French share the position of second most taught language, depending on geographical location.

A major problem highlighted in many meetings is a pro-English public perception of language priorities. In many countries where English is favored as the first foreign language, this appears to work as a brake on the take-up of other languages, thereby countering the avowed policy goal of MT + 2. France and Germany, for example, indicate how popular demand for English impedes the encouragement of diversity, but if parents were guaranteed that English as a third language were offered on entry to secondary education, they could be persuaded of the advantages of linguistic diversity in primary education.

In order to promote linguistic diversity, member-state experts were invited to provide examples of what they themselves considered as illustrations of good practice, so as to inform others of initiatives taken in different countries. Below are a few illustrations:

Table 9.1   Illustrations of Good Practice

Country	Brief Description	Policy Impact
Austria	Promoting linguistic diversity at the primary level through the development of teaching materials for less widely used and learnt languages (e.g. neighboring, minority, migrant languages)	Awareness raising
France	Promotion of eight of the less popular languages for 11–15-year-olds via incentives (extra funding)	Diversity
Germany	*Spotkanie* project for stimulating cross-border languages (German–Polish) by encouraging contacts and exchange visits involving sixty-four schools	Neighboring languages

Bilingual Education: CLIL/EMILE

The promotion of some form of bilingual education has developed into one of the major preoccupations of the European Commission since the 1990s, thereby increasing awareness about its nature and potential, and gradually decreasing apprehensions and hostility. In the field of bilingual education highly varied initiatives have been and are being implemented.

Some form of bilingual education has long existed in certain parts of Europe. In Luxembourg bilingual education was established in 1843 (Davis, 1994) and trilingual education for the entire school population has been in place since 1913 (Berg, 1993). In Malta too, bilingual education has existed since the nineteenth century, while in Bulgaria the first bilingual upper-secondary school was founded in 1950 with considerable expansion since the 1960s. Similarly, in Estonia bilingual schooling has been a long-standing tradition since the 1960s. Germany began its first bilingual German–French schools in 1969 (Eurydice, 2006) and the multilingual European School network for the children of European civil servants was founded in 1953 (Swan, 1996).

CLIL/EMILE

The European Union has coined two acronyms intended to clearly distinguish European bilingual education efforts from other similar programs elsewhere (CLIL for Content and Language Integrated Learning and EMILE for *Enseignement d'une matière intégrée à une langue étrangère*). There are at least thirty-three different designations for some type of "bilingual education," which may be the term used in some countries but which tends to be avoided at the European level, given that in certain countries it has a negative connation. The term "immersion," though used in some countries, is not favored either, given that this tends to be associated with the Canadian efforts, whereas many of the European initiatives either pre-dated the immersion phenomena or were developed independently and with very different goals and methodologies. Luxembourg has no special designation for its trilingual system of education for all, since this is taken for granted as just the normal mode of education. The European initiatives grouped under the acronyms CLIL/EMILE take on varied forms. (European Commission, 2002; Marsh, 2002. For more information, see http://ec.europa.eu/education/policies/lang/teach/clil_en.html.)

CLIL is an umbrella term that embraces any type of program where a second language is used to teach non-linguistic content-matter. This generic term encompasses what already existed under different forms in many countries; it does not, however, cover language maintenance for minority or lesser-used languages, where the entire curriculum is given in these languages for their speakers, for example, Welsh-language schools in Wales for children where Welsh is the home language. Although non-native-speaker children may be present in such schools, thereby undergoing an early total immersion experience, the program itself is not considered as a CLIL initiative. Nor would children of immigrant language backgrounds undergoing a monolingual submersion experience in a mainstream language be considered as participating in a CLIL curriculum.

CLIL is envisioned as having a social-impact potential. A poignant illustration is the comment by a teenager in a technical school in Scotland who believed that language-learning was for intellectuals and not for more practically minded people such as himself. But after the introduction of a very modest form of CLIL, with a limited amount of learning of content matter through French, he claimed that the experience had "changed his life." He felt more confident in his own language learning capacities, discovered he could put the language to use in his immediate school environment, and was looking forward to travel and contact with native speakers.

This example is reinforced in Marsh, Marsland, and Stenberg's (2001) detailed practical guide based on VocTalk, a European Commission-supported initiative for teacher and institutional development programs aimed to introduce CLIL in vocational and professional education (secondary and tertiary) using electronic media and published materials. CLIL has brought about social and pedagogical changes, as it has promoted linguistic capacities, partial or advanced, for lifelong learning. As the European Commissioner Ján Fígel said: "Without lifelong learning there will be little lifelong earning."

CLIL and Canadian immersion

Although Canadian immersion research has had considerable influence on certain types of European bilingual education programs, it cannot be directly transferable to other social contexts. The European Commission (2002: 56) refers to this, stating:

> What has clearly been hugely successful and popular in Canada however does not necessarily transpose easily into European contexts [. . .]. Briefly, the Canadian context, unique as most contexts are, allowed immersion to flourish in an environment in which certain situational and operational variables were fairly constant. This was particularly the case in terms of pedagogical doctrine, supply of bilingual teachers, *homogeneity of language starting levels* and socioeconomic status of children (our italics).

A difference between many CLIL-type programs and Canadian immersion is in their goals. Full immersion offers intensive contact with the target language and aims for native or near-native competence, at least in receptive skills of comprehension and reading. However, many early total Canadian immersion pupils, even by the end of the program, continue to reveal striking grammatical inaccuracies in their speaking and writing (Hammerly, 1991; Swain, 1985). Most CLIL-type programs offer less intensive contact with the target language: instruction through the students' second language does not take extensive portions of curriculum time. CLIL-type programs aim at achieving a functional competence in both receptive and productive skills, particularly when the target language takes a low portion of curriculum time, as in vocational or professional training (Muñoz, 2002). The heavier CLIL programs, that is, those that use the students' second language in instruction for a significant portion of the curricular time, do produce very high productive and receptive skills, as witnessed in the interviews of learners in the information films produced for the European Commission – *Intertalk* (1998) and *CLIL for the Knowledge Society – Using Languages to Learn* (2006).

Another major difference is that, right from the beginning, CLIL programs have always tended to include the teaching of the target language as a subject parallel to its being used as a vehicle for content-matter learning, in order to enhance accuracy and to help assimilate the target language rules and norms. In many cases in secondary education, though not all, this involves different teachers who work in tandem, a language teacher and a subject teacher who conveys the content through the same language as that used by the language teacher. According to Wolff (2002), this two-pronged approach, whether supplied by one and the same teacher or not, provides a learning environment that is more authentic, both for content and interaction. The authentic material used for the content-matter subject relates to the real world, whereas the traditional language classroom tends to talk about pseudo-real and fictitious content.

An example from a communicative exercise in a traditional English-language lesson illustrates this point. The teacher asks students to sit in small groups and give their opinions in the foreign language on a subject such as "euthanasia." Setting aside the anecdote that some students might have misunderstood and thought that they should give opinions on "youth in Asia," it is doubtful that students would volunteer opinions on euthanasia even in their own language and in real life. Bringing the real world into the classroom may be difficult without authentic material (Marsh and Langé, 1999).

On the other hand, analyzing tables, maps, or diagrams in a geography lesson, or reading historical sources and discussing them in a history lesson help lead the learner to a certain degree of autonomy in using the second language, which is more difficult to achieve in a traditional second-language lesson. And as learners realize the relevance of some of the activities in the purely language lessons, this increases the motivation to acquire the language and then apply it in content-matter lessons. Many comments from teachers and learners involved in CLIL programs underline this heightened motivation aspect. A student explains: "CLIL is taking two birds with one stone" (*CLIL-AXIS*, 2006: 18).

An important feature of CLIL-type programs is that they place both language and non-language content on a continuum, without implying preference for one or the other. Both aspects have a joint curricular role by means of a variety of methods and this integrated approach has brought about considerable changes in general teaching practice, particularly in diminishing the role of frontal teaching and stimulating interactive group work.

The propagation of CLIL responds to the growing need for efficient linguistic skills, bearing in mind that the major concern is about *education*, not about becoming bilingual or multilingual, and that multiple language proficiency is the "added value" which can be obtained at no cost to other skills and knowledge, if properly designed. As Fishman (1989: 447) has said: "Bilingual education must justify itself philosophically as education."

Research

Research by Gajo and Mondada (2000) and Gajo and Serra (2002) has addressed the major questions recurrent in all debates about plurilingual education. Questions asked all over the world concern the following:

1. *The L1 problem*: Will the first language develop normally despite a significant amount of instruction time being conducted in another language?
2. *The L2 problem*: Will the second language really develop better if a significant amount of instruction time is conducted in it?
3. *The subject problem* (school knowledge): Does the second language complicate the subject learning and slow down progress in the curriculum subject?
4. *The sociopsychological problem*: Is bilingual education appropriate for all students?

Research has tended to produce findings answering questions 1, 3, and 4 in the affirmative, and question 2 in strong positive terms. Bilingual education in fact improves general language-learning and -teaching.

The latest trend of research focuses on question 3 (the content subject problem) and tries to ascertain whether bilingual education will provide added value in the form not only of greater second language proficiency, but also subject knowledge. The question can be reformulated as follows: *What is the impact of bilingual education on subject teaching and learning?* This question is fundamental, not only for learning issues, but also for educational policies. Bilingual education must have the support of, and commitment from, subject teachers who "lend" their discipline for language goals. These teachers have to develop new methods of teaching their subject. Language and subject must take advantage of each other for more general educational progress.

Gajo and Serra (2002) investigated the teaching of mathematics through a second language, French, to Italian pupils in the Val d'Aoste region of Italy. The assumption that underpinned this research, well established in the literature on bilingualism in education, was that any content or linguistic knowledge built up in the classroom is mainly elaborated through verbal interaction. Negotiation of meaning and of form promotes deep processing of the input. The scaffolding of basic cognitive operations, such as selecting information, making connections, mapping, and problem solving operations, has to be implemented by focusing on the language structures in the first and the second language that organize or underlie them (for more on this, see Chapters 13 and 14 on bilingual instructional practices). By investigating how mathematics was taught in a bilingual class and comparing the results with those in a monolingual class, Gajo and Serra (2002) found that overall the results were slightly more positive for the bilingual group, but that there were differences. The monolinguals and the bilinguals developed different ways of processing subject knowledge, the strength of the monolinguals being informational knowledge, while for bilinguals it is operational knowledge. Informational knowledge refers to the capacity to memorize knowledge, or "knowing that," while operational knowledge refers to the ability to transfer and apply knowledge to new situations, or "knowing how." Further studies have confirmed these findings, including investigations of children at the primary level as absolute beginners with the second language.

Interestingly, the Gajo and Serra study (2002) incidentally also improved mathematics teaching to monolingual groups as the teachers involved in the experimental comparisons became aware of the specific nature of the language of mathematics and paid more attention to making sure that the concepts were clearly understood, as was the case with those teachers working through the second language. Muñoz (2002) claims that using the second language as medium of instruction and communication makes the teacher more aware of the learners' linguistic needs, and it triggers tuned-in strategic language behavior (for example, teachers' strategies to make input comprehensible and context-embedded). Also, the need for constant comprehension checks on the part of the teacher results in high levels of communication both between teachers and learners, and among learners themselves. In this way, CLIL fosters *fluency* where typical foreign-language teaching tends to focus on accuracy.

Research on CLIL-type bilingual education in primary schools in the Val d'Aoste region of Italy has focused on measures of cognitive skills based on analyzing text materials in the strongest language, Italian, and the weaker target language, French. Certain, but obviously not all, logical and strategic measures revealed better results on the parallel tests in the second language than in the first language. For certain cognitive operations, for example, those that require identification of key points, there was no difference between first- and second-language scores. Measures requiring co-ordination of cognitive skills, such as sorting out and producing a hierarchy, and synthesizing materials, were stronger in the Italian first language. But in tasks that could not be immediately grasped, which were "more difficult" and required higher cognitive skills, results were paradoxically better in the French second language. In the Italian measures it appeared that the learners relied on general, global comprehension skills, leading to impressionistic reactions and less accurate responses. When working through the French materials they appeared to concentrate more on the detail, thereby providing more accurate results on the test questions (Assuied and Ragot, 2004).

What recent European investigations have taught us is to move away from the unilingual frame of reference in bilingual programs by underlining that *bilingualism is never an all-or-nothing phenomenon*, that the outcome of bilingual education is not a reduplication of monolingualism, but that it is a "more or less" proficiency in more than one language. And as the Luxembourg experience can testify, everyone can obtain some benefit from content-and-language integrated learning without expecting every schoolgoer to achieve the same level of high proficiency in several languages.

As investigation into CLIL-type programs progresses, research is looking into four aspects or principles that have been called the four Cs – content, communication, cognition, and culture/citizenship (Coyle, 2002: 27–8):

- *Content* – At the very heart of the learning process lies successful content or subject learning, and the acquisition of knowledge, skills, and understanding inherent to that discipline. As Coyle (2002: 27) says: "The symbolic relationship between language and subject understanding demands a focus on how subjects are taught whilst working with and through another language rather than in another language."
- *Communication* – Language is learned through using it in authentic and un-rehearsed yet "scaffolded"[6] situations to complement the more structured approaches common to foreign language lessons.
- *Cognition* – CLIL provides a setting for rich developing thinking skills in conjunction with both basic interpersonal communication skills (BICS) and cognitive-academic language proficiency (CALP) (Coyle, 2002).
- *Culture/citizenship* – CLIL provides an opportunity for students to operate in alternative cultures through studies in an alternative language. For Coyle (2002) this element is fundamental to fostering European understanding and making citizenship a reality.

As Dieter Wolff (2005) has said, CLIL is about "learning by construction, rather than learning by instruction."

Challenges

As enthusiasm for embarking on some type of CLIL program gathers momentum in Europe, several problems are being encountered, which may endanger successful expansion unless properly addressed. Among the challenges is that, apart from a small number of institutions in Austria, Germany, Italy, and England, there is very little specific training for teachers who combine language and content-matter, so that many teachers of CLIL/EMILE have learnt how to cope "on the job." One teacher said: "It's been hard work, and at the beginning I thought it was almost ridiculous, but then I began to feel good, sort of 're-vitalized' because after 15 years of teaching, this was a big leap in terms of professional development" (Marsh, Marsland, and Stenberg, 2001: 30). There is an inadequate supply of teachers with the necessary qualifications in both the subject-matter and the target language, except in Austria and Germany where all graduate teachers are expected to train to teach two subjects and many combine a language and a non-linguistic subject for their diplomas. The question of teacher language competence has been addressed in Finland (Nikula and Marsh, 1999) where it has been found that native-speaker-like com-petence is not necessarily the best qualification for CLIL programs, often because if the native speakers came from another country they are not familiar with the educational traditions or syllabus content of the country where the language is being used for part of the program. This can also be important for the culture/citizenship aspect of bilingual education. In many cases it has been found that subject teachers can cope adequately with the target language, even though they may not be the most fluent speakers of that language. Teachers are increasingly aware of this, as attested in the following four quotes:

> I was also worried about my language skills in doing CLIL until I realized that I didn't need to be a perfect model, like a native speaker. I don't think such perfection actually exists. (Marsh, Marsland, and Stenberg, 2001: 45)

> I personally have felt sometimes that my insufficient language skills have even encouraged the pupils. It is my aim to show that you do not always have to be a diamond to have the courage to try – glass can sparkle in a nice way sometimes too. (Marsh, Marsland, and Stenberg, 2001: 149)

> Words and beautiful speech in perfect sentences don't build bridges. (Marsh, Marsland, and Stenberg, 2001: 148)

> In CLIL the teachers provide the linguistic bricks and communication cement to get the student prepared for the "doing" side of his or her occupational expertise in later life. (Marsh, Marsland, and Stenberg, 2001: 37).

There is also an inadequate supply of teaching materials available, since foreign language materials produced abroad may not cover syllabus requirements in a different country, and may be linguistically too complex in the earlier stages of the program. Consequently, many teachers have to improvise their own materials.

The problem of assessment on the language side of the equation is an important area for implementers of CLIL programs, since although research findings may provide information of discrete and fragmentary types, schools often require standardized measurements which are easy to apply in order to regulate progress in the school curriculum. A teacher talks about the difficulties in using standardized measures to assess progress in CLIL: "We tried testing students who had gone through quite a lot of CLIL, and found big problems, not with the youngsters but with the tests. It's like the old joke about intelligence not being what intelligence tests measure! A language test needs to focus on the 'doing' part of how the student performs and not just the 'knowing'" (Marsh, Marsland, and Stenberg, 2001: 47). Another teacher talks about the problem of using standardized measures before the student gets into the program: "Some of the students who got a lot out of CLIL would never have been accepted onto the programme if they had been language tested beforehand" (Marsh, Marsland, and Stenberg, 2001: 117).

Assessment specifically attuned to taking bilingual education into account is problematic (see more on this in Chapter 15). Most countries apply monolingual exit criteria, which fail to take the bilingual program into account, or even insist on national, monolingual examinations which in fact negate the spirit and essence of the bilingual program pupils have followed. In Britain one school has succeeded in negotiating the right to present part of the secondary school exit examination (GCSE) in the foreign language in which the subject was taught, but this is exceptional. In the Netherlands the very authorities that support content-matter instruction in a foreign language also insist that final examinations be presented in Dutch.

The German *Länder*, or states, that promote bilingual programs, require the ability to handle content-matter in both German and the foreign language. However, assessments focus on accurate knowledge of the content-matter, but allow infelicities in the target language. Successful manipulation of the foreign language receives a special mention on exit certificates as a bonus. There may well be very cogent reasons for the different policies with regard to certification, but it is clear that careful consideration of the link between bilingual secondary programs and exit criteria is required. Inconsistencies between language of examination and language of instruction could well be a major stumbling block to the expansion of bilingual education, though it seems reasonable to expect those undergoing bilingual education to be able to handle the knowledge acquired in the language of their environment.

The rapid expansion of CLIL education can lead to less than satisfactory results if the necessary precautions are not taken. As Kaplan and Baldauf (1997: 134) state:

> Many teachers may be uncomfortable with a new methodology because they do not understand the theoretical assumptions upon which it is founded, or because the assumptions underlying it contradict the ways in which they were trained, or because the method differs from the way they learned the target language, which they know by definition works, or simply because the exemplary materials for the new methodology are poorly constructed.

This may well result in a teacher trying hard to satisfy certification requirements, building up an excellent rapport with the class, creating an illusion of producing the results proposed in the bilingual classroom, yet failing to integrate the language and content learning in any useful, productive fashion. The result may be that the use of the other language in content-matter subjects actually stimulates "reactive" rather than "active" pupil output, slot-filling reactions to teacher questions, and minimal genuine use of the target language.

In an analysis of bilingual classrooms in Brunei, where all children undergo bilingual education in Malay and English, Martin (1997) illustrated a case where a fifty-minute geography lesson in English produced the following pattern: thirty-five one-word responses, four two-word responses, three nods of the head, one shake of the head, one inaudible response, and one attempt with no response – not a single sentence was produced by a child in the lesson!

Similar misapplications of teaching strategies determined by bilingual programs have been noted elsewhere. For example, teachers have been informed that limited code-switching could be tolerated as a short-cut to lexical precision in the early stages of bilingual content-matter learning. But an analysis of actual classroom practice revealed how a misunderstanding of this tolerance led a teacher to use the stronger first language for all explanations and the target second language for labeling new concepts; in other words, without being aware of it, the teacher was teaching the content mainly through the first language and providing a word-list in a second language, yet was under the illusion that he was providing content and language integrated instruction (Baetens Beardsmore, 1999).

The problems inherent to mainstreaming attempts of what, until now, are still mainly exceptional programs have not discouraged European policy-makers who have supported many international conferences. During the Luxembourg Presidency of the Council of the European Union, the Ministry of Education hosted a symposium entitled "The Changing European Classroom – the Potential of Plurilingual Education" (March 2005). At this conference, chief stakeholders from the education world throughout the European Union examined ways in which the study of non-linguistic subjects, such as history, geography, or biology, and the acquisition of vocational skills through a second language, could increasingly be incorporated in the member states' education and training.

Another initiative was the "Conference on Regional and Minority Languages in Education Systems," held in Brussels in 2006 (March 27–8) aimed to give an official European Union boost to some form of bilingual education for the highly diversified groups targeted. Colin Baker provided the most striking conclusion to this meeting when he asked the question: "Is any child not educated bilingually in Europe being disadvantaged?" (2006b).

Conclusion

In contrast to the previous chapter which discussed the at times tolerant, at times restrictive, language policy in the United States, this chapter presents recent policy efforts by two supra-national bodies of the European Union – the Council of Europe and the European Commission – to promote bilingualism in its plurilingual dimensions. Although these initiatives support bilingual education in majority and minority languages, the languages of immigrants are not included.

This chapter also focuses on the major educational policy innovation of recent years in Europe, that is, the promotion of CLIL/EMILE for all European students. The chapter discusses CLIL programs, their efficacy, as well as the challenges in adopting this educational approach to teach all children in the European Union.

Questions for Reflection

1. Compare the language policies of the U.S. discussed in Chapter 8 with those of the European supra-national institutions in this chapter. What are the similarities and/or differences? How do European language policies differ from those in the context in which you live or work?
2. How can the ideologies that impact on language policy in Europe be interpreted? What are the differences with the United States?
3. What are the similarities and/or differences between the CLIL/EMILE programs in Europe and the current bilingual education programs in the U.S.?
4. What are the possible educational implications of the language policies in Europe for classroom teachers, practitioners, and scholars?

Further Reading

Baetens Beardsmore, H. (ed.) (1993) (ed.). *European Models of Bilingual Education*. Multilingual Matters, Clevedon.

Beacco, J.C., and Byram, M. (2004). *Guide for the Development of Language Education Policies in Europe: From Linguistic Diversity to Plurilingual Education*. Council of Europe, Language Policy Division, Strasbourg. Available at www.coe.int/t/dg4/linguistic/default_en.asp.

Cenoz, J., and Genesee, F. (1998). *Beyond Bilingualism. Multilingualism and Multilingual Education*. Multilingual Matters, Clevedon.

Council of Europe (2006). *Plurilingual Education in Europe: 50 Years of International Cooperation*. Council of Europe, Language Policy Division. Strasbourg. Available at www.coe.int/t/dg4/linguistic/Source/PlurinlingalEducation_EN.pdf.

Coyle, D., and Baetens Beardsmore, H. (eds.) (2007). "Research on Content and Language Integrated Learning (CLIL)." *International Journal of Bilingual Education and Bilingualism* 10(5) (Special issue).

Extra, G., and Gorter, D. (2001). *The Other Languages of Europe: Demographic, Sociolinguistic and Educational Perspectives*. Multilingual Matters, Clevedon.

Holt, M., and Gubbins, P. (eds.) (2002). *Beyond Boundaries. Language and Identity in Contemporary Europe*. Multilingual Matters, Clevedon.

Phillipson, R. (2003). *English-Only Europe? Challenging Language Policy*. Routledge, London.

Important Websites

CILT (Centre for Information of Language Teaching and Research) (UK) www.cilt.org.uk/
Council of Europe. Language Policy Division www.coe.int/t/dg4/linguistic/default_EN.asp
European Bureau for Lesser Used Languages www.eblul.org/
European Centre for Modern Languages www.ecml.at
Eurydice www.eurydice.org/portal/page/portal/Eurydice
Mercator www.mercator-central.org/

10

Monoglossic Bilingual Education Policy

Bilingüe es mejor, porque si no entiendes inglés, cómo te van a enseñar?
(Bilingual is better because if you don't understand English, how are they going
to teach you?)

U.S. Latino fifth-grader girl, Trinity School,
New Rochelle, NY, October 2007

The more languages you know the better and better.

Fifth-grader girl, U.S.

Overview

In this chapter, we will discuss monoglossic bilingual education policies and
programs:

- Policies for transition: transitional BE:
  - the United States;
  - Indigenous peoples;
  - Latin America;
  - Sub-Saharan Africa;
  - China;
  - the Foyer Project in Brussels.
- Policies for maintenance and enrichment of minorities: maintenance BE:
  - Indigenous peoples;
  - U.S. Latinos;
  - community schools;
  - Western Thrace;
  - Sønderjylland/Nordschleswig.

- Policies for enrichment of social elite: prestigious BE:
  - all-day private bilingual schools;
  - international schools.
- Policies for enrichment of majorities: immersion BE:
  - Quebec and immersion;
  - other contexts.

Introduction

Chapters 8 and 9 reviewed language policy in education in the United States and the European Union. This chapter and the next move beyond the United States and Europe and consider other international contexts. But in so doing, Chapters 10 and 11 make evident how bilingual education is a form of language planning, as well as how the sociopolitical and sociocultural contexts shape these efforts. Chapters 10 and 11 do not provide an exhaustive treatment of bilingual education efforts by country. Instead, they give examples of how different groups (national, supranational, social, ethnolinguistic, cultural) have planned for the bilingualism and multilingualism of their children by developing different types of bilingual education programs.

All education programs, including bilingual ones, are a result of choices that political authorities or social groups make in educating their children. Every society or group has to choose languages of instruction and is therefore involved in some kind of language planning. As Fettes (2003: 13) says:

> The choice of [. . .] languages of instruction in schools presupposes the existence of language varieties suitable for the task. [. . .] such a language of instruction is expected to be highly standardized (so that many different schools can use the same curricular and human resources) and both prestigious and widely used (so that education promotes economic mobility and intergroup communication). These are not "natural" characteristics for any language; *they are the result of the more-or-less conscious influence of various powerful groups and institutions on sociolinguistic norms.* In its most conscious, explicit and rationalized form, such influence is known as *language planning* (our italics).

If monolingual schools have to choose a language of instruction, bilingual schools have to do the same for two or even more languages, as well as the varieties of those languages. This means that the possibility of varieties of programs is amplified, as different social groups, regions, states, and families make choices. And despite the fact that bilingual education may give more options than monolingual education, it is still the purview of school, an institution whose major role is to influence sociolinguistic norms. Language-in-Education Policy (LiEP), whether enacted by states, families, or educators, is important because using a language as medium of instruction may raise its status and expand its corpus, as new language users come about and new language uses evolve (King and Benson, 2004).

All countries make language education policies for the teaching and assessment of official or national languages, as well as, at times, of other languages. Sometimes those policies are enacted *from the top down*,[1] with the official educational authorities mandating curricula, assessment, and even books and methodology throughout all or part of a given territory. At other times they grow *from the bottom up*, with parent pressure groups or local authorities making decisions about curricula, the educational resources used to teach their children, and the ways of assessing their learning; all, of course, in negotiation with the region or state (Hornberger, 1996). Yet at other times, language education policies grow *from side to side*, with educational experiments and projects, often funded externally, impacting on and modifying over time, national or official educational programs (Dutcher, 2004).[2] We purposely include and mix in this chapter and the next, bilingual education efforts espoused by *national policies* with *local efforts* that sometimes go against established policies and accepted practices. And yet, it is the state and their corresponding national policies that provide most of the organizational framework for this chapter.

We look at different *bilingual education planning and policies* efforts. We discuss these policies and attempts in the context of states because education is mostly in their hands. However, the policy is occasionally discussed in the context of its implementation for a specific group, for example, the Deaf or the Rom (Roma). We consider how each context, in implementing a policy, has adopted (and most times adapted) specific types of bilingual education. Many of the policies roughly correspond to types of bilingual education, but not always. *The two chapters are not an exhaustive treatment of language policy and planning in education around the world or by all ethnolinguistic groups.* We start out by describing a well-known social context, sometimes a state or a geographical region, sometimes the local effort of a group. We follow the first example with other examples as a way to illustrate how bilingual education policy is carried out by *many actors* – sometimes by the region or state, other times by the community itself; sometimes led by the interests of the majority, other times of the minority, and at times of both.

We have organized these two chapters according to bilingual education policies that parallel the frameworks of bilingual education considered in Chapter 6. The reader is warned, however, that sometimes bilingual education policies as enacted by states or willed by ethnolinguistic groups or communities of parents do not correspond neatly to types of bilingual education. It is also not possible to assign only one bilingual education policy to a specific society. Different actors in the same society or the same ethnolinguistic group may have different wishes for the education of their children, and the types of bilingual programs developed are therefore different even in the same local context.

In this chapter, we include examples of bilingual education policies that emanate from *monoglossic beliefs and practices* that view the multiple languages of bilinguals in isolation from each other. Thus, all these bilingual education types fall under a Subtractive Theoretical Framework or Additive Theoretical Framework, as displayed in Table 10.1:

Table 10.1   Language Policies and Bilingual Education Types: Monoglossic Beliefs

Language Policies	Bilingual Education Types
Subtractive Theoretical Framework	
Policy for transition to a dominant or colonial language	Transitional
Additive Theoretical Framework	
Policy for maintenance and enrichment of language minorities	Maintenance
Policy for enrichment of social elite	Prestigious
Policy for enrichment of language majorities	Immersion

Policy for Transition: Transitional Bilingual Education

Although these bilingual education policies promote the transition to a majority or colonial language, it is most important to point out that they also provide a respite from ineffective monolingual education for powerless language minorities. Dutcher (2004), speaking of the developing world and of education through English, has remarked that *there are no examples in the world of a language of wider communication, English or any other, being successful in educating children of underserved groups.* When children are taught exclusively in a language they do not understand, that is, in a foreign language, they cannot learn. They sit in classes without understanding. They are not promoted, and soon drop out (Dutcher, 2004). (For insightful examples of how this happens, see Martin [2005] for rural schools in Malaysia, and Bunyi [2005] for schools in Kenya.) Thus, although the programs that these transitional bilingual education policies support are only temporary and promote transition to a majority language, *they are useful pedagogical approaches to the education of language minorities.*

The United States[3]

No country has had more deliberate educational policies in transitioning their immigrant, refugee, and Native American populations to monolingualism as the United States. As we have seen in Chapter 8, in 1968 and as a result of the increased ethnic consciousness that came about in the Civil Right Era, Title VII of the Elementary and Secondary Education (the Bilingual Education Act) was passed. It supported the use of the child's home language in education until s/he gained English proficiency.

August and Hakuta (1998: 19–20) define transitional bilingual education in the United States by saying: "[English-language learners] receive some degree of instruction through the native language; however, the goal of the program is to transition to English as rapidly as possible, so that even within the program, there is a *rapid shift* toward using primarily English" (our italics). Transitional bilingual education is the program that has been most frequently used throughout the United States to teach immigrants,[4] especially recently arrived Latino students. The program attempts to assimilate children linguistically as early as possible. Typically, there are many kindergarten and first-grade transitional bilingual education class-rooms, with children quickly transferred to monolingual classrooms by the third grade. In the upper grades, as well as in middle and secondary schools, most stu-dents in transitional bilingual education are recently arrived immigrants, although there always remain some who, because of issues other than those of second-language development, fail to pass the language proficiency examinations required to enter monolingual classrooms. As a specialized program serving only immigrant mono-lingual students who are mostly immigrant students of color, it is easy to under-stand how children and teachers in these programs become stigmatized, often relegated to the basement of the school building or to portable units in the school grounds (for more on the inequities surrounding the education of language minority children in the United States, see García, Kleifgen, and Falchil, 2007).

Transitional bilingual education programs are mostly of the *early exit* kind requir-ing that children be transferred out of the program within three years. Although the early exit programs are the ones supported by the U.S. Federal Government, research has shown that children in late exit programs (those in which children stay throughout their elementary years or for a minimum of five years)[5] score higher in English, as well as other academic subjects (Ramirez, 1991; Thomas and Collier, 1997, 2002). In recent years, Late Exit Transitional Bilingual Education programs have become almost non-existent, as Federal regulations in the United States have required that immigrant children be assessed and transferred to mono-lingual instruction after three years in a bilingual education program.[6]

As we said in Chapter 8, despite the limitations of transitional bilingual education programs, these programs provide immigrant children with support and familiarity in an educational context that is foreign to them (García, 2006b; Hernández-Chávez, 1978). The often-used alternative, providing immigrant students with instruction in English only, is not in any way an improvement. The bilingualism that English-only schooling develops, as students acquire English, is not superior to that acquired in bilingual programs. In fact, as we have argued in Chapter 8, transitional bilingual education programs have been found to be more effective in educating language minority students than English-only programs (see Thomas and Collier, 2002; Willig, 1985). And the insistence that educators not use the most effective pedagogical resource in initial second-language acquisition – the language in which student can make meaning – robs students and educators of educational possibilities.[7]

For example, one transitional bilingual education program that supports the students' transition to English as they educate effectively is the one in the Dr. Sun Yat Sen Middle School, IS 131 in Chinatown, New York. Working with teachers, Danling Fu (2003) has developed writing practices that allow students to trans-language in writing as they develop English proficiency. Says Fu (2003: 79): "writing in their first language enabled these new immigrant students to express what was deep in their hearts and helped them make the transition into this new world, but it also gave them a personal meaning for their school learning." Fu (2003: 74) explains the importance of using the child's first language, if only for a short time:

> If we let our students express themselves and present their ideas in their primary language, we give them opportunities to continue the development of their thinking.

With this development uninterrupted, they are able to write well in a second language once they develop proficiency in it. If we let them wait until their English is good enough, their thinking and writing skills will not only have stopped developing but will have diminished – especially damaging for those students who don't yet have good writing skills in their first language.

The following text boxes offer some descriptions of transitional bilingual education programs in the United States:

La Esperanza Middle School, San Pablo, California

Upon entry into the school, students' language skills are assessed; students whose proficiency in English is limited are placed in bilingual classrooms. In the first two grades, bilingual classes provide early reading instruction in Spanish, and teach mathematics, social studies, art, and so on in Spanish, but they also include intensive instruction in oral and written English. In grades 3 and 4, children learn to read English and are instructed in their other subjects in a mixture of Spanish and English. By the fifth grade, reading in Spanish has been phased out, and most of the instruction in other subjects is conducted in English. In fact, with some exceptions, Mexican American and Anglo fifth-graders are integrated into the same classrooms and taught by the same teachers, most of whom are monolingual English speakers.

In Bull, Fruehling and Chattergy, 1992: 60–1

Malden, MA High School, Cantonese Chinese Bilingual Program

The Cantonese transitional bilingual program in my high school [. . .] offers content courses such as math, science, and social studies in Cantonese [. . .] My students also take English-as-a-Second-Language classes, and as their English proficiency improves, they begin to be partially mainstreamed – that is, they take some content classes with monolingual English teachers and some with me.

In Kwong, 2000: 44

Indigenous peoples

Most bilingual education programs for Indigenous peoples are still of the transitional kind. For example, in Canada, since the 1960s, the Northwest Territories of Canada have used Athapaskan and Inuktitut in teaching. The purpose of these programs has been to teach in the Indigenous languages whilst English is fully acquired. But children are mainstreamed into English classes as they reach higher grades. Despite the transition, these transitional bilingual education programs are more beneficial than monolingual education.

In the remote province of Ratanakiri in northwest Cambodia, there are villages where children have never had any education. Although 90 percent of the population of Cambodia are Khmer, the children speak minority languages of the Mon-Khmer group, especially Tampuen and Kreung. In 2003, a three-year program of bilingual education was piloted, a result of the cooperation between the Cambodian Ministry of Education, Youth and Sport, and CARE (Noorlander, Samal, and Sohout, 2003). School boards have been established by the communities following traditional decision-making processes and teachers have been trained. The same year (2003), the Draft Law for Education was passed, giving language minorities the right to use their languages in school. The law states: "The Khmer language will be the official language of instruction in public schools. The ethnic minority peoples have the right to use their own language in the public schools for at least primary grades 1 and 2" (Chapter 7, Article 44, p. 61, as cited in UNESCO, 2005: 19).

In Australia, when European colonization began in 1788, there were 300,000 Aboriginal people speaking about 260 languages. Fifty ancestral languages are still spoken today in the sparsely populated northern and central areas. The largest ancestral language, Yolngu Matha, has about 3,000 speakers. Still approximately 150,000 indigenous Australians speak Aboriginal English, and 20,000 use Kriol, an Indigenous Creole (Harris, 1990).

Bilingual Education started in the Northern Territory of Australia in 1973 with four schools that followed a transitional bilingual education model. The Aboriginal language was used half the time in school, and it decreased from pre-school to Year 7, while use of English increased from 10 percent of the time in Year 1 to 80 percent of the time after Year 5 (Harris and Devlin, 1997).

From 1990 on, these schools increasingly came under aboriginal control and more aboriginal teachers were hired. A slogan of "two-way" or "both ways" schooling demanding equal time for the two languages from Year 1 to 7 was adopted (Harris, 1990). In the beginning, these bilingual education programs followed traditional forms, but soon more dynamic language use was accepted. Harris and Devlin (1997: 12) explain: "For a time White academics debated whether code-switching threatened language maintenance, but with increased Aboriginal control this has become less of an issue." This is an important statement for what it says about the flexible use of languages in schools with language minorities. We will return to this topic in Chapter 12.

Indigenous language minorities are slowly being granted the right to an education in their language (see for example UNESCO, 2005, for the situation in Asia). The fact that there are many examples of bilingual education efforts of Indigenous peoples under either planning for maintenance in this chapter or planning for revitalization in the next, is evidence of their renewed strength, interconnectedness, and determination to revitalize their languages.

Latin America

In Latin America there are over 30 million Indigenous peoples who speak one of over 1,000 autochthonous languages. For example, in Bolivia 62 percent and in

Guatemala 41 percent of the population use Indigenous languages (López, 2006). Except in Paraguay, and despite recent efforts to officialize them, the Indigenous languages of Latin America remain marginalized.

It was the conquerors themselves who first started to use the languages of the Indigenous population to teach. Spanish clerics resorted to those Indigenous languages believed to be "more general," *lenguas generales,* to transmit the Catholic faith and evangelize them, as they promoted *castellanización,* or the teaching of the Spanish language with the subsequent suppression of the mother tongue (García, 1999; López, 2006; Valdiviezo, 2006).

It was not until the 1970s that Latin America started to acknowledge its Indigenous languages. For example, in Peru, a National Bilingual Education Policy was passed in 1972 promoting *bilingual education of a transitional kind.* The law stated: "[There is] a need to overcome the present violent Hispanicization and disparagement of the aboriginal languages by means of the system of bilingual literacy teaching as a preliminary process to *easier, more sure and permanent Hispanicization* and the understanding and recognition of the cultural patterns of each group" (quoted in Hornberger, 1988: 24) (our italics). In Puno, Peru, a bilingual education program, *PEB-P,* was implemented in 1977 (Hornberger, 1988) for Quechua speakers. Funded by the German technical assistance agency GTZ (Deutsche Gesellschaft für Technische Zusammenarbeit), the PEB-P folded in 1991 when the government could not maintain the efforts nor scale it up nationally.

The advent of Intercultural Bilingual Education programs in the late twentieth century aimed to recognize the *rights of Native populations,* especially with regards to language and culture, and to foster cross-cultural understanding (Hornberger, 1996; King, 2001; López, 2005; López, 2006). In fact, the selection of the term "intercultural" over "multicultural" pointed to renewed efforts to shape and educate the entire population, Indigenous and non-Indigenous, to each other's ways. Since the 1990s and democratization, eleven countries – Argentina, Bolivia, Brazil, Colombia, Ecuador, Guatemala, Mexico, Nicaragua, Paraguay, Peru, and Venezuela – have passed laws recognizing their multiculturalism and multilingualism. Especially the Andean countries with significant Indian populations – Ecuador, Bolivia, and Peru – have developed intercultural bilingual education programs. However, these efforts often still depend on sponsor organizations from abroad and most programs are of a transitional kind.

In Guatemala, 5 out of 12 million Guatemalans speak a Mayan language and most of the population is bilingual in one or more Mayan languages and Spanish. In 1991, the Educational Law acknowledged the right of Guatemalan Indigenous peoples to education in their mother tongue, and in 2003 a National Language Act was passed. There are around 1,200 primary schools offering an early transitional bilingual education especially in the first three grades, with Spanish-only education by grades 4 or 5. It is important to remember, however, that Guatemalan Indian children do not go to school beyond grades 3 or 4, so the issue of *whether bilingual education is transitional or not does not really apply* (López, 2006). The Mayan Indigenous movement has been implementing its own Mayan educational model (Ogulnick, 2006), stressing traditional Mayan knowledge, philosophy, spirituality, and community involvement, and providing more maintenance bilingual education.

Only 40 percent of the people of Bolivia are Spanish monolinguals; there are approximately 1.5 million Aymara speakers and slightly over 2 million Quechua speakers (López, 2006). The Bolivian Reform of 1994 focused on changing the entire educational system to recognize the country's own interculturality. The law also requires Spanish-speakers to learn an additional Indian language. The development of *intercultural bilingual education* in Bolivia, especially the efforts of the Indigenous population, or the *población originaria* (founding or original, as they prefer to be called) has been studied by López (2006). In reality, and despite the election in early 2006 of Evo Morales Aima, the first Indian president, the bilingual education programs remain transitional in nature, and few monolingual Spanish speakers of European descent are learning Aymara or Quechua.

Unlike Bolivia, Peru conceptualized intercultural bilingual education simply as a model for the education of Indian people, not including those of European descent (López, 2005). In 1979, the Peruvian Constitution officialized Quechua and Aymara and declared in Article 35: "The State promotes the study and knowledge of the aboriginal languages. It guarantees the right of Quechua, Aymara and other communities to receive primary education in their own tongue" (quoted in Hornberger, 1988: 30). The new constitution of 1993 declared the state's obligation to promote intercultural and bilingual education depending on the character of each region.

Ecuador, declaring itself a multinational state in its constitutional reform of 1998, developed an intercultural bilingual education policy focusing only on using Indigenous languages while having the Indian population learn Spanish, and resulting in more bilingual education programs.

In introducing Quechua into the schools of Bolivia, Peru, and Ecuador, a battle over the standardization of Quechua has been ongoing between those who want to use the *auténtico*, spoken by elderly and rural dwellers, and those who want the *unificado*, promoted by educators. With 8 to 12 million Quechua-speakers throughout Peru, Bolivia, Ecuador, Argentina, Colombia, and Chile, there are many varieties of the language (Hornberger and Coronel-Molina, 2004). The issue of whether Quechua should be written with five vowels as in Spanish, or with three vowels has been most important in all discussions (Valdiviezo, 2006). Standardization of Quechua seems inevitable and necessary for its use in mass education. And yet, Luykx (2000) has warned that this standardization undermines the meaningful use of Quechua in schools because it distances it from its speakers. The Quechua spoken by people today has much Spanish-language influence and differs greatly from the traditional Quechua of the past.

In Latin America, only Paraguay seems to have truly gone beyond transitional bilingual education in its intercultural bilingual education efforts. A landlocked country, Paraguay was not ravaged by Spanish Conquerors. As such, it remained a stronghold of Guaraní, the language spoken by the Indigenous population. But the Jesuit Missions established in the 1600s ensured that Spanish was learned as a way to learn the lessons of Catholicism. Today, Paraguay is officially bilingual and at least half of the population, most of whom are descendants of the Indigenous population, is also bilingual in Spanish and Guaraní. Until 1973, Paraguay had an exclusively Spanish-only system of education, but in that same year, the Educational Reform recommended a controversial *transitional bilingual education* program that used Guaraní for the first three years in rural areas to facilitate the students' transition to study in Spanish (Corvalán, 1989). Twenty years later, the Banco Interamericano de Desarrollo (1993) still recommended transitional bilingual education and the development of reading ability in Jopará, a form of Guaraní characterized by code-switching, code-mixing, and/or language borrowing from Spanish, that is, translanguaging that reflects its strong bilingualism.

Paraguay, however, has ambitions of more developmental kinds of bilingual education. As early as 1974, Paraguay implemented the study of Guaraní as a subject in the first three years of secondary education. And the New Educational Reform of 1992 requires the teaching of Spanish and Guaraní in the educational curriculum with the purpose of proficiency and literacy in both languages. For the first time in the history of Paraguay, Guaraní has started to serve as a language of instruction in the regular educational system, although the standardization of written Guaraní continues to be controversial (Corvalán, 1989). According to Corvalán (2000) the major problem in the provision of adequate bilingual education lies in the difference between national requirements imposing one variety of Guaraní over another and local needs and uses.

When linguists started to work on *corpus planning*, the issue of which variety of Guaraní to select for school came to the forefront. Guaraní had changed much in the centuries in which it had not been standardized or used in any official function. So it turned out that the original Guaraní which linguists wanted to use in education had little to do with the ways in which Guaraní-speakers languaged. The controversy means that there are insufficient Guaraní language educational materials to be used by teachers. It has also left many feeling that their Guaraní practices are not authentic, are not real, are not correct, leading to greater linguistic insecurity.

Sub-Saharan Africa[8]

As a result of the Phelps B. Stokes reports (see Jones, 1922, 1925) the British colonial education system recommended using African indigenous languages at the lower levels of primary education in ways that resemble today's transitional bilingual education. The *Memorandum on Education Policy in British Tropical Africa* of 1925 (referred to in Phillipson, 1992: 118), laid down principles of African education among which were a focus on African languages, and that "education should be adapted to the mentality, aptitudes, occupations, and traditions of the various peoples, conserving as far as possible all sound and healthy elements in the fabric of their social life."

The 1953 UNESCO resolution giving it as axiomatic that children be taught to read in their home language propelled the experimentation with transitional bilingual education throughout Africa in colonial times. The resolution stated: "pupils should begin their schooling through the medium of the mother tongue because they understand it best and because to begin their school life in the mother tongue will make the break between home and school as small as possible." In postcolonial situations, European languages generally continue to be preferred as media of instruction (Bamgbose, 2000; Mazrui, 2004; Vavrus, 2002). Africa continues to struggle with the legacy of colonialism in education. As Ngugi wa Thiong'o (1986: 17) has said: "The language of an African child's formal education was foreign. The language of the books he read was foreign. Thought in him took the visible form of a foreign language."

In the 1970s and 1980s some African countries, with external support, experimented successfully with transitional bilingual education. Perhaps the best known example is that of Nigeria. The Nigerian state of Ife, with funding from the Ford Foundation, started to use Yoruba in 1970 in all levels of primary education. The results of the IFE Primary Education Research project were very encouraging (Afolayan, 1976), although the project ended in 1978 when funding stopped. The 1977 National Policy on Education, officialized the use of African indigenous languages in pre-primary education, although in practice much remains to be done.

In Africa today, even when indigenous African languages are used, they are often limited to the first primary grades, usually grades 1 to 3, and to adult literacy programs (Bamgbose, 1991, 2000). Thus, most bilingual education programs in Africa focus on the eventual transition to a former colonial language. It is important to underline that the use of students' home languages, even in primary grades, is not by any means universal throughout Africa, and that transitional bilingual education is an important, albeit still limited, pedagogical tool. And we would be remiss if we did not point out that even after mother-tongue instruction has stopped, African classrooms display much multilingualism, as the children continue to speak and answer in languages other than the one selected as medium of instruction.

In Kenya, Ghana, and Malawi, English is the sole medium of instruction after the first three years of school. In Uganda, Zambia, and Nigeria, English is used as medium of instruction after four years of primary school, although English is taught as a subject from the start. Tanzania, Lesotho, Ethiopia, and Somalia introduce English as a medium of instruction at the start of secondary school.

Kenya, with over forty different indigenous languages, the majority belonging to the Bantu family, developed a language education policy that uses "the language of the catchment area" (the school's neighborhood) as a medium of instruction in the first three years of primary education, when English, which is studied as a subject from the beginning, becomes the sole medium of instruction. Kiswahili is taught as a subject throughout school (Bunyi, 1997). In looking at the teaching of primary science through English in Kenya, Cleghorn, Merritt, and Abagi (1989) have shown that teachers have difficulties explaining abstract scientific concepts in English. They also add that using English in education only benefits the children of elites who have access to English at home.

In Tanzania, a country with over 120 languages, the Arusha Declaration of 1967 was passed after independence in 1961, declaring Kiswahili the medium of instruction in primary schools as an instrument of Education for Self-Reliance, the policy of Julius Nyerere, with English taught as a subject. Nyerere's policies of egalitarianism were responsible for the spread of Kiswahili among the population, with approximately 90 percent of the population speaking it today, especially in urban areas. Children begin learning English in the third year of primary school, for about four hours per week. In secondary school, there is a switch to English only as the only medium of instruction, with Kiswahili continuing to be taught as a subject. Secondary education, however, remains out of reach for most children in Tanzania. Criper and Dodd (1984) report that throughout secondary school, little or no subject information gets across to about 50 percent of students and only about 10 percent of students in secondary school have a level of competence which might make it reasonable to use English as medium of instruction. Mtesigwa (2006) has referred to this use of foreign language-in-education in Tanzania as "the education of the few."

Botswana's education system is claimed to be one of the best in Africa. Setswana, the national language, is spoken by over 90 percent of the population, although there are approximately twenty-seven languages spoken (Nyati-Ramahobo, 2006). Setswana is used as medium of instruction until the fourth grade, with English taught as a subject. English becomes the medium of instruction from fifth grade on, and Setswana is taught as a subject. Although the policy has been successful in that 84 percent of children in Botswana now reach fifth grade, many complain that Setswana is ultimately irrelevant for success in society (Nyati-Ramahobo, 2006). Nyati-Ramahobo (2006) documents how in one such bilingual school, Estha 6, children have problems participating effectively in discussion and understanding the teacher. Furthermore, the teaching is not really only in Setswana and then only in English, but other languages are used by both children and teachers, and during the English only part (from grade 6 on), Setswana and other African languages form part of the discursive practices of the children.

In South Africa, where the South African Constitution of 1996 declared eleven languages official – Zulu, Xhosa, Afrikaans, Pedi, English, Tswana, Sesotho, Tsonga, Swazi, Venda, Ndebele – the government encourages a "structured bilingual approach" with initial instruction through the home language, and a gradual transition to English (Alexander, 2002; Heugh, 2000). Although the policy encourages multilingualism, and the use of home languages in instruction, in reality most of the schools start in English. The popularity of English-medium education in South Africa has much to do with the history of apartheid when Bantu language education was used to separate and discriminate (Heugh, 1995). And, yet, initial instruction in English means that many South African children continue to be poorly educated (Alexander, 2004; C. Van der Walt, November 10, 2006, personal communication).

The former French colonies have also experimented with transitional bilingual education. In Niger the Écoles Experimentales, in Mali the Écoles de la Pédagogie Convergente and in Burkina Faso the Écoles Satellites, have used children's mother tongues in the first three years, with French taught as a subject and used as a medium of instruction from the fourth grade (Alidou, 2004).

Cameroon is a French–English bilingual country made up of a multilingual ethnic population, where French is far more prevalent than English (Tchoungi, 2000). The sole languages of education, from primary to tertiary, are the official languages – French and English – not home languages of many Cameroonians. In spite of official policy promoting French–English bilingualism in education, the Indigenous languages are omni-present and often used in classrooms (Tchoungi, 2000).

In 1990, in the Jomtien Declaration of Education for All by 2000, African countries announced the promotion of African languages as media of instruction as one of the best strategies for effective learning. But African countries have mostly relied on international aid to establish experimental transitional bilingual education programs through UNICEF, the German Technical Cooperation Agency (GTZ), the German Foundation for International Development (DSE), or the Unites States Agency for International Development (USAID). There has been little institutionalization of bilingual education in African countries.

Africa continues to struggle with its educational language policy especially as a result of the growing demand for privatization and structural adjustment by the International Monetary Fund (IMF) and the World Bank (Benson, 2000). In West Africa, Alidou (2004) observes that even though the World Bank values the use of children's mother tongues as media of instruction, particularly in the primary level of schooling, it rarely funds bilingual schools. And Mazrui (2004) points out that its loans to African countries come with conditions that textbooks be purchased from western countries.

China

During the 1990s, the Chinese government implemented limited transitional bilingual education programs in an effort to curb the high dropout rate among the language minority groups that comprise eight percent of the population. Besides the Han majority that speaks many dialects[9] of Chinese, there are two minorities that speak other dialects of Chinese (the Hui and Manchu), and then fifty-three minorities that speak over eighty languages from five different language families (Zhou, 2001). According to Jing Lin (1997), the bilingual education effort for Chinese language minorities was beneficial not only to the minorities who received a better education, but also to China which was able to enhance political stability in these regions by declaring them "autonomous" in language and culture. Lin (1997) cautions that even when minority languages are used in the education of minority groups, they are most often included in instructional explanations, while Chinese texts are used. The minority languages are used temporarily as oral media of instruction according to the spirit of the Constitution and current laws. Transitional bilingual education for Chinese minority ethnic groups has sufficient legal support, which is deemed "as the best solution for minority language problems in China" (Blachford, 1999: 167).[10]

The only official bilingual education efforts in China seem to be to educate some language minorities. However, in practice, there is much use of home languages other than the official standard Putonghua (standard Mandarin based on the Beijing dialect) in the early grades; for example, in Shanghai or Canton where other Chinese dialects are broadly spoken. By the end of the first year in school, however, most classroom subjects are discussed only in Putonghua by the teacher.

Ramsey (1987) points out that for Chinese children, using Putonghua in education is often a form of *immersion* (we would say *submersion*) for those who do not speak it as a home language. The intent of this language education policy is to homogenize language practices and spread the use of Putonghua (meaning: "common language"). But most southerners still speak the same dialects as their parents and grandparents, and use their local dialects for everything outside of the public sphere. And, spoken Cantonese, for example, has its own written form of the language. However, in the southern part of China, the language of the government, Putonghua, tends to be used for all public activities. For schoolchildren, this often means that in school they use Putonghua, while outside school they continue to use the home language.

The Foyer Project in Brussels[11]

One highly unusual transitional bilingual education program for immigrants exists in ten primary Dutch-language schools of Brussels. Three of these schools have programs oriented to Italian immigrant children, three to Turkish children, two to Moroccan children, one to Spanish children, and one to Aramean Turkish[12] children (Byram and Leman, 1990). The programs aim at the gradual integration of immigrant children in the host school environment while preserving and reinforcing the child's mother tongue and cultural identity in the early years of kindergarten and the first two years of elementary school. Gradually, Dutch as a second language is built onto what is learned through the mother tongue, and over time it occupies an ever greater place in the timetable. Although the program is transitional in nature, it does not linguistically isolate immigrant children, but provides for separate instructional time in the home language, separate instructional time in the second language, and *integrated instructional time* in the second language with Dutch-speaking children.

Immigrant children are restricted to 30 percent of the school population; they are taught part of the time (30%) separately in their first language in kindergarten, and for 70 percent of the time together with the Flemish children through the medium of Dutch. In the first year of elementary school they are taught separately (30% of the time) in the first language for specific courses, 25 percent of the time separately in Dutch as a second language, and 45 percent of the time together with the Flemish children through the medium of Dutch. From the third year onwards, the immigrant children spend 90 percent of the time with the Flemish children in Dutch, spend a few hours per week separately in the first language and start learning French for a few hours a week, as imposed by the law. Often the immigrant children achieve better results in French, their third language in the program, than their Flemish counterparts for whom it is the second language, probably because it is the language of the street outside school, which they have picked up, whereas the Flemish children interact less frequently in French outside school.

The aim of the Foyer Project is to enable these children to reach the same average levels for insertion into standard, Dutch-medium secondary schools by the end of primary education, a goal achieved according to research results. An interesting anecdotal element around these schools is that one of the grandchildren of the King of the Belgians attended a Foyer Project school, the example intending to show support for this initiative from the Head of State.

Policy for Maintenance and Enrichment: Maintenance Bilingual Education

Groups actively speaking minority languages who have gained some measure of agency, or who live in social contexts that are supportive of their bilingualism, may be able to influence educational authorities or organize their own schools. Maintenance bilingual education programs were originally conceptualized for ethnolinguistic minorities whose children were not fully proficient in the dominant language of society and for whom the development of such proficiency was important. At the same time, these bilingual education policies and programs were cognizant of the value of the first language as a tool to educate deeply. These programs support children's bilingualism, as well as the ethnolinguistic groups' aspirations of self-determination. Beyond the sociolinguistic goals of these policies, the educational programs they encourage provide meaningful education experiences for language minorities who otherwise might be left out of the educational process.

Indigenous peoples

An example of a program to educate Indigenous peoples while maintaining their Native American language was the first American Indian community-controlled school in the United States – Rough Rock School on a Navajo/Diné[13] reservation in Arizona (Holm and Holm, 1990; McCarty, 2002). The Rough Rock Demonstration Project, as it was first called, started in 1966 when only one child in the school spoke English. The school was organized around principles of kinship, family, and communalism, and a bilingual-bicultural program that used both Navajo and English in instruction. Students were organized into pre-school, beginning, Phase I, and Phase II. Instruction was entirely in Navajo up to the end of Phase I with bilingual teachers, except for a daily oral English program. McCarty (2002: 93) describes: "Phase I students remained in self-contained classrooms throughout the day, receiving instruction from both their classroom teacher and specialists who rotated from class to class. Phase II students moved from a base classroom to specialized classes in Navajo language and social living, physical education, science, industrial arts, and home economics." Because of the rapid rate of language shift in the Navajo community in the last few decades, by 1990 only 70 percent of students entering the school spoke Navajo as their primary language. Diné bilingual education programs are therefore increasingly of the immersion revitalization type that will be further discussed in Chapter 11.

Another example of a bilingual education program that responded to enriching and maintaining the Native American community was the one developed in the Navajo/Diné U.S. community of Rock Point in the 1970s. Spolsky (1978: 281) described the efforts in the late 1970s:

> Rock Point is a Navajo community in the midst of the reservation that is strongly traditional with very little English outside the school. Almost all of the children start school speaking only Navajo [. . .]. In the early 1970s, the school became independent, under the control of a locally elected school board, and also started to implement what is referred to as a "coordinate bilingual program". Essentially, the program puts two teachers in each classroom: a Navajo language teacher to introduce new conceptual material in Navajo, and an English language teacher to concentrate on the teaching of English as a second language.

McCarty (2002) reminds us that although in 1975, the United States Congress passed the Indian Self-Determination and Educational Assistance Act (P.L. 93–638) giving local control to Indian tribes and communities, in 1974 the Bilingual Education Act took on a remedial emphasis, limiting educational efforts to transitional bilingual education, and making it difficult to secure funding for Native American maintenance bilingual programs.

U.S. Latinos

Although U.S. Latinos make up half of the 700,000 to 1 million immigrants that enter the United States annually (more if the undocumented are included), not all Latinos are immigrants. As we have mentioned above, Spanish-speakers co-settled what was to be the United States, along with the British. Kloss (1977) maintains that the status of Spaniards as solitary original settlers in the Southwest and Florida extends language rights to Spanish beyond those of other groups. Kloss (1977: 19) states: "Demands and esteem are highest in the case of the solitary original settlers and lowest for the late cosettlers." In the mid-1960s, as civil rights became the cry of the land, Mexican American Chicano activists who claimed Aztlán, the mythical place of origin of the Aztecs and the portion of Mexico that was appropriated by the United States after the Mexican American War, as their homeland, organized maintenance bilingual education schools. By 1974, when the reauthorization of the Bilingual Education Act explicitly funded only transitional bilingual education programs, these schools started facing an up-hill struggle. Bilingual education programs with the explicit purpose of enriching the education of U.S. Latinos solely and maintaining their Spanish are becoming rare.

A current example of a successful bilingual education program in the United States that responds to this policy of enrichment and maintenance is Gregorio Luperón High School in New York City (García and Bartlett, 2007). Gregorio Luperón School is a public high school for Latino immigrant newcomers. Because these students are already of secondary-school age and have just recently moved from Spanish-speaking countries, mostly from the Dominican Republic, they are proficient and literate in Spanish, although their literacy in Spanish varies considerably. But graduating from U.S. secondary schools requires passing high-stakes tests that rely on developed English literacy proficiency. To accomplish that, the school uses Spanish to teach academic subjects, as well as the metalinguistic skills needed to pass the English language exam. The success of this program in educating recent U.S. Latino immigrants is the result of what García and Bartlett (2007) call the "speech community model" of bilingual education, in which the education targets the cultural, social and linguistic needs of this specific U.S. Latino population. English-language acquisition in this school, where all students speak Spanish natively, follows a process of "macroacquisition," as described by Brutt-Griffler (2002), with the entire speech community undergoing the development of bilingualism at the same time and with few monolingual models.

Community schools

Bilingual education has been carried out for a long time by ethnolinguistic communities themselves all over the world. In some societies, as in Canada, these bilingual day schools are fully supported by the state. In other societies, such as the United

States, these bilingual day schools are financed by the ethnolinguistic group itself, often in the form of tuition charged to parents. These schools recognize that developing the bilingualism of an ethnolinguistic group is enriching for their cognitive, social, and educational growth.

In the United States these independent schools in the early part of the twentieth century were referred to as "ethnic-community mother-tongue schools" (Fishman, 1979, 1980a, b; García, 1988). Lately, the literature increasingly refers to all these efforts as "heritage language schools." In the United States, the Center for Applied Linguistics under the Alliance for the Advancement of Heritage Languages is compiling an online collection of profiles of heritage language programs and related resources within and beyond the formal U.S. education system. Creese, Martin, Blackledge, Li, and Lytra (2008) are conducting studies in four complementary community schools in Great Britain. Some of these schools are after-school and weekend schools,[14] but many of these schools are all-day bilingual schools.

In Canada, Alberta was the first Canadian province in 1971 to permit languages other than English or French to be taught in elementary schools, and shortly afterwards, in 1973, the Ukrainian–English bilingual program in Edmonton where elementary school students were taught in English and Ukrainian interchangeably became the first Heritage Language Program in Canada. Heritage language programs started as Cultural Enrichment Programs in 1977, and grew as a result of Canada's Multiculturalism Act in 1988. Until 1990, most of those programs were in Quebec, Ontario, and the Prairie Provinces (Cummins and Danesi, 1990). Although making a strong contribution to the development of bilingualism among Canadian children, they are, for the most part, supplementary programs (after-school or weekend) that teach the heritage language only, and therefore cannot be considered bilingual education programs per se.

Bilingual day schools run by ethnolinguistic groups, especially those with religious affiliations, are popular throughout the world. A well-known example is that of the Hebrew day schools which grew after World War II especially in the United States, South America, Great Britain, South Africa, and Australia. In Modern Orthodox Hebrew day schools, Jewish children are, with some variations, taught to read the Torah in classical Hebrew and to discuss the texts (such as the Talmud, Mishnah, and Gemara) in modern Hebrew. They use the language of the society in which the school is located for secular subjects.

Children attending Muslim day schools in countries other than those where Arabic is an official language speak many varieties of Arabic. It is common for children to receive an education in Fuṣ'ḥá, standard varieties of Arabic, although many Arabic vernaculars are spoken, depending on the children's and teachers' country of origin. Both Fuṣ'ḥá varieties are used, with Classical Arabic used to read the Qu'ran, and Modern Standard Arabic used to teach Arabic values and subjects. The language of the society is then used to teach secular subjects. An example is the King Fahd Academy, a private bilingual school in London, serving children of Arab expatriates. This school teaches Islamic studies and Arabic language, and prepares students for the British General Certificate of Secondary Education (GCSE) and the Advanced-level (A-level) examinations in science and art. According to the website "The English curriculum followed by the academy helps its graduates to proceed to higher studies in England without losing their Arab and Islamic identities" (www.kingfahdbinabdulaziz.com/main/m102.htm).

It is interesting to note that in the cases described above, education is not simply in two languages, as children not only learn classical and modern varieties of Hebrew and Arabic. In the Jewish case, different scripts, such as the Rashi script are taught in order to read commentaries. In some schools, the emphasis is not on developing speaking skills per se, but in getting children to read classical Hebrew and Arabic in order to read the Torah and the Qu'ran. Thus, although some schools aim to develop the biliteracy and even multiliteracy of their students, they are not as keen to ensure their bilingualism.

Greek day schools and Armenian day schools throughout the world fulfill similar functions. In these schools, Greek and Armenian continue to be taught as subjects and are used in teaching history, culture, religion, and literature. And although sometimes the heritage language is used only for an instructional period, the esteem in which the language is held by the school community – principals, teachers, parents – is high enough that children develop bilingual and even biliterate proficiencies.

An example of heritage language schools for U.S. Latinos are the Cuban American schools in Miami, Dade County, established in the 1960s, with some of them still in existence today (García and Otheguy, 1985, 1988). In the 1980s when they were studied extensively, these schools were still providing maintenance bilingual education to Cuban children whose parents were hopeful of a return to Cuba. These Cuban American schools have undergone transformation as the community has become ethnically and linguistically heterogeneous, and as life in the United States continues.

Western Thrace

After the Greek–Turkish war (1923), around 130,000 Muslims remained in Western Thrace, Greece, and the Treaty of Lausanne granted them the right to establish and control, at their own expense, schools where they would be free to practice their Muslim religion and maintain their Turkish (Dragonas and Frangoudaki, 2006). These minority schools are bilingual, with Turkish language, mathematics, physics, chemistry, religion (the Qur'an), art, and physical education taught in Turkish; and Greek language, history, geography, environmental studies, and civic education taught in Greek. Since 1997 efforts have focused on improving the methodology and educational material to teach Greek to the Turkish-speaking children (Dragonas and Frangoudaki, 2006).

Sønderjylland/Nordschleswig

Another example of a maintenance bilingual education policy is that followed by the school in the border region of Sønderjylland/Nordschleswig (Southern Jutland, Denmark) for the German minority. The school's philosophy is expressed in its mission:

1. Our school is a German school. It intends to introduce its pupils in the German language to the German cultural world and reinforce the German sense of community.

2. Our school is a German school in the Danish state. It intends therefore to intro-
    duce its pupils to the Danish cultural and language world and to prepare them
    for life as citizens of this state. (Byram, 1986: 23)

In the first two years, all subjects but Danish are taught in German, with Danish
used in informal "play lessons" and no attempt made to teach written Danish, except
after the third year by which time children are already literate in German. At the
end of the school system, children are trilingual in German, Standard Danish, and
the local vernacular (Byram, 1986). A few schools have introduced co-ordinated
teaching in German and Danish in the first three classes and some social sciences
and mathematics are also taught in Danish. The leaving examinations of the
German schools in this area are recognized in both Denmark and the Federal Republic
of Germany (Kühl and Pedersen, 2006). In this bilingual education program in a
border region, the group's language, but especially its culture, is maintained.

Policy for Enrichment of Social Elite: Prestigious Bilingual Education

All-day bilingual private schools for the children of the social elite where children
are instructed in two languages have always existed and abound today (for more
on this, see especially Carder, 2007; Mejía, 2002). Many of these bilingual private
schools, especially pre-schools, have adopted immersion-type bilingual education
in which only the child's second language is used initially. We will discuss this
type in the next section. In the last two decades there has also been a growth
of international bilingual schools where two languages are used as medium of
instruction.

All-day private bilingual schools

All-day private bilingual schools have been a favorable option for the education of
the elite especially in the developing world. They are prevalent in Latin America,
Africa, and many parts of Asia. In Latin America, for example, American, British,
German, and French private bilingual schools offer parents the option of not
having to worry about low teachers' salaries and low budgets in the public schools
(Mejía, 2002). In Argentina, the English Speaking Scholastic Association of the
River Plate (ESSARP) brings together more than 100 schools that provide private
bilingual education (Banfi and Day, 2005). The same occurs in Asia and Africa,
where private bilingual schools, especially in English, French, and German, are on
the rise. They serve the local population and not expatriates.

International schools

International schools are not new. In fact, the English International Schools were
established in the first part of the twentieth century (Carder, 1991; 2007). Their

growth in the last two decades has accelerated, promoted mostly by international business and the rise of global organizations. In 1998, there were 850 international schools in over ninety countries. Following Hayden and Thompson (1998), Mejía (2002: 14) refers to two types of International Schools:

1. Schools designed to be "national schools away from home," such as French Lycées, German Gymnasia, and English Grammar schools. These are mono-lingual schools that serve as linguistic and cultural islands. For example, the British School of Brussels is situated in Dutch-speaking territory outside Brussels. Although it teaches French as a foreign language, as they do in Britain, it does not teach Dutch at all, and the instruction is in English. The American School of Asunción, Paraguay, is also conducted mainly in English, although the students are, for the most part, Paraguayans of high socioeconomic status. In fact, in Latin America, the American Overseas Schools (AOS) are mainly for elite Latin American children (Spezzini, 2005).

2. Schools that "base an education on the emerging principles for global human development arising from, for example, the League of Nations and, later the United Nations" (Hayden and Thompson, 1998: p. iv) and that use the language of the host country and an additional language. The Chinese International School in Hong Kong is one school where two languages – English and Mandarin – are successfully used as media of instruction.

It is only the second type of international school that is bilingual. Bilingual inter-national schools teach in both the host-country language and the language of the school, often English (Carder, 2007).

Policy for Enrichment of Language Majorities: Immersion Bilingual Education

Quebec

Canadian immersion bilingual education programs were originally developed specifically to meet the needs of Anglophone parents in Quebec who wanted their children to become fluent speakers of French. The Official Languages Act of 1969 had declared Canada to be bilingual in English and French. The policy of "multi-culturalism within a bilingual framework" stipulated that there were two official languages and no official culture, with no ethnic group taking precedence over any other. The Anglophone numerical minority in Quebec, mostly Protestants, enjoyed a higher standard of living than the majority Francophone Catholics. The Anglophones controlled government, business, and real estate in Quebec, and often did not know French. Upward social mobility for Francophones required they become bilingual, although the same was not true for Anglophones. In 1974, after the Québecois party won the elections for the first time in the history of the province, French was made official in Quebec. Bill 101, the Charter of the French Language, passed in 1977, made French the language of work, business, and education in Quebec

(Ricento and Burnaby, 1998). Officializing French was a way to redress the power and privilege imbalance in favor of the Francophone numerical majority. The Anglophones responded by taking steps to ensure that their children would become bilingual so as not to lose out to the Francophones.

Under the leadership of Wallace Lambert from McGill University, an early immersion bilingual education program came into being in St. Lambert, a suburb in Montreal, in 1965 (Lambert and Tucker, 1972). This initiative was at the request of a group of English-speaking parents who were concerned with the low level of French attained by their children in monolingual Anglo schools providing traditional French as a Second Language Program.[15] In the St. Lambert experiment, French only was used in the first year, with English Language Arts taught in grades 2 or 3 for approximately an hour a day, and thereafter each language being taught for 50 percent of the time.

Over time, immersion programs expanded all over Canada and have received extensive attention in the research literature. All studies confirm that immersion bilingual education programs have been most effective in developing the bilingualism of Anglophone children. Anglophone children who are schooled in immersion programs have not only French language skills comparable to those of Francophone children and better than those of Anglophones who receive French as a Second Language instruction, but also have better English-language skills than their Anglophone counterparts who are schooled in English-only systems. They also have better math skills than all their counterparts (Lambert and Tucker, 1972; Swain, 1978). In addition, these children have better attitudes towards Francophones than those who have not experienced immersion bilingual education (Swain and Lapkin, 1982; Lambert and Tucker, 1972).

Despite the success of immersion bilingual education programs in Canada, there are critics who claim that language skills could be improved by teaching the second language explicitly and formally. Studying the difference in second-language acquisition between immersion bilingual education in Quebec and the multilingual European Schools for civil servants (more on these later), Baetens Beardsmore and Swain (1985) claim that the accompanying explicit second-language instruction in the European Schools, on top of the use of the target language as a medium of instruction, is responsible for the greater accuracy in production of their students over those in the immersion programs. Research has repeatedly shown that although the receptive ability in both listening and reading in French of Anglophone students in Canadian immersion bilingual education programs is native-like, the productive ability lags behind those of native Francophones. That is, in speaking and writing, Anglophones who have gone through immersion bilingual education show many differences from native-born students (Swain, 1997).

Because of the discrepancy created by Bill 101 in Quebec, the Official Languages Act was revised in 1988 for the whole of Canada. The clamor for language rights for Canadian Indigenous groups (numbering approximately 1 million in 2006; Mackey, 2003), as well as the many languages of immigrants to Canada, has meant that English–French bilingualism has continued to be negotiated and that Canadian bilingual education is shifting and changing.

Other contexts

Immersion bilingual education programs have grown in the last decade especially for the *early schooling* of language-majority children in societies for which a global language has become important. For example, pre-schools in places as different as Taiwan and Argentina are experimenting with immersion bilingual education in English. The results of these programs have been mixed. For the most part, these pre-school programs are private businesses, often moved by profit and not an educational interest in the child. They lack, unlike the case of the Canadian French programs, a cohesive and immediate societal need.

Mejía (2002) describes two pre-school English–Spanish immersion private schools for upper-middle-class children on the outskirts of Cali, Colombia, that use a partial immersion program. We quote a description of one of the programs here to show how adaptations have been made to the original model:

> In the first year of schooling the pupils had initially 80% of their teaching and learning in Spanish (the first language) and 20% in English (the foreign language). In their second school year, however, this ratio was reversed, so that the children had around 70% of their schooling in English and 30% in Spanish, thus approximating more to an Early Partial Immersion model. (Mejía, 2002: 86)

In general, pre-schools, being child-centered, are seldom of the early total immersion type. Most use the other language only at times. The fact that they insist on calling themselves "immersion schools" has much to do with associating, for marketing purposes, with the positive results achieved by Canadian immersion programs.

An example of a private immersion school in Latin America is the Colegio Menor San Francisco de Quito in Ecuador. The school begins in pre-school and continues through high school. Students are Ecuadorian Spanish-speakers of high socioeconomic status who want to acquire English. The pre-school teachers speak and plan all activities in English, although students are allowed to speak in Spanish. First- and second-grade students receive five hours of Spanish a week, taught in another classroom by a different teacher. Beginning in third grade, the number of Spanish hours increases until they reach middle school where half the classes are in English and half are in Spanish. At high school, a third language is offered.[16] Yet another example is the Markham College in Lima, Peru which has both a Lower and Upper School and uses English as the main language of instruction at both levels (see www.markham.edu.pe). The school's motto is "We do everything in English."

Another example of an immersion bilingual education program to acquire English is the Doha Academy in Qatar. This private bilingual school immerses Qatari children in English, while at the same time giving them a strong program in Islamic religious studies and Arabic language and values. It follows the British National Curriculum, as well as the Qatar Ministry of Education and Higher Education Curriculum Guidelines. Although mostly an English-medium school, the school instills strong Muslim and Arabic values. For example, boys and girls are separated, and the school week is from Saturday through Wednesday. This school also includes French in the curriculum from the first grade onwards. By the time children graduate, they are trilingual.

The number of immersion bilingual programs in the United States is also grow-ing. According to the Center for Applied Linguistics, there were 353 immersion education programs in the United States in 2006 – fifty-one in pre-schools, 180 in elementary schools, eight-six in middle schools, and thirty-six in high schools. Most programs are in Louisiana, followed by Hawaii, Oregon, Virginia, and then Minnesota. Although most programs are in Spanish (130 accounting for 42% of all programs), there are 90 programs in French (29%), twenty-six in Hawaiian (8%), twenty-two in Japanese (7%), twelve in Mandarin (4%), and ten in German (4%). There are also one to two programs in other languages (for information, see www. cal.org/resources/immersion/Doc/PercentageofImmersionProgramsbyLanguageofI nstruction.pdf). Only 42 percent of all immersion programs in the United States are of the total kind.

It is important to reiterate that immersion education is *bilingual*, using two lan-guages in instruction. The growing number of all-English-medium schools through-out the world cannot be considered under this rubric, unless two languages are used in instruction. For example, in Pakistan, there are many private schools which claim to be English-medium schools. Rahman (2001) states that such schools are found in areas ranging from the most affluent (and run by the state itself as elitist institutions in the name of defense, modernization, and efficiency) to poor and even rural areas. In the non-elitist private schools, however, and in the poorer areas "a pretense is made of teaching most subjects in English but the teachers themselves are neither from English schools nor otherwise qualified to teach anything but English of a rudimentary kind through rote-learning and spoon-feeding methods" (Rahman, 2001: 248). And thus, although English is poised as giving access to the most lucrative and powerful jobs, it remains an instrument to close the ranks of the elite. Because it gives power, people are desperate to acquire it, and yet, because schooling through English is not the same everywhere, people resent it. Rahman (2001: 59) concludes: "English, therefore, serves to maintain the present power struc-ture which disempowers most of our people." Although, in theory, these English-medium schools might be considered immersion bilingual schools if they also used the other language as medium for some subjects, in practice, the poor performance of these immersion schools do not fit into any regular category.

Conclusion

This chapter gives examples of different bilingual education policies and the types of programs enacted by different social groups and states when they hold monoglossic beliefs. In general, the following *three principles* emerge from this discussion:

1. If a dominant social group wants to ensure that a non-dominant group under-goes language shift, *transitional bilingual education programs* are established. In transitional bilingual education the non-dominant language is used as medium of instruction for a short period of time, as the dominant language takes up more and more curricular time until it becomes the exclusive medium of instruc-tion. Monolingualism is the goal as language shift is encouraged. The minor-itized language is considered a problem and the educational program aims to

also impose the monoculture of the dominant group on the language minority children.

2. If a non-dominant social group has gained enough agency as to insist on the maintenance of their language, *maintenance bilingual education programs* are established. Maintenance bilingual education programs use two languages throughout a child's education. Each language does not necessarily have equal time in the curriculum, although both languages are ensured a role. The minoritized language is considered a source of enrichment for the group and a bicultural stance is promoted.

3. If a dominant social group wants to ensure that their children become bilingual, two kinds of bilingual education programs may be established – *prestigious bilingual education programs* or *immersion bilingual education programs*. Prestigious bilingual education programs often look like maintenance bilingual education programs in that the two languages are used throughout a child's education to different degrees, depending on the group's wishes. The children, however, are mostly members of dominant groups. Immersion bilingual education differs from prestigious bilingual education programs in that in the former one language is exclusively used as medium of instruction for a period of time, whereas in the latter both languages are used at all times to different degrees. Immersion bilingual education eventually devotes equal time to the two languages.

Table 10.2 summarizes for the reader the different characteristics of these four types of bilingual education programs, as well as the examples discussed in this chapter:[17]

Table 10.2 Types of Monoglossic Bilingual Education and Characteristics

Type	Transitional BE	Maintenance BE	Prestigious BE	Immersion BE
Language use	Initially, child's home language. Increasingly, child's second language. Eventually, exclusively child's second language	Both languages throughout to different degrees	Both languages throughout to different degrees	Initially, child's second language. Eventually both languages throughout
Linguistic goal	Monolingualism	Bilingualism	Bilingualism	Bilingualism
Linguistic ecology	Shift	Maintenance	Addition	Addition
Bilingual orientation	Problem	Enrichment	Enrichment	Enrichment
Cultural ecology	Monoculturism	Biculturism	Biculturism/ Monoculturism	Biculturism
Type of Children	Minority	Minority	Majority	Majority
Examples in this chapter	• U.S. • Indigenous • Latin America • Africa • China • Foyer Project	• Indigenous • U.S. Latinos • Community Education • Western Thrace • Border, Denmark	• All-day private • International	• Quebec • Other

As we will see, in contexts where language-minority groups have acquired more language rights or in contexts where language-majority groups have espoused the power of bilingualism and multilingualism for all children, these types of bilingual programs have been extended and adapted. The bilingual education policies that we will consider in Chapter 11 respond to more heteroglossic beliefs and practices, as well as to theoretical frameworks of recursive bilingualism and dynamic bilingualism. It is important, however, for the reader to realize that some of the examples given in this chapter and in the next could have been described as one type or another, since all bilingual education policy, whether drawn by states, ethnolinguistic minorities, or parents and educators, in practice only approximates a theoretical ideal.

Questions for Reflection

1. Identify how monoglossic beliefs impact on the planning of different types of bilingual education programs. Explain how it is possible to have bilingual programs that respond to monoglossic beliefs.
2. Discuss some of the ways in which different states or groups have planned for the education of their children in ways that incorporate bilingual education.
3. In educating language-minority children, what is the difference between planning for their transition to a majority language and planning for the maintenance of their minority language? How do programs differ? Is there ever a time in which transitional bilingual education programs are appropriate?
4. This chapter considered examples of indigenous intercultural bilingual education in Latin America as transitional bilingual education. Do you agree? What is the reality at present?
5. How does the planning for the bilingual education of language majorities and social elite tend to differ from that of language minorities?
6. What are some of the characteristics of Canadian immersion programs; how did they come about; and how do they differ from other immersion programs?

Further Reading

August, D., and Hakuta, K. (eds.) (1997). *Improving Schooling for Language-Minority Children. A Research Agenda.* National Academy Press, Washington, DC.

Bamgbose, A. (2000). *Language and Exclusion: The Consequences of Language Policies in Africa.* Lit Verlag, Munich.

Brock-Utne, B. (2000). *Whose Education for All? The Recolonization of the African Mind.* Falmer Press, London.

Carder, M. (2007). *Bilingualism in International Schools. A Model for Enriching Language Education.* Multilingual Matters, Clevedon.

Feng, A. (ed.) (2007). *Bilingual Education in China. Practices, Policies and Concepts.* Multilingual Matters, Clevedon.

García, O., and Baker, C. (eds.) (2007). *Bilingual Education: An Introductory Reader.* Multilingual Matters, Clevedon.

García, O., Skutnabb-Kangas, T., and Torres-Guzmán, M. (eds.) (2006). *Imagining Multilingual Schools: Languages in Education and Glocalization.* Multilingual Matters, Clevedon.

Hornberger, N. (ed.) (1996). *Indigenous Literacies in the Americas. Language Planning from the Bottom Up.* Mouton de Gruyter, Berlin.

Lin, A.M.Y., and Martin, P.W. (eds.) (2005) *Decolonisation, Globalisation. Language-in-Education Policy and Practice.* Multilingual Matters, Clevedon.

Mejía, A.M. de (2002). *Power, Prestige and Bilingualism. International Perspectives on Elite Bilingual Education.* Multilingual Matters, Clevedon.

—— (ed.) (2005). *Bilingual Education in South America.* Multilingual Matters, Clevedon.

Ouane, A. (ed.) (2003). *Towards a Multilingual Culture of Education.* UNESCO Institute for Education, Hamburg.

Swain, M., and Lapkin, S. (1982). *Evaluating Bilingual Education: A Canadian Case Study.* Multilingual Matters, Clevedon.

UNESCO (2005). *First Language First: Community-Based Literacy Programs for Minority Language Contexts in Asia.* UNESCO Asia and Pacific Regional Bureau of Education, Bangkok, Thailand.

11

Heteroglossic Bilingual Education Policy

by Ofelia García and Hugo Baetens Beardsmore, with contributions by Debra Cole and Zeena Zakharia

Education in many countries of the world takes place in multilingual contexts. Most plurilingual societies have developed an ethos which balances and respects the use of different languages in daily life. From the perspective of these societies and of the language communities themselves, multilingualism is more a way of life than a problem to be solved. The challenge is for education systems to adapt to these complex realities and provide a quality education which takes into consideration learners' needs, whilst balancing these at the same time with social, cultural and political demands. While uniform solutions for plural societies, may be both administratively and managerially simpler, they disregard the risks involved both in terms of learning achievement and loss of linguistic and cultural diversity.

UNESCO, 2003: 12

It is not deaf children that need remediation; it is the system that educates them.
Mahshie, 1995: 179

Overview

In this chapter, we will discuss heteroglossic bilingual education policies and programs:

- Policies for language revitalization: immersion revitalization bilingual education:
  - Māori;
  - Hawaii;
  - Navajo;
  - Canadian First Nations;
  - Sámis.

- Policies for development of minority languages: developmental bilingual education:
  - the European Union:
    - Spain: Catalonia, Galicia, and the Basque Community (Euskadi);
    - the UK: Wales and Scotland;
    - the Republic of Ireland;
    - Friesland;
    - Roma;
  - the United States;
  - the Deaf community.
- Policies for plurilingualism across groups: poly-directional / two-way bilingual education (dual language):
  - the United States;
  - European Schools for Civil Servants;
  - Berlin;
  - Israel;
  - Vienna;
  - international schools.
- Policies for plurilingualism within groups: CLIL and CLIL-type bilingual education:
  - CLIL:
    - Europe;
  - CLIL-type:
    - Asia;
    - Malaysia;
    - Shanghai, China.
- Policies for multiple languages: multiple multilingual education:
  - the European Union:
    - Luxembourg;
  - Asia:
    - the Philippines;
    - India;
    - Hong Kong;
    - Singapore;
    - Brunei Darussalam;
    - the Arab Middle East and North Africa.

Introduction

As movements of people have increased, and technology has brought all of us closer together, communities have started to become aware of the fact that it is not necessary for one language or one identity to take over a competing one, but that it is possible to hold on to multiple languages, to engage in multiple communicative and literacy practices, and to have multiple identities.[1] Ethnolinguistic groups that had experienced language shift and had *relinguified*, or were experiencing language loss, have started again to claim their heritage languages as their right, and as part of multiple identities. Bilingualism has now become an important requirement in order to communicate and have meaningful human and business relationships with others, as well as to engage in the global citizenship of the twenty-first century. English, Mandarin Chinese, Arabic, French, and Spanish have become important global languages. Community languages are increasingly important to educate, especially in the developing world (UNESCO, 2005). And acquiring competence in two languages through education is simply not enough, as recognition is made of the multiplicity of languaging throughout the world.

Romaine (2006) has pointed out that bilingual schools, even more than homes and families, are becoming a most important way of transmitting home languages, when there has been large language shift. For example, Romaine reminds us that more children are learning Basque (Euskara) and Irish through the education system than at home as a native language. Thus, maintenance of societal bilingualism often has more to do with, as Romaine (2006) says, "the capacity of the *schools* to produce competent bilinguals than to the capacity of the bilingual community to reproduce itself." This in itself has significantly changed who a speaker of a language is, how the language is used, and in turn how bilingual and multilingual schools are organized.

In this chapter, we consider different bilingual education policies emanating from *heteroglossic beliefs and practices* that view the multiple languages of bilinguals as multiple and co-existing. All these policies therefore fall under a Recursive Theoretical Framework or Dynamic Plurilingual Theoretical Framework (see Chapter 6), as in Table 11.1:

Table 11.1   Planning Language and Bilingual Education Types: Heteroglossic Beliefs

Planning Language	Bilingual Education Types
Recursive Theoretical Framework	
Planning for revitalization of endangered minority languages	Immersion revitalization
Planning for the development and recovery of expanding minority languages	Developmental
Dynamic Theoretical Framework	
Planning for plurilingualism across groups	Poly-directional / two-way (dual language)
Planning for plurilingualism within groups for all	CLIL and CLIL-type
Planning for the development of multiple languages	Multiple multilingual

In most cases, these policies and the types of bilingual education programs that are supported, are designed and handed down by states or regions that want to educate their children bilingually for various reasons. But in other cases bilingual education has been designed by educators or communities themselves, responding to interests and motivations of parents and societies. These bilingual education policies have led to greater complexity of types of programs than in the past, with ever more language practices, all responding to local interests, ideologies, and contexts.

Although they are discussed here as exclusive types, it is important for the reader to keep in mind that these types are constantly expanding and taking on different characteristics, as their societal goals shift. The banyan tree of bilingual education grows ever more complex.

Policies for Language Revitalization: Immersion Revitalization Bilingual Education

Motivated by the success of the Canadian immersion bilingual education programs, ethnolinguistic minorities who have experienced language shift away from their heritage languages have adapted the Canadian model to fit their needs.[2] Perhaps the best-known educational effort to reverse the language shift of an ethnolinguistic group is the one that has taken place in Aotearoa/New Zealand among the Māoris since the 1970s.

Māoris[3]

When the Māoris of Aotearoa/New Zealand surrendered their sovereignty to the British Crown in 1840, they signed the Treaty of Waitangi, guaranteeing them "their lands, their homes and all their treasured possessions (*taonga*)" (May, 2004: 22). In 1913, 90 percent of Māori schoolchildren could speak Māori, by 1975 the figure was less than 5 percent (Durie, 1997). Māori was designated an official language, and a *taonga* in the Māori Language Act of 1987. It was around this time that New Zealanders started a type of immersion bilingual education as a desperate attempt to get elderly grandparents to pass on the language to their grandchildren. Te Kōhanga Reo programs, or "language nests" as they were called, involved pre-school children under the age of five in centers where the *whānau*, or extended family, impart Māori spiritual values, language, and culture. The concept of *whānau* also includes clusters of values: virtues of *aroha* (caring, sharing, and empathy), *whānaungatanga* (family responsibilities), *rangimarie* (peacefulness), and *manaaki* (kindness) (Fleras, 1992). By 1995, close to 50 percent of all Maori pre-schoolers attended Te Kōhanga Reo, and the New Zealand government now funds all programs. Te Kōhanga Reo is much more than simply an immersion program. It is closely linked to the concept of nation-building and Māori cultural sovereignty (Black, Marshall, and Irwin, 2003).

The success of Te Kōhanga Reo was such that Kura Kaupapa Māori programs (bilingual education programs at the elementary level) started to be developed. In these schools, children who had been immersed in Māori in *Te* Kōhanga Reo were now instructed through the medium of Māori (Benton, 2007). Recently, Whārekura programs,[4] Māori medium education at the secondary level, and Whāre Wananga programs, Māori medium tertiary institutions have been implemented (May, 2004). The continuum of Te Kōhanga Reo coupled with Kura Kaupapa and Whārekura is an instance of immersion revitalization bilingual education,[5] successful not only in making individual children speakers of Māori, but in so doing, regenerating the heritage language of all the Māori people. Although many Māori children attend Te Kōhanga Reo programs, only 2.3 percent of Māori students are enrolled in a *kura* (May, 2004), demonstrating the difficult task of using a revitalized heritage language in the higher grades.

Increasingly there are other Māori–English bilingual education options for children. In some Te Reo Māori programs, Māori is taught as a separate subject. In Taha Māori, or Māori-enriched programs, both the language together with the philosophy and way of life are taught.

May (2006) points out that despite the advances of Māori-medium education, there have been few efforts to support the bilingual education of the Pasifika population in Aotearoa/New Zealand, that is, the Pacific Island[6] migrants who live in Aotearoa/New Zealand, as well as that of recent Asian immigrants.

Hawaii

The Hawaiian language was banned in public schools after annexation to the U.S. in 1898. In 1978 the Hawaiian language was again made official in the state and taught in public schools. Since the 1980s, native Hawaiians have had an Immersion Revitalization Bilingual program – Pūnana Leo[7] – modeled after that of Māoris in New Zealand. By then, most native speakers of Hawaiian were over seventy years old. In these pre-schools, only Hawaiian is used. The success of these programs has led to the establishment of Hawaiian-medium schools, the Kula Kaiapuni Hawai'i (Hawaiian immersion public schools) where children are educated in Hawaiian through the fifth grade, when English is introduced as a subject. Children also learn a third language (Wilson and Kamanā, 2001). The website for Aha Pūnana Leo, the leading organization for language revitalization, expresses the educational wishes of parents and community:

> We sought full education through Hawaiian from preschool through high school. We sought teaching English as a second language beginning in fifth grade and having English taught through the medium of Hawaiian if the school so chose. We sought a guarantee that any Hawaiian speaking child would be guaranteed the right to education through the Hawaiian medium in the same way that any English speaking child had the right to be educated in English in Hawai'i. We sought the hiring of teachers who were certified as having fluency in Hawaiian that was equal to the level of English fluency required in the English medium classrooms. We sought text books and other teaching materials in Hawaiian. We sought the right to bus service to Kula Kaiapuni Hawai'i for all children attending in the same way that children attending English language schools all have the right to bus transportation to their schools. We sought testing in Hawaiian for our children in the same way that children in English schools had their children tested through the language of the school. Finally we sought to establish total Hawaiian medium schools where the principal, librarian, cooks, and entire staff spoke Hawaiian. (Cited in www.ahapunanaleo.org/MU.htm)

Navajo/Diné

The efforts of Māori and Hawaiian communities to revitalize their languages have spread to other Indigenous communities. Rawlins, a Hawaiian language advocate, explains the impact in Native American communities in the U.S. (Rawlins, 2003: 5–6):

> We have developed a web of relationships with other Native American communities throughout the United States interested in language revitalization. We have helped groups with information to their tribal councils and school boards. We have provided information on developing specialized fonts and computer programs [. . .]. We have sponsored resolutions. [. . .] We have even sent teachers to teach in their schools. Our biggest impact has been through hosting visitors. Hosting visitors is part of traditional Hawaiian culture. In the past five months alone we have hosted members of the Cheyenne, Crow, Navajo, Alutiiq, Central Yup'ik, Onondaga, Mohawk, Cayuga and Squamish peoples [. . .]. We can save for future generations of our own peoples and for all the peoples of the world, the great beauty of the languages and cultures that our elders left for us, and with those languages develop high quality education that will assure our children will be fully a part of an interconnected world.

In 1988, P.L. 100–297 provided funding for community-controlled schools. But as many have remarked, these Native American schools increasingly concern themselves today with meeting English-only standards of No Child Left Behind that leave little time for local languages and knowledge (McCarty, 2002; McCarty, Romero, and Zepeda, 2006).

One example of efforts and resistance is the development of the Navajo/Diné immersion program at Fort Defiance, Arizona. Between kindergarten and grade 3, more than half of classroom time is spent in Navajo, and the rest of the time in English. After grade 4, there is one hour of daily Navajo instruction. McCarty (2002) refers to the success of this program in promoting proficiency in the Indigenous language at no cost to the students' proficiency in English.

Canadian First Nations

Canadian educational policy for its Indigenous minorities has been similar to that followed in the United States, and thus, much language loss has resulted. For example, the Indian Act of 1920, and its ensuing amendments, made attendance compulsory in residential schools where instruction was only in English.

In the 1980s, immersion programs became increasingly used as a way to revitalize some of the Indigenous languages. For example, the Kahnawake community in Quebec developed and implemented an Immersion Revitalization Mohawk school in 1979. Mohawk is used in the first three years; English instruction is introduced in grade 4, and, by grade 6, English is used for 50 percent of the instruction. Lambert, Genesee, Holobow, and McGilly (1984) have evaluated the results of this program and concluded that, by grade 4, the children are increasingly literate in Mohawk, and their achievement in English standardized tests is comparable to that of their non-immersion peers (Assembly of First Nations, 1988).

Another example is the Mohawk and Cayuga immersion schools in the Grand River Territory in Ontario, Canada.[8] To revitalize the languages of the Six Nations, parents organized in 1985 the Kawenni:io/Gaweni:yo, FLA (First Language Academy). The K/G, FLA was the beginning of the language immersion programs. The elementary immersion schools and the Kawenni:io/Gaweni:yo High School are run as independent schools with their own school board within the territory. Students are taught only in the Mohawk or Cayuga language from kindergarten to sixth grade. In grades 7 and 8, 50 percent is taught in English and 50 percent in Mohawk or Cayuga. In high school, Mohawk/Cayuga is used 40 percent of the time, and English is used 60 percent of the time. Throughout the four years of high school, the students take one semester of Mohawk or Cayuga, and a second semester of Native Studies taught through the Indigenous language. The purpose of transmitting the language and culture is to continue the traditional way of life, as well as to prepare the children for the greater society beyond The Grand River Territory.

Sámis[9]

The Sámis, speaking several Sámi languages, live mainly in Norway, but also in Finland, Sweden, and Russia. The loss of Sámi traditional ways of life and the influx of non-Sámi speakers has resulted in the endangerment of Sámi languages. Not all Sámis have been equally successful in developing immersion revitalization bilingual education programs. (See Aikio-Puoskari, 2005; Magga and Skutnabb-Kangas, 2003; see also www.galdo.org/web/index.pho?sladja=43&giella1=eng.)

In 1967, Norway initiated Sámi-medium transitional bilingual education as a way to educate Sámis and develop their proficiency in Norwegian. But in 1987 the Norwegian Parliament passed the Sámi Act, and in 1988 an amendment to the Norwegian Constitution recognized the Sámis as Indigenous people with their own language and culture, and made the language co-official with Norwegian. In 1992, six municipalities were defined as bilingual territories, with one more added in 2006. As such, in the bilingual territories, Sámis have the right to be taught through the medium of Sámi in primary school, although Norwegian is a compulsory subject (for details, see Niemi, 2006; Özerk, 2006, forthcoming). A Sámi University College, funded by the state, was established in 1989, where bilingual teachers are educated.[10]

In Finland, Sámi Language Acts were approved by voters in 1992 and 2003, aimed to enable the Sámi to maintain their own language and culture. The Acts included the right to use Sámi as languages of instruction and to receive day-care in Sámi. According to the Finnish Comprehensive Schools Act, "Mother-tongue tuition will take place either in Finnish, Swedish or in Sámi, according to the language of education of the pupil. The tuition in mother tongue can also take place in Romani, sign language or another mother tongue spoken by the pupil" (Myntti and Nuolijärvi, 2006: 193). Within the Sámi homeland, pupils whose first language is Sámi receive most of their education in Sámi. There is strong state financial support in order to increase the use of Sámi in upper secondary schools and vocational education (Myntti and Nuolijärvi, 2006).

Sweden has had legislation since the 1970s supporting the right of students to be schooled in their own language. Legislation in 1985 and 1990–1991 required that one or both parents have a language other than Swedish as their mother tongue and that this language be used by the child in everyday life. But this restriction does not apply to Sámi, children of Roma extraction (more on these below), or

Tornedalians (speakers of Meänkieli and descendants of Finns who settled in Northern Sweden), even if they do not actually use their traditional language in everyday life and at home (Åkermark and Huss, 2006). In spite of legislation, there are limited bilingual education programs because there are few teachers for such programs. There are a handful of special Sámi-language schools (*Sameskolan*) where bilingualism is an explicit goal of education, and Sámi is the main language of instruction until the third grade. But most Sámi children in Sweden only have one or two hours a week of Sámi language instruction in public schools.

Policies for Development of Minority Languages: Developmental Bilingual Education

Immersion revitalization bilingual education, of the kind described above, is important in planning to reverse the language shift of group whose language is *deeply threatened*. Often these groups are Indigenous. Because these ethnolinguistic groups have had a great degree of language shift as a result of violence, there is much linguistic homogeneity. Immersing learners in the minoritized language is the only way to reverse their language shift.

In this section, we consider bilingual education programs that are designed for ethnolinguistic groups whose languages are *expanding*, often gaining speakers not only of that ethnolinguistic group, but also of others. Often these are autochthonous ethnolinguistic groups with a great degree of agency. In some cases, they are immigrant groups that are numerous and whose language is expanding in that society. In the case of the Deaf, it signals a group that is changing status – from one seen in the past as having a medical disability to one considered today as being linguistically and culturally different. Because of the greater linguistic heterogeneity involved in these group, the developmental bilingual education efforts offer much more flexibility and a greater range of possibilities, with most programs using both the threatened and the dominant language simultaneously from the beginning. In some cases, however, the focus is on the threatened language. These bilingual education programs are designed to *recover functions and status* of languages that are expanding, but that have hereto not had a rightful place in school.

The European Union

The regional and minority languages of Europe have fared better than immigrant languages and Indigenous languages, although their status and fate have depended on the state in which they are situated. Especially since the 1980s, developmental bilingual education has been increasingly used to support the survival of these languages among their speakers and among those who reside in these areas. As we saw in Chapter 9, in 1993, the Council of Europe proposed the Charter on Regional and Minority Languages, giving ethnolinguistic minorities the right to use their languages in education, the media, and public administration, at least in those countries that ratified the Charter (Ager, 2001; Clyne, 1997; Council of Europe, 1993). Developing the expansion of "lesser-used languages" of Europe by using them in education is one of the goals of the European Commission. (See for example the website of the European Bureau for Lesser-Used Languages [EBLUL, 2007].) Thus, bilingual education in Europe is gaining strength. More information about other regional and minority languages used in bilingual education in the European Union can be gained by consulting the Mercator (2007) website. We offer below only a few examples.

Spain: Catalonia, Galicia, and the Basque Community (Euskadi)

Since the end of the Spanish Civil War in 1936, and until the end of Francisco Franco's dictatorship, all languages other than Spanish were banned in all schools in Spain. Although Catalan, a Romance language, was not taught in the schools of Catalonia, Catalan families continued to use it in the home, in speech, as well as in reading and writing, since the language had an extensive literary tradition. Yet, at the time of the 1978 Spanish Constitution, only 25 percent of the population of Catalonia had knowledge of Catalan (Ager, 2001). In 1983 the Law of Linguistic Normalization was passed, aimed at regulating the use of Spanish and promoting the other languages. Catalan was declared the only official language in regional government and required for graduation from secondary school. Bilingual education programs have been crucial for the successful regeneration of Catalan, claimed today by half the population as their mother tongue (Ager, 2001).

Today Catalan is used as the only teaching medium at all levels of the education system in Catalonia and is also taught as a subject, with Spanish taught only as a subject throughout the grades. In addition, Spanish is used as a medium of instruction in one content area from grade 3, and two content areas from grade 6 (Artigal, 1997). There is, of course, variety in the implementation of these programs, with much Spanish informally present in the curriculum, even when instruction is supposedly solely in Catalan. The Generalitat de Catalunya (Catalan Autonomous Government) has full control over the elementary schools, the secondary schools, and the nine universities in the region.

Galician was the Romance language spoken in the entire western part of the Iberian Peninsula. Spoken in the geographically isolated and rural community of Galicia, and without the benefits of standardization and schooling afforded to what became Portuguese, Galician was maintained throughout the Franco regime. It was spoken mostly by the women who remained more monolingual in Galician than the men who served in the army. Galician was passed on inter-generationally, although children were unable to read and write it. Today, through the advent of bilingual education programs, Galician children are biliterate, reading and writing the extensive literature that is being produced and published in Galicia. Education in the first two years is either in Galician or Spanish, depending on the students' home languages. From the age of 8 to 14, education is in Spanish with Galician used as a medium for at least one school subject.

The Basque Autonomous Community of Spain (*Euskadi*) had undergone more extensive language shift than either Catalonia or Galicia. Unlike Catalan and Galician which are Romance languages, Basque or Euskara is a language isolate with no known genealogical relationship with other languages. In the 1960s, a special arrangement was made between the Catholic Church and the central government in Madrid to allow the church to provide Euskara-medium education to Euskara-speaking children in *ikastolas*, Euskara-medium schools (Arzamendi and Genesee, 1997). In 1983, with the passage of Spain's Law of Linguistic Normalization, Basque started to once again be used in public education.

Euskadi has three bilingual education programs:

- Model A: instruction is carried out in Spanish. Euskara has the status of a language subject taught for a stipulated number of hours.
- Model B: schooling is carried out in equal proportions through two languages (Euskara and Spanish), and in addition both languages are taught as subjects.
- Model D:[11] schooling is carried out in Euskara, and Spanish is taught as a subject (Etxeberria, 1999).

Although in the 1980s most students were enrolled in Model A, today only 8.1 percent of students are in Model A, 30.5 percent are in Model B, and 61.4 percent in Model D, a tribute to the gains of Euskara in the region (Etxeberria, 2006). At this writing, there is discussion of whether to discontinue Model A.

The United Kingdom: Wales and Scotland

In Wales the Education Act of 1870 required Welsh children to learn English and prohibited them from speaking Welsh at school. However, in the 1940s Welsh-speaking parents succeeded in establishing Welsh-medium schools with state funding. By the 1960s these schools started also to attract Anglophone children, motivated especially by the increase in the use of Welsh in public sector employment (Jones and Martin-Jones, 2004).

The Education Reform Act of 1988 established the National Curriculum in England and Wales, with Welsh becoming a core subject in all Welsh-medium schools, and a foundation subject in all other schools (Jones and Martin-Jones, 2004). In 1993, the Welsh Language Act declared that Welsh and English were to be treated "on an equal basis of equality" in Wales. This legislation has done much to spur the growth of bilingual education in Wales. Welsh immersion centers have been developed for children between 2 and a half and 5 years of age (Jones and Martin-Jones, 2004). Designated Bilingual Schools (*Ysgolion Cymraeg*) which offer immersion in Welsh-medium education and are primarily for Anglophone students are growing (Jones and Martin-Jones, 2004). There are also Traditional or Natural Bilingual schools for Welsh speakers, mostly in the rural heartland. In these Traditional or Natural Bilingual Schools children are taught in Welsh initially, and from the age of 7 they study English, with both languages used as medium of instruction throughout the primary years (Jones and Martin Jones, 2004). Many Welsh and non-Welsh children today attend schools in which subjects are taught through the medium of English and Welsh, with more emphasis on each of the languages depending on family choice (Ager, 2001).

In Scotland, Gaelic is spoken by slightly over 1 percent of the population. The majority of Gaelic-speakers reside in what were formerly known as the Western Isles (*Na h-Eileanan*) and the Highland Region. Developmental bilingual education programs in Gaelic–English have existed since 1985.

The Republic of Ireland
The case of the Irish language in the Republic of Ireland is somewhat unique in Europe in that it is the official first language of the Republic of Ireland, yet, at the same time, it is a minority language. Irish is losing ground in the native speaker community of the Gaeltacht[12] in the west, and it is only spoken by about 5 percent in the English-speaking part of the rest of the country (Ó Laoire, 2005). The official government strategy since independence has been a dual policy of maintenance of the language in areas where it is a community language, that is to say, the Gaeltacht, and its revitalization in all other areas.

The burden of sustaining and revitalizing the Irish language depends almost exclusively on schools in Ireland. In the Gaeltacht where many children are Irish-speaking, there are Irish-medium primary and secondary schools, with English used only in some curricular areas. There are also Irish-medium developmental bilingual schools in the rest of Ireland, especially at the primary level (Mac Donnacha, Ní Chualáin, Ní Shéaghdha, and Ní Mhainín, 2005). These bilingual education programs have grown considerably over recent years, from fourteen in 1975 to 114 in 1999, though this still represents only 3.6 percent of total primary schools in Ireland (Ó Laorie, 2005). In English-medium schools, Irish is an obligatory subject for the entire population throughout compulsory schooling, and the emphasis is primarily on oral language use.

France
One of the European countries which has been least supportive of linguistic minorities has been France. From the sixteenth century until 1950 France had a policy of oppression of their regional languages especially Basque, Breton, Corsican, and Occitan (also known in the English-speaking world as Provençal, although that term is often reserved for the variety of Occitan spoken in Provence) (Ager 1999, 2001). French had been considered the only language in which to express the rights of man.

In 1951, the Loi Deixonne allowed the four regional languages to be taught in school, although it has taken much effort to implement (Hélot and Young, 2006). Since 2002 bilingual education in the regional languages has been promoted. In Brittany, some immersion programs in Breton have been implemented under the name of Diwan since 1977. The Diwan network consists of a few kindergarten and primary schools, three lower secondary establishments, known as *collèges* in France, and one upper secondary school or *lycée*. Although partially subsidized by the state, they depend much on the commitment of the parents and private associations for their survival and meet with considerable lack of cooperation from the official French controlling authorities. In 2005, there were over 2,200 students in Diwan schools throughout Brittany. Students are immersed in Breton from pre-school until they are 8 or 9 years of age. Throughout the rest of primary school, students are taught in both French and Breton. In middle school, a third language is also used as medium of instruction.

Friesland
Frisian, which in linguistic structure is the nearest language to English, has been spoken in the northern province of Friesland in the Netherlands (approximately

600,000 inhabitants) for generations. About 94 percent of the Frisian population can understand it, 73 percent speaks it, 65 percent reads it, and 10 percent can write the language (Gorter, Jelsma, de Vos, and van der Plank, 1988). Today Frisian is acknowledged by the Dutch government as an official language of the Netherlands, alongside Dutch.

As early as 1907, the provincial government offered a grant supporting extra-curricular Frisian lessons after school. In 1955 the teaching of Frisian and its use as a medium of instruction in primary school was approved, and in 1980 it was made obligatory as a subject throughout primary school in the province. Bilingual education in Friesland was promoted and a Frisian Center for Bilingual Schooling established (Zondag, 1991). In 1991 all secondary schools in the province were obliged to teach Frisian in the first three years of their curriculum (Ytsma and de Jong, 1993).

Yet, most primary schools spend only one lesson a week on education in Frisian and at least one fifth of the primary schools do not use it at all as a medium. There is little interest in teaching writing in Frisian, and more than a third of the teachers cannot write the language. Over time, the use of Frisian as a medium of instruction has declined as the student population has become more mixed in origin, with fewer children of Frisian background in the classrooms. In spite of legislation and official support, "the legally permitted educational opportunities are far too minimally exploited" (Ytsma and de Jong, 1993: 45).

Roma[13]

The Rom or Roma is a minority group who have been discriminated against and neglected for centuries. The languages of the Rom are referred to by the International Romani Union under the term Romani Chib, which includes all Romani varieties and languages (Winsa, 1999). The Rom are often, though not always, itinerant, non-sedentary populations (travelers) living in areas that straddle national borders, particularly numerous countries in Central Europe, although they are present in nearly all European countries. Many have no official citizenship. Estimates as to the size of this group are extremely difficult to obtain, but they are thought to represent several millions across Europe.

According to the OSCE (Organisation for Security and Cooperation in Europe, 2000) discrimination and exclusion are fundamental features of the Roma experience. There is no unified, standardized Romani language, few written materials in any of the varieties that exist, and very few educated teachers from Rom communities. The lifestyle of many of the Rom is difficult to reconcile with accepted school organization, which implies regularity and codified time allocation.

The Gandhi Project, initiated in Hungary and serving as a model for adaptations in other countries in Central Europe such as the Czech Republic and Slovakia, pro-vides insight into one of the more interesting examples of how to meet the linguistic and educational needs of this population. In contrast to the segregated Roma schools established by public authorities, this model envisages schools created and admin-istered by Roma themselves, ideally with state support. The leading example of such a school – and a model that has inspired Romani activists in other countries – is the Gandhi Gimnázium in Pécs, Hungary, which began operating in February 1994, provides insight into one of the most interesting examples of how to meet the linguistic and educational needs of this population (Katz, 2005).

Its founders conceived of the Gandhi Gimnázium as a vehicle for fostering the development of a Roma intelligentsia through high-quality education aimed principally at Roma students. The school's aim is to educate a significant number of Roma professionals who will be capable of reorganizing the disintegrated communities. To these ends, the Gimnázium seeks to prepare students to attend university. But while providing education of the highest academic standards, the Gandhi Gimnázium also offers a program that fosters pride in students' ethnic identity and develops a pan-Roma identity. Although the language of instruction is Hungarian, the curriculum includes courses in the two languages spoken by the Roma of Hungary – Lovári and Beás[14] – as well as courses in Romani history and culture.[15]

The very establishment of the Gandhi Gimnázium is, in the eyes of its supporters, a powerful symbol of achievement. Observers have noted that in addition to providing a quality education to Roma students, the school also "educates" the broader population. People living in Pécs can see that Roma children are capable of achievement, and that having a Roma school in the city can also be a source of pride. Recently, Pécs was honored with a UNESCO award for multiculturalism (OSCE, 2000).

The United States

In the United States today, the use of the term "maintenance" bilingual education has been completely substituted by "developmental" (see Table 8.9). Developmental bilingual education is used to educate children, mostly immigrants and refugees, who stay in the bilingual education program usually until the end of elementary education. The website of the National Clearinghouse of English Language Acquisition (www.ncela.gwu.edu/expert/faq/22models.html) equates the term "late-exit bilingual education" with developmental bilingual education. Although researchers (Ramirez, 1992; Thomas and Collier, 2002) have repeatedly shown their efficacy, developmental bilingual education programs for language minorities in the United States remain rare.

The Deaf community
by Debra Cole

Educating the Deaf bilingually has at its core the use and development of multiple languages. One of those languages is a sign language, which, as we have seen, is at the very bottom of the language hierarchy in terms of power (Skutnabb-Kangas, 2006).

Bilingual education for the Deaf developed only since the 1980s. In 1983, the Swedish Parliament passed a law requiring schools to educate deaf children bilingually (Baker, 1999). Danish Sign Language is now part of the curriculum for all deaf children in Denmark (Mahshie, 1995). But many schools around the world even today insist on oralism, focusing on the development of speech skills, and forbidding the use of sign language at school. There are other schools that use some manual system of communication that differs significantly from sign languages in that the signs produced follow the syntax of the majority spoken or written language. Examples of these are Signed French, and Linguistics of Visual English (LOVE). But in bilingual programs for the Deaf, both the sign language and the language of the speaking community are acknowledged, and used in educating children. As a result, children acquire at least the language of the speaking community and sign language, although usually they have multilingual competence. Bilingual education for the Deaf is always bimodal (Cole, forthcoming).

Strong (1995) emphasizes that no two bilingual programs for the Deaf are the same. In some schools, a sign language may only be used as a medium of instruction, and never taught as a subject. In other schools, sign language is not only used as a medium, but also taught explicitly in order to enhance the student's ability to conduct metalinguistic analyses of both languages.

Studies of bilingual education for the Deaf have shown positive results with regards to both academic and effective components. Strong and Prinz (1997), Ramsey and Padden (1998), and Wilbur (2000) have shown that Deaf children who have a strong foundation in a sign language are more likely to have stronger academic abilities in the written language than other Deaf children. Using a sign language as the medium of instruction has also been shown to develop literacy skills across the curriculum (Hoffmeister, 2000; Mahshie, 1995). Deaf students also have more self-esteem and a healthier attitude towards education in bilingual programs that acknowledge their Deaf identity and sign-language use (La Sasso and Metzger, 1998).

Deaf students around the world, as mentioned before, are also becoming more diverse and are moving and immigrating. And their schooling is going beyond one written language and one sign language to include many written languages and many sign languages. Deaf people of various language groups are also communicating with each other much more than in the past and in increasingly diverse forms. Thus, bilingual Deaf education is also becoming more complex, with multiple ways of using languages for communication and learning.

Policy for Plurilingualism across Groups: Poly-Directional or Two-Way Bilingual Education (Dual Language)

Poly-directional or two-way bilingual education programs (dual language education in the U.S.) are certainly not new, but they have never been very popular because they require two or more ethnolinguistic groups who are comfortable being educated in each other's languages. These programs build on theories of second-language acquisition which propose that native- and non-native-speaker interactions are essential (Ellis, 2000; Pica, 1994), and that such relationships are also important in developing cross-cultural understandings (Cohen, 1994; Slavin, 1985). Genesee (1999: 37) points to their benefits since "native language models are available in the classroom for both groups of second language learners."

The United States

As early as 1969, Rudolf Troike said that two-way bilingual schools that aim to make students of two different linguistic background fluent and literate in two languages were rare and were likely to remain so. The earliest and best-known two-way bilingual education public-school program in the United States in the second half of the twentieth century is Coral Way, established in Miami, Dade County, Florida in 1963. The model was based on the principles of elite and binational bilingual schools in Europe and Latin America. At its founding, 50 percent of the children had recently arrived from Cuba after the Cuban Revolution of 1959, and needed to develop English-language proficiency, but also the Spanish-language proficiency that would be necessary to re-enter the Cuban educational system in what they thought would be just a few years. But the remainder of the children were Anglo American (Mackey and Beebe, 1977). (For more on this story, see Chapter 8.)

The Coral Way School adopted the following principles:

1. that the Dade County Curriculum Scope and Sequence be followed and the time allocations for each skill area be observed;
2. that each child receive his instruction for a part of the day in his vernacular with a native teacher of his language;
3. that each child receive his instruction for a part of the day in his second language with a native teacher of the second language;
4. that he spend a part of each day in a mixed group, at which time both or either language might be used;
5. that second-language materials be purchased or developed to reinforce or supplement vernacular instruction.
   (Cancela, 1975: 51)

A description of the Coral Way School, as portrayed in Castellanos (1983) appears in the text box below.

Coral Way Elementary School, Miami, Dade County, Florida, U.S.

During half of the school day subjects were taught in the pupils' native language –in Spanish to Spanish-speaking children by native Cuban teachers, and in English to English-speaking children by American teachers. During the other half of the school day, the concepts which had been introduced in the native language were reinforced in the pupils' second language. Once the children had acquired adequate control of the second language, concepts were introduced in the native language of the teacher regardless of the native language of the student. The cultures of both Spanish- and English-speaking groups were incorporated in the instruction that all received. From the beginning the children were mixed on the playground as well as for lunch, music, and art. They were to speak either language.

In Castellanos, 1983: 72

Because of the silencing of the word "bilingual" in the U.S. in the last decade (for more on this, see Chapter 8), and also recognizing their poly-directionality and not just their two-way direction,[16] these programs have been increasingly called "dual language education." These programs are also known as two-way immersion. August and Hakuta (1998: 20) define them thus: "About half of the students in these programs are native speakers of English, and the other half are English-language learners from the same language group. The goal of the program is to develop proficiency in both languages for both groups of students."

Lindholm-Leary (2001) identifies three goals of these dual language programs:

1. learn the language of the others as well as their own language;
2. achieve academically through and in both languages;
3. come to appreciate each others' languages and cultures.

Lindholm-Leary (2001) also lists criteria for their success. Besides those that are important in any school – qualified personnel, home-school collaboration, and a challenging core curriculum – she adds that successful dual language education programs should:

1. provide a minimum of four to six years of bilingual instruction;
2. provide optimal language input including quality language-arts instruction in both languages;
3. use the language other than English for instruction a minimum of 50 percent of the time (to a maximum of 90 percent in the early grades). English should be used at least 10 percent of the time;
4. include a balance of students from the language other than English and English backgrounds who participate in instructional activities together;
5. give all students an opportunity to learn a second language while continuing to develop their native language proficiency;
6. facilitate positive interactions by using co-operative learning strategies.

In the United States dual-language education has experienced a growth spurt in the last decade, although, as Troike predicted in 1969, programs remain rare. In 1995, there were just 182 programs of this kind nationwide (Christian and Whitcher, 1995). But the Center for Applied Linguistics (2006) identified 329 in March 2006. The vast majority of these programs were in Spanish (312), but there were also a handful of dual-language education programs in other languages (nine in French, four in Cantonese, four in Korean, four in Navajo, two in Mandarin, one in Japanese, and one in French/Spanish/German). It is important to note that these numbers pale in comparison to the many thousands of transitional bilingual education programs in the United States in the last three decades.

Many have warned that the substitution of two-way bilingual education types for transitional bilingual education in the United States, without a substantial increase in these types of programs, may lead to the demise of bilingual education over time for language-minority children (García, 2006b; Reyes, 2006b; Valdés, 1997). Krashen (2004) concludes that dual-language education programs show some promising results, but research has not yet demonstrated that they are the best possible programs.

A well-known example of a two-way bilingual education school is the Oyster Bilingual School in Washington, DC, which values both Spanish and English as equal languages. At Oyster School there are two bilingual teachers – one Spanish-dominant and the other English-dominant – in every classroom. There is a 50:50 two-way model with students addressing each teacher in one language only, and teachers speaking only their language. Even though the school's focus is on respecting linguistic diversity and equality, Freeman (1998) observes how English has higher prestige. For example, code-switching from Spanish to English was much more common than the reverse, and students graduated with greater proficiency in written and oral English than in written and oral Spanish. The success of the program, however, is in that it "crosses language, cultural and class lines" (Freeman, 1998: 123). Two-way dual bilingual education questions "the mainstream U.S. assumption of monolingualism in Standard English for the majority of the U.S. population" (Freeman, 1998: 11). The text box that follows includes a description of the Oyster Bilingual School.

Oyster Bilingual School, Washington, DC

the students are 58% Hispanic, 26% White, 12% Black, and 4% Asian, with the children representing over 25 countries [. . .]. Because there are two teachers in each class, one Spanish-dominant who ideally speaks and is spoken to only in Spanish and one English-dominant who ideally speaks and is spoken to only in English, sometimes one classroom may be used for two separate classes at the same time, one conducted in Spanish and the other in English. At other times, the Spanish-dominant teacher may teach the entire class in Spanish, and later in the day the English-dominant teacher may teach the entire class in English [. . .]. The students are generally organized to work together in small groups in the classroom, or in the hallway, or wherever there is space.

In Freeman, 1998: 21, 23

In their longitudinal study of the Amigos Two-Way Immersion program in Cambridge, MA, Cazabón, Lambert, and Hall (1999) found that students, Latinos and non-Latinos, had less prejudicial attitudes towards the other group, and non-Latinos were positive about the value of Spanish in the U.S. However, Cohen and Roper (1972) caution that equal status of languages and groups must be constructed by teachers, rather than assumed. Cohen and Lotan (1995) have consistently found that contact among different groups without deliberate interventions to increase equal status and positive interactions will increase, rather than reduce, intergroup tensions.

Hadi-Tabassum (2006) has examined how language, space, and power intersect in one fifth-grade two-way bilingual classroom. Dual-language education programs bridge bilingual education types for language-minority children with those for the majority (García, 2006b; García, forthcoming). And thus this type of bilingual education program is better able to accommodate the linguistic and cultural hybridities of our globalized world. Potowski (2007) describes the language and identity negotiations of children involved in dual-language classrooms.

European Schools for civil servants

The European Schools for civil servants were founded in 1953. Although specifically designed to accommodate children of European civil servants, these schools may contain up to forty-two nationalities, and provide up to eleven (not all in the same school) mother-tongue sections as the basis of their trilingual development (Baetens Beardsmore, 1995, Müller and Baetens Beardsmore, 2004). In this way, these schools go beyond two languages and two linguistic groups: they are true examples of poly-directional multilingual education.

The European Schools support the children's mother tongue, as well as their cultural, religious, and linguistic identity. They do this by providing a strong education in the child's so-called "first" language. Children also receive explicit instruction in an additional language (English, French, or German) from grade 1 of primary school, and gradually lessons are taught in the child's additional language (Baetens Beardsmore, 1996). In the upper grades of middle school, the study of a third language is required. In order to promote sociocultural and sociolinguistic integration, there are communal lessons (European Hours) where children of different language groups are brought together. These lessons are mostly project-oriented (Müller and Baetens Beardsmore, 2004). Baetens Beardsmore reports that the students' success rate on entrance examinations for universities has been above 90 percent, demonstrating the schools' success (Baetens Beardsmore, 1993c, 1995).

Although most two-way bilingual education programs in the United States keep children of different language abilities together during instruction, European Schools initially separate the children, especially for initial literacy instruction in their home language, but bring them together for more communal lessons as they progress through the program. This is a major distinction between most U.S. dual-language programs and European poly-directional programs.

Begegnungsschule in Berlin

Another interesting example of two-way bilingual education comes from Berlin, where there are *Begegnungsschule* (Encounter Schools) that involve about 3,500 learners. These cover kindergarten, primary, and secondary levels of education and the target languages are English, French, Russian, Spanish, Italian, Portuguese, Polish, Turkish, and Greek. A 50:50 principle is followed in terms of curricular time devoted to each language, to pupil make-up, and to teachers who come from both cultural and language backgrounds involved in the program in a particular school. Teachers use their home language following the principle of one teacher, one language. Reading and writing are first taught in the strongest language in primary schools, but pupils are expected to become equally literate in both languages by the end of year 8. Initially language groups are separate, before being merged, with ever more mixing occurring as they move up through the school system (see Housen and Baetens Beardsmore, 1987).

In the Berlin schools, the other language in the program is known as the "part-ner language," a good non-discriminatory term. At primary level, mathematics is always taught in German, whereas "topic work" (for instance, environmental stud-ies) is always done in the partner language. In later years the language distribution depends on the availability of teachers with the requisite language and subject specialization, either in the home language or the partner language. On exit from the secondary school, learners can get special recognition on their school leaving certificates for the bilingual competence attained.

Although the research on these programs to date is fragmentary, parental satis-faction is high. There is considerable pressure to expand these programs because of their strong intercultural dimension and their relevance to the changing ethno-linguistic profiles of so many large cities.

Examples in Israel

Although Hebrew and Arabic are recognized as official languages of Israel, Hebrew is clearly the dominant language, and bilingualism in these two languages is not widespread. Almost 5 million Israelis have functional competence in Hebrew, but only 2 million speak Arabic (Spolsky and Shohamy, 1999). Hebrew is the language of instruction in most Jewish schools, whereas Arabic is the language of instruction in all Arab schools. Hebrew is taught as a second language in Arabic schools from third grade on, whereas Arabic is studied as an additional language by some Jewish children (Amara, 2005).

An exception to this educational policy is the three integrated schools developed by the Hand-in-Hand Association where Jewish and Arabic children study together. Both languages are used as languages of instruction for every subject. Every class-room has an Arab and Jewish teacher who team-teach, allocating equal time to each language irrespective of the subject. The schools also have a Jewish and Arab co-principal. An effort is made to maintain a numerical balance of Jewish and Arabic children in the school.

Despite these efforts, Amara (2005) has found that Hebrew continues to be more salient and that bilingual education is more successful among Arab students. Many factors account for the difference, the most important one having to do with the power of Hebrew in Israeli society. In practice, although Arab teachers are fully bilingual, the Jewish teachers are not, and thus, Arab teachers tend to use both languages in interactions with students, whereas Jewish teachers use only Hebrew.

Neve-Shalom / Wahat Al-Salam is a two-way dual-language school in Israel that aims to integrate minority Arab children while promoting peaceful co-existence and multiculturalism between the Hebrew-speaking majority students and the Arabic-speaking minority students. The school employs both Israeli and Arab teachers; school publications and bulletin boards include both Arabic and Hebrew language and Islamic and Jewish cultural elements. Conflict, crisis, and peace efforts are import-ant themes in the curriculum. The philosophy of the school is based on Freirian (Freire, 1970) concepts of education and social change. Still, as Feuerverger (2001) makes evident, Hebrew enjoys a hegemonic position because the school is in Israel and, even though Arab teachers speak Hebrew, the reverse is not true. Jewish Israeli children do not develop Arabic skills as quickly as Arabic Israeli children develop their Hebrew. To solve this problem, the school has developed a language center: "The center is a large room, comfortable and attractively designed, in which pupils independently choose learning tasks that are well defined and explained so that students can work with a minimum of guidance. The center supplements the regular language courses by providing an enjoyable, unpressured learning atmosphere, which raises the pupils' motivation to take initiative in language learning" (Feuerverger, 2001: 72).

Border school in Vienna

A model of cross-border schooling in Central Europe involves Vienna (Austria), Bratislava (Slovakia), Brno (Czech Republic), and Györ-Moson-Sopron (Hungary). The school could be considered a poly-directional bilingual education program. Pupils from Bratislava, Brno, and Györ either stay in Vienna during the week or commute to school on a daily basis where a full range of language classes is provided.

The goals of the school are:

1. to fulfill the requirements of the national curricula;
2. to promote language-learning in three languages: mother tongue, English, and a second modern language, particularly the languages of the partner regions;
3. to encourage an understanding of the European dimension through a newly created subject field called "European Studies," using English as a working language, and to implement various trans-regional projects;
4. to promote intercultural understanding and tolerance.

In so doing, the school meets the three goals for education outlined by the European Commission:

1. it promotes the mother tongue plus two additional languages, MT + 2;
2. it promotes regional and minority languages;
3. it addresses diversity.

Poly-directional international schools

Increasingly, there is greater diversity of students in international schools, and also greater mobility. To deal with that diversity, poly-directional and two-way bilingual international schools are slowly growing, although they are not prevalent. They most often offer a two-track program where children from the host country can learn the language and cultures of the other, and where the children of the expatriates can learn the language and culture of the host country. In some ways these bilingual international schools can be considered two-way or poly-directional dual bilingual education programs. One example is the Lycée International de Saint-Germain-en-Laye outside Paris. This international school has five sub-sections subsidized by the state – German, Spanish, Dutch, Italian, and Portuguese – and five sub-sections privately endowed – American, British, Danish/Norwegian, Swedish, and Japanese. Children are taught through their first language at native-speaker levels, but are also constantly mixed together for communal instruction through the medium of French. This school also specifically caters to the children of returning French expatriates who may not have been educated through the French system abroad (for more information, see Duverger and Maillard, 1996).

Policies for Plurilingualism within Groups: CLIL and CLIL-Type Bilingual Education

CLIL is an umbrella term that embraces any type of program where an additional language is used to teach non-linguistic content-matter to all the children in a school. It is always accompanied by explicit language instruction. Unlike other types of bilingual education, CLIL instruction does not take up a large amount of time in the curriculum, and it is often limited to one or two periods of instruction.

CLIL in Europe

All recent European initiatives of bilingual education are grouped under the acronyms CLIL/EMILE (CLIL for Content and Language Integrated Learning and EMILE for its French translation, Enseignement d'une matière intégrée à une langue étrangère) and take on varied forms (European Commission, CLIL/EMILE, 2002; Coyle and Beatens Beardsmore, 2007). The reader is referred to Chapter 9 which devotes close attention to CLIL programs in the European Union. Two examples, one from France and one from Austria follow.

In secondary schools in France under the title of *sections européennes*, CLIL programs involve about 2,500 schools, of which 134 are vocational training schools. The target languages are predominantly English, German, Spanish, or Italian, though other languages are being encouraged, such as Russian, Dutch, and Chinese. The amount of exposure is either low (5–15%) or medium (15–50%) curricular time. Any subject can be taught through the target language except the French language and compulsory philosophy. Only part of a particular subject or part of the curriculum is taught through the target language, which brings about changes in teaching practice. For example, the hours taught in the home language are devoted to knowledge-intensive teaching, whereas the CLIL hours focus on activities permitting the use of the target language, consolidating knowledge, and using it in various communicative activities.

In primary education an interesting case comes from Austria. Known as the Salzburg model, a second language is obligatory from the first grade (age 6) and is taught in short daily sequences which are integrated into all subjects except the teaching of German. Although English predominates, the target language may be French, Italian, Croatian, Czech, Slovakian, Slovenian, or Hungarian. Exposure to the language is low, 5–15 percent of teaching time, yet interdisciplinarity is high. This model is viewed as preparing learners for formal language instruction, and it also enhances awareness of the home language, since pupils learn to compare and conceptualize in both languages.

CLIL-type

Bilingual education programs that develop proficiency in a global language, including immersion-type programs, are clearly on the rise throughout the world. But as we said before, there are no examples in the developing world of a language of wider communication, English or any other, being successful in educating children of underserved groups (Dutcher, 2004). That is, immersion bilingual education is not appropriate for language-minority groups. And yet, in the developing world, as Canagarajah (2005b) has observed, decolonization which led to rejection of colonial languages was quickly followed by globalization which renewed the need for colonial languages, with English, French, Spanish, and Portuguese being the most popular.

One of the most important issues for the developing world today is then how to develop proficiency in global languages for all of their children, while meaningfully educating them. One way to do so is to teach one or two subjects in a global language. We refer to this type of arrangement as CLIL-type bilingual education, borrowing the term as used in the European Union. Two conditions need to be present:

- it does not take up a large amount of time in the curriculum, and is often limited to one to two subjects and one to two periods of instruction;
- it includes all children.

Asia: Malaysia

In Malaysia, at least one hundred languages are spoken over two land masses – Peninsular Malaysia and the states of Sabah and Sarawak on the island of Borneo. There are three main groups in Malaysia – Malays and other indigenous groups (58%), Chinese (24%) speaking a number of Chinese languages, Indians (8%) speaking a number of Indian languages (Wong and James, 2004). Bahasa Malaysia (also known as Bahasa Melayu or Malay) was selected as the national language upon independence in 1957, and in 1968 all primary schools started to be converted to Malay-medium. This process was completed by 1976 for elementary schools, and by 1985 for secondary schools (Gill, 2004).

By 1995, when the Malay medium in education policy was declared fully implemented, a new Education Bill was passed that reaffirmed Malay as necessary for nation-building, but insisted that English also was necessary for economic reasons. Although Malay was reaffirmed as the medium of instruction and taught as a subject five hours a week in primary schools and four hours in secondary schools, English was required to be taught for at least three and a half hours a week in both primary and secondary schools. David and Govindasamy (2003: 217) describe the language education policy in Malaysian schools: "Malay is the medium of instruction. English is a compulsory second language in such schools, and English lessons are conducted daily from the start of compulsory schooling in Standard 1. In addition, the teaching of Chinese or Tamil languages as a subject is made available if requested by the parents of at least 15 children in the school." David and Govindasamy (2003: 223), commenting on the Kuala Lumpur bilingual mixed discourse, say: "One reason for such a code-mixed variety of Malay and English discourse is because such a mix, especially English/Malay, is also used by teachers in the English-language classroom and this influences the input students receive."

In 2003, a new education plan was announced promoting the use of English in teaching mathematics and science starting in primary schools. Gill (2004) points to one of the reasons for this policy implementation – the impossibility of competing with scientific publications in English. Now that Bahasa Malaysia is secure, the attention of educational policy has shifted to how to promote bilingual education that would also develop the English of Malays (David, 2007).

Asia: Shanghai, China

An interesting developing situation inside China refers to the bilingual education project for students in public schools of Shanghai, which is a government-organized project targeting Han-Chinese students in its public school system and involving using English as a medium of instruction for limited periods (Wei, 2005). As we saw in Chapter 10, bilingual education for minority ethnic groups has some legal support, but for majority-language students, that is, Han students, laws specify that Putonghua is the only legitimate medium of instruction. Accordingly, the practice of using an additional language to Putonghua has been discouraged or prohibited. Putonghua had been the sole oral medium of instruction for the majority Han students in public schools in Shanghai at least since the late 1980s.

At the beginning of this millennium the Shanghai Education Commission (SHEC) officially initiated a project to develop bilingual education using English. As of December 2004, over 300 primary and secondary schools have participated in the project, involving about 2,800 teachers and 70,000 students. The project plans to target "half a million" (about 30 percent) of the total student population in the next five years (Zhu, 2004; *News Morning Post*, 2003). Shanghai became the first region to implement government-organized bilingual education despite the fact that, first, it is clearly stipulated in laws that Modern Standard Chinese (MSC) using Putonghua should be the basic medium of instruction for all Han Chinese, and, second, the sociolinguistic milieu remains Chinese-speaking.

Recently, China reformed the College Entrance Examination to "Three plus X," meaning that everyone will have to pass exams in three major subjects – Chinese, mathematics, and English (Feng, 2007). Private and joint venture Chinese and English bilingual learning centers are developing (Fangni Zhang, personal communication, October 17, 2006). It is too early yet to analyze the effects of this massive implementation of a form of bilingual education involving English in China, and developments on this scale should be well worth watching.

Policies for Multiple Languages: Multiple Multilingual Education

The increased understanding and recognition of global multilingual situations have also spurred the adoption of bilingual education policies that develop and spread multiple languages among its citizens, as schools use more than two languages to educate. In these cases, the aim of bilingual education is not simply to recover minority languages that are expanding, but to develop multiple languages and spread them throughout an entire population. An education in two languages is not sufficient, and trilingual and multilingual education is becoming more important.[17] Often these programs weave languages in and out of the curriculum, dropping them, expanding them, and using them for one function or the other, depending on particular instructional circumstances. Many times, these programs are composites of two kinds – transitional bilingual education and developmental bilingual education. The children's home languages and varieties are sometimes used only in the initial grades, followed by the use of a national one and a global one. Other times, multiple languages are used throughout.

Luxembourg

The Grand Duchy of Luxembourg is one of the most experienced countries in bilingual education, with a developed and complex trilingual education system applied to the whole school-going population. In Luxembourg the national language, Luxemburgish, which is only partially standardized since it is mainly used for oral communication, is the home language of the indigenous population, and represents the major marker of its distinctive identity. Schools, however, develop trilingualism for the entire population through a multiple multilingual education program (Baetens Beardsmore and Lebrun, 1991; Hoffman, 1998; Lebrun and Baetens Beardsmore, 1993). When children enter schools, they are first taught in the home language, Luxemburgish; but very soon the same teacher introduces German, which is genetically related to Luxemburgish, for initial reading and writing. Subsequently, the primary school teacher responsible for all subjects introduces French as a subject. In secondary education French is increasingly used as a medium of instruction, and depending on their orientation and age, all children receive their education through the medium of Luxemburgish, German, and French, in that order (Baetens Beardsmore and Lebrun, 1991; Clyne, 1997; Lebrun and Baetens Beardsmore, 1993). Throughout schooling the three languages are used as a medium for non-linguistic content-matter. The schedules for languages as a subject reflects the importance given to this aspect of the program, which takes up almost 40 percent of the curriculum in primary education (see Table 11.2) and from 36 percent to 50 percent in general secondary education (see Table 11.3), less in technical and professional schools.

Table 11.2 Primary School Program: Number of Hours Devoted to Language as Subject

Grade	1	2	3	4	5	6
Luxemburgish	1	1	1	1	1	1
French	–	3	7	7	7	7
German	8	8.5	5	5	5	5

Table 11.3   Lower Secondary School Program: Language as Subject Lessons per Grade

	Grade 7	*Grade 8*	*Grade 9*
French	6	6	4.5–5.5
German	4	4	3.0–3.5
Luxemburgish	1	0	3.5–5.5
English/Latin	0	6	English 3.5–5.5
			Latin 4.5
TOTAL	11 of 30 lessons	16 of 30 lessons	14.5–15.5 of 30 lessons

As for the distribution of languages as a medium for non-linguistic subjects, this may vary according to the grade and the orientation chosen in secondary education. For example, history is taught in German or in French, depending on the grade. Philosophy is taught in French when handling French texts, and in German or French when handling German texts. French is used to teach political economy, civics, mathematics, physics, and chemistry; but biology and geography is taught in German in the lower grades and in French in the higher grades. Economics is taught through the medium of French, whereas arts and music are taught through either German or French, depending on the grade.

Lebrun and Baetens Beardsmore (1993) have pointed out that Luxembourg's trilingualism-through-education policy for all is generally successful because of particular circumstances. The complex system is considered a political choice based on economic, cultural, and political foundations. The country is small and the three languages have important complementary functions for all citizens – Luxemburgish for reasons of identity, French and German for contact with large neighboring countries. Trilingualism is understood and accepted by all citizens, including the representatives of immigrant organizations (Grand Duchy of Luxembourg, 2005–2006). Education is generously funded with teacher salaries being among the highest in Europe. All teachers are adequately trained to operate through three languages, and moreover, all of them, like the children's parents, have been through the trilingual system themselves, since it has been in operation since 1912. Finally, there is careful lock-step phasing of each language in the curriculum.

One of the major challenges facing the Luxembourg education system is the large number of immigrant children, with 39 percent of the total population in 2004 being made up of foreigners and 36 percent of the workforce coming from across the international borders daily (Grand Duchy of Luxembourg, 2005–2006). The children of this large immigrant population, primarily of Portuguese origin, have to be integrated into this complex system and do not necessarily speak Luxemburgish as the first home language.

In a critical self-appraisal of the language education policy in Luxembourg, produced as a country profile in collaboration with Council of Europe expertise (see Chapter 9 for more information on this procedure), the Luxembourg authorities have analyzed the strengths and weaknesses of their unique system (Grand Duchy of Luxembourg, 2005–2006). This report gives invaluable insights into the role of the home language in educational success, the problems of selection for moving up through the system, the different types of difficulties encountered by immigrants and nationals in adapting to school requirements, and a commitment to modify teaching practice to face the ever more complex linguistic situation brought about by migration, globalization, and technological advances. There is no question, however, of eliminating the avowed political goal of developing trilingualism for all through schooling.

Asia

The Philippines

In the Philippines, the 1967 Constitution declared Pilipino to be the national language, a non-existent language that was envisioned to blend all the different national languages of the archipelago (some 171 living languages, according to Grimes, 2000). The eight major languages of the Philippines are Tagalog, Ilocano, Pampangan, Bicolano, Cebuano, Ilonggo (Hiligaynon), Waray, and Pangasinan. In reality, however, Pilipino, since 1987 referred to as Filipino, is a dialect of Tagalog. In an effort to promote and spread Pilipino, as well as English, throughout the archipelago, the Philippines passed their Bilingual Education Policy in 1974, which stated:

> Bilingual education is defined operationally as the separate use of Pilipino and English as media of instruction in definite subject areas. Arabic shall be used in the areas where it is necessary. The use of English and Pilipino as Medium of Instruction begins in grade I in all schools. The vernacular is an auxiliary medium of instruction in grades I and II. English and Pilipino are taught as subjects in elementary and secondary schools. (Sibayan, 1978: 302)

Although teachers were allowed to use the local languages in the early grades especially for literacy, Pilipino/Filipino was imposed as the language in which to teach social studies/social sciences, music, arts, physical education, home economics, practical arts, and character education. In addition, it was decided that math, science, and technology were to be taught in English.

In 1987, the Bilingual Education policy of 1974 was modified and vernaculars were forcefully restored as auxiliary teaching languages in the initial grades of schools. A trilingual system is now used in the early grades, with the vernaculars, Filipino, and English used up to grade 3, at which point the use of the auxiliary languages ceases. During this transitional stage a *bimedial system* of instruction is used. The instructor gives the gist of the lesson in the language prescribed – Filipino or English – and then explains to students in the local vernacular (Gonzalez, 1998). The policy continues to be controversial, especially among speakers of Cebuano and Ilocano, two of the other most prevalent Filipino languages.

Research has confirmed the damaging effects of the use of English on Filipino student learning, especially among the poor and the middle class. Bernardo (1999, 2004) has summed up the findings of empirical research over the last twenty years on the damaging effects of English on learning:

First, students learn better in their mother tongue. Second, students do not learn as well in English; in some cases, they do not learn at all. Third, using English as the medium of instruction in some subject areas prevents students from learning as much as they could if the mother tongue were used. In some cases, specific obstacles to learning are clearly associated with difficulties with the English language. Fourth, the ones who will benefit most from education in the English language are those who have good levels of proficiency in English to begin with and/or those who grow up in environments where English language inputs, materials and resources are abundant. (Bernardo, 2004: 27)

While public schools in the Philippines continue to be under-funded, overcrowded, and staffed by poorly paid teachers, private schools for elite families offer a high-quality bilingual system of education. Graduates of elite private schools have major advantages, including superior English proficiency (Tollefson, 2002).

India

The multilingualism of India is complex, with the number of languages in the thousands and at least thirty languages being spoken by over a million native speakers (Mohanty, 2006). The Official Languages Act of 1967 provided for the use of Hindi as the language of communication between the center and the Hindi-speaking states, and the use of English for communication between the center and non-Hindi-speaking states (Brass, 1994). At the federal level, there were then two official languages, Hindi and English, although there were fifteen official languages at the state level – Telugu, Bengali, Marathi, Tamil, Urdu, Gujarati, Kannada, Malayalam, Oriya, Punjabi, Kashmiri, Sindhi, Assamese, Konkani, and Sanskrit. In December 2003, the 100th constitutional amendment to the Constitution of India (eighth schedule) officially recognized twenty-two languages, along with English, as the associate official language (Mohanty, 2006).

Mohanty (2006) has described the very different multilingual nature of India: widespread bilingualism at the grassroots level; maintenance norms supported by the non-competing roles of languages and their complementarities in the lives of people; the multiplicity of linguistic identities; and bilingualism and multilingualism as a positive force.

In 1957, a formula known as the Three-Language Formula for education was adopted, which recommended:

1. regional languages or mother tongue as the first teaching language for five years;
2. Hindi in non-Hindi areas and any other Indian language in Hindi areas as the second language (as a school subject) for three years (i.e., the sixth to eighth years in school);
3. English as third language subject from the third year onwards (as cited in Mohanty, 2006: 273).

In 1964 this formula was modified making Hindi no longer compulsory for non-Hindi areas, and English able to be taught in place of Hindi. English eventually became the most common second-language subject in all states.

Only 11 percent of the population in India has completed ten years of education (Annamalai, 2004). Although there are thirty-three languages used in education in India, including English, and there are forty-one languages available for study in school (NCERT, 1999), education in India, as Mohanty (2006: 279) says, is not really bilingual: "education in India is only superficially multilingual, and it remains monolingual at an underlying level. The official three-languages formula is more abused and less used." Pattanayak (1997) has also referred to the lack of bilingual education programs in India. Of course, as Mohanty points out, much use of other languages in education occurs. For example, although a lesson may be read in the official medium of instruction, it may be explained, discussed, or clarified in another language.

Mohanty (2006: 279) describes a transitional bilingual education program for tribal groups designated as a *Bilingual Transfer Model* and developed by the Central Institute of Indian Languages in Mysore:

> The program begins with use of tribal language as medium of instruction in the first year of schooling, along with oral communication in the regional language. Instructional time for the regional language is progressively increased as that for the tribal language is reduced so that, by the beginning of the fourth year of schooling, the child is ready for instruction in regional language only.

The MLE (Multilingual Education) program in the tribal areas of Orissa, directed by Mahendra Kumar Mishra, provides instruction in ten tribal languages in 195 schools.[18] The distribution of the tribal language, Oriya, and English appears in Table 11.4:

Table 11.4 Curriculum Framework 2007–2012 Orissa

	Grade 1 Age 5+	Grade 2 Age 6+	Grade 3 Age 7+	Grade 4 Age 8+	Grade 5 Age 9+
Tribal lang.	80% oral and written	70% oral and written	50% oral and written	40% oral and written	30% oral and written
Oriya	20% oral	30% oral and transfer to written	40% oral and written	50% oral and written	60% oral and written
English			10% oral	10% oral introduction to written	10% oral and written

As in other parts of the world, the growth of private schools with tuition has encouraged the growth of bilingual education programs. Annamalai (2004) recounts how urban middle-class families often send their children to bilingual schools in which science subjects are taught through English and other subjects through Hindi. Even though these Indian children do well, these schools are well funded and these students would have been academically successful anyway. Annamalai warns against the trend in Asia, Africa, and the Arabic-speaking world of teaching math and science through English. He says (2004: 191):

> the bilingual model that associates Indian languages with "soft," (i.e., non-science) subjects will have adverse effects on the development of Indian languages as vehicles of scientific knowledge. The ideological conflict – between empowering people with English and empowering them with their native languages by using the latter in domains of power such as science and technology – must be taken into consideration when making decisions on medium of education.

Hong Kong

The citizens of the Hong Kong Special Administrative Region (HKSAR) do not speak either of the entity's two official languages as a first language – Standard Mandarin Chinese and English. According to Article 9 of the Basic Law adopted in 1990 and in effect in 1997, "In addition to the Chinese language, English may also be used as an official language by the executive authorities, legislature and judiciary of the Hong Kong Special Administrative Region." The term "Chinese language" is deliberately left undefined. English reflects the colonial status of Hong Kong until 1997. Putonghua / Mandarin Chinese represents the cultural norm before and after the creation of the Hong Kong Special Administrative Region, although is not a commonly spoken medium.

According to the 1991 census, 96 percent of Hongkongers speak Cantonese, 32 percent speak English, and 18 percent speak Mandarin (Ngai-Lai, 2004). The use by all official instances of "Chinese" in Hong Kong is ambiguous to the outsider, since it refers to both Putonghua, the standard language of the whole of China, and to Cantonese. Within Hong Kong, Cantonese is taken to be a type of spoken Chinese with official status in certain contexts. It is very distinct, has a rich oral and written tradition, is used in the press and audio-visual media, the youth culture (via "Cantopop" music) and is omnipresent both within and outside the education system. To some extent, this is comparable to the use of the term "German" in Switzerland, which can refer to the standard language of all the German-speaking countries, but which is very distinct from the Helvetian variety known as *Schwyzertütsch*.

Purely by coincidence, the linguistic reality of Hong Kong means that the education system confronts youngsters with the principle of "mother tongue plus two modern languages." According to the policy of the present government, mother tongue is understood to be Cantonese in spoken form and Modern Standard Chinese in written form. After the change of sovereignty, the government espoused a language education policy of biliteracy and trilingualism, that is, Cantonese, Mandarin, and English (Tsui, 2007).

In primary schools, children interact mainly in Cantonese, which shares the same standardized written characters as Mandarin (though the older, more complex system of traditional characters is used in Cantonese print material).[19] They also receive instruction in and of Mandarin, and English as a foreign language, though often the level of proficiency attained in these languages may not be as high as desired.

At the secondary level, two distinct systems exist. The majority of schools operate in Chinese as medium of instruction (whether this means most activities occur in Cantonese or in Mandarin appears to be left deliberately ambiguous in almost all studies: see So, 2004; Tsui, 2007). Secondary schools can only offer instruction through English after having been judged capable of effectively using this medium. About 80 percent of pupils attend the Chinese-medium schools, and 20 percent the English-medium schools.

The policy of Chinese as medium of instruction in secondary schools that went into effect when the former colony was handed over to China has been controversial, with parents and the business sectors objecting vehemently. Yet, four years after the implementation, there was evidence that students benefited from learning in Chinese. A study by Marsh, Hau, and Kong (2000) showed that although English-medium secondary schools had positive effects on English proficiency, they had negative effects on mathematics achievement, and very negative effects on achievement in geography, history, and science. Other studies have shown that there were differences in teacher–student interaction between classrooms that used English as a medium of instruction and those that used Chinese. In those classrooms where Chinese was used, different types of questions were asked and there were more responses elicited. Students were also more engaged in collaborative construction of knowledge, and the language used by the teacher and the student was more precise (Tsui, 2004).

The majority of universities in Hong Kong officially operate through English as medium of instruction. The reality of what happens in secondary education (and to some extent in universities) is that Cantonese is prevalent as the spoken medium, regardless of the institution's official language status. Many non-language subjects resort to massive code-switching between Cantonese and the official language, and it is proving difficult to activate the use of the target languages as exclusive media in education. This may be because of a variety of reasons, including lack of teacher proficiency in the official target languages, lack of training on how to operate in a bilingual teaching context, and the vigor and strength of Cantonese in the general environment. Classroom observations in Hong Kong also show that many secondary teachers, especially science and mathematics teachers, translanguage when teaching in English because of their own language difficulties and those of the students (Tsui, 2004).

Hong Kong is still adapting to the presence of a trilingual school environment. As So (2002) has clearly indicated, there is a mismatch in Hong Kong between official policy to promote Chinese medium instruction as a priority, and perceived needs by parents and employers for an efficient form of education that offers high levels of proficiency in both Mandarin and English and takes into account the omnipresent Cantonese.

Singapore

Singapore, independent since 1964, is a multi-ethnic nation with four official languages – Mandarin, Malay, Tamil, and English. The "national language" is Malay, and it is used for commands in the armed forces and in the national anthem, but English is the *de facto* major language for the entire population. The ethnic breakdown consists of approximately 76 percent Chinese, 14 percent Malay, 8 percent Indian, and 2 percent other residents (Pakir, 2004). The Chinese population consists of speakers of mainly Hokkien, Teochew, Cantonese, Hainanese, and Hakka, while the Indian population may be speakers of Indian languages other than Tamil, for example, of Malayalam and Punjabi (Pakir, 2004).

Since 1979, English has been the medium of instruction in schools. But the learning of an official "ethnic mother tongue," according to the father's ethnicity, is also compulsory in all schools in Singapore. All children are expected to learn in school their official ethnic language, develop language and literacy skills in that language, as well as cultural values associated with that ethnicity (Pakir, 2004). In Singapore's highly centralized education system, the official policy is that all children become bilingual and biliterate in English and one other official language (Malay, Mandarin, or Tamil) as determined by their ethnic origin (Pakir, 2004). Fraser Gupta (1997) points out, however, that there is virtually no opportunity for learning cross-ethnic languages in Singapore schools, meaning, for example, that Malays cannot study Mandarin, and Chinese cannot study Malay in school. Nevertheless, Singaporean schools provide for the development of multiple languages for Singaporean society, if not for individuals. Pakir (2004: 129) calls Singapore, an "ascendant English-knowing bilingual community for a globalized world."

Singapore, however, seems to have been undergoing massive language shift away from a multiplicity of languages because there is no education in local languages (UNESCO, 2005). Parallel to the shift to English as a major language of education, secondary language shift has occurred from other dialects of Chinese towards Mandarin (Baetens Beardsmore, 1998). Vigorous "Speak Mandarin" campaigns aimed at the Chinese ethnic group have been in place for twenty-five years and there is continuous adjustment of the teaching and examining criteria for Mandarin to improve levels of competence and usage (Chew, 2007).

Malay speakers are the ones that are least likely to abandon their "ethnic mother tongue," partially because of its prevalence in the neighboring countries (Malaysia where it is known as Bahasa Malay or Bahasa Melayu, Indonesia where it is known as Bahasa Indonesia, and Brunei). Continuous monitoring of language issues is a permanent concern of the Singapore government, with regular press interventions on the promotion of Standard English over *Singlish*, an English variety used in informal interaction, encouraging the use and knowledge of Mandarin, pointing out the usefulness of Malay, and anchoring Singapore identity (Chew, 2007).

Singaporeans have different levels of linguistic proficiency in English and the official ethnic tongues. In families, each generation may have proficiency in different languages. For example, grandparents may be monolingual speakers of Hokkien. The Chinese-educated parents may be dominant in Mandarin and proficient in English. And the third-generation children may be dominant in English with restricted proficiency in school-transmitted Mandarin. All three generations, however, are capable of interfamily communication via translanguaging strategies. They have receptive competence in many languages and varieties (Pakir, 2004).

Brunei Darussalam

Situated on the northeastern coast of Borneo, Brunei has a population of approximately 300,000 inhabitants of whom 70 percent are Malays, 17 percent are

Chinese, 11 percent are expatriate workers, and 6 percent are non-Malay indigenous people (Henry, Rohaniah, and Metussin, 1999). The largest indigenous language is Malay. The Chinese population uses a variety of Chinese dialects. Other Indigenous languages are Tutong, Belait, Dusun Bisaya, Murat (Austronesian languages), Iban, and Penan (North-Sarawak languages) (Jones, Martin, and Ozóg, 1993).

In 1984 the Government of Brunei introduced an official *dwibahasa* (two-languages) policy for the entire school system. Malay became the medium of instruction in the first three years of primary school, accompanied by English-as-a-subject lessons. Starting from the fourth grade, geography, mathematics, and science are taught in English, while civics, Brunei history, religious knowledge (Islam), physical education, and art, are taught in Standard Malay (Saxena, 2007). Because the majority of Bruneians are also Muslims, most children in primary schools are also initiated in Arabic during religious instruction. Given that both Arabic and Malay in Brunei use the Arabic script (*Jawi*), this implies that the majority of children are confronted with three official languages in primary education (Malay, English, and Arabic) and two scripts: the Roman alphabet for both English and Malay, together with the Arabic script for both Malay and Arabic. Children who attend Chinese schools in Brunei Darussalam are taught in Mandarin Chinese (which is usually not the Chinese child's home language), English, and Malay, and acquire literacy using the Roman alphabet and Chinese characters. For the majority of children, none of the official school languages may be their home language, which may be a non-standard variety of Brunei Malay, a so-called Chinese dialect such as Cantonese, or a non-Malay language such as Iban. Despite Brunei's linguistic diversity, there are no provisions for the use of local languages in education (UNESCO, 2005).

The ideological basis for Brunei society is based on the concept of Melayu Islam Beraja, or the Malay Islamic Monarchy. Brunei has overcome the potentiality for language and cultural shift through a bilingual education system, maintaining Malay as the language of initial schooling and its use throughout education as a medium for some subjects. Luxembourg's trilingual program provides the nearest European comparison to Brunei in language education policy.

The outcome of Brunei's policy can be assessed on several levels. Rapid development, modernization, and bilingualism do not appear to threaten the Indigenous culture. There is no apparent cultural shift apart from the inevitable consequences of semi-urbanization, mass media-provision and greater general wealth. The fact that the *dwibahasa* policy does not engender the abandonment of Malay means that no significantly indigenized variety of Brunei English has developed. This contrasts with Singapore, where because English has become the *de facto* language of most of the population, a new variety of English, disparagingly known as Singlish, has developed.

In Brunei the goal is full bilingualism and full biliteracy in Malay and English and minimal trilingualism with triliteracy in Arabic. In other words, the education system aims at producing people who can read, write, understand, and speak Malay and English at levels which match their specific needs. Adults should be able to read and write Malay either with the Romanized alphabet or with the Arabic script.

Arabic is expected to be sufficient for religious purposes and for reading the Qur'an.

The Arab Middle East and North Africa[20]
by Zeena Zakharia

The Arabic language has held symbolic and functional significance in Arab religious and secular discourse, and continues to be the fundamental criterion in defining the national self (Suleiman, 1994; Zakharia, 2005). In many ways, all education in Arabic is multilingual, or at least multi-dialectal. Both Fuṣ'ḥá varieties are used – with Classical Arabic used to read the Qur'an, and Modern Standard Arabic used to teach values and curricular subjects. In addition, local spoken vernaculars are used in classroom communication and in non-formal situations at school. However, Fuṣ'ḥá is nobody's home language, and the differences between Fuṣ'ḥá, standardized in the eighth and ninth centuries, and the local spoken vernaculars, have increased over the centuries. Moroccan Arabic, for example, has Berber influence, and thus, it is difficult to understand by speakers of colloquial Arabic in Syria or Saudi Arabia. Small neighboring countries such as Lebanon, Syria, Palestine, and Jordan speak a mutually intelligible colloquial Arabic, and spoken vernaculars diverge increasingly across geographic distances, from Morocco in the West, to Iraq in the East.

The average student in an Arabic-dominant Islamic school will therefore employ at least three varieties of Arabic throughout his or her schooling, and the average student in a non-Islamic school will employ at least two varieties, making Arabic language education policies at least bilingual. Until recently, little attention has been given to this taken-for-granted phenomenon and its impact on children's literacy and achievement during their first years of schooling, where, without the introduction of a "recognized" foreign language, students are already immersed in a bilingual setting, and expected to learn curricular subjects in an Arabic variety that is "foreign" to the young learner, rather than in the familiar home variety.

The era of colonization and missionary enterprises introduced foreign languages into schools in parts of the Arab world as early as the mid-nineteenth century. This influence grew after World War I with the carving up of the Ottoman Empire largely into British and French mandates and protectorates. In the Maghreb, for example, the French and Italian languages gained preeminence, while in the Levant, French and English gained ground in accordance with the language of the mandatory power. As Arab states gained independence after World War II, a policy of Arabization in education spread throughout the region with the rise of Arab nationalism, and in response to western imperialism. New countries in the Arabian Gulf established formal systems of schooling in the latter half of the twentieth century, incorporating the teaching of English into their development plans, in part because of British and American influence, and in part because of an influx of diverse peoples from around the world during the oil boom and the rapid industrialization and urbanization that followed. The development of multiple languages in schools in these three regions of the Arab Middle East and North Africa – the Maghreb, the Levant, and the Arab Gulf – evolved from very different historical, social, political, cultural, and economic circumstances and periods, some as recent as the last decade. Today multilingualism is highly valued across the region for a variety of reasons. All Arab students who finish government schooling have been exposed to instruction in Arabic and at least some English and/or French, to varying degrees. In addition, minority languages such as Tamazight (Berber languages), Kurdish, Armenian, and Aramaic continue to survive through community-run schools.

The following discussion focuses on planning for the development of multiple languages, beyond Arabic, in selected educational systems across the region, comprising twenty-two states in which Arabic is the official language, beginning with the Maghreb to the West, then moving East to the region known as the Levant, and further East and South to the Arab Gulf. This discussion is intended to provide an overview of systems-wide initiatives in bilingual education and does not cover every state in these geographic blocks. Rather, through a handful of cases, it serves to highlight the commitment to various forms of bilingual education across the region arising from different historical, social, and developmental realities, and with varying success.

The Maghreb

The Maghreb, comprising Morocco, Algeria, Tunisia, and Libya, share a similar linguistic and religious history, with Arabic introduced during the eighth- and ninth-century Islamic conquest, and French and Italian introduced with European colonization in the nineteenth century. The Indigenous Berber languages (also known collectively as Tamazight) survived and are spoken today by a significant portion of the population (for example three dialects of Berber account for approximately 45% of Moroccan speakers), but are not generally used in the schooling of Berber children. After independence from colonial rule in the latter half of the twentieth century, a policy of Arabization established Arabic as the sole official language of Algeria, Morocco, and Tunisia; however, French continued to dominate non-religious areas of public life as the unofficial second language.

In Morocco today, Arabic is the main language of instruction, with French introduced as the second language in grade 3 for eight hours a week. A third language is introduced in the tenth grade and given an equal number of teaching hours as Arabic and French. National education reforms introduced in late 2002 established English in public schools from grade 4 onward, alongside Arabic and French. Similarly, in Tunisia, students begin school in Arabic, and French is introduced from grade 3 (nine hours per week) and English from grade 7 (two hours per week). Otherwise all subjects are taught in Arabic until the secondary level, where mathematics and sciences begin being taught in French in order to prepare students for university studies.

Algeria began to Arabize its curriculum in the early 1960s, replacing French with Arabic as the language of instruction at the primary level. Later this was moved up to the secondary level. Today all subjects are taught in Arabic except for the teaching of additional languages. In 1992 English was introduced from grade 4 as a first additional language option (five hours per week) alongside French, and students choose between these two languages. In grade 8, students choose the other language (French or English) as their second additional language (four hours per week) and some students study a third additional language as part of their curriculum in the secondary cycle. In 2003, Tamazight were also permitted in schools.

The Levant

The sociolinguistic history of the Levant, comprising Lebanon, Jordan, Syria, and Palestine, differs from the Maghreb. Under centuries of Ottoman occupation, culminating in missionary activity in the educational arena during the nineteenth century, and French and British mandatory control after World War I, the region was historically exposed to multiple languages in education. Except for Syria, in which a monolingual educational policy was established with Arabization after independence from France, the countries of this region maintained the already-integrated missionary and colonial languages of their school systems, particularly in the private sector, after World War I.

Lebanon has a long history of bilingual educational practices and is an interesting case. First established with Christian missionary schools in the first half of the nineteenth century, bilingual educational practices developed along the lines of their European and American missionary sponsors (Shaaban and Ghaith, 2003), thus spreading along sectarian lines during the late Ottoman period and prior to World War I. The French mandate (1920-1943) established French and Arabic as official languages, imposed the French educational system and language, and encouraged the establishment of private French schools and French missionary institutions. After independence (1943), Arabic was made the sole official language; however, French continued to dominate private institutions and public life. In 1946 English was officially introduced as an alternative additional language option to French in schools, and while all subjects were to be taught in Arabic in grades 1 to 6, students could sit for government examinations in mathematics and sciences in Arabic, English, or French.

Today, based on this legacy, the national curriculum, which governs public and private schools, operates in Arabic, French, and English for all students, in different combinations. Arabic and either French or English are introduced from the first grade, and the second additional language (French or English) is introduced from grade 7. Half of the curriculum (humanities and social sciences) is taught in Arabic, and the other half (mathematics and sciences) is taught in the first additional language. In practice, most private schools, which account for the large majority of students, introduce the second additional language as early as the primary grades, but with lesser weight. Arabic and the first additional language are given equal weight in terms of number of language-teaching hours, and number of hours in each language of instruction. Approximately 70 percent of schools function with French as the first additional language of instruction (used to teach mathematics and sciences) and 30 percent function with English as the first additional language of instruction. In addition, a number of private schools also teach in Armenian and other European languages such as German and Italian. All schools, however, teach Arabic as the common denominator for all while being in different degrees bilingual, and choice of language-medium for public and private schooling is left up to parents (Zakharia, 2005).

The Arab Gulf
In the Arab Gulf, comprising the United Arab Emirates, Saudi Arabia, Qatar, Bahrain, Kuwait, and Oman, the establishment of formal systems of education and ministries of education is relatively new, and generally accompanied the discovery of oil and the rapid industrial development and urbanization that followed in the early 1970s. As a result, growth in enrollment and literacy has been phenomenal in recent years. Today, a large percentage of Gulf country residents are non-nationals, or expatriates, both from Arab and non-Arab countries. Thus school systems were established in a relatively short period to cater to the languages and cultures of diverse peoples.

For example, the educational system of the United Arab Emirates (UAE) was established in the early 1970s, and includes a large network of public, private, and international schools. Non-UAE nationals represent 70–80 percent of the resident population of the UAE. All schools are licensed by the Ministry of Education and operate in accordance with government policy, which stipulates that all schools offer Islamic education and the Arabic language as core subjects for students of Arab origin, and as non-core subjects for non-Arab students.

Until recently, bilingual education in the UAE was primarily the domain of elite private and international schools, with literature and humanities taught in Arabic, and mathematics and sciences taught in English. These schools, alongside private schools offering bilingual education and curricula for expatriate communities (mainly British, American, Indian, Pakistani, French, Russian, German, Iranian), account for over 40 percent of the student population. Public, or free-tuition government schools, on the other hand, teach all subjects in Arabic and introduce English language as a limited subject from the primary grades. At the end of grade 12, all students of Arab origin – public or private – are required to pass a national terminal examination in Arabic and religion (Islamic education), with a pass mark of 40 percent (a special version of this examination is required of Arab nationals whose mother is a non-Arab native).

The recent educational development strategy by year 2020, however, entails a shift in language education policy for all public schools in line with the modernizing objectives of the government. The elaborate series of five-year plans involves development of the educational infrastructure through public–private school partnerships and model schools in which mathematics and sciences are taught in English for all students within the coming years. The reform initiative launched its pilot program in late 2006 and involves the development of English-language skills for elementary students, in collaboration with Zayed University, starting from grade 1, at four model schools, with the goal of universal implementation by 2020. A central component of the plan is the "Emiratization" of the teaching staff in government schools to ensure Islamic principles and traditions. In order to meet the twin objectives of increasing the numbers of UAE teachers to 90 percent of the teaching staff by 2020, and teaching mathematics and science subjects in English, the UAE government is focusing a large component of its teacher training on developing English-language skills within the teaching profession.

The educational system of Saudi Arabia grew out of a history of religious and basic literacy teachings in mosques during the 1930s, when the first formal secular primary schools were founded. Established in the 1950s, the Ministry of Education oversees all government and local private schools and supervises the operation of private and international schools. The vast majority of students are educated in government schools whose primary emphasis is on Arabic language and Islamic studies, which together account for up to eighteen hours per week, or over half the number of hours of classroom study. At present, English is introduced as a second language in grade 7 and continues through grade 12 for all students, whether enrolled in General Secondary, Religious Secondary, or Technical Secondary School curricula. The public-sector schools provide for Saudi and other Arab nationals who share language and religion.

The large majority of foreign and international private schools, which cater to diverse expatriate groups, operate largely in English and offer other foreign languages. These include British, American, Indian, Pakistani, and Filipino schools. In addition, elite bilingual schools operate in French, German, and Japanese. The large number of expatriates working in Saudi Arabia has made English a lingua franca.

Saudi Arabia's ten-year plan for education (2004 to 2014) aims at improving the quality and quantity of education for a growing student population, and in line with state development plans for "preparing human resources that are capable of creating and achieving comprehensive social development for the community in the various aspects of its social and economic life" (Kingdom of Saudi Arabia, 2005: 5). A portion of this initiative is dedicated to improving the quality of English-language teaching and introducing English from the primary grades.

Qatar wants to ensure that Qatari children are educated in Islamic and other local cultural values, and the government is increasingly interested in having all children develop proficiency in English. They are thus experimenting with bilingual forms of education, with math and science being taught in English (Al-Thani, 2004; García, 2004). The education reform initiative of Qatar, "Education for a New Era," calls for new innovative schools, "guided in their teaching by internationally competitive curriculum standards in *Arabic, English*, mathematics and science" (Education for a New Era. Fact Sheet, 2004; my italics).

As we have seen, a number of models exist for the development of multiple languages in the Arab Middle East and North Africa, stemming from diverse historical, social, religious, and economic circumstances. While Arabic is used as the vehicle for everyday expression and communication throughout the region, other languages, especially English, are increasingly needed for economic and technical domains, and educational planning reflects these imperatives. Because of the distance between local vernaculars, Modern Standard Arabic, and Classical Arabic, coupled with a renewed interest in proficiency in English and/or French, all education in Arab countries develops the ability of children to successfully use multiple languages and engage in translanguaging practices.

Conclusion

This chapter has looked at how bilingual education policies have expanded the types of bilingual education programs presented in Chapter 10, as they adapt to different ideologies, wishes, and local circumstances. So that the reader understands the intricacies and complexities of how bilingual education policy is enacted, we have focused in this chapter on language education policies of states and nations, although we have also included some examples of policy of specific communities, and even of particular schools.

In general, the following *five principles* emerge from this discussion:

1. If a non-dominant social group wants to reverse their extreme degree of language shift and revitalize their endangered language, *immersion revitalization bilingual education* programs are established. In immersion revitalization bilingual education, the endangered language is used as the main medium of instruction and takes up most of the time in the curriculum, although the other language is also used. Revitalizing the language and bilingualism is the goal of such programs. In practice, there is much translanguaging in these classrooms as bits and pieces of the ancestral language are recovered. As a result of this education, the group develops bicultural multiplicity, allowing access to the overlapping and separate features of the two or more cultures that come in and out as needed.

2. If a language-minority group has recovered some measure of agency and has been able to obtain its right to use the language in the education of their children, *developmental bilingual education* programs are established. There is a much broader range of bilingualism in these communities than in those that establish immersion revitalization programs. This has to do with two factors: first, the language shift has not been as extensive, and, thus, there are more members of the community that are bilingual; second, the language-minority community is now more politically, economically, and socially powerful than in the past, so it is able to attract speakers of dominant languages to become bilingual. Developmental bilingual education programs generally use two languages throughout a child's education, although often there is more emphasis on the threatened language. But because of the greater bilingual range of these communities, there are often other types of bilingual education that exist side by side with these developmental kinds so as to fulfill the sociolinguistic need of all speakers. There is also a greater range of flexibility with how the language is used instructionally and how students translanguage. As a result of this education, the group develops bicultural multiplicity, allowing access to the overlapping and separate features of the two or more cultures that come in and out as needed.

3. When two or more groups want to learn each other's languages and want to benefit from their close contact and sharing of cultures, *poly-directional or two-way (dual-language) bilingual education* programs are established. Bilingualism is shared across groups as the two or more languages are used in instruction, mostly in integrated groups, but initially in separate groups for literacy acquisition. This is possible when bilingualism is considered a resource. Across the groups there is much bilingual heterogeneity and there is no expectation of becoming a balanced bilingual. Rather plurilingualism is valued as children language differently. If conducted appropriately, these poly-directional or dual-language bilingual education efforts encourage transculturalism.

Table 11.5 Types of Heteroglossic Bilingual Education and Characteristics

Type	Immersion Revitalization	Developmental	Poly-Directional or Two-Way (Dual Language)	CLIL-Type	Multiple Multilingual
Language use	Threatened language predominantly	Emphasis on threatened language; both languages throughout to different degrees	Both languages throughout across groups	Two languages throughout for few subjects within groups	More than two languages used in curriculum, often weaved in and out
Linguistic goal	Bilingualism	Bilingualism	Bilingualism	Bilingualism	Bilingualism
Linguistic ecology	Revitalization endangered language	Revitalization expanding language	Plurilingualism	Plurilingualism	Plurilingualism
Bilingual orientation	Right	Right	Resource	Resource	Resource
Cultural ecology	Bicultural multiplicity	Bicultural multiplicity	Transcultural	Transcultural	Transcultural
Type of children	Language minority; different points of bilingual continuum	Language minority; different points of bilingual continuum	Multiple groups; different points of bilingual continuum across groups	All; different points of bilingual continuum within groups	All; different points of bilingual continuum
Examples in this chapter	• Māori • Hawaii • Navajo/Diné • Canada First Nations • Sámis	• EU: Catalonia; Galicia; Basque Country; Wales; Scotland; Republic of Ireland; Friesland (Roma, Gandhi Project)[21] • U.S. • Deaf community	• U.S. dual language • European schools • Berlin ex. • Israel ex. • Vienna border ex. • Poly-directional international	• CLIL Europe • CLIL-type: Malaysia; Shanghai	• Luxembourg • Asia: Philippines; India; Hong Kong; Singapore; Brunei; Arab Middle East and North Africa

4. When a group considers multilingualism, or at least bilingualism, as a resource for all their children, *CLIL-type bilingual education* programs are established. The language other than that of the national curriculum is used as a medium of instruction for one to two subjects. These types of bilingual education programs have been increasingly supported in the European Union in order to meet the mandate of MT + 2 for all children. But these same types of bilingual education programs are increasingly substituting traditional foreign-language programs throughout the world, especially with regards to using global languages in education.

5. When entire nation-states acknowledge the linguistic and cultural multiplicity and complex languaging of its population, *multiple multilingual education* is developed. These complex multilingual education programs use more than two languages in education and often have movable parts – that is, languages are weaved in and out of the curriculum as needed. Multilingualism is considered a resource for all children in the society. As a result of the inclusion of all children, there is considerable variation in bilingual proficiency; translanguaging is therefore a common feature of this education. Transculturalism is promoted, as not only languages, but also cultures, are blended.

Table 11.5 summarizes for the reader the different characteristics of these types of bilingual education programs, as well as the examples discussed in this chapter.[22]

It is important, however, for the reader to keep in mind that some of the examples given in this chapter (and in Chapter 10) do not fit neatly within the boxes, since all bilingual education policy, whether drawn by states, ethnolinguistic minorities, or parents and educators, in practice only approximates a theoretical ideal and the local situation is much more complex. It is also difficult to categorize these efforts because there is often tension between top-down policies and bottom-up practices. In reality, there is much more dynamism and push/pull than what can be captured in this linear book.

The complexity of bilingual education types has also been made more relevant as bilingual education types continue to gravitate towards the last category, that of multiple multilingual education. As social groups develop increased experience with bilingual education and come to recognize the benefits of bilingualism, comfort with bilingualism, translanguaging, and bilingual education grows. This renewed comfort promotes a renewed flexibility about the end goals of bilingualism and tolerance towards translanguaging in education. Increasingly, social groups face the fact that two languages simply do not reflect the linguistic complexity of a global world or of local communities. As a result, more hybrid types of multiple multilingual education are growing throughout the world, combinations of all the types that we have here described.

The cursory review of bilingual education planning efforts and policies in this chapter and Chapter 10 leads us to agree with Tucker (1998: 338):

The cumulative evidence from research conducted over the last three decades at sites around the world demonstrates conclusively that cognitive, social, personal, and economic benefits accrue to the individual who has an opportunity to develop a high level of bilingual proficiency when compared with a monolingual counterpart. The message for educators is clear: Draw upon community resources and involve diverse stakeholders in all phases of program planning and implementation, implement carefully planned and well-articulated sequences of study, utilize trained and committed teachers, and begin innovative language-education programs that will lead to bilingual or multilingual proficiency for participants as early as possible. The graduates of such programs will be culturally rich, linguistically competent, and socially sensitive individuals prepared to participate actively in our increasingly global economy.

How this can be accomplished is the subject of Part IV of this book where we look at practices and strategies used by bilingual educators around the world in developing their children's bilingualism.

Questions for Reflection

1. Explain how heteroglossic beliefs impact on the planning of different types of bilingual education programs.
2. Discuss the language nest movement. Give examples from different contexts.
3. What is the difference between planning for an endangered minority language and a recovering and expanding minority language? How does the difference impact on the type of bilingual education program? Give examples.
4. Discuss some of the ways in which different states or groups have planned for the education of their children in ways that incorporate bilingual education and that act on their heteroglossic beliefs.
5. Discuss two-way or poly-directional bilingual education. What are the opportunities and the challenges? Give examples.
6. Why is multiple multilingual education important? Give examples. Why are there more and more examples of this type of bilingual education?

Further Reading

Baetens Beardsmore, H. (ed.) (1993). *European Models of Bilingual Education*. Multilingual Matters, Clevedon.

Cenoz, J., and Genesee, F. (1998). *Beyond Bilingualism. Multilingualism and Multilingual Education*. Multilingual Matters, Clevedon.

Cloud, N., Genesee, F., and Hamayan, E. (2000). *Dual Language Instruction. A Handbook for Enriched Education*. Heinle and Heinle, Boston, MA.

Faltis, C.J., and Hudelson, S.J. (1998). *Bilingual Education in Elementary and Secondary School Communities. Toward Understanding and Caring*. Allyn and Bacon, Boston, MA.

Feng, A. (ed.) (2007). *Bilingual Education in China. Practices, Policies and Concepts*. Multilingual Matters, Clevedon.

Freeman, R.D. (1998). *Bilingual Education and Social Change*. Multilingual Matters, Clevedon.

Johnson, R.K., and Swain, M. (eds.) (1997). *Immersion Education: International Perspectives*. Cambridge University Press, New York.

Kam, H.W., and R.Y.L. Wong (eds.) (2004). *Language Policies and Language Education. The Impact in East Asian Countries in the Next Decade*, second edn. Eastern Universities Press, Singapore.

Lessow-Hurley, J. (2005). *The Foundations of Dual Language Instruction*, fourth edn. Pearson, Boston, MA.

Lindholm-Leary, K. (2001). *Dual Language Education*. Multilingual Matters, Clevedon.

Mansoor, S. (ed.) (2003). *Language Policy, Planning and Practice: A South Asian Perspective*. Oxford University Press, Oxford.

Phillipson, R. (2003). *English-Only Europe? Challenging Language Policy*. Routledge, London.

Tollefson, J.W., and A.B.M. Tsui (eds.) (2004). *Medium of Instruction Policies. Which Agenda? Whose Agenda?* Lawrence Erlbaum, Mahwah, NJ.

Tsui, A.B.M., and Tollefson, J. (eds.) (2007). *Language Policy, Culture, and Identity in Asian Contexts*. Lawrence Erlbaum, Mahwah, NJ.

Part IV
Bilingual Education Practices

12

Bilingualism in the Curriculum

[C]ommand of language turns out to be useless without respect for language. If I respect your words that means that I give myself to responding meaning-fully to what you say [. . .]. Talking entails care and care-taking. This is part of what respecting one another means.

Hearne, 1986: 21

Overview

In this chapter, we will consider how language is allocated, arranged, practiced, and used in the bilingual curriculum:

- Bilingual allocation.
- Bilingual arrangements:
  - strict separation;
  - flexible convergent;
  - flexible multiplicity.
- Bilingual practices.
- Models of bilingual teaching:
  - convergent;
  - immersion;
  - multiple.

Introduction

As Van Lier (2005) has established for language education, bilingual education is a transdisciplinary endeavor that requires an ecological and sociocultural perspective. Parts I and II of this book have looked at how views surrounding language and bilingualism, as well as structures of bilingual education programs, respond to sociopolitical interests. Because schools are most often under the influence of the state, issues of the different degrees of power of different languages are most important to consider in any bilingual education enterprise. Part III reviewed different types of bilingual education programs and language education policies that favor one type or another. But even after decisions are made in selecting one type of bilingual education program or another, consideration of curriculum and pedagogy must be made.

This part of the book will focus on the core of bilingual education practices – the structure and processes of curriculum and its pedagogy. As we discuss pedagogy, we take into consideration not only the individual learners with their identities, wishes, needs, and lives, but also the state in which they live and are educated, which has much to do with the ways in which schools are organized. Only in the relationship between curriculum, pedagogies, individual learners, and communities of learners can bilingual development be enhanced.

What makes bilingual education complex is that one has to think not only of pedagogy, approaches, and methodology, but also of how to allocate, arrange, and use the two or more languages in instruction. As the previous two chapters, this is a chapter about language policy. Whereas the last two were on language policy at the state and social level on the kinds of bilingual education programs that were to be developed, this one is about language policy at the school and classroom level. All decisions about how languages in bilingual classrooms are allocated, arranged, and used in the curriculum are language policy choices. This chapter is specifically about the ways in which bilingualism is planned and used in the curriculum.

Bilingual Allocation

Bilingual allocation refers to the time allotments given to one language or the other in bilingual education. Every school has to decide how many class periods will be dedicated to instruction through one language or the other. The most equitable distribution of languages (although not necessarily the most adequate) is, of course, a 50:50 allocation, where half the subjects are taught in one language, and half in the other. The most extreme, but perhaps one of the most popular ones is a 90:10 distribution, with one language used 90 percent of the time, and the additional language used only 10 percent of the time. This is the case, for example, of the CLIL and CLIL-type programs, where most of the instruction takes place in the school's dominant language. The additional language is used for one to two periods of instruction.

Most of the time, bilingual education programs have a *sliding bilingual allocation.* What we mean by this is that as bilingualism develops, the allocation of time to different languages changes. For example, transitional bilingual education programs may start out with a 90:10 allocation, with the minority language being used 90 percent of the time while the second language is acquired. As children become more proficient, the instruction is increasingly done through the child's second language. By the time the child exits the transitional bilingual education program, the time allotment for the language might have completely flip-flopped, with the majority language being used 90 percent of the time, and the minority language being used only for one subject, usually literacy.

Immersion bilingual education also uses a sliding bilingual allocation. In total immersion types, 100 percent of the time is initially allocated to the majority child's second language. But the child's home language is increasingly used until the two languages are equally divided in a 50:50 relationship.

Developmental bilingual education programs also often use a sliding allocation. The initial instruction usually follows a 90:10 relationship with the minoritized language used for 90 percent of the curricular time while it is strengthened. But as the power of the languages equalize, the other language may be allocated equal time in the curriculum. But there are also developmental bilingual education programs which are 50:50 or that allocate the two languages in different combinations.

Bilingual allocation, especially in multiple multilingual education, is often even more complex, with languages being weaved in and out. For example, a bilingual education program in India might start out with a 90:10 allocation, with 90 percent of the time devoted to a tribal language, and 10 percent of the time to the regional language in the earliest primary grade. But soon afterwards, the tribal language might be phased out, and English introduced. Although the regional language might be prevalent at first, English might eventually be used 90 to 100 percent of the time, especially in tertiary education.

In reality all bilingual allocation arrangements are much more flexible than what we describe here since, as we will see below, the languaging bilingually of students and teachers greatly alter these percentages. Still, all bilingual education programs must make decisions about the bilingual allotment in their curriculum. The variability of bilingual allocation in bilingual education programs has to do with the resources available, including teachers and material, as well as societal goals. No one allocation is better than another. And despite the myth that a 50:50 allocation is best, research has shown that as long as the two languages are respected and given their appropriate value, bilingualism could be developed with a very unequal time allocation. Equity between languages does not always mean equality in time allocation.

Bilingual Arrangements

Even after languages have been allocated, educators must make decisions about how languages will be used or arranged in the curriculum. The languages of a bilingual education curriculum can be arranged either by strictly separating them or by using the two languages flexibly. Flexible language arrangements can be of two types – those which lead to *convergence*, which is the result of the dominance of one language over the other, and those which lead to *multiplicity* of languages. Thus, we treat here three different types of language arrangements:

1. strict separation;
2. flexible convergence;
3. flexibility multiplicity.

Strict separation

Bilingual education programs following *additive* bilingual frameworks usually follow this structure. This is usually what happens, for example, in prestigious bilingual education, immersion bilingual education, and maintenance bilingual education programs. In the United States, two-way bilingual education programs also tend to have a policy of strict language separation on the grounds that concurrent language use ends up favoring the majority language. It is also thought that if teachers can use the child's home language in instruction, they are less likely to adapt instruction in the second language (Cloud, Genesee, and Hamayan, 2000; Freeman, Freeman, and Mercuri, 2005).

Decisions as to how the languages are to be separated follow one of four strategies:

* time-determined separation;
* teacher-determined separation;
* place-determined separation;
* subject-determined separation.

We turn now to how administrators and teachers make decisions on each of these arrangements.

Time-determined

In this case, the school makes a decision as to when one language or the other is used. There are different alternatives as to how the languages are divided:

* half- or part-day;
* alternate-day;
* alternate-week.

Schools that choose especially the half- or part-day alternative have to decide whether to keep the time of day always associated with one language or the other, or to switch the time in which the language is used. Some educators feel that children should be able to work in one language or another in the morning when they are fresher as opposed to the afternoon when they are more tired. And some educators believe that it is important for students to continue to work in the same language on the following day for at least a period of time, in that way offering continuity and reinforcement. For these reasons, schools often choose what is commonly called a *roller-coaster arrangement with language alternation*, with languages switching time of day for instruction. Other educators, however, feel that it is important for the same language to be used during the same time of day, thus providing consistency. In that case, there is simply *language alternation*.

If there is only one bilingual teacher per grade, a time-determined separation of languages is preferable, with the teacher switching languages at specific times. The advantage of this arrangement is that teachers teach only one group of students. The disadvantages, however, are that teachers have to be quite literate and professionally educated in two languages and have to prepare material in more than one language. Another disadvantage is that children often have a difficult time understanding the language to be used, especially if the language of instruction keeps changing time. To avoid children's confusion, one kindergarten teacher we know uses a different color apron which she wears for each language. So when the kindergarteners come in and see her wearing her red apron, they know she is teaching in Spanish; and when they see she is wearing a blue apron, they know she is teaching in English. Most teachers have a chart on the door and the board which signals the language being used during the day. Another teacher we know changes "TV channels" (and also languages) on a monitor she displays in the front of the room.

Often early childhood bilingual education classrooms use the language alternation arrangement. Good early childhood practices support the practice of one teacher staying with the same children throughout the day in order to give them the personal support that young children need.

Teacher-determined

Here one teacher speaks only one language, and the second teacher solely speaks the other language. There are different manifestations of teacher-determined language-structuring:

Two teachers, two classrooms. This is the strictest of this teacher-determined separation. It combines *teacher-determined*, with *time determined* separation. Here one teacher teaches in one language at some time of day, while at the same time another teacher teaches in the other language. At an alternate time, the two teachers switch children. For example, in a bilingual Chinese–Italian school, teacher A teaches group A in Chinese which consists of twenty-five children. At the same time, teacher B teaches another twenty-five children in Italian, group B. At some determined time (afternoon, the next day, the next week) teacher A teaches group B in Chinese, whereas teacher B teaches group A in Italian. This arrangement is known as *side-by-side* and requires, at the primary level, two teachers who are bilingual but who in effect function as a monolingual teacher. One advantage of the side-by-side teaching arrangement is that teachers use only one language in teaching, and only need to prepare in one language. Another advantage is that the teachers' bilingualism and biliteracy do not need to be fully developed. That is, it is possible to use two bilingual teachers who are only receptive bilinguals, able to understand the children and texts, but not completely literate to teach in two languages. The disadvantage of this arrangement at the elementary level is that teachers teach two groups of students, and thus, have to teach double the number of children. For example, teacher A above will teach a total of fifty children, instead of twenty-five.

Two teachers, one classroom. Another arrangement is to have *two teachers within one classroom* who speak only one language to the students but are able to facilitate their learning in the other language because they themselves are bilingual. This is the usual arrangement when there are enough resources, especially in early childhood. The advantage of this is that it provides language separation, while always ensuring that children are supported in the language they know best. A disadvantage, of course, is cost.

Sometimes this arrangement is carried out with a teacher and a teacher-aide (para-professional) with each individual speaking a different language within the class-room. One disadvantage of this arrangement is that, when there is a minority language, the teacher-aide is often the person who speaks it. Thus, the professional teacher raises the status of the majority language, while the teacher aide further stigma-tizes the minority language. Because of the importance that all schools attach to the development of the majority language, the opposite arrangement, that is, with the teacher-aide or paraprofessional representing the majority language, is seldom used.

Place-determined

This refers to situations where one particular classroom is used for instruction in one language, and a different classroom for instruction in the other. This is the structure used in many European classrooms and also in many Canadian immer-sion bilingual education programs. It is also used in kura kaupapa Māori programs where English is often taught in a different building! This arrangement is considered useful because it enables the linguistic landscape of the classroom, that is, the decoration, the signs, the books, to be consistent with the language of instruction. In each room, only one language is displayed and used by the teacher and the children. Most secondary schools also use this arrangement.

The advantage of this arrangement is that it provides a "language-surround," a context in which children's language development is supported by enabling them to only hear, see, read, and write in that particular language. The disadvantage is that the children have to change rooms, difficult in early primary education. Another disadvantage is that it discourages contrastive analyses of the two languages, a strategy that might be useful in the later stages of bilingual development.[1] Most often, place-determined separation is done in conjunction with an arrangement that is teacher-determined. That is, the teacher stays in one room, teaches only in one language, and it is the children who change rooms. But it is also possible to have a teacher change classrooms.

It is important to point out that when there is no place-determined separation, it is useful for some clear demarcation of languages to be physically established in a classroom. In some classrooms, the left side is for one language, the right for the other. In others, different colors are used for the two languages. For example, in the United States it is quite common, as we have said, for teachers to write in blue for English and red for Spanish. Whichever way the languages are separated, it is also important to build upon understandings that are developed through their contrastive analyses in later stages of bilingual development, especially when lan-guages belong to the same families and share script.[2] In this way, children develop not only their own bilingualism, but awareness of multilingualism in general.

Subject-determined

This occurs when different subjects are taught through one or another language. Bilingual secondary schools most often use this arrangement – with some teachers teaching an academic subject in one language, and others teaching other subjects in the other language.

Often there are entire societies that prescribe the use of one language or the other for different subjects. For example, in Chapter 11 we saw how in the Philippines, Filipino is used for social studies / social sciences, music, arts, physical education, home economics, practical arts, and character education, while math, science, and technology are taught in English. In fact, many countries are increasingly teaching math, science, and technology in English. This is the case, for example, of Malaysia since 2003 (David and Govindasamy, 2007; Martin, 2005). Another example is that of bilingual education programs of ethno-religious groups where the religious subjects are taught in the sacred language, while the other subjects are taught in the state's language.

Although some bilingual education programs teach all subjects in the two languages to all students, this may not be necessary. In fact, Fishman (1976) has pointed out that teaching all subjects in the two languages, the kind of program that Fishman calls *Full Biliterate Bilingualism* does not reflect societal reality because balanced competence is, as we have seen in Chapter 3, a theoretical impossibility. Thus, a *Partial Biliterate Bilingual* program where some subjects are taught in one language, and others in another, might be more suitable.

Because bilingual education programs in the twenty-first century often serve children of different ethnolinguistic groups, many programs follow a *mixture of the full and partial kinds*; that is, all subjects, although *not* the same content material, are taught in both languages. This requires a lot of teacher collaboration, especially in programs with two teachers who share students.

Flexible convergent

The flexible use of languages in bilingual classrooms has been little considered and researched (for an early exception, see Jacobson, 1981; see also Jacobson and Faltis, 1990). And yet, language in all bilingual classrooms is most often used flexibly, a result of the languaging bilingually or translanguaging which is present in all bilingual context (for more on this concept, see Chapter 3). The fact that *suppleness* is required in all of these uses is the reason why flexible language arrangements and practices are so often misunderstood and stigmatized in bilingual education circles.

Flexible language use that drives towards *convergence*, that is, whose goal is to encourage language shift is used in *subtractive* bilingual frameworks, and generally follows two patterns:

- random code-switching;
- monoliterate bilingualism.

Random code-switching

It is well recognized that bilingual communities code-switch as a way to achieve their full range of expression. That is, just as monolingual communities style-switch from more formal to more informal registers, bilingual communities code-switch because they have at their disposal more than one code. As we have seen before, at times bilingual communities code-switch for specific communicative reasons or social motivations (Gumperz, 1982), but at other times code-switching is simply a discourse style (Zentella, 1997), often signaling multiple identities or membership in the many cultures that the languages index (Myers-Scotton, 2006). Indeed, bilinguals who code-switch have also been shown to have a high degree of cognitive control over various languages simultaneously (Zentella, 1997). Without any awareness about language use in education, teachers who are members of bilingual communities will use their two languages in classrooms in ways similar to those in which they use them in the community.

But the randomness of those switches which potentialize the effect of communication in communities is not always appropriate in educational settings where the development of academic language is necessary. Random code-switching is often the way in which bilingual teachers use languages in transitional bilingual education classrooms. That is, they use two languages to teach the same content *concurrently*, with frequent shifting back and forth between the two languages within a lesson, and with little thought as to why they are doing so. This way of using code-switching in the classroom is often referred to as *Concurrent Translation*, signaling that teachers go back and forth randomly. Sometimes code-switching responds to what Zentella (1997: 19) has called "following the child," as the teacher switches languages to imitate the language which the child has used. Yet, other times, teachers code-switch to engage emotionally with the child or take disciplinary actions.

Cummins and Swain (1986) provide evidence that a "mixing" approach produces weaker academic results than a "separation" approach. However, in recent years, CLIL/EMILE research in Europe has shown how code-switching, if properly understood and suitably applied, can in fact enhance cognitive skills for the content-matter of non-language subjects such as mathematics or history (Gajo, 2007; Serra, 2007). (More on this type of flexible multiple bilingual arrangement below.)

In random code-switching, teachers do not have clear control of why a switch is made. Thus, bilingual teachers might also, in effect, promote the shift to the more powerful language, and erase, rather than develop, bilingualism. Especially in cases where the two languages have clearly unequal value in an educational setting, it is important to pay some attention to how the languages are to be used. If not, this random code-switching erodes the minority language as the majority language takes over, encouraging language shift. This language arrangement is thus common in types of bilingual education programs with a subtractive bilingual framework (O. García, 1993).

In the late 1980s, Rodolfo Jacobson (see Jacobson and Faltis, 1990) attempted to develop a pedagogy that used code-switching as a pedagogical tool. Known as the *New Concurrent Approach* (in opposition to Concurrent Translation which we refer to here as "random code-switching"), Jacobson's approach taught teachers never to use *intrasentential switches* (those switches that occur within a sentence and which are most common in bilingual communities), but instead to use *only intersentential switches* (between sentences) as a way of providing conceptual reinforcement and review. Although signaling the idea that code-switching as a pedagogical tool was not always a bad idea, the New Concurrent Approach failed to spread because it was based on an artificial bilingual use which could not be sustained in classrooms, and which teachers resisted.

Monoliterate bilingualism

This bilingual arrangement requires that literacy be reserved only for the dominant language (Fishman, 1976). An example of a monoliterate bilingual arrangement is presently used in the Philippines with regards to the local vernaculars: the instructor gives the gist of a lesson in either Filipino or English, and then explains it to the students in the local vernacular (Gonzalez, 1998). The local vernacular is never read or written; it is merely used to support understandings and instruction.

Another example of this monoliterate bilingual arrangement is the one used in Mali. Since 1994, Malian teachers have used what they call *pédagogie convergente* (convergent pedagogy) in which there is convergence, or simultaneous use of both the children's mother tongues and French. During the first stages and until fifth grade, when French becomes the medium of instruction, the thirteen national languages – Bambara and Fulfulde being the most prevalent– are used to encourage dialogue and storytelling, with French only used in written expression (Traore, 2001).

Flexible multiplicity

The conception of bilingualism as linear and solely as $1 + 1 = 2$ rejects any bilingual languaging which violates traditional concepts of language as an autonomous system. But if we accept the more recursive and dynamic model of bilingualism introduced in this book, then we are given the possibility of building on bits and pieces of languaging practices. In this book, we argue that flexible bilingual arrangements in the classroom are not in themselves bad. The problem is that often these practices are put to the service of the majority language, as we have seen before, encouraging switching towards the dominant language only, and used progressively to take space and time away from the minority language until it disappears completely.

Bilingual practices in the bilingual classrooms, and in particular code-switching, have been looked upon as bad practice (see, for example, Camilleri, 1996; O. García, 1993; González and Maez, 1980; Milk, 1981, Potowski, 2007). Scholars and educators have repeatedly held that code-switching violates diglossia and creates a linguistic hegemony that favors the language of power, thus leading to language shift.

But as we have said, bilingualism for the twenty-first century must be more than the knowledge of two languages. Abilities such as translation, language switching and designing information bilingually will be increasingly important, abilities that are supported by the community's translanguaging. The recursivity and dynamism of bilingualism today, that is, its adaptive nature to an increasingly socially complex context, demands bilingual skills that are much more than just monolingual skills in two separate contexts. If we focus then not on separate languages as we have done in the past, but on the bilingual or multilingual discourse practices that we need and that are readily observable in bilingual classrooms, we can see that bilingual arrangements that build on translanguaging, in the broad sense as defined in Chapter 3, is indeed the only way to build the plurilingual abilities that we will need in the future.

Duverger (2005) makes a useful distinction between *micro-alternation* and *macro-alternation* in bilingual education. Macro alternation refers to a certain number of courses, or of lessons which form a didactic unity, taught primarily in one or the other language and where the use of a given language across the curriculum is clearly identifiable and highly visible. This does not mean that the "other" language may never occur in the slot where one language is the preferred mode. The "other language" could occur as complementary information, additions, openings, or extensions of subject matter, but should be limited and carefully controlled by the teacher. This type of alternation is useful in cases where one wants to underline the bilingual nature of a program and where no subject is ever treated exclusively in one language, even if, at certain stages of the curriculum, one language is clearly and deliberately dominant. In this mode of macro-alternation one is clearly underlining the bilingual mode of education, which is not reduced by the system to the sum of two monolingual educations (Duverger, 2005).

Micro-alternation occurs when a course, which is predominantly handled in one language, makes use of elements of the other language. This type of code-switching is a reflection of what occurs naturally in bilingual communities and has long been considered taboo by the language-teaching profession. And, yet, Duverger tells us that *if controlled and understood by teachers* it can help de-dramatize the concentration on language "purity" which often reduces learners to silence. As Duverger (2005: 93) says: "Macro-alternation is programmed, institutionalized, demanding; micro-alternation adds suppleness, flexibility, and efficiency. The combination of the two is subtle."

What is important is to understand that it is not a flexible bilingual arrangement itself that leads to language shift or language maintenance or addition, but *the uses to which these practices are put*. Bilingual education programs which have monolingualism as a goal encourage language mixing in ways that lead to language shift. But bilingual education programs which develop bilingualism not as the full wheels of a bicycle but as an all-terrain vehicle adjusting to the ridges and craters of multilingual communication (see Chapter 1), build on translanguaging practices that ensure the functional interrelationship of the languages used in school. We describe here how this takes place in bilingual classrooms.

Five flexible multiple bilingual arrangements can develop the multiplicity of multilingual practices that are important today:

- responsible code-switching both ways;
- preview/view/review;
- translanguaging;
- co-languaging;
- cross-linguistic work and awareness.

Responsible code-switching both ways

The negative associations with code-switching in the classroom have been increasingly questioned by scholars. For example, Ferguson (2003: 193) says that the evidence suggests that: "CS [code-switching] is a useful resource for mitigating the difficulties of learning through a foreign language. There is a good case, then, for moderating official hostility to CS, for acknowledging its prevalence and, indeed, for incorporating awareness of CS as a resource into teacher education curricula." Likewise, research in Europe on CLIL bilingual education has shown how code-switching, if properly understood and suitably applied, can in fact enhance cognitive skills for the content matter of non-language subjects such as mathematics or history (Gajo, 2007; Serra, 2007). Merrit, Cleghorn, Abagi, and Bunyi (1992) have found that teachers use code-switching to focus or regain students' attention and to clarify or reinforce lesson material. Lin (1996), Arthur (1996), Bunyi (2005), and Bloom (2008) have observed that code-switching is a scaffolding technique in bilingual classrooms, making the additional language more comprehensible. Gutiérrez and her colleagues (1999a, 1999b, 2001) have suggested that the "commingling of and contradictions among different linguistic codes and registers" offer significant resources for learning (Gutiérrez, Baquedano-López, and Tejada, 1999b: 289). As Martin-Jones and Saxena (1996) have established, it is not necessarily code-switching that is bad, but rather how language is used, and by whom, that shapes the students' perceived value of the two languages in a bilingual classroom.

Especially in the context of Africa and Asia, where multilingualism is common, the use of what Van der Walt, Mabule, and De Beer (2001) have coined as "responsible code-switching" is being promoted. Van der Walt, Mabule, and De Beer (2001: 129) argue that code-switching is a way of strengthening the connection to the students' home language and of providing meaningful input. The students' home language, as we have been arguing, is an important resource to solve problems in the additional language and to develop that language (Cummins, 1979; 2000). Thus, it stands to reason that banishing the students' home language when instruction is taking place in a language they do not know well (even for half a day) is not appropriate.

Van der Walt, Mabule, and De Beer (2001) caution, however, that teachers must monitor both the quantity and the quality of their code-switching. In terms of quantity, the main part of classroom instruction needs to take place in the language being developed. As to quality, teachers should code-switch to offer meaningful instructional support and not merely to give orders, instructions, call attention, discipline, or follow the language input of the child. That is, code-switching cannot be simply random.

O'Neill and Velasco (2007) give three ways in which code-switching to the child's home language could be a useful and responsible pedagogical technique:

* when providing the definition of a word;
* when providing a linguistic summary;
* when providing a summary of a lesson in one language so that the child can derive more meaning, as well as focus on the language structures.

According to Gutiérrez, Baquedano-López, and Alvarez (2001: 128), "hybrid language use is more than simple code-switching as the alternation between two codes. It is more a systematic, strategic, affiliative, and sense–making process." Hybrid language use in the bilingual classroom builds on the use and study of languages cross-linguistically to expand students' oral and written expression.

Fu (2003) provides a powerful description of how two languages – Chinese and English – can be used to expand the oral and written abilities of Chinese immigrant children new to the United States. By encouraging students to use Chinese in writing English, not only do students new to English develop writing faster, but explicit cross-linguistic analysis can occur. For example, teachers in the school described by Fu contrast the structure of Chinese with that of English, but, most importantly, they point out the different strategies that Chinese students use to learn to read Chinese and English. Chinese students in this school become aware of the fact that English, unlike Chinese, has verb tenses, and that English verbs, unlike Chinese, change endings. And they are explicitly made aware of the fact that English has subject and object forms of pronouns, whereas Chinese does not. But besides all these comparisons, Chinese children are taught to reflect on their own development as Chinese readers – on the role of graphic memory in remembering Chinese characters and in the relationship between shape and meaning. And Chinese children reflect on the other strategies they use as English readers – phonics and meaning-based approaches.

Manyak (2001, 2002), working in a primary classroom of Latino Spanish speakers in California post-227 documented that in this "supposedly" English-only class, Spanish was frequently used in order to have students make sense of the material. He examined the blending of not only Spanish and English but also home and school registers this classroom. He found that, although useful, a hybrid literacy pedagogy did not benefit all students equally.

Gajo and Serra (1999) have conducted research in the Val d'Aoste region of Italy where an Italian–French bilingual program has been in operation for the entire school population for several years, paying particular attention to the "bilingual mode" of teaching, and where macro- and micro-alternation form an integral part of the curriculum.[3] In this autonomous region of Italy, bilingual education for all was introduced at kindergarten in 1983, at primary school in 1988, and in the middle school (ages 10 to 13) in 1994, backed up by extensive research from Italian, French, and Swiss specialists. In this program, teachers and students take advantage of both the languages. Teachers and learners alternate between languages in order to eliminate linguistic obstacles, but also to better confront the obstacle in question. By exploiting both languages intelligently and in a relaxed fashion for pedagogic reasons, teachers use code-switching effectively. The goal is not to teach code-switching, but to capitalize on its natural occurrence in order to transmit knowledge and skills.

In the Val d'Aoste bilingual programs some reading and writing also occurs in a micro-alternating mode. For example, students are encouraged to write in one language and continue in the other language when they have difficulty or when they prefer. Also, tests sometimes may have instructions in one language and questions in the other (Aymond, Cavalli, Coste, *et al.*, 2006).

An evaluation of the bilingual skills of 13-year-olds in the middle school of Val d'Aoste reveals how code-switching used in macro- and micro-alternation neither impairs language acquisition of French, has ill effects on Italian, the majority language, nor impairs the development of cognitive skills and strategies.

In situations of unequal power between languages, however, it is not enough to allow the use of minority languages in responsible code-switching when instruction is taking place in the majority language. For responsible code-switching to lead to bilingual abilities there must also be space for classroom instruction in the minority language itself even if translanguaging is allowed there. In situations of unequal power, when instruction is in the minority language, responsible code-switching into the majority language should be minimized by the teacher, so as to protect the minority language.

In our globalized world, the ability to use two or more languages flexibly is a must. But when there is unequal power between the languages, then Fishman's warning (1991) to protect the minority language is still very relevant. While it is important to put the minority language alongside the majority language, thus ensuring for it a place in powerful domains, it is important to preserve a space, although not a rigid or static place, in which the minority language does not compete with the majority language. In all cases, however, it is important to remember that responsible code-switching is an instrument to develop students' metalinguistic understandings and metacognitive awareness, important for today's bilingually educated individuals.

Preview/view/review

The bilingual curriculum sometimes uses one of the two languages to preview the lesson, another one to view the lesson, and either language to review it. When the language chosen to preview, view, and review varies, it can be considered an instance of convergent multiple arrangements. Throughout the world, this is a popular arrangement at the secondary level. The instructor gives the gist, the preview, most often in the home language of the students, then teaches the lesson in a second language, and then reviews in a language understood by the students. But sometimes this process is reversed, especially when students are at the initial stages of the emergent bilingual period. Teachers then preview the lesson in the students' second language, giving them specialized disciplinary vocabulary in that language, then teach the lesson in the language understood by students, and finally review in the second language. This has the benefit of explicitly teaching specialized lexicon, important in understanding content-matter especially at the secondary and tertiary levels.

Translanguaging

Another way in which a more dynamic bilingualism can be nurtured in students, is by following bilingual curriculum that uses the methodology that Cen Williams has called "translanguaging."[4] According to Baker (2001), translanguaging, developed specifically as a curriculum arrangement by Cen Williams in Wales, involves the hearing, signing, or reading of lessons in one language, and the development of the work (the oral discussion, the writing of passages, the development of projects and experiments) in another language. That is, the input and output are deliberately in different languages.

Cen Williams sees four advantages to translanguaging – deeper understanding of the subject matter, development of competence in the weaker language, home–school co-operation, and integration of fluent speakers with early-level learners (as discussed by Baker, 2001). Baker (2001) clarifies that translanguaging is not about code-switching, but rather about an arrangement that normalizes bilingualism without functional separation.

What makes translanguaging different from the monoliterate language arrangement discussed above is that the assignment of one language to be input or output is systematically *varied* so that students get an opportunity to use both languages receptively (understanding and reading) and productively (reading and writing). Baker adds that this kind of deliberate and systematic concurrent use of two languages is especially useful at the secondary and tertiary level.

In most bilingual curriculum, translanguaging is even more flexible than what Cen Williams describes. For example, in an advanced biology class given to secondary school students recently arrived in the U.S. from Spanish-speaking countries, the main text is in English. The students use that text alongside one written in Spanish that offers complementary material on the same topic. The instructional dialogue between teacher and students takes place mostly in Spanish. But because students have to write the Advanced Placement examination in English, students write in both languages. Spanish is used most of the time in writing. But English essays, based on those first drafted in Spanish, are carefully prepared.

In a fifth-grade dual-language classroom in the United States, the children learn social studies in Spanish. And although the New York State test is offered in both English and Spanish, all, except for one of the students in this class, choose to answer the exam in English.[5] Thus, for the extensive review that takes place for a month, the curriculum follows a translanguaging arrangement. The readings that have been done during the entire class time, and the accompanying notes, are in Spanish. During the review sessions the discussion is in English, since the teacher follows old English language tests. The students look up their notes written in Spanish, and consult their Spanish-language textbooks. But all this knowledge is then rendered into English as they write their practice exams.

Co-languaging

Teaching technology affects the ways in which curriculum is structured and instruction is delivered. For example, PowerPoint enables Deaf students and hearing students who speak different languages to follow a lecture by presenting multiple languages in a co-languaging arrangement. For example, the text below shows a PowerPoint slide of an instructor at Stellenbosch University in South Africa.[6] The university's efforts to integrate students and include non-Afrikaans-speaking students rest on delivering the curriculum in a bilingual mode, with Afrikaans and English co-present. Having both languages present on the screen, each in a different color, enables the inclusion of all students while reserving room for Afrikaans, the language traditionally used in the university. Especially at the secondary and tertiary level, co-languaging is becoming a familiar curricular language arrangement when the content has to be delivered to different language groups simultaneously.

WETENSKAPLIKE TAALONDERSOEK
SCIENTIFIC LANGUAGE INVESTIGATION

- *Wat is Wetenskaplike Taalondersoek?*
  What is Scientific Language Investigation?
- *Waaruit bestaan dit? (komponente)*
  What does it consist of? (components)
- *Hoe word dit gedoen? (verloop, stappe)*
  How is it done? (progress/course, steps)

Hierdie kursus fokus op die wetenskaplike ondersoek van twee taalkundige
verskynsels:
  This course focuses on the scientific investigation of two such phenomena:
die taalvermoë van kinders (aangebore of aangeleer?)
  the language capacity of children (nature or nurture?)
die taalvermoë van die mens (waar kom dit vandaan?)
  the human language capacity (where does it come from?)

Co-languaging is also used when the history teacher shows a video documentary in one language with subtitles in another. Sometimes, students work side by side in different languages, through computer-assisted instruction. In the primary classroom they often listen to books on tape in the two languages, sometimes different students listening to different languages, other times the same students going back and forth to one or the other language in co-languaging ways.

Cross-linguistic work and awareness
Many bilingual education programs blend language-separation arrangements with flexible convergence types. Although some subjects are taught through one or the other language, a part of the curriculum is reserved for bringing the two or more languages together for contrastive analysis. Here, vocabulary, structures, and discourse patterns are contrasted. At other times, there is an instructional space for bilingual children to do cross-linguistic work which allows them to translanguage, using both languages flexibly, in much the same way as experienced bilingual authors, and bilingual communities, often do. For example, much attention is paid to how bilingual literary authors use cross-linguistic strategies for different effects, as the students' abilities to reproduce these in writing are expanded. Other times, actual languaging of bilingual communities is critically examined, as children reflect on this cross-linguistic use and its purpose and effect.

The importance of this cross-linguistic work and space is that it is possible to go beyond the languages of bilingual instruction, creating space for the many language practices that are present in the classroom and the community, and the many languaging patterns of the students. This arrangement makes it possible to build *linguistic tolerance* towards all varieties of languages and ways of languaging, acknowledging its valuable use beyond the classroom. This is crucial in developing *multilingual awareness* (García, 2007c).

It has been found that the metalinguistic and metacognitive exercises offered in cross-linguistic work strengthen the students' languages. They also develop important associations between languages that learners can then draw on (August, Calderon, and Carlo, 2001; Carlo, August, McLaughlin *et al.*, 2004). Overall, these strategies also develop students' multilingual awareness, important in our globalized world (see Hélot and Young, 2006).

Bilingual Practices: Translanguaging

Despite curricular arrangements that separate languages, the most prevalent bilingual practice in the bilingual education classrooms is that of translanguaging. Because of the increased recognition of the bilingual continuum that is present in schools and communities that are revitalizing their languages, or schools where more than one language group is present, linguistically integrated group work is prevalent in many bilingual classrooms. Here, students *appropriate* the use of language, and although teachers may carefully plan when and how languages are to be used, children themselves use their entire linguistic repertoires flexibly. Often this language use appropriation by students is done *surreptitiously*. For example, many two-way bilingual education classrooms in the United States carefully compartmentalize languages and have a clear policy of language separation. But when children with different linguistic profiles are involved in group work, children violate the language use norms of the classroom, using languages flexibly to support their understandings and building conceptual and linguistic knowledge. This language use in two-way bilingual classrooms has been referred to as transdiglossic in García (2006b) or transglossic (in this volume). It provides for a *blending* of language separation with language integration, and, as such, reflects the dynamic bilingual use of the twenty-first century. Language flexibility is built in, as the children appropriate both the content and the language.

Translanguaging in a New York kindergarten

In a kindergarten dual-language class in New York students of different language groups are learning through English and Spanish.[7] The kindergarten separates languages by having an English-medium and a Spanish-medium teacher side by side. Students go from one classroom to the other during the day, sometimes in separate language groups (that is, those who receive more support in English or Spanish through second-language classes), but at other times as integrated language groups (for example, for homeroom and playtime). Despite the language separations, children translanguage constantly to co-construct meaning, to include others, and to mediate understandings. And it is perhaps this translanguaging, more than any other language arrangement, that is responsible for children's bilingual acquisition. We give below a few examples of how this takes place.

The two participants in the example that follows are having snack during home-room. A Spanish-speaking boy, Adolfo, whose bilingualism is at the very beginning stages is snacking alongside Beatriz, a Spanish-speaking girl whose bilingualism is more advanced, although still emerging:

A: [Looking out the window and talking to himself.]
Está lloviendo mucho. (It is raining a lot.)
Look [telling the others]. It's washing. There's washing *afuera* (outside).
B: *Está lloviendo?* [She asks him.]
[Turning to me] He says raining. He speaks Spanish, only Spanish
[Turning to boy] Adolfo, raining.
A: Raining.

Although Adolfo had no word for "raining," and used "washing" to commun-icate, the translanguaging that occurred allowed a meaningful interaction between Adolfo, Beatriz, and myself, and enabled Adolfo to acquire the lexical item that he needed without any intervention from the teacher. Thus, translanguaging in the classroom enables language acquisition without having to wait for the teacher to assume her role.

In the example that follows, Aaron, an English-speaking boy whose bilingualism is at the very beginning stages is counting pumpkin seeds during an activity fol-lowing Halloween. Aaron is working with Bima, an English-speaking girls whose bilingualism is a bit more advanced because her father, although not her mother, is Mexican:

A: I have *veinticinco y* I need *dos más*, no *tres*, look.
[Counts to twenty-five in Spanish.]
I only have *veintitrés*, now [. . .] *Veinticinco.* I need *dos*!
B: *Necesitas una? Toma ése* (Do you need one? Take this one) [. . .]
Yo tiene una más. Se cayó. (I have another one. It fell.)
A: *Necesita una más.* (I need another one.)

This translanguaging event enabled Aaron to produce the Spanish that he had acquired, mainly numbers. But the intervention of Bima, despite the inaccuracies of her Spanish, enables Aaron to acquire more than numbers, as children co-construct meaning.

That translanguaging is important for children to develop bilingualism is evident in the next example. T, the teacher, has taken the ESL children outside and is showing them the trees and teaching them how to compare them. Alicia, a Spanish-speaking emergent bilingual girl tries it out under her breath:

T: This tree is bigger. That tree is smaller.
A: [Tries out under her breath] This tree is *grander*.

In this two-way bilingual kindergarten, children with different linguistic profiles often work, learn, and play together. Playtime becomes a translanguaging negotiation event and the only way in which activities can continue across the different languages. In the example that follows, there is an interaction between Alice, an English-speaking emergent bilingual girl, Bruno, a Spanish-speaking emergent bilingual boy, and Carolina, a bilingual girl:

A: Are you done? [As she tries to take over the block area from B and C who have been speaking in Spanish]
B: Yes, I done. [As he starts to walk away]
C: [To A] Do you want to play with us? [They start playing, translanguaging.]

The only way of including the great range of linguistic differences in this classroom in order to accommodate both Alice and Bruno is to translanguage.

Finally, there is no simpler translanguaging than that which takes place in translations. It turns out that effective two-way dual-language classrooms rely on these in order for children to make sense of what is being taught. In this kindergarten class, one particular bilingual boy, Aristides, has an important function. He frequently provides interpretations and translations, often direct translations, for teachers and for children. The three examples that follow provide evidence of his ability to translanguage in order to co-teach.

T: I'm getting angry at you [. . .] [to Iris, a Spanish-speaking emergent bilingual]
A: *¡Qué tienes que escuchar a la maestra, Iris!*
      (That you have to listen to the teacher, Iris!)

T: Sit up!
A: In Spanish, it's *siéntate arriba* [says to the whole class]

B: How do you say snowball in Spanish?
A: Right Ms T. *que* snowball *es nieve bola*?

In the first example, Aristides interprets that the teacher's getting angry means that Iris has to listen, and tells her so. In the second and third example, he translates directly, first for the whole group, and then for a specific student. This is evidence not only of Aristides' ability to translanguage comfortably, but of his understandings that bilingualism is a precious ability that is appreciated, nurtured, and developed in this bilingual classroom. Despite the social and academic issues that a kindergartener such as Aristides may manifest, in this classroom the message is clear – he has an advantage by being bilingual and he displays his translanguaging ability with pride and confidence.

Translanguaging in the European School of Brussels[8]

An investigation into language behavior of multilingual adolescents, all of whom must learn and use a minimum of three languages in the school program in the European School of Brussels, shows how the language repertoire of all pupils oscillates between the exclusive use of the official languages of their lessons at the appropriate times, and translanguaging in unmonitored, informal interactions (Baetens Beardsmore and Anselmi, 1991). The examples that follow are from the European School of Brussels where students learn and use three languages (Baetens Beardsmore and Anselmi, 1991). The three participants in the first example are all Italian and there is no external clue in the social context to justify the change of B's language from Italian to French (underlined), provoking the ironic comment by C:

A: *Ma allora, dove hai messo la borsa?*
B: *Ma è <u>là sur le palier</u>.*
C: *Senti quello come parla bene l'italiano.*

(A: Well then, where have you put your bag?
B: It's over <u>there on the landing</u>.
C: Just listen to how well he speaks Italian!)

The second example is between a Spanish girl (A), an Italian girl (B), and a Dutch girl (C), who cross over from one language to another (underlined) in their informal interaction.

A: *¿Lo meto?*
B: *Si, dentro . . . un accendino, un portachiavi, una spilla?*
A: *Tengo 30 francos.*
B: *OK. Grazie! <u>Qu'est-ce que vous faites? Don't you want to buy anything?</u> [. . .] É
     60 franchi . . . <u>Achète quelque chose. Un bic? Un porte-clefs? It's for human rights!</u>*
C: I know. Look, I'm not going to sign this if I don't even know why.
B: <u>Why don't you read it?</u>

(A: Shall I put it in here?
B: Yes, inside . . . a lighter, a key-ring, a pin?
A: I have 30 francs.
B: OK. Thanks. <u>What are you doing? Don't you want to buy anything?</u> [. . .] It's 60
     francs . . . <u>Buy something. A pen? A key-ring? It's for human rights!</u>
C: I know. Look, I'm not going to sign this if I don't even know why.
B: <u>Why don't you read it?</u>)

B's competence in Spanish is almost nil, so she answers A's question in Italian, which is frequent accepted behavior between Italian and Spanish peers in the European School of Brussels. The switches to French and Italian correspond to a change of addressee, French and Italian pupils respectively, while switching to English is reserved for the Dutch girl, C, on the basis of a tacit agreement which takes into account the girl's preference for English.

Considerations

Despite the stigma attached to translanguaging practices in bilingual communities and classrooms, this data makes clear that translanguaging is indeed a powerful mechanism to construct understandings, to include others, and to mediate understandings across language groups. It is important for bilingual educators and bilingual students to recognize the importance and value of translanguaging practices. Too often bilingual students who translanguage suffer linguistic shame because they have been burdened with monoglossic ideologies that value only monolingualism. The result of this linguistic shame is always the shift towards the dominant language and monolingualism, robbing students of the possibility to develop their bilingualism. And too often bilingual teachers hide their natural translanguaging practices from administrators and others because they have been taught to believe that only monolingual ways of speaking are "good" and valuable. Yet, they know that to teach effectively in bilingual classrooms, they must translanguage. Accepting their own translanguaging would raise their status as bilingual teachers, as they learn to use its power to support their children's learning. In all of this, it would do us well to remember that Einar Haugen (1972) once said that it is better to bend than to break. Bending and blending ways of languaging bilingually will be increasingly important in the twenty-first century.

Models of Bilingual Teaching

As we have been discussing, bilingual curricula have to consider language *allocation* and language *arrangements*, and allow for translanguaging *practices*. But even after all of that is done, there are still different ways of teaching bilingually. When people speak about teaching bilingually, they can be referring to one of three teaching models of bilingual teaching:

1. convergent teaching;
2. immersion teaching;
3. multiple teaching.

Convergent

What characterizes convergent bilingual teaching is the use of the two languages concurrently in ways that *subordinate* one language to the other following a flexible convergent arrangement. The teacher's intent is always to develop a language of power or to make content in the majority language understood. Thus, when the minority language is used, its only purpose is to support instruction in the majority language. Most of the time, neither the school nor the teacher has a language policy nor any understanding of how language is to be used. There is clarity, however, that the language integration is only allowed temporarily and only to support the child's transition to the majority language. As we saw before, there are many ways of carrying out convergent bilingual instructional practices, but two languages are always used within the same lesson.

The goal of instruction of convergent bilingual teaching is the development of academic proficiency in the dominant language. While there is much emphasis on instructional strategies to develop the dominant language, little interest exists in pedagogy for the home language.

Immersion[9]

The belief here is that the two languages are best developed in isolation. What characterizes this model of bilingual teaching is the explicit carving out of a space for both languages so that each would function with the privilege of a majority language. Thus, all schools using this bilingual teaching have a clear and explicit language policy of teaching monolingually for bilingualism.

This immersion bilingual teaching is often used when the minority language has to be protected because of the encroachment of the majority language, or in cases where one of the languages is being revitalized. It is important to point out that although we refer to this here as *immersion bilingual teaching*, this practice also characterizes types of bilingual education programs other than immersion and immersion revitalization bilingual education. For example, it is often used in prestigious bilingual education, maintenance bilingual education, and developmental bilingual education programs. And it is also used in many poly-directional and two-way bilingual education programs. The alternate names for these programs – bilingual immersion and two-way immersion – denote precisely the immersion instructional practice of teaching monolingually in two languages. CLIL and CLIL-type programs may also use this model of bilingual teaching. As we said before, however, immersion bilingual teaching always contains bilingual elements and examples of translanguaging can be found in all types of programs that use immersion bilingual teaching.

Multiple

Schools that adopt multiple bilingual teaching have a clear language policy that includes not only the development of bilingual proficiency, but also *the translanguaging practices and plurilingual values* of today – multilingual awareness and linguistic tolerance. Thus, the two or more languages are always used in combination – neither concurrently nor separately, but in a *blending* of the two practices. Oftentimes this is accomplished by having a separate bilingual arrangement but nurturing and building upon translanguaging practices in the classroom. Deaf bilingual education is always multiple.

As we have seen, in some schools, such as some two-way bilingual education schools, the teachers separate the languages, while the integrated student body mixes them during collaborative group work. In other schools, teachers use teaching material in both languages, interchanging them often as students are asked to go from one language to the other. In schools that use these multiple bilingual instructional practices, there is emphasis in developing students' metalinguistic skills in contrasting the two languages and comparing them to others. The development of multilingual awareness, as well as multilingual competence, is an important component in these schools.

Conclusion

Table 12.1 displays the different bilingual arrangements and models of bilingual teaching, as well as the *most likely* bilingual education framework and type that

Table 12.1   Bilingual Arrangements, Strategies and Models of Teaching

Bilingual Arrangement	Flexible Convergent	Strict Separation			Flexible Multiple
Bilingual Strategies	• Random code-switching • Monoliterate	• Time-determined • Teacher-determined • Place-determined • Subject-determined			• Responsible code-switching • Preview/view/review • Translanguaging • Co-languaging • Cross-linguistic practices
Models Bilingual Teaching	Convergent	Immersion			Multiple
Theoretical Framework	Subtractive	Additive	Recursive		Dynamic
Types	• transitional	• maintenance • prestigious • immersion	• immersion revitalization • developmental		• poly-directional two-way (dual); • CLIL and CLIL-type; • multiple multilingual.

correspond to each. In reality, there is much fluidity especially between the recursive and dynamic types of bilingual education, indicated by arrows in the table.

Because of the complexity of the decisions on the bilingual curriculum, school leadership that understands issues of bilingualism for bilingual schools is crucial (Hunt, forthcoming). The education of school leaders and administrators for bilingual schools is an area that needs extensive attention. Also important is the education of bilingual teachers, for it is the teachers themselves who will, through their pedagogical practices, deliver the curriculum. The next two chapters consider the pedagogy of bilingual education, paying close attention to biliteracy itself in Chapter 14.

Questions for Reflection

1. What are some of the time separation arrangements used for teaching in two languages? What are signs and signals that teachers use to distinguish what language they are teaching in? Why might teachers want to give these signs?
2. What is the difference between random code-switching and responsible code-switching? Is code-switching always a poor instructional strategy in bilingual classrooms? When is it beneficial and when is it harmful?
3. What is *translanguaging* as a pedagogical strategy? When might a teacher use it?

4. How might you engage in cross-linguistic practices such as bringing two or more languages together for contrastive analysis? Give an example of how and why you would do this.
5. What is the difference between translanguaging as a pedagogical strategy and translanguaging practices in bilingual classrooms? Do translanguaging practices have a role?

Further Reading

Baker, C. (2006). *Foundations of Bilingual Education and Bilingualism*. Fourth edn. Multilingual Matters, Clevedon. First edn. 1993; second edn. 1996; third edn. 2001.

Brisk, M.E. (2006). *Bilingual Education. From Compensatory to Quality Schooling*, second edn. Lawrence Erlbaum, Mahwah, NJ.

Faltis, C.J. (1997). *Joinfostering. Adapting Teaching for the Multilingual Classroom*. Second edn. Merrill, Upper Saddle River, NJ.

13

Bilingual Education Pedagogy and Practices

[T]o teach from strength is to teach in the light of the student's preferred learning mode, according to the shape of his or her thought, and with attention to what is of deep interest and value to the student. This is observable wherever the learning environment provides the student with the opportunity to make choices and state preferences; the opportunity to engage with a range of media and materials to which the student can give shape and form; and the opportunity to contribute ideas and raise questions that will be heard and responded to.

Carini, 1986: 19–20. (The word "children"
in the original has been substituted by "student.")

Overview

In this chapter, we will discuss:

- Bilingual education approaches and methods:
  ○ grammatical;
  ○ communicative;
  ○ cognitive.
- Principles and practices of bilingual education pedagogy:
  ○ social justice;
  ○ social interaction.
- A bilingual pedagogical strategy: scaffolding.

Introduction

It is important to remember that, as Fishman (1989: 447) has said: "Bilingual education must justify itself philosophically as education." It is teachers who implement the bilingual education policies imposed from above or constructed by communities and educators. As such, bilingual education pedagogy is the heart of the matter. Sometimes this pedagogy supports and follows the language policy,[1] but most of the time, teachers create, contest, change, and transform policies, as they enact their pedagogy.

This chapter and the one that follows look at bilingual education pedagogy, considering approaches and methods, as well as instructional strategies. Bilingual education pedagogy enacts beliefs about bilingualism, teaching, and learning. Like all pedagogies, bilingual education pedagogy is an art, as well as a science. Sometimes, it is carried out well by experienced teachers, whereas other times it fails. Just as bilingual classrooms contain multiple language practices and develop two or more languages, bilingual teachers must have multiple pedagogical practices (approaches, methodologies, strategies), as they teach children with different linguistic profiles, sometimes in their home languages or following their home language practices, other times not.

Pedagogical traditions depend greatly on the sociocultural context in which the school is located. For example, some states are aligned with more traditional teacher-centered pedagogies, what are often called *transmission models* of education. Other states recognize more constructivist pedagogies where the children are actively involved. These pedagogies are often referred to as "transformative" (Cummins, 2001).

Transmission pedagogy is built on a western empirical tradition which views knowledge as separate from the knower and as a collection of facts and concepts. Learning is viewed as the consumption, storage, memorization, and reproduction of information. Thus, students are perceived as empty vessels or buckets (Freire, 1970) that have to be filled, as they receive knowledge from teachers and textbooks. Teachers break down information into small pieces and proceed in a linear fashion, attempting to cover content and going from the most basic to the most complex (Oakes and Lipton, 1999).

Constructivist pedagogy, on the other hand, is built on the conviction that learning should involve social negotiation and interaction with others in authentic contexts that are relevant to the learner. In this tradition, teachers serve primarily as facilitators of learning (Cummins, 2001; Villegas and Lucas, 2001).

Bilingual education must always make space for different pedagogical traditions, much the same way as it makes space for different languaging and cultural content. As John Dewey, the most influential pedagogue in the U.S. in the twentieth century, has said: "the *social life of the child* is the basis of concentration, or correlation, in all his training or growth. The social life gives the unconscious unity and the background of all his efforts and of all his attainments" (Dewey, 1897: 79, our italics). Thus, one cannot ignore the society in which a child lives and his or her social and community context in considering pedagogy. Before we describe the heart of the matter – the principles of a bilingual education pedagogy – we consider approaches and methods that have been frequently used in bilingual education programs.

Bilingual Education Approaches and Methods

This section will review some of the popular ways in which different philosophical orientations are translated into professional practice. Bilingual education blends approaches towards education in general with approaches that are specific to language education. That is, bilingual education always integrates language and content. As Faltis (1997) has indicated, bilingual instruction is always a *joinfostering* of balancing support for development of both the home and the additional language, as well as content learning. In bilingual education, the construction of new understandings in curriculum always goes hand in hand with the development of language, especially of the additional language (Gibbons, 1998). Snow, Met, and Genesee (1989) suggest that bilingual development is promoted when the language is used as medium of instruction because of three reasons (cited in Lessow-Hurley, 2005: 91):

- cognitive development and language development are inextricably tied;
- such a link allows students to develop the kind of language that is used in school;
- school subjects are what children need to talk about in school, so it provides the motivation and opportunity for meaningful communication.

Because of the complexity of educating while developing bilingualism, bilingual education approaches are not as clear cut as foreign-language and second-language approaches. But in teaching through an additional language, especially for emergent bilinguals, bilingual education often combines three approaches that are well known in language education: 1. *a grammatical approach*, with 2. *a communicative approach*, with 3. *a cognitive approach*.

Grammatical

The grammatical approach emphasizes the rules and structure of the language that is being acquired. Students are explicitly taught language rules and sentence structures and are engaged in much practice. In general, the grammatical approach relies on three distinct methodologies – the *grammar-translation method*, the *direct method*, and the *audiolingual method*.

The grammar-translation method has fallen into disuse. It focuses on translation of complex texts and grammatical accuracy. In contrast, the direct method and the audiolingual method are still widely used. Both the direct and the audiolingual methods focus less on explicit instruction of grammar. Students infer grammar structures as they repeat language patterns (Herrera and Murry, 2005). In the direct method, translation is avoided, and teachers model language patterns that students then repeat. In the audiolingual method, students practice patterns and dialogues to develop particular language structures.

Communicative

The communicative approach towards language teaching emerged in the 1960s as a way to go beyond the grammatical approach. Whereas the grammatical approach was based on a *behaviorist* theoretical framework, the communicative approach is derived from a *constructivist* theoretical framework that suggests that language learning occurs as students draw meaning from experience and interpersonal interaction. It was the burgeoning of bilingual education in the second half of the twentieth century that laid the groundwork for the development of what have become the two most important language learning methods under the communicative approach – *immersion instruction* and *integrated content-based instruction* (ICB).

Immersion methodology[2] became popular as a result of the growth of immersion bilingual education in Canada in order to develop bilingualism in a minority language. Pedagogically, teachers plan content and language objectives concurrently. The method promotes the use of *language that is slow and simplified, with guarded vocabulary and short sentences*, while the grade level curriculum is used, although *modified*. Teachers generally use thematic instruction. Immersion methodology is also used throughout the world for revitalization of languages.

But the immersion instruction method is also used in countries that do not support bilingualism and has become most popular in monolingual instruction for immigrants and refugees, under the label "sheltered instruction."[3] A protocol for this sheltered instruction method that has become popular in the United States in programs that teach language minorities only in English is the SIOP (Sheltered Instruction Observation Protocol) developed by Echevarria, Vogt, and Short (2000) (for more information, see www.siopinstitute.net). As an immersion or sheltered instruction method, SIOP features the following characteristics:

- content and language objectives that are developed concurrently;
- comprehensible input that uses guarded speech, clear explanation of tasks, and visuals or modeling of lesson in the form of graphic organizers;
- the linking of concepts to students' background and emphasizing key vocabulary;
- supporting students' understanding and use of questions that promote higher order thinking;
- providing opportunities for interaction and sufficient wait time, as well as co-operative learning.

It is interesting that despite the "sheltered" instruction aspects of SIOP, this approach supports the use of the students' native language to clarify concepts and assignments. Echevarria, Vogt and Short (2004: 107) state: "we believe that clarification of key concepts in students' L1 by a bilingual instructional aide, peer, or through the use of materials written in the students' L1 provides an important support for the academic learning of those students who are not yet fully proficient in English."

Integrated content-based instruction (ICB) refers to a method of teaching language and content concurrently. It is an adaptation of immersion methodology. Whereas the emphasis in the immersion method is on the acquisition of content knowledge alongside second-language development, the emphasis of ICB is more on the development of language and literacy in a second language. As such, it relies usually on language teachers, rather than content teachers. Therefore, teachers are not usually bilingual educators, although they may work in bilingual programs. Like immersion teachers, ICB teachers also plan content and language objectives concurrently. During instruction, the key vocabulary is usually pre-taught. Much emphasis is placed on building the background to a lesson and using visual and other contextual support. It is prevalent in many bilingual education programs throughout the world.

Cognitive

The *cognitive approach* emerged in the 1980s as a view of learning based on the process of children's construction of meaning by using thinking and reasoning strategies. That is, learning is recognized to be as much cognitive, as it is social and interactive. The emphasis on this approach is on the learner's *metacognitive processes*, that is, the active control over the cognitive processes that are used in learning (Flavell, 1979). The cognitive approach also emphasizes the students' interactions with text and discourse structures present in the classroom. It distinguishes between three types of knowledge: *declarative knowledge*, what we know; *procedural knowledge*, what we know how to do; and *conditional knowledge*, the knowledge of when, why, or where to use information and skills. Learning occurs in the interaction between these three types of knowledge which are stored in long-term memory frameworks or *schemata* (in the case of declarative and conditional knowledge), or in *production systems* (in the case of procedural knowledge).

The cognitive approach supports the transfer of knowledge stored as schemata or production systems in one language to the learning of new tasks in a second language. As such, it is very prevalent in bilingual education programs that use the two languages with greater flexibility. It is prevalent, for example, in two-way bilingual education programs in the United States and CLIL programs in Europe. Methods that fall under this approach generally integrate cognitive theory with communicative strategies and child-centered constructivist perspectives.

The cognitive approach sees language as a process, and *what we do with language* as an integral aspect of our thinking, meaning-making selves. The learners' agency, that is their motivation and autonomy, emerges from, and results in, action-movement, perception, and understanding. Van Lier (2006) remarks that language learning as agency involves learning to perceive "affordances," which he defines as relationships of possibility within communicative events. Van Lier explains affordances by saying that it is an ecological term that suggests that one sees things from different perspectives because of one's own activity: it is the relationship between what is out there and the learner.

One popular method of bilingual learning based on the cognitive approach and used in some bilingual classrooms in the United States is *CALLA or the Cognitive Academic Language Learning Approach* (Chamot and O'Malley, 1994). As with the methods under the communicative approach, CALLA combines the teaching of content with language learning. As such, it offers much visual and contextual support and builds background knowledge. However, the emphasis in this method is on the development of *academic language abilities*. This is accompanied by explicit instruction in *metacognitive learning strategies* for both content and academic language and literacy development. For example, CALLA explicitly teaches learning strategies, such as the following:

- skimming the text to identify the main organizing concept and find specific information;
- listening or reading selectively (*selective attention*) by attending to key words and linguistic markers;
- engaging with the material by taking notes and summarizing;
- asking clarifying questions.

Students work with other students in co-operative groups to solve problems with the assistance of the teacher and peers. Thus, students learn to manage their own language and content learning (Lessow-Hurley, 1991). There is also emphasis on students' reflection on learning, and in the ability to integrate new and existing knowledge. The Biliteracy Workshop that we describe in Chapter 14 is another example of a cognitive methodology.

Comparison

Both the cognitive approach and the communicative approach to teaching through an additional language, as well as a home language, support learning that happens through *guided or independent construction of meaning*. For both the cognitive and communicative approaches, language learning is *inductive* (that is, from general to specific) and driven through *interaction*.

The difference between both approaches is that whereas communicative approaches support language learning through authentic communication as social construction, the cognitive approach believes also in the explicit teaching and modeling of learning strategies and language. Thus, the intent of the cognitive approach is to develop the learner's metacognitive processes and their capacity for introspection, which they can then use in learning both language and content. Table 13.1 displays the comparison of approaches and methods:

Table 13.1   Instructional Approaches and Methods in Bilingual Education

Approach	*Grammatical Approach*	*Communicative Approach*	*Cognitive Approach*
Theoretical framework	Behaviorist	Constructivist	Constructivist and metacognitive
Strategies	Explicit teaching of rules and structures or drill and practice	Drawing from experience; interpersonal interaction	Drawing from knowledge as schemata or production systems; learners' agency in action and understanding
Methods; examples	Grammar translation; direct; audiolingual	Immersion instruction; Integrated Content-Based instruction (ICB)	Cognitive Academic Language Learning Approach (CALLA); Biliteracy Workshop

Principles and Practices of Bilingual Education Pedagogy

Regardless of different pedagogical traditions, theoretical framework of bilingualism, or language use arrangement, bilingual education teachers must be mindful of the two basic principles of bilingual pedagogy:

- social justice;
- social practice.

Table 13.2 outlines the corresponding dimensions of the two principles of bilingual education pedagogy. The sections that follow describe each of the dimensions and propose instructional practices that correspond to each:

Table 13.2   Bilingual Education Pedagogy Principles

Social Justice	*Social Practice*
1. Equity	1. Interactions and involvement
2. Language of child / language tolerance	2. Language
3. Expectations and rigor	3. Collaboration and group work
4. Assessment	4. Relevance

Cummins (1986) has named the pedagogy that derives from the intersection of these two principles *reciprocal interactional-oriented pedagogy*, and, on a more recent occasion (2000), *transformative pedagogy*. Good pedagogy that ignores the social justice principle is ineffective for bilingual instruction. And good pedagogy that falls only under the social justice principle without potentializing learning as social practice is also ineffective for students who are developing bilingualism.

Social justice

Social justice is a most important principle of bilingual education pedagogy since bilingual teaching combines two or more languages and cultures. It is thus important for equity between the two languages and content to be established, and for students of all linguistic and cultural backgrounds to be recognized as knowers (Freire, 1970). Schecter and Cummins (2003: 9) have said: "In contexts of cultural, linguistic, or economic diversity, where social inequality inevitably exists, these interactions are never neutral: they either challenge the operation of coercive relations of power in the wider society or they reinforce those power relations." This principle values the strength of bilingualism and bilingual students. It enables the creation of a learning context which is not threatening to the students' identities but that builds multiplicities of language uses and linguistic identities, while maintaining academic rigor and upholding high expectations. A *cultural and linguistically responsive pedagogy* falls within this principle (Au, 2006; Villegas and Lucas, 2001). Another important element of this principle relates to advocating for assessment that is valid for bilingual students. We comment on each of the four dimensions of the social justice principle below, as we describe instructional practices that are appropriate for each category.[4]

Equity

Meaningful bilingual pedagogy revolves around the issue of *equity* – equity for the students, their languages, and their cultures and communities. This means that the teacher ensures that all students, regardless of language backgrounds or proficiency, participate equally. To support this equality of participation, the teacher uses group work, individual work, as well as whole class instruction. And s/he allows students to participate in different ways in classroom activities according to their linguistic and conceptual abilities – sometimes drawing, sometimes writing and reading in their home language, other times in the second language. The emphasis is on creating ways of having a democratic classroom where everyone has an equal opportunity to participate (Gonzalez, Moll, and Amanti, 2005).

Collaborative descriptive inquiry, described by García and Traugh (2002), is an equitable and democratic pedagogical practice, especially for students at the secondary level. Students put their voices, opinions, and texts alongside each other. The teacher goes around the room, allows each student the opportunity to participate (in whichever language) or pass, and does not interrupt with questions, comments or discussions. Instead, she pulls the threads of thought that have been generated by the group together at the end of the student participation. Traugh (notes, September 18, 1999) describes collaborative descriptive inquiry as having three components:

- *Descriptive* and based on each student describing a text or a work. It means trying to stay out of the realms of judging other students' work or words.
- *Collaborative*, as students often work in groups and pay close attention to what the teacher and the other students have to say. Putting a shared reading or text alongside individual work allows teachers and students to understand the large ideas more completely and see some of the meaning in the class's peculiarities.
- *Disciplined* in that there is a process that is used. Being descriptive is also a discipline.

Pedagogy that is based on equity ensures that bilingual students have access to all curricula and programs, including programs for gifted students. It also means ensuring that bilingual students are not overrepresented in programs for students with disabilities. Furthermore, equity demands that bilingual students not be tracked academically. In the case of bilingual minority students, an equity pedagogy demands that students not be segregated. There are exceptions in cases where this is done to ensure a meaningful and targeted education, for example, in the secondary school for Latino newcomers to New York City that García and Bartlett (2007) have described.

Equity of languages does not simply mean that 50 percent of the instructional time is spent in one language and 50 percent in the other. Equity of languages can be achieved by giving the two languages respect and status within the curriculum despite uneven use. Actual language use in the curriculum, as we have seen, often responds to the sociolinguistic context in which the school exists, societal wishes and aspirations of parents, and differences in instructional material and teachers. Most important is a pedagogy that treats the two languages equitably and respectfully. An equitable pedagogy under no circumstances forbids a student to use either language.

Language of child / language tolerance

Effective bilingual pedagogy builds on the students' linguistic strengths – their home language practices – to build meaning and to enable students to co-construct their understandings. As John Dewey (1897: 78) has said: "the school life should grow gradually out of the home life; [. . .] it should take up and continue the activities with which the child is already familiar in the home. [. . .] It is the business of the school to deepen and extend his sense of the values bound up in his home life."

In using the home language and acknowledging the children's language practices, the teacher follows pedagogy that is consistent and purposeful. That is, s/he does not continuously change the ways in which the students' home language is used, but plans carefully the ways in which it is included. The teacher makes available books in the children's home languages and sometimes uses tapes at listening centers. The children's home languages are also clearly displayed in the classroom and around the school, and there are plenty of books in the two languages, as well as bilingual books. In addition, the teacher understands that bilingualism and biliteracy develop slowly and jointly.

It is most important that the home language used in school includes the language practices of the children and their varieties. It is simply not enough to teach in Quechua, if the Quechua used differs significantly from the language practices of the community. In cases where the bilingual school is promoting the standard variety of the children's home language, it is most important that attention is paid to developing plurilingual tolerance, and pupils' appreciation for different practices regardless of whether they are used in school or not.

Beyond the use of the students' home language, an effective bilingual pedagogy builds on *multilingual awareness* (Hawkins, 1984; García, 2007c). That is, a bilingual pedagogy must not only focus on how language works and how students use and learn languages, but also on the understanding of the social, political, and economic struggles surrounding the use of two languages – what has become known as "critical language awareness" (see Fairclough, 1992, 1999).

Expectations and rigor

Tending to the social justice principle in pedagogy also means having high expectations and promoting academic rigor. In these classrooms, there is mutual respect, and all students, regardless of skill or proficiency, are encouraged to achieve. Furthermore, the teacher communicates clearly to students that it is necessary to work hard and take risks in order to master challenging academic work (Walqui, García, and Hamburger, 2004).

Teachers do not focus on drill and remediation, and the bilingual curriculum is not narrowed to language only. Instead, the teacher focuses on ideas that can be applied or extended and that form the basis for future learning. The teacher presents these ideas in their complexity and interrelatedness and in no way simplifies the content. In addition, teachers engage students in combining ideas to synthesize, generalize, explain, hypothesize, or arrive at some conclusion or interpretation (Walqui, García, and Hamburger, 2004).

Effective bilingual pedagogy also develops students' metacognitive skills, that is, plans of attack that enable learners to successfully approach academic tasks and that monitor our thinking (Baker and Brown, 1984; Walqui, 2006). It teaches critical thinking and study skill development.

According to Dermody and Speaker (1995), *metacognition* is characterized by four factors:

- matching thinking and problem-solving strategies to particular learning situations;
- clarifying purposes for learning;
- monitoring one's own comprehension through self-questioning;
- taking corrective action if understanding fails.

Pedagogy that develops metacognition includes such things as *think-alouds*, in which students explain the way in which they have gone about thinking of an issue or problem. Students are also taught to self-assess their learning.

A good rule of thumb to use in the teaching of bilingual students is to, as Walqui (2006) says: "Amplify, do not simplify." In maintaining academic rigor, it is important to amplify the language used and the concepts included. A meaningful bilingual pedagogy contextualizes conceptual understandings through visuals and other materials and includes language that is tautological, that is, says the same thing twice in different ways to enhance understandings. Teachers scaffold instruction for students – they offer high support for the lesson (more on the concept of scaffolding below).

Beyond scaffolding, there is also explicit overt instruction to develop awareness and understanding of practice (New London Group, 1996). Explicit language instruction in combination with language used in content has proven to be most effective in expanding bilingual competence (Baetens Beardsmore and Lebrun, 1991; Beatens Beardsmore, 1993b, c). If instruction only revolves around implicit processes, students may understand the messages without having to focus on the form–function analysis, and will therefore never develop accurate speaking and writing.

There are syntactic structures and lexicon that must be taught explicitly. For example, all disciplines have different linguistic registers, and students must be made aware of such differences. In all languages, the discourse of history is marked by chronological steps, as well as cause–effect, and may call for irregular past-tense verb forms infrequently used in everyday language (Gibbons, 2002). In Spanish, French, and English, science discourse uses the passive voice. There are also transition words which must be explicitly taught for academic discourse; for example, in English, the words "nonetheless," "therefore," "consequently." Mini-lessons (more on these in the next chapter) provide an effective way of teaching something explicitly, while also reviewing key background concepts, introducing vocabulary, and engaging in "text walk," that is, getting to know the text prior to reading, speaking, or writing, so as to make the student's work more meaningful (Vogt, 2000).

Vocabulary has been found to be a most important ingredient in teaching for bilingualism. Vocabulary has to be taught directly and systematically, focusing on both meaning and form (Lapkin and Swain, 1996). Teachers ought to focus both on technical words and high-frequency academic words. For example, words such as "analyze" or "define" are high-frequency academic words that are found in content-area texts and must be explicitly taught (O'Neill and Velasco, 2007). One way of building vocabulary is to emphasize cognates, that is, words that are similar in the two languages of the child, whenever they are present.

An effective bilingual pedagogy is careful with corrections. The Luxembourg Ministry of Education has given instructions to primary school teachers working through the additional language introduced first (German) or introduced later (French) not to interrupt children as they try to express themselves, in an effort to encourage continuous discourse, and not to correct excessively when they speak, under the fear that "You can correct a child until you get a silence that is grammatically perfect" (Baetens Beardsmore, personal communication, April 5, 2007).

Although an effective bilingual pedagogy does not overcorrect, it does make students aware of errors and engages them in self-correction. For emergent bilinguals,[5] the focus should be on meaningful communication (Cloud, Genesee, and Hamayan, 2000), but effective bilingual pedagogy brings students to focus also on form. Recasts, in which the teacher reformulates what the student has said, minus the error, is the most used feedback technique and probably the most useful (Lyster, 1998a). Besides recasts, teachers also elicit the right word or phrase by eliciting students to complete a sentence or reformulate, or they can request clarification, by asking, for example, "What do you mean by x?" Teachers also can provide metalinguistic cues, for example by saying, "There's an error. Can you find it?" or with older students, "The word is masculine, not feminine." Finally, teachers can also explicitly correct errors, although Lyster (1998a) found that this was the least-used feedback strategy by teachers.

Assessment

There cannot be meaningful pedagogy without valid assessment. Assessment is so important that it merits an entire chapter (Chapter 15). Bilingual teachers must engage in formative assessment, that is, constant evaluation of students' learning that helps shape pedagogical practices and curriculum. Instruction and assessment must be planned simultaneously. Teachers must learn to observe, to engage students in conferencing, to review learning logs and student journals, and to construct equitable and valid tests. They must be able to evaluate "how and what students know and can do in real-life performance situations" (Darling-Hammond, 1994:

6). This type of assessment is known as *performance assessment* and it is used to inform instruction.

There are simple integrative tests that are effective for bilingual students. For example, research indicates that *dictation* is helpful to measure a person's overall language ability (Lessow-Hurley, 2005) since it requires understanding meaning. Another simple integrative technique for assessing language ability is *cloze testing* where words in a passage have been left out. Usually every fifth, sixth, or seventh word is deleted from the text, keeping the first and the last sentences intact.

But in an era of high-stakes tests and increasing accountability measures in most countries of the world, teachers must also prepare students to take *summative assessments* that are increasingly standardized on a mostly monolingual population. Thus, teachers must also become advocates for their children (Cummins, 1986, 2000, 2001) and raise constant questions about the validity of assessment that is in one language or the other, ignoring the potential of bilingualism and translanguaging practices. We will return to assessments in Chapter 15.

Social practice

The social practice principle of bilingual pedagogy places learning through an additional language as a result of collaborative social practices in which students try out ideas and actions (Lave and Wenger, 1991), and thus socially construct their learning (Vygotsky, 1978). Learning is seen as occurring through doing (Dewey, 1897). Thus, an *action-based pedagogy* falls within this principle. In the field of language education, this is often referred to as *task-based pedagogy* (Ellis, 2003). We expand on the dimensions of this principle below, and comment on different instructional practices that may be appropriate.

Interactions

Meaningful instruction for bilingual students includes quality interactions. This means that the dialogue is not scripted, is not dominated by the teacher, and there is sharing of ideas to promote understanding of concepts. The dialogue is highly focused on the subject matter and generative to support future development of understanding.

Tharp, Estrada, Dalton, and Yamauchi (2000) have shown how teaching through conversation, or what they call "instructional conversations," is most effective. The discourse of whole-class teacher-led instruction is usually one of Initiation–Response–Feedback (IRF) (Mehan, 1979; Sinclair and Coulthard, 1975). That is, the teacher makes the first move, called *initiation*, the second move or *response* is done by the student, and the third move, *feedback*, by the teacher, leaving little room for conversation. However, instructional conversations build upon understandings. A student says something and the other builds upon what was just said or asks for clarification (O'Neill and Velasco, 2007). Teacher questions are most important in promoting conversation. O'Neill and Velasco (2007) give us a list of such important questions to initiate conversation:

- What do you think this might mean?
- What similarities and differences do you see?

- What parts seem to be related to one another? How?
- What might be the reason for this?
- Why do you think this happened?
- What can you conclude from this?
- What did you find out?

To encourage conversations, teachers often ask students to "turn and talk," as student pairs talk about and try out what they are learning and thinking, in the language of their choice.

There is an art in talking to children, especially bilingual children. Gibbons (2002) encourages teachers to observe three steps:

1. Start with an open question.
2. Slow down the dialogue by increasing wait time and allowing more turns before evaluating or recasting what the learner has said by asking them to explain or expand more.
3. Respond to the meaning of what is being said: listen carefully.

Language focus
Meaningful pedagogy for bilingual students also focuses on the practice of disciplinary and academic language. It promotes the ways in which the discipline uses language to express key concepts and processes. Lessons engage students in sustained discussions of how specific written and spoken texts are structured and how they work. Students practice how oral and written production of text begin, unfold, and end.

Table 13.3 provides a list of *language functions* (Gibbons, 1991; Halliday, 2001) that teachers must plan for, as well as some examples of each objective.

Table 13.3   Language Objectives for the Bilingual Classroom

Language Objectives	Examples of Language Functions
• Vocabulary of discipline • Discourse structure of discipline	(Differs by discipline) • Requesting information • Justifying opinions • Summarizing information • Making comparisons • Defending an argument • Persuading others • Asking for clarification • Classifying • Comparing • Giving instructions • Planning and predicting • Synthesizing information from two texts

Table 13.3 (*continued*)

Language Objectives	Examples of Language Functions
• Reading abilities of discipline	• Reading comprehension skills • Predicting • Inquiring/Questioning • Evaluating • Inferring • Drawing conclusions • Finding main idea • Remembering facts and details • Understanding sequence • Describing how a character is feeling • Comparing and contrasting plots • Analyzing author's intent • Criticizing • Negotiating meaning and questioning one's own meaning of text • Summarizing the plot

• Writing abilities of discipline	• The writing process:
	  ○ outlining;
	  ○ drafting;
	  ○ revising;
	  ○ editing and completing a text.
	• Writing mechanics (e.g. capitalization)
	• Writing functions:
	  ○ justifying opinions;
	  ○ providing detailed explanations;
	  ○ stating conclusions;
	  ○ summarizing information;
	  ○ making comparisons;
	  ○ supporting one's own opinions;
	  ○ hypothesizing;
	  ○ identifying;
	  ○ persuading others;
	  ○ agreeing and disagreeing;
	  ○ denying;
	  ○ describing;
	  ○ reporting;
	  ○ sequencing.

• Research abilities of discipline	• Expressing process or research • Expressing results of research • Justifying opinions • Stating theories • Providing detailed explanations • Articulating predictions or hypotheses • Stating conclusions • Summarizing information

Compiled from Brisk, 2006; Gibbons, 1991; and Menyuk and Brisk, 2005.

An effective bilingual pedagogy thus incorporates the notion of *Design* proposed by the New London Group (1996), that is, the available designs such as grammars or genres with which students must become familiar, and also the notion of *Redesign* in which students create transformed designs to express new meanings. We will return to this in the next chapter.

Co-operative learning

Co-operative learning has been shown to be a highly effective component of bilingual pedagogy (Slavin, 1990). Grouping can take many forms. For example, for reading there could be *book clubs and literature circles* where groups of four to five students discuss books together; *shared reading* where a group of students works with the teacher; *read-alouds* where the teacher reads aloud to the whole class (more on this in Chapter 14). Two kinds of groupings can be established – *homogeneous grouping*, useful when practicing a particular language structure, and *heterogeneous grouping* for greater linguistic support.

Collaborative grouping does not only develop talk that is useful for learning. It has also been shown to encourage students to focus on form and function of language. Gibbons (2002) gives us seven reasons why group work is important, especially in bilingual teaching:

1. Students get to hear more language with greater variety and more is directed to them: there is more comprehensible input (Krashen, 1985).
2. Students get to interact more; getting more turns and engaging with more responsibly. That is, there is more output (Swain, 1985).
3. The language used is more contextualized: it is heard and used in appropriate contexts.
4. There is more "message redundancy."
5. Students have increased opportunities to ask questions.
6. Group work has positive affective consequences, thus lowering the affective filter (Krashen, 1985) which is sometimes responsible for the anxiety that prevents learning.
7. Students construct the talk jointly, and talk is scaffolded by contributions of group.

One technique that involves group work that specifically develops syntactic and morphological awareness is the *dictagloss*. For the dictagloss, the teacher reads a short, difficult passage at normal speed in a second language to students who are emergent bilinguals. Students take notes. Then they work in groups to reconstruct the text. Since it is likely that the notes students have taken only include vocabulary and phrases, the group reconstruction often focuses on structural and linking elements. The group versions are then presented to the whole class and analyzed.

Gibbons (2002) reminds us that effective grouping should involve all children in cognitively demanding tasks that are embedded in the curriculum topic that the children are studying. To encourage children's need to talk there must be an authentic purpose. One way of encouraging talk in collaborative groups is to set it up so that not all children initially share all information. That is, there must be a built-in information gap that children must solve. An example of this kind of task is the *Jigsaw* where students, for example, read different kinds of information about the subject they are studying, and then share with each other.

Relevance that is high

An effective pedagogy for bilingual students is also *highly relevant*. It includes what the New London Group (1996) has called *Authentic Situated Practice*, that is, immersing students in practice. It also includes *interconnecting* the world of ideas to that of the students' world, whether it is their experiences as learners, in the public world, or their personal experiences, including their cultures, language practices, and identities. This means that pedagogy must include the students' diverse experiences.

Cummins (2006) speaks of the inclusion of *identity texts* in which students relate their stories using any of the languages. Children create stories in their own language that are then translated with the help of older students, parents, and teachers into the other languages. These multilingual stories are then published on the web, accompanied by images, spoken, musical, and dramatic renderings, or combinations of these in multimodal form. Cummins (2006) claims that what he calls *maximum identity investment* on the part of students is key to optimal academic development. According to Cummins (2000: 246) *empowerment* or the *collaborative creation of power* results from "classroom interactions that enable students to relate curriculum content to their individual and collective experience and to analyze broader social issues relevant to their lives." Cummins concludes (2000: 254) that "the process of identity negotiation is fundamental to educational success for all students, and furthermore that this process is directly determined by the micro-interactions between individual educators and students." Cummins' *transformative pedagogy* engages students' cognitive and linguistic abilities while creating a context of empowerment where student identities are affirmed as they participate academically.

García and Traugh (2002) describe how they have used *double entry journals* as a way to help language minority students put their stories, texts, and voices alongside those of the academic text of which they are making sense. In that way, the students' diverse histories and voices are included. That is, teachers build from the students' own texts, as they enlarge the understandings of the academic texts.

Many teachers, especially in elementary schools, start out the day with a group meeting in which the children share their daily news (Cappellini, 2005). As the students share their news, the teacher writes down the students' sentences, allowing all the children to compose grammatically correct texts. In this way, the material through which children learn is highly relevant.

Another way to provide interconnectedness is for pedagogical practices to include parents and communities. Moll (1992) has described pedagogy that uses the community's *funds of knowledge*, often different from those of school. By bringing parents' experiences and expertise into the classroom, the pedagogy becomes highly relevant to students from diverse backgrounds. Parents, grandparents, and other members of the community can be invited to read and tell stories in their own languages, share what they know, or simply to participate.

One of the challenging tasks of bilingual teachers is that, more than other kinds of teachers, they are often teaching through languages that the parents do not know. Bilingual teachers cannot blame parents for failing to provide bilingual and biliteracy practices for their children. But because of the importance of parental participation in a child's education, teachers need to engage parents and the community. For example, teachers must make explicit to parents who do not share the language of schooling or the literacy practices in which their children are engaged, the different academic literacy practices of school (Edwards and Nwenmely, 2000). Bringing the parents into the classrooms is one way of making them familiar with schools' language and literacy practices, even when they do not share the language of the lesson.

Summary

Bilingual pedagogy must always incorporate two important principles – attention to social justice and to social practice. But it is often difficult for bilingual teachers to know how to act on these two principles. The section above has reviewed the dimensions and the instructional practices that are necessary to act on these principles of bilingual education pedagogy. Table 13.4 provides a summary of the dimensions and some of its elements:

Table 13.4   Principles and Dimensions of Bilingual Pedagogy

Social Justice Principle
1. Equity:
    - provide equity in participation structures;
    - give access to the same curriculum, practices and programs for all.
2. Language of child and language tolerance:
    - include the home languages;
    - build plurilingual tolerance and multilingual awareness.
3. Expectations and academic rigor:
    - support a community of achievement and mutual respect;
    - encourage higher order thinking skills;
    - develop metacognitive skills:
        ○ amplify, do not simplify;
        ○ support lesson; that is, scaffold;
        ○ provide explicit overt instruction;
        ○ correct errors explicitly but in context.
4. Assessment that is valid and equitable:
    - provide valid bilingual assessments;
    - give reasonable time for completion and provide other accommodations;
    - have reasonable outcome expectations.

Social Practice Principle
1. Interactions of quality:
    - sustain reciprocal dialogue;
    - provide generative talk.
2   Language focus
    - provide discourse practice on language, texts and genres.

Table 13.4   (*continued*)

3. Cooperative learning:
    *   encourage collaborative group work.
4. Relevance that is high:
    *   use authentic situated practice;
    *   interconnect to students' world and identities:
        o   encourage the development of identity texts;
        o   include parents and community.

Strategies: Scaffolding

Initial considerations

The core of bilingual pedagogical strategies especially for emergent bilinguals in the beginning stages is "scaffolding," a term that has been abused in the literature and is little understood. Often used to signal the structure of support that bilingual learners need, scaffolding was originally coined to also include *the process of taking away the structure* in which learning is advanced (Walqui, 2006). Bruner and Sherwood (1975) used "scaffold" to refer to the non-rule part of a peek-a-boo game. That is, in a peek-a-boo game the parent repeatedly hides their face, and then shows it to the child. But the scaffold refers not to the rule, but the instance in which the parent stops the game and there are no rules. The scaffold refers specifically to the "point of rupture," to the taking away of the structure so that learning can take place. As Walqui (2006) repeats, what is important is not just the external structure, but the *process* in which learning is "handed over" to the child.

Scaffolding is related to Vygotsky's *Zone of Proximal Development* (ZPD) which he defines as (1978: 86) "the distance between the actual developmental level as determined by independent problem solving and the level of potential development as determined through problem solving under adult guidance or in collaboration with more capable peers." Because scaffolding can only occur in the ZPD, scaffolding is *contingent*, that is, it depends on other actions; it is *collaborative* and jointly achieved; and it is *interactive* because two or more people are mutually engaged (Walqui, 2006). Students move through four phases:

*   A *tutorial phase* in which the teacher explicitly models and guides instruction.
*   A *contingent phase* which is teacher-student based and it is students' learning that provokes the teacher's feedback, modeling, and questions.
*   An *interactive phase* which is student-based. This is what happens when students "turn and talk" to another student or work in pairs.
*   An *independent phase* when students themselves decide which strategies are more appropriate for the specific academic task (Walqui, 2006).

Cummins' model of bilingual pedagogy (2000: 71) makes clear that "language and content will be acquired most successfully when students are challenged cognitively but provided with the *contextual and linguistic supports or scaffolds* required for successful task completion." Cummins' pedagogical model includes two axes – one of cognitive demands, the other of contextual support as in Figure 13.1:

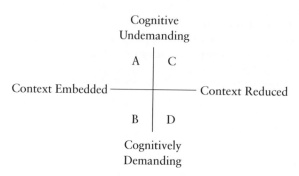

Figure 13.1   Cognitive Demands and Contextual Support in Bilingual Pedagogy

From Cummins (2000: 68, figure 3.1)

Cummins argues that optimal instruction for linguistic, cognitive, and academic growth of emerging bilingual students occurs in *Quadrant B* with content that is highly *cognitively demanding* – academically difficult – but that is presented in *context-embedded ways* – supported by visuals, manipulatives, through co-operative learning, and project-based lessons. Language is context-embedded when it is very dependent on what is happening in the immediate situation (Gibbons, 1991). As we have said above, Cummins tells us that contextual support has *internal and external dimensions.* Internal contextual support refers to attributes of the student – his or her prior experience and understandings. For example, if a student knows a lot about chemistry, reading a chemistry text in a second language will be less difficult than if he or she is ignorant of chemistry. External contextual support refers to aspects of the language input. For example, a lesson in which the teacher speaks clearly with a lot of redundancy and paraphrasing provides good contextual support (Cummins, 2000).

The task of the teacher is to progressively take away the structure provided by the context-embeddedness, while keeping the high cognitive demands of the lesson. Thus, competent bilingual students can increasingly be faced with instruction in which tasks are not only cognitively demanding, but have little contextual support. By providing bilingual students with high contextual support, meaningful bilingual pedagogy enables students to increasingly perform tasks such as the reading of complicated texts and completing standardized assessments, tasks that fall under *Quadrant D* and that are *context reduced*, that is, they rely solely on *linguistic cues* for meaning.

Gibbons (1998: 99) also supports pedagogy that builds on context-embeddedness, and says: "children's current understandings of a curriculum topic, and their use of familiar 'everyday' language to express these understandings, should be seen as the basis for the development of the unfamiliar registers of school."

Structures

We describe below some of the *scaffolding structures* for bilingual learning, although we caution that, as Van Lier (2006) explains, *pedagogy* is a combination of *constraining with structure and releasing with process*. We provide here the planning, the routine, and the ritual (the structure), but as Van Lier (2006) points out, pedagogy also involves *innovation, exploration and improvisation*, aspects that rely on teachers' imagination and abilities and that cannot be simply summarized here.

Scaffolding structures, or structures that provide contextual and linguistic support, are summarized in Table 13.5 and then explained:

Table 13.5   Scaffolding Structural Components

- Routines
- Contextualization
- Modeling
- Bridging and schema-building
- Multiplicities – multiple entry points

Routines

The teacher establishes routines which she follows consistently and predictably. She repeats language patterns. She uses language clearly, paraphrasing and summarizing consistently throughout the lesson. The teacher checks the students' comprehension frequently. She also repeats and explicitly teaches basic phrases that students can use continuously. Some of these phrases might be:

For linguistic help:

   "How do you say X?"
   "I don't understand." "What does it mean?"
   "Can you repeat that?" "Can you say that again?"

For content help:

   "Can I have Y?"
   "Please, can you help me?"

For support help:

   "Excuse me."
   "May I come in?"
   "May I go to the bathroom?"

The teacher also has routines for the classroom and students learn to negotiate the changes in instructional space without difficulty. Because these transitions have been established as routines, the teacher has little need to say much in order to have the children act.

Contextualization

A most important tool to contextualize instruction is the use of the *students' home language*. Teachers should understand both of the students' languages. She often allows emerging bilinguals to speak or write in their home language while encouraging them to use the other language.

The teacher also contextualizes language through other paralinguistic strategies, that is, approaches to understand linguistic messages that fall outside of language itself. For example, she uses *body language* and *gestures*. The teacher also uses *visuals* such as pictures, as well as *manipulatives* and *realia* that help students comprehend. To contextualize, these pedagogical practices are often *technologically* enriched, using films, tapes, the internet, and drawing from multimedia experiences. The teacher also keeps *word walls* where she displays vocabulary and phrases that are important for the students to build their own texts.

Charts, diagrams, and maps are used copiously by these teachers. *Graphic organizers* are used to help students arrange the information in visual form. Among the different kinds of *graphic organizers*, we find:

- *Semantic mapping* which display words, ideas or concepts in categories, and then show how they are related to each other. They are usually constructed through brainstorming with the entire class.
- *Story maps* which display in graphic form the components of a story – the title and the author, the setting, the main characters, the beginning, middle and end of the story, the problem, the solution, and some of the important events.
- *Venn diagrams* which allows text comparisons.
- *Double entry forms* where students write out parts of the text and then in the other column tell how this text relates to themselves.
- *Timelines* where the chronological pace of the story is laid out.[6]

Graphic organizers can be used as a prereading or prewriting activity to build background, but they can also be used as postreading activity so that students can demonstrate their comprehension of a topic and record personal understandings and responses (Buehl, 2001).

Teachers can also contextualize instruction by supporting the learning of content with fictional literature. Because of the aesthetic response that literature produces in readers, there is a possibility of a deeper *transactional experience* (Rosenblatt, 1991), allowing for deeper understanding of concepts.

Modeling

The teacher models all routines and engages in *think-alouds*, that is, she verbalizes the actions and processes of the lesson (Baumann, Jones, and Seifert-Kessell, 1993). For example, the teacher may model writing in front of the class and say "Now, what should I put next?" The teacher provides oral and written scripts for students to use.

A way of modeling reading is for the teacher to do *read-alouds* from a variety of texts. Teachers demonstrate the steps or directions needed to complete the tasks, as well as the language used. I reproduce here a teaching moment of a mini-lesson of a fourth-grade *reading workshop* (more on this in the next chapter) in the United States focusing on empathizing with characters:

Mini-Lesson: Reading Workshop

[Teacher speaks to the students]

A few days ago we read *Peter's Chair* during our read-aloud. However, sometimes when we pick a book up again that we haven't read in a little while, it is a good idea to just quickly take a walk through to remind ourselves what it is about. (The teacher demonstrates this by flipping through the pages and retelling it to herself.) Now, I am going to read a part of *Peter's Chair* by Ezra Jack Keats and I want you to pay close attention to how I empathize with Peter and his situation. [Teacher reads a part and then continues . . .]

I'm concerned that Peter might be starting to feel jealous that his sister has his crib and they painted it pink. I can relate to Peter because when my sister was born I remember looking into her room like Peter did, and guess what I saw? The room which used to be my white room was now painted pink. I felt really jealous, just like Peter. I am concerned that all the things that used to be Peter's are now his sisters and I know this is making Peter feel sad, just like it made me feel sad.

So readers, did you notice how as I read, I stopped, and I looked at the prompts, and I said how I was concerned with Peter, and then I explained how I can relate to Peter by bringing in my personal connection? Because I did this, I was able to "empathize with Peter" and I did that by putting myself in his shoes.

Example provided by D. Zamir, March 29, 2006

Another way of modeling is asking questions so that students can learn to think of important questions to raise. Gibbons (1991) lists eight types of questions that are important in bilingual pedagogy and that teachers need to model. We reproduce them here with one example:

Type of Question	An Example
Classifying	How are these things similar/different?
Describing	How would you describe . . . ?
Evaluating	Do you agree with this? Why ?
Explaining	Why does . . . ?
Generalizing	What have you found out about . . . ?
Inferring	What do you think might be happening here?
Predicting	What might happen if . . . ? / What would you do if . . . ?
Recalling information	How many . . . ?

Bridging and schema building

The teacher uses pedagogy that supports learning in the present but evokes the past, since, as Faltis and Hudelson (1998) have pointed out, learning and interactions rely on meaning and images that have already happened. New concepts and language are only learned if they are built on previous knowledge. Schema, or clusters of meaning that are interconnected, that is, *knowledge of the world*, are how we organize knowledge and understanding. Building understanding is a matter of weaving new information into pre-existing structures of meaning (Walqui, 2006).

To do this, teachers usually *preview* the material to be taught. For example, they may do a "picture walk" before reading where the students and the teacher talk about the picture that accompanies a story. She then asks students to think of how the picture relates to their lives and other texts they might have read or understandings that they may have had. Teachers might also review terms before introducing new concepts as a way to build schema. They might preview the entire text, noting the title and subtitles, the charts and graphics.

Another important strategy for bridging and schema building is to use two- or three-column *anticipatory guides*, with one column for what students *know* about the story or the subject about which they are going to read and what they would *want* to know. After they read, students fill out the column labeled "what I *learned*." In the United States, these anticipatory guides are often referred to by their acronym – KWL.

Yet another strategy is what is known as SQP2RS (Vogt, 2000, 2002). This strategy which is useful for teaching content with expository texts includes six steps (Echevarria, Vogt, and Short, 2004):

1. surveying (scanning the text for one to two minutes);
2. questioning (having students generate questions);
3. predicting (stating one to three things students think they will learn);
4. reading (searching for answers to questions and confirming/disconfirming predictions);
5. responding (answering questions and formulating new ones);
6. summarizing (orally or in writing).

Students are also given an opportunity to actively engage with the lesson by using "turn-and-talk." That is, after the teacher's modeling, the students get an opportunity to try it out in a non-threatening supportive context with another peer. Students are free to use any of their languages.

To bridge the two languages, cognates are used. And the two languages are often compared and contrasted. The teacher pays special attention to cross-linguistic text features (Grabe and Kaplan, 1989) and to the different writing conventions, rhetorical patterns and text organization of the students' two or more languages. It is also important for the teacher to pay attention to the different expectations for literacy, and the purposes for literacy of the students' different cultures (Alderson, 2000). For example, the reading of the Qur'an does not encourage the expression of personal opinions, whereas this is often the core of western secular literacy.

Thematic planning
This is yet another good way of both bridging and contextualizing, because vocabulary is repeated naturally in lessons that are related through a theme (Freeman and Freeman, 2000). Themes such as cultural differences and language are broad enough and very applicable for bilingual classrooms.

Multiple entry points
Because of the different linguistic levels in all bilingual education programs, it is most important for the teacher to provide multiple entry points into the lesson. What this means is that some children in the class might be able to use the language of instruction fully without adaptation, while others might have to use their first language or a mixture of the two, and others might only be able to draw a picture. The teacher not only allows students to demonstrate their understandings in different ways, but s/he also differentiates instruction. For example, for some students, s/he uses books on tapes, rather than have them read individually. For others, s/he provides sentence starters or a chart to fill in, rather than expect them to write an essay. Still others are expected to narrate orally, while others are asked to write. Especially in the emerging bilingual stage, teachers allow for a silent stage in which students engage cognitively with instruction, although they are not expected to produce oral or written texts in the target language.

Even when bilingual students are approximately at the same stage of bilingual development, teachers are cognizant of the eight kinds of Gardner's multiple intelligences (1993):

1. linguistic intelligence: being word smart;
2. logical-mathematical intelligence: being number or reasoning smart;
3. spatial intelligence: being picture smart;
4. bodily-kinesthetic intelligence: being body smart;
5. musical intelligence: being music smart;
6. interpersonal intelligence: being people smart;
7. intrapersonal intelligence: being self-smart;
8. naturalist intelligence: being nature smart.

Thus, teachers use a wide variety of activities besides traditional lessons – music, art, role-playing, going on field trips, engaging in inner reflection.

Multiple entry points also allow the teachers to *conference* with children. During conferences, teachers focus on helping the students express meaning by explicitly asking questions such as "Can you remember how we said that when we were writing together?" (Gibbons, 1991: 108).

Conclusion

This chapter offers educators guides to pedagogical strategies to support bilingualism. But the best bilingual pedagogical approaches and methodologies will not work unless instruction is mindful of social justice and social interaction. Oftentimes, schools pay a lot of attention to techniques and strategies while ignoring the social justice aspects of bilingual pedagogy. All education should be grounded on social justice, but bilingual education, more than any other, needs to pay special attention to issues of equity. Bilingual teachers thus need to be much more than good technicians; effective bilingual educators must also be advocates for equity and justice.

With this said, it is important to recognize that advocacy by itself will not in any way advance bilingualism. Thus, bilingual teachers must develop practices that encompass both principles – that of social justice *and* that of social practice. It is in the blending of the two, in much the same way as in the blending of languages and cultures that is a result of bilingual education, that bilingual teachers can be effective.

Questions for Reflection

1.   What is the pedagogical framework for developing bilingualism discussed in this chapter? Identify the two principles. Why is it important to pay attention to the two principles? How does this framework inform philosophies of teaching and learning?
2.   What is the difference between the grammatical approach, the communicative approach, and the cognitive approach in bilingual education?
3.   Identify the principles of bilingual pedagogy and discuss the practices associated with them.
4.   What are some ways of scaffolding instruction for emergent bilingual learners?

Further Reading

Cloud, N., Genesee, F., and Hamayan, E. (2000). *Dual Language Instruction. A Handbook for Enriched Education.* Heinle and Heinle, Boston, MA.

Echevarria, J., Vogt, M.E., and Short, D.J. (2000). *Making Content Comprehensible for English Learners. The SIOP Model,* second edn. Allyn and Bacon, Needham Heights, MA.

Gallagher, E. (2008). *Equal Rights to the Curriculum: Many Languages, One Message.* Multilingual Matters, Clevedon.

Gibbons, P. (1991). *Learning to Learn in a Second Language.* Heinemann, Portsmouth, NH.

—— (2002). *Scaffolding Language, Scaffolding Learning. Teaching Second Languages in the Mainstream Classroom.* Heinemann, Portsmouth, NH.

—— (2006). *Bridging Discourses in the ESL Classrooms: Students, Teachers and Researchers.* Continuum, London.

Herrera, S.G., and Murry, K.G. (2005). *Mastering ESL and Bilingual Methods: Differentiated Instruction for Culturally and Linguistically Diverse (CLD) Students.* Allyn and Bacon, Boston, MA.

14

Biliteracy Practices and Pedagogy

A text, whether written on paper, or on the soul (Plato), or on the world (Freire), is a loaded weapon. The person, the educator, who hands over the gun, hands over the bullets (the perspective), and must own up to the consequences. There is no way out of having an opinion, an ideology, and a strong one, as did Plato, as does Freire. Literacy education is not for the timid.

Gee, 1996: 39

Overview

In this chapter, we will discuss biliteracy practices, and consider:

- a sociocultural approach;
- the continua of biliteracy;
- models of biliteracy use;
- biliteracy sequencing;
- written language and texts;
- instructional approaches;
- the biliteracy workshop.

Introduction

The previous chapter addressed bilingual education pedagogies important for all types of bilingual education programs. This chapter will focus more specifically on *biliteracy*, that is, "any and all instances in which communication occurs in two or more languages *in or around writing*" (Hornberger, 1990: 213, my italics). As Hudelson (1994: 102) has said, "Literacy is language and language is literacy." All language processes of reading, writing, listening and speaking or signing are interrelated and mutually supportive. Thus, they need to be developed holistically. The previous chapter and this one should be read in interdependent ways. That is, the bilingual education pedagogical principles discussed in the last chapter also apply to biliteracy/practices, as is evident from the earlier discussion.

Not all bilingual education programs are concerned with the *development of biliteracy*, since, as we saw in Chapter 12, some programs only use one of the languages orally. Also, the child's home language may not have a written standard or any written materials, as is the case with many Indigenous languages in Borneo. And Deaf students may, or may not, develop biliteracy in more than one written language. But *all* bilingual education programs must take into account the *concept of biliteracy practices*, since even if written texts are only in one language, the communication that occurs around writing, often in the language of the child – written or signed – and different from the one in which the text is written, is most important for developing literacy in the language of the text. Thus, all bilingual education program types engage in *biliteracy practices* even when the educational goal is only monoliteracy.[1]

Because reading and writing are such important language abilities for school, and especially for assessment, we expand on *school-based biliteracy* practices here. Written *academic* texts have different characteristics than those of other written texts. Thus, the development of reading and writing abilities and the engagement of students in literacy practices, especially in an additional language, are most often the purview of schooling.[2] For these reasons, we have decided to devote one chapter to *school-based biliteracy practices*, while acknowledging that there are many literacy practices in the home that interact with those of school.

A Sociocultural Approach

Unfortunately, most schools adhere to the concept of *literacy as an autonomous skill* (Street, 1984, 1993), that is, a cognitive set of skills that are universal and culturally neutral. As such, schools focus on developing *functional literacy*, the plain mastery of skills needed to read and write as measured by standardized forms of assessment.

When bilingual schools refer to biliteracy, many (fortunately, not all) are adopting this functional definition of literacy as they consider the autonomous skills of reading and writing in two languages. For example, in *transitional bilingual education* classrooms, even when the two languages are used in reading and writing, the language of lower prestige is often used only according to the norms and practices of the more powerful language. This is often the case of Spanish–English transitional bilingual classrooms in the United States, where Spanish reading is taught following the literacy practices of English. Although teaching to read in Spanish in countries where Spanish is the dominant language relies on a syllabic approach, with children first learning to decode syllables (ma–me–mi–mo–mu, etc.), in the United States teaching children to read in Spanish is most often taught phonetically (/m/), a strategy that is useful only for English reading. Thus, Spanish literacy, according to its different discourse and sociocultural norms, is simply not in any way used or developed. Spanish literacy is only a springboard to English functional literacy.

In many bilingual education programs that follow an *additive bilingual theoretical framework* (such as maintenance, prestigious and immersion bilingual education programs), there is also a tendency to define biliteracy according to this autonomous concept of literacy as two single separate languages. And thus, bilingual children may sometimes fall short of accomplishing this functional competence in two separate languages as if they were two monolingual individuals.

But as we said in the beginning of this chapter, biliteracy is much more than the plain mastery of reading and writing in two languages. Biliteracy is "any and all instances in which *communication occurs in two or more languages in or around writing*" (Hornberger, 1990: 213). *Sociocultural studies of literacy* (Street, 1984, 1993) have demonstrated that literacy practices are influenced by social, cultural, political, and economic factors, and that literacy is not an *autonomous* skill. Literacy learning and use varies by situation and entails complex social interactions. Making meaning from and with print varies according to different sociocultural contexts (Hornberger, 1989; Kenner, 2000, 2004; Martin-Jones and Jones, 2000; Pérez, 1998). As Pérez (1998: 22) says: "[Literacy] is a technology or tool that is culturally determined and used for specific purposes. Literacy practices are culture-specific ways of knowing." As such, biliteracy practices are most appropriately studied within an *ideological* framework (Street, 1984).

Basing his understandings on Street's work, Lüdi (1997: 207) has proposed a broad definition of *biliteracy* as: "the possession of, or access to, the competences and information required to accomplish literacy practices which an individual wishes to – or is compelled to – engage in everyday situations in two languages, with their corresponding functions and in the corresponding cultural contexts." In an effort to emphasize the co-existence of not just two, but multiple languages and literacies, Martin-Jones and Jones (2000) have proposed the term "multilingual literacies." Multilingual literacies refer to the multiplicity of individual and group repertoires, and the varied communicative purposes for which groups use different spoken, signed, and written languages. The term also focuses attention on the multiple ways in which people draw on, and combine codes in their communicative repertoire when they speak,[3] sign, and write. Biliteracy practices entail complex social interactions and are influenced by sociopolitical and socioeconomic factors.

In previous work, García, Bartlett, and Kleifgen (2007) have argued for the extension of multilingual literacies to the concept of *pluriliteracy practices*.[4] Literacy practices are not only associated with different cultural contexts and social structures, but also with different channels or modes of communication. Literacy practices are increasingly *multimodal* – that is, written–linguistic modes of meaning are intricately bound up with other visual, audio, and spatial semiotic systems (Cope and Kalantzis, 2000; Kress, 2003; New London Group, 1996). In the twenty-first century, new media are occasioning increased variation in multimodal discourses. Biliteracy practices are thus often carried out, in an *integrated* fashion, as Coste (2001) has said. The *pluriliteracy practices* approach moves away from the dichotomy of the traditional L1/L2 pairing, emphasizing instead that language and literacy practices are interrelated and flexible, positing that all literacy practices have equal value, and acknowledging the *agency* involved in communicating around writing. Although grounded in the social and the political, pluriliteracy practices have the potential for *transformation and change*, precisely because of the dynamism and flexibility of integrated hybrid practices and the agency of those involved. What is important in pluriliteracy practices is that students develop the agency to use both languages in an integrated or separate fashion, depending on the sociocultural context in which they perform the literacy practice. But pluriliteracy practices encourage students to use any of their languages or modes of meaning at their disposal in order to make sense of all kinds of texts.

Gutiérrez and her colleagues (Gutiérrez, Baquedano-López, Alvarez, and Chiu, 1999a; Gutiérrez, Baquedano-López, and Tejada, 1999b; Gutiérrez, Baquedano-López, and Alvarez, 2001), as well as Reyes (1992, 2001) have demonstrated the diversity of, and interplay between, linguistic codes and literacy practices in multilingual classrooms. Gregory and Williams (2000) show how Gujarati children living in London mix and blend practices from home and school. These children bring family literacy practices that are different from those considered essential in the mainstream school literacy literature. For example, instead of having been read good bedtime stories, these children have developed excellent capacities for memorization, a product of their practices with Qur'anic reading. They also bring experience of working in larger groups and concentrating over an extended period of time. Kalmar (2001) demonstrates how Latino migrants construct hybrid alphabets to make sense of their new language.

Pluriliteracy practices thus include four principles:

- an emphasis on *literacy practices in their appropriate sociocultural contexts*, as influenced by different cultural contexts and various social relations;
- the *hybridity* of literacy practices, especially as afforded by new technologies;
- the increasing *interrelationship of semiotic systems*, a product of new technologies;
- *increased valuing of different literacy practices*, including those that have no place in school, and the drawing on different literacy practices to develop school-based literacy (García, Bartlett, and Kleifgen, 2007).

The Continua of Biliteracy

Nancy Hornberger's continua of biliteracy (2003) identifies the major social, linguistic, political, and psychological issues that surround the development of biliteracy, as they relate to each other. It builds on the *differences* that are the result of at least five factors – the degree to which groups or societies: 1. have power; 2. live in monolingual or bilingual societies; 3. speak languages that have literacies or not, or that have similar/dissimilar language structures or scripts; 4. have schools in which their languages are used or taught; 5. have opportunities to receive or produce texts with different varieties of diverse languages. That is, bilingual schools not only have to take into account the theoretical framework which they adopt in order to determine their biliteracy approach, but also must carefully consider the social, linguistic, political, and psychological issues addressed in Hornberger's continua.

The most recent version of the continua of biliteracy model (Hornberger and Skilton-Sylvester, 2003) emphasizes that not only are all points in a particular continuum interrelated, but that all points across the continua are also interrelated. This revision integrates a *critical perspective*, positing that there tends to be a privileging of one end of the continua over the other because of differences in power relations, and that biliteracy is better obtained when learners can draw on all points of the continua (Hornberger, 1989). The interrelated nature of Hornberger's continua supports the potential for positive transfer across literacies, but its nested nature also shows how transfer can be promoted or hindered by different contextual factors (Hornberger, 2003).

In the continua of biliteracy model included in Figure 14.1 (Hornberger and Skilton-Sylvester, 2003), the left represents the less powerful, and the right the more powerful, end of the continuum:

Contexts of biliteracy

micro ——————————————— macro
oral ——————————————— literate
bilingual ——————————————— monolingual

Biliterate development in the individual

reception ——————————————— production
oral language ——————————————— written language
L1 ——————————————— L2 transfer

Media of biliteracy

simultaneous ——————————————— successive exposure
dissimilar ——————————————— similar language structures
divergent ——————————————— convergent scripts

Content of biliteracy

minority ——————————————— majority
vernacular ——————————————— literacy
contextualized ——————————————— decontextualized language texts

Figure 14.1 Continua of Biliteracy

The model of pluriliteracy practices described in the previous section (García, Bartlett, and Kleifgen, 2007) falls within Hornberger's continua of biliteracy framework, and reinforces the recognition that there could be simultaneous and integrated use of both ends of each and every continuum. For example, in a single communication around text, pluriliteracy practices may include both the oral and the literate, multiple languages, and divergent media as well as scripts. The García, Bartlett, and Kleifgen (2007) model of pluriliteracy practices pays attention to translanguaging, the hybridity of language use and literacy practices that is essential for today's globalized world, as well as the more traditional ways of languaging in local contexts, and especially in schools.

Models of Biliteracy Use

Bilingual schools must make decisions about how to use languages in literacy practices. Four models of language and literacy use in biliteracy practices can be identified:

1. A *convergent monoliterate model* which uses the two languages in communication to transact[5] with a text written in one language, usually a dominant one.
2. A *convergent biliterate model* which uses the two languages in communication to transact with a text written in each of the two languages, but with minority literacy practices calqued on majority literacy practices.
3. A *separation biliterate model* which uses one language or the other to transact with a text written in one language or the other according to their own socio-cultural and discourse norms.
4. A *flexible multiple model* which uses the two languages in communication to transact with texts written in both languages and in other media according to a bilingual flexible norm, capable of both integration and separation.

Convergent monoliterate

The convergent monoliterate model is used mostly to teach language minority students in languages that either are not written or that have very low status in society. Teachers and students communicate in the two languages *around writing* in the majority language, but the minority language is *not used in writing*. This is often the case of instruction in many African countries, where the vernaculars of students are used, alongside other languages, in making sense of print written in a more powerful language. It corresponds to subtractive theoretical frameworks of bilingualism and is prevalent in transitional bilingual education. Only the majority language is assessed. It can be diagrammed as in Figure 14.2:

Language A and Language B ⟶ Language B written text

Figure 14.2 Convergent Monoliterate Model

Convergent biliterate

The convergent biliterate model of biliteracy practices is also used in transitional bilingual education classrooms in which literacy is expected and assessed only in the majority language, but minority literacy is used to assist in that development. In these cases, the minority literacy practices are calqued on (or copied from) those of majority literacy practices. It can be diagrammed as in Figure 14.3:

Language B, and Language A calqued on Literacy B ⟶ Language B written text

Figure 14.3 Convergent Biliterate Model

Separation biliterate

This model is used to communicate in one or the other language when writing in the same language. Thus, children and teachers *match* the language in which they are communicating around writing to the language of the written text. Students are encouraged to "think" in the language in which they are reading or writing. Only one language or the other is used around writing and in writing in the same language. Both languages are assessed and it is expected that students engage in literacy practices in one or the other language according to monolingual standards. Bilingual education programs that follow the additive theoretical framework use this model which is displayed here in Figure 14.4:

Language A ⟶ Language A written text

Language B ⟶ Language B written text

Figure 14.4 Separation Biliterate Model

Flexible multiple

This model of biliteracy practices allows for *crossovers and supports translanguaging.* That is, both languages and media are used in literacy practices around a text in one or the other language or in multiple media. Teachers encourage children to use all linguistic codes and modes as resources in order to engage in literacy practices in one or the other language. For example, when planning to write in English in the U.S., Latino children use Spanish to build the background, to question the text, to think about strategies; and they use not only print, but also signs, images, videos. This is also the biliteracy practice most used in Deaf bilingual education programs where ASL is used to develop literacy about Deaf histories, experiences and cultures that then support the development of literacy in the written language. In this flexible multiple model of biliteracy both languages might be assessed, but it is expected that students' engagement with written texts would differ from that of their monolingual counterparts. Usually, bilingual education programs that fall within the dynamic bilingual education framework or the recursive bilingual education framework are likely to permit this approach, although many insist on following the separation biliterate approach. The flexible multiple model can be diagrammed as in Figure 14.5:

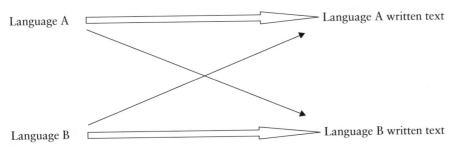

Language A ⟶ Language A written text

Language B ⟶ Language B written text

Figure 14.5 Flexible Multiple Model

Table 14.1   Biliteracy Models, Goals and Bilingual Education Frameworks

Biliteracy Models	*Convergent* (convergent monoliterate and convergent bilingual)	*Separation*	*Flexible Multiple*
Biliteracy Goal	Functional literacy with monoliteracy goal	Full biliteracy	Functional biliteracy
BE Theoretical Framework	Subtractive	Additive	Recursive and dynamic
Types	• transitional	• maintenance • prestigious • immersion	• immersion revitalization • developmental • poly/two-way • CLIL-type • multiple multilingual

Table 14.1 summarizes the different biliteracy models and goals that are pertinent to bilingual education classrooms. They are placed here according to the theoretical framework of the bilingual education program which is *most likely* to support one or the other approaches to biliteracy.[6]

Biliteracy Sequencing[7]

Bilingual schools must make decisions about when to introduce literacy practices in two or more languages. Whether schools are following a model of language use around biliteracy practices that is convergent, separate, or flexible, and in cases where both written languages are used, decisions must be made as to whether written texts in the two languages are presented in instruction simultaneously or sequentially. Usually schools develop biliteracy practices using either a *sequential mode or a simultaneous mode*.

Sequential

In 1953 UNESCO declared that there were advantages in using the child's mother tongue to teach initial literacy. A *sequential view of biliteracy* posits that literacy in the additional language should not be introduced until a child has competence in speaking, reading, and writing a first language (Wong Fillmore and Valadez, 1986). This is consistent with research findings on the academic failure of Indigenous peoples and immigrants, who most often are given their initial reading instruction in a second language (Francis and Reyhner, 2002; Skutnabb-Kangas, 1981, 2000). The idea in these programs is often not to develop biliteracy per se, but rather to advance literacy in the dominant societal language by teaching children first to read and write in a language they understand. Full transition to reading and writing in the child's second language is only made after the child has oral proficiency in the language to be read, as shown in Figure 14.6:

| Literacy in L1 and oral proficiency in L2 | → | Literacy in L2 and oral proficiency in L2 |

Figure 14.6 Literacy Education in Transitional Bilingual Education Programs

Cummins (1981b, 1991), writing about second-language acquisition, and Bernhardt and Kamil (1995), writing about second-language reading research, have proposed that there is an interdependence across languages. As we have seen before, Cummins refers to this as the *Common Underlying Proficiency* and the *Developmental Interdependence Hypothesis*. Bernhardt and Kamil speak of the *Linguistic Interdependence Hypothesis*. Both hypotheses posit that successful readers in a first language must reach a *threshold* of second-language competence for transferability of literacy skills to occur (Bossers, 1991; Brisbois, 1995). They argue that there should be fluency and literacy in a first language before starting literacy instruction in a second one; that is, *sequential biliteracy* is necessary (Hakuta, 1986; Wong Fillmore and Valadez, 1986). Many correlational studies have indeed shown that at least reading proficiency transfers between languages (Carson, Carrell, Silberstein, *et al.*, 1990; Elley, 1984; Goldman, Reyes, and Varnhagen, 1984; Groebel, 1980; Reyes, 1987; Tregar and Wong, 1984). Heath (1986) has referred to this same concept as "transferable generic literacies."

Simultaneous

But there are those who argue that children can learn to read in two languages at once, even as they are still developing cognitive-oral skills in a second language (Barrera, 1983; Edelsky, 1986; Hudelson, 1984; Reyes, 2001). Dworin (2003: 179) posits the *bidirectionality* of biliteracy development, pointing to the "dynamic, flexible process in which children's transactions with two written languages mediate their language learning for both languages." The success of immersion bilingual education programs in Canada where Anglophone children learn to read in French, a second language, without any adverse effects has challenged the position that literacy in a first language is essential to acquire literacy in a second one (Cummins, 1979; Lambert and Tucker, 1972). Furthermore, in his studies of ethnic mother-tongue schools, Fishman (1980b) found that children were able to *simultaneously* acquire literacy in two languages, even when the languages differed significantly in script and discourse mode. Similar findings have resulted from studies of community language classes and complementary schools in Great Britain (Gregory, 1996; Kenner, 2000, 2004), as well as heritage language programs in Canada (Beynon and Toohey, 1991).

In the Val d'Aoste bilingual programs, students are also introduced to the two written codes (Italian and French) simultaneously. This co-alphabetization is possible because, as we said earlier, children are allowed to alternate written codes when writing, as they develop biliteracy. The same can be said of the Chinese American children in the bilingual school that Fu (2003) studied.

Sequential or simultaneous?

The view of sequential or simultaneous biliteracy holds that each language develops separately, even if simultaneously, and thus each literacy should be taught as monolingual literacy. Most handbooks for teaching biliteracy propose reading and writing approaches that are similar to those that are used to teach literacy in one or the other language. Most texts focus on teaching literacy in a majority language, most often English, to second-language learners, especially immigrants (Gibbons, 2002; Gregory, 1996; Peregoy and Boyle, 2001). It is more difficult to find studies and texts that describe how biliteracy is simultaneously and integratively acquired (for an exception, see Fu, 2003) because bilingual schools are usually not organized in ways that allow this.

Hornberger (2002) and Cummins (2000) suggest that findings that a stronger first language leads to a stronger second language do not necessarily imply that the first language must be fully developed before literacy in the second language is introduced. Rather, they argue that the first language must not be abandoned before it is fully developed, whether the second language is introduced simultaneously or successively, early or late, in that process.

Written Language and Texts

Although, as we have said, literacy and biliteracy practices are not solely about reading and writing, it is the written text that is the focus of attention as communication takes place. This section describes some properties and differences of written language and written texts that are important to take into account when thinking about biliteracy practices.

Writing systems and scripts

Because script plays such an important role in written texts, and because bilingual education often uses texts written in different scripts, we briefly describe here the complexity of scripts. Writing systems have been around for a long time – the earliest in Egypt and Asia Minor, China, and what is today Mexico. Perhaps the earliest writing system, known as cuneiform, developed in Mesopotamia in modern-day Iraq around the fourth millennium BC to write Sumerian. It was later adapted by others.

Today's systems of writing, even those based on ideographic representations, such as Chinese, link representation of speech through abstract symbolization to the sounds of words. This is precisely why meaning in reading often comes from the reader's knowledge of the spoken form of the language.

There are different types of scripts and many different scripts. (For more on this, see Coulmas, 2003; Rogers, 2005. Also visit the website of Omniglot.) English, the language of this book, is written in *Roman script* which uses an *alphabetic type* of writing that denotes consonants and vowels with separate characters. The Roman alphabet (a b c) and the Greek alphabet (α β γ) are different scripts, but they both belong to the category of alphabetic writing systems. Cyrillic is yet another alphabetic script used to write some of the Slavic languages, for example, Russian, Bulgarian, and Serbian, among others. Alphabetic writing systems generally use one symbol arbitrarily to represent one sound. Symbols are written together to stand for a word.

The Arabic script and Hebrew script use *Abjad* or *consonantal type* of writing in which only the consonants are generally written. The Arabic script is used not only in the Arabic language, but also in such languages as Urdu, Punjabi, Malay,

Pashto, and Persian, among many. On the other hand, Hindi uses an *Abugida type* of writing in its Devanagari script in which each character represents a consonant followed by a specific vowel.

Chinese, however, uses a *logosyllabary or morphemic type* of writing (also known as *logographic*), meaning that characters, known as *hànzi* denote a syllable with meaning and a subset of these characters are used for their phonetic syllabic values without regard to their semantic values. Chinese characters consist of a combination of a *radical*, symbols representing meaning, and a *phonetic complement*, which indicates the sound by means of an analogy. There are also *syllabary types* of scripts used, for example in Japanese *kana*, where the characters denote syllables.

Hangul, the script used for Korean is of a *featural type*, meaning that the shape of each of the characters has a systematic relation to the phonetic features of its sound. Each Hangul letter begins with a consonant symbol and the vowel symbols are added, while an additional consonant symbol may or may not be added as the final sound (Ann, 1998). Sign Writing, a system of writing the movements and handshapes of sign languages can also be considered featural.

Table 14.2 summarizes the different types of scripts with examples of scripts under each, as well as languages:

Table 14.2   Types of Scripts and Languages

Type of Script	Description of type of script	Example of names of scripts	Example of languages	Examples of scripts
Alphabetic	Consonants and vowels with separate characters	Roman script; Greek script	English; Greek	a b c α β γ
Logosyllabary or morphemic	Characters denote morphemes and subset used for phonetic syllabic values	Hànzi or Chinese script	Chinese	漢字
Syllabary	Characters denote syllables	Kana script in Japanese	Japanese	ひらがな (Hiragana) カタカナ (Katakana)
Featural	Shape of character has relation to phonetic features	Hangul script	Korean	한글
Abjad or consonantal	Only consonants written	Arabic script	Arabic languages, Urdu, Punjabi, Persian, Malay	المريبه
Abugida or syllabic type	Each character represents consonant and specific vowel	Devanagari script	Hindi	देपनागरी

There are languages such as Japanese which combine a logosyllabary type – the *kanji*, as Japanese call the Chinese characters – with two syllabary types – *hiragana*, a syllabic system of fifty-six items used for grammatical patterns, and *katakana*, used for words of foreign origin.

Some languages can be written in more than one script. For example, *Azeri* can be written in Latin, Cyrillic, or Arabic scripts. In Azerbaijan, where it is the official language, it is now written in Roman script, although prior to the collapse of the Soviet Union, Azeri was written in Cyrillic. In Iran, however, Azeri is written in Arabic script. When it is written in Roman or Cyrillic scripts, Azeri is written left to right; when it is written in the Arabic script, it is written right to left.

Script has also played an important role in drawing differences between languages and people's language identities. For example, it is mostly the Devanagari script of Hindi and the Perso-Arabic script of Urdu that differentiates these two languages (King, 2001). To turn attention to the West, Kemal Atatürk replaced the Arabic script of Turkish with the Roman one in 1928. And after the collapse of the Soviet Union, Uzbekistan, Turkmenistan, Kazakhstan and Kyrgyzstan shifted from Cyrillic to Roman script, while Tajikistan shifted to Arabic script (Schlyter, 2003).

In the People's Republic of China, Chinese is written in *simplified Chinese script*. But in Taiwan and Hong Kong, a *traditional Chinese script* is used. Learning to read Chinese in Mainland China, children are first taught to read *Hanyu Pinyin*, a Roman alphabet. But in Taiwan, Chinese phonetic symbols known as *Zhu Yin Fu Hao* are used to teach children to read. Both *Pinyin* and *Zhu Yin Fu Hao* help children who have to learn from 4,000 to 6,000 Chinese characters during their years of schooling (Ingulsrud and Allen, 1999).

Different writing systems have different levels of *phonological transparency*, meaning that they provide different amount of phonological information. Alphabetic, syllabic, featural and abugida writing systems (which represent each phoneme/syllable of the language) are more phonologically transparent than consonantal or abjad writing systems (which do not represent vowels). In turn, these are more phonologically transparent than morphemic or logosyllabary writing systems (which represent phonology only indirectly). Thus, children learning to read phonological transparent languages can rely on grapho-phonemic cues, that is, cues that are letter- and shape-based. In contrast, children learning to read phonological opaque languages cannot rely on grapho-phonemic cues. This is the case of children learning to read Chinese. They must rely more on the semantic (meaning-based) or visual cues since the character can only be read by recognizing it and knowing its meaning and pronunciation.

Languages that use the same writing system may have different degrees of phonological transparency. For example, English and Spanish are both written with the Roman alphabet, but Spanish is much more phonologically transparent than English. Spanish can be read and spelled letter by letter, so children learning to read Spanish can rely on grapho-phonemic cues much more than those learning to read English. In fact, it has been noted that native speakers of a language such as English or French, which both have very opaque writing systems, often learn initial reading and writing more easily through a second language such as Spanish, Italian, or Dutch, where the sound–symbol correspondence is far more consistent, leading to a rapid transfer of reading skills to their home language.

To learn a new script one must also learn a new *handwriting* – a different way of holding the pen or pencil, of drawing graphemes or symbols, or of joining graphemes. For example, writing Japanese *kanji* often requires starting with the horizontal line. Thus, Japanese learners of English usually handwrite the horizontal line in "t" before the vertical line.

Different writing systems may have different *punctuations* or different punctuation conventions. And even in the same writing systems, punctuation rules may be divergent. In Modern Greek, a question is marked by a semicolon. The use of the comma, for example, differs enormously between French, English, and Dutch. Writing systems also have different *spacing*. For example, in Spanish and English, it is words that are separated by spacing. The Hebrew writing system also separates words, but nouns and prepositions are joined. Chinese does not separate words.

Scripts are also read and written in different directions. Most scripts are written *left to right*. This is the case of the Roman script, the Greek script, the Devanagari script, and the Cyrillic script, for example. But there are also many languages that are written *right to left*, for example, Arabic and Hebrew. There are other languages that are written *top to bottom and right to left* such as Chinese, Japanese, and Korean. But recently and because of western influence, Chinese, Japanese, and Korean are increasingly written left to right. There are also languages that are written *bottom up, left to right* – for example, Tagalog. In some languages directionality is variable and depends on the writer. This is the case, for example, of Tamazight (Berber languages).

Students learning to read or write a language in which print is read in a different direction from that of their home language, will have to be explicitly taught *print directionality*. And because each language has different *grammar* and *orthographic* features, those have to be explicitly taught as well. Different languages also *structure stories* differently and employ different *rhetorical devices*. It is therefore also important for these to be taught directly. Finally, and most importantly, *vocabulary* needs to be explicitly taught. It has been shown that lack of vocabulary remains one of the major obstacles for bilingual readers (Birch, 2002).

Written language is structured differently in various cultures. For example, English writing is much more linear and hierarchical than other writing. Japanese writing is much more circular. Spanish writing includes digression and commentaries (Pérez, 1998). That is, different languages have different discourse rules, as well as rules of cohesion and coherence.

Languages also differ morphosyntactically, leading to differences in the ways in which written language is expressed. For example, whereas Chinese is a topic-prominent language, English is a subject-prominent language based on actors and actions. English has verb tenses and inflections in word endings. Chinese does not mark tense or mood and has no articles. Chinese adds morpheme characters rather than modify the form of the character. The use of gender-specific pronouns is not required in Chinese, and neither are sentences or punctuation. Graphically, Chinese spoken words are displayed without word boundaries (Chang, 1998).

There is much evidence of reading transfer from a language that one has learned to read first to a second one if the writing systems are similar (Alderson and Urquhart, 1984; Coady, 1979; Muljani, Koda, and Moates, 1998). Literacy concepts such as the meaningfulness of print and metacognitive strategies used in reading and writing (for example, skimming and predicting in reading; using dictionaries in writing) are transferable. But because of language differences, much has to be taught explicitly.

In a study of Hebrew–English bilingual children, Abu-Rabia (1997) shows how although syntactic and working memory skills are correlated, phonological and ortho-graphic tasks showed no positive correlation. Birch (2002) summarizes these findings by saying that strategies do transfer from a first to a second language, espe-cially if the knowledge and processing strategies are similar in the two languages, but that if there are differences, these could cause inefficiency in reading.

Written texts

Written language is also used in many ways even within a single culture, some of which are given below (Ramirez, 1994):

- *enumerative texts*, such as signs and addresses that involve recognition of memorized elements;
- *orientational texts*, such as travel forms, schedules, menus, brief messages which require skimming and scanning;
- *instructive texts*, such as labels, instructions, and directions which require decoding and classifying processes;
- *expressive personal texts*, similar to informal talk;
- *transactional writing*, writing that shares information often to inform or persuade;
- *evaluative texts*, such as editorials, analyses, and biographies which require inferring, hypothesizing, and interpreting;
- *projective texts* such as art critiques, literary or poetic texts, philosophical papers, and argumentation, which require the ability to analyze, verify, extend, imagine, and hypothesize.

To this list we can add *scientific texts* such as the ones used to report scientific findings. These texts often have a rigid and fixed organization. Although all readers can have experience practicing the first four kinds of texts enumerated above outside of school, it is the school that most often engages students in writing transactional, evaluative, projective and scientific texts.

Depending on the social context of the bilingual school, children may have more or less access to texts in different languages outside of school. For example, a Latino child residing in New York City may see Spanish-language print in advertisements, labels, directions, press. But a Bengali-speaking child living in New York City may have little access to such texts in Bengali. Likewise, prestigious bilingual education programs often expose children to languages that they seldom see in print outside of school.

Written texts are always *transactional* (Rosenblatt, 1978). That is, readers always attempt to make meaning, as they transact with the author through the influence of reader and text in the making of meaning. Readers then develop a purpose or stance along a continuum from *efferent*, that is, to acquire information, to understand what the text is saying, to *aesthetic*, that is, to evoke individual meaning that is pleasurable to the senses. Thus, teachers must not only encourage students to read written texts in order to acquire information, but also to evoke individual aesthetic meaning.

Academic written texts are more linear and non-repetitive than other texts. Syntactically, they exhibit balance and tightness. In Spanish and English, they also use extensive modals, conditionals, counterfactuals, and quantifiers in order to promote inference, deduction, and concept formation. Ramirez (1994) tells us that academic written texts have constraints that make them different from other texts.

Gibbons (1991) identifies at least five different types of written texts used in schools:

- *narratives*, about specific people and events;
- *recount*, also about specific people and events, but personal;
- *report*, intended to inform;
- *procedure*, about processes and intended to inform;
- *argument*, aiming to persuade.

Each of these text types has a different organizational structure in the different cultures. In English, for example, narratives start with an *orientation* which sets the scene, introduces the characters, and says when and where the narrative is set. Next, the narrative describes *events* which lead to a problem or a *complication*. Finally, the problem is resolved in *resolution* (Gibbons, 2002). Besides this organizational structure, narratives in English are usually written in the past tense and they contain many action verbs, as well as many "saying" verbs in the dialogue. Furthermore, because there is a sequence of time in narratives, conjunctions and connectives become important (Gibbons, 2002). Narratives in other languages are structured differently.

Instructional Approaches

Our sociocultural focus on biliteracy/pluriliteracy practices requires that students be immersed, that is, *apprenticed* as a member of biliterate social practices. As the New London Group (1996) has shown us, people read and talk about texts in certain ways, hold certain attitudes and values about them, and socially interact with them in certain ways. One learns biliteracy practices in *embodied action*, by being immersed in reading and writing practices in two languages. But beyond this immersion, more is needed, especially for emergent bilinguals who are developing literacy skills in a second language.

The New London Group (2000) has identified four factors in a meaningful pedagogy to develop literacy practices:

1. *authentic situated practice* and immersion of students in such practice;
2. *overt instruction* to develop awareness and understanding of practice;
3. *critique of practices* so that meanings are related to their social contexts and purposes;
4. *transformed practice* in which students transfer and re-create their designs of meaning from one context to another through experimentation with innovative practices.

As Freebody and Luke (1990) have shown us, effective literacy pedagogy draws on a repertoire of practices that allow learners, as they engage in reading and writing activities to:

- *break the code* of written texts by recognizing and using fundamental features of the language itself, including structural conventions and patterns and where appropriate, the alphabet, the sounds in the words, and the spelling;
- *participate in understanding and composing* meaningful written, visual, and spoken and signed texts, taking into account their available knowledge and their experiences of other cultural discourses, texts, and meaning systems;
- *use texts* functionally by knowing about and acting on the different cultural and social functions that various texts perform inside and outside school;
- *critically analyze and transform texts* by acting on knowledge that texts are not ideologically natural or neutral – that they represent particular points of views while silencing others, and that their designs and discourses can be critiqued and redesigned in novel and hybrid ways.

As Freire and Macedo (1987) have said, "reading the world precedes reading the word," and reading the word implies continually reading the world. Thus, *critical literacy* or the ability to understand oneself and one's relationship to the world in terms of the relationship between power and knowledge in society is important in transacting with written texts. *Social constructivist theories of literacy*, which emphasize the social context of literacy practices and learning and the importance of making meaning from print according to distinct individual and sociocultural resources, are equally important. The social justice axis and the social practice axis that we identified as essential for bilingual education pedagogies in Chapter 13 are equally relevant here. Critical literacy or "reading the world" is associated with the social justice axis, whereas social constructivist theories of literacy or "reading the word" is associated with the social practice axis.

But because of the *different worldviews and sociocultural contexts* of the two or more languages used in bilingual schools, biliteracy practices and teaching must also *read and write two or more different worlds* (Martin-Jones, 2000). Teachers in bilingual education must pay attention to the social justice principle no matter what language is being used for instruction. But teachers must also ensure that they engage in social literacy practices that reflect, explore, and question different worlds. The principles must be interrelated and recursive, as in Figure 14.7:

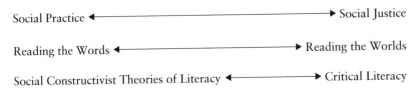

Figure 14.7   Transaction with Written Texts

If one of the functions of schooling is to develop literacy practices that conform to standard language use, then children must have opportunities to do two things: engage in the full processes of reading and writing the standard language according to sociocultural norms; and study parts of reading and writing in the standard language. But this cannot be done without building on the literacy practices that the children bring from home (Au, 2006). After all, all readers make sense of reading by using not only text-based features, that is syntactic, lexical, and phonemic/graphemic recognition, but also extra-text base components such as their prior knowledge and their languaging practices (Ramirez, 1994, 1995).

For *emergent bilingual students* – students who are developing their bilingualism – the *building of background knowledge* is doubly essential in order to make up for any cueing system that they may not yet fully possess. For example, in English, there are three cueing systems that readers use:

1. *Graphophonic cues* tapping into the reader's knowledge of representing spoken language through written systems. For example, in the case of English this is the sound–letter relationships.
2. *Semantic cues* relying on knowledge of words and the particular type of text.
3. *Syntactic cues* building on knowledge of the structure of the language.

But *reading in a second language* is, like Gregory (1996) says, like using fingers in a hand. Like fingers, some cueing systems can compensate for any that are missing and still developing. Bilingual readers and writers use cues in different combinations from monolingual readers and writers. This is particularly so in the case of Deaf bilingual children who must rely on being visual learners.

Teachers of bilingual readers must then:

- expand the students' background knowledge for improved comprehension, and develop students' abilities to relate the text to prior experiences or learning;
- activate three types of schemata – *linguistic* schemata, based on prior language development; *content* schemata, based on prior knowledge of content; and *text* schemata, based on knowledge of rhetorical structure of the text (Carrell, 1987);
- provide students with *explicit instruction* in such literacy strategies as previewing, skimming, adjusting reading rate, recognizing the author's purpose, making inferences, and separating fact from opinion (Jensen, 1986);
- teach vocabulary and other structural characteristics of the language and the text explicitly;
- encourage students to *read extensively* to become productive readers.

The Biliteracy Workshop

The *balanced literacy workshop method* of reading and writing instruction combines language and literature-rich authentic activities aimed at enhancing meaning, understanding, and the love of language and literacy, with explicit teaching skills (Honig, 1996). It refers to an approach that does not privilege either *top-down processing* (where high-level processing strategies[8] are privileged to make predictions about text and inferences about characters and events in a text) or *bottom-up processes* (starting with precise bits of knowledge about language, writing and processing strategies that permit readers to "turn the squiggles on the page into meaningful symbols": Birch, 2002: 2). Balanced literacy attempts to develop readers who are adept at both bottom-up and top-down processing. It makes reading interactive in three ways:

- interaction of top-down strategies, as well as bottom-up processing strategies, along with the knowledge base;
- interaction of the reader's mind with the written text;
- interaction of the reader indirectly with the writer of the text across time and space, as the writer communicates, and the reader grasps the information (Birch, 2002: 4).

The balanced literacy workshop approach has been proven to be effective in teaching literacy in English-speaking countries, although it *may be irrelevant to teach literacy practices that follow different sociocultural norms*. We have observed, for example, very effective bilingual schools in which the teaching of English proceeds according to the balanced literacy workshop method, and yet the teaching of Chinese, Japanese, or Spanish follows very traditional literacy methodology, more in keeping with cultural and linguistic stances. Another difficulty of implementing a balanced literacy workshop approach throughout the world is that it relies not only on good practices by teachers, but also on the economic resources that would keep the number of students in classrooms small, and the quality and quantity of instructional material high. We caution, therefore, that the *biliteracy workshop* model that we describe below has only partial relevance for some language groups in some societal contexts.

In contrast to the "balanced" literacy workshop, the biliteracy workshop extends bottom-up strategies as it attempts to make the text explicit for the emergent bilingual. It allows the tapping of the students' different languaging practices, as well as the inclusion of multimodal texts in different languages and scripts. It *stretches* the *predictable structures* that are the hallmark of balanced literacy instruction (Calkins, 1994; Graves, 1983), thus allowing for the more direct and explicit instruction that bilingual readers and writers may need, and for the translanguaging texts that bilingual children produce. For Gibbons (2002: 60), *teaching explicitly* means that:

> students are encouraged to reflect on how language is used for a range of purposes and with a range of audiences, and that teachers focus explicitly on those aspects of language that enable students to do this. Explicit teaching is related to real-life use,

so that understanding about language is developed in the context of actual language use. It aims to foster active involvement in learning, independence in writing, and the ability to critique the ways that language is used in authentic contexts, such as the ways it is used to persuade and control.

Gibbons (2002) adds that entering a new culture is easier if information about appropriateness of behavior is explicit. Likewise, it is important to point out the linguistic nature of texts, as they are produced within appropriate social contexts and for various purposes. Rather than attempt to balance the two languages, the biliteracy workshop calls for giving students autonomy in the selection of languages and ways of languaging, leaving it up to the students to select which language to use when, where and for what literacy event, and when translanguaging is appropriate. In other words, the biliteracy workshop responds to sociolinguistic norms of authentic languaging, rather than the artificial language use that schools often impose. Of course, monoliterate practices, as well as pluriliterate practices have to be developed in schools. With the guidance of the teacher, bilingual students can then act on their agency as to which language should be used when, and in which combination, for which literacy event.

For emergent bilingual students, the biliteracy workshop allows for more explicit instruction. It also regulates the time through which students have to work through their weaker language, ensuring that students develop literacy practices in that language.

The structure of the biliteracy workshop allows for the handing over of the instruction to the students through group and independent work. It also encourages students to use all linguistic codes, modes, and practices at their disposal to make sense of the text. In so doing, its balanced literacy and balanced linguistic nature is challenged, with the students capturing the agency to create the dynamism of its instruction.

Like balanced literacy, the *biliteracy workshop method* uses a *predictable* structure and organization – a mini lesson, followed by the workshop itself.

The mini-lesson

During the initial mini-lesson for the whole class, the teacher models through signing, the home language, and sometimes the additional language, effective metacognitive processes, discourse structures, and interactions with texts (Au, 2006; Calkins, 1986). But the mini-lesson of the biliteracy workshop is *stretched* especially for emergent bilinguals. The mini-lesson starts with a *teacher-made connection* in which the teacher explicitly tells students what she will be teaching and how it fits into the work they are doing. Next, there is *explicit teaching* as the teacher models a strategy. Then, there is opportunity for *children's active engagement* by trying out what they have been taught or imagining themselves trying it. This often involves talking or signing with a partner in what Calkins (1986) calls "turn-and-talk." In bilingual classrooms, this "turn-and-talk" is often done in the language of preference of the children, sometimes different from the one in which the teacher is conducting the mini-lesson. Finally, there is a *teacher-made link* of the mini-lesson to the workshop for the day.

Some of the appropriate higher- and lower-level reading strategies that teachers may teach in any language during a literacy mini-lesson appear in Table 14.3:

Table 14.3   Strategies for Mini-Lessons during Shared Reading

Higher-Level Strategies

Literary elements	*Expanding meaning*

Fiction
- character development
- concept of time
- problem/solution
- plot development

- inferring
- summarizing
- analyzing
- author's purpose

Nonfiction
- table of contents
- glossary
- index
- headings
- captions
- reading graphics

- comparing/contrasting
- connecting
- reflecting
- evaluating

Word/Language Study – Functions and Patterns
- script
- phonology
- syntax
- morphology

- sentence structure
- asking questions
- answering questions
- making statements
- using dialogue

Lower-Level Strategies

Print awareness	*Sustaining meaning*

- tracking
- pointing to words
- return sweep
- noticing spaces
- following the text
- using illustrations

- solving words
- monitoring
- predicting
- self-correcting
- rereading a sentence
- cross-checking

Capellini, 2005: 125. Used with permission of Stenhouse Publishers.

Birch (2002) insists that strategies to learn *vocabulary* must be explicitly taught to emergent bilinguals. She recommends teaching the following strategies:

- Look at the word carefully to form an image.
- Look at the syntactic and meaning context and try to determine the new word's structural characteristics and definition.
- For production: for hearing students, pronounce it several times even if incorrect to store it in long-term memory, so as to form a phonological image; for all,

associate the sound of the second-language word with a similar word in the home language and relate them through a visual image or sentence.

Au (2006) cautions that when teaching the whole class, it is most important to be mindful of linguistic, discourse, and cultural differences. For example, it has been shown that African American students use choral responses (Hollins, 1982), whereas Native American students participate infrequently (Erickson and Mohatt, 1982). Students who are learning through an additional language are often more hesitant to participate than those who are learning through their own home language. Whereas some students volunteer freely, others are cautious. Having students discuss their ideas with a partner or a small group in their own language and participating through the use of whatever languaging they have at their disposal helps to go beyond the inequities of participation that are prevalent in whole-class lessons.

The workshop

During the workshop, the most substantial part of the process, children work as either groups of approximately six students, as pairs, or as individuals. Again, there is much interaction that takes place in the languages that children are comfortable with, often translanguaging. There are *teacher-led small groups* in which the teacher acts as a coach, and there are *student-led small groups*. Individual work time gives teachers an opportunity to conduct individual consultations and conferences. At all times, children are encouraged to tap into their own linguistic resources, and translanguaging is encouraged. At the end of the workshop period of independent work, the teacher engages students in *sharing* what they have done.[9]

Reading and writing are interconnected. They are both meaning-making processes, they are both transactional processes (Rosenblatt, 1978), and they involve the creation of an original text. They also both involve a public act of sharing. However, we discuss each of these practices separately here, starting first with reading.

Reading

In general, *reading activities* to develop biliteracy practices should not only help the readers understand the particular text they are reading in the specific language and mode of the text, but they must also help readers develop good reading strategies for reading other texts in different multimodalities and languages. For this reason, what the teacher does is extremely important. Planning for *before, during,* and *after* reading activities is a must (Gibbons, 2002; Peregoy and Boyle, 2001).

Before reading. Teachers who develop effective reading practices first become familiar with the meaning of the text and prepare for linguistic, cultural, and conceptual difficulties. They also activate the children's prior knowledge, and build the sense of the text's overall meaning with students (Gibbons, 2002). To do this, they engage with children in predicting from the title, the first sentence, or the pictures what the book might be about. Mindful of the multimodalities of texts in the twenty-first century, the teacher includes images and electronically generated material that connects to the text. Sometimes the text is in printed traditional form; other times it is electronic. Sometimes it includes only script; other times it is accompanied by images and sounds. Sometimes it is in one language or the other; other times the text is bilingual either side-by-side or hybrid.[10]

Students are asked to share any experiences that they have had with the topic and to recall any previous knowledge or experience with the topic, the author, or the book, prior to reading (Ada, 2003). Teachers also encourage children to draw, speak, sign, or write from experiences that they have had in other languages, cultures, and even countries.

If the students are emergent bilinguals, the teacher might first tell the story in the students' home languages. In the event that this is not possible, the teacher tells the story with appropriate contextualization. The teacher would also identify what would be unfamiliar language for the students – vocabulary, phrases, and idioms. To help the students predict these meanings, the teacher might encourage the students to develop a *semantic web* with the different lexical items or ideas associated with the unfamiliar language. Particular attention might be paid to such features as connectives, conjunctions, and pronouns, in languages which exhibit these.

The teacher would also encourage talk or signing, with students acting on their agency by using their home languages, or the language of the lesson, or both languages. Cazden (1988) reminds us that oral talk with peers acts as a catalyst to learn and problem-solve, and it is exploratory rather than final, encouraging the languaging and exploration that bilinguals need.

During reading. The teacher then follows what Cappellini (2005) calls "the to, with, and by model." That is, the teacher reads to the children in the form of *read-alouds or read-performances* for Deaf students; she reads with the children in the form of *shared reading*; and there is then reading by the children in the form of *guided reading*, and eventually *independent reading*.

The teacher models reading strategies. She does read-alouds or read-performances; that is she reads out loud or signs the reading. In so doing, she constantly interrogates and interacts with the text. That is, she performs think-alouds of important reading strategies. For example, this third-grade teacher[11] wants to make sure that her students who are all emergent bilinguals visualize what is happening in a reading in English about Native Americans. She says:

> Last night I took this book home because I wanted to learn more about the longhouses. And I was reading. It was really interesting. I was learning a lot. I had a great picture in my mind, and then, guess what happened? I lost it. All of a sudden, I got to a part where there was no more picture in my mind. Nothing. I said, Oh no!
>
> So, what I'm going to do today is show you what you should do when that happens. You can't just keep reading without understanding what's going on. So let me show the page that gave me a little bit of trouble last night.
>
> When I got to the part where there was no more picture, I stopped. That's the first thing I did, I stopped. And then, I went back and I read it again. That's the first thing you want to do. Just stop. Because you want to get the picture back in your mind. Then, I looked at the pictures here to try to help me. And then I thought to myself, Ms. Celic, what would make sense here? What is it telling me from some of the clues? And if it's a word that's dark black, a bold word, you can always look it up in the glossary to help you. If you already know it, then you already have the picture in mind and you can then keep on reading.

The teacher also predicts what is coming as she reads aloud. She makes explicit the interactive nature of reading by making connections, building on what the class knows, inferring, analyzing. For example, the teacher might think aloud: "I wonder what they're going to find?" or "I wonder why the author chose the word x? Is it because of this?" Sometimes these think-alouds may be done in children's home or additional language, while the story is read in a different language.

Ada (2003) says that one of the best ways of bringing children and books together is by reading aloud. For emergent bilinguals, this gives them the opportunity of listening to the language of written texts in their second language. For all bilingual students, this practice of hearing written texts in both languages is extremely important, for it turns out that bilingual children are often less exposed to literacy in one language than the other.

Gibbons (2002) recommends that the teacher *models* reading with expression. And that she models for the students how to *skim*, that is find the main idea, as well as *scan*, that is, find particular information. The teacher also models how to re-read for details, how to make note of the words or phrases that are not clearly understood, and how to use technology to find further context. While the modeling of reading with expression is done in the language of the lesson, the teacher may use the children's additional language to model particular reading strategies.

It is also important to model ways of finding out the meaning of unknown vocabulary. For example, the teacher models how it is important to carefully read the language that surrounds a word in the text, to read to the end of the sentence, to think about what students know about similar words, to look for familiar word parts, and to recognize cognates (Gibbons, 2002).

Beyond read-alouds or read-performances, the teacher also does *shared reading*. For shared reading, the teacher uses a *Big Book* in the early grades or a text in an overhead projector or screen for later grades. She reads or signs the text several times with expression. The children follow, and later on read or sign jointly with the teacher. Finally, the children read the text alone. During shared reading, there is a lot of choral reading or signing and the text is read many times. Shared reading can be done in groups or as a whole-class activity. It is particularly important for children who are learning to read, as well as all emergent hearing bilinguals who are also struggling with pronunciation of a new language. Throughout the shared reading, the teacher is *modeling* reading strategies. For example, she pauses to encourage students to predict what is going to happen or what they would do if they were the character of the book.

Teachers who use shared reading practices effectively always have a ritual, a special place in which shared reading takes place (Ada, 2003). Ada (2003) reminds us that poetry, song, and folklore are important elements in shared reading. And it is important to draw from literature originally written in any of the two or more languages and other multicultural texts. In the case of emergent hearing bilinguals, it is also possible to do *shadow reading*, whereby the children read aloud along with a tape, either a commercial one or one that the teacher has recorded.

There are times when the teacher engages in *guided reading*. During guided reading, the children read an unfamiliar text by themselves at their instructional level with guidance from teacher. Students have their own copies of the book and read individually, either silently or in a low voice. They generally work in small homogeneous groups of about six, using reading strategies and language patterns they have learned. The children mix languages during the discussion. Although the teacher does not actually read the book to or with the children, she engages them in prior conversations about the text, sometimes in a language different from that of the text. The teacher acts as a coach.

The structure of guided reading is given by Fountas and Pinnell (1996). There is first an introduction and orientation to the text by the teacher. Sometimes this can be done in a language other than that of the text. Next, the children do a first reading of the text and possible a rereading. Finally, there is a discussion about what was learned, in which children language in their own ways.

Sometimes guided reading takes the form of *Literature Circles* where older children read and discuss the literature in small heterogeneous groups of four to six. The teacher assists them when necessary, and peers provide other assistance, again sometimes using a language other than that of the text. At the end of the session, there usually is a closing community share where different book clubs speak about what they have discussed, their interactions, and any problems they may have encountered.

Finally, there is also room for *independent reading*. The children select texts at their reading level in one language or the other and work independently. Students keep track of what they have read and in what language by filling out reading logs and journals.

Although the structure of the biliteracy approach is the same as that of the balanced literacy approach, the blocks of time devoted to each of the reading activities varies. In the biliteracy approach, more time is devoted to read-alouds and shared readings than to independent reading because bilingual students, and especially emergent bilinguals, need special scaffolding when reading in an additional language. And the children's home languages are used freely to make sense of the text. However, every workshop lesson should engage *all* bilingual children in both guided reading and independent reading. What emergent bilinguals do during this time might be different from what fluent bilingual and monolingual students do, but all students have to be immersed in the practice of independent reading. And all students, regardless of bilingual ability, need time with oral and shared reading, although the emphasis might be different, as in Figure 14.8:

Oral reading
Shared reading

Guided reading

Independent reading

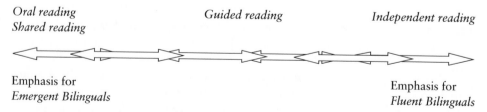

Emphasis for
Emergent Bilinguals

Emphasis for
Fluent Bilinguals

Figure 14.8 Emphasis of Reading Activities with Emergent vs. Fluent Bilinguals

After reading. At this time, children are allowed opportunity to focus more deeply on information in the text or to give the same information in a *different mode or a different language.* For example, the students may put on a performance, puppet show, or engage in readers' theater. They can create art, a cartoon strip, a poster, a story map, draw a diagram, or create a time line. Or they can do a PowerPoint presentation after conducting web-based research. They can also use a web-based translation tool such as Babelfish to render a translation into another language. A meaningful activity for language development is for students to be engaged in some story innovation. For example, the characters could be changed or the story could be told from someone else's perspective, from another cultural context, in another language, or during a different historical time period.

Ada (2003) describes the five phases of a creative reading process:

1. *Descriptive phase* in which the reader discovers the who, what, when, where, how, and why of the text.
2. *Personal/interpretive phase* in which the reader connects to his or her memories, concerns, feelings and emotions.
3. *Critical/multicultural/antibias phase* in which the reader looks for the author's intentions, that is, for the consequence of what the text implies.
4. *Move to action* in which readers discover things that make them more understanding, more generous.
5. *Creative/transformative phase* in which the reader takes action and adopts attitudes that will improve their own lives.

Texts to read

In choosing texts for bilingual students to read, it is important that they be "authentic" and not be specifically written to teach reading. Gibbons (2002) points out that "learn to read texts" are more difficult to read than an authentic complete story because it is difficult to predict what comes next, forcing students to rely on cues that are not about reading. In most languages, this means that students will have to rely on visual characteristics of words, which lead away from understanding the text as a coherent whole. These "reading books" are usually devoid of rich language and there is little interesting meaning in them. It is important to remember that authentic texts are not always print-based texts, although print is usually an important component of these texts.

Because emergent bilingual students interact with written texts in ways that are not the same as those of students who are fluent bilinguals, it is important for teachers to select books that have certain characteristics. Gibbons (2002) says that for early reading, it is important to select books that have clear print and illustrations, but that are not too busy. But in addition, the language should be repetitive or there should be a repetitive event that builds up into a cumulative story. For older students, it is important that texts be well organized and that they have clear signaling devices: that there are titles, clear topic sentences, and that the written text is cohesive. There should be, however, conceptual density that matches the interest of these older students.

There should be books of the same quality in both languages of instruction. Bilingual books, of both the side-by-side, as well as integrated (hybrid) kind, are especially helpful (see note 10). But it is important that students not always choose bilingual books, but also books in one language or the other so that they practice using their own inner resources to make sense of the print.

It is most important that bilingual classrooms have original texts in both languages, rather than just translations. It is also important that the texts relate to the students' backgrounds and that they reflect the bilingual realities of students' lives and their multiculturalism. And it is crucial that bilingual classrooms use the text resources available on the internet to ensure that all modes of communication (visual, as well as auditory), are fully exploited. The internet brings the entire world closer, and bilingual children must develop the ability to go beyond nationally produced printed texts that the local school provides.

Writing

As with reading, children learn *to write* when they are encouraged to do so frequently and are able to use their own expressive language, whatever code or mode it includes. Children also need to have a context with a real audience to be able to share their writing (Graves, 1983). But beyond social practice, students need to have knowledge of three things:

1. the symbols of the writing systems;
2. the ways in which writing differs from speech;
3. the different text types or genre prototypes (Gibbons, 1991).

Thus, writing must also be explicitly taught, especially to language-minority children (see for example Delpit, 1988, for a criticism of process approaches in the teaching of literacy to minority children).

Derewianka (1990) has identified four stages of *explicit literacy teaching* of what she calls the *Curriculum Cycle for writing* that are especially important for emergent bilinguals and bilinguals in general:

1. *Building the field.* During this stage, teachers and students build background knowledge. There is much speaking, listening, reading, information-gathering, note-taking, and reading in one language and the other in order to build the field. Sometimes, individuals in groups are assigned different aspects of the topic that they then share. Much is done in two languages.
2. *Modeling the text type.* During this stage, students and teachers make decisions about the ways in which they are going to use written language: are they going to write in one language or the other, or in both? Students become familiar with the purpose, the overall structure, and the linguistic features of the type of text they are going to write. The teacher models texts on an overhead projector or large sheets or finds models in the internet. She guides students in the study of these model texts, paying particular attention to their organizational structure, and the structure of the language. The teacher might also

contrast how the same text type is written in another language broadly spoken by the students.

3. *Joint construction.* During this cycle, the teacher and the students write the text together. The teacher *scribes* or takes down the text and guides the discussion of the linguistic and the discourse aspects of the text. For example, she might say, "How should we start? Is that the best way to say it? Can anyone think of a better word than that? Can anyone see anything that needs fixing up? What do you think we should talk about next?" The students contribute the ideas, sometimes using a language other than the one in which the text is written. When the draft is complete, the teacher rewrites it.

4. *Independent writing.* During this cycle, students write individually or in pairs. The teacher reminds them of the process. They will first write a draft. Then they will self-edit the first draft. Next, they will discuss the draft with their friends and teacher. And finally, they will produce a published text (in print or electronic) that will be exhibited in the class or made into a book that the class can use afterwards.

It is important to understand that throughout all four stages, there are plenty of opportunities for students to speak, read, and listen in both languages, often crossing from one language to the other.

These four stages of the cycle have been adapted in the balanced literacy writing workshop. Calkins (1994) identifies its five components, described here with the adaptations that are essential for the biliteracy workshop approach that bilingual students require:

1. *The mini-lesson,* when students gather in a close circle and teachers teach about writing skills and strategies, such as re-reading one's work or keeping an image of one's topic in mind. Often, the teacher introduces a strategy that they may write on a class chart. All languages of the class are used. For emergent bilinguals, the mini-lessons are longer than the usual ten to fifteen minutes, lasting between twenty minutes to a half hour because the modeling has to be extensive, and students have to have more opportunities to "turn and talk" so that they can make sense of what the teacher is modeling in their own languages. Charts where the teacher writes down the strategy are always used and are displayed throughout the classroom, sometimes in different languages.

2. *Work time* (prewriting, writing, and conferring). Students go to their desks and they work on ongoing projects. Sometimes the whole class works on a genre study (for example, poetry). Everyone writes, sometimes in the language of instruction, sometimes in their home languages, other times going back and forth across the two languages. Sometimes children write short sentences and illustrate them. In some classrooms, computers are used. With emergent bilinguals, children might copy from a chart in the room or from a semantic web, and then illustrate their text. Other times, they may write in their home language, or use a mixture of both. The teacher moves among individuals, conferring with them. Students plan and prewrite. They then write, revise, and edit.

3. *Peer-conferencing and/or response groups*. Groups of four to six students meet daily for at least twenty minutes. The students share their drafts and what they are grappling with. The group contributes ideas. The students' home languages are used extensively for this conferencing; translanguaging as they share their products is allowed.

4. *Share sessions*. The students share their progress in public. They read their entries out loud and solicit responses. Sometimes they share about the process of writing itself. Other times, they put their texts up on the web and encourage online feedback.

5. *Publication celebrations*. The students' work is published and celebrated. Sometimes, the teacher publishes an anthology with the class's work either in print or electronically. Sometimes, she invites parents to have students read their work. Throughout the year, these publication celebrations include texts written in both languages.

It is important for teachers and students to understand that writing is a complex, recursive process (Calkins, 1994; Graves, 1983). Good writers do not simply follow a linear process of planning, writing, revising, editing, and publishing. Instead good writers go back and forth because through writing we discover what we think and know (Smith, 1978).

Conclusion

This chapter has reviewed how today's literacy practices are increasingly *multilingual and multimodal* – interaction around written text makes use of different languages, translanguaging, and different modes of expression. And written texts themselves are increasingly multilingual and multimodal. The meanings of biliteracy practices are not only bound up with more than one language and cultural system, but also with other visual, audio, and spatial semiotic systems. And yet this chapter also makes clear that literacy practices in schools hardly accommodate these complexities. The biliteracy workshop approach gives a glimpse of how this might be done, although in practice even enlightened educators often fall short. This has to do with the realities of schooling, and the fact that literacy practices often respond to, and reflect, the traditional format of assessment instruments. It is then assessment itself that is the topic of our last and concluding chapter.

Questions for Reflection

1. What is the difference between the autonomous view of biliteracy and the ideological view of biliteracy?
2. How would you define biliteracy? What is the difference between this concept and that of pluriliteracy practices?
3. What is Hornberger's continuum of biliteracy? How would you apply it to your present situation?

4. What are the four models of biliteracy use in bilingual education classrooms considered in this chapter? What is the objective of each? When is one or the other more appropriate?
5. What are some ways that written texts are used in bilingual schools?
6. What are some ways that learners interact with texts as explained in Luke and Freebody's four resources model? How does this apply to bilingual learners?
7. Discuss the biliteracy workshop approach. What adaptations would you have to make for your students?

Further Reading

Ada, A.F. (2003). *A Magical Encounter: Latino Children's Literature in the Classroom*, second edn. Allyn and Bacon, Boston, MA.

Au, K. (2006). *Multicultural Issues and Literacy Achievement*. Lawrence Erlbaum, Mahwah, NJ.

Brisk, M.E., and Harrington, M. (2000). *Literacy and Bilingualism*. Lawrence Erlbaum Associates, Mahwah, NJ.

Gibbons, P. (2002). *Scaffolding Language, Scaffolding Learning. Teaching Second Languages in the Mainstream Classroom*. Heinemann, Portsmouth, NH.

Gregory, E. (1996). *Making Sense of a New World. Learning to Read in a Second Language*. Paul Chapman Publishers, London.

Gregory, E., Long, S., and Volk, D. (eds.) (2004). *Many Pathways to Literacy. Young Children Learning with Siblings, Grandparents, Peers and Community*. Routledge, London.

Hornberger, N. (ed.) (2003). *Continua of Biliteracy. An Ecological Framework for Educational Policy, Research, and Practices in Multilingual Settings*. Multilingual Matters, Clevedon.

Kenner, C. (2004). *Becoming Biliterate: Young Children Learning Different Writing Systems*. Trentham Books, Stoke-on-Trent and Sterling, VA.

Martin-Jones, M., and Jones, K. (2000). *Multilingual Literacies. Reading and Writing Different Worlds*. John Benjamins, Amsterdam.

Pérez, B. (ed.) (1998). *Sociocultural Contexts of Language and Literacy*. Lawrence Erlbaum, Mahwah, NJ.

—— (2004). *Becoming Biliterate. A Study of Two-Way Bilingual Immersion Education*. Lawrence Erlbaum, Mahwah, NJ.

15

Assessment of Bilinguals

by Ofelia García and Hugo Baetens Beardsmore

[Pay] close attention to how a child goes about learning or making some-thing, and not only to assessment of what the child learned, made or did [. . .]. It is when a teacher can see this process, the child in motion, the child in activities meaningful to her, that it is possible for the teacher to gain the insights needed to adjust her or his own approaches to the child accordingly.

Carini, 2000: 9, her emphasis

Overview

In this chapter, we will discuss:

- assessment development and use;
- assessment of bilinguals;
- democratic assessment for bilinguals.

Introduction

Earlier chapters have hinted that assessment measures for children undergoing some form of bilingual education have been beset with problems. Several reasons account for this, perhaps the most important being that bilingual education operates mostly in monolingual educational systems. Even those bilingual programs that have benefited from extensive research support and official encouragement, as is the case with Canadian immersion initiatives, have almost always relied on measurements designed from a monolingual normative perspective.

Bilingual schools and programs are faced with the enormous difficulty of assessing their students' learning and proficiencies in ways that take their bilingual and cultural specificities into account, while also, most times, satisfying criteria of a monolingual centralized assessment system that often acts as gatekeeper. Thus, assessment is an area of concern for bilingual education. While students in bilingual education learn to function as bilingual individuals and professionals, assessment most often ignores their bilingualism and assesses their abilities and knowledge only as if they were monolinguals in the languages of dominance and power. And not all societies assess the two languages of students. For example, except for Scandinavian countries, assessment of sign languages is never the experience of any Deaf child, even if bilingually educated. In the United States, the Spanish of students in bilingual education programs is assessed only in few cases, and the performance of students has no real consequence on achievement or promotion.

Bilingual education must prepare students to use their bilingualism fully and as a complex single ability. But students in bilingual education must also demonstrate in "official" assessments, which are often conducted only in the dominant language of schooling, that they have adequate abilities in that language. In many ways, bilingual education must promote the development of bilingualism for the students' full life, while teaching them ways of *masking their bilingual abilities and their translanguaging* in monolingual assessment. This chapter describes different ways of assessing bilinguals, while pointing to the tension that is often present between the bilingualism of the classroom and the monolingualism of most assessments.

The Power of Assessment

Assessment is always a political act, and as Foucault (1979) has indicated, a way to exercise power and control. Testing is not neutral since it is a product and agent of ideological agendas. It is often under the control of official, national, or regional authorities, and it is based on specific cultural and pedagogical traditions. Foucault (1979: 18) explains: "The examination combines the technique of an observing hierarchy and those of normalizing judgment. It is a normalizing gaze, a surveillance that makes it possible to quantify, classify and punish. It establishes over individuals a visibility through which one differentiates and judges them."

Shohamy (2001) indicates that the power of tests comes from being able to determine the future of individuals. As such, tests dominate curriculum, textbooks, and teaching. Shohamy (2001) identifies the features of tests that make them have such power:

1. Tests are administered by powerful institutions.
2. Tests use the language of science.
3. Tests use the language of numbers.
4. Tests use written forms of communication.
5. Tests rely on documentation.
6. Tests use objective formats.

Shohamy (2001) shows us how in Israel, for example, tests of reading comprehension of Arabic and English as foreign languages serve as mechanisms through which bureaucratic agendas are carried out, rather than simply being language tests.

Development and use

Perhaps one of the first attestations of using assessment to sort people was the use of the word "shibboleth" to separate the conquered from the victorious in the *Book of Judges* (see Chapter 2). Since then, tests have been used for power and control. It was the Chinese who invented the "examination" in 210 BC to select the senior officials for the Emperor (Spolsky, 1995). Madaus (1993) recounts how the Jesuits brought the examination system to Europe precisely to control the school curricula and the classroom.

Since Alfred Binet developed his intelligence testing methods in the early twentieth century, tests have been used to label and misclassify students, especially those who are culturally and linguistically diverse. For example, the Stanford–Binet test developed by Lewis Terman for the U.S. population was used to "prove" that "[Indians, Mexicans, and Negroes] should be segregated in special classes [. . .]. They cannot master abstractions, but they can often be made efficient workers" (Terman, cited in Oakes, 1985: 36).

The original aim of tests was to sort and rank students for purposes of comparison and placement. Tests are therefore constructed so that only the items that can discriminate between high and low scorers are included (Taylor, 1994). The history of assessment has been entangled from the very beginning with racism and linguicism (Wiley, 1996b). Testing has been used, and continues to be used, to allocate educational and employment benefits, rather than as a means for informing teaching and developing learning, in the ways described by Pat Carini in the quote at the beginning of this chapter.

Glaser (1990) distinguishes between testing and assessment. *Testing*, he says, is precisely to predict success at learning, and select and place students. *Assessment*, on the other hand, is supposed to measure the results of a course of learning. Stefanakis (2002) reminds us that *assess* comes from the Latin *assidere*, which means "to sit beside," so that assessment is literally "to sit beside the learner." In reality and for education, there is no difference between testing and assessment.

Shohamy (2001) distinguishes between three different purposes of assessment: *formative, summative,* or *predictive*. Formative assessment refers to what teachers do on an ongoing basis which is part of learning in a classroom. Summative assessment tests evaluate whether students have acquired the material in the curriculum. Finally, predictive testing predicts the future performance of the test-taker.

Standardized tests are administered and scored in a predetermined, standard way; accordingly, their administration, content, format, language, and scoring procedures are the same for all test-takers. They are usually used in large-scale assessments organized by educational authorities.

Standardized tests have been traditionally *norm-referenced* – they compare individual students to the cohort taking the test. But in the last decade or so, *criterion-referenced* standardized tests have become prevalent. In these assessments, students are graded according to whether they have met defined criteria or standard (thus, criterion-referenced assessments are standards-based). There are *content standards* that determine what students should know and be able to do in various subject areas. There are also *performance standards* which tell us the various levels of proficiency that students can achieve in the content standards. The assumption is that all students can achieve the standards, although performance may differ as advanced, proficient, basic, or novice (Taylor, 1994). Criterion-referenced assessments are usually used to establish students' competence, and not to compare them with each other.

Standardized tests of both norm-referenced and criterion-referenced kind can have *multiple-choice questions* or *performance-assessment questions*. Performance-assessment questions focus on the ability of students to solve a problem and be able to generate responses. They target how and what students know, and are able to do. Although performance-based assessment questions have been traditionally used only to inform instruction, they are increasingly being incorporated into large-scale accountability assessment programs.

Standardized assessment instruments have to have *reliability* and *validity*. Reliability has to do with the degree to which the test yields the same results on repeated trials. Validity relates to the degree to which a test measures what it intends to measure. *Content validity* is the ability to understand what student performance reveals about learning, a most important component of performance assessment (Lachat, 1999). Messick (1989) and Cronbach (1989) have broadened the definition of validity to include the social consequences of assessment, its *consequential validity*, emphasizing that results are not valid when assessments are inappropriate, or when the use of test results deprives certain students from having access to high-quality learning environments. Fair assessment must have consequential validity, that is, positive consequences both for the teaching and learning process, and for students who may experience different educational opportunities as a result of test-based placements (Glaser, 1990).

Throughout the world, test-oriented accountability has grown since the 1970s as a way to strengthen the curriculum, educational resources, and teaching quality. In reality, this narrow vision of accountability has resulted in assessment being exclusively concerned with measuring and reporting data for outside audiences (Wolf, LeMahieu, and Eresch, 1992). In the United States, test-oriented accountability has been accompanied by an increase in rote learning, and a decline of teaching methods that encourage higher-order thinking skills, the writing of essays, and conducting research (Goodlad, 1984). As a result, there has been a decrease in U.S. standing in international studies of achievement (McKnight, Crosswhite, Dossey et al., 1987).

Research suggests that what appears on tests is what teachers teach (Resnick and Resnick, 1991). Therefore, assessments have been increasingly redesigned to include what students ought to be learning – for example, oral, and written expression, and complex problem-solving and analysis (Resnick and Resnick, 1991; Darling-Hammond, 1994). Nevertheless, there continues to be a disparate impact of high-stakes testing today among different groups of students. Heubert and Hauser (1999) remind us that in the United States minority students and poor students are failing state graduation tests at alarming rates.

Assessing Bilinguals

Every assessment is an assessment of language (American Educational Research Association, American Psychological Association, and National Council on Measurement in Education, 1985). This is most important especially in thinking about testing the content knowledge of emergent bilinguals who are still learning the language of the test. The difficulty in offering fair and equitable assessment for bilinguals has to do with being able to understand the interrelationship between *language proficiency* and *content proficiency* – two important objectives in all testing.

Language proficiency has been traditionally tested by focusing on discrete language skills, such as vocabulary and grammar (McLaughlin, 1984). But it is also possible to test language proficiency through more authentic and holistic means, such as oral interviews, story retellings, picture cues, teacher observation checklists, and portfolios (Rivera, 1984; Wong Fillmore, 1982b; Valdez Pierce and O'Malley, 1992).

In schools, emphasis is paid on assessing academic language proficiency, which usually entails three criteria, according to Gottlieb (2006: 25):

1. Comprehension and use of specialized or technical vocabulary and language patterns associated with content.
2. Linguistic complexity (length and variety of sentences and discourse), register (formality), organization, and cohesion of oral interaction or writing.
3. Demonstration of understanding or usage of the sound system (phonology), the grammatical structure (syntax), and the meaning (semantics) of the language.

Content proficiency refers to whether the student has actually acquired understandings of the subject matter. Testing content proficiency independently of language proficiency is complex. To avoid this, sometimes bilingual students are assessed using translations in their native language (see more on the difficulties of translations below) or for Deaf students using sign language. Besides the difficulties inherent in identifying the native language of bilingual students (see Chapters 2 and 3), native language assessments have other problems. It is sometimes difficult to determine the regional variety that is to be used, especially if the students come from different geographical regions. If the emergent bilingual has been schooled poorly,[1] the student may not have developed sufficient literacy in the native language. Likewise, if the language is not used for instruction, then assessment for content proficiency in the students' native language may be counterproductive. Finally, there is the problem of the nonequivalence of vocabulary difficulty between languages, making comparisons for content proficiency between tests given in different languages totally inappropriate (August and Hakuta, 1998).

Shepard (1996) has argued that a fair assessment framework should integrate two dimensions – *language proficiency* and *content proficiency*. Performance of bilinguals should be seen as a continuum that is related to language acquisition, so that the language of the assessment should be adapted according to the place of the continuum in which the student is situated.

Duverger (2005) suggests that a double scale of criteria operate: criteria relating to the *discipline* being delivered, and criteria relating to the *language* being used. Depending on the type of bilingual education program that the student attends or the purpose of assessment, one or the other criteria might be assigned a higher coefficient. When the purpose of bilingual education is simply to teach another language, the language proficiency should receive a higher coefficient. But where the primary goal is the learning of content-matter through a weaker language, subject-matter knowledge should have a higher coefficient and language errors should never mask satisfactory handling of the content. In these situations, the language should be at the service of the content-matter and should take second priority.

It is important for all bilingual students to be *included* in all assessments. But in order for results to be equitable, bilingual students must be included in the design and piloting of the assessments. In this way, the *norming* of the test would not be biased, and the test would have both validity and reliability for bilingual students (Abedi and Lord, 2001).

Content bias is another important issue in assessment of bilinguals. Content bias occurs when the test reflects the language structure and shared knowledge of one culture or when test items do not include activities, words, or concepts from both of the worlds of bilingual students (Mercer, 1989).

Another important issue in testing bilinguals is the *purpose for doing it* – is it to sort them, to promote them, to retain them? Because of inadequate assessment, many bilingual students are misdiagnosed. In the United States, inadequate assessment has resulted in a disproportionate assignment of bilinguals to lower curriculum tracks and over-referral to special education classes (Cummins, 1984; Ortiz and Wilkinson, 1991).

It is also important to develop *scoring criteria* that can differentiate between subject-matter knowledge and abilities, and the language in which the students respond (La Celle-Peterson and Rivera, 1994). In the case of performance assessments, individuals who are knowledgeable about the cultural and linguistic characteristics of the students being assessed should participate in the development of rubrics for scoring student work.

The problem with assessment of bilinguals is linked to the increasing emphasis on the assessment *of* learning, instead of the assessment *for* learning. It is the latter kind of assessment – formative assessment – that is most important for emergent bilingual students. But with the increased emphasis on high-stakes tests for accountability purposes, the development and use of formative assessments for bilinguals has been neglected (Fleming, 2007).

Testing as bilinguals

Because large-scale standardized summative assessment is in the hands of educational authorities that rarely recognize the bilingualism of students, most standardized tests are conducted as if students were monolingual. Yet we know that the child's home language is a strength that could be built upon not only to learn, but also to show what has been learned. There could be ways in which all assessment, including large-scale standardized assessment, could be done in bilingual ways.

Translanguaging mode

Students being educated bilingually could be *assessed via a translanguaging mode*, a way of rendering the child's bilingual competence an accepted part of his or her identity and knowledge. For example, questions may be put in one language and responses requested in the other. Or written tests can have the question in language

A and the responses could be provided in language B. Or the written text could be produced by the learner in language A and the oral or signed presentation in language B. This would provide the teacher with a measure of productive skills across two media and for both languages, and would give the child the opportunity to use both language A and language B in different contexts, for different purposes. In this way, this translanguaging mode of assessment would give educators not only a better picture of what students really know without having language as an intervening variable, but would also offer a much clearer picture of students' languaging capacities.

Bilingual tap mode

In cases where school authorities would be interested in students' production of only one language, students being educated bilingually could also be *assessed via a bilingual tap mode*, a way of tapping their home language practices in order to produce the target language. That is, rather than negate the students' bilingualism, this type of assessment would, for example, give instructions and questions in the child's home or sign languages and ask students to respond solely in the other language. In this way, the child's home or sign language would be used to activate knowledge for assessment in much the same that any bilingual child uses his or her home language and culture to make sense of texts. This bilingual tap assessment builds on recent work on bilingual language processing by Dufour and Kroll (1995) and Kecskes and Papp (2005). Van der Walt (2006, 2007) has shown how an explicit bilingual task positively affects the performance of a group of bilingual higher-education students in South Africa, compared to another group of bilingual students who were given the same, but monolingual task. Although rarely used, bilingual tap assessment holds much promise.

Performance-based

It has been shown that *performance-based assessment* is better for bilingual students because they provide a wider range of opportunities for bilingual students to show what they know and can do in both language and content areas (Estrin and Nelson-Barber, 1995; Navarrete and Gustke, 1996). Because the assessment is connected to meaningful context, it makes it easier to demonstrate what bilinguals know and can do. Also because both students and teachers are involved in performance-based assessment, it may be possible for teachers to tap into children's bilingual resources. They can also use the information about student learning to adapt instruction to individual students more effectively (García and Pearson, 1994). By offering a range of contexts – including opportunities to work alone, in pairs, or in groups – teachers can vary assessment settings to reflect student preferences, and also evaluate the impact of these contexts on particular students' progress (García and Pearson, 1994). García and Pearson (1994) support the notion that performance-based assessment should be *dynamic*, in the sense that it should find out what the student can do with or without the help of the teacher. In this way, teachers are able to evaluate the kind of support that bilinguals need to complete tasks (Peña, Quinn, and Iglesias, 1992).

Performance-based assessments also offer bilingual children different ways to display their knowledge and abilities, including drawing on their multiple intelligences and enabling the use of different modes such as movement through dance and gestures, as well as visual/artistic renderings (Genishi and Borrego-Brainard, 1995). Because the students show how they solve problems, teachers can then differentiate between language proficiency and content proficiency. More importantly, the interpretation of the performance assessments rely on the judgment of those scoring the tests (Lachat, 1999), making it possible to integrate performance on the assessment with language proficiency.

An example of a performance-based formative assessment tool that is useful for bilingual students in the United States is the *Primary Language Record*, an observational tool for teachers to document student language and literacy development in different performance contexts. Studies of the use of this observational tool reveal that it develops teachers' capacities to look closely at students' work and develop strategies to support their learning (Darling-Hammond, Ancess, and Falk, 1995). Another important assessment tool for everyone is the process that Carini (2000) has called "Descriptive Review of Students." Teachers describe students fully under five headings: physical presence and gesture, disposition and temperament, connections with others (both children and adults), strong interests and preferences, and modes of thinking and learning (Carini, 2000). Parents are also often engaged in this process. The purpose is to "build a layering narrative account, developed over time, of a child's learning" (2000: 9). The process of Descriptive Review has been shown to be highly effective in assessing bilingual students and including their translanguaging practices (García and Traugh, 2002). It is also very useful for analyzing students' production of multimodal texts and for developing a multidimensional portrait of bilingual learners.

Instructionally embedded assessment is particularly relevant for bilingual children. Information is collected from a variety of sources, such as student observations, classroom products, and conversations with family members. For example, observations during science experiments, dramatization of historical events, and math problems may be collected. A portfolio is then developed and in turn that information is used to inform curriculum and teaching (McLaughlin and Vogt, 1997).

Portfolios should mirror standards, curriculum, and the languages of instruction in proportion to their use. Gottlieb (2006: 178) suggests that the following be included:

- a summary sheet with student goals and summary in list form of student work;
- original samples of student work with feedback;
- multimedia entries;
- quizzes and tests;
- reflection on portfolio.

These portfolios should always include samples, entries, and tests in both languages. They should be developed with the teacher's help and shared with family members.

A European case

In German secondary-school bilingual programs, operating through French and German since 1972, the examination system has been developed so as to enable a win–win situation for those who enroll voluntarily for this type of education (Mäsch,

1993). In these schools, there are traditional language lessons in the second language which are assessed using the same criteria and instruments as those used to assess second-language development in monolingual schools. But there are also certain subjects taught through the medium of the second language. At the end of the program students can *select* to take the examination either in their first language or the second language. Those who decide to take the examination through the second language must satisfy the criteria for content knowledge along the same lines as students who have followed the monolingual program. But linguistic errors will not affect the pass mark for the content matter. On the other hand, if the second language used in the test is of a satisfactory level of accuracy and appropriateness, it receives special recognition, or a "bilingual mention" on the final diplomas. These official diplomas dispense those who hold them from taking language examinations to assess suitability for tertiary education in the country where the target language is used. Thus, this is a win–win situation which encourages students to take the risk of doing the examination in the target language at little cost.

Encouraging bilingualism in Europe

There are bilateral agreements between different European countries which recognize the language competence of those who have followed part of their secondary schooling in a bilingual mode. For example, in Germany, there are agreements with the French authorities which allow students to take special language examinations in French as a foreign language which will dispense with any further requirements of proof of ability to benefit from higher education in France. Bilateral agreements between France and Germany also enable students in bilingual programs to take a specially developed final examination giving access to universities in both Germany and France under the form of a mutually recognized final certificate, combining elements of the German school-leaving certificate, the Abitur, and the French one, the Baccalaureate. Such initiatives are designed to encourage learners to embark on bilingual education programs.

Under international treaty, the European school network has its own specific secondary school final examination diploma, known as the European Baccalaureate, which gives access to higher education anywhere in the world. All school leavers in the European schools must present their final Baccalaureate examination through the medium of two languages. Apart from specific language tests, developed to measure ability in the three languages that are compulsory components of the curriculum, certain content-matter subjects are evaluated through the medium of the language in which the subject was taught: French, German, or English, depending on students' choice of their compulsory additional language. Examination questions for language or non-linguistic content-matter subjects exist in parallel versions, irrespective of the language being used, and in theory are marked along the same criteria, whether the student is using one or the other language. In practice, however, some tolerance on lower linguistic diversity or lexical richness is applied if the candidate is using a language other than that of their home.

Perhaps the most important European initiative to use assessment to encourage bilingualism is the development of the *language portfolio*, an initiative of the Council of Europe that has been fully described in Chapter 9. The portfolio encourages pupils, in co-operation with teachers, to observe their developing multilingualism and describe varied levels of competence.

Despite these European advances, it is important to note that immigrant students are subjected to assessment solely in the dominant school language. For example, in French schools, children who speak Turkish or Swahili rarely benefit from the same indulgence as French–English bilinguals do.

Testing as monolinguals

Unfortunately, most bilingual students even in the best bilingual education systems are often asked to perform as two monolinguals. Many educational systems provide *accommodations* for emergent bilingual students when tested in their non-dominant language as if they were monolinguals. Most accommodations have to exist because of the little interest in developing appropriate bilingual assessment, as the ones described above. In the United States, and as a result of the new accountability systems that are a result of the No Child Left Behind act of 2001, a number of accommodations have been implemented to test emergent bilinguals who are in the process of developing English proficiency (Rivera and Stansfield, 2000):

1. *Presentation* – permits repetition, explanation, simplification, test translations into students' home languages, or test administration by a bilingual specialist.
2. *Response* – allows a student to dictate his/her answers, and to respond in his/her home language or to display knowledge using alternative forms of representation.
3. *Setting* – includes individual or small group administration of the test, or administration in a separate location or multiple testing sessions.
4. *Timing/scheduling* – allows for additional time to complete the test or extra breaks during administration.
5. *Reinforcement* – permits use of dictionaries and glossaries.

Because of the culture of disability that continues to surround the education for the Deaf, Deaf students are also provided with accommodations for assessment. As with all bilingual students, these accommodations cannot substitute for appropriate bilingual assessments nor can they provide fair ways of assessing what Deaf students know. Despite accommodations, tests normed in an English-proficient hearing population continue to lack validity for Deaf children or those who even the Government categorizes as "Limited English Proficient" or "English Language Learners."[2]

Abedi, Lord, and Plummer (1997) show how linguistic modification with test items that are shorter and less complex results in significant differences in math performance among bilinguals in the United States. In fact, additional research has shown that the only accommodation that narrows the gap between emergent bilinguals and other students is *linguistic modification of questions* with excessive language demands. Other accommodations such as providing extra time, using a glossary of key terms on the test, or reducing the language complexity of the test questions increase scores for *all* students, and therefore do not narrow the gap between bilinguals and others (Abedi, 2004; Abedi, Hofstetter, and Lord, 2004).

Another accommodation that is sometimes provided to emergent bilinguals is to use *translations* of the tests. But this is neither always feasible nor appropriate. Some students may not be literate in their native language, especially if they are immigrant students who have not had access to bilingual education. And living bilingually means that tests in one or the other language do not fully capture the complexity of the linguistic repertoire of bilinguals. Furthermore, assessments conducted in different languages are not psychometrically equivalent (Anderson, Jenkins, and Miller, 1996). Maintaining construct equivalence is difficult when the test is either translated directly from one language to another or when tests in two languages are developed. The "Standards for Educational and Psychological Testing" state:

> Psychometric properties cannot be assumed to be comparable across languages or dialects. Many words have different frequency rates or difficulty levels in different languages or dialects. Therefore, words in two languages that appear to be close in meaning may differ radically in other ways important for the test use intended. Additionally, test content may be inappropriate in a translated version (American Educational Research Association, American Psychological Association, and National Council on Measurement in Education, 1985: 73).

In addition, translations are only appropriate if the student has been taught through the language of the test. Abedi (2004) concludes that the language of the assessment needs to match the student's primary language of instruction.

Another problem with translations has to do with the fact that unless bilinguals have been effectively educated in their home language, they may have limited academic literacy in that language. Sometimes, emergent bilinguals are allowed to use both the home-language version and the dominant-language version. But developing and validating equivalent versions of a test (two monolingual versions side by side) is difficult and costly (Anderson, Jenkins, and Miller, 1996). Furthermore, research on this issue has repeatedly shown substantial psychometric discrepancies in students' performance on the same test items across both languages (August and Hakuta, 1997). This means that test items are not measuring the same underlying knowledge.

Transadaption is different from translations because tests are developed in the other language from the beginning. Transadaptions are developed and normed on the bilingual population that will be using them, and thus, are much better than translations. This type of testing is now in effect in Texas in the United States where schools are using standardized tests in Spanish. A transadapted test, as such, works to eliminate cultural biases (Johnston, 1997). However, the linguistic issues dealing with testing bilinguals with a monolingual test remain.

"Fox" strategies

As large-scale assessments are increasingly used for accountability purposes all over the world, teachers have to find ways of having their emergent bilinguals do well in monolingual assessments in a language other than their home language. An ESL teacher in a New York City secondary school for newcomers, Jakob Clausen, suggested to García at a staff development session (March 3, 2004): "We have to be like the fox – this is the back door, this is the way you can get in." The group of teachers then elaborated "fox strategies" that would enable their students to do well in the English language test:

1. Contextualize: Work from the inside out. Start with something students are familiar with. Read the works in the home language of the students, but have them practice talking and writing about the books in English. Teach them to use cognates smartly.
2. Provide models: Give students prepared essays, skeleton paragraphs, samples of concluding sentences, transitions. Make sure that students know the vocabulary (for example, "clearly state," interpretation, analysis), useful words and terms for the test.
3. Build up predictability and redundancy: Practice with old tests. Have students know the tests well, what they are being asked to do, how questions are to be answered, what each question requires. Take the test directions and have students develop topic sentences from that. Have them rephrase the instructions.
4. Keep it simple: Show students how to take the easier way out. For example, disagree in an essay, rather than agree so that you can make better arguments.
5. Look elsewhere for meaning: If multiple choice questions, have students first look at the questions before they read, so that they know what they are looking for.
6. Look closely: Teach students to follow directions closely, doing what tasks request of them. Teach them to proofread carefully. Have them ask themselves, "Have I answered it?"

Although we must question the effects of this type of instruction on students' learning and development, unless students pass the English-language test for which these teachers are preparing them, they will not be able to graduate from secondary school. Given that there is an unfair assessment system for these emergent bilinguals, it is then important to consider what is the worse consequence – teaching to the test in reductionist ways, or letting students fail the test and thus be left out of any further educational and economic opportunity in the future? For these dedicated teachers, the answer in an unfair assessment system is clear.

To *discourage bilingualism: the U.S.*
The No Child Left Behind act of 2001 (NCLB) mandates all states to evaluate the achievement of all students, including emergent bilinguals[3] in meeting the state's English reading/language arts academic standards, if the student has attended school in the U.S. for one academic year (Menken, 2006, 2008). NCLB also expects that by the 2013–2014 school year, all students must achieve the level of "proficient" in state assessment systems.

The devastating effect of high-stakes testing in English for language minority students in the United States has been well documented (Amrein and Berliner, 2002; Valenzuela, 1999, 2000). Valenzuela and McNeil (2001), for example, argue that high-stakes testing in Texas has been the most detrimental policy for Latinos and emergent bilinguals and that there should be local control over assessment. As Menken (2008) has shown, mandating high-stakes tests in English for all has acted as language policy, effectively devastating bilingual education programs in the United States and the potential for the development of bilingualism. As a result, bilingual students are being "pushed out" of school and dropping out. Gutiérrez, Asato, Santos, and Gotanda (2002) have also shown that California schools have found it difficult to retain bilingual instruction when the sole measure of accountability is performance on a state test that is offered in English only.

Democratic Assessment for Bilinguals

It is important that flexible assessments be used with bilingual students. This means that bilingual students should be given the opportunity to show their proficiency in both languages, both academically and socially, and both separately and demonstrating their translanguaging abilities. This also means that bilingual students should be given the choice of demonstrating their academic achievement in content areas in any of their two languages. Substantive content must be differentiated from language proficiency (La Celle-Peterson and Rivera, 1994).

In assessing bilinguals, care must also be taken to differentiate one end of the bilingual continuum, the emergent bilingual stage in which the student is still developing proficiency in the second language, from other points in the continuum. For emergent bilinguals, an expectation of proficiency in the target language is an impossibility, since productive skills take much longer to develop than receptive skills. So speaking and listening or signing, as well as reading and writing must be assessed. Comparing test scores of emergent bilinguals in the dominant language with those of monolinguals, and even with bilinguals at other points of the language continuum is never fair. The assessment of emergent bilinguals should focus on their progress over time towards established goals (La Celle-Peterson and Rivera, 1994).

It is clear that the best way to assess bilingual students is for teachers to observe and listen to their students, and to record these observations systematically over long periods of time. Authentic, formative assessments are much better ways of obtaining valid, reliable information that then informs our teaching.

No area in bilingual education is in more need of development than that of bilingual assessment. Without large-scale bilingual assessment that would take into consideration the bilingual continuum in which bilingual children operate, as well as the integrated nature of their language proficiency and content knowledge, bilingual children will never be able to demonstrate their strength. There is also urgent need to develop assessment that can tap the pluriliteracies of multimodal texts which bilingual children must produce in the twenty-first century.

Conclusion

This book has been about the power of bilingualism in extending knowledge and intercultural understandings. But in all schools, the power of assessment looms larger than the power of bilingualism. Unless true bilingual assessments (and not assessments in two languages) are adopted as ways to show what bilingual children know and are able to do both conceptually and linguistically, the power of bilingualism in schools will not be sufficient to change the monoglossic ideology with which monolingual schools (and even some bilingual schools) continue to operate. And unless multimodal assessments (and not only assessments of print-based texts) are designed and used, today's schools will continue to value and reproduce knowledge that may be outdated for a future in which localized and globalized understandings, as well as traditional and technological knowledge, will be needed.

Questions for Reflection

1. How is testing and assessment related to power? How do different ways of testing make a difference for bilingual educators and students?
2. What are the differences between *formative, summative,* and *predictive* assessments in terms of their purposes? How do they impact on bilingual students differently?
3. How do *norm-referenced* and *criterion-referenced* assessments compare, especially for bilingual students? Give examples of different types of tests and tell if they are the former or the latter.
4. Explain what the difference is between assessing bilingual students as bilinguals and assessing bilingual students as monolinguals. What are the consequences?
5. Discuss the difference between a translanguaging mode of assessment and a bilingual tap assessment.
6. What are the problems with translations and accommodations in assessing bilingual students?
7. What is the concept behind democratic assessment for bilinguals?

Further Reading

Abedi, J., Hofstetter, C.H., and Lord, C. (2004). "Assessment Accommodations for English Language Learners: Implications for Policy-Based Empirical Research." *Review of Educational Research* 74, 1–28.

Gottlieb, M. (2006). *Assessing English Language Learners: Bridges from language Proficiency to Academic Achievement.* Corwin Press, Thousand Oaks, CA.

Menken, K. (2008). *English Language Learners Left Behind: Standardized Testing as Language Policy.* Multilingual Matters, Clevedon.

O'Malley, J.M., and Valdez-Pierce, L. (1996). *Authentic Assessment for English Language Learners.* Addison-Wesley, Reading, MA.

Shohamy, E. (2001). *The Power of Tests: A Critical Perspective on the Uses of Language Tests.* Longman, Harlow.

Part V

Bilingual Education for the Twenty-first Century

Conclusion

La educación es como un árbol: se siembra una semilla y se abre en muchas ramas. Hombres recogerá quien siembre escuelas.

(Education is like a tree: You plant a seed and many branches sprout. Men will be the crop of those who plant schools.)

Martí, 1975: vol. VII, p. 15

El abono se puede traer de otras partes; pero el cultivo se ha de hacer conforme al suelo.

(You can bring the fertilizer from other parts; but you must cultivate it according to the soil.)

Martí, 1975: vol. XX, p. 147

Para los niños trabajamos, porque los niños son los que saben querer, porque los niños son la esperanza del mundo.

(We work for the children, because children are the ones who know how to love, because children are the hope of the world.)

Martí, 1975: vol. XVIII, p. 302

La enseñanza ¿quién no lo sabe? es ante todo una obra de infinito Amor.
(Teaching is, who doesn't know it? it is above all work of infinite Love.)

Martí, 1975: vol. X, p. 23

This book has tried to show the complexity of bilingual education in the twenty-first century. By introducing different societal contexts, and including different states' and people's wishes, the text shows us that bilingual education is complex. But, as the previous words of the Cuban writer and patriot José Martí remind us, bilingual education is, above all, an enterprise of love for the children of the world who will be the men and women of the future. Martí also reminds us that each local context needs to cultivate its own soil, its own bilingual education programs, and educate and nurture their own men and women.

The image of the banyan tree serves well to explain what has happened to bilingual education, as it has developed in time, and as it has expanded from one society to the other, and to the multiple ways in which people language throughout the world. But the banyan trees of bilingual education are multiple, adjusting to the many soils, contexts, and resources in which they develop.

What makes this book different from others that have tackled this subject before? Traditionally, bilingual education has been studied from a western perspective, mostly North American. This book tries to expand on this vision and to turn it upside down, incorporating the complex multilingualism of most the world. As an activity that is mostly organized by states that seek to control the way in which people language, bilingual education has also been perceived and studied from a monolingual perspective. What we call here a monoglossic ideology has hereto dominated even the bilingual education field, with educators calling for equal and balanced proficiencies as outcomes of bilingual education. In this book, we adopt a heteroglossic perspective, putting bilingualism and language differences at the center of the endeavor and considering it the norm. Thus, the treatment of bilingual education in this book doesn't accommodate to monolingual standards and ways of using language in education. Bilingual education is here seen in its own right.

What are the consequences of including the perspective of the developing world alongside that of the developed world with regards to bilingualism? And of including language minorities alongside language majorities? We are immediately confronted with the idea that language as a bound autonomous system has little to do with the ways in which people "language." Languaging as a concept is given attention in this book, and we treat academic language, the purview of bilingual education, as one more languaging event. Including the developing world brings multilingualism to the forefront of all languaging events. Multilinguals throughout the world translanguage in order to make sense of their world. It is only when they get to school that their language complexity becomes stigmatized. Schools attempt to control this gift of translanguaging, marking the more fluid languaging practices of society as "incorrect," or "corrupt." But bilingual education in the ways conceived in this book has the possibility of building on this translanguaging and to transform it as a useful resource for the twenty-first century.

Putting these translanguaging practices of multilinguals alongside the models of additive and subtractive bilingualism, models that the scholarship on bilingualism have made popular in the last fifty years, has enabled us to question these also. We have thus expanded on these models of bilingualism to capture the linguistic complexity of the world. To the traditional subtractive and additive models of bilingualism, we have added a recursive and dynamic bilingual model. The recursive model recognizes that because of the language dominance of many, the bilingualism of minoritized language groups is recursive. The ancestral language cannot be added whole, but its bits and pieces can be recovered and reconstituted for new functions within a bilingual context. Dynamic bilingualism also recognizes that bilingualism doesn't develop as a linear sum, but as a multiple trajectory that operates at different levels. In this book, we consider dynamic bilingualism to be similar to plurilingualism, although we take it beyond the borders of the European Union to encompass the multiple multilingualism of societies such as India.

If bilingualism cannot be considered as simply two wholes – a simple addition of $1 + 1 = 2$ – then bilingual education theoretical frameworks cannot be simply additive or subtractive. To the traditional ones that the literature has studied so well, we add two other theoretical frameworks of bilingual education – a recursive one and a dynamic bilingual one. These two theoretical frameworks recognize recursive and dynamic bilingualism as important goals for bilingual education in the twenty-first century. These theoretical frameworks also build on the heteroglossic language practices that are prevalent in the twenty-first century among most bilingual communities. They are not ways of approximating monolingualism in either language. Rather they promote bilingualism in its own right and shape.

Although we find the idea of bilingual education models problematic because bilingual education is never a tight system, we provide the readers with nine different types of bilingual education that correspond to the four theoretical frameworks proposed in this book. Each of these types has different characteristics, goals, and types of children. We describe the types fully. We start with those that were originally developed following monoglossic ideologies that considered bilingualism a problem of the developing world and of the poor, or a privilege of the elite – transitional, maintenance, prestigious, or immersion bilingual education. We then pay particular attention to those types of bilingual education that were developed as bilingualism started to be considered a right by Indigenous and autochthonous minorities, and a resource for a globalized world. These five types respond to more heteroglossic ideologies – immersion revitalization, developmental, as well as poly-directional or two-way, CLIL and CLIL-type, and multiple multilingual education. Because they were developed later, these are based on the earlier monoglossic types of bilingual education, although they extend and complicate them. Although all types of bilingual education are growing throughout the world, those that respond to a dynamic bilingual framework – poly-directional or two-way, CLIL and CLIL-type, and multiple multilingual education – are exploding, as people increasingly understand the need for bilingualism across groups, for all children, and beyond two languages. Thus, all types of bilingual education are extending towards the last type – multiple multilingual –, as many more groups attempt to develop trilingualism and other more flexible ways of translanguaging multilingually. The traditional bilingual education types simply do not suffice in the twenty-first century.

The development and implementation of different bilingual education types is the realm of language-in-education policy, and in the third part of the book, we look at how it is imposed and managed from the top, usually by the government of the national state. Because we know that different contexts require changes and transformations to bilingual education types, we provide a full treatment of the different variables that must be considered, features that could be ignored, accepted, or emphasized, as the bilingual education program is designed and implemented.

Bilingual education policy throughout the world is described in the book. Because bilingual education continues to be an important and controversial topic in North America and Europe, we devote an entire chapter to the U.S. context, and another one to the European contexts. These two chapters, read side by side, can enlighten the reader about how different developed societies make different decisions about bilingual education policy, depending on their histories and their sociopolitical stances. Whereas bilingual education in the United States, despite its controversies, continues to be mostly for immigrants, in the European Union, immigrants are not included in their very liberal bilingual education policy for all. Beyond the U.S. and the European Union, different states and societal entities plan bilingualism for different reasons and end up adopting different types of bilingual education programs. This book reviews some of the best-known in order to serve as examples of how different societies have shaped bilingual education programs for their differing needs. The treatment is also not air-tight. For example, different societies adopt various types of bilingual education for different groups. Different groups within a society might develop bilingual education types to fit their needs which might be contrary to those of a centralized government. Thus, although this part of the book mostly considers bilingual education policies as enacted by states, it also includes those negotiated by different language groups and communities. Because bilingual education policy almost always translates into a bilingual education type, Chapters 10 and 11 provide further descriptions of the different bilingual education types as they match up to different policy and planning decisions.

Bilingual education policy, however, does not simply refer to how states or social groups plan and implement their programs; it also refers to the practices that collectively describe how to teach bilingually. This book makes clear that bilingual education for the twenty-first century must do much more than separate languages, as was the ideology of additive monoglossic bilingual types. By considering language arrangements in the classroom that support flexible language uses, and specifically translanguaging, this book gives options to the educators that have hereto not been available. Translanguaging is here validated as an important language practice in the bilingual classroom, and flexible multiple language arrangements and models of multiple bilingual teaching are supported in this book. But the book also describes the many different language arrangements and models of bilingual teaching that characterize all types of bilingual education programs that correspond to different theoretical frameworks.

Finally, the book provides educators with pedagogical practices that are important for any societal context wishing to develop bilingual education programs. Bilingual education is much more than a technique or a pedagogy. Bilingual education is education, and it is also a way of equalizing opportunities. It rests on principles of social justice, and supports social practices for learning. With these two principles – social justice and social practice – bilingual education pedagogy is constructed and described in this book. Although not all bilingual education programs concern themselves with literacy, literacy is important in many educational contexts, and the book devotes one chapter to explore how to develop biliteracy among students.

The issue of assessment is perhaps the most thorny issue in bilingual education contexts. Besides pointing out the difficulties of monolingual assessment for bilingual students and the inequities in comparing bilingual children to a monolingual child in one of the languages, this book also offers some types of bilingual assessment that recognize and tap the students' bilingual abilities.

The five parts of this book are interrelated, although meant to address different components important to the bilingual education enterprise. Part I acts as an introduction to the book and reminds us that bilingual education is for all children.

Part II explores the dimensions of bilingualism, developing the notion of languaging bilingually or translanguaging and proposing two new models of bilingualism – recursive and dynamic. Part III then turns to bilingual education itself, exploring policy and types, and paying particular attention to the new types of bilingual education that have been developed as a result of different theoretical frameworks with regards to bilingual education, the recursive and dynamic framework. It will be useful to educational policy-makers – official ministries, but also families and communities – as they struggle to decide on how to design a bilingual education program. Part IV then turns to the practices of bilingual education, the aspects of language policy that educators must understand and deliver. From the design of Part III, this part moves to implementation. It will be of particular interest to those that have to enact the curriculum and the pedagogy. In considering the practices and pedagogy of bilingual education, this part makes evident that the new theoretical frameworks of bilingual education require new language arrangements and new pedagogical practices. In so doing, this part questions venerable assumptions that have been associated with bilingual education, and particularly the notion that code-switching is always "bad." Finally, Part V acts as a conclusion, summarizing for the reader how it is that bilingual education must be considered in the twenty-first century.

Throughout the entire book, emphasis is made on the fact that different societies have different aspirations and wishes for their citizens and children, and unequal resources. All theoretical frameworks and types of bilingual education program therefore co-exist, and are here considered. It is important to repeat that bilingual education should be the only option to teach all children in the twenty-first century in equitable ways. But we cannot require that all societies and groups, unequal to begin with, implement the same kinds of bilingual education for their children. No one type of bilingual education is better than another if we consider the entire world and the social conditions of different educational systems. In societies where children are not being schooled beyond the first three years, fighting for developmental bilingual education might not be relevant. And with groups that speak tribal languages or minoritized languages, developing two-way bilingual education programs might not be realistic. Every society and group has to make choices that are relevant for its children. And we must all ensure that those choices are fair and the best that could be had, given the societal resources.

If bilingual education is going to reach its transformative potential, we are going to have to let go of monoglossic beliefs and practices that continue to view two languages through monolingual lenses. Instead, we need to break visions of whole languages so that we can construct new ones that are more inclusive of differences, of the translanguaging that is so extensive in bilingual communities and classrooms. Bilingualism must be accepted as an all-terrain vehicle, adapting to the ridges and the craters of communication that encompass technologically enriched interactions in the global sphere and in very local exchanges. Bilingual education could be a mechanism to develop this communicative capacity for the twenty-first century. The challenge will be whether states can let go of their language–identity–allegiance associations, and allow children to build multiple identities, as they construct abilities to translanguage and use multiple languages in the flexible ways of the future. We hope that this book will be a guide to those who want to ensure that bilingual education bring further equity and hope to language minorities, immigrants, and underserved children, and further understandings and tolerance of linguistic differences and development of bilingual and multilingual abilities to language majorities. Only by equalizing languaging possibilities for all groups will we be able to create a more just multilingual world in the future where translanguaging is not only supported, but is used to build connections among groups.

Table 16.1 below acts as the integrating element that pulls together aspects that we have considered throughout the book – the theoretical frameworks of bilingual education, the language arrangements and pedagogies in the bilingual curriculum, and the types of bilingual education. Although here, and elsewhere throughout the book, it appears in linear and box form, it is important to remember that in practice there is much fluidity. Bilingual education can only be understood with the image of the banyan tree. While it expands its roots horizontally and vertically, it makes connections and reaches out to different realms, but in so doing it respects and protects the temple that is the child. So it turns out that despite its global connections, bilingual education is ultimately a local endeavor, focused on educating the individual child with multiple possibilities and deep respect.

Table 16.1   Integrative Table: Bilingual Education

Theoretical Framework (*see Chapters 3 and 6*)	Subtractive	Additive	Recursive	Dynamic
Language Goal (*see Chapter 6*)	Monolingualism; monoglossic	Bilingualism; monoglossic	Bilingualism; heteroglossic	Bilingualism; heteroglossic
Literacy Goal (*see Chapter 14*)	Monoliteracy	Full biliteracy	Functional biliteracy	Functional biliteracy
Cultural Goal (*see Chapter 6*)	Monocultural	Bicultural	Bicultural multiplicity	Transcultural
Initial Linguistic Position of Children (*see Chapter 6*)	Monolingual	Monolingual	Different points of bilingual continuum	Different points of bilingual continuum
Language Arrangement (*see Chapter 12*)	Flexible convergent	Strict separation	Separation to flexible multiple	Flexible multiple to separation
Models of Bilingual Pedagogy (*see Chapter 12*)	Convergent	Immersion	Immersion	Multiple

Table 16.1 (*continued*)

Models of Biliteracy Pedagogy (*see Chapter 14*)	Convergent	Separation	Flexible multiple	Flexible multiple
Type of Bilingual Education (*see Chapters 6, 10, and 11*)	Transitional BE	Maintenance BE; Prestigious BE; Immersion BE	Immersion Revitalization BE; Developmental BE	Poly-directional/ two-way (dual language), CLIL and CLIL-type; Multiple Multilingual

Appendix
Myths and Realities

by Cristina Muir, Yesenia Morales, Lori Falchi, and Ofelia García

Bilingual Education: What It Is

Bilingual education uses two or more languages in instruction.

Bilingual education *does not* focus on the acquisition of a second language at the expense of one's native language.

Myths and Facts across the Globe

Myth: Bilingual Education does not work.

Fact: Literally hundreds of scientific studies over the past half century have shown that bilingual education – when well designed and well implemented – is an effective approach for educating language minorities and language majorities who want to learn an additional language. These findings have been consistent across numerous national borders, languages of instruction, and types of students, all pointing to the conclusion that bilingual education "works" (www.nabe.org/education/effective.html).

Moreover, research reveals that "A variety of cognitive advantages have been reported in associations with bilingualism" (Cummins and Swain, 1986: 10). Furthermore, "A positive association has also been reported between bilingualism and both general intellectual skills and divergent thinking" (Cummins and Swain, 1986: 10).

Inconsistent labels of bilingual education programs have resulted in many generalizations and misconceptions around the effectiveness of bilingual education. No single program fits all students, and bilingual education encompasses many types of programs, and is therefore often difficult to assess.

Myth: There are few benefits that come with bilingual education.

Fact: "The cognitive, linguistic and cultural goals of bilingual education are interrelated and are, in turn, closely linked to the affective goals. The importance of self-image may, in the final analysis, be the single most important outcome of bilingual education" (Von Maltitz, 1975). Bilingual education therefore gives notice to both cultural and linguistic practices of pupils. When pupils' cultures and languages are equally validated, there is a rise in both self-confidence and school performance. There are also multiple social and economic advantages to bilingualism in an increasingly globalized world.

Myth: Education through the use of two languages (at once) confuses children; and therefore bilingual education programs mix up children.

Fact: There is no evidence suggesting that bilingual education confuses children, nor is there any evidence that a bilingual upbringing confuses children. In fact, there is much evidence that there are cognitive advantages for bilingual children (Bialystok, 2001) and that children that are educated in more than one language develop better literacy in their two languages, as well as deeper content knowledge (Genesee, Lindholm-Leary, Saunders, and Christian, 2006).

Myth: Bilingual education delays students' acquisition of an additional language.

Fact: On the contrary, one of the major goals of bilingual education is the development of an additional language, with an emphasis on having the support of the home language.

Examination of bilingual programs has indicated that when students are instructed bilingually they tend to perform as well as their monolingual counterparts in both language skills and content areas. Unlike monolinguals that are solely instructed in one language, bilingual students develop language skills in both languages as a result of bilingual education (Hosch, 1984: 5). Furthermore, if the students' home languages are used to make lessons meaningful, students will learn more language, and more subject matter, too (Crawford, 1998: 4).

Myth: Bilingual education programs are for minority students.

Fact: "Bilingual Education should not be a special form of education for a minority, but rather the normal curriculum for all students" (Hosch, 1984: 29). Even more, it must cease to be a program for "disadvantaged minorities" (Center for Applied Linguistics, 1977: 57). "It is estimated that between 60 and 75 percent of the world is bilingual, and bilingual education is a common educational approach used throughout the world. It may be implemented in different ways for majority and/or minority language populations, and there may be different educational and linguistic goals in different countries" (http://education.stateuniversity.com/pages/1788/Bilingual-Education.html).

Myth: It is easier for children to learn an additional language than it is for adults.

Fact: Language acquisition in relation to the age of the learner is contingent upon many critical factors. Young children simply have more opportunities to practice language in a meaningful context, which facilitates rapid language acquisition. "Differences in the context in which language is used [also] help to account for some of the reasons why younger children may be seen as better language learners" (Davies Samway and McKeon, 1999: 20). "The context of language use refers to the degree to which the environment is rich with meaningful clues that help the language learner decipher and interpret the language being used" (Davies Samway and McKeon, 1999: 20).

Additionally, young children and adults process language structures differently. Research shows that different parts of the brain are responsible for specific skills in language acquisition, thus indicating that both young children and adults find particular skills easier to learn than their respective counterparts.

Myth: Bilingual education is part of the problem in today's schools; it is not the solution.

Fact: There is much evidence in the literature to show that the goals of bilingual education are compatible with the goals of general education (Center for Applied Linguistics, 1997: 3). Moreover, bilingual education offers students an additional resource to their overall education by allowing them to acquire additional multiple languages.

Myth: The best way to become bilingual is to be immersed in that language in school.

Fact: Using a child's home language as a primary vehicle of instruction and resource effectively facilitates the acquisition of understandings and of an additional language. Furthermore, developing literacy in the home language is a short-cut to literacy in an additional language. "It is easier to learn to read in a language you understand; once you can read in one language, this knowledge transfers rapidly to any other language you learn to read" (Krashen at www.rethinkingschools.org/special_reports/bilingual/Bi152.shtml). Thus, by supporting the balance between students' language practices, educators create meaningful learning environments.

Myth: Bilingual education programs are expensive.

Fact: A study commissioned by the California legislature in the U.S. examined a variety of well-implemented program models and found no budgetary advantage for English-only approaches. The incremental cost was about the same each year ($175 to $214) for bilingual and English immersion programs, as compared with $1,198 for English as a second language (ESL) "pullout" programs. The reason was simple – the pullout approach requires supplemental teachers, whereas in-class approaches do not (Parrish, 1994; Crawford, 1998: 4).

Furthermore, it is important to highlight that there have been minimal studies on the costs of bilingual education programs, in part due to the number of differential factors that are associated with particular programs and program types. This suggests the importance of assessing programs on a case-by-case basis, as bilingual education programs successfully operate according to local context and individual student needs.

"[O]n the other side of the coin, not providing bilingual education can be costly in human terms" (Davies Samway and McKeon, 1999: 13). "[T]he economic benefits of producing truly bilingual citizens may far outweigh any programmatic costs incurred" (Davies Samway and McKeon, 1999: 14). In examining the costs of bilingual education, we must look at the bigger picture, and consider the long-term implications in *not* providing bilingual education. Bilingual education offers a brighter future for both our students and the global community.

Myth: Transitional programs are the most effective bilingual programs, and the fastest way to learn a second language.

   Fact: Although transitional bilingual education programs have been and continue to be successful, the success is dependent on the particular school context and factors that influence that circumstance. Even though the home language of minority students is transitionally supported by the program model, most transitional programs favor a goal of instruction in the other language as soon as it is feasible (Genesee, 1999; Ovando and Collier, 1998). Thus, transitional models aim to just use the additional language as the language of instruction and therefore move away from bilingual education. Bilingual education should strive towards development of bilingualism (Center for Applied Linguistics, 1977: 57).

Myth: There is no relationship between learning an additional language and the home language.

   Fact: Cummins (1981) argues that although the two languages may seem separate on the surface, they are actually quite interdependent at the deeper level of cognitive functions. For example, it is a well-established finding that students who learn to read and write in their first language are able to readily transfer those abilities to a second language (Krashen, 1996; Cummins, 1992). Both languages nurture each other when the educational environment permits children access to both languages (www.iteachilearn.com/cummins/mother.htm).

Myth: Deaf students cannot be bilingual, and thus do not need bilingual education.

   Fact: The bilingual-bicultural perspective in Deaf education advocates the use of sign language as a language of classroom instruction and introduces the other language in print form only (a visually accessible form) to Deaf students (Digello, Singelton, Morgan, Wiles, and Rivers, 2004: 650). Bilingual education of Deaf and hard-of-hearing children allows children to use sign language and the other language and it supports the acquisition of both.

Myth: Bilingual education only concerns urban environments.

   Fact: As people continue to migrate and immigrate to various countries and cities throughout the world, all teachers will sooner or later encounter emergent bilingual students. Moreover, all teachers will inevitably be required to receive some sort of education in bilingual education and/or to teach emergent bilinguals. UNESCO states: "Education in many countries of the world takes place in multilingual contexts. Most plurilingual societies have developed an ethos which balances and respects the use of different languages in daily life." Furthermore, "The challenge is for education systems to adapt to these complex realities and provide a quality education which takes into consideration learner's needs, and political demands" (http://portal.unesco.org/education/en/ev.php-URL_ID=13126&URL_DO=DO_TOPIC&URL_SECTION=201.html).

Myth: Bilingual education is a threat to majority languages, and especially to the English language in the United States.

Fact: There is nothing within the philosophy of bilingual education that diminishes the reality of the importance of majority languages or English in the United States (Hosch, 1984: 57). With its economic power, English has never been "threatened." In two or three generations immigrant and Indigenous minorities have learned English and have often lost their native languages (www.nabe.org/education/politics.html). Equally important to recognize is that "Today, more than ever, we need multilingual skills to enhance national security and prosper in a global economy" (www.nabe. org/education/politics.html).

Notes

Note to the Preface

1. In this book we capitalize the word "Deaf" to indicate a community or someone who culturally identifies as a Deaf person and to be consistent with Deaf scholarship on this topic.

Notes to Chapter 1

1. In this book we capitalize the word "Indigenous" to indicate a land-based group and to be consistent with Indigenous scholarship on this topic (see Sumida, forthcoming).
2. In this book, we use the term "minoritized" to indicate that the minority status has been conferred to it as a form of oppression. In so doing, we indicate that the minority status has nothing to do with numbers or viability, but with lack of power and control (for more on this, see McCarty, 2004, and Romaine, 2006).
3. This is often the situation in some countries of Africa where children continue to be schooled in the colonial language.
4. When we refer to language-teaching programs we mean both foreign-language and second-language teaching programs per se. Foreign-language programs usually refer to learning a language in a national context other than where it is spoken. Second-language programs most likely refer to programs that teach the language in the context in which it is spoken, and, thus, the communicative demands are greater and more immediate than when a language is perceived as being foreign. The differences between the two approaches, however, are beginning to blur in the context of globalization, especially for global languages such as English.
5. As we will see, some bilingual education programs do this more than others, but by using more than one language in instruction, all of them show greater respect for language diversity than those that use only a majority language.
6. There are types of bilingual education that use the students' home language to provide a meaningful education to language minorities that cannot comprehend instruction. Likewise, there are types of bilingual education for language majorities that use the students' additional language to provide an education that the society would consider

meaningful and beneficial because its citizens would become bilingual. In both cases, albeit with different goals, the education that bilingual education provides is more meaningful than a monolingual education.

7. For more on the concept of monoglossic and heteroglossic ideologies, see Del Valle, 2000, 2006.

8. We are aware that not all societies are involved in these multimodal networks, and thus throughout this book we make room for bilingual education options that can also function in isolated and rural contexts.

9. We borrow the image of the banyan tree from Makoni and Pennycook (2007). We thank R. Werner for his images.

10. Ghettoization refers to the separation and segregation of students.

11. We use the term "Latino" to refer to people in the U.S. of Latin American background. The U.S. government uses the term "Hispanic" to refer to the same people. However, we prefer the use of "Latino" because it is the term used by the people themselves, and because it links to a history of civil rights struggle which is important when considering bilingual education in the U.S.

12. We distinguish here between "state" and "nation". We use nation to refer to what Fishman (1972a: 3) refers to as nationalities: "sociocultural units that have developed beyond primarily local self-concepts, concerns, and integrative bonds that do not necessarily have their own autonomous territory." States, however, refer to political-territorial units, often without a single nationality.

13. For more on this, see chapter 8. See also, E. García, 2005; O. García 2006b; Hornberger, 2006.

14. For more on this, see chapter 9.

15. We are aware of the full import of the term "education," and of the many agents, including communities and parents, who are responsible for educating children, and even educating them bilingually. In this book, however, we focus on the school as the main agent in developing the bilingualism of children.

16. Bilingual education has been used by states to teach a global language such as English (see, for example, the case of Singapore [Pakir, 2003]), and to spread a national language (see, for example, the case of the Philippines [Gonzalez, 1998; Sibayan, 1994; Nical, Smolicz, and Secombe, 2004] and Botswana [Nyati-Ramahobo, 2006]). Bilingual education has also been used by nations trying to gain legitimacy, such as the case of the Basque Country (Cenoz, 1998).

17. Bilingual education, like monolingual education, also has the potential to restrict access. See, for example, García's foreword in Makoni and Pennycook (2007).

18. Cuneiform script is one of the earliest written forms, and was created by Sumerians around the fourth century BC.

19. For more on the concept of the imagined nation-state, see Anderson (1983).

20. Although this conceptualization of language is now popular, there have always been scholars who have seen bilingualism as a resource. This is the case of, for example, Fishman who proposed (1966) that languages were important resources for U.S. society.

21. In 1972 Einar Haugen proposed the term "language ecology" to refer to the interactions that exist within and between different ethnolinguistic communities. Mühlhäusler (1996) used the same concept, calling it "linguistic ecology" in his study of the Pacific region. But Fettes (2003) proposes that the language ecology of the twenty-first century must go beyond the study of linguistic interactions, referring instead to the balance that makes possible the co-existence of many languages for efficiency, equity, and integration, and responding to both local and global contexts.

22. A much more elaborated version of this table appears in García and Tsai, 2008.

Notes to Chapter 2

1. "Accountable talk" is classroom talk that is considered responsible for children's learning. It is based on the belief that children learn more from talking about what they are learning than just by listening or copying down what the teachers have said. It is a most important ingredient in workshop-type approaches to education, further considered in Chapters 13 and 14.

2. We use the term "emergent bilingual" to refer to students who are in the beginning stages of moving along a bilingual continuum.

3. These activities have been subsumed under the field of language policy and planning, to which we devote much attention in Chapter 4.

4. See note 18 below.

5. *De jure* is Latin for "by right" or "legally." In contrast, *de facto* means "in fact but not in law." Thus, there are education systems that operate in official languages legally constituted, and others that use languages that are official by the mere nature of their being used.

6. According to Nettle and Romaine (2000: 32), over 70 percent of the languages of the world are found in just 20 nation-states, most of them in Africa, Asia and Latin America – Papua New Guinea (860 languages), Indonesia (670), Nigeria (427), India (380), Cameroon (270), Australia (250), Mexico (240), the Democratic Republic of the Congo (former Zaïre) (210), Brazil (210), the Philippines (160), Malaysia (137), Tanzania (131), Vanuatu (105), Laos (92), Vietnam (86), Ivory Coast (73), Ghana (72), Solomon Islands (66), Benin (51), Togo (43).

7. Elizabeth Sumida, personal communication, December 18, 2006. For more information on APTN see www.aptn.ca/content/view/21/189/.

8. There is a difference between close-captioning and subtitling. Close-captioning can be viewed only if a certain device is turned on and is more sensitive to hearing-impaired viewers. It lets the viewers know when a phone is ringing, whether a speaker is talking with a British accent, or when music is playing. Captions are also placed in different areas of the screen to indicate who is speaking. Subtitles are just words placed at the bottom in the center all the time and they do not appear when the native language is used.

9. Video relay is a system a Deaf person can use to call a hearing person through an interpreting service.

10. The term was coined by Japanese economists in the *Harvard Business Review* in the late 1980s. It was introduced into English in an article by the British sociologist Roland Robertson (1995), and has since been developed by Zygmunt Bauman. For more on glocalization, see the website of the Glocal Forum and World Bank, http://topics.developmentgateway.org/glocalization/index.do, as well as http://searchcio.techtarget.com/sDefinition/0,,sid182_gci826478,00.html.

11. This was the dominant religion in much of Greater Iran, still practiced by some today in Iran and India.

12. Our gratitude to Elizabeth Huaman Sumida, who taught us so much about Indigenous ways.

13. See www.sign-lang.uni-hamburg.de/bibweb/ for different sign languages from around the world.

14. This view fits within the theoretical posturing of postmodernism. Postmodernism is a theory and way of thinking that rejects the received canon of knowledge, the linearism of Enlightenment notions of progress, and the hegemony of western thought. Instead, it favors situated knowledge and thought that is politically engaged so that claims to

"the truth" are untenable because they mask how power operates. Language and discourse are thus not mere reflections of the world. In fact, they are primary sites of how the social, economic, and political world is organized.

15. By "discourse" we mean ways of talking or writing within a context; thus, the context influences how language is constructed. Stubbs (1983: 1, my italics) defines discourse analysis as "the linguistic analysis of *naturally occurring connected speech or written discourse* [. . . it] is also concerned with *language use in social contexts*, and in particular with *interaction* or dialogue between speakers."

16. The Basque language is also known as *eusquera* or *euskera*. Recently the Basque term, Euskara, has gained popularity especially in the Basque Country. It is the term we use in this book.

17. *Ikastolas* were illegal Basque schools often run by parents in basements.

18. The name of the language, "Spanish," is often contested on the grounds that there are other Spanish languages. Castilian is then the desired designation. In this book we use the term "Spanish" because we refer to the language of all Spanish-speaking people throughout the world and especially in the Americas, and not just to those who speak Spanish in Castile and other regions of Spain. Castilian has also been used, especially in the United States, in opposition to Latin American Spanish to denigrate the Spanish of U.S. Latinos. In selecting the term "Spanish," we reconceptualize this traditional hierarchical relationship.

19. Derek Bickerton has proposed the Language Bioprogram Hypothesis (1984) which states that the transition from pidgin to creole was made possible by a genetically inscribed innate grammar.

20. Tamazight refers to the northern Berber languages spoken mainly in Morocco and Algeria.

21. The variety of English that many African Americans speak is referred to as African American Vernacular English (AAVE), Ebonics, African American English, African American Language, Black English and Black Vernacular English (BVE).

Notes to Chapter 3

1. To learn about descriptive reviews, an important and detailed way of observing and describing children by teachers, see Carini, 2000.

2. For an exhaustive review of the literature on bilingualism, see May, Hill, and Tiakiwai, 2005.

3. Haugen, a Norwegian, conducted his studies of bilinguals among Norwegian immigrants in the Midwest U.S. Weinreich, a Yiddish scholar, studied especially the Jewish immigrant community in the Northeast of the U.S.

4. For more on this, see Chapter 4.

5. For an excellent and comprehensive, up-to-date study of sociolinguistics as speakers' choice, see Coulmas, 2005.

6. Haugen (1953) and Weinreich (1953) were the pioneers in the study of language contact. Most of this discussion owes much to their work.

7. Markedness refers to a code that has social meaning because it has been changed to give special meaning. In contrast, the *unmarked choice* is just the normal meaning.

8. Pragmatics studies how people produce and comprehend sentences in a concrete speech situation, usually conversations, by paying attention to context.

9. By "second generation" we mean those born in the host country, in this case the United States. The third generation refers to their children.

10. The Council of Europe groups forty-eight nation-states at its seat in Strasbourg, France.
11. For an incisive discussion of this issue, see the *Modern Language Journal* 89(4) (2005), and especially Garcia 2005b.
12. See Peyton, Ranard, and McGinnis, 2001, for papers of the first conference. See also the web page of the Heritage Language Initiative at www.cal.org/heritage.
13. We are conscious that literacy abilities encompass much more than reading and writing, but we are limiting ourselves here to traditional skills. For more on literacy itself, see Chapter 14.
14. This is the term used by Nover and Andrews, 1999.
15. "Indigenous peoples" refers to descendants from the population which inhabited the place at the time of conquest or colonization. "Autochthonous minorities" refer to a group which is smaller in number than the rest of the population of a state with different ethnic, religious, or linguistic features. For a more focused discussion see, Skutnabb-Kangas, 2000: 487–92.
16. One of the first parental guides was by Saunders (1982), focusing on middle-class children with highly literate and professional parents at least one of whom is bilingual. In 1986, Harding and Riley published their handbook for parents, and a year later, Arnberg (1987) published the first guide for immigrant families. And there are guidebooks for raising Deaf children to be bilingual (Adams, 1997; Marscharck, 2003). Combining the wisdom of what to tell parents, as well as teachers, Baker's guide to bilingualism appeared in 1995; and King and Mackey (2007) give parental advice on how to raise a bilingual child. In 2006, Waho published a guide for Māori parents.
17. One example in France is www.enfantsbilingues.com, which is a forum for discussion linked to a book by Barbara Abdelilah-Bauer (2006).
18. According to these authors, in the first stage the girls operate with one lexical system and do not have a choice of lexical item for the same entity. When the girls move to multiword utterances, they appear to have two lexical systems. Finally, there is growing separation of the two languages, as they develop awareness that there are two languages and that a particular language is associated with certain individuals.
19. As will be explained in Chapter 6, the difference between early-immersion and late-immersion programs have to do with the age at which students are taught solely through the medium of a second language before the first language is used for instruction.
20. Dichotic listening refers to presenting two different stimuli simultaneously in each ear; tachistoscopic presentations refers to presenting visual stimuli to one hemisphere of the brain only.

Notes to Chapter 4

1. Diglossia is defined in the next section.
2. Some of this section and the one on language shift referring to Fishman's work are based on García, Peltz, and Schiffman, 2006.
3. Although Ferguson is credited for the term "diglossia," in 1885 a French specialist of Greek, Jean Psichari in his *Essais de grammaire néo-grecque* borrowed the term *diglossia* (or rather, *diglossie*) from an article in a popular review, *Acropolis*, to distinguish the classical standard of Greek, known as *Katharevusa*, from popular, spoken, modern Greek, known as *Demitokon*. Diglossia was given a clear definition by Hubert Pernot in 1897 in his *Grammaire grècque moderne* and made more widely known in a French

article published by Psichari in 1928 in the magazine *Mercure de France*. Ferguson acknowledges the Psichari source.

4. The change of letter to annotate these languages, from H/L (High/Low) to X, Y indicates the more neutral value of the languages vis-à-vis each other.

5. Some of this section is based on García (2007b).

6. We agree with Wright that these are examples of nationalist ideologies, even if there are historical reasons why these issues are important to those who pursue it.

7. *Mestizaje* is a Spanish word which refers to the fusion of cultures and races that is common in Latin America.

8. An important website for accessing language policies in different countries is Jacques Leclerc's (2001) http://www.tlfq.ulaval.ca/axl/index.shtml, available in French, and the Language Policy Research Unit (2007), www.language-policy.org.

9. According to Calvet (1987, trans. 1998) the term "language planning" was first used by Einar Haugen in 1959. It was Joshua A. Fishman who in 1970 added the phrase "language policy." Different scholars have used these two phrases differently. For Kaplan and Baldauf (1997: xi) language planning is the activity to promote systematic linguistic change which consists of beliefs, practices and laws, and regulations (which they call policy). For Kaplan and Baldauf planning is broader than policy, which is only about laws and regulations. This is also the definition given by Tollefson (1991: 16) of language policy as "language planning done by Governments." Likewise Ager (2001) considers language planning to be any unofficial influence exercised by individuals and communities; and reserves the term "language policy" for any official influence.

10. Shohamy (2006a) talks about Language Education Policy (LEP). Because of the meaning of this acronym in the United States as Limited English Proficient, we prefer LiEP.

11. These early planners consisted of Einar Haugen, Joshua A. Fishman, Joan Rubin, Björn Jernudd, Jyotirindra Das Gupta, among others.

12. Nahir (1984) identified eleven goals for language planning – language purification, language revival, language reform, language standardization, language spread, lexical modernization, terminological unification, stylistic simplification, interlingual communication, language maintenance, and auxiliary code standardization.

13. And yet these languages are mother tongues of only 17 percent of the Malay, Indian, and Chinese population. Malay is the mother tongue of 12 percent of Malays, Tamil of 5 percent of Indians, and Mandarin of 0.1 percent of the Chinese population (Rubdy, 2005: 57).

14. We have altered slightly Skutnabb-Kangas's hierarchy to reflect the Deaf community as a language minority. We also caution that in societies like Latin America, a white immigrant may have many more rights than Indigenous peoples, even if not codified into law.

15. The signatories of this declaration were the nine high-population development countries – Bangladesh, Brazil, China, Egypt, India, Indonesia, Mexico, Nigeria, and Pakistan.

Notes to Chapter 5

1. The term "transculturation" was coined by Cuban ethnologist Fernando Ortiz. In his *Contrapunteo Cubano del Tabaco y del Azúcar*, Ortiz wrote(1978: 96, my translation): "We understand that the word *transculturation* better expresses the different phases of the transitive process of one culture to another, because this consists of not only acquiring a different culture, which is really what the Anglo-American word *acculturation* means, but the process also necessarily implies the loss or lack of hold of a first culture, that which can be called a partial deculturation, and it also points to the consequent

creation of new cultural phenomena that could be called neoculturation. In effect, as the Malinowski school claims, in all embraces of cultures there is something of what happens in the genetic copulation of individuals: the child always has something of both progenitors, but it is always different from each of them."

2. For an insightful review of ethnicity, see May, 2001: 19–51.

3. Discourse (Foucault, 1972) refers here to the historically situated uses of language practices so as to formulate knowledge.

4. Cummins also posits that there is a first threshold of linguistic competence that must be passed in at least one language so that there are no detrimental cognitive effects.

Notes to Chapter 6

1. Baetens Beardsmore (1993b) has remarked that bilingual education scholarship has often ignored the long-standing efforts of European bilingual education, as well as bilingual education efforts in the developing world.

2. A typology is a classification of types of bilingual education programs that have common characteristics. The literature on bilingual education often uses the term "model" interchangeably with type. A model is broader and refers to the representation of a system that allows for its investigation. Because, as we will see, bilingual education programs are not tight systems, but vary in characteristics, we use in this text the term "type," although, as we will see, even a typology proves illusory at times.

3. Bakhtin (1981) opposes to the traditional concept of monoglossia, a heteroglossia; that is, the multiplicity of languages and rhetorical forms that make up linguistic interaction. The opposition between monoglossia and heteroglossia is considered in Del Valle, 2000 and 2006, and we refer to it in Chapter 1.

4. This is not always beneficial, as in, for example, many inclusive programs where the Deaf are not served or emergent bilinguals are ignored. In such cases, a separate specialized program may serve this population better.

5. This transculturalism is similar to that expressed by Oksaar, 1989 (see Chapter 5). For more on transculturation, see Chapter 5, note 1.

6. Baker (1996) distinguished between weak forms and strong forms of bilingual education to indicate those that aimed at bilingualism and those that used two languages in instruction but that led to monolingualism.

7. For examples of the interaction between language policy institutionalization and program development and practices as acted out every day, see especially Freeman, 2004; Hornberger and Johnson, 2007; Skilton-Sylvester, 2003; Stritikus, 2002.

8. Baker (1993) assigns the term "Weak Bilingual Education" to transitional types, reserving the term "Strong Bilingual Education" for all other types here considered. By "Weak Bilingual Education" Baker means educational programs that use two languages but whose goal is not bilingualism.

9. Elsewhere (1997a) I have called these programs "developmental maintenance programs" because it is difficult in practice to differentiate between the two. Baker also refers to these programs as developmental maintenance.

10. Like prestigious bilingual education, immersion bilingual education is also for language-majority children. The difference, however, is that in prestigious bilingual education the child's additional language is never used exclusively to teach, whereas immersion bilingual education insists on this exclusive use at some point.

11. The purpose of immersion programs is to have children become bilingual. Thus the educational programs in immersion education have been carefully designed, with a clear

role for the child's home language and parental opting-in. On the other hand, the purpose of submersion programs is to impose the language of power and monolingualism, with no use at any point of the child's language.

12. The term "partial immersion" is problematic because programs under this label sometimes cannot be differentiated from other programs. For example, Lambert, Genesee, Holobow, and McGilly (1984) refer to the Mohawk program in the Kahnawake school system near Montreal, where children are taught both in Mohawk and French, as partial immersion. We would refer to this program as developmental bilingual education. In general, Canada prefers to refer to bilingual education programs as immersion programs.

13. In reality, children are often from the same language group, although they exhibit differing degrees of bilingualism upon entering the school.

14. We are grateful to Debra Cole for insisting on this integrative position and reminding us that Deaf children are bilingual, like any other. We also thank her for providing the information that follows.

15. International Sign is a new form of communication where a unique system of signing is established based on what is deemed universal across signed languages around the world (see Rosenstock, 2004, for an excellent discussion of International Sign as a unique social phenomenon).

Notes to Chapter 7

1. This is a revised and expanded version of Baetens Beardsmore, 1997b.
2. An in-depth review of language policies in the United States and the European Union appears in Chapters 8 and 9 respectively. Chapters 10 and 11 address language policies in other contexts and the ensuing types of bilingual education programs promoted.
3. Because of the localized and internal nature of the operational factor, we do not include it in this integrative discussion which relates more to societal variables and wishes.

Notes to Chapter 8

1. For an important collection of official documents to complement this history, see especially Crawford, 1992. This chapter owes a great deal to the work of Jim Crawford which is cited throughout.
2. The difference between promotion-oriented rights and tolerance-oriented rights was first made by Heinz Kloss (1977).
3. Decreolization refers to the loss of creole features that is the result of contact with a powerful language, in this case, English.
4. Some of the early history of Spanish-language teaching is based on García, O. (1993).
5. A thorough timeline of these developments appears in Crawford, 2004: 124–5 and 147.
6. For a list of these schools, see Castellanos, 1983: 73.
7. No one has done more to help us understand the history of bilingual education policy and its situation today than Jim Crawford. His website http://ourworld.compuserve.com/homepages/JWCRAWFORD/ has essential information. For a simple chronology of the Official English movement, see Draper and Jiménez, 1992, as well as other documents in Crawford, 1992.

8. 7 S.J. Res. 72. 1981. 97th Cong., 1st Sess., 27 April. http://ourworld.compuserve.com/homepages/JWCRAWFORD/ela97.htm.

9. The reader is warned of the inadequacies of using census data, all of which is based on self-report.

10. In a paper co-authored with JoAnne Kleifgen and Lori Falchi (2008), García proposes the term "Emergent Bilingual" in lieu of English Language Learner, arguing that the denial of these children's emergent bilingualism as they acquire English is the cause of much misguided educational and assessment policy. Limited English Proficient is the term preferred by the U.S. government.

11. The U.S. Department of Education counts all 5- to 17-year-olds who claim to speak English less than very well as English Language Learners or Limited English Proficient Students for purposes of allocating funds through No Child Left Behind. We have adopted here a broader definition of bilingualism.

12. The reader is reminded that these figures differ from the way in which English Proficient and Limited English Proficient students are calculated by the US federal government. The United States Department of Education considers LEP anyone who speaks English less than very well, that is, those who speak English well, not well, and not at all. In our calculations, we use a broader definition of bilingualism and consider English Proficient Bilinguals anyone who claims to speak English very well and well.

13. One of the difficulties in establishing these numbers is that each state determines how to designate students as English Language Learners through a standardized test that may, or may not, be the same for other states.

14. The title of Stephen Krashen's insightful book on this subject is *Under Attack: The Case against Bilingual Education* (1996).

15. Structured Immersion programs in English Only are not considered in this book because, despite the name, they have nothing to do with Immersion bilingual education programs or Immersion Revitalization bilingual education programs. Baker (1993) considers them a form of submersion education.

16. The reader is warned that as in much of the discussion of types of bilingual education programs, there is much more variation than displayed in this table. For example, there are programs such as those used in the International High Schools in New York for immigrant newcomers, where the teachers do not use the child's first language explicitly in instruction because of the large language heterogeneity, but support the child's native language use and development in instruction. California has many Newcomer Centers for immigrant students who have had lack of access to schooling in their home country. There are also ESL self-contained classrooms which make considerable use of the child's native languages and where the children are likewise encouraged to make use of their native languages in their education (García has called these elsewhere "stretched ESL," see García and Celic, 2006).

17. Increasingly in the United States the preferred term for these programs, which mix children linguistically, is "Dual Language." Dropping the two-way label recognizes that often these classrooms include not two ethnolinguistic groups but one, most often Latinos with different linguistic profiles. It also acknowledges that in the greater heterogeneity of the twenty-first century, groups are not holistically constituted and cannot be referred to as one or two.

18. These included the ITBS, CTBS, Stanford 9, and Terra Nova.

19. English total reading refers to the subtest measuring academic problem-solving in English across the curriculum – math, science, social studies, literature.

20. NCE is the Normal Curve Equivalent. NCE are standard scores with a mean of 50 and a standard deviation of 21.06.

21. The reader is reminded that developmental bilingual programs in the United States that are one-way are often labeled "Dual Language." Regardless of what they're called, such programs are few.

22. Spanish Total Reading refers to the subtest measuring academic problem-solving in Spanish across the curriculum – math, science, social studies, literature. The nationally standardized tests used were Aprenda 2, and SABE.

23. The Panel's report was not released by the government. But the authors were given the copyright and the report was published by Lawrence Erlbaum.

24. We thank Leah Mason for this information.

Notes to Chapter 9

1. As we said before, Heinz Kloss (1977) first distinguished between tolerance-oriented language rights and promotion-oriented language rights. It is important to repeat that this promotion of bilingualism in the European Union does not in any way include the languages of immigrants.

2. Further information can be obtained by consulting the website www.coe.int/lang. See also the European Centre for Modern Languages, situated in Graz, Austria, which works under the auspices of the Council of Europe and concentrates on the teaching aspects of modern languages, at www.ecml.at.

3. Also known by its Italian name, Val d'Aosta.

4. In the case of Estonia, this reluctance does not imply that there is no provision for the Russian language minority. Mehisto and Asser (2007) illustrate the programs co-ordinated by the Estonian Language Immersion Centre to have Russian minority students achieve: 1. grade-appropriate levels of academic achievement in all subjects taught through Estonian and in those subjects taught through Russian; 2. age-appropriate functional proficiency in listening, speaking, reading, and writing in Estonian, as well as Russian; 3. an understanding and appreciation of the cultures associated with the Estonian and Russian languages.

5. Rom is also referred to as Roma. They are considered further in Chapter 11.

6. For more on the processes of scaffolding, see Chapters 13 and 14.

Notes to Chapter 10

1. These are referred to by Spolsky (2004) as "language management."

2. These side-by-side LiEPs have much to do with inability to introduce change to a very centralized authoritarian educational system in any other way.

3. For more in-depth information about the U.S. language policy, see Chapter 8 of this book.

4. U.S. education is highly decentralized. Although transitional bilingual education is the most prevalent type, there are also many other kinds of bilingual education programs.

5. As we said in Chapter 8, these programs are also known as developmental bilingual education programs.

6. The exception to this is if there are English-speaking children in the bilingual classroom, as in dual language bilingual programs. In reality, dual language programs often include only children of one ethnolinguistic group, for example, U.S. Latinos, although they have different linguistic profiles.

7. Increasingly ESL programs are "stretched" and support the use of the students' native language in initial instruction to make meaning. See for example, Echevarria, Vogt,

and Short (2004) and the SIOP model. For more on "Stretched ESL" see García and Celic (2006).

8. We describe bilingual education in Sub-Saharan Africa as being of the transitional kind, although, as this description shows, there are many differences among countries. For example, South Africa has adopted a multilingual education policy. Botswana spreads Setswana and English. Thus, many of the examples here described could be considered under Multiple Multilingual Education in the next chapter. We have chosen to describe them here only because although in practice the African context is, along with Asia, a complex multilingual situation, the ideology in education circles is still monoglossic because of the strong position of the colonial languages.

9. The Chinese refer to these as "dialects" because there is one written form. However, they are mutually unintelligible and could be considered languages in their own right.

10. This policy, however, is left to regional governments who do not always implement it, as is the case of the most remote rural areas such as Xinjiang and Yunnan.

11. Hugo Baetens Beardsmore contributed this section.

12. Aramean Turks are descendants of Aramaic-speaking groups who once ruled Mesopotamia. They adopted Christianity and suffered discrimination and persecution under the Ottoman Empire.

13. Native Americans are reclaiming their Indigenous names for themselves. The Navajo are also called Diné which is what they call themselves in their own language.

14. Although supplementary or complementary educational programs cannot be considered instances of bilingual education because they teach only in one language, they contribute to the development of bilingualism. In the United States, for example, the Chinese American community and the Korean American community have an extensive system of Chinese and Korean language schools, both after school and on weekends. These schools function both as ways to transmit the parents' language and culture to the children, as well as a way to instill Chinese and Korean values, although within a U.S. context. Protestant Evangelical churches, as well as Catholic ones in the United States, have started to exert an important influence in serving as means of providing bilingual education. Catering especially to immigrant communities, these churches use home languages to read and study the Bible, the prayers, and the hymnals. Children involved in these church services often attend classes in which speaking the heritage language and reading and writing it are important activities. This is the case of the many churches catering to Latinos in the United States.

15. Similar parental initiatives were at the origin of other bilingual schooling initiatives elsewhere, as with the founding of the European School model for state employees in Luxembourg in the 1950s (note supplied by Hugo Baetens Beardsmore).

16. This information was provided by Cristina Loftus, a past teacher at the school.

17. Table 6.5 provided the reader with a summative treatment of all the types of bilingual education and their characteristics. This figure only considers the four monoglossic types included in this chapter.

Notes to Chapter 11

1. Such multiple language practices have always been prevalent in Africa, Asia, and Latin America, and even in Europe in the past, as, for example, at the time of the Austro-Hungarian Empire before World War I. But they have come to the forefront today. More on this is explored in Chapters 2, 3, and 4 especially.

2. We insist in not grouping these under immersion programs because they serve a different purpose and have different characteristics, especially the fact that they serve children of language minority groups.

3. For more on bilingual/immersion education in Aotearoa/New Zealand, see especially the special issue of the *International Journal of Bilingual Education and Bilingualism* 8(5) (2005), edited by Stephen May. In November 2008 I had the pleasure of staying with Tainui Māori who taught me much about these programs. I am indebted to Cath Rau, Robyn Hata, and Iria Whiu, among many other Māori educators.

4. Whārekura o Rakaumanga is the largest Kura Kaupapa.

5. Aotearoa/New Zealand language education policy differentiates between immersion (high levels of immersion) and bilingual education (lower levels of immersion).

6. Pasifika migrants is the pan-ethnic term to refer to those coming from Samoa, Tonga, Cook Islands, Niue, Tokelau and Tuvalu, and other Pacific nations.

7. Meaning "Nest of Voices."

8. Kanerahtahere (Michelle Davis) contributed greatly to this paragraph.

9. Sámis are often called Lapps or Laplanders. Sámi or Saami is the way in which the group refers to themselves and it is the way in which we refer to them in this book.

10. We are grateful to Kamil Özerk for his observations on this section.

11. Because there is no letter "C" in Basque, this model is known as "D."

12. The Gaeltacht refers to any of the seven historically Irish-speaking regions in Ireland along the western seaboard. In the map below, the Gaeltacht regions are shaded:

13. The Roma are popularly known as Gypsies. Although this is not in itself an example of an expanding language and the Gandhi project is not an example of bilingual education per se, it is discussed here because the Roma have received very little educational attention.

14. According to Katz (2005), Lovári is a Romani dialect, but Béas is a language spoken by Roma of southern Hungary and is distinct from Romani.

15. We include the Gandhi project here although it is not, strictly, a bilingual education program. But the presence of languages of Roma in school is so exceptional that it can be considered an example of policy to develop and recover expanding minority languages.

16. As we explained in Chapter 6, this has to do with the fact that children in these programs are not simply from two language groups but represent the entire bilingual continuum. Sometimes they are from the same ethnolinguistic group although they are linguistically heterogeneous, with some being speakers of one language, others of the other, and yet others of both.

17. For how some of the European developmental bilingual education programs described in the previous section are evolving and expanding into trilingual education programs that develop a local language, a dominant language, and a global language, especially English, see Cenoz and Genesee, 1998.

18. The tribal languages used in instruction are: Saura, Kuvi, Kui, Kisham, Oram, Munda, Santali, Bonda, Koya, and Juang.

19. In the 1960s the People's Republic of China simplified its Chinese characters. Both Taiwan and Hong Kong are still using traditional Chinese characters.

20. For more on bilingualism in the Arab world, see the special issue of the *International Journal of Bilingual Education and Bilingualism* 9(1), 2006, edited by Mahmoud A. Al-Khatib.

21. Although this is not an example of developmental bilingual education, it is included here because of its significance.

22. Table 6.5 provided the reader with a summative treatment of all the types of bilingual education and its characteristics. This figure only considers the heteroglossic types included in this chapter.

Notes to Chapter 12

1. The children's metalinguistic awareness should automatically be raised by the presence of two languages in their school environment and may occur spontaneously. At the early stages of bilingual development, contrastive analysis may not be necessary.

2. We are aware that this practice is polemical. There is no evidence that this is useful at the early stages of bilingualism, although we think that it may encourage metalinguistic and multilingual awareness at the later stages of bilingualism.

3. Hugo Baetens Beardsmore provided most of the information for this case.

4. We remind the readers that this is not the sense in which the term "translanguaging" is being used in this book. For more on this, see Chapter 3. See also the section of this chapter titled Bilingual Practices: Translanguaging.

5. In practice, the children are allowed to use both language exams side by side, although they can only answer one or the other.

6. We thank Christine Anthonissen for sharing this slide with us. This lesson was observed at Stellenbosch University by García on April 18, 2006.

7. We take this opportunity to thank the administrators and the teachers of Jefferson School in New Rochelle, N.Y. for giving García access to this classroom during the fall of 2007, and to the children for sharing their translanguaging with García. I learned so much from all of you. This data is part of a large dataset that was collected through the support of a Teachers College Dean's grant. All names are pseudonyms.

8. Hugo Baetens Beardsmore provided this example.

9. We distinguish here between immersion as a type of bilingual education, and the way it is being used here as an approach to teaching.

Notes to Chapter 13

1. As Shohamy (2006a) reminds us, this policy could be explicit as when it is prescribed by states as described in some of the examples in Chapters 10 and 11, or implicit, as supported by mechanisms such as tests, the subject of Chapter 15.
2. Notice that the term immersion is associated in this book with three different concepts: 1. as a type of bilingual education (see Chapters 6 and 10); 2. as a model of bilingual teaching (see Chapter 12); 3. as a methodology (see Chapter 13). They often, although not always, correspond to each other.
3. Again, we warn readers that we refer to a method, not to a type of educational program.
4. Some of these elements and the language used in describing them have been directly taken from the observation instrument developed for WestEd by García, Walqui, and Hamburger (Walqui, García, and Hamburger, 2004). WestEd is a research and service educational agency that does educational development work in the US.
5. A reminder that we consider emergent bilinguals new learners of a second language who are still in the process of becoming bilingual.
6. For examples of these graphic organizers, see Brisk (2006).

Notes to Chapter 14

1. The reader might be wondering how this could be true in the context of many Indigenous languages. This has to do with our concept of pluriliteracy practices considered below.
2. For an interesting counter-example to this, see Kalmar (2001) who desmonstrates how Latino adult migrants developed their own hybrid writing system that uses the Spanish alphabet to capture English speech sounds.
3. We use "speak" in an inclusive way throughout much of this chapter, including, of course, sign languages.
4. Some of what follows under this section was originally conceived and proposed in García, Bartlett, and Kleifgen (2007).
5. We use "transact" here in the ways given to us by Rosenblatt (1978). For more on this, see page 351.
6. We are not making any value judgment about which is better or worse, since different groups and societies need various types of language and literacy skills for different purposes. We also caution the reader that the program types that appear here under flexible multiple approach often prefer and insist on separation biliterate approaches.
7. Some of what follows in this section was also originally proposed in García, Bartlett, and Kleifgen (2007).
8. These strategies refer to making meaning out of stories, paragraphs, or sentences.
9. Much of this information is drawn from our familiarity with the Reading and Writing Workshop model developed by Lucy Caulkins at Teachers College, Columbia University.

10. In side-by-side bilingual texts, one page contains one language, and the opposite page has the translation into another language. In hybrid bilingual texts, both languages are used, usually with one dominating.
11. This excerpt comes from a lesson taught by Christina Celic, November 9, 2005.

Notes to Chapter 15

1. This is the case of many immigrant and refugee students who have attended school systems that have been torn by war and extreme poverty.
2. No Child Left Behind calls these students LEP (Limited English Proficient) while most of the bilingual education literature in the United States calls them ELL (English Language Learners). We prefer to call them emergent bilinguals because as García, Kleifgen, and Falchi (2008) have said, it is the lack of understanding that these students will be bilingual that leads to much "miseducation" of these students in the U.S.
3. A reminder that NCLB calls these students "Limited English Proficient students."

Bibliography

Abdelilah-Bauer, B. (2006). *Le Défi des enfants bilingues: Grandir et vivre en parlant plusieurs langues*. La Découverte, Paris.

Abdulaziz-Mkilifi, M. (1978). "Triglossia and Swahili–English bilingualism in Tanzania." In J.A. Fishman (ed.). *Advances in the Study of Societal Multilingualism*. Mouton de Gruyter, The Hague, pp. 129–49.

Abedi, J. (2004). "The No Child Left Behind Act and English Language Learners: Assessment and Accountability Issues." *Educational Researcher* 33(1), 4–14.

Abedi, J., Hofstetter, C.H., and Lord, C. (2004). "Assessment Accommodations for English Language Learners: Implications for Policy-Based Empirical Research." *Review of Educational Research* 74, 1–28.

Abedi, J., and Lord, C. (2001). "The Language Factor in Mathematics Tests." *Applied Measurement in Education* 14(3), 219–34.

Abedi, J., Lord, C., and Plummer, J.R. (1997). *Final Report of Language Background as a Variable in NAEP Mathematics Performance* (CSE Tech. Rep. No. 429). National Center for Research on Evaluation, Standards, and Students, University of California, Los Angeles, CA.

Abu-Rabia, S. (1997). "Verbal and Working Memory Skills of Bilingual Hebrew-English Speaking Children." *International Journal of Psycholinguistics* 1, 25–40.

Abutalevi, J., Cappa, S.F., and Perani, D. (2001). "The Bilingual Brain as Revealed by Functional Neuroimagining." *Bilingualism: Language and Cognition* 4, 179–80.

Ada, A.F. (2003). *A Magical Encounter: Latino Children's Literature in the Classroom*, second edn. Allyn and Bacon, Boston, MA.

Adams, J. (1997). *You and Your Deaf Child: A Self-Help Guide for Parents of Deaf and Hard of Hearing Children*. Gallaudet University Press, Washington, DC.

Afolayan, A. (1976). "The Six-Year Primary Project in Nigeria." In Bamgbose, A. (ed.). *Mother Tongue Education: The West African Experience*. UNESCO Press, London, pp. 113–14.

Ager, D. (1999). *Identity, Insecurity and Image. France and Language*. Multilingual Matters, Clevedon.

—— (2001). *Motivation in Language Planning and Language Policy*. Multilingual Matters, Clevedon.

Aikio-Puoskari, U. (2005). *The Education of the Sámi in the Comprehensive Schooling of Three Nordic Countries: Norway, Finland and Sweden*, ed. Magne Ove Varsi.

Guovdageaidnu, The Resource Center for the Rights of Indigenous Peoples. Two separate publications, one in North Saami, one in English.

Åkermark, S., and Huss, L. (2006). "Ten Years of Minority Discourse in Sweden." In S. Åkermark, L. Huss, S. Oeter, and A. Walker (eds.). *International Obligations and National Debates: Minorities around the Baltic Sea.* The Åland Islands Peace Institute, Mariehamn, pp. 545–87.

Al-Khatib, M. ed. (2006). "Aspects of Bilingualism in the Arab World." *International Journal of Bilingual Education and Bilingualism* 9(1) (special issue).

Al-Thani, S.T.B.H. (2004). "Forum on Education for a New Era." Doha, March 15, 2004.

Albert, M., and Obler, L.K. (1978). *The Bilingual Brain: Neuropsychological and Neuro-linguistic Aspects of Bilingualism.* Academic Press, New York.

Alderson, J. (2000). *Assessing Reading.* Cambridge University Press, Cambridge.

Alderson, J., and Urquhart, A.H. (1984). *Reading in a Foreign Language.* Longman, London.

Alexander, N. (2002). "Linguistic Rights, Language Planning and Democracy in Post-Apartheid South Africa." In S.J. Baker (ed.). *Language Policy: Lessons from Global Models.* Monterey Institute of International Studies, Monterey, CA.

—— (2004). "Socio-political Factors in the Evolution of Language Policy in Post-Apartheid South Africa." Paper presented at the 30th International LAUD Symposium: Empowerment through Language, 12–19 April, 2004. Available at www.linse.uni-essen.de/linse/laud.

Alidou, H. (2004). "Medium of Instruction in Post-Colonial Africa." In J.W. Tollefson and A.B.M. Tsui (eds.). *Medium of Instruction Policies. Which Agenda? Whose Agenda?* Lawrence Erlbaum, Mahwah, NJ, pp. 195–214.

Amara, M. (2005). *A New Model of Bilingual Education, Summary.* The Center for Jewish-Arab Education in Israel, Hand in Hand, Jerusalem. Available at www.handinhand12.org/index.cfm?content.displayandpageID=110.

American Educational Research Association, American Psychological Association, and National Council on Measurement in Education (1985). *National Council on Measurement in Education Standards for Educational and Psychological Testing.* American Psychological Association, Washington, DC.

Amrein, A.L., and Berliner, D.C. (2002). "High-Stakes Testing, Uncertainty, and Student Learning." *Education Policy Analysis Archives,* 10(18), available at http://epaa.asu.edu/epaa/v10n18/.

Anderson, B. (1983). *Imagined Communities: Reflections on the Origin and Spread of Nationalism.* Rev. edn. Verso, London. Second edn. 1991.

Anderson, N.E., Jenkins, F.F., and Miller, K.E. (1996). *NAEP Inclusion Criteria and Testing Accommodations: Findings from the NAEP 1995 Field Test in Mathematics.* Educational Testing Service, Princeton, NJ.

Ann, S. (1998). "Korean Language Efficiency Improvement (Meaning Density) and the Necessity of the Traditional CI: Hangul Hybrid Writing Usage." *Ohak Yonku/Language Research* 34(3), 509–20.

Annamalai, E. (2004). "Medium of power: The question of English in education in India." In J.W. Tollefson and A.B.M. Tsui (eds.). *Medium of Instruction Policies. Which Agenda? Whose Agenda?* Lawrence Erlbaum, Mahwah, NJ, pp. 177–94.

—— (2005). "New Approach to Language Policy." In F. Martí, P. Orega, I. Idiazabal, A. Barreña, P. Juaristi, C. Junyent, B. Uranga, and E. Amorrortu (eds.). *Words and Worlds. World Languages Review.* Multilingual Matters, Clevedon, pp. 111–17.

Anzaldúa, G. (1987). *Borderlands / La Frontera: The New Mestiza.* Aunt Lute Books, San Francisco, CA.

Appadurai, A. (1996). *Modernity at Large: Cultural Dimensions of Globalization.* University of Minnesota Press, Minneapolis, MN.

Apple, M. (1982). *Education and Power*. Routledge, London.

Arnberg, L. (1987). *Raising Children Bilingually: The Pre-School Years*. Multilingual Matters, Clevedon.

Aronin, L., and Ó Laoire, M. (2003). "Exploring Multilingualism in Cultural Contexts: Towards a Notion of Multilinguality." In C. Hoffman and J. Ytsma (eds.). *Trilingualism in Family, School and Community*. Multilingual Matters, Clevedon, pp. 11–29.

Arthur, J. (1996). "Code Switching and Collusion: Classroom Interaction in Botswana Primary Schools." *Linguistics and Education* 8(1), 17–33.

Artigal, J. (1993). "Catalan and Basque immersion programmes." In H. Baetens Beardsmore (ed.). *European Models of Bilingual Education*. Multilingual Matters, Clevedon, pp. 30–53.

—— (1997). "The Catalan Immersion Program." In R.K. Johnson and M. Swain (eds.). *Immersion Educational Perspectives*. Cambridge University Press, Cambridge, pp. 133–50.

Arzamendi, J., and Genesee, F. (1997). "Reflections on Immersion Education in the Basque Country." In R.K. Johnson and M. Swain (eds.). *Immersion Educational Perspectives*. Cambridge University Press, Cambridge, pp. 151–66.

Assembly of First Nations (1988). "Tradition and Education: Towards a Vision of Our Future." *National Review of First Nations Education*. Vols. 1, 2, and 3, Assembly of First Nations, Ottawa.

Assessorat à l'Éducation et à la Culture (2007). *Profil de la politique linguistique éducative: Vallée d'Aoste – Rapport Régional*, Aoste (Report).

Assuied, R., and Ragot, A.-M. (2004). *Penser et apprendre en deux languages*. Aoste, Italy, Institut régional de recherche éducative de la Vallée d'Aoste.

Au, K. (2006). *Multicultural Issues and Literacy Achievement*. Lawrence Erlbaum, Mahwah, NJ.

Auer, P. (1995). "The Pragmatics of Code-Switching: A Sequential Approach." In L. Milroy and P. Muysken (eds.). *One Speaker, Two Languages: Cross-disciplinary Perspectives on Code-Switching*. Cambridge University Press, Cambridge.

August, D., Calderon, M., Carlo, M. (2001). *The Transfer of Skills from Spanish to English: A Study of Young Learners*. NABE News (March/April 2001) summarized from a study conducted jointly in 1998–2001 by the Center for Applied Linguistics, Harvard University, and Johns Hopkins University.

August, D., and Hakuta, K. (eds.) (1997). *Improving Schooling for Language-Minority Children. A Research Agenda*. National Academy Press, Washington, DC.

—— (eds.) (1998). *Educating Language-Minority Children*. National Academy Press, Washington, DC.

August, D., and Shanahan, T. (eds.) (2006). *Developing Literacy in Second-Language Learners. Report of the National Literacy Panel on Language-Minority Children and Youth*. Lawrence Erlbaum, Mahwah, NJ.

Aymond, P., Cavalli, M., Coste, D., Dematteis, F., Porté, G., Rosina, M., and Sciacqua, C. (2006). *Langues, apprentissages, identités: Actualiser dans la continuité l'éducation bi-/plurilingue*. IRRE-VDA, Aoste.

Baetens Beardsmore, H. (1982). *Bilingualism: Basic Principles*. Multilingual Matters, Clevedon. Second edn. 1986.

—— (1992). "Bilingual Education." In J. Lynch, C. Modgil, and S. Modgil (eds.). *Cultural Diversity and the Schools*, vol. 1. Falmer Press, London, pp. 273–84.

—— (1993a). "Belgium." In U. Ammon, K. Mattheier, and P. Nelde (eds.). *Mehrsprachigkeitskonzepte in den Schulen Europas/Multilingual Concepts in the Schools of Europe, Sociolinguistica*, vol. 7. Max Niemeyer Verlag, Tübingen, pp. 12–21.

—— (1993b). "European Models of Bilingual Education: Practice, Theory and Development." In G.M. Jones and A.C. Ozog (eds.). *Bilingualism and National Development*. Multilingual Matters, Clevedon, pp. 103–21.

—— (ed.) (1993c). *European Models of Bilingual Education*. Multilingual Matters, Clevedon.

—— (1993d). "Report to the Ministry of Education of Brunei Darussalam on the Visit to Schools and Discussions with Ministry Officials." Unpublished document.

—— (1994). "Language Shift and Cultural Implications in Singapore." In S. Gopinathan, Ho Wah Kam, A. Pakir, and V. Saravanan (eds.). *Language, Education and Society in Singapore: Issues and Trends*. Times Academic Press, Singapore, pp. 47–64.

—— (1995). "The European School Experience in Multilingual Education." In T. Skutnabb-Kangas (ed.). *Multilingualism for All*. Swets and Zeitlinger, Lisse, pp. 21–68.

—— (1996). "Reconciling Content Acquisition and Language Acquisition in Bilingual Classrooms." *Journal of Multilingual and Multicultural Development* 17, 114–22.

—— (1997a). "Bilingual Education in Secondary Schools: Learning and Teaching Non-Language Subjects through a Foreign Language." *Language Teaching* October 1997, 235–9.

—— (1997b). *Manipulating the Variables in Bilingual Education (or: You Can't Beat Them All)*, Report on the Conference on European Networks in Bilingual Education, Alkmaar, Europees Platform voor het Nederlandse Onderwijs, pp. 8–16.

—— (1998). "Language Shift and Cultural Implications in Singapore." In S. Gopinathan, Ho Wah Kam, A. Pakir, and V. Saravanan (eds.). *Language, Education and Society in Singapore: Issues and Trends*, second edn. Times Academic Press, Singapore, pp. 85–98.

—— (1999). "La consolidation des expériences en éducation plurilingue / Consolidating Experience In Plurilingual Education." In D. Marsh and B. Marsland (eds.). *CLIL Initiatives for the Millennium*. University of Jyväskylä, Jyväskylä, pp. 24–30.

—— (2002). "The Significance of CLIL/EMILE." In D. Marsh (ed.). *CLIL/EMILE – The European Dimension. Actions, Trends and Foresight Potential* (Public Services Contract DG EAC 36 – 1 Lot 3). University of Jyväskylä, Jyväskylä, pp. 20–6.

—— (2003). "Who's Afraid of Bilingualism?" In J. Dewaele, A. Housen, and Li Wei (eds.). *Bilingualism: Beyond Basic Principles*. Multilingual Matters, Clevedon, pp. 10–27.

Baetens Beardsmore, H., and Anselmi, G. (1991). "Code-Switching in a Heterogeneous, Unstable, Multilingual Speech Community." In *Papers for the Symposium on Code-Switching in Bilingual Studies; Theory, Significance and Perspectives*, vol. ii. European Science Foundation, Strasbourg, pp. 405–36.

Baetens Beardsmore, H., and Lebrun, N. (1991). "Trilingual Education in the Grand Duchy of Luxembourg." In O. García (ed.). *Bilingual Education. Focusschrift in Honor of Joshua A. Fishman on the Occasion of his 65th birthday*, vol. 1. John Benjamins, Strasbourg, pp. 107–22.

Baetens Beardsmore, H., and Swain, M. (1985). "Designing Bilingual Education: Aspects of Immersion and 'European School' Models." *Journal of Multilingual and Multicultural Development* 6(1), 1–15.

Baker, C. (1988). *Key Issues in Bilingualism and Bilingual Education*. Multilingual Matters, Clevedon.

—— (1995). *A Parents' and Teachers' Guide to Bilingualism*. Multilingual Matters, Clevedon.

—— (1999). "Sign Language and the Deaf Community." In J. Fishman (ed.). *Handbook of Language and Ethnic Identity*. Oxford University Press, Oxford and New York, pp. 122–39.

—— (2001). *Foundations of Bilingual Education and Bilingualism*. Third edn. Multilingual Matters, Clevedon. First edn. 1993; second edn. 1996; fourth edn. 2006.

—— (2006). "Changing Perspectives in Bilingual and Multilingual Education." Paper presented at the Conference on Regional and Minority Languages in Education Systems, Brussels, April 27–28, 2006. Also available online at: http://64.233.161.104/search?q=cache:2cU7LNljxkkJ:ec.europa.eu/education/policies/lang/conferenceprog.pdf+Conference+on+Regional+and+Minority+Languages+in+Education+Systems,+Brussels,+Bakerandhl=enandgl=usandct=clnkandcd=1.

Baker, C., and Hornberger, N. (eds.) (2001). *An Introductory Reader to the Writings of Jim Cummins*. Multilingual Matters, Clevedon.

Baker, C., and Prys Jones, S. (1998). *Encyclopedia of Bilingualism and Bilingual Education*. Multilingual Matters, Clevedon.

Baker, K.A., and de Kanter, A.A. (1981). *Effectiveness of Bilingual Education: A Review of the Literature*. U.S. Department of Education, Washington, DC.

Baker, L., and Brown, A.L. (1984). "Metacognitive Skills and Reading." In P.D. Pearson (ed.). *Handbook of Reading Research*. Longman, New York.

Bakhtin, M. (1981). *Dialogic Imagination: Four Essays*. University of Texas Press, Austin, TX.

Bamgbose, A. (1991). *Language and the Nation: The Language Question in Sub-Saharan Africa*. Edinburgh University Press for the International African Institute, Edinburgh.

—— (1994). "Pride and Prejudice in Multilingualism." In R. Fardon and G. Furniss (eds.). *African Languages, Development and the State*. Routledge, London, pp. 32–43.

—— (2000). *Language and Exclusion: The Consequences of Language Policies in Africa*. Lit Verlag, Munich.

Banfi, C., and Day, R. (2005). "The Evolution of Bilingual Schools in Argentina." In A. de Mejía (ed.). *Bilingual Education in South America*. Multilingual Matters, Clevedon, pp. 65–78.

Barrera, R. (1983). "Bilingual Reading in the Primary Grades: Some Questions about Questionable Views and Practices." In T.H. Escobedo (ed.). *Early Childhood Bilingual Education: A Hispanic Perspective*. Teachers College Press, New York, pp. 164–83.

Barth, F. (1969). *Ethnic Groups and Boundaries: The Social Organization of Culture Difference*. Little, Brown and Co., Boston, MA.

Batibo, H.M. (2005). *Language Decline and Death in Africa. Causes, Consequences and Challenges*. Multilingual Matters, Clevedon.

Baugh, J. (1997). "Research on Race and Social Class in Language Acquisition and Use." In N. Hornberger and D. Corson (eds.). *Research Methods in Language and Education*. Kluwer Academic, Boston, MA, pp. 111–21.

Baumann, J., Jones, L., and Seifert-Kessell, N. (1993). "Using Think-Alouds to Enhance Children's Comprehension Monitoring Abilities." *The Reading Teacher* 47(3), 184–93.

Baynton, D. (2006). "The Undesirability of Admitting Deaf-Mutes: US Immigration Policy and Deaf Immigrants 1882–1924." *Sign Language Studies* 6(4), 391–415.

Beacco, J.C. (2005). *Languages and Language Repertoires: Plurilingualism as a Way of Life in Europe*. Council of Europe, Strasbourg.

Beacco, J.C., and Byram, M. (2004). *Guide for the Development of Language Education Policies in Europe: From Linguistic Diversity to Plurilingual Education*. Council of Europe, Language Policy Division, Strasbourg. Available at www.coe.int/t/dg4/linguistic/default_en.asp.

Bejarano, C.L. (2005). *¿Qué onda? Urban Youth Cultures and Border Identity*. University of Arizona Press, Tuscon, AZ.

Ben-Zeev, S. (1977). "The Influence of Bilingualism on Cognitive Strategy and Cognitive Development." *Child Development* 48, 1009–18.

Bennett, W. (1985). "The Bilingual Education Act: A Failed Path." In J. Crawford (ed.) *Language Loyalties. A Source Book on the Official English Controversy*. University of Chicago Press, Chicago, IL, pp. 358–63.

Benson, C. (2000). "The Primary Bilingual Education Experiment in Mozambique, 1993 to 1997." *International Journal of Bilingual Education and Bilingualism* 3(3), 149–66.

Bentahila, A. (1983). *Language Attitudes among Arabic–French Bilinguals in Morocco*. Multilingual Matters, Clevedon.

Bentolila, A., and Gani, L. (1981). "Langues et problèmes d'éducation en Haiti." *Langages* 61, 117–27.

Benton, R.A. (2007). "*Mauri* or Mirage? The Status of the Māori Language in Aotearoa New Zealand in the Third Millennium." In A.B.M. Tsui and J.W. Tollefson (eds.). *Language Policy, Culture, and Identity in Asian Contexts*. Lawrence Erlbaum, Mahwah, NJ, pp. 163–84.

Berg, G. (1993). *Mir Wëlle Bleiwe, Wat Mir Sin: Soziolinguistische und sprachtypologische Betrachtungen zur Luxemburgischen Mehrsprachigkeit*. Niemeyer, Tübingen.

Bernardo, A.B.I. (1999). "Overcoming Obstacles to Understanding and Solving Word Problems in Mathematics." *Educational Psychology* 19(2), 149–63.

—— (2004). "McKinley's Questionable Request: Over One Hundred Years of English in Philippine Education." *World Englishes* 23(1), 17–31.

Bernhardt, E., and Kamil, M. (1995). "Interpreting Relationships between L1 and L2 Reading: Consolidating the Linguistic Threshold and the Linguistic Interdependence Hypotheses." *Applied Linguistics* 16, 15–34.

Beykont, Z. (ed.) (2002). *The Power of Culture. Teaching across Language Difference*. Harvard Education Publishing Group, Cambridge, MA.

Beynon, J., and Toohey, K. (1991). "Heritage Language Education in British Columbia: Policy and Programmes." *Canadian Modern Language Review* 47(4), 606–16.

Bhabha, H. (1990). "The Third Space: Interview with Homi Bhabha." In J. Rutherford (ed.). *Identity: Community, Culture, Difference*. Lawrence and Wishart, London, pp. 207–21.

—— (1994). *The Location of Culture*. Routledge, London.

Bialystok, E. (1987). "Influences of Bilingualism on Metalinguistic Development." *Second Language Research* 3(2), 154–66.

—— (2001). *Bilingualism in Development: Language, Literacy, and Cognition*. Cambridge University Press, New York.

—— (2004). "Language and Literacy Development." In T.K. Bhatia and W.C. Ritchie (eds.). *The Handbook of Bilingualism*. Blackwell, Malden, MA, pp. 577–601.

Bickerton, D. (1984). "The Language Bioprogram Hypothesis." *Behavioral and Brain Sciences* 7(2), 173–222.

Birch, B.M. (2002). *English L2 Reading. Getting to the Bottom*. Lawrence Erlbaum, Mahwah, NJ.

Birdsong, D. (1999). *Second Language Acquisition and the Critical Period Hypothesis*. Lawrence Erlbaum, Mahwah, NJ.

Blachford, D.R. (1999). "Language Planning and Bilingual Education for Linguistic Minorities in China: A Case Study of the Policy Formulation and Implementation Process." PhD thesis, University of Toronto.

Black, T., Marshall, P., and Irwin, K. (2003). *Māori language nests in New Zealand: Te Kohanga Reo, 1982–2003*. Paper presented at the United Nations Permanent Form on Indigenous Issues conference, May 20, 2003. Also available online at http://www.kohanga.ac.nz.

Blom, J.P., and Gumperz, J.J. (1972). "Social Meaning in Linguistic Structures: Code-switching in Norway." In J.J. Gumperz and D. Hymes (eds.). *Directions in Sociolinguistics*. Holt, Rinehart and Winston, New York, pp. 407–34.

Blommaert, J. (1999). "The Debate Is Open." In J. Blommaert (ed.). *Language Ideological Debates*. Mouton de Gruyter, Berlin, pp. 1–38.

Bloom, J. (2008). "Pedagogical Code-Switching: A Case Study of Three Bilingual Content Teachers' Language Practices." Unpublished EdD dissertation, Teachers College, Columbia University.

Bloom, L., and Tinker, E. (2002). *The Intentionality Model and Language Acquisition. Engagement, Effort and the Essential Tension in Development*. Blackwell, Oxford.

Bloomfield, L. (1933). *Language*. Holt and Company, New York.

Blondin, C. (2003). "L'immersion linguistique dans l'enseignement fondamental en communauté française de Belgique: L'état de la question." *Journal de l'immersion* 25(2), 19–31.

Bossers, B. (1991). "On Thresholds, Ceilings and Short-Circuits: The Relation between L1 Reading, L2 Reading and L2 Knowledge." *AILA Review* 8, 45–60.

Bosso, E., and Kuntze, M. (1994). "Literacy for Deaf Students: Freire and Macedo's Model." In B. Snider (ed.). *Post-Milan ASL and English Literacy: Issues, Trends and Research.* Gallaudet University College for Continuing Education, Washington, DC, pp. 37–44.

Boswell, T. (2000). "Demographic Changes in Florida and Their Importance for Effective Educational Policies and Practices." In A. Roca (ed.). *Research on Spanish in the United States: Linguistic Issues and Challenges.* Cascadilla Press, Somerville, MA, pp. 406–31.

Boulet, J. (2006). "Bad in Any Language. HR 4766 Needs to Be Blocked." September 27, 2006. Available at http://article.nationalreview.com/?q=ZjBkYzBjM2RmMGMzOTI3Z DgxZDRhMGYxZGUyMWI3ZTk=.

Bourdieu, P. (1991). *Language and Symbolic Power.* Harvard University Press, Cambridge, MA.

Boysson-Bardies, B. (1999). *How Language Comes to Children: From Birth to Two Years.* MIT Press, Cambridge, MA.

Branaman, L., and Rhodes, N. (1997). *Foreign Language Instruction in the United States: A National Survey of Elementary and Secondary Schools.* Center for Applied Linguistics, Washington, DC.

Brandt, E.A., and Ayoungman, V. (1989). "A Practical Guide to Language Renewal." *Canadian Journal of Native Education* 16(2), 42–77.

Brass, P. (1994). *The Politics of India since Independence. The New Cambridge History of India*, Part IV, vol. 1. Second edn. Cambridge University Press, Cambridge, pp. 157–91.

Braunmüller, K. (2002). "Semicommunication and Accommodation: Observations from the Linguistic Situation in Scandinavia." *International Journal of Applied Linguistics* 12, 1–23.

—— (2006). "On the Relevance of Receptive Multilingualism in a Globalised World: Theory, History and Evidence from Today's Scandinavia." Paper read at the First Conference on Language Contact in Times of Globalization, September 28, 2006. University of Groningen.

Brejle, W. (1999). Global Perspectives on the Education of the Deaf in Selected Countries. Butte Publications, Inc., Hillsboro, Oregon.

Breton, A. (1978). *Le Bilinguisme: Une approche économique.* C.D. Howe Institute, Montreal.

Brinton, D., Snow, M.A., and Wesche, M. (1989). *Content-Based Second Language Instruction.* Newbury House, New York.

Brisbois, J.E. (1995). "Connections between First- and Second-Language Reading." *Journal of Reading Behavior* 27, 565–84.

Brisk, M.E. (2006). *Bilingual Education. From Compensatory to Quality Schooling*, second edn. Lawrence Erlbaum, Mahwah, NJ.

Brisk, M.E., and Harrington, M. (2000). *Literacy and Bilingualism.* Lawrence Erlbaum Associates, Mahwah, NJ.

Brock-Utne, B. (2000). *Whose Education for All? The Recolonization of the African Mind.* Falmer Press, London.

Bruck, M. (1984). "The Suitability of Immersion Education for Children with Special Needs." In C. Rivera (ed.). *Communicative Competence Approaches to Language Proficiency Assessment: Research and Application.* Multilingual Matters, Clevedon, pp. 123–31.

Bruner, J.S., and Sherwood, V. (1975). *Peekaboo and the Learning of Rule Structures.* In J.S. Bruner, A. Jolly, and K. Sylva (eds.). *Play: Its Role in Development and Evolution.* Penguin Books, Harmondsworth, pp. 277–85.

Brutt-Griffler, J. (2002). *World English: A Study of Its Development.* Multilingual Matters, Clevedon.

Buehl, D. (2001). *Classroom Strategies for Interactive Learning.* Second edn. Wisconsin State Reading Association, Madison, WI.

Bull, B.L., Fruehling, R.T., and Chattergy, V. (1992). *The Ethics of Multicultural and Bilingual Education*. Teachers College Press, New York.

Bunyi, G.W. (1997). "Language in Education in Kenyan Schools." In J. Cummins and D. Corson (eds.). *Encyclopedia of Language and Education*, vol. 5: *Bilingual Education*. Kluwer, Dordrecht, pp. 33–43.

—— (2005). "Language Classroom Practices in Kenya." In A.M.Y. Lin and P.W. Martin (eds.). *Decolonisation, Globalisation. Language-in-Education Policy and Practice*. Multilingual Matters, Clevedon, pp. 131–52.

Byram, M. (1986). *Minority Education and Ethnic Survival. Case Study of a German School in Denmark*. Multilingual Matters, Clevedon.

Byram, M., and Leman, J. (eds.) (1990). *Bicultural and Trilingual Education. The Foyer Model in Brussels*. Multilingual Matters, Clevedon.

California Department of Education (2005). *Language Census, 2004–05 (R30-LC)*. Educational Demographics Office, Sacramento, CA.

—— (2006a). *Number of English Learner Students Enrolled in Specific Instructional Settings*. Retrieved January 29, 2007 from the California Department of Education's website at http://dq.cde.ca.gov/dataquest/ElP2_State.asp?RptYear=2005–06andRptType=ELPart2_1b.

—— (2006b). *English Learners, Instructional Settings and Services*. Retrieved January 29, 2007 from the California Department of Education's website at www.dq.cde.ca.gov/dataquest/ELP2_State.asp?RptYear=2004–05andRPTType=ELPart2_1a.

Calkins, L. (1994). *The Art of Teaching Writing*, second edn. Heinemann, Portsmouth, NH.

Calvet, L.J. (1987). *La guerre des langues et les politiques linguistiques*. Payot, Paris. Translated by M. Petheram (1998). *Language Wars and Linguistic Politics*. Oxford University Press, Oxford.

—— (1993). *La Sociolinguistique*. Presses universitaires de France, Paris.

Camilleri, A. (1995). *Bilingualism in Education: The Maltese Experience*. Julius Groos Verlag, Heidelberg.

—— (1996). "Language Values and Identities: Code Switching in Secondary Classrooms in Malta." *Linguistics and Education* 8(1), 85–103.

Canagarajah, S. (1999). *Resisting Linguistic Imperialism in English Teaching*. Oxford University Press, Oxford.

—— (2005a). "Accommodating Tensions in Language-in-Education Policies: An Afterword." In A.M.Y. Lin and P. Martin (eds.). *Decolonisation, Globalisation. Language-in-Education Policy and Practice*. Multilingual Matters, Clevedon. UK, pp. 194–202.

—— (2005b). *Reclaiming the Local in Language Policy and Practice*. Lawrence Erlbaum, Mahwah, NJ.

Cancela, G. (1975). "Bilingual Education in Dade County." In L. Ortega (ed.). *Introduction to Bilingual Education*. Anaya-Las Americas, New York, pp. 47–65.

Candelier, M. (ed.) (2003). *Evlang – L'éveil aux langues à l'école primaire*. De Boeck-Duculot, Brussels.

Cappellini, M. (2005). *Balancing Reading and Language Learning. A Resource for Teaching English Language Learners, K-5*. Stenhouse Publishers, Portland, ME.

Capps, R., Fix, M., Murray, J., Ost, J., Passel, J.S., and Herwantoro, S. (2005). *The New Demography of America's Schools: Immigration and the No Child Left Behind Act*. Urban Institute, Washington, DC.

Carder, M. (1991). "The Role and Development of ESL Programmes in International Schools." In P.L. Jonietz and D. Harris (eds.). *The World Yearbook of Education*. Kogan Page, London, pp. 108–24.

—— (2007). *Bilingualism in International Schools. A Model for Enriching Language Education*. Multilingual Matters, Clevedon.

Carini, P. (1986). "Building from Children's Strengths." *Journal of Education* 168, 19–20.

—— (2000). "Prospect's Descriptive Processes." In M. Himley and P. Carini (eds.). *From Another Angle: Children's Strengths and School Standards. The Prospect Center's Descriptive Review of the Child.* Teachers College Press, New York, pp. 8–20.

Carlo, M.S., August, D., McLaughlin, B., Snow, C.E., Dressler, C., Lippman, D.N., Lively, T., and White, C.E. (2004). "Closing the Gap: Addressing the Vocabulary Needs of English-Language Learners in Bilingual and Mainstream Classrooms." *Reading Research Quarterly* 39, 188–215.

Carreira, M. (2000). "Validating and Promoting Spanish in the US. Lessons from Linguistic Science." *Bilingual Research Journal* 24: 333–52.

Carrell, P.L. (1987). "Content and Formal Schemata in ESL Reading." *TESOL Quarterly* 21: 461–81.

Carson, J.E., Carrell, P.L., Silberstein, S., Kroll, B., and Kuehn, P.A. (1990). "Reading–Writing Relationships in First and Second Language." *TESOL Quarterly* 24(2), 245–66.

Casanova, U. (1991). "Bilingual Education: Politics or Pedagogy?" In O. García (ed.). *Bilingual Education.* John Benjamins, Amsterdam, pp. 167–80.

Casserly, M. (2006). *Beating the Odds: A City-by-City Analysis of Student Performance and Achievement Gaps on State Assessments, 2004–2005 School Year.* Council of Great City Schools, Washington, DC. Available at www.cgcs.org/publications/BeatingtheOdds6_profiles.aspx.

Castellanos, D. (1983). *The Best of Two Worlds. Bilingual-Bicultural Education in the U.S.* New Jersey State Department of Education, Trenton, NJ.

Castles, S. (2000). *Ethnicity and Globalization: From Migrant Worker to Transnational Citizen.* Sage, London.

Cazabón, M., Lambert, W., and Hall, G. (1999). *Two-Way Bilingual Education: A Report on the Amigos Program.* Center for Applied Linguistics, Washington, DC.

Cazden, C.B. (1972). *Child Language and Education.* Holt, Rinehart and Winston, New York.

—— (1988). *Classroom Discourse: The Language of Teaching and Learning.* Heinemann, Portsmouth, NH.

Cazden, C.B., and Snow, C.E. (eds.) (1990). *English Plus: Issues in Bilingual Education. The Annals of the American Academy of Political and Social Science* 508. Sage, London.

Cenoz, J. (1998). "Multilingual Education in the Basque Country." In J. Cenoz and F. Genesee (eds.). *Beyond Bilingualism. Multilingualism and Multilingual Education.* Multilingual Matters, Clevedon, pp. 175–91.

Cenoz, J., and Genesee, F. (1998). *Beyond Bilingualism. Multilingualism and Multilingual Education.* Multilingual Matters, Clevedon.

Cenoz, J., Hufeisen, B., and Jessner, U. (2001). *Cross-Linguistic Influence in Third Language Acquisition: Psycholinguistic Perspectives.* Multilingual Matters, Clevedon.

Center for Applied Linguistics (1977). "Bilingual Education: Current Perspectives." *Center for Applied Linguistics* 5, 1–57.

—— (2006). *Directory of Two-Way Bilingual Immersion Programs in the U.S.* Available at www.cal.org/twi/directory.

Chamot, A.U., and O'Malley, J.M. (1994). *The CALLA Handbook. Implementing the Cognitive Academic Language Learning Approach.* Addison-Wesley Publishing Company, Reading, MA.

Chang, J. (1998). "Language and Literacy in Chinese American Communities." In B. Pérez (ed.). *Sociocultural Contexts of Language and Literacy.* Lawrence Erlbaum Associates, Mahwah, NJ, pp. 163–88.

Chew, P.G.-L. (2007). "Remaking Singapore: Language, Culture, and Identity in a Globalized World." In A.B.M. Tsui and J.W. Tollefson (eds.). *Language Policy, Culture, and Identity in Asian Contexts.* Lawrence Erlbaum, Mahwah, NJ, pp. 73–94.

Christ, I. (1996). "Bilingual Teaching and Learning in Germany." In G. Fruhauf, D. Coyle, and I. Christ (eds.). *Teaching Content in a Foreign Language*, Stichting Europees Platform voor het Nederlandse Onderwijs, Alkmaar, pp. 81–100.

Christensen, K.M., and Delgado, G.L. (eds.) (2000). *Deaf Plus: A Multicultural Perspective.* Dawn Sign Press, San Diego, CA.

Christian, D., and Whitcher, A. (1995). *Directory of Two-Way Bilingual Programs in the United Status*, rev. edn. National Center for Research on Cultural Diversity and Second Language Learning, Santa Cruz, CA.

Cioran, E.M. (1995). *Œuvres*. Gallimard, Paris.

Cleghorn, A., Merritt, M., and Abagi, J.O. (1989). "Language Policy and Science Instruction in Kenyan Primary Schools." *Comparative Education Review* 33(1), 21–39.

CLIL-AXIS (2006). *Content and Language Integrated Learning Team Teaching.* Laurea University of Applied Sciences, Vantaa Tikkurila. Available online at www.clil-axis.net.

CLIL/EMILE (2002). *The European Dimension*. European Commission, Brussels.

Cloud, N., Genesee, F., and Hamayan, E. (2000). *Dual Language Instruction. A Handbook for Enriched Education.* Heinle and Heinle, Boston, MA.

Clyne, M. (ed.) (1997). *Undoing and Redoing Corpus Planning*. Mouton de Gruyter, Berlin.

—— (2003a). *Dynamics of Language Contact. English and Immigrant Languages.* Cambridge University Press, Cambridge.

—— (2003b). "Towards a More Language-Centred Approach to Plurilingualism." In J.M. Dewale, A. Housen, Li Wei (eds.). *Bilingualism: Beyond Basic Principles*. Multilingual Matters, Clevedon, pp. 43–55.

Coady, J. (1979). "A Psycholinguistic Model of the ESL Reader." In R. Mackay, B. Barkman, and R. Jordan (eds.). *Reading in a Second Language: Hypotheses, Organization, and Practice*. Newbury House, Rowley, MA, pp. 179–86.

Cohen, E.G. (1994). *Designing Group Work: Strategies for the Heterogenous Classroom*, second edn. Teachers College Press, New York.

Cohen, E.G., and Lotan, R.A. (1995). "Producing Equal-Status Interaction in the Heterogeneous Classroom." *American Education Research Journal* 32, 99–120.

Cohen, E.G., and Roper, S.S. (1972). "Modification of Interracial Interaction Disability: An Application of Status Characteristic Theory." *American Sociological Review* 37, 643–57.

Cole, D.L. (2008). "English as a Foreign Language for Deaf Adult Students: Rethinking Language Learning amidst Cultural and Linguistic Diversity." In C.J. Kellett Bidoli and E. Ochse (eds.). *English in International Deaf Communication*. Peter Lang, Bern, pp. 179–92.

—— (forthcoming). "Bilingual Education and the Deaf." In J. González (ed.). *Encyclopedia of Bilingual Education*. Sage Publications, Thousand Oaks, CA.

Collier, V. (1995). "Acquiring a Second Language for Schools." *Directions in Language and Education* 1(4), 1–12 (National Clearinghouse for Bilingual Education).

Combs, M.C. (1992). "English Plus: Responding to English-Only." In J. Crawford (ed.). *Language Loyalties. A Source Book on the Official English Controversy*. University of Chicago Press, Chicago, IL, pp. 216–24.

Cook, V.J. (1992). "Evidence for Multicompetence." *Language Learning* 42(4), 557–91.

Cooper, R.L. (1989). *Language Planning and Social Change*. Cambridge University Press, Cambridge.

Cope, B., and Kalantzis, M. (2000). *Multiliteracies. Literacy Learning and Design of Social Futures*. Routledge, London.

Corson, D. (2001). *Language Diversity and Education*. Lawrence Erlbaum, Mahwah, NJ.

Corvalán, G. (1989). *Política lingüística y educación*. Centro Paraguayo de Estudios Sociológicos, Asunción.

—— (2000). "Asunción." In W. Mackey (ed.). *Espaces urbains et coexistence des langues*, Special Issue of *Terminogramme* 93–4, 187–215.

Coste, D. (2001). "La notion de compétence plurilingue et ses implications possibles." In *L'Enseignement des langues vivantes. Perspectives. Coll. 'Les Actes de la DESCO'*, CRDP de l'Académie de Versailles, 29–38.

Coulmas, F. (2003). *Writing Systems: An Introduction to Their Linguistic Analysis*. Cambridge University Press, Cambridge.

—— (2005). *Sociolinguistics. The Study of Speakers' Choice*. Cambridge University Press, Cambridge.

Council of Europe (1993). *European Charter for Regional or Minority Languages*, Council of Europe, Strasbourg.

—— (2000a). *Common European Framework of Reference for Languages: Learning, Teaching, Assessment*. Language Policy Division, Strasbourg. Available at www.coe.int/t/dg4/linguistic/CADRE_EN.asp.

—— (2000b). *European Language Portfolios*. Available at: www.coe.int/t/dg4/portfolio/Default.asp?L=EandM=/main_pages/welcome.html.

—— (2003a). *Guide for the Development of Language Education Policies in Europe*. Council of Europe, Strasbourg.

—— (2003b). Recommendation 1598. Protection of Sign Languages in the Member States of the Council of Europe. Available at http://assembly.coe.int/Documents/AdoptedText/ta03/EREC1598.htm.

—— (2004). *Language Education Policy Profiles. Guidelines and Procedures*. Council of Europe, Language Policy Division, Strasbourg. Available at www.coe.int/t/dg4/linguistic/Source/GuidelinesPol_EN.pdf.

—— (2006). *Plurilingual Education in Europe: 50 Years of International Cooperation*. Council of Europe, Language Policy Division. Strasbourg. Available at www.coe.int/t/dg4/linguistic/Source/PlurinlingalEducation_EN.pdf.

—— (2007). From Linguistic Diversity to Plurilingual Education. Language Policy Division, Strasbourg. www.coe.int/t/dg4/linguistic/Source/Guide_Main_Beacco2007_EN.doc.

Coyle, D. (2002). "Against All Odds: Lessons from Content and Language Integrated Learning in English Secondary Schools." In D.W.C. So and G.M. Jones (eds.) *Education and Society in Plurilingual Contexts*. VUB Brussels University Press, Brussels, pp. 37–55.

Coyle, D., and Baetens Beardsmore, H. (eds.) (2007). "Research on Content and Language Integrated Learning (CLIL)." *International Journal of Bilingual Education and Bilingualism* 10(5) (Special issue).

Crawford, J. (1991). *Bilingual Education: History, Politics, Theory, and Practice*. Crane, Trenton, NJ.

—— (ed.) (1992). *Language Loyalties: A Sourcebook on the Official English Controversy*. University of Chicago Press, Chicago, IL.

—— (1998). "Ten Common Fallacies about Bilingual Education." *Center for Applied Linguistics*, available at www.cal.org/resources/digest/crawford01.html.

—— (2000). *At War with Diversity. U.S. Language Policy in an Age of Anxiety*. Multilingual Matters, Clevedon.

—— (2003a). *A Few Things Ron Unz Would Prefer You Didn't Know about English Learners in California*. http://ourworld.compuserve.com/homepages/JWCRAWFORD/castats.htm.

—— (2003b). *Hard Sell: Why is BE So Unpopular with the American Public?* Language Policy Research Unit website of Arizona State University, www.asu.edu/educ/epsl/LPRU/features/brief8.htm.

—— (2004). *Educating English Learners: Language Diversity in the Classroom*, fifth edn. (Formerly *Bilingual Education: History, Politics, Theory, and Practice*.) Bilingual Educational Services, Los Angeles, CA.

—— (2006a). *Frequently Asked Questions about Official English*. Language Policy Web Site and Emporium, http://users.rcn.com/crawj/OfficialEnglishFAQ.pdf.

—— (2006b). "Getting 'Accountability' Right. High Stakes for English Language Learners." Paper presented at the 2nd Annual Conference on Educating English Language Learners. September 15, 2006. Hostos Community College.

—— (2007). "The Decline of Bilingual Education: How to Reverse a Troubling Trend." *International Multilingual Research Journal* 1(1), 33–7.

—— (2008). *Advocating for English Learners*. Multilingual Matters, Clevedon.

Creese, A., Martin, P., Blackledge, A., Li Wei, and Lytra, S. (2008). "Investigating Multilingualism in Complementary Schools in Four Communities." Reports available at www.esrcsocietytoday.ac.uk/esrcinfocentre/viewawardpage.aspx?awardnumber=RES-000–23–1180.

Criper, C., and Dodd, N. (1984). *Report on the Teaching of English Language and Its Use as a Medium in Education in Tanzania*. British Council, Dar es Salaam.

Cronbach, L.J. (1989). "Construct Validation after Thirty Years." In R.L. Linn (ed.). *Intelligence: Measurement Theory and Public Policy*. University of Illinois Press, Urbana, IL.

Crystal, D. (1997). *English as a Global Language*. Cambridge University Press, Cambridge. Second edition 2003.

Csovcsics, E., and Solymosi, J. (2006). "The Ghandi Project – Hungary." Paper presented at the Conference on Regional and Minority Languages in Education Systems, 27–28 April, 2006, European Commission, Brussels.

Cummins, J. (1979). "Linguistic Interdependence and the Educational Development of Bilingual Children." *Review of Educational Research* 49, 222–51.

—— (1981a). "Four Misconceptions about Language Proficiency in Bilingual Education." *NABE Journal* 5, 31–45.

—— (1981b). "The Role of Primary Language Development in Promoting Educational Success for Language Minority Students." In California State Department of Education (ed.). *Schooling and Language Minority Students: A Theoretical Framework*. Evaluation, Dissemination and Assessment Center, Los Angeles, CA.

—— (1984). *Bilingualism and Special Education: Issues in Assessment and Pedagogy*. Multilingual Matters, Clevedon.

—— (1986). "Empowering Minority Students: A Framework for Intervention." *Harvard Educational Review* 56, 18–36.

—— (1991). "Conversational and Academic Language Proficiency in Bilingual Contexts." *AILA Review* 8, 75–89.

—— (2000). *Language, Power and Pedagogy: Bilingual Children in the Crossfire*. Multilingual Matters, Clevedon.

—— (2001). "Assessment and Intervention with Culturally and Linguisitically Diverse Learners." In S.R. Hurley and J.V. Tinajero (eds.). *Literacy Assessment of Second Language Learners*. Allyn and Bacon, Boston, MA, pp. 115–29.

—— (2003). "Bilingual Education." In J. Bourne and E. Reid (eds.). *Language Education. World Year of Education*. Kogan Page, London, pp. 3–21.

—— (2006). "Identity Texts: The Imaginative Construction of Self through Multiliteracies Pedagogy." In O. García, T. Skutnabb-Kangas, and M. Torres-Guzmán (eds.). *Imagining Multilingual Schools: Languages in Education and Glocalization*. Multilingual Matters, Clevedon, pp. 51–68.

Cummins, J., and Danesi, M. (1990). *Heritage Languages. The Development and Denial of Canada's Linguistic Resources*. Our Schools/Our Selves Education Foundation, Toronto.

Cummins, J., and Swain, M. (1986). *Bilingualism in Education: Aspects of Theory, Research and Practice*. Longman, London.

Danesi, M., McLeod, K., and Morris, S. (eds.) (1993). *Heritage Language and Education. The Canadian Experience*. Mosaic Press, Oakville.

Danoff, M.N. (1978). *Evaluation of the Impact of ESEA Title VII Spanish–English Bilingual Education Programs*. Technical Report. American Institutes for Research, Washington, DC.

Darling-Hammond, L. (1994). "Performance-Based Assessment and Educational Equity." *Harvard Educational Review* 64, 5–30.

Darling-Hammond, L., Ancess, J., and Falk, B. (1995). *Authentic Assessment in Action: Case Studies of Students and Schools at Work*. Teachers College Press, New York.

David, M.K. (2007). *A Guide for the English Language Teacher: A Malaysian Perspective*. Strategic Information and Research Development Centre, Petaling Jaya.

David, M.K., and Govindasamy, S. (2003). "Language Education and Nation-Building in Multilingual Malaysia." In J. Bourne and E. Reid (eds.). *Language Education. World Year of Education*. Kogan Page, London, pp. 215–25.

—— (2007). "The Construction of National Identity and Globalization in Multilingual Malaysia." In A.B.M. Tsui and J.W. Tollefson (eds.). *Language Policy, Culture, and Identity in Asian Contexts*. Lawrence Erlbaum, Mahwah, NJ, pp. 55–72.

Davies Samway, C., and McKeon, D. (1999). *Myths and Realities: Best Practices for Language Minority Students*. Heinemann, Portsmouth, NH.

Davis, K. (1994). *Language Planning in Multilingual Contexts: Policies, Communities and Schools in Luxembourg*. John Benjamins, Amsterdam.

De Bot, K., and Clyne, M. (1994). "A 16-Year Longitudinal Study of Language Attrition in Dutch Immigrants in Australia." *Journal of Multilingual and Multicultural Development* 15, 17–28.

De Cohen, C.C., Deterding, N., and Chu Clewell, B. (2005). *Who's Left Behind? Immigrant Children in High and Low LEP Schools*. Program for Evaluation and Equity Research, Urban Institute, Washington, DC.

De Graff, M. (1999). *Language Creation and Language Change: Creolization, Diachrony, and Development*. MIT Press, Boston, MA.

De Houwer, A. (1990). *The Acquisition of Two Languages from Birth: A Case Study*. Cambridge University Press, Cambridge.

—— (2006). "Bilingual Language Development: Early years." *Encyclopedia of Languages and Linguistics*, second edn. Elsevier, Oxford, pp. 781–7.

de Swaan, A. (2001). *Words of the World: The Global Language System*. Polity Press, Cambridge.

Delhi Declaration and Framework for Action, 1993 (2003) UNESCO, Paris, Education for All Summit, December 16, 1993, available at www.unesco.org/education/pdf/DELHI.PDF.

Del Valle, J. (2000). "Monoglossic Policies for a Heteroglossic Culture: Misinterpreted Multilingualism in Modern Galicia." *Language and Communication* 20, 105–32.

—— (2006). "U.S. Latinos, *la hispanofonía*, and the language ideologies of high modernity." In C. Mar-Molinero and M. Stewart (eds.). *Globalisation and the Spanish-Speaking World*. Palgrave, New York, pp. 27–46.

Del Valle, J., and Gabriel-Stheeman, L. (eds.) (2002). *The Battle over Spanish between 1800 and 2000: Language Ideologies and Spanish Intellectuals*. Routledge, London.

Del Valle, S. (2003). *Language Rights and the Law in the United States*. Multilingual Matters, Clevedon.

Delpit, L. (1988). "The Silenced Dialogue: Power and Pedagogy in Educating Other People's Children." *Harvard Educational Review* 58, 280–98.

Department of Education (1995). *English in the National Curriculum*. HMSO, London.

Derewianka, B. (1990). *Exploring How Texts Work*. Heinemann, Portsmouth, NH.

Dermody, M., and Speaker, R. (1995). "Effects of Reciprocal Strategy Training in Prediction, Clarification, Question Generation, and Summarization on Fourth Graders' Reading Comprehension." In K.A. Hinchman, D. Leu, and C.K. Kinzer (eds.). *Perspectives on Literacy Research and Practice*. National Reading Conference, Chicago, IL.

Deuchar, M., and Quay, S. (2000). *Bilingual Acquisition: Theoretial Implications of a Case Study*. Oxford University Press, Oxford.

Devonish, H., and Carpenter, K. (2005). *Full Bilingual Education in a Creole Language Situation: The Jamaican Bilingual Primary Education Project*. Department of Linguistics, University of the West Indies, Mona, Kingston.

Dewey, J. (1897). "My Pedagogic Creed." *School Journal* 54, 77–80.

Dicker, S. (2003). *Languages in America. A Pluralist View*, second edn. Multilingual Matters, Clevedon.

Diebold, A.R. (1964). "Incipient Bilingualism." In D. Hymes (ed.). *Language in Culture and Society*. Harper and Row, New York, pp. 495–511.

Digello, E., Singelton, J.L., Morgan, D., Wiles, J., and Rivers, R. (2004). "Vocabulary Use by Low, Moderate, and High ASL-Proficient Writers Compared to Hearing ESL and Monolingual Speakers." *Journal of Deaf Studies and Deaf Education* 9, 86–103.

Dorian, N. (1999). "Linguistic and Ethnographic Fieldwork." In J.A. Fishman (ed.). *Handbook of Language and Ethnic Identity*. Oxford University Press, Oxford, pp. 25–41.

Dragonas, T., and Frangoudaki, A. (2006). "Educating the Muslim Minority in Western Thrace." *Islam and Christian–Muslim Relations* 17(1), 21–41.

Draper, J.B., and Hicks, J.H. (2002). *Foreign Language Enrollments in Public Secondary Schools, Fall 2000*. American Council on the Teaching of Foreign Languages, Yonkers, New York.

Draper, J.B., and Jiménez, M. (1992). "A Chronology of the Official English Movement." In J. Crawford (ed.). *Language Loyalties. A Source Book on the Official English Controversy*. University of Chicago Press, Chicago, IL, pp. 89–93.

Drexel-Andrieu, I. (1993). "Bilingual Geography: A Teacher's Perspective." In H. Baetens Beardsmore (ed.). *European Models of Bilingual Education*. Multilingual Matters, Clevedon, pp. 173–82.

Dufour, R., and Kroll, J.F. (1995). "Matching Words to Concepts in Two Languages: A Test of the Concept Mediation Model of Bilingual Representation." *Memory and Cognition* 23(2), 166–80.

Durie, A. (1997). "Maori–English bilingual education in New Zealand." In J. Cummins and D. Corson (eds.). *Encyclopedia of Language and Education*, vol. 5: *Bilingual Education*. Kluwer, Dordrecht, pp. 15–23.

Dutcher, N. (2004). *Expanding Educational Opportunities in Linguistically Diverse Societies*, second edn. Center for Applied Linguistics, Washington, DC.

Duverger, J. (2005). *L'Enseignement en classe bilingue*. Hachette, Paris.

Duverger, J., and Maillard, J.P. (1996). *L'Enseignement bilingue aujourd'hui*. Albin Michel, Paris.

Dworin, J. (2003). "Insights into Biliteracy Development: Toward a Bidirectional Theory of Bilingual Pedagogy." *Journal of Hispanic Higher Education* 2, 171–86.

Echevarria, J., Vogt, M.E., and Short, D.J. (2004). *Making Content Comprehensible for English Learners. The SIOP Model*, second edn. Allyn and Bacon, Needham Heights, MA.

Edelsky, C.K. (1986). *Writing in a Bilingual Program. Había una vez*. Ablex Publishing, Norwood, NJ.

Education for a New Era. Fact Sheet (2004). Qatar Education Reform Initiative, Supreme Education Council, Doha.

Edwards, J. (1994). *Multilingualism*. Routledge, London.

—— (2004). "Foundations of Bilingualism." In T.K. Bhatia and W.C. Ritchie (eds.). *The Handbook of Bilingualism*. Blackwell, Malden, MA.

Edwards, V., and Newcombe, L.P. (2006). "Back to Basics: Marketing the Benefits of Bilingualism to Parents." In O. García, T. Skutnabb-Kangas, and M. Torres-Guzmán (eds.). *Imagining Multilingual Schools: Languages in Education and Glocalization*. Multilingual Matters, Clevedon, pp. 137–49.

Edwards, V., and Nwenmely, H. (2000). "Language, Literacy and World View." In M. Martin-Jones and K. Jones. *Multilingual Literacies. Reading and Writing Different Worlds*. John Benjamins, Amsterdam, pp. 91–102.

Elenes, A. (2002). "Border/Transformative Pedagogies at the End of the Millennium: Chicana/o Cultural Studies and Education." In A.J. Aldama and N. Quiñones (eds.). *Decolonial Voices: Chicana and Chicano Cultural Studies in the 21st Century*. Indiana University Press, Bloomington, IN, pp. 245–61.

Elley, W.B. (1984). "Exploring the Reading Difficulties of Second Language Learners and Second Languages in Fiji." In C.J. Alderson and A.H. Urquhart (eds.). *Reading in a Foreign Language*. Longman, London, pp. 281–97.

Ellis, R. (2000). "Theoretical Perspectives on Interaction and Language Learning." In R. Ellis (ed.). *Learning a Second Language through Interaction*. John Benjamins, Philadelphia, pp. 3–32.

—— (2003). *Task-Based Language Learning and Teaching*. Oxford University Press, Oxford.

Enote, J. (2002). "Maintaining Our Identity and Language Is the Heart of the Landscape." *Native Americas: Hemispheric Journal of Indigenous* 19(3 and 4), 28–30.

Epstein, N. (1977). *Language, Ethnicity and the Schools: Policy Alternatives for Bilingual-Bicultural Education*. The Georgetown University Institute for Educational Leadership, Washington, DC.

Erasmus (2007). "Frequently Asked Questions." http://www.erasmus.ac.uk/students/faq.html?item=6.

Erickson, F., and Mohatt, G. (1982). "Cultural Organization of Participation Structures in Two Classrooms of Indian Students." In G.B. Spindler (ed.). *Doing the Ethnography of Schooling: Educational Anthropology in Action*. Holt, Rinehart, and Winston, New York, pp. 132–74.

Eriksen, T. (1993). *Ethnicity and Nationalism: Anthropological Perspectives*. Pluto Press, London.

Erikson, F. (1996). "Transformation and School Success: The Politics and Culture of Educational Achievement." In E. Jacob and C. Jordan (eds.). *Minority Education: Anthropological Perspectives*. Ablex, Norwood, NJ, pp. 27–52.

Errington, J. (2001). "Colonial Linguistics." *Annual Review of Anthropology* 30, 19–39.

Escamilla, K. (2006). "Monolingual Assessment and Emerging Bilinguals: A Case Study in the US." In O. Garcia, T. Skutnabb-Kangas, and M. Torres-Guzmán (eds.). *Imagining Multilingual Schools: Languages in Education and Glocalization*. Multilingual Matters, Clevedon, pp. 184–99.

Estrin, E., and Nelson-Barber, S. (1995). *Issues in Cross-Cultural Assessment: American Indian and Alaska Native Students*. Far West Laboratory Knowledge Brief 12. Far West Laboratory, San Francisco, CA.

Etxeberria, F. (1999). *Bilingüismo y Educación en el País del Euskara*. Erein, San Sebastian/Donostia.

Etxeberria-Sagastume, F. (2006). "Attitudes towards Language Learning in Different Linguistic Models of the Basque Autonomous Community." In O. García, T. Skutnabb-Kangas, and M. Torres-Guzmán (eds.). *Imagining Multilingual Schools: Languages in Education and Glocalization*. Multilingual Matters, Clevedon, pp. 111–33.

Eurobarometer (2000). *Europeans and Languages: A Eurobarometer Special Survey*. European Commission, Luxembourg.

Euromosaic III (2004). *The Presence of Regional and Minority Language Groups' Languages in the New Member States*. European Commission, Brussels.

European Bureau of the Lesser-Used Languages. EBLUL (2007). Available at www.eblul.org/.

European Commission (2002). *CLIL/EMILE – The European Dimension: Actions, Trends and Foresight Potential*. European Unit, Brussels, Public Services Contract 2001 – 3406/ 001–001.

—— (2003). *Promoting Language Learning and Linguistic Diversity: An Action Plan 2004– 2006*. European Unit, Brussels. Also available online at: http://ec.europa.eu/education/ doc/official/keydoc/actlang/act_lang_en.pdf.

—— (2006). *Languages of Europe*. Available at www.europa.eu.int/comm/education/poli-cies/lang/languages/index_en.html.

European Union (2006). DVD. *CLIL for the Knowledge Society*.

Eurydice (2005). *Key Data on Teaching Languages at School in Europe*. Eurydice, Brussels. Available at: www.eurydice.org/ressources/eurydice/pdf/0_integral/049EN.pdf.

—— (2006). *Content and Language Integrated Learning (CLIL) at School in Europe, 2006*. Eurydice, Brussels.

Expert Group on Future Skills Needs (2005). *Languages and Enterprise. The Demand and Supply of Foreign Language Skills in the Enterprise Sector*. Forfás, Dublin.

Extra, G., and Gorter, D. (2001). *The Other Languages of Europe: Demographic, Sociolinguistic and Educational Perspectives*. Multilingual Matters, Clevedon.

Extra, G., and Yagmur, K. (2002). "Language Diversity in Multicultural Europe. Comparative Perspectives on Immigrant Minority Languages at Home and at School." Management of Social Transformation (MOST). Discussion Paper 63. UNESCO, Paris, www.unesco. org/most/dp63extra.pdf.

Fabbro, F. (1999). *Neurolinguistics of Bilingualism: An Introduction*. Taylor and Francis, Philadelphia, PA.

Fagerlind, I., and Saha, L.J. (1989). *Education and National Development: A Comparative Perspective*. Pergamon Press, Oxford.

Fairclough, N, (ed.) (1992). *Critical Language Awareness*. Longman, London.

—— (1999). "Global Capitalism and Critical Awareness of Language." *Language Aware-ness* 8(2), 71–83.

Faltis, C.J. (1997). *Joinfostering. Adapting Teaching for the Multilingual Classroom*. Second edn. Merrill, Upper Saddle River, NJ.

Faltis, C.J., and Hudelson, S.J. (1998). *Bilingual Education in Elementary and Secondary School Communities. Toward Understanding and Caring*. Allyn and Bacon, Boston, MA.

Fasold, R. (1984). *The Sociolinguistics of Society*. Blackwell, Oxford.

Feng, A. (ed.) (2007). *Bilingual Education in China. Practices, Policies and Concepts*. Multilingual Matters, Clevedon.

Ferguson, C. (1959). "Diglossia." *Word* 15, 325–40.

Ferguson, G. (2003). "Classroom Code-Switching in Post-colonial Contexts: Functions, Attitudes and Policies." *AILA Review* 16(1), 38–51.

—— (2006). *Language Planning and Education*. Edinburgh University Press, Edinburgh.

Fettes, M. (2003). "The Geostrategies of Interlingualism." In J. Maurais and M. Morris (eds.). *Languages in a Globalising World*. Cambridge University Press, Cambridge, pp. 37–46.

Feuerverger, G. (2001). *Oasis of Dreams: Teaching and Learning Peace in a Jewish-Palestinian Village in Israel*. Routledge, London.

Finegan, E., and Rickford, J.R. (eds.) (2004) *Language in the USA*. Cambridge University Press, Cambridge.

Finlayson, R., and Slabbert, S. (1997). " 'I'll Meet You Halfway with Language': Code-Switching within a South African Urban Context." In M. Putz (ed.). *Language Choices: Conditions, Constraints and Consequences*. John Benjamins, Amsterdam, pp. 381–421.

Fishman, J.A. (1965). "Who Speaks What Language to Whom and When?" *La Linguistique* 2, 67–88.

—— (1966). *Language Loyalty in the United States. The Maintenance and Perpetuation of Non-English Mother Tongues by American Ethnic and Religious Groups*. Mouton, The Hague.

—— (1972a). *Language and Nationalism. Two Integrative Essays*. Newbury House, Rowley, MA.

—— (1972b). *Language in Sociocultural Change. Essays by Joshua A. Fishman*. Stanford University Press, Stanford, CA.

—— (1976). *Bilingual Education: An International Sociological Perspective*. Newbury House, Rowley, MA.

—— (1977a). "The Establishment of Language Education Policy in Multilingual Societies." In B. Spolsky and R. Cooper (eds.). *Frontiers in Bilingual Education*. Newbury House, Rowley, MA, pp. 94–106.

—— (1977b). "The Social Science Perspective." In *Bilingual Education: Current Perspectives*. Social Science Center for Applied Linguistics, Arlington, VA, pp. 1–49.

—— (1978a). "Positive Bilingualism: Some Overlooked Rationales and Forefathers." In J.E. Alatis (ed.). *Georgetown Roundtable on Languages and Linguistics*. Georgetown University, Washington, DC, pp. 42–52.

—— (1978b). "Talking about Bilingual Education." *Newsletter (BESC)* 5, 1–2.

—— (1979). "The Significance of the Ethnic Community Mother Tongue School: Introduction to a Study." *National Association of Bilingual Education/NABE Journal* 3(3), 39–47.

—— (1980a). "Ethnic Community Mother Tongue Schools in the USA: Dynamics and Distributions." *International Migration Review* 14, 235–47.

—— (1980b). "Ethnocultural Dimensions in the Acquisition and Retention of Biliteracy." *Journal of Basic Writing* 3: 48–61.

—— (1985a). *The Rise and Fall of the Ethnic Revival*. Mouton de Gruyter, Berlin.

—— (1985b). "The Societal Basis of the Intergenerational Continuity of Additional Languages." *Scientific and Humanistic Dimensions of Language. Festchrift for Robert Lado*. John Benjamins, Amsterdam, pp. 551–8.

—— (1989). *Language and Ethnicity in Minority Sociolinguistic Perspective*. Multilingual Matters, Clevedon.

—— (1991). *Reversing Language Shift. Theoretical and Empirical Foundations of Assistance to Threatened Languages*. Multilingual Matters, Clevedon.

—— (1996). *In Praise of the Beloved Language: A Comparative View of Positive Ethnolinguistic Consciousness*. Mouton de Gruyter, Berlin.

—— (ed.) (1999). *Handbook of Language and Ethnic Identity*. Oxford University Press, New York.

—— (2000). "The Status Agenda in Corpus Planning." In R.D. Lambert and E. Shohamy (eds.). *Language Policy and Pedagogy: Essays in Honor of A. Ronald Walton*. John Benjamins, Amsterdam, pp. 43–51.

—— (ed.) (2001). *Can Threatened Languages Be Saved?* Multilingual Matters, Clevedon.

—— (2006). *Do Not Leave Your Language Alone. The Hidden Status Agendas within Corpus Planning in Language Policy*. Lawrence Erlbaum, Mahwah, NJ.

Fishman, J.A., Conrad, A.W., and Rubal-López, A. (eds.) (1996). *Post-Imperial English. Status Change in Former British and American Colonies, 1940–1990*. Mouton de Gruyter, Berlin.

Fishman, J.A., Cooper, R.L., Ma, R., *et al.* (1971). *Bilingualism in the Barrio*. Language Science Monographs 7. Indiana University Press, Bloomington, IN.

Fishman, J.A., and Lovas, J. (1970). "Bilingual Education in Sociolinguistic Perspective." *TESOL Quarterly* 4, 215–22.

Fitouri, C. (1983). *Biculturalisme, bilinguisme et éducation*. Delachaux et Niestlé, Neuchâtel-Paris.

Flavell, J. (1979). "Metacognition and Cognitive Monitoring: A New Area of Cognitive-Developmental Inquiry." *American Psychologist* 34, 906–11.

Fleischman, H.L., and Hopstock, P.J. (1993). *Descriptive Study of Services to Limited English Proficient Students*, vol. 1: *Summary of Findings and Conclusions*. Development Associates, Arlington, VA.

Fleming, M. (2007). "The Challenges of Assessment within Language(s) of Education." In W. Martyniuk (ed.). *Evaluation and Assessment within the Domain of Language(s) of Education*. Council of Europe, Strasbourg, pp. 9–15.

Fleras, A. (1992). *The Nations Within. Aboriginal–State Relations in Canada, United States, and New Zealand* (with J.L. Elliott). Oxford University Press, Toronto.

Foucault, M. (1972). *The Archaeology of Knowledge*. Pantheon, New York.

—— (1979). *Discipline and Punish: The Birth of the Prison*. Vintage Books, New York.

—— (1991). "Governmentality." In G. Burchell, C. Gordon, and P. Miller (eds.). *The Foucault Effect: Studies in Governmentality*. University of Chicago Press, Chicago, IL, pp. 87–104.

Fountas, I., and Pinnell, G.S. (1996). *Guided Reading: Good First Teaching for All Children*. Heinemann, Portsmouth, NH.

Francis, D.J., Lesaux, N., and August, D. (2006). "Language of Instruction." In D. August and T. Shanahan (eds.). *Developing Literacy in Second-Language Learners. Report of the National Literacy Panel on Language-Minority Children and Youth*. Lawrence Erlbaum, Mahwah, NJ, pp. 365–414.

Francis, N., and Reyhner, J. (2002). *Language and Literacy Teaching for Indigenous Education: A Bilingual Approach*. Multilingual Matters, Clevedon.

Fraser Gupta, A. (1997). "When Mother-Tongue Education Is *Not* Preferred." *Journal of Multilingual and Multicultural Development* 18(6), 496–506.

Freebody, P., and Luke, A. (1990). "Literacies Programs: Debates and Demands in Cultural Context." *Prospect: Australian Journal of TESOL* 5(7), 7–16.

Freeman, R.D. (1998). *Bilingual Education and Social Change*. Multilingual Matters, Clevedon.

—— (2004). *Building on Community Biligualism*. Caslon Publishing, Philadelphia, PA.

Freeman, D.E., and Freeman, Y.S. (2000). *Teaching Reading in Multilingual Classrooms*. Heinemann, Portsmouth, NH.

Freeman, Y.S., Freeman, D.E., and Mercuri, S.P. (2005). *Dual Language Essentials for Teachers and Administrators*. Heinemann, Portsmouth, NH.

Freire, P. (1970). *Pedagogy of the Oppressed*. Herder and Herder, New York.

Freire, P., and Macedo, D. (1987). *Literacy: Reading the Word and the World*. Bergin and Garvey, South Hadley, MA.

French, B. (1999). "Imagining the Nation: Language Ideology and Collective Identity in Contemporary Guatemala." *Language and Communication* 19, 277–87.

Fruhauf, G. (1996). "Bilingual Education in the Netherlands." In G. Fruhauf, D. Coyle, and I. Christ (eds.). *Teaching Content in a Foreign Language*. Stichting Europees Platform voor het Nederlandse Onderwijs, Alkmaar, pp. 113–33.

Fu, D. (2003). *An Island of English: Teaching ESL in Chinatown*. Heinemann, Portsmouth, NH.

Gajo, L. (2007). "Linguistic Knowledge and Subject Knowledge: How Does Bilingualism Contribute to Subject Development?" *International Journal of Bilingual Education and Bilingualism* 10(5), 563–81.

Gajo, L., and Mondada, L. (2000). *Interactions et aquisitions en contexte.* Éditions Universitaires, Fribourg.

Gajo, L. and Serra, C. (2002). "Bilingual Teaching: Connecting Language and Concepts in Mathematics." In D. So and G. Jones (eds.). *Education and Society in Plurilingual Contexts.* VUB Brussels University Press, Brussels, pp. 75–95.

Gal, S. (1989). "Language and Political Economy." *Annual Review of Anthropology* 18, 345–67.

Gallagher, E. (2008). *Equal Rights to the Curriculum: Many Languages, One Message.* Multilingual Matters, Clevedon.

Gallaudet Research Institute (2006). *Annual Survey 2004–2005. Regional and National Summary.* Available at http://gri.gallaudet.edu/Demographics/2005_National_Summary.pdf.

García, E. (2005). *Teaching and Learning in Two Languages. Bilingualism and Schooling in the United States.* Teachers College Press, New York.

García, G., and Pearson, P. (1994). "Assessment and Diversity." In L. Darling-Hammond (ed.). *Review of Research in Education* 20, 337–91.

García, O. (1988). "The Education of Biliterate and Bicultural Children in Ethnic Schools in the United States." *Essays by the Spencer Fellows of the National Academy of Education* 4, 19–78.

—— (1993). "Understanding the Societal Role of the Teacher in Transitional Bilingual Education Classrooms: Lessons from Sociology of language." In K. Zondag (ed.). *Bilingual Education in Friesland: Facts and Prospects.* Gemeenschappelijk Centrum voor Onderwijsbegeleiding, Leeuwarden, pp. 25–37.

—— (1995). "Spanish Language Loss as a Determinant of Income among US Latinos: Implications for Language Policy in Schools." In J.W. Tollefson (ed.). *Power and Inequality in Language Education.* Cambridge University Press, New York, pp. 142–60.

—— (1997a). "Bilingual Education." In F. Coulmas (ed.). *The Handbook of Sociolinguistics.* Blackwell, Oxford, pp. 405–20.

—— (1997b). "From Goya Portraits to Goya Beans: Elite Traditions and Popular Streams in U.S. Spanish Language Policy." *Southwest Journal of Linguistics* 12 (1993), 69–86.

—— (1999). "The Forging of a Latin American Ethnolinguistic Identity: Between the Written and Oral Word." In J. Fishman (ed.). *Handbook of Language and Ethnic Identity.* Oxford University Press, Oxford, pp. 226–43.

—— (2003). "Nouvelles Espérances et barrières dans le domaine de l'éducation aux États-Unis." *Hommes et migrations* 1246, 17–27.

—— (2004). "Language-in-Education Policies: Global Perspectives. Considerations for Qatar." October 2004. Unpublished report submitted to Adel Al-Sayed.

—— (2005a). "Minority Language Education." In K. Brown (ed.). *Encyclopedia of Language and Linguistics,* vol. 8. Elsevier, Oxford, pp. 159–63.

—— (2005b). "Positioning Heritage Languages in the United States." *Modern Language Journal* 89(4), 601–5.

—— (2006a). Foreword. *Disinventing and Reconstituting Languages,* ed. by S. Makoni and A. Pennycook. Multilingual Matters, Clevedon, xi–xv.

—— (2006b). "Lost in Transculturation: The Case of Bilingual Education in New York City." In M. Pütz, J.A. Fishman, and N.-V. Aertselaer (eds.), *Along the Routes to Power: Exploration of the Empowerment through Language.* Mouton de Gruyter, Berlin, pp. 157–78.

—— (2007a). "Constructing Plural Language Practices in Education." Keynote presentation at the Language, Education and Diversity conference. University of Waikato, New Zealand. November 24, 2007.

—— (2007b). "Lenguas e identidades en mundos hispanohablantes. Desde una posición plurilingüe y minoritaria." In M. Lacorte (ed.). *Lingüística aplicada del español*. Arco, Madrid, pp. 377–400.

—— (2007c). "Multilingual Language Awareness and Teacher Education." In J. Cenoz and N. Hornberger (eds.). *Encyclopedia of Language and Education*, second edn, vol. 6. Knowledge about Language. Springer, Berlin.

—— (ed.) (2008a). *Spanish as a Global Language. The International Multilingual Research Journal* 2(1).

—— (2008b). "Teaching Spanish and Spanish in Teaching in the U.S.: Integrating Bilingual Perspectives." In C. Hélot and A.-M. de Mejía. *Forging Multilingual Spaces: Integrating Majority and Minority Bilingual Education*. Multilingual Matters, Clevedon, pp. 31–57.

García, O., and Baker, C. (eds.) (2007). *Bilingual Education: An Introductory Reader*. Multilingual Matters, Clevedon.

García, O., and Bartlett, L. (2007). "A Speech Community Model of Bilingual Education: Educating Latino Newcomers in the U.S." *International Journal of Bilingual Education and Bilingualism* 10, 1–25.

García, O., Bartlett, L., and Kleifgen, J. (2007). "From Biliteracy to Pluriliteracies." In P. Auer and Li Wei (eds.). *Handbooks of Applied Linguistics*, vol. 5: *Multilingualism*. Mouton de Gruyter, Berlin, pp. 207–28.

García, O., and Celic, C. (2006). "Stretching ESL for Immigrant Students in the US with Home Languages." Keynote presentation at the 26th Annual Bilingual Conference at William Patterson College, NJ, December 8, 2006.

García, O., Kleifgen, J.A., and Falchi, L. (2008). *Equity in the Education of Emergent Bilinguals: The Case of English Language Learners*. The Campaign for Educational Equity Research Review Series 1. Teachers College, New York. Available at www.tc.columbia.edu/i/a/document/6468_Ofelia_ELL_Final.pdp.

García, O., and Mason, L. (forthcoming). "Where in the World is U.S. Spanish? Creating a Space of Opportunity for U.S. Latinos." In W. Harbert, W. McConnell-Ginet, A. Miller, and J. Whitman (eds.). *Language and Poverty*. Multilingual Matters, Clevedon.

García, O., and Menken, K. (2006). "The English of Latinos from a Plurilingual Transcultural Angle: Implications for Assessment And Schools." In S. Nero (ed.). *Dialects, Other Englishes, and Education*. Lawrence Erlbaum, Mahwah, NJ, pp. 167–84.

García, O., Morín, J.L., and Rivera, K. (2001). "How Threatened Is the Spanish of New York Puerto Ricans? Language Shift with *vaivén*." In J.A. Fishman (ed.). *Can Threatened Languages Be Saved? Reversing Language Shift Revisited*. Multilingual Matters, Clevedon, pp. 44–73.

García, O., and Otheguy, R. (1985). "The Masters of Survival Send Their Children to School: Bilingual Education in the Ethnic Schools of Miami." *Bilingual Review. Revista Bilingüe* 12, 3–19.

—— (1988). "The Bilingual Education of Cuban American Children in Dade County's Ethnic Schools." *Language and Education* 1, 83–95.

—— (1994). "The Value of Speaking a LOTE in U.S. Business." *Annals of the American Academy* 532(1994), 99–122.

García, O., Peltz, R., and Schiffman, H. (eds.) (2006). *Language Loyalty, Continuity and Change: Joshua A. Fishman's Contributions to International Sociolinguistics*. Multilingual Matters, Clevedon.

García, O., Skutnabb-Kangas, T., and Torres-Guzmán, M. (eds.) (2006). *Imagining Multilingual Schools: Languages in Education and Glocalization.* Multilingual Matters, Clevedon.

García, O., and Traugh, C. (2002). "Using Descriptive Inquiry to Transform the Education of Linguistically Diverse U.S. Teachers and Students." In Li Wei, J. Dewaele, and A. Housen (eds.). *Opportunities and Challenges of (Societal) Bilingualism.* Walter de Gruyter, Berlin, pp. 311–28.

García, O., and Tsai, P.J. (2008). "Bilingual Education and Language Policy in Global Perspective". In J. González (ed.). *Encyclopedia of Bilingual Education.* Sage, London, pp. 435–8.

Gardner, H. (1993). *Multiple Intelligences: The Theory in Practice.* Basic Books, New York.

Gardy, P., and Lafont, R. (1981). "La diglossie comme conflit: L'exemple occitan." *Langages* 16, 75–91.

Gee, J.P. (1996). *Social Linguistics and Literacies. Ideology in Discourses.* Taylor and Francis, London.

Gellner, E. (1983). *Nations and Nationalism. New Perspectives on the Past.* Blackwell, Oxford.

Genesee, F. (1978). "Is There an Optimal Age for Starting Second Language Instruction?" *McGill Journal of Education* 13, 145–54.

—— (1981). "A Comparison of Early and Late Second Language Learning." *Canadian Journal of Behavioral Science* 13, 115–27.

—— (1988). "Neuropsychology and Second Language Acquisition." In L. Beebe (ed.). *Issues in Second Language Acquisition.* Newbury House. Rowley, MA, pp. 32–57.

—— (1994). "Double Immersion Programs in Canada." In II Jornadas Internacionales de Educación Plurilingüe, November 3–4, 1994. *Vitoria-Gasteiz, Fundacion Gaztelueta,* 1–23.

—— (1999). *Program Alternatives for Linguistically Diverse Students.* Center for Research on Education, Diversity and Excellence, Santa Cruz, CA, and Washington, DC. Available at www.cal.org/crede/pubs/edpractice/EPR1.pdf.

—— (2003). "Rethinking Bilingual Acquisition." In J.M. Dewaele (ed.). *Bilingualism: Challenges and Directions for Future Research.* Multilingual Matters, Clevedon, pp. 204–29.

—— (2004). "What Do We Know about Bilingual Education for Majority Language Students?" In T.K. Bhatia and W. Ritchie (eds.). *Handbook of Bilingualism and Multiculturalism.* Blackwell, Malden, MA, pp 547–76.

Genesee, F., and Hamayan, E.V. (1994). "Classroom-Based Assessment." In F. Genesee (ed.). *Educating Second Language Children: The Whole Child, the Whole Curriculum, the Whole Community.* Cambridge University Press, New York.

Genesee, F., Lindholm-Leary, K., Saunders, W.M., and Christian, D. (eds.) (2006). *Educating English Language Learners.* New York: Cambridge University Press.

Genesee, F., Tucker, G.R., and Lambert, W.E. (1975). "Communication Skills in Bilingual Children." *Child Development* 46, 1010–14.

Genishi, C., and Borrego Brainard, M. (1995). "Assessment of Bilingual Children: A Dilemma Seeking Solutions." In E. Garcia and B. McLaughlin (eds.). *Meeting the Challenge of Linguistic and Cultural Diversity in Early Childhood Education.* Teachers College Press, New York, pp. 49–63.

Gerner de Garcia, B., (1992). Diversity in Deaf Education: What can we learn from bilingual and ESL education? In: Martin, D. and Mobley, R. (eds.) *Proceedings of First International Symposium on Teacher Education in Deafness.* Gallaudet University Press, Washington, DC.

—— (1993). "Addressing the Needs of Hispanic Deaf Children." In K.M. Christensen and G.L. Delgado (eds.). *Multicultural Issues in Deafness.* Longman Publishing, New York.

Gibbons, P. (1991). *Learning to Learn in a Second Language*. Heinemann, Portsmouth, NH.

—— (1998). "Classroom Talk and the Learning of New Registers in a Second Language." *Language and Education* 12, 99–118.

—— (2002). *Scaffolding Language, Scaffolding Learning. Teaching Second Languages in the Mainstream Classroom*. Heinemann, Portsmouth, NH.

—— (2006). *Bridging Discourses in the ESL Classrooms: Students, Teachers and Researchers*. Continuum, London.

Gibson, H., Small, A., and Mason, D. (1997). "Deaf Bilingual Bicultural Education." In J. Cummins and D. Corson (eds.). *Encyclopedia of Language and Education*, vol. 5: *Bilingual Education*. Kluwer Academic Publishers, Dordrecht, pp. 231–40.

Giddens, A. (1984). *The Nation State and Violence*. University of California Press, Berkeley, CA.

Gill, S.K. (2004). "Medium-of-Instruction Policy in Higher Education in Malaysia: Nationalism versus Internationalization." In J.W. Tollefson and A.B.M. Tsui (eds.). *Medium of Instruction Policies: Which Agenda? Whose Agenda?* Lawrence Erlbaum, Mahwah, NJ, pp. 135–52.

Glaser, R. (1990). *Testing and Assessment: O tempora! O mores*. University of Pittsburgh, Learning Research and Development Center, Pittsburgh, PA.

Glazer, N., and Moynihan, D. (1975). *Ethnicity: Theory and Experience*. Harvard University Press, Cambridge, MA.

Goldman, S.R., Reyes, M., and Varnhagen, C.K. (1984). "Understanding Fables in First and Second Languages." *NABE Journal* 8, 35–66.

Gonzalez, A. (1998). "The Language Planning Situation in the Philippines." *Journal of Multilingual and Multicultural Development* 19, 487–525.

González, G., and Maez, L.F. (1980). "To Switch or Not to Switch: The Role of Code-Switching in the Elementary Bilingual Classroom." In R.V. Padilla (ed.), *Theory in Bilingual Education: Ethnoperspectives in Bilingual Education Research*. US Department of Foreign Languages and Bilingual Studies, Bilingual Programs, Ypsilanti, MI, vol. ii, pp. 125–35.

González, J. (2008). *Encyclopedia of Bilingual Education*. Sage, Thousands Oaks, CA.

Gonzalez, N., Moll, L.C., and Amanti, C. (2005). *Funds of Knowledge. Theorizing Practices in Households, Communities, and Classrooms*. Lawrence Erlbaum, Mahwah, NJ.

Goodlad, J. (1984). *A Place Called School: Prospects for the Future*. McGraw-Hill, New York.

Goot, A. (1999). *Bilingual Education in Aosta Valley: Differentiation Strategies in Primary Education*. Fryske Akademy/ Mercator-Education, Ljouwert/Leeuwarden.

Goral, M., Levy, E., Obler, L., and Cohen, E. (2006). "Cross-Language Lexical Connections in the Mental Lexicon: Evidence from a Case of Trilingual Aphasia." *Brain and Language* 98: 235–47.

Gordon, R.G., Jr. (ed.) (2005). *Ethnologue – Languages of the World*. SIL International, Dallas, TX. 15th edn., 2 vols.; available at www.ethnologue.com.

Gorter, D., Jelsma, G.H., de Vos, K., and van der Plank, P.H. (1988). *Language in Friesland* (English summary of "Taal yn Fryslân," a survey of language use and language attitudes in Friesland, the Netherlands). Fryske Akademy, Ljouwert.

Gottlieb, M. (2006). *Assessing English Language Learners: Bridges from language Proficiency to Academic Achievement*. Corwin Press, Thousand Oaks, CA.

Grabe, W., and Kaplan, R.B. (1989). "Writing in a Second Language. Contrastive Rhetoric." In D. Johnson and D. Roen (eds.). *Richness in Writing: Empowering ESL Students*. Longman, New York, pp. 253–62.

Graddol, D. (1997). *The Future of English?* The British Council, London.

—— (2006). *English Next. Why Global English May Mean the End of 'English as a Foreign Language.'* The British Council, London. Available at: www.britishcouncil.org/learning-research-english-next.pdf.

Gramsci, A. (1971). *Selections from the Prison Notebooks*. Q. Hoare and G.N. Nowell-Smith (trans. and eds.). International Publishers, New York.

—— (1988). *An Antonio Gramsci Reader: Selected Writings, 1916–1935*. Ed. by D. Forgacs. Schocken Books, New York.

Grand Duchy of Luxembourg (2005–2006). *Language Education Policy Profile – Grand Duchy of Luxembourg*, Council of Europe and Government of the Grand Duchy of Luxembourg, Strasbourg.

Graney, S. (1997). *Where Does Speech Fit In? Spoken English in a Bilingual Context*. Laurent Clerc National Deaf Education Center, Washington, DC.

Graves, D. (1983). *Writing: Teachers and Children at Work*. Heinemann, Portsmouth, NH.

Gregory, E. (1996). *Making Sense of a New World. Learning to Read in a Second Language*. Paul Chapman Publishers, London.

Gregory, E., Long, S., and Volk, D. (eds.) (2004). *Many Pathways to Literacy. Young Children Learning with Siblings, Grandparents, Peers and Community*. Routledge, London.

Gregory, E., and Williams, A. (2000). "Work or Play? 'Unofficial' Literacies in the Lives of Two East London Communities." In M. Martin-Jones and K. Jones (eds.). *Multilingual Literacies. Reading and Writing Different Worlds*. John Benjamins, Amsterdam, 37–54.

Grimes, B.F. (2000). *Ethnologue – Languages of the World*. SIL International, Dallas, TX. 14th edn., 2 vols. Available at www.ethnologue.com.

Grin, F. (2002). *Using Language Economics and Education Economics in Language Education Policy*. Council of Europe, Strasbourg.

—— (2003). "Language Planning and Economics." *Current Issues in Language Planning* 4(1), 1–66.

Grin, F., and Moring, T. (2002). *Support for Minority Languages in Europe, Final Report to the European Commission*. European Commission, Brussels, Contract No. 2000–1288/001–001 EDU-MLCV.

Groebel, L. (1980). "A Comparison of Students' Reading Comprehension in the Native Language with Their Reading Comprehension in the Target Language." *English Language Teaching Journal* 35, 54–9.

Grosjean, F. (1982). *Life with Two Languages*. Harvard University Press, Cambridge, MA.

—— (1997). "The Bilingual Individual." *Interpreting: International Journal of Research and Practice in Interpreting* 2(1 and 2), 163–87.

—— (2004). "Studying Bilinguals: Methodological and Conceptual Issues." In T. Bhatia and W.C. Ritchie (eds.). *The Handbook of Bilingualism*. Blackwell, Malden, MA, pp. 32–64.

Guibernau, M. (1996). *Nationalisms: The Nation-State and Nationalism in the Twentieth Century*. Polity Press, Cambridge.

Gumperz, J. (1982). *Discourse Strategies*. Cambridge University Press, Cambridge.

Gutiérrez, K., Asato, J., Santos, M., and Gotanda, N. (2002). "Backlash Pedagogy: Language and Culture and the Politics of Reform." *The Review of Education, Pedagogy, and Cultural Studies* 24(4), 335–51.

Gutiérrez, K., Baquedano-López, P., and Alvarez, H.H. (2001). "Literacy as Hybridity: Moving beyond Bilingualism in Urban Classrooms." In M. Reyes and J.J. Halcón (eds.). *The Best for Our Children: Critical Perspectives on Literacy for Latino Students*. Teachers College Press, New York, pp. 122–41.

Gutiérrez, K., Baquedano-López, P., Alvarez, H.H., and Chiu, M.M. (1999a). "Building a Culture of Collaboration through Hybrid Language Practices." *Theory into Practice* 38 (2), 87–93.

Gutiérrez, K., Baquedano-López, P. and Tejada, C. (1999b). "Rethinking Diversity: Hybridity and Hybrid Language Practices in the Third Space." *Mind, Culture and Activity* 6(4), 286–303.

Hadi-Tabassum, S. (2006). *Language, Space and Power. A Critical Look at Bilingual Education*. Multilingual Matters, Clevedon.

Hakuta, K. (1986). *Mirror of Language: The Debate on Bilingualism*. Basic Books, New York.

Hakuta, K., and Diaz, R. (1985). "The Relationship between Degree of Bilingualism and Cognitive Ability: A Critical Discussion and Some New Longitudinal Data." In K.E. Nelson (ed.). *Children's Language*, vol. 5. Lawrence Erlbaum, Hillsdale, NJ, pp. 319–44.

Hall, S. (1996). "Introduction: Who Needs 'Identity'?" In S. Hall and P. du Gay (eds.). *Questions of Cultural Identity*. Polity Press, Cambridge, pp. 273–326.

Halliday, M. (2001). "New Ways of Meaning: The Challenge to Applied Linguistics." In A. Fill and P. Mühlhausler (eds.). *The Ecolinguistic Reader: Language, Ecology and Environment*. Continuum, London.

Hamel, R.E. (2003). "Regional Blocs as a Barrier against English Hegemony? The Language Policy of Mercosur in South America." In J. Maurais and M. Morris (eds.). *Languages in a Globalising World*. Cambridge University Press, Cambridge, pp. 111–41.

Hamers, J.F., and Blanc, M.H.A. (1983) [1989 English translation]. *Bilinguality and Bilingualism*. Cambridge University Press, Cambridge.

Hammerly, H. (1991). *Fluency and Accuracy: Toward Balance in Language Teaching and Learning*. Multilingual Matters, Clevedon.

Harding, E., and Riley, P. (1986). *The Bilingual Family. A Handbook for Parents*. Cambridge University Press, Cambridge.

Harley, B., Allen, P., Cummins, J., and Swain, M. (eds.) (1990). *The Development of Second Language Proficiency*. Cambridge University Press, Cambridge.

Harley, B., and Wang, W. (1997). "The Critical Period Hypothesis: Where Are We Now?" In A.M.B. de Groot and J.F. Kroll (eds.). *Tutorials in Bilingualism: Psycholinguistic Perspectives*. Lawrence Erlbaum, Mahwah, NJ, pp. 19–51.

Harris, S. (1990). *Two-Way Aboriginal Schooling: Education and Cultural Survival*. Aboriginal Studies Press, Canberra.

Harris, S., and Devlin, B. (1997). "Bilingual Programs Involving Aboriginal Languages in Australia." In J. Cummins and D. Corson (eds.). *Encyclopedia of Language and Education*, vol. 5: *Bilingual Education*. Kluwer, Dordrecht, pp. 1–14.

Hassani, J. (2001). "Language Loss among Second-Generation Moroccan Immigrants in Brussels." Unpublished doctoral thesis, Vrije Universiteit Brussel.

Haugen, E. (1953). *The Norwegian Language in America: A Study in Bilingual Behavior*. University of Pennsylvania Press, Philadelphia, PA.

—— (1972). *Ecology of Language*. Stanford University Press, Stanford, CA.

Hawkins, E. (1984). *Awareness of Language: An Introduction*. Cambridge University Press, Cambridge.

—— (1986). *Language Awareness*. Cambridge University Press, Cambridge.

Hayden, M., and Thompson, J. (1998). "Changing Times: The Evolution of the International School." In D. Bingham (ed.). *The John Catt Guide to International Schools*. John Catt Educational, Suffolk.

Hearne, V. (1986). *Adam's Task: Calling Animals by Name*. Knopf, New York.

Heath, S.B. (1976). "A National Language Academy? Debate in the New Nation." *International Journal of the Sociology of Language* 11, 9–43.

—— (1986). "Sociocultural Contexts of Language Development." In Evaluation, Dissemination and Assessment Center (ed.). *Beyond Language: Social and Cultural Factors in Schooling Language Minority Students*. California State University, Los Angeles, CA, pp. 145–86.

Heindler, D., and Abuja, G. (1996). "Forms of Bilingual Education in Austria." In G. Fruhauf, D. Coyle, and I. Christ (eds.). *Teaching Content in a Foreign Language*. Stichting Europees Platform voor het Nederlandse Onderwijs, Alkmaar, pp. 13–30.

Heller, M. (1982). "Negotiations of Language Choice in Montreal." In J. Gumperz (ed.). *Language and Social Identity.* Cambridge University Press, Cambridge, pp. 108–18.

—— (1987). "The Role of Language in the Formation of Ethnic Identity." In J. Phinney and M. Rotheram (eds.). *Children's Ethnic Socialization.* Sage, Newbury Park, CA, pp. 180–200.

—— (1995). "Language Choice, Social Institutions, and Symbolic Domination." *Language in Society* 24, 373–405.

—— (1999). *Linguistic Minorities and Modernity: A Sociolinguistic Ethnography.* Longman, London.

—— (ed.) (2007). *Bilingualism. A Social Approach.* Palgrave Macmillan, New York.

Hélot, C. (2003). "Language Policy and the Ideology of Bilingual Education in France." *Language Policy* 2(3), 255–77.

—— (2006). "Bridging the Gap between Prestigious Bilingualism and the Bilingualism of Minorities. Towards an Integrated Perspective of Multilingualism in the French Education Context." In M. O'Laoire (ed.). *Multilingualism in Educational Settings.* Schneider Verlag Hohengehren, Baltmannsweiler, pp. 49–72.

—— (2007). *Du bilinguisme en famille au plurilinguisme à l'école.* L'Harmattan, Paris.

Hélot, C., and Young, A. (2006). "Imagining Multilingual Education in France: A Language and Cultural Awareness Project at Primary Level." In O. García, T. Skutnabb-Kangas, and M. Torres-Guzmán (eds.). *Imagining Multilingual Schools: Languages in Education and Glocalization.* Multilingual Matters, Clevedon, pp. 69–90.

Henry, A., Rohaniah, D.H., and Metussin, P.H. (1999). "An Investigation into the Levels of Difficulty of Certain Semantic Word Classes in a Bilingual Setting." *International Journal of Bilingual Education and Bilingualism* 2(1), 13–29.

Herdina, P., and Jessner, U. (2000). "Multilingualism as an Ecological System: The Case for Language Maintenance." In B. Ketterman and H. Penz (eds.). *ECOnstruction, Language, Nature and Society: The Ecolinguistic Project Revisited. Essays in Honour of Alwin Fill.* Stauffenburg Verlag, Tubingen, pp. 131–44.

Hernández-Chávez, E. (1978). "Language Maintenance, Bilingual Education, and Philosophies of Bilingualism in the United States." In J.E. Alatis (ed.). *Georgetown University Round Table on Languages and Linguistics.* Georgetown University Press, Washington, DC, pp. 527–50.

—— (1984). "The Inadequacy of English Immersion Education as an Educational Approach for Language Minority Students in the United States." In *Studies on Immersion Education: A Collection for United States Educators.* Dissemination and Assessment Center, Los Angeles, pp. 144–83.

Herrera, S.G., and Murry, K.G. (2005). *Mastering ESL and Bilingual Methods: Differentiated Instruction for Culturally and Linguistically Diverse (CLD) Students.* Allyn and Bacon, Boston, MA.

Heubert, J., and Hauser, R.M. (eds.) (1999). *High Stakes: Testing for Tracking, Promotion and Graduation.* National Academy Press, Washington, DC.

Heugh, K. (1995). "From Unequal Education to the Real Thing." In K. Heugh, A.P. Siegruhn, and P. Pluddermann (eds.). *Multilingual Education for South Africa*, Heinemann, Johannesburg, pp. 42–52.

—— (2000). *The Case against Bilingual and Multilingual Education in South Africa.* PRAESA, Cape Town.

Hinton, L. (2001). "Language Revitalization: An Overview." In L. Hinton and K. Hale (eds.). *The Green Book of Language Revitalization in Practice.* Academic Press, San Diego, CA, pp. 3–18.

—— (2002). *How to Keep Your Language Alive.* Heyday Books, Berkeley, CA.

—— (2003). "Language Revitalization." *Annual Review of Applied Linguistics* 23, 44–57.

Hinton, L., and Hale, K. (eds.) (2001). *The Green Book of Language Revitalization in Practice.* Academic Press, San Diego, CA.

Hoffman, C. (1991). *An Introduction to Bilingualism.* Longman, London.

—— (1998). "Luxembourg and the European Schools." In J. Cenoz and F. Genesee (eds.). *Beyond Bilingualism. Multilingualism and Multilingual Education.* Multilingual Matters, Clevedon, pp. 143–74.

Hoffman, C., and Ytsma, J. (eds.) (2004). *Trilingualism in Family, School and Community.* Multilingual Matters, Clevedon.

Hoffmeister, R. (2000). "A Piece of the Puzzle: The Relationship between ASL and English Literacy in Deaf Children." In C. Chamberlain, R. Mayberry, and J. Morford (eds.). *Language Acquisition by Eye.* Lawrence Erlbaum, Mahwah, NJ, pp. 143–63.

Hollins, E.R. (1982). "The Marva Collins Story Revisited." *Journal of Teacher Education* 33(1), 37–40.

Holm, A., and Holm, W. (1990). "Rock Point, a Navajo Way to Go to School: A Valediction." *Annals AAPSS* 508, 170–84.

Holt, M., and Gubbins, P. (eds.) (2002). *Beyond Boundaries. Language and Identity in Contemporary Europe.* Multilingual Matters, Clevedon.

Honig, B. (1996). *Teaching Our Children to Read: The Role of Skills in a Comprehensive Reading Program.* Corwin Press, Thousand Oaks, CA.

Hopper, P. (1998). "Emergent Grammar." In M. Tomasello (ed.). *The New Psychology of Language.* Lawrence Erlbaum, Mahwah, NJ, pp. 155–75.

Hornberger, N. (1988). *Bilingual Education and Language Maintenance. A Southern Peruvian Quechua Case.* Foris Publications, Dordrecht.

—— (1989). "Continua of Biliteracy." *Review of Educational Research* 59, 271–96.

—— (1991). "Extending Enrichment Bilingual Education: Revisiting Typologies and Redirecting Policy." In O. García (ed.). *Bilingual Education. Focusschrift in honor of Joshua A. Fishman,* vol. 1. John Benjamins, Philadelphia, PA, pp. 215–34.

—— (ed.) (1996). *Indigenous Literacies in the Americas. Language Planning from the Bottom Up.* Mouton de Gruyter, Berlin.

—— (2002). "Multilingual Language Policies and the Continua of Biliteracy: An Ecological Approach." *Language Policy* 1, 27–51.

—— (ed.) (2003). *Continua of Biliteracy. An Ecological Framework for Educational Policy, Research, and Practices in Multilingual Settings.* Multilingual Matters, Clevedon.

—— (2006). "Nichols to NCLB: Local and Global Perspectives on U.S. Language Education Policy." In O. García, T. Skutnabb-Kangas, and M. Torres-Guzmán (eds.). *Imagining Multilingual Schools: Languages in Education and Glocalization.* Multilingual Matters, Clevedon, pp. 223–37.

Hornberger, N., and Coronel-Molina, S. (2004). "Quechua Language Shift, Maintenance and Revitalization in the Andes: The Case for Language Planning." *International Journal of the Sociology of Language* 167, 9–67.

Hornberger, N.H., and Johnson, D.C. (2007). "Slicing the Onion Ethnographically: Layers and Spaces in Multilingual Language Education Policy and Practice." In V. Ramanathan and B. Morgan (eds.). Special issue on *Language Policies and TESOL: Perspectives from Practice. TESOL Quarterly* 41(3), 509–32.

Hornberger, N., and Skilton-Sylvester, P. (2003). "Revisiting the Continua of Biliteracy: International and Critical Perspectives." In N. Hornberger (ed.). *Continua of Biliteracy. An Ecological Framework for Educational Policy, Research, and Practices in Multilingual Settings.* Multilingual Matters, Clevedon, pp. 35–70.

Hosch, H. (1984). *Attitudes toward Bilingual Education: A View from the Border.* Texas Western Press, El Paso, TX.

Housen, A. (2002). "Second Language Achievement in the European School System of Multilingual Education." In D. So and G. Jones (eds.). *Education and Society in Plurilingual Contexts*. VUB Brussels University Press, Brussels, pp. 96–127.

—— (2007). "European Schools' Achievement." Paper presented at the Language, Education and Diversity Symposium. University of Waikato, New Zealand, November 22, 2007.

Housen, A., and Baetens Beardsmore, H. (1987). "Curricular and Extra-curricular Factors in Multilingual Education." *Studies in Second Language Acquisition* 9(1), 83–102.

Howard, E.R., and Christian, D. (2002). *Two-Way Immersion 101: Designing and Implementing a Two-Way Immersion Education Program at the Elementary School Level* (Educational Practice Report 9). Center for Research on Education, Diversity and Excellence, Santa Cruz, CA.

Howard, E.R., Sugarman, J., Christian, D., Lindholm-Leary, K.J., and Rogers, D. (2007). *Guiding Principles for Dual Language Education*, second edn. Center for Applied Linguistics, Washington, DC. Available at www.cal.org/twi/Guiding_Principles.pdf.

Hudelson, S. (1984). "Kan yu ret and rayt en Ingles: Children become literate in English as a second language." *TESOL Quarterly* 18: 221–38.

Huebener, T. (1961). *Why Johnny Should Learn Foreign Languages*. Chilton Co., Philadelphia, PA.

Hunt, V. (forthcoming). "Transformative Leadership: A Comparative Case Study in Established Dual Language Programs." Unpublished doctoral dissertation. Teachers College, Columbia University, New York.

Hymes, D. (1967). "Models of the Interaction of Language and Social Setting." *Journal of Social Issues* 23(2), 8–38.

Ianco-Worrall, A. (1972). "Bilingualism and Cognitive Development." *Child Development* 43, 1390–400.

Igoa, C. (1995). *The Inner World of the Immigrant Child*. Lawrence Erlbaum, Mahwah, NJ.

Ingulsrud, J.E., and Allen, K. (1999). *Learning to Read in China: Sociolinguistic Perspectives on the Acquisition of Literacy*. Edwin Mellen Press, New York.

Irvine, J. (1998). "Ideologies of Honorific Language." In B. Schieffelin, K. Woolard, and P. Kroskrity (eds.). *Language Ideologies: Practice and Theory*. Oxford University Press, New York, pp. 251–62.

Irvine, J., and Gal, S. (2000). "Language Ideology and Linguistic Differentiation." In P. Kroskrity (ed.). *Regimes of Language: Ideologies, Polities and Identities*. School of American Research Press, Santa Fe, NM, pp. 34–84.

Jacobson, R. (1981). "The Implementation of a Bilingual Instructional Model: The New Concurrent Approach." In P. Gonzalez (ed.). *Proceedings of the Eighth Annual International Bilingual Bicultural Education Conference at Seattle*. National Clearinghouse for Bilingual Education, Rosslyn, VA.

Jacobson, R., and Faltis, C. (1990) (eds.). *Language Distribution Issues in Bilingual Schooling*. Multilingual Matters, Clevedon.

Jensen, L. (1986). "Advanced reading skills in a comprehensive course." In F. Dubin, D.E. Eskey, and W. Grabe (eds.). *Teaching Second Language Reading for Academic Purposes*. Addison-Wesley, Reading, MA, pp. 103–24.

Jewett, C., and Kress, G. (2003). *Multimodal Literacy*. Peter Lang, New York.

Johnson, R.K., and Swain, M. (eds.) (1997). *Immersion Education: International Perspectives*. Cambridge University Press, New York.

Johnston, P. (1997). *Knowing Literacy: Constructive Literacy Assessment*. Stenhouse Publishers, York, ME.

Johnstone, R. (2002). *Immersion in a Second or Additional Language at School: A Review of the International Research*. Scottish Centre for Information on Language Teaching, Stirling. Available online at www.scilt.stir.ac.uk/pubs.htm#067.

Jones, B.M. (1995). "Schools and Speech Communities in a Bilingual Setting." In B.M. Jones and P.A. Singh Ghuman (eds.). *Bilingualism, Education and Identity*. University of Wales Press, Cardiff, pp. 79–107.

Jones, D., and Martin-Jones, M. (2004). "Bilingual Education and Language Revitalization in Wales: Past Achievements and Current Issues." In J.W. Tollefson and A.B.M. Tsui (eds.). *Medium of Instruction Policies. Which Agenda? Whose Agenda?* Lawrence Erlbaum, Mahwah, NJ, pp. 43–70.

Jones, G., Martin, P., and Ozóg, C. (1993). "Multilingualism and Bilingual Education in Brunei Darussalam." In G. Jones and C. Ozóg (eds.). *Bilingualism and National Development, Special Issue of the Journal of Multilingual and Multicultural Development* 14, 39–58.

Jones, T.J. (1922). *Education in Africa: A Study of West, South and Equatorial Africa by the African Education Commission under the Auspices of the Phelps-Stokes Fund and the Foreign Missions Societies of N. America and Europe*. Phelps-Stokes Fund, New York.

—— (1925). *Education in East Africa: A Study of East, Central and South Africa by the Second African Education Commission under the Auspies of the Phelps-Stokes Fund, in Cooperation with the International Education Board*. Phelps-Stokes Fund, New York.

Kachru, B.B. (1985). "Standards, Codification and Sociolinguistic Realism: The English Language in the Outer Circle." In R. Quirk and H.G. Widdowson (eds.). *English in the World: Teaching and Learning the Language and Literatures*. Cambridge University Press, Cambridge, pp. 11–30.

Kalmar, T.M. (2001). *Illegal Alphabets and Adult Biliteracy. Latino Migrants Crossing the Linguistic Barrier*. Lawrence Erlbaum, Mahwah, NJ.

Kam, H.W., and R.Y.L. Wong (eds.) (2004). *Language Policies and Language Education. The Impact in East Asian Countries in the Next Decade*, second edn. Eastern Universities Press, Singapore.

Kaplan, R., and Baldauf, R. (1997). *Language Planning: From Practice to Theory*. Multilingual Matters, Clevedon.

Karim, K. (1996). "Economic Dimensions of Minority and Foreign Language Use. An International Overview." *The Official Languages and the Economic Perspective: New Reality and New Thinking*. Canadian Heritage. Available at www.pch.gc.ca/offlangoff/perspectives/english/econo/part2a.htm.

Katz, S.R. (2005). "Emerging from the Cocoon of Romani Pride: The First Graduates of the Gandhi Secondary School in Hungary." *Intercultural Education* 16(3), 247–61.

Kecskes, I., and Papp, T. (2007). Foreign language learning affecting mother tongue. Actas do i Simposio Internacional sobre o Bilinguismo. At http://webs.uvigo.es/ssl/actas1997/03/Kecskes.pdf. As on 09/03/2007.

Kendler, A.C. (2002). *Survey of the States' Limited English Proficient Students 2000–2001*. Office of English Acquisition, Language Enhancement and Academic Achievement for Limited English Proficient Students, U.S. Department of Education, Washington, DC.

Kenner, C. (2000). "Biliteracy in a Monolingual School System? English and Gujarati in South London." *Language, Culture and Curriculum* 13, 13–30.

—— (2004). *Becoming Biliterate: Young Children Learning Different Writing Systems*. Trentham Books, Stoke-on-Trent and Sterling, VA.

King, K., and Mackey, A. (2007). *The Bilingual Edge. Why, When, and How to Teach Your Child a Second Language*. HarperCollins, New York.

King, K.A. (2001). *Language Revitalization Processes and Prospects: Quichua in the Ecuadorian Andes*. Multilingual Matters, Clevedon.

King, K.A., and Benson, C. (2004). "Indigenous Language Education in Bolivia and Ecuador: Contexts, Changes and Challenges." In J.W. Tollefson and A.B.M. Tsui (eds.). *Medium of Instruction Policies. Which Agenda? Whose Agenda?* Lawrence Erlbaum, Mahwah, NJ, pp. 241–61.

Kingdom of Saudi Arabia (2005). *The Executive Summary of the Ministry of Education Ten-Year Plan 1425–1435 H (2004–2014)*. Second edn. Ministry of Education, Riyadh.

Kipp, D. (2002). "Okoyi: To Have a Home." *Native Americas: Hemispheric Journal of Indigenous Issues* 19(3 and 4), 17–18.

Klein, D., Milner, B., Zatorre, R., Evans, A., and Meyer, E. (1994). "Functional Anatomy of Bilingual Language Processing: A Neuroimaging Study." *Brain and Language* 47, 464–6.

Kloss, H. (1977). *The American Bilingual Tradition*. Newbury House, Rowley, MA.

Krashen, S. (1981b). *Second Language Acquisition and Second Language Learning*. Pergamon, Oxford.

—— (1982). *Principles and Practice in Second Language Acquisition*. Pergamon, Oxford.

—— (1985). *The Input Hypothesis*. Laredo Publishing Company, Beverly Hills, CA.

—— (1994). "Bilingual Education and Second Language Acquisition Theory." In Bilingual Education Office (ed.). *Schooling and Language Minority Students: A Theoretical Framework*, second edn. California State University, National Evaluation, Dissemination and Assessment Center, Los Angeles, CA, pp. 47–75.

—— (1996). *Under Attack: The Case against Bilingual Education*. Language Education Associates, Burlingame, CA.

—— (1999). *Condemned without a Trial: Bogus Arguments against Bilingual Education*. Heinemann, Portsmouth, NH.

—— (2004). "The Acquisition of Academic English by Children in Two-Way Programs: What Does the Research Say?" Paper presented at NABE 2004. Albuquerque, NM.

Krashen, S., Long, M., and Scarcella, R. (1979). "Age, Rate, and Eventual Attainment in Second Language Acquisition." *TESOL Quarterly* 13, 573–82.

Krashen, S., and McField, G. (2005). "What Works? Reviewing the Latest Evidence on Bilingual Education." *Language Learner* 1(2), 7–10, 34. Available at http://users.rcn.com/crawj/langpol/Krashen-McField.pdf.

Krashen, S., Rolstad, K., and MacSwan, J. (2007). Review of "Research summary and bibliography for structured English immersion programs" of the Arizona English Language Learners Task Force, October 2007. Institute for Language and Education Policy, Tacoma Park, MD.

Krauss, M. (1992). "The World's Languages in Crisis." *Language* 68, 6–10.

Kress, G. (2003). *Literacy in the New Media Age*. Routledge, London and New York.

Kroll, J.F., and de Groot, A.M.B. (eds.) (2005). *Handbook of Bilingualism: Psycholinguistic Approaches*. Oxford University Press, Oxford.

Kroon, S. (2003). "Mother Tongue and Mother Tongue Education." In J. Bourne and E. Reid (eds.). *Language Education. World Year of Education*. Kogan Page Limited, London, pp. 35–47.

Kühl, J., and Pedersen, M. (2006). "The German Minority in Denmark." In S. Äkermark, L. Huss, S. Oeter, and A. Walker (eds.). *International Obligations and National Debates: Minorities around the Baltic Sea*. The Åland Islands Peace Institute, Mariehamn, pp. 39–107.

Kwong, K.M.-K. (2000). "Bilingual Equals Access: The Case of Chinese High School Students." In Z. Beykont (ed.). *Lifting Every Voice. Pedagogy and Politics of Bilingualism*. Harvard Education Publishing Group, Cambridge, MA, pp. 43–52.

La Celle-Peterson, M.W., and Rivera, C. (1994). "Is It Real for All Kids? A Framework for Equitable Assessment Policies for English Language Learners." *Harvard Educational Review* 64(1) (spring), pp. 55–75.

La Sasso, C., and Metzger, M. (1998). "An Alternate Route for Preparing Deaf Children for Bi-Bi Programs." *Journal of Deaf Studies and Deaf Education* 3(4), 264–89.

Labov, W. (1972). *The Logic of Non-Standard English*. In P. Giglioli (ed.). *Language and Social Context*. Penguin, Harmondsworth.

Labrie, N. (1993). *La Construction linguistique de la Communauté Européenne*. Champion, Paris.

Lachat, M.A. (1999). *What Policymakers and School Administrators Need to Know about Assessment Reform for English Language Learners*. Northeast and Islands Regional Educational Laboratory at Brown University, Providence, RI.

Lagabaster, D. (1998). "The Threshold Hypothesis Applied to Three Languages in Contact at School." *International Journal of Bilingual Education and Bilingualism* 1(2), 119–33.

Lakoff, R. (1973). "Language and Women's Place." *Language in Society* 2, 45–79.

Lambert, W.E. (1955). "Measurement of the Linguistic Dominance in Bilinguals." *Journal of Abnormal and Social Psychology* 50, 197–200.

Lambert, W.E., Genesee, F., Holobow, N.E., and McGilly, C. (1984). *An Evaluation of a Partial Mohawk Immersion Program in the Kahnawake Schools*. McGill University, Montreal.

Lambert, W.E., and Tucker, G.R. (1972). *The Bilingual Education of Children*. Newbury House, Rowley, MA.

Language Policy Research Unit (2007). www.language-policy.org.

Lapkin, S., and Swain, M. (1996). "Vocabulary Teaching in a Grade 8 French Immersion Classroom: A Descriptive Case Study." *The Canadian Modern Language Review* 53(1), 242–56.

Laroussi, F. (2003). "Arabic and the New Technologies." In M.A. Morris and J. Maurais (eds.). *Languages in a Globalising World*. Cambridge University Press, Cambridge, pp. 250–9.

Lave, J., and Wenger, E. (1991). *Situated Learning: Legitimate Peripheral Participation*. Cambridge University Press, Cambridge.

Lebrun, N., and Baetens Beardsmore, H. (1993). "Trilingual Education in the Grand Duchy of Luxembourg." In H. Baetens Beardsmore (ed.). *European Models of Bilingual Education*. Multilingual Matters, Clevedon, pp. 101–20.

Leclerc, J. (2001). *L'Aménagement linguistique dans le monde*, available at www.tlfq.ulaval.ca/axl/index.shtml.

Leibowitz, A.H. (1980). *The Bilingual Education Act: A Legislative Analysis*. InterAmerica Research Associates, Rossly, VA.

Leman, J.L. (1993). "Bicultural Programmes in the Dutch-Language School System in Brussels." In H. Baetens Beardsmore (ed.). *European Models of Bilingual Education*. Multilingual Matters, Clevedon, pp. 86–100.

Leopold, W.F. (1939). *Speech Development of a Bilingual Child: A Linguist's Record*. Volume 1: *Vocabulary Growth in the First Two Years*. Northwestern University Press, Evanston, IL.

—— (1947). *Speech Development of a Bilingual Child: A Linguist's Record*. Volume II: *Sound Learning in the First Two Years*. Northwestern University Press, Evanston, IL.

—— (1949). *Speech Development of a Bilingual Child: A Linguist's Record*. Volume III: *Grammar and General Problems*. Northwestern University Press, Evanston, IL.

—— (1952). *Speech Development of a Bilingual Child: A Linguist's Record*. Volume IV: *Diary from Age 2*. Northwestern University Press, Evanston, IL.

—— (1961). "Patterning in Children's Language Learning." In S. Sapporta (ed.). *Psycho-linguistics*. Holt, Rinehart and Winston, New York.

Le Page, R.B., and Tabouret-Keller, A. (1985). *Acts of Identity: Creole-Based Approaches to Language and Ethnicity*. Cambridge University Press, Cambridge.

Lepore, J. (2002). *A is for American: Letters and Other characters in the Newly United States*. Knopf, New York.

Lessow-Hurley, J. (2005). *The Foundations of Dual Language Instruction*, fourth edn. Pearson, Boston, MA.

Levy, E.S., Goral, M., and Obler, L.K. (1999). "Neurolinguistic Perspectives on Mother Tongue: Evidence from Aphasia and Brain Imaging." *Les Cahiers Charles V* 27, 141–57.

Lewis, E.G. (1977). "Bilingualism and Bilingual Education – The Ancient World to the Renaissance." In B. Spolsky and R.L. Cooper (eds.). *Frontiers of Bilingual Education*. Newbury House, Rowley, MA.

—— (1981). *Bilingualism and Bilingual Education*. Pergamon Press, Oxford.

Li Wei (2000). *The Bilingualism Reader*. Routledge, London.

Lieberson, S. (1969). "How Can We Describe and Measure the Incidence and Distribution of Bilingualism?" In L.G. Kelly (ed.). *Description and Measurement of Bilingualism*. University of Toronto Press, Toronto.

Liebkind, K. (1999). "Social Psychology." In J.A. Fishman (ed.). *Handbook of Language and Ethnic Identity*. Oxford University Press, New York, pp. 140–51.

Lin, A.M.Y. (1996). "Bilingualism or Linguistic Segregation? Symbolic Domination, Resistance and Codeswitching in Hong Kong Schools." *Linguistics and Education* 8(1), 49–84.

Lin, A.M.Y., and Martin, P.W. (eds.) (2005) *Decolonisation, Globalisation. Language-in-Education Policy and Practice*. Multilingual Matters, Clevedon.

Lin, J. (1997). "Policies and Practices of Bilingual Education for the Minorities of China." *Journal of Multilingual and Multicultural Development* 18(3), 193–205.

Lindholm-Leary, K.J. (2001). *Dual Language Education*. Multilingual Matters, Clevedon.

Linton, A. (2003). *Is Spanish Here to Stay? Contexts for Bilingualism among U.S.-born Hispanics*. Center for Comparative Immigration Studies Summer Institute, University of California – San Diego.

Long, M.H. (1990). "Maturational Constraints on Language Development." *Studies in Second Language Acquisition* 12, 251–85.

López, L.E. (2005). *De Resquicios a Boquerones. La educación intercultural bilingüe en Bolivia*. PROEIB Andes, La Paz.

—— (2006). "Cultural Diversity, Multilingualism and Indigenous Education." In O. García, T. Skutnabb-Kangas, and M. Torres-Guzmán (eds.). *Imagining Multilingual Schools: Languages in Education and Glocalization*. Multilingual Matters, Clevedon, pp. 238–61.

Lüdi, G. (1997). "Towards a Better Understanding of Biliteracy." In C. Pontecorvo (ed.). *Writing Development: An Interdisciplinary View*. John Benjamins, Amsterdam, pp. 205–19.

—— (2003). "Code-switching and Unbalanced Bilingualism." In J.H. Dewaele, A. Housen, and Li Wei (eds.). *Beyond Basic Principles*. Multilingual Matters, Clevedon, pp. 174–88.

Luke, A., McHoul, A., and Mey, J. (1990). "On the Limits of Language Planning. Class, State and Power." In R. Baldauf and A. Luke (eds.). *Language Planning and Education in Australia and the South Pacific*. Multilingual Matters, Clevedon, pp. 25–44.

Luykx, A. (2000). "Gender Equity and Inteculturalidad: The Dilemma in Bolivian Education." *The Journal of Latin American Anthropology* 5(2), 150–78.

Mac Donnacha, S., Ní Chualáin, F., Ní Shéaghdha, A., and Ní Mhainín, T. (2005). "A Study of Gaeltacht Schools 2004. Dublin, An Chomhairle um Oideachas Gaeltachta and Gaelscolaíochta." www.cogg.ie/downloads/Gaeltacht%20achoimre2.pdf.

Mackey, W. (1967). *Bilingualism as a World Problem / Le Bilinguisme: Phenomène mondial*. Harvest House, Montreal.

—— (1970). "A Typology of Bilingual Education." *Foreign Language Annals* 3, 596–608.

—— (1972). *Bilingual Education in a Binational School*. Newbury House, Rowley, MA.

—— (1978). "The Importation of Bilingual Education Models." In J. Alatis (ed.). *Georgetown University Round Table on Languages and Linguistics*. Georgetown University Press, Washington, DC, pp. 1–18.

—— (2003). "Forecasting the Fate of Languages." In M.A. Morris and J. Maurais (eds.). *Languages in a Globalising World*. Cambridge University Press, Cambridge, pp. 64–81.

Mackey, W.F., and Beebe, V.N. (1977). *Bilingual Schools for a Bicultural Community: Miami's Adaptation to the Cuban Refugees*. Newbury House, Rowley, MA.

Madaus, G. (1993). "A National Testing System: Manna from Above? An Historical/Technical Perspective." *Educational Assessment* 1(1), 9–26.

Magga, O.H., and Skutnabb-Kangas, T. (2003). "Life or Death for Languages and Human Beings – Experiences from Saamiland." In L. Huss, A. Camilleri Grima, and K. King (eds.). *Transcending Monolingualism: Linguistic Revitalisation in Education*. Lisse, Swets and Zeitlinger, pp. 35–52.

Mahoney, K., MacSwan, J., and Thompson, M. (2005). *The Condition of English Language Learners in Arizona: 2005*. Education Policy Studies Laboratory, Tempe, AZ.

Mahshie, S. (1995). *Educating Deaf Children Bilingually*. Laurent Clerc National Deaf Education Center, Washington, DC. Available online at http://clerccenter.gallaudet.edu/products/B442.html.

Makoni, S., and Pennycook, A. (2007). *Disinventing and Reconstituting Languages*. Multilingual Matters, Clevedon.

Mamouri, M. (1998). "Language Education and Human Development: Arabic Diglossia and Its Impact on the Quality of Education in the Arab region." Paper presented at the World Bank's The Mediterranean Development Forum, Marrakech, September 3–6, 1998.

Mansoor, S. (ed.) (2003). *Language Policy, Planning and Practice: A South Asian Perspective*. Oxford University Press, Oxford.

Manyak, P. (2001). "Participation, Hybridity, and Carnival: A Situated Analysis of a Dynamic Literacy Practice in a Primary-Grade English Immersion Class." *Journal of Literacy Research* 33(3), 423–65.

—— (2002). " 'Welcome to Salon 110': The Consequences of Hybrid Literacy Practices in a Primary-Grade English Classroom." *Bilingual Research Journal* 26(2), 421–42.

Mar-Molinero, C., and Stewart, M. (eds.) (2006), *Globalisation and the Spanish-speaking World*. Palgrave Macmillan, New York.

Marscharck, M. (2003). *Raising and Educating a Deaf Child*. Oxford University Press, Oxford.

Marsh, D. (ed.) (2002). *CLIL/EMILE. The European Dimension. Actions, Trends and Foresight Potential* (Public Services Contract DG EAC 36 01 Lot 3). University of Jyväskylä, Jyväskylä.

Marsh, D., and Langé, G. (1999). *Implementing Content and Language Integrated Learning*. University of Jyväskylä, Jyväskylä.

Marsh, D., Marsland, B., and Stenberg, K. (2001). *Integrating Competencies for Working Life*. University of Jyväskylä, Jyväskylä.

Marsh, H.W., Hau, K.T., and Kong, C.K. (2000). "Late Immersion and Language Instruction in Hong Kong High Schools: Achievement Growth in Language and Non-Language Subjects." *Harvard Educational Review* 70(3) 302–46.

Martí, F., Orega, P., Idiazabal, I., Barreña, A., Juaristi, P., Junyent, C., Uranga, B., and Amorrortu, E. (eds.) (2005). *Words and Worlds. World Languages Review*. Multilingual Matters, Clevedon.

Martí, J. (1975). *Obras Completas*. Vols. VII, X, XVIII, XX. Editorial de Ciencias Sociales, Havana.

Martin, P.W. (1997). "Accomplishing Lessons Bilingually in Three Primary Classrooms in Negara Brunei Darussalam: Insights into the Dwibahsa Programme." Unpublished doctoral dissertation, University of Lancaster.

—— (2003). "Bilingual encounters in the classroom." In J.M. Dewaele, A. Housen, and Li Wei (eds.). *Bilingualism: Beyond Basic Principles. Festchrift in Honour of Hugo Baetens Beardsmore*. Multilingual Matters, Clevedon, pp. 67–88.

—— (2005). "'Safe' Language Practices in Two Rural Schools in Malaysia: Tensions between Policy and Practice." In A.M.Y. Lin and P.W. Martin (eds.). *Decolonisation, Globalisation: Language-in-Education Policy and Practice*. Multilingual Matters, Clevedon, pp. 73–97.

Martin-Jones, M., and Jones, K. (eds.) (2000). *Multilingual Literacies. Reading and Writing Different Worlds*. John Benjamins, Amsterdam.

Martin-Jones, M., and Saxena, M. (1996). "Turn-Taking, Power Asymmetries and the Positioning of Bilingual Participants in Classroom Discourse." *Linguistics and Education* 8(1), 105–23.

Martínez, G.A. (2006). *Mexican Americans and Language. Del Dicho al Hecho*. University of Arizona Press, Tucson, AZ.

Mäsch, N. (1993). "The German Model of Bilingual Education: An Administrator's Perspective." In H. Baetens Beardsmore (ed.). *European Models of Bilingual Education*. Multilingual Matters, Clevedon, pp. 155–72.

Mashie, S. (1995). *Educating Deaf Children Bilingually: With Insights and Applications from Sweden and Denmark*. Gallaudet University Press, Washington, DC.

Mason, L. (2006). "Graduation and Global Requirements: Expanding Foreign Language Education in the United States." Unpublished Masters thesis. Teachers College, Columbia University.

Maurais, J., and Morris, M.A. (eds.) (2003). *Languages in a Globalising World*. Cambridge University Press, Cambridge.

May, S. (2001). *Language and Minority Rights. Ethnicity, Nationalism and the Politics of Language*. Pearson, Essex.

—— (2004). "Māori-Medium Education in Aotearoa/New Zealand." In J.W. Tollefson and A.B.M. Tsui (eds.). *Medium of Instruction Policies. Which Agenda? Whose Agenda?* Lawrence Erlbaum, Mahwah, NJ, pp. 21–41.

—— (2006). "Language Policy and Minority Rights." In T. Ricento (ed.). *An Introduction to Language Policy. Theory and Method*. Blackwell, Malden, MA, pp. 255–72.

May, S., Hill, R., and Tiakiwai, S. (2004). *Bilingual/Immersion Education: Indicators of Good Practice. Final Report to the Ministry of Education*. Ministry of Education, Weillington. Available online at http://educationcounts.edcentre.govt.nz/publications/schooling/bilingual.html.

Mazrui, A. (2004). *English in Africa after the Cold War*. Multilingual Matters, Clevedon.

McCarty, T.L. (2002). *A Place to Be Navajo. Rough Rock and the Struggle for Self-Determination in Indigenous Schooling*. Lawrence Erlbaum, Mahwah, NJ.

—— (2004). "Dangerous Difference: A Critical-Historical Analysis of Language Education Policies in the United States." In J.W. Tollefson and A.B.M. Tsui (eds.). *Medium of Instruction Policies. Which Agenda? Whose Agenda?* Lawrence Erlbaum, Mahwah, NJ, pp. 71–93.

McCarty, T.L., Romero, M.E., and Zepeda, O. (2006). "Reclaiming Multilingual America: Lessons from Native American Youth." In O. García, T. Skutnabb-Kangas, and M. Torres-Guzmán (eds.). *Imagining Multilingual Schools: Languages in Education and Glocalization*. Multilingual Matters, Clevedon, pp. 69–90.

McCarty, T.L., and Watahomigie, L.J. (1999). "Community-based Indigenous Language Education in the USA." In S. May (ed.). *Indigenous Community-Based Education.* Multilingual Matters, Clevedon, pp. 79–96.

McKnight, C.C., Crosswhite, F.J., Dossey, J.A., Kifer, E., Swafford, S.O., Travers, K.J., and Cooney, T.J. (1987). *The Underachieving Curriculum: Assessing U.S. School Mathematics from an International Perspective.* Stipes, Champaign, IL.

McLaughlin, B. (1984). *Second Language Acquisition in Childhood,* 2nd edn. Lawrence Earlbaum Associates, Hillsdale, NJ.

McLaughlin, M., and Vogt, M.E. (1997). *Portfolios in Teacher Education.* International Reading Association, Newark, DE.

McLuhan, M. (1967). *The Gutenberg Galaxy: The Making of Typographic Man.* University of Toronto Press, Toronto.

Mehan, H. (1979). *Learning Lessons.* Harvard University Press, Cambridge, MA.

Mehisto, P., and Asser, H. (2007). "Stakeholder Perspectives: CLIL Programme Management in Estonia." *International Journal of Bilingual Education and Bilingualism* 10(5), 683–701.

Meisel, J. (1989). "Early Differentiation of Languages in Bilingual Children." In K. Hyltenstam and L. Obler (eds.). *Bilingualism across the Lifespan.* Cambridge University Press, Cambridge, pp. 13–40.

—— (2004). "The Bilingual Child." In T.K. Bhatia and W.C. Ritchie (eds.). *The Handbook of Bilingualism.* Blackwell, Malden, MA, pp. 91–113.

Mejía, A.M. de (2002). *Power, Prestige and Bilingualism. International Perspectives on Elite Bilingual Education.* Multilingual Matters, Clevedon.

—— (ed.) (2005). *Bilingual Education in South America.* Multilingual Matters, Clevedon.

Menken, K. (2005). "When the Test Is What Counts: How High-Stakes Testing Affects Language Policy and the Education of English Language Learners in High School." Unpublished doctoral dissertation. Teachers College, Columbia University.

—— (2006). "Teaching to the Test: How Standardized Testing Promoted by the No Child Left Behind Act Impacts Language Policy, Curriculum, and Instruction for English Language Learners." *Bilingual Research Journal,* 30(2), 521–46.

—— (2008). *English Language Learners Left Behind: Standardized Testing as Language Policy.* Multilingual Matters, Clevedon.

Menyuk, P., and Brisk, M.E. (2005). Language Development and Education: Children with Varying Language Experience. Palgrave, New York.

Mercator (2007). European Research Centre on Multilingualism and Language Learning. www.mercator-education.org.

Mercer, J.R. (1989). "Alternative Paradigms for Assessment in a Pluralistic Society." In J.A. Banks and C.M. Banks (eds.). *Multicultural Education.* Allyn and Bacon, Boston, MA, pp. 289–303.

Merrit, M., Cleghorn, A., Abagi, J.O., and Bunyi, G. (1992). "Socializing Multilingualism: Determinants of Codeswitching in Kenyan Primary Classrooms." *Journal of Multilingual and Multicultural Development* 13(1–2), 103–21.

Messick, S. (1989). "Validity." In R.L. Linn (ed.). *Educational Measurement,* third edn. American Council on Education and National Council on Measurement in Education, Washington, DC, pp. 13–103.

Met, M. (1994). "Teaching Content through a Second Language." In F. Genesee (ed.). *Educating Second Language Children: The Whole Child, the Whole Curriculum, the Whole Community.* Cambridge Univesity Press, Cambridge, pp. 159–82.

Miles, M. (2005). "Deaf People Living and Communicating in African Histories, c. 960s–1960s." *Disability and Society* 19, 531–45.

Milk, R. (1981). "An Analysis of the Functional Allocation of Spanish and English in a Bilingual Classroom." *CABE Research Journal* 2(2), 11–26.

Miller, K.F. (2002). "Children's Early Understanding of Writing and Language: The Impact of Character and Alphabetic Orthographies." In Li Wei, J.S. Gaffney, and J.L. Packard (eds.). *Chinese Children's Reading Acquisition. Theoretical and Pedagogical Issues.* Kluwer Academic Publishers, Boston, MA, pp. 17–30.

Milroy, L., and Muysken, P. (eds.) (1995). *One Speaker, Two Languages: Cross-Disciplinary Perspectives on Code-Switching.* Cambridge University Press, Cambridge.

Miniwatts Marketing Group (2008). "Internet World Stats. Usage and Population Statistics." www.internetworldstats.com/stats7.html.

Mohanty, A.K. (1994). "Bilingualism in a Multilingual Society: Psychosocial and Pedagogical Implications." Central Institute of Indian Languages, Mysore.

—— (2006). "Multilingualism of the unequals and predicaments of education in India: Mother tongue or other tongue?" In O. García, T. Skutnabb-Kangas, and M. Torres-Guzmán (eds.). *Imagining Multilingual Schools: Languages in Education and Glocalization.* Multilingual Matters, Clevedon, pp. 262–83.

Moll, L.C. (1992). "Bilingual Classroom Studies and Community Analysis." *Educational Researcher* 21(2), 20–4.

Moll, L.C., Amanti, C., Neff, D., and Gonzalez, N. (1992). "Funds of Knowledge for Teaching: Using a Qualitative Approach to Connect Homes and Classrooms." *Theory into Practice* 31(2), 132–141.

Moody, B. (2002). "International Sign: A Practitioner's Perspective." *Journal of Interpretation*, 1–47.

Mtesigwa, P. (2006). "Kiswahili in the Globalization Era: Perspectives, Challenges and Prospects." Paper presented at the International Symposium on African and Diasporic Languages and Education. October 5, 2006. Teachers College, Columbia University.

Mühlhäusler, P. (1996). *Linguistic Ecology. Language Change and Linguistic Imperialism in the Pacific Region.* Routledge, London.

—— (2000). "Language Planning and Language Ecology." *Current Issues in Language Planning* 1(3), 306–67.

—— (2002). "Ecology of Languages." In R.B. Kaplan (ed.). *The Oxford Handbook of Applied Linguistics.* Oxford University Press, Oxford, pp. 374–87.

Muljani, D., Koda, K., and Moates, D. (1998). "The Development of Word Recognition in a Second Language." *Applied Psycholinguistics* 19, 99–113.

Müller, A., and Baetens Beardsmore, H. (2004). "Multilingual Interaction in Plurilingual Classes – European School Practice." *International Journal of Bilingual Education and Bilingualism* 7(1), 24–42.

Muñoz, C. (2002). "Aprendizaje integrado de contenidos y lengua extranjera." In D. Marsh (ed.). *CLIL/EMILE – The European Dimension: Actions, Trends and Foresight Potential* (Public Services Contract 2001–3406/001–001, pp. 33–6). University of Jyväskylä, Jyväskylä.

Muysken, P. (1988). "Are Creoles a Special Type of Language?" In F.J. Newmeyer (ed.). *Linguistics: The Cambridge Survey.* Vol. 2: *Linguistic Theory: Extensions and Implications.* Cambridge University Press, Cambridge, pp. 285–301.

Myers-Scotton, C. (1990). "Intersections between Social Motivations and Structural Processing in Code-Switching." In *Papers for the Workshop on Constraints, Conditions and Models* (held in London, September 27–29, 1990). European Science Foundation, Strasbourg, pp. 57–82.

—— (1993). *Dueling Languages: Grammatical Structure in Codeswitching.* Clarendon Press, Oxford.

—— (2006). *Multiple Voices. An Introduction to Bilingualism.* Blackwell, Malden, MA.

Myntti, K., and Nuolijärvi, P. (2006). "The Case of Finland." In S. Äkermark, L. Huss, S. Oeter, and A. Walker (eds.). *International Obligations and National Debates: Minorities around the Baltic Sea.* The Åland Islands Peace Institute, Mariehamn, pp. 171–225.

Nahir, M. (1984). "Language Planning Goals: A Classification." *Language Problems and Language Planning* 8, 294–327.

National Center for Education Statistics (1997). *A Profile of Policies and Practices For Limited English Proficiency Students.*

National Clearinghouse for English Language Acquisition and Language Instruction Educational Programs (2007). www.ncela.gwu.edu.

National Council of State Supervisors for Languages (2006). *State and Question Matrix Report,* www.ncssfl.org/reports/state_question_matrix.php.

Navarrete, C., and Gustke, C. (1996). "A Guide to Performance Assessment for Linguistically Diverse Students." *National Clearinghouse for Bilingual Education.* EAC West, Albuquerque, NM. Available at www.ncbe.gwu.edu/miscpubs/eacwest/perform.htm.

NCERT (1999). *Sixth All India Educational Survey: Main Report.* National Council for Educational Research and Training, New Delhi.

Nettle, D., and Romaine, S. (2000). *Vanishing Voices: The Extinction of the World's Languages.* Oxford University Press, Oxford.

New London Group (1996). "A Pedagogy of Multiliteracies: Designing Social Futures." *Harvard Educational Review* 66(1), 60–92.

—— (2000). "A Pedagogy of Multiliteracies. Designing Social Futures." In B. Cope and M. Kalantzis (eds.). *Multiliteracies. Literacy Learning and the Design of Social Futures.* Routledge, London, pp. 9–37.

New York City Department of Education (2006). *ELLs in New York City: Student Demographic Data Report,* available at http://schools.nycenet.edu/offices/teachlearn/ell/DemoPerformanceFINAL_10_17.pdf.

News Morning Post (2003). "Shanghai Will Provide Bilingual Education to Half a Million Students by 2010." October 28, 2003. *Shanghai Morning Post.*

Ngai-Lai, C. (2004). "Hong Kong SAR." In H.W. Kam and R.Y.L. Wong (eds.). *Language Policies and Language Education. The Impact in East Asian Countries in the Next Decade,* second edn. Eastern Universities Press, Singapore, pp. 100–14.

Nical, I., Smolicz, J., and Secombe, M. (2004). "Rural Students and the Philippine Bilingual Education Program on the Island of Leyte." In J.W. Tollefson and A.B.M. Tsui (eds.). *Medium of Instruction Policies. Which Agenda? Whose Agenda?* Lawrence Erlbaum, Mahwah, NJ, pp. 153–76.

Niemi, E. (2006). "National Minorities and Minority Policy in Norway." In S. Äkermark, L. Huss, S. Oeter, and A. Walker (eds.). *International Obligations and National Debates: Minorities around the Baltic Sea.* The Åland Islands Peace Institute, Mariehamn, pp. 397–451.

Nikula, T., and Marsh, D. (1999). "Case Study: Finland." In D. Marsh and G. Langé (eds.). *Implementing Content and Language Integrated Learning.* Continuing Education Centre, Jyväskylä, pp. 17–72.

Noorlander, J., Samal, K., and Sohout, K. (2003). "Highland Children's Education Project (HCEP). Ranakiri Province, Cambodia." Available at www.sil.org/asia/ldc/parallel_papers/noorlander_%20samal_and_%20sohout.pdf.

Norton, B. (2000). *Identity and Language Learning: Gender, Ethnicity and Educational Change.* Longman; Pearson Education, London.

Norton, B., and Toohey, K. (2001). "Changing Perspectives on Good Language Learners." *TESOL Quarterly* 35(2), 307–22.

Nover, S.M., and Andrews, J.F. (1999). *Critical Pedagogy in Deaf Education: Bilingual Methodology and Staff Development. USDLC Star Schools Project Report No. 2, Year Two 1998–1999.* New Mexico School for the Deaf, Santa Fe, NM.

—— (2000). *Critical Pedagogy in Deaf Education: Bilingual Methodology and Staff Development. USDLC Star Schools Project Report, Year 3 (1999–2000).* New Mexico School for the Deaf, Santa Fe, NM.

—— (2001). *Critical Pedagogy in Deaf Education: Bilingual Methodology and Staff Development. USDLC Star Schools Project Report, Year 4 (2000–2001).* New Mexico School for the Deaf, Santa Fe, NM.

Nyati-Ramahobo, L. (2006). "The Long Road to Multilingual Schools in Botswana." In O. García, T. Skutnabb-Kangas, and M. Torres-Guzmán (eds.). *Imagining Multilingual Schools: Languages in Education and Glocalization.* Multilingual Matters, Clevedon, pp. 200–22.

Ó Laoire, M. (2005). "An Overview of Bilingualism and Immersion Education in Ireland: Complexity and Change." In X.P. Rodríguez-Yáñez, A.M. Lorenzo-Suárez, and F. Ramallo (eds.). *Bilingualism and Education: From the Family to the School.* Lincom Europa, Munich, pp. 275–82.

Oakes, J. (1985). *Keeping Track: How Schools Structure Inequality.* Yale University Press, New Haven, CT.

Oakes, J., and Lipton, M. (1999). *Teaching to Change the World.* McGraw Hill, Boston, MA.

Ochs, E. (1992). "Indexing Gender." In A. Duranti and C. Goodwin (eds.). *Rethinking Context.* Cambridge University Press, Cambridge, pp. 335–58.

Ogbu, J.U. (1998). "Voluntary and Involuntary Minorities: A Cultural-Ecological Theory of School Performance with Some Implications for Education." *Anthropology and Education Quarterly* 29(2), 155–88.

Ogulnick, K. (2006). "Popular Education and Language Rights in Indigenous Mayan Communities: Emergence of New Social Actors and Gendered Voices." In O. García, T. Skutnabb-Kangas, and M. Torres-Guzmán (eds.). *Imagining Multilingual Schools: Languages in Education and Glocalization.* Multilingual Matters, Clevedon, pp. 150–70.

Oksaar, E. (1989). "Psycholinguistic Aspects of Bilingualism." *Journal of Multilingual and Multicultural Development* 10(1), 33–46.

Oller, D.K., and Eilers, R. (eds.) (2002). *Language and Literacy in Bilingual Education.* Multilingual Matters, Clevedon.

O'Malley, J.M., and Valdez-Pierce, L. (1996). *Authentic Assessment for English Language Learners.* Addison-Wesley, Reading, MA.

Omniglot. Writing systems and languages of the world. www.omniglot.com/writing.

O'Neill, J., and Velasco, P. (2007). "Understanding the Power of Scaffolds." Unpublished manuscript.

Orellana, M.F., Reynolds, J., Dorner, L., and Meza, M. (2003). "In Other Words: Translating or 'Paraphrasing' as a Family Literacy Practice in Immigrant Households." *Reading Research Quarterly* 38(1), 12–34.

Organisation for Security and Co-operation in Europe. OSCE (2000). *Report on the Situation of Roma and Sinti in the OSCE Area.* Available at www.osce.org/search/.

Ortiz, A.A., and Wilkinson, C.Y. (1991). "Assessment and Intervention Model for the Bilingual Exceptional Student (AIM for the BESt)." *Teacher Education and Special Education* 14, 35–42.

Ortiz, F. (1978). *Contrapunteo Cubano del Tabaco y el Azúcar*. Ayacucho, Caracas. (Original worked published in 1940.)

Ostler, N. (2005). *Empires of the Word: A Language History of the World*. HarperCollins, London.

Otheguy, R. (1995). "When Contact Speakers Talk, Linguistic Theory Listens." In E. Contini-Morava and B. Sussman Goldberg (eds.). *Meaning as Explanation: Advances in Linguistic Sign Theory*. Mouton de Gruyter, Berlin, pp. 213–42.

—— (2001). "Simplificación y adaptación en el español de Nueva York." *Ponencias del II Congreso Internacional de la Lengua Española*. Centro Virtual Cervantes, Madrid, http://cvc.cervantes.es/obref/congresos/valladolid/ponencias/unidad_diversidad_del_espanol/3_el_espanol_en_los_EEUU/otheguy_r.htm.

—— (2003). "Las piedras nerudianas se tiran al norte: Meditaciones lingüísticas sobre Nueva York." *Insula* 679–80, July–August.

Otheguy, R., and García, O. (1993). "Convergent Conceptualizations as Predictors of Degree of Contact in U.S. Spanish." In A. Roca and J.M. Lipski (eds.). *Spanish in the United States: Linguistic Contact and Diversity*. Mouton de Gruyter, Berlin, pp. 135–54.

Otheguy, R., and Otto, R. (1980). "The Myth of Static Maintenance in Bilingual Education." *Modern Language Journal* 64, 350–7.

Ouane, A. (ed.) (2003). *Towards a Multilingual Culture of Education*. UNESCO Institute for Education, Hamburg.

Ovando, C. and Collier, V. (1998). *Bilingual and ESL Classrooms: Teaching in Multicultural Contexts*. McGraw-Hill, Boston, MA.

Özerk, K. (2006). *Fra språkbad til språkdrukning* (From Immersion to Submersion). Oplandske Bokforlag, Vallset.

—— (forthcoming). "Attempts at Revitalization of a Threatened Indigenous Language – a case of Sámi People in Norway."

Padden, C.A. (2003). "The Expansion of Sign Language Education." In J. Bourne and E. Reid (eds.). *Language Education. World Year of Education*. Kogan Page, London, pp. 49–60.

Pakir, A. (1993). "Two Tongue Tied: Bilingualism in Singapore." In G. Jones and C. Ozóg (eds.). *Bilingualism and National Development, Special Issue of the Journal of Multilingual and Multicultural Development* 14, 73–90.

—— (2003). "Singapore." In J. Bourne and E. Reid (eds.). *Language Education. World Year of Education*. Kogan Page, London, pp. 268–80.

—— (2004). "Medium-of-Instruction Policy in Singapore." In J.W. Tollefson and A.B.M. Tsui (eds.). *Medium of Instruction Policies. Which Agenda? Whose Agenda?* Lawrence Erlbaum, Mahwah, NJ, pp. 117–33.

Pang, V.O., and Cheng, L. (eds.) (1998). *Struggling to Be Heard: The Unmet Needs of Asian Pacific American children*. SUNY Press, Albany, NY.

Paradis, M. (ed.) (1983). *Readings on Aphasia in Bilinguals and Polyglots*. Didier, Montreal.

Paradis, J., and Genesee, F. (1996). "Syntactic Acquisition in Bilingual Children: Autonomous or Interdependent?" *Studies in Second Language Acquisition* 18, 1–25.

Parrish, T. (1994). "A Cost Analysis of Alternative Instructional Models for Limited English Proficient Students in California." *Journal of Education Finance* 19, 256–78.

Pattanayak, D.P. (1997). *Language Curriculum for Teacher Educators*. National Council of Teacher Education, New Delhi.

Paulston, C.B. (1992). *Sociolinguistic Perspectives on Bilingual Education*. Multilingual Matters, Clevedon.

—— (2000). "Ethnicity, Ethnic Movements, and Language Maintenance." In G. Kindell and M.P. Lewis (eds.). *Assessing Ethnolinguistic Vitality: Theory and Practice*. SIL International, Dallas, TX, pp. 27–38.

Pavlenko, A. (2002). "Poststructuralist Approaches to the Study of Social Factors in Second-Language Learning and Use." In V. Cook (ed.). *Portraits of the L2 User*. Multilingual Matters, Clevedon, pp. 277–302.

—— (2005). *Emotions and Multilingualism*. Cambridge University Press, Cambridge.

—— (ed.) (2006). *Bilingual Minds. Emotional Experience, Expression and Representation*. Multilingual Matters, Clevedon.

Pavlenko, A., and Blackledge, A. (eds.) (2004). *Negotiation of Identities in Multilingual Contexts*. Multilingual Matters, Clevedon.

Peal, E., and Lambert, W. (1962). "The Relation of Bilingualism to Intelligence." *Psychological Monographs* 76(546), 1–23. Reprinted 1972 in R. Gardner and W. Lambert (eds.). *Attitudes and Motivation in Second-Language Learning*. Newbury House, Rowley, MA.

Pearson, B.Z., Fernandez, M.C., and Oller, D.K. (1992). "Measuring Bilingual Children's Receptive Vocabularies." *Child Development* 63, 1012–221.

—— (1993). "Lexical Development in Bilingual Infants and Toddlers: Comparison to Monolingual Norms." *Language Learning* 43, 93–120.

Pedraza, P. Jr., Attinasi, J., and Hoffman, G. (1980). "Rethinking Diglossia." In R.V. Padilla (ed.). *Ethnoperspectives in Bilingual Education Research: Theory in Bilingual Education*. Department of Foreign Languages and Bilingual Studies. Eastern Michigan University, Ypsilanti, MI, pp. 76–97.

Peet, R., with Hartwick, E. (1999). *Theories of Development*. Guilford Press, New York.

Peña, E., Quinn, R., and Iglesias, A. (1992). "The Application of Dynamic Methods to Language Assessment: A Nonbiased Procedure." *Journal of Special Education* 26, 269–80.

Pennycook, A. (1998). *English and the Discourses of Colonialism*. Routledge, London.

—— (2000). "English, Politics, Ideology: From Colonial Celebration to Postcolonial Performativity." In T. Ricento (ed.). *Ideology, Politics and Language Policies: Focus on English*, John Benjamins, Amsterdam, pp. 107–19.

—— (2002). "Language Policy and Docile Bodies: Hong Kong and Governmentality." In J.W. Tollefson (ed.). *Language Policies in Education: Critical Issues*. Lawrence Erlbaum, Mahwah, NJ, pp. 91–110.

—— (2003). "Global Englishes, Rip Slyme, and Performativity." *Journal of Sociolinguistics* 7(4), 513–33.

Pepper, S. (1996). *Radicalism and Education Reform in 20th Century China*. Cambridge University Press, Cambridge.

Peregoy, S.F., and Boyle, O.F. (2001). *Reading, Writing and Learning in ESL: A Resource Book for K-8 Teachers*, second edn. Longman, New York.

Pérez, B. (ed.) (1998). *Sociocultural Contexts of Language and Literacy*. Lawrence Erlbaum, Mahwah, NJ.

—— (2004). *Becoming Biliterate. A Study of Two-Way Bilingual Immersion Education*. Lawrence Erlbaum, Mahwah, NJ.

Perkins, J.A. (1980). "Strength through Wisdom: A Critique of U.S. Capability. A Report to the President from the President's Commission on Foreign Languages and International Studies." November 1979. *Modern Language Journal* 64, 9–57.

Peyton, J.K., Ranard, D.A., and McGinnis, S. (eds.) (2001). *Heritage Languages in America: Preserving a National Resource*. CAL/ERIC/Delta Systems Inc., Washington, DC.

Phillipson, R. (1992). *Linguistic Imperialism*. Oxford University Press, Oxford.

—— (2003). *English-Only Europe? Challenging Language Policy*. Routledge, London.

Pica, T. (1994). "Research on Negotiation. What Does It Reveal about Second Language Learning Conditions, Processes, and Outcomes?" *Language Learning* 44(3), 493–527.

Platt, J. (1977). "A Model for Polyglossia and Multilingualism (with Special Reference to Singapore and Malaysia)." *Language in Society* 6, 361–78.

Poleschuk, V., and Helemäe, J. (2006). "Estonia – In Quest of Minority Protection." In S. Äkermark, L. Huss, S. Oeter, and A. Walker (eds.). *International Obligations and National Debates: Minorities around the Baltic Sea*. The Åland Islands Peace Institute, Mariehamn, pp. 109–70.

Portes, A., and Rumbaut, R. (1996) *Immigrant America: A Portrait*, second edn. University of California Press, Berkeley, CA.

—— (eds.) (2001a). *Ethnicities: Children of Immigrants and America*. University of California Press, Berkeley, CA.

—— (2001b). *Legacies: The Story of the Immigrant Second Generation*. University of California Press, Berkeley, CA.

Posner, R. (1991). "Der ployglotte Dialog." *Der Sprachreport* 3(91), 6–10.

Potowski, K. (2007). *Language and Identity in a Dual Immersion School*. Multilingual Matters, Clevedon.

Pratt, M.L. (1991). "Arts of the Contact Zone." *Profession. Association of Departments of English Bulletin* 91, 33–40.

Profile on Language Education Policy: Ireland (2008). Council of Europe, Strasbourg.

Prucha, F.P. (1976). *American Indian Policy in Crisis: Christian Reformers and the Indian, 1865–1900*. University of Oklahoma Press, Norman, OK.

Pütz, M. (1992). "The Present and Future Maintenance of German in the Context of Namibia's Official Language Policy." *Multilingua* 11(3), 293–324.

Rahman, T. (2001). "English-teaching Institutions in Pakistan." *Journal of Multilingual and Multicultural Development* 22(3), 242–61.

Ramirez, A.G. (1994). "Literacy Acquisition among Second-Language Learners." In B. Ferdman, R.M. Weber, and A. Ramirez (eds.). *Literacy across Languages and Cultures*. State University of New York Press, Albany, NY, pp. 33–102.

—— (1995). *Creating Contexts for Second Language Acquisition: Theory and Methods*. Longman, White Plains, NY.

Ramirez, D. (1992). "Executive Summary." *Bilingual Research Journal* 16: 1–62.

—— (1991). *Final Report: Longitudinal Study of Structured English Immersion Strategy, Early-Exit and Late-Exit Transitional Bilingual Education Programs for Language Minority Children*. http://www.ncela.gwu.edu/miscpubs/ramirez/longitudinal.html.

Ramsey, C., and Padden, C. (1998). "Natives and Newcomers: Gaining Access to Literacy in a Classroom for Deaf Children." *Anthropology and Education Quarterly* 29(1), 5–24.

Ramsey, S.R. (1987). *The Languages of China*. Princeton University Press, Princeton, NJ.

Rassool, N. (2007). *Global Issues in Language, Education and Development. Perspectives from Postcolonial Countries*. Multilingual Matters, Clevedon.

Rawlins, N. (2003). Testimony of Namaka Rawlins: Hearing before the Senate Committee on Indian Affairs on S. 575, the Native American Languages Act on May 15, 2003. Retrieved December 2, 2005 from the United States Senate Committee on Indian Affairs website at: www.indian.senate.gov/2003hrgs/051503hrg/rawlins.PDF.

Resnick, L.B., and Resnick, D.P. (1991). "Assessing the Thinking Curriculum: New Tools for Educational Reform." In B.R. Gifford and M.C. O'Connor (eds.). *Changing Assessments: Alternative Views of Aptitude, Achievement, and Instruction*. Kluwer, Boston, MA, pp. 37–75.

Reyes, L. (2006a). "The Aspira Consent Decree: A Thirtieth Anniversary Retrospective of Bilingual Education in New York City." *Harvard Education Review* 76, 369–400.

—— (2006b). "How Are ELLs Doing in New York City?" Paper presented at the Conference on Latino High School Dropouts, May 26, 2006. Hunter College, New York.

Reyes, M. (1987). "Comprehension of Content Area Passages: A Study of Spanish/English Readers in Third and Fourth Grade." In S. Goldman and H. Trueba (eds.). *Becoming Literate in English as a Second Language*. Ablex, Norwood, NJ, pp. 107–26.

—— (1992). "Challenging Venerable Assumptions: Literacy Instruction for Linguistically Different Students." *Harvard Educational Review* 62, 427–46.

—— (2001). "Unleashing Possibilities. Biliteracy in the Primary Grades." In M. Reyes and J.J. Halcón (eds.). *The Best for Our Children: Critical Perspectives on Literacy for Latino Students*. Teachers College Press, New York, pp. 245–8.

Reyhner, J., and Eder, J. (1989). *A History of Indian Education*. Billings, MT, Eastern Montana College.

Ricciardelli, L.A. (1992). "Creativity and Bilingualism." *Journal of Creative Behavior* 26(4), 242–54.

Ricento, T. (2003). "The Discursive Construction of Americanism." *Discourse and Society* 14(5), 611–37.

—— (ed.) (2006). *An Introduction to Language Policy. Theory and Method*. Blackwell, Malden, MA.

Ricento, T., and Burnaby, B. (eds.) (1998). *Language Politics in the U.S. and Canada: Myths and Realities*. Lawrence Erlbaum, Mahwah, NJ.

Riquet, M. (1984). "Attitudes et perceptions liées à l'emploi du bilinguisme: Analyse du cas tunisien." Publ. de la Sorbonne, Paris.

Rivera, C. (ed.) (1984). *Placement Procedures in Bilingual Education. Education and Policy Issues*. Multilingual Matters, Clevedon.

Rivera, C., and Stansfield, C. (2000). *An Analysis of State Policies for the Inclusion and Accommodation of English Language Learners in State Assessment Programs during 1998–1999* (executive summary). The George Washington University, Center for Equity and Excellence in Education, Washington, DC.

Rivera, K., and Huerta-Macías, A. (2007). *Adult Biliteracy: Sociocultural and Programmatic Responses*. Lawrence Erlbaum, Mahwah, NJ.

Robertson, R. (1995). "Glocalization: Time-Space and Homogeneity-Heterogeneity." In M. Featherstone, S. Lash, and R. Robertson (eds.). *Global Modernities*. Sage, London, pp. 25–44.

Rogers, H. (2005). *Writing Systems: A Linguistic Approach*. Blackwell, Oxford.

Rolstad, K., Mahoney, K., and Glass, G. (2005). "The Big Picture: A Meta-Analysis of Program Effectiveness Research on English Language Learners." *Educational Policy* 19(4), 572–94.

Romaine, S. (1989). *Bilingualism*. Blackwell, Oxford. Second edn. 1995.

—— (1994). *Language in Society: An Introduction to Sociolinguistics*. Oxford University Press, Oxford. Second edn. 2001.

—— (2006). "Planning for the Survival of Linguistic Diversity." *Language Policy* 5(4), 443–75.

Romero, M.E., and McCarty, T. (2006). *Language Planning Challenges and Prospects in Native American Communities and Schools*. Arizona State University College of Education, Education Policy Studies Laboratory, Tempe, AZ. Available online at http://epsl.asu.edu/epru/documents/EPSL-0602-105-LPRU-exec.pdf.

Ronjat, J. (1913). *Le Développement du langage observé chez un enfant bilingue*. Champion, Paris.

Roots, J. (1999). *The Politics of Visual Language: Deafness, Language Choice, and Political Socialization*. Carleton University Press, Ottawa.

Rosenblatt, L.M. (1978). *The Reader, the Text, the Poem: The Transactional Theory of the Literary Work*. Southern Illinois Press, Carbondale, IL.

—— (1991). "Literacy Theory." In J. Flood, J.M. Jensen, D. Lapp, and J. Squire (eds.). *Handbook of Research in the English Language Arts*. Macmillan, New York, pp. 57–62.

Rosenstock, R. (2004). "An Investigation of International Sign: Analyzing Structure and Comprehension." Unpublished doctoral dissertation. Gallaudet University, Washington, DC.

Roy, J.D. (1987). "The Linguistic and Sociolinguistic Position of Black English and the Issue of Bidialectism in Education." In P. Homel, M. Palij, and D. Aaronson (eds.). *Childhood Bilingualism: Aspects of Linguistic, Cognitive and Social Development.* Erlbaum, Mahwah, NJ, pp. 231–42.

Rubdy, R. (2005). "Remaking Singapore for the New Age: Official Ideology and the Realities of Practice in Language-in-Education." In A. Lin and P.W. Martin (eds.). *Decolonisation, Globalisation. Language-in-Education Policy and Practice.* Multilingual Matters, Clevedon, pp. 55–73.

Ruiz, R. (1984). "Orientations in Language Planning." *NABE Journal* 8 (2), 15–34.

Rumberger, R. and Gándara, P. (2000). "The Schooling of English Learners." In E. Burr, G. Hayward, B. Fuller, and M. Kirst (eds.). *Critical Issues in California Education.* University of California and Stanford University Policy Analysis for California Education, Berkeley, CA, pp. 1–34.

Sacchetti, M., and Tracy, J. (2006). "Bilingual Law Fails First Test: Most Students Not Learning English Quickly." *Boston Globe*, May 21, 2006. Retrieved January 15, 2008, from http://www.boston.com/news/local/articles/2006/05/21/bilingual_law_fails_first_test/?page=full.

Saer, D.J., Smith, F., and Hughes, J. (1924). *The Bilingual Problem.* Hughes and Son, Wrexham.

SALAD (1985). "Not English Only, English Plus! Bilingual Education Issue Analysis." A press release by Spanish American League against Discrimination in Miami, December 4, 1985.

Saldívar-Hull, S. (1997). *Border Matters: Remapping American Cultural Studies.* University of California Press, Los Angeles, CA.

Samarin, W. (1996). Review of Adegbija Efurosibina, *Language Attitudes in Sub-Saharan Africa: A Sociolinguistic Overview. Anthropological Linguistics* 38(2), 389–95.

Saunders, G. (1982). *Bilingual Children: Guidance for the Family.* Multilingual Matters, Clevedon.

Saxena, M. (2007). "Multilingual and Multicultural Identities in Brunei Darussalam." In A.B.M. Tsui and J.W. Tollefson (eds.). *Language Policy, Culture, and Identity in Asian Contexts.* Lawrence Erlbaum, Mahwah, NJ, pp. 143–62.

Schecter, S., and Cummins, J. (eds.) (2003). *Multilingual Education in Practice. Using Diversity as a Resource.* Heinemann, Portsmouth, NH.

Schieffelin, B., Woolard, K., and Kroskrity, P. (eds.) (1998). *Language Ideologies: Practice and Theory.* Oxford University Press, New York, pp. 3–47.

Schlyter, B. (2003). "Sociolinguistic Changes in Transformed Central Asian Societies." In J. Maurais and M.A. Morris (eds.). *Languages in a Globalising World.* Cambridge University Press, Cambridge, pp. 157–87.

Serra, C. (2007). "Assessing CLIL at Primary School: A Longitudinal Study." *International Journal of Bilingual Education and Bilingualism* 10(5), 582–602.

Shaaban, K., and Ghaith, G. (2003). "Effect of Religion, First Foreign Language and Gender on the Perception of the Utility of Language." *Journal of Language, Identity and Education* 2(1), 53–77.

Sharwood Smith, M., and Kellerman, E. (1986). *Crosslinguistic Influence in Second Language Acquisition.* Pergamon Press, New York.

Shepard, L.A. (1996). "Research Framework for Investigating Accommodations for Language Minority Students." Presentation made at CRESST Assessment Conference, UCLA, 1996.

Shin, S.J. (2005). *Developing in Two Languages: Korean Children in America.* Multilingual Matters, Clevedon.

Shohamy, E. (2001). *The Power of Tests: A Critical Perspective on the Uses of Language Tests*. Longman, Harlow.

—— (2006a). "Imagined Multilingual Schools: How Come We Don't Deliver?" In O. García, T. Skutnabb-Kangas, and M. Torres-Guzmán (eds.). *Imagining Multilingual Schools: Languages in Education and Glocalization*. Multilingual Matters, Clevedon, pp. 171–83.

—— (2006b). *Language Policy: Hidden Agendas and New Approaches*. Routledge, London.

Sibayan, B. (1978). "Bilingual Education in the Philippines: Strategy and Structure." In J. Alatis (ed.). *Georgetown University Round Table on Languages and Linguistics*. Georgetown University Press, Washington, DC, pp. 302–29.

—— (1994). "Philippine Language Problems." In J.E. Acujia (ed.). *The Language Issue in Education*. Congressional Oversight Committee in Education, Congress of the Republic of Philippines, Manila, pp. 47–86.

Simon, P. (2001). "Beef up the Country's Foreign Language Skills." *The Washington Post*, October 23, 2001, p. A23.

Sinclair, J.M., and Coulthard, R.M. (1975). *Towards an Analysis of Discourse: The English Used by Teachers and Pupils*. Oxford University Press, London.

Singleton, D. (2001). "Age and Second Language Acquisition." *Annual Review of Applied Linguistics* 21, 77–89.

Skilton-Sylvester, E. (2003). "Legal Discourse and Decisions, Teacher Policymaking and the Multilingual Classroom: Constraining and Supporting Khmer/English Bilitracy in the United States." *International Journal of Bilingual Education and Bilingualism* 6(3 and 4), 168–84.

Skutnabb-Kangas, T. (1981). *Bilingualism or Not: The Education of Minorities*. Multilingual Matters, Clevedon.

—— (1987). "Are the Finns in Sweden an Ethnic Minority – Finnish Parents Talk about Finland and Sweden." Roskilde University Centre, Institute VI, Roskilde, Denmark (unpublished manuscript).

—— (2000). *Linguistic Genocide in Education – or Worldwide Diversity and Human Rights?* Lawrence Erlbaum, Mahwah, NJ.

—— (2006). "Language Policy and Linguistic Human Rights." In T. Ricento (ed.). *An Introduction to Language Policy. Theory and Method*. Blackwell, Malden, MA, pp. 273–91.

Skutnabb-Kangas, T., and García, O. 1995. "Multilingualism for All? General Principles." In T. Skutnabb-Kangas (ed.). *Multilingualism for All*. Swets and Zeitlinger, Lisse, pp. 221–56.

Skutnabb-Kangas, T., and Phillipson, R. (eds.) (1994). *Linguistic Human Rights: Overcoming Linguistic Discrimination*. Mouton, Berlin.

Skutnabb-Kangas, T., and Toukomaa, P. (eds.) (1976). *Teaching Migrant Children's Mother Tongue and Learning the Language of the Host Country in the Context of the Sociocultural Situation of the Migrant Family*. Report written for UNESCO. Research Reports 15. Department of Sociology and Social Psychology, University of Tampere.

Slavin, R.E. (1985). "Cooperative Learning: Applying Contact Theory in Desegregated Schools." *Journal of Social Issues* 41(3), 45–62.

—— (1990). *Cooperative Learning: Theory, Research, and Practice*. Prentice-Hall, Englewood Cliffs, NJ.

Slavin, R.E., and Cheung, A. (2005). "A Synthesis of Research on Language of Reading Instruction for English Language Learners." *Review of Educational Research* 75(2), 247–84.

Smith, F. (1978). *Understanding Reading: A Psycholinguistic Analysis of Reading and Learning to Read*. New York: Holt, Rinehart and Winston, 1978.

Snow, M.A., Met, M., and Genesee, F. (1989). "A Conceptual Framework for the Integration of Language and Content in Second/Foreign Language Instruction." *TESOL Quarterly* 23: 201–17.

So, D. (2002). "Whither Bilingual Education in Hong Kong: Views of the Stakeholders on the Way Forward, 1974–1999." In D. S. and G. Jones (eds.) *Education and Society in Plurilingual Contexts*. Brussels, Brussels University Press.

Spezzini, S. (2005). "English Immersion in Paraguay: Individual and Sociocultural Dimensions of Language Learning and Use." In A. de Mejía (ed.). *Bilingual Education in South America*. Multilingual Matters, Clevedon, pp. 79–98.

Spolsky, B. (1978). "Bilingual Education in the United States." In J. Alatis (ed.). *Georgetown University Round Table on Languages and Linguistics*. Georgetown University Press, Washington, DC, pp. 268–84.

—— (1995). *Measured Words: The Development of Objective Language Testing*. Oxford University Press, Oxford.

—— (2004). *Language Policy*. Cambridge University Press, Cambridge.

Spolsky, B., Green, J., and Read, J. (1974). *A Model for the Description, Analysis and Perhaps Evaluation of Bilingual Education*. Navajo Reading Study Progress Report 23. University of New Mexico, Albuquerque, NM.

Spolsky, B., and Shohamy, E. (1999). *The Languages of Israel: Policy, Ideology and Practice*. Multilingual Matters, Clevedon.

Stavans, I. (2004). *Spanglish: The Making of a New American Language*. Rayo, New York.

Stefanakis, E. (2002). *Whose Judgment Counts? Assessing Bilingual Children, K-3*. Heinemann, Portsmouth, NH.

Steiner, G., and Ladjali, C. (2003). *Éloge de la transmission*. Hachette, Paris.

Street, B. (1984). *Literacy in Theory and Practice*. Cambridge University Press, Cambridge.

—— (ed.) (1993). *Cross-cultural Approaches to Literacy*. Cambridge University Press, Cambridge.

Stritikus, T. (2002). *Immigrant Children and the Politics of English-Only*. LFB Scholarly Publishing LLC, New York.

Strong, M. (1995). "A Review of Bilingual/Bicultural Programs for Deaf Children in North America." *American Annals of the Deaf* 140(2), 84–94.

Strong, M., and P. Prinz (1997). "A Study of the Relationship between American Sign Language and English Literacy." *Journal of Deaf Studies and Deaf Education* 2(1), 37–46.

Stubbs, M. (1983). *Discourse Analysis: The Sociolinguistic Analysis of Natural Language*. Blackwell, Oxford.

Suleiman, Y. (2004). *A War of Words: Language and Conflict in the Middle East*. Cambridge Middle East Studies. Cambridge University Press, Cambridge.

Sumida, E.H. (forthcoming). "'Our Wealth and Our Poverty': A Comparative Study of Indigenous Ecological Traditions and Native Language Transmissions to Youth in Huanca and Pueblo Indian Communities." EdD dissertation. Teachers College, Columbia University.

Swain, M. (1972). "Bilingualism as a First Language." Unpublished doctoral. dissertation. University of California, Irvine.

—— (1978). "Bilingual Education for the English-speaking Canadian." In J. Alatis (ed.). *Georgetown University Round Table on Languages and Linguistics*. Georgetown University Press, Washington, DC, pp. 141–54.

—— (1985). "Communicative Competence: Some Roles of Comprehensive Input and Comprehensible Output in its Development." In S. Gass and C. Madden (eds.). *Input in Second Language Acquisition*. Newbury House Publishers, Cambridge, MA, pp. 235–53.

—— (1996a). "Discovering Successful Second Language Teaching Strategies and Practices." *Journal of Multilingual and Multicultural Development* 17(2–4), 89–104.

—— (1996b). "Integrating Language and Content in Immersion Classrooms: Research Perspectives." *The Canadian Modern Language Review* 52, 529–48.

—— (1997). "French Immersion Programs in Canada." In J. Cummins and D. Corson (eds.). *Encyclopedia of Language and Education*, vol. 5: *Bilingual Education*. Kluwer, Dordrecht, pp. 261–70.

—— (2006). "Languaging, Agency and Collaboration in Advanced Second Language Learning." In H. Byrnes (ed.). *Advanced Language Learning: The Contributions of Halliday and Vygotsky*. Continuum, London, pp. 95–108.

Swain, M., and Lapkin, S. (1982). *Evaluating Bilingual Education: A Canadian Case Study*. Multilingual Matters, Clevedon.

Swan, D. (1996). *A Singular Pluralism: The European Schools 1984–1994*. The Institute of Public Administration, Dublin.

Tannen, D. (1990). *You Just Don't Understand. Women and Men in Conversation*. William Morrow, New York.

Taylor, C. (1994). "Assessment for Measurement or Standards: The Peril and Promise Of Large-Scale Assessment Reform." *American Educational Research Journal* 31, 231–62.

Tchoungi, G. (2000). "Yaoundé." In W. Mackey (ed.). *Espaces urbains et coexistence des langues*, Special issue of *Terminogramme* 93–4, 59–84.

Tharp, R.G., Estrada, P., Dalton, S.S., and Yamauchi, L.A. (2000). *Teaching Transformed: Achieving Excellence, Fairness, Inclusion and Harmony*. Westview Press, Boulder, CO.

Thiong'o, N. Wa (1986). *Decolonizing the Mind: The Politics of Language in African Literature*. James Currey, London.

Thomas, W., and Collier, V.P. (1997). *School Effectiveness for Language Minority Students*. National Clearinghouse for Bilingual Education, Washington, DC.

—— (2002). *A National Study of School Effectiveness for Language Minority Students' Long Term Academic Achievement: Final report*. http://crede.berkeley.edu/research/llaa/1.1_final.html.

Timmermans, N. (2005). *The Status of Sign Languages in Europe*. Council of Europe, Strasbourg.

Todd, L. (1984). "Language Options for Education in a Multilingual Setting." In C. Kennedy (ed.). *Language Planning and Language Education*. Allen and Unwin, London, pp. 160–71.

Toer, P.A. (1975) [1990, English translation]. *The Earth of Mankind*. Penguin, New York.

Tollefson, J.W. (1991). *Planning Language, Planning Inequality*. Longman, London.

—— (2002). "Limitations of Language Policy and Planning." In R.B. Kaplan (ed.). *The Oxford Handbook of Applied Linguistics*. Oxford University Press, Oxford, pp. 416–25.

Tollefson, J.W., and A.B.M. Tsui (eds.) (2004). *Medium of Instruction Policies. Which Agenda? Whose Agenda?* Lawrence Erlbaum, Mahwah, NJ.

Traore, S. (2001). "La pédagogie convergente et son impact sur le système d'éducation." (The Convergent Pedagogy and Its Impact on the Educational System.) *Prospects: Quarterly Review of Comparative Education* 31(3), 353–71.

Tregar, B., and Wong, B.F. (1984). "The Relationship between Native and Second Language Reading Comprehension and Second Language Oral Ability." In C. Rivera (ed.). *Placement Procedures in Bilingual Education; Education and Policy Issues*, Multilingual Matters, Clevedon, pp. 152–64.

Troike, R.C. (1978). "Research Evidence for the Effectiveness of Bilingual Education." *NABE Journal* 3(1), 13–24.

Tsai, P. (2005). "Theoretical Issues and Approaches to Language Policy and Language Planning in Taiwan." Unpublished specialization exam essay (July 1, 2005), Teachers College, Columbia University.

T'sou, B. (1980). "Critical Sociolinguistic Realignment in Multilingual Societies." In E. Afendras (ed.). *Patterns of Bilingualism*. Singapore University Press, Singapore, pp. 261–86.

Tsui, A.B.M. (2004). "Medium of Instruction in Hong Kong: One Country, Two Systems, Whose Language?" In J.W. Tollefson and A.B.M. Tsui (eds.). *Medium of Instruction Policies. Which Agenda? Whose Agenda?* Lawrence Erlbaum, Mahwah, NJ, pp. 97–116.

—— (2007). "Language Policy and the Social Construction of Identity: The Case of Hong Kong." In A.B.M. Tsui and J.W. Tollefson (eds.). *Language Policy, Culture, and Identity in Asian Contexts*. Lawrence Erlbaum, Mahwah, NJ, pp. 121–42.

Tsui, A.B.M., and Tollefson, J. (eds.) (2007). *Language Policy, Culture, and Identity in Asian Contexts*. Lawrence Erlbaum, Mahwah, NJ.

Tucker, G.R. (1998). "A Global Perspective on Multilingualism and Multilingual Education." In J. Cenoz and F. Genesee. *Beyond Bilingualism. Multilingualism and Multilingual Education*. Multilingual Matters, Clevedon, pp. 3–15.

Tunmer, W.E., Pratt, C., and Herriman, M.L. (eds.) (1984). *Metalinguistic Awareness in Children: Theory, Research and Implications*. Springer-Verlag, Berlin.

UNESCO (2003). *Education in a Multilingual World*. Education Position Paper. Paris: UNESCO. Available at: http://unesdoc.unesco.org/images/0012/001297/129728e.pdf.

—— (2005). *First Language First: Community-Based Literacy Programs for Minority Language Contexts in Asia*. UNESCO Asia and Pacific Regional Bureau of Education, Bangkok, Thailand.

Urciuoli, B. (1996). *Exposing Prejudice. Puerto Rican Experiences of Language, Race, and Class*. Westview Press, Boulder, CO.

U.S. Census Bureau (2000, 2002). *Current Population Survey*. Washington, DC.

Valdés, G. (1997). "Dual-Language Immersion Programs: A Cautionary Note Concerning the Education of Language-Minority Students." *Harvard Educational Review* 67, 391–429.

—— (2002). *Expanding Definitions of Giftedness: The Case of Young Interpreters from Immigrant Countries*. Erlbaum, Mahwah, NJ.

Valdés, G., and Figueroa, R.A. (1994). *Bilingualism and Testing: A Special Case of Bias*. Ablex Publishing, Norwood, NJ.

Valdés, G., Fishman, J., Chávez, R., and Pérez, W. (2006). *Developing Minority Language Resources. The Case of Spanish in California*. Multilingual Matters, Clevedon.

Valdez Pierce, L., and O'Malley, J.M. (1992). *Performance and Portfolio Assessment for Language Minority Students*. NCBE Program Information Guide Series. National Clearinghouse for Bilingual Education, Washington, DC.

Valdiviezo, L.A. (2006). "The Construction of Interculturality: An Ethnography of Teachers' Beliefs and Practices in Peruvian Quechua Schools." Unpublished doctoral dissertation. Teachers College, Columbia University.

Valenzuela, A. (1999). *Subtractive Schooling: U.S.-Mexican Youth and the Politics of Caring*. State University of New York Press, New York.

—— (2000). "The Significance of the TAAS Test for Mexican Immigrant and Mexican American Adolescents: A Case Study." *Hispanic Journal of the Behavioral Sciences* 22(4), 524–39.

Valenzuela, A., and McNeil, L. (2001). "The Harmful Impact of the TAAS System of Testing in Texas: Beneath the Accountability Rhetoric." In M. Kornhaber and G. Orfield (eds.). *Raising Standards or Raising Barriers? Inequality and High Stakes Testing in Public Education*. Century Foundation, New York, pp. 127–50.

Van der Walt, C. (2006). "University Students' Attitudes towards and Experiences of Bilingual Classrooms." *Current Issues in Language Planning* 7(2, 3), 359–76.

—— (2007). "Bilingual Assessment Strategies in Higher Education." Unpublished manuscript.

Van der Walt, C., Mabule, D.R., and De Beer, J.J. (2001). "Letting the L1 in by the Back Door: Codeswitching and Translation in Science, Mathematics and Biology Classes." *SAALT Journal* 35(2 & 3), 170–84.

Van Lier, L. (2005). *The Ecology and Semiotics of Language Learning*. Kluwer Academic, Dordrecht.

—— (2006). "Action-Based Teaching: Autonomy and Identity." Lecture, University of Groningen, October 2, 2006.

Vavrus, F. (2002). "Postcoloniality and English: Exploring Language Policy and the Politics of Development in Tanzania." *TESOL Quarterly* 36(3), 373–97.

Villa, D. (2000). "Languages Have Armies, and Economies, Too: The Presence of U.S. Spanish in the Spanish-speaking World." *Southwest Journal of Linguistics* 19: 143–54.

Villegas, A.M., and Lucas, T. (2001). *Educating Culturally Responsive Teachers: A Coherent Approach*. SUNY Press, Albany, NY.

Vogt, M.E. (2000). "Content Learning for Students Needing Modifications: An Issue of Access." In M. McLaughlin and M.E. Vogt (eds.). *Creativity and Innovation in Content Area Teaching: A Resource for Intermediate, Middle, and High School Teachers*. Christopher-Gordon Publishers, Norwood, MA.

—— (2002). "SQPRS: Increasing Students' Understandings of Expository Text through Cognitive and Metacognitive Strategy Application." Paper presented at the 52nd Annual Meeting of the National Reading Conference.

Volterra, V., and Taeschner, T. (1978). "The Acquisition and Development of Language by Bilingual Children." *Journal of Child Language* 5, 311–26.

Von Malitz, F. (1975). *Living and Learning in Two Languages: Bilingual-Bicultural Education in the United States*. McGraw-Hill, New York.

Vygotsky, L.S. (1962). *Thought and Language*. E. Hanfmann and G. Vakar (eds. and trans.). MIT Press, Cambridge, MA.

—— (1978). *Mind and Society*. Harvard University Press, Cambridge, MA.

Waho, T. (2006). "Te Reo o te Whānau. The Intergenerational Transmission of the Māori Language: Supporting Parents to Nurture Māori-Language Families." Unpublished manuscript.

Walqui, A. (2006). "Scaffolding Instruction for English Learners. A Conceptual Framework." *International Journal of Bilingual Education and Bilingualism* 9(2), 159–80.

Walqui, A., García, O., and Hamburger, L. (2004). "Quality Teaching for English Language Learners." In *Classroom Observation Scoring Manual*. WestEd, San Francisco, CA.

Walsh, C. (1991). *Pedagogy and the Struggle for Voice: Issues of Language, Power and Schooling for Puerto Ricans*. Bergin and Garvey, New York.

Walters, J. (2005). *Bilingualism: The Sociopragmatic-Psycholinguistic Interface*. Lawrence Erlbaum, Mahwah, NJ.

Weber, M. (1946). *From Max Weber: Essays in Sociology*. Oxford University Press, New York.

—— (1978). *Economy and Society: An Outline of Interpretive Sociology*. University of California Press, Berkeley, CA.

Wee, L. (2002). "When English Is Not a Mother Tongue: Linguistic Ownership and the Eurasian Community in Singapore." *Journal of Multilingual and Multicultural Development* 23(4), 282–95.

Wei, R.N. (2005). "A Critical Review of Bilingual Education for the Han Chinese in the Public School System of Shanghai with Reference to Factors Related to Teachers,

Students and Parents." Paper presented at the Seminar on Bilingual Education at the Vrije Universiteit Brussel, June 15, 2005, Brussels.

Weinreich, U. (1953). *Languages in Contact, Findings and Problems*. Linguistic Circle of New York, New York.

Wenger, E. (1998). *Communities of Practice*. Cambridge University Press, Cambridge.

Wesche, M., Towes-Janzen, M., and MacFarlane, A. (1996). *Comparative Outcomes and Impacts of Early, Middle and Late Entry French Immersion Options: Review of Recent Research and Annotated Bibliography*. OISE/UT Press, Toronto.

Wilbur, R. (2000). "The Use of ASL to Support the Development of English and Literacy." *Journal of Deaf Studies and Deaf Education* 5(1), 81–104.

Wilcox, S., and Peyton, J.K. (1999). *American Sign Language as a Foreign Language*. Center for Applied Linguistics, Washington, DC.

Wiley, T.G. (1996a). "Language Planning and Policy." In S.L. McKay, M.H. Long, and N.F. Hornberger (eds.). *Sociolinguistics and Language Teaching*. Cambridge University Press, Cambridge, pp. 103–47.

—— (1996b). *Literacy and Language Diversity in the United States*. Center for Applied Linguistics, Washington, DC. Second edn. 2005.

—— (1999). "Comparative Historical Analysis of U.S. Language Policy and Language Planning: Extending the Foundations." In T. Huebner and K.A. Davis (eds.). *Sociopolitical Perspectives on Language Policy and Planning in the USA*. John Benjamins, Amsterdam, pp. 17–37.

Wiley, T., and Wright, W. (2004). "Against the Undertow: Language Minority Education Policy and Politics in the 'Age of Accountability.'" *Educational Policy* 18(1), 142–68.

Williams, G. (1992). *Sociolinguistics. A Sociological Critique*. Routledge, London.

Willig, A.C. (1985). "A Meta-Analysis of Selected Studies on the Effectiveness of Bilingual Education." *Review of Educational Research* 55(3), 269–317.

Willis, L. (2002). "Language Use and Identity among African-Caribbean Young People in Sheffield." In P. Gubbins and M. Holt (eds.). *Beyond Boundaries. Language and Identity in Contemporary Europe*. Multilingual Matters, Clevedon, pp. 126–44.

Wilson, W.H., and Kamanā, K. (2001). "*Mai loko mai o ka 'i'ni*: Proceeding from a dream. The 'Aha Punana Leo connection in Hawaiian language revitalization." In L. Hinton and K. Hale (eds.). *The Green Book of Language Revitalization in Practice*, Academic Press, San Diego, CA.

Winsa, B. (1999). "Language Planning in Sweden." *Journal of Multilingual and Multicultural Development* 20(4 and 5), 376–473.

Wolf, D.P., LeMahieu, P.G., and Eresch, J.A. (1992). "Good Measure: Assessment as a Tool for Educational Reform." *Educational Leadership* 49(May), 8–13.

Wolff, D. (2002). "On the Importance of CLIL in the Context of the Debate on Plurilingual Education in the European Union." In D. Marsh (ed.). *CLIL/EMILE – The European Dimension: Actions, Trends and Foresight Potential* (Public Services Contract 2001–3406/001–001). University of Jyväskylä, Jyväskylä, pp. 44–8.

—— (2005). "Integriertes Inhalts- und Sprachlernen: Ein innovatives Kozept in den Erziehungs- und Bildungssystemen der Europäischen Union" (The Changing European Classroom – the Potential of Plurilingual Education), Paper presented in Luxembourg, March 10–11, 2005.

Wong, R.Y.L., and James, J.E. (2004). "Malaysia." In H.W. Kam and R.Y.L. Wong (eds.). *Language Policies and Language Education. The Impact in East Asian Countries in the Next Decade*, second edn. Eastern Universities Press, Marshall Cavendish, pp. 207–39.

Wong Fillmore, L. (1982b). "Language Minority Students and School Participation: What Kind of English Is Needed?" *Journal of Education* 164, 143–56.

Wong Fillmore, L., and Valadez, C. (1986). "Teaching Bilingual Learners." In M.C. Wittrock (ed.). *Handbook of Research on Teaching.* New York: Macmillan, New York, pp. 648–85.

Woolard, K.A. (1998). "Introduction: Language Ideology as a Field of Inquiry." In B. Schieffelin, K. Woolard, and P. Kroskrity (eds.). *Language Ideologies: Practice and Theory.* Oxford University Press, New York, pp. 3–47.

Woolard, K.A., and Schieffelin, B.B. (1994). "Language Ideology." *Annual Review of Anthropology* 23, 55–82.

Wright, S. (2004). *Language Policy and Language Planning. From Nationalism to Globalisation.* Palgrave, New York.

Wright, W.E., and Pu, C. (2005). "Academic Achievement of English Language Learners in Post Proposition 203 Arizona." Education Policy Studies Laboratory, Language Policy Research Unit, Tempe, AZ. Available at www.asu.edu/educ/epsl/EPRU/documents/EPSL-0509–103-LPRU.pdf.

Yip, V., and Matthews, S. (2007). *The Bilingual Child. Early Development and Language Contact.* Cambridge University Press, Cambridge.

Yngve, V. (1996). *From Grammar to Science: New Foundations for General Linguistics.* John Benjamins, Amsterdam.

Young, A., and Hélot, C. (2006). "Parent Power: Parents as a Linguistic and Cultural Resource at School." In A. Camillieri (ed.). *ENSEMBLE: Whole-School Language Profiles and Policies.* Council of Europe, European Centre for Modern Languages, Graz, pp. 14–28.

Ytsma, J., and de Jong, S. (1993). "Frisian." In G. Extra, and L. Verhoeven (eds.). *Community Languages in the Netherlands.* Swets and Zeitlinger, Amsterdam, pp. 29–49.

Zakharia, Z. (2005). "Language and Education Policy in Lebanon." Unpublished specialization exam essay, Teachers College, Columbia University.

Zampini, M.L., and Green, K.P. (2001). "The Voicing Contrast in English and Spanish: The Relationship between Perception and Production." In J. Nicol (ed.). *One Mind, Two Languages: Bilingual Language Processing.* Blackwell, Oxford, pp. 23–48.

Zehler, A., Fleischman, H., Hopstock, P., Stephenson, T., Pendizick, M., and Sapru, S. (2003). *Descriptive Study of Services to LEP Students and LEP Students with Disabilities,* Vol. 1: *Research Report.* [Electronic Version] from http://www.ncela.gwu.edu/resabout/research/descriptivestudyfiles/vol1_research_fulltxt.pdf.

Zentella, A.C. (1997). *Growing up Bilingual.* Blackwell, Malden, MA.

Zhou, M. (2001). "The Politics of Bilingual Education and Educational Levels in Ethnic Minority Communities in China." *International Journal of Bilingual Education and Bilingualism* 4(2), 126–50.

Zhu, P. (2004). "Perspectives on Bilingual Education in Its Initial Stage in Shanghai." Paper presented at the National Conference on Bilingual Education in Shanghai.

Zondag, K. (1991). "Bilingual Education in Friesland from the Innovator's Point of View." In O. García (ed.). *Bilingual Education: Focusschrift in Honor of Joshua A. Fishman on the Occasion of His 65th Birthday,* Vol. 1. John Benjamins, Amsterdam, pp. 123–34.

Author Index

Subject Index

Printed and bound by CPI Group (UK) Ltd, Croydon, CR0 4YY